Boston's Immigrants

1790–1880

Boston's Immigrants

A STUDY IN ACCULTURATION

Revised and Enlarged Edition

By

OSCAR HANDLIN

Professor of History, Harvard University

*originally published by The Belknap Press of
Harvard University Press*

ATHENEUM

New York

1975

Published by Atheneum
Reprinted by arrangement with Harvard University Press
Copyright © 1941, 1959 by the President and Fellows of Harvard College
All rights reserved
Library of Congress catalog card number 59-7653
ISBN 0-689-70086-5
Manufactured in the United States of America by
The Murray Printing Company, Forge Village, Massachusetts
Published in Canada by McClelland & Stewart Ltd.
First Atheneum Printing January 1968
Second Printing January 1969
Third Printing September 1969
Fourth Printing September 1970
Fifth Printing November 1970
Sixth Printing September 1971
Seventh Printing January 1972
Eighth Printing November 1972
Ninth Printing January 1974
Tenth Printing February 1975

TO

MY MOTHER AND FATHER

Preface to the Revised Edition

THIS work was originally published in 1941 as Volume L of the Harvard Historical Studies. The exhaustion of the first edition some years ago suggested the advisability of a reprinting. I refrained from preparing a revision despite the gratifying reception accorded the volume at its first appearance, in the hope that I might some day be able to extend this study to the present and thus to tell the whole story of the development of the population of an important American metropolitan community. With that objective in view, I was encouraged by the Department of Social Relations at Harvard University for several years to offer a course on the Boston Community. In the preparation of that course I hoped to assemble the materials for that larger history.

Other tasks, however, delayed the completion of the studies required to trace in detail the recent ethnic history of Boston. The assumption of a major new responsibility in 1958 made it seem unlikely that I could complete those studies in the near future. I have therefore decided to reissue the work in essentially its original form. The whole volume has, however, been thoroughly revised; and a new section brings it up to 1880, a more justifiable stopping point than the original, 1865. In preparing this revision, I have also been able to take account of recent scholarship in the fields bearing upon this subject and have incorporated references to new works where relevant.

In my work upon this edition, I have found particularly helpful the papers written for me, over many years, by the students in my seminar in the History of Immigration and in the Boston Community. I am also grateful to the Department of History, Harvard University, for relinquishing its rights in the original book. Mary Flug Handlin collaborated as devotedly in the tasks of revision as in those of composition; and Dorothy Summers helped prepare the manuscript.

O. H.

Cambridge, Massachusetts
October, 1958

Foreword

Not of the mighty! not of the world's friends
Have I aspired to speak within these leaves;
These best befit their joyful kindred pens —
My path lies where a broken people grieves. . . .[1]

THE origins of a social process of any importance must be sought "in the internal constitution of the social *milieu*."[2] The character of the environment — the community in its broadest sense — is particularly important in the study of the contact of dissimilar cultures. It is the field where unfamiliar groups meet, discover each other, and join in a hard relationship that results in either acculturation or conflict. As such, the qualities of the environment subtly condition all the forces involved and often exercise a determining influence upon their evolution.

Only by considering immigrant adjustment on the local scale can the influence of the *milieu* be given full weight. Comprehending that, the practical sociologists heretofore most directly concerned with these matters have produced a number of excellent community studies. But since restrictive legislation has pushed the immigration problem into his sphere, the historian now faces the primary obligation of analyzing it. In the study of the community, however, he meets peculiar difficulties. Lacking the sociologist's or anthropologist's direct access to the subject by questionnaires or observation, he must piece together his story from widely diversified sources, and, tethered within the limits of that which is known, impale upon a rigid page the intimate lives and deepest feelings of humble men and women who leave behind few formal records.

Between 1790 and 1880, thousands of these humble men and women transferred their residences to Boston. This study describes historically their settlement in the community. From a consideration of the society the immigrants * found on arrival and the society they left behind, it attempts to explore the basic factors influencing their economic, physical, and intellectual adjustment, and seeks in the character of that adjustment the forces promoting or discouraging group consciousness and group conflict.

This work thus extends into a "relatively unformulated field of social science." Working in a poorly charted field, I was fortunate to be able to draw upon the friendly guidance and stimulating advice of Arthur Meier Schlesinger, who has in his own work done much to widen the scope of the historical discipline and to break down the parochial boundaries between the various social sciences. Mr. Schlesinger suggested the subject of the doctoral dissertation of which this study is an outgrowth and carefully criticized each step of its progress. Only those who have profited similarly from his guidance can truly appreciate the impelling drive that comes from his conscientious teaching and from the stimulus of his vigorous scholarship. More important, contact with a deeply

* "Immigrant" refers, in this study, to persons of whatever nationality who transferred their residence to Boston from outside it, though primary attention is directed to newcomers from Europe.

human personality revealed the realm of history that transcends immediate questions of techniques and the accumulation of material, and lies in the sphere of the understanding.

At the close of a long task it is good to remember the assistance from many sources that lightened the inevitable drudgeries of research. Much of this work was carried on under scholarships and fellowships offered by the Department of History and the Graduate School of Arts and Sciences at Harvard University for which I am deeply grateful. The criticisms of many kind friends clarified a host of problems. Paul H. Buck read the entire manuscript twice, and Hans Rosenberg, David V. Glass, and Samuel J. Hurwitz let me profit from their opinions on various sections. The late Marcus L. Hansen was free with his advice in a field of which he was master. Robert D. White assisted me with the drawings. George O'Brien helped me find my way in the Irish materials; Father Thomas T. McAvoy allowed me to use the Brownson papers; Father John Sexton made available the files of the *Pilot* in St. John's Ecclesiastical Seminary before those were microfilmed; and the custodians of all the libraries mentioned on page 266 cheerfully allowed me to use their collections.

And I owe a particular debt to Mary Flug Handlin for devoted collaboration.

O. H.

Cambridge, Massachusetts
September, 1941

Contents

ILLUSTRATIONS

Illustrations

TABLES

Tables

Social Boston

1790–1845

There is a city in our world upon which the light of the sun of righteousness has risen. There is a sun which beams in its full meridian splendour upon it. Its influences are quickening and invigorating the souls which dwell within it. It is the same from which every pure stream of thought and purpose and performance emanates. It is the city that is set on high. "It cannot be hid." It is Boston. The morality of Boston is more pure than that of any other city in America.[1]

THE Boston merchants who with their allies masqueraded as Indians and flavored the waters about Griffin's Wharf with the fine strong tea of the East India Company were scarcely aware that in protecting their immediate interests they were destroying the foundations of their prosperity. Few realized that the impending breach between the Crown and its colonies was to widen steadily in the following two years, and lead inevitably to separation; and even fewer foresaw the full economic implications of separation. There was a blustering bravado about these men, a feeling of self-confidence, engendered by years of smuggling in defiance of royal officials, which enabled them to speak bravely enough of independence. But all too soon, they understood that they themselves would suffer most thereby.

For normally, before 1763, Boston functioned as an integral part of the British imperial system, subsisting largely by reason of her position as purveyor of rum to Africa and of slaves to the West Indies in the great triangular traffic. This had been the keystone of her economy ever since John Winthrop had warned her to "look out to the West Indies for a trade." [2] All her commerce was concentrated in it; she had not even the "bread trade" with which a fertile back country had endowed New York and Philadelphia. Even Boston's industry, consisting either in the conversion of West Indian sugar into rum or, to a considerable extent, in the manufacture of naval stores to outfit ships, was involved directly or indirectly in this commerce. With the possible exception of fishing, there was but one other important source where the Boston merchants might seek profits — in the evasion of duties accepted elsewhere. That smuggling was an activity of long standing in the Bay Colony finds ample confirmation in the plaintive reports of John Randolph.[3] But after 1763 the attempts to introduce the "new colonial system" inordinately stimulated such enterprises; as Boston's position in the trade with the islands weakened, merchants shifted to the principal alternative open to them.[4]

Reforms in the collection of revenue and revision of duties downward, however, rendered even illicit profits precarious, and drove the traders into the hazardous course of revolution.[5] The independence that followed destroyed the city's principal occupations. Commerce languished under

2

hostile British legislation, while sharply curtailed imports and an efficient customs service rendered smuggling both unprofitable and impracticable. By a series of acts culminating in that of 1788, the English reserved the trade of their colonies for their own bottoms. The rejection by Congress of Article XII of Jay's Treaty nullified the few British concessions and completely eliminated the possibility of reviving trade with the West Indies. For some time vestiges of commerce with the French and Spanish islands persisted, but, because of the turmoil of the war years 1791–1815, always sporadically and uncertainly. The prohibition of the slave trade and, finally, the abolition of slavery in the British possessions, removed an essential commodity and ended any hopes that might have remained for the restoration of the triangular traffic.[6]

Independence also destroyed Boston's share in the direct trade between England and the North American continent. The Orders in Council of 1783 limited imports from America to naval stores and a few other commodities. The government of Massachusetts retaliated with prohibitive duties on English shipping. But since no other state did likewise, commerce merely shifted to other American ports. As a result, the English could boast that "the 600,000 tonnage of shipping usually employed in that trade are now entirely English bottoms whereas before they were nearly one-half American."[7]

The resultant decrease in Boston's business threatened to continue indefinitely.[8] But there were providential turnings in the ways of commerce; and eventually the merchants recouped their losses in new markets. Profits from privateering and from neutral trading tided them over while they vigor-

3

ously pursued the quest for unknown trade routes. Venturesome Boston skippers, pushing their boats down the South Atlantic and through the Straits, traced the first of these and founded the great China trade. Although New York and Salem had made contact with the Orient in the 1780's, trade had been handicapped at first by the absence of a commodity for which there was a demand in China. But on August 9, 1790, the *Columbia,* captained by Robert Gray, returned from a three-year voyage in which she had circumnavigated the globe, with the news that furs, which brought so high a price in the river marts of Canton, could be acquired for trifling trinkets along the coast of Oregon. This discovery effected a revolution in Boston's economic prospects; by 1792 a new triangular traffic was well established. Carrying cargoes of copper, cloth, iron, and clothes, ships left the city each autumn, arriving at the Columbia River the following spring. There they remained from eighteen to twenty months, bargaining their wares for furs. Then they were off across the Pacific, generally stopping at the Sandwich Islands (Hawaii) for sandalwood, or at California to make illicit deals with the Spaniards. In Canton, they disposed of their stock, and, by way of the Cape of Good Hope, returned with Chinese teas, textiles and porcelain. Bostonians rushed into this enormously profitable trade so quickly that among the Chinooks and other West Coast Indians "Boston-men" soon became synonymous with Americans.[9]

At about the same time, the foundations were laid for a new triangular trade with Russia in which Bostonians exchanged West Indian sugar for linens and iron. This business developed such proportions during the troubled period of the

4

continental blockade, when the Czar permitted "the free admission of nankin in Russian ports," that Bostonians declared John Quincy Adams' mission to Saint Petersburg "of the utmost importance to the commerce of the United States, and the most honorable appointment abroad that is in the gift of our government. . . ." [10]

Although commerce with China and Russia lasted throughout this period, it encountered serious obstacles arising out of the fact that Boston was never more than an entrepôt. All the essential commodities of this trade were drawn from far-off ports as accessible to other cities as to Boston. Based upon the enterprise and initiative of Boston merchants rather than upon the city's advantageous position or natural resources, this commerce had no permanent or durable roots. The prosperity arising from it was superficial and temporary, confined largely to those immediately engaged in it. Its uncertainty became especially apparent in the 1820's when Chinese exports shifted almost exclusively to tea, for which New York was a better market than Boston, and in the 1830's when the supply of northwest furs began to fall off. [11] To some extent, cheap textiles from the Merrimac replaced otter skins from the Columbia, but Lowell and Lawrence could not compete with Manchester and Birmingham. Thereafter Boston's position declined steadily and only the extension of the ice trade to the Far East in the same decade saved the Boston merchants from complete collapse. [12]

A staple product for export, or a wide New England market for imports, alone could firmly ground the roots of trade in Boston's economic life; and both depended upon the back country. But while the hinterland of the other great ports —

New York, Philadelphia, Baltimore, and New Orleans — constantly expanded, Boston's was contracting. Trade with the backwoods of Connecticut and Massachusetts whence had come a limited number of agricultural staples, and, to a certain extent, with the Maine and New Hampshire forests from which were drawn the timber and naval stores for old and New England, had never been important as compared with the triangular traffic, and had declined after 1790.[13] The completion of the Erie Canal in 1825 immediately diverted the produce of large sections of western Massachusetts to New York and ultimately established a link between that city and the fertile plains of the trans-Allegheny west which all the subsequent efforts of commercial Boston proved incapable of breaking.[14] Geographically, Boston could not profit by the use of canals. The only rivers in Massachusetts that might be used advantageously were the Connecticut, the Blackstone, and the Merrimac. But the first two would benefit Hartford or Providence, and, indirectly New York; the third, Portsmouth.[15] Even the advent of the railroads, despite Boston's pioneer role, brought no solution. Contemporaries soon pointed out that *"Boston* is not a thriving, that is, not an increasing town. It wants a fertile back country, and it is too far removed from the western states to be engaged in the supply of that new and vast emporium. . . ."[16]

Bostonians had not failed to realize that "the city is derived from the country" and ever since 1791, when they projected a canal to Worcester, Massachusetts legislators had sought to extend the back country.[17] The Erie Canal forced upon the state the realization that "some decisive measures are *necessary* to facilitate the intercourse between Boston and . . .

Albany," and a railroad was recommended.[18] But not until 1831 was the first line chartered in Massachusetts, and not until 1835 was the first ready for traffic. Although the Western Railroad opened in December, 1841, Bostonians proved singularly inept in the management of their own affairs, and not until after the Civil War was there a direct connection between the Boston wharves and Chicago. By that time the other great ports had already effected permanent contact with the west and had preëmpted its trade.[19]

For a time, tremendous expansion in the industrial hinterland compensated for Boston's shrinking agricultural environs. The period directly following the War of 1812 witnessed the amazing growth of textile centers at Lowell, Fall River, and the mill towns of the Merrimac. For these factories and for the shoe industries about Lynn, Boston became the entrepôt through which goods flowed to all quarters of the continent. On the basis of these enterprises, a flourishing coasting business in which shoes and cotton goods were exchanged for corn and cotton developed with the south.[20] Ultimately, this trade too acquired triangular features. The excess cotton from the slave-tilled fields of the south which New England mills could not absorb found a ready market in Liverpool, and the transatlantic leg of the process tended to become increasingly important.[21] Eventually, however, Boston's failure to develop links to the hinterland undermined her position as carrier even for New England manufacturers. These found it more profitable to exchange their products in New York for the wheat of the west and the cotton of the south already being brought there. Following the trend, many Boston merchants like the Tappans set up

7

branches in New York, and many more sent their ships to swell the commerce that flowed up the Hudson.[22] In this trade, as elsewhere, Boston's commerce rested upon an extremely uncertain base, though it grew steadily if not sensationally.[23]

Nevertheless, the resultant prosperity, though impermanent and derived from external sources, had an important effect upon the city's integral economic life; it made Boston a powerful financial center and the greatest money market in America in these years, its "available capital . . . being even greater than that of New York." [24] Previously, some surplus funds had accrued from land, particularly from real estate within the city limits, and some, from amassment started in the colonial period — though on a rather small scale. But, essentially, Boston capital blossomed forth in the federal period in the fortunes of the China princes whose risky ventures yielded large profits in lump unsteady sums which could not be immediately reinvested.[25]

This surplus led to a phenomenal development in banking which continued to the Civil War in spite of successive depressions. In 1790 Boston had only one bank. By 1800 she had three — a branch of the Bank of the United States, the Union Bank, and the Massachusetts Bank — with a combined capital of less than $2,000,000. The last named had been uniformly successful since its foundation in 1784, often paying as much as 16 per cent interest on its capital of $300,000.[26] After the War of 1812 growth was sensational: in the decade 1810–20 six new banks were incorporated with a combined capital of $8,500,000. Thereafter, in a startling spurt, there were six new incorporations in 1822, three in 1825, two in

1826, one in 1827, six in 1828, six in 1831, six in 1832, five in 1833, and sixteen new incorporations or expansions in 1836 alone. By 1830 Boston was second only to New York in financial strength and resources, and, when the panic of 1837 intervened, was ready to surpass her rival. Progress in the following years, while not as extraordinary, continued steadily until the panic of 1857 and the Civil War upset the money market.[27]

These huge resources, seeking an outlet, promoted the development of industry and transportation in the interior of Massachusetts in the decades following the War of 1812. Between 1780 and 1840, some 2,254 corporations were founded in the state with an aggregate capital of $238,139,222.66, largely raised in Boston. Of these, by far the most important were those devoted to manufacturing. The power of $100,-000,000 of Boston money gave Boston capitalists a solid grip upon the factories of Haverhill, of Waltham, of Lowell, and of Fall River, from which they drew a steady stream of dividends.[28] Their money also sponsored great railroads, first across Massachusetts and New England, and finally across the whole continent.[29]

However, while Boston capital built great industries outside of Boston, it failed to develop them at home. In 1790 Boston was a village of small artisans and handicraftsmen, its industry centered in the need for satisfying the home market. Tailors and cobblers, butchers and grocers, went about the business of feeding and clothing the Bostonians much as they had a hundred years earlier. Whatever other enterprise there was, grew out of and was subsidiary to the commercial activities of the city. Chandlers and ropemakers, duck weavers and sparmakers there were, but of autonomous industrial activity there was no sign.[30] A boom in shipbuilding in the 1790's soon collapsed, and Boston was replaced by the towns of the lower Merrimac and the North River, not regaining her position as the shipbuilder for Massachusetts until well into the 1840's when Donald McKay began to mold the trim figures of his clipper ships in the East Boston yards of Enoch Train.[31]

Even in 1845, whatever industry existed in the city was small in scale and local in character. By far the majority of those engaged in industry at that date were employed either in establishments of ten or less or were unclassifiable, that is, worked in their homes.[32] In 1845, the whole number of industrial workers, including the last group, was less than 10,-000 in a population of 165,000.[33] Only the manufacture of glass and of iron, which needed considerable labor and lacked the inventions which made possible a mechanized factory system located in the suburbs of Boston.[34]

Two factors caused Boston capitalists to invest their money not in Boston, but in the new towns around it. In the first place, in at least two major industries inventions had not yet enabled the factory system to replace the domestic or putting-out system which operated most economically in rural districts. Thus Miss Martineau found that "shoe-making at Lynn is carried on almost entirely in private dwellings, from the circumstance that the people who do it are almost all farmers or fishermen likewise. . . . The whole family works . . . during the winter; and in the summer the father and sons turn out into the fields, or go fishing." [35] The towns near Boston "attracted masons, carpenters and other workmen, in the winter season, when their own professions were dull, to pursue shoemaking. . . ." [36] This system also characterized the manufacture of ready-made clothing and shirts, in which the sewing was given out in all parts of New England to women who worked for pin-money in spare moments.[37]

Even industries in which the factory system prevailed did not flourish in Boston. Machines depended upon water power, for the fee simple of a good site "would not cost the annual expense of a steam engine." [38] Yet despite the efforts of Uriah Cotting and other Bostonians to harness the Mill Dam for manufacturing, the swift waters of the Merrimac and the upper Charles offered superior attractions. Furthermore, Boston offered no advantages as to labor supply. Within the city there were no appreciable numbers of men ready and willing to work at wages low enough to foster the establishment of profitable new enterprises. But in the country areas, farm girls whose families found it increasingly difficult to eke a living out of the hard New England soil, gladly spent a few years in the mills before marriage in order to help out financially at home, and to gather a dowry as well. More tractable, more exploitable, and more plentiful than any labor source then in Boston, they stimulated the diversion of capital away from the city.

Except for fishing, which fluctuated in significance and never in this period became as important as elsewhere in Massachusetts, there was no other economic activity of any proportions.[39] Boston remained in 1845 a town of small traders, of petty artisans and handicraftsmen, and of great merchant princes who built fortunes out of their "enterprise, intelligence, and frugality," and used the city as a base for their far-flung activities.[40] Commercially, Boston's foundations were unstable, and the eastern trade which constituted the whole of its glittering superstructure had already slipped into a decline. Industrially, there seemed little to look forward to, for large-scale ventures failed to locate there. The field of handicrafts was limited and the prospects of the agricultural environs of Boston were meager indeed.[41]

As against the promise of the broad fields and the new cities of the west and south, Boston offered few opportunities to those who lacked the twin advantages of birth and capital. Enterprising young men who made no headway chose to depart, and led a steady stream of emigration from the city. Although to observers it seemed the most homogeneous American community, throughout this period the proportion of native Bostonians was actually dwindling. By 1850, only half the descendants of the Bostonians of 1820 still lived there. Consequently, Boston receded steadily from its third place in 1790 on the roster of American cities. Although its absolute numbers increased slowly, its rate of growth was small compared to that of its rivals. And that its population did not decline absolutely was due in fact, not to the maintenance of its native stock, or to migrations from abroad, but to incursions in the 1820's and 1830's from the depressed rural areas of New England.[42]

Though wealth stimulated only finance and banking in Boston, it nevertheless was put to interest there in many other ways. The merchant's contact with the world exerted a profound influence upon the whole social character of the city, transforming it from John Hancock's theaterless town of 1790 to the gracious cosmopolitan Hub of Ticknor and

Bancroft in 1845. Absence of business activity and of heavy industries requiring a large proletariat obviated the development of slums and blighted areas. And windfall money fortuitously acquired was benevolently parted with for urban improvements. The enhancement of the city accentuated Bostonians' civic consciousness and pride. They seriously accepted their responsibilities as citizens and actively concerned themselves with solving municipal problems.

In 1790 Bulfinch's Pillar replaced the old Beacon Hill light, blown down the preceding year, initiating a process which levelled the three heights of Beacon Hill, nibbled at the fastness of Fort Hill, filled in the old Mill Pond with their sands, threw the famous Mill Dam across the sluggish waters of the Back Bay, doubled the town's area by filling in flats along its waterfront, and united it with its neighbors by a row of sturdy bridges. Levelling the hills was primarily a matter of real estate investments, as was the filling of the Mill Pond. The Mill Dam united a project to benefit by tolls and to utilize the waters of the Back Bay for industrial purposes. The bridges across the Charles and the ferry to East Boston likewise were constructed by men who hoped to make money from tolls, as was the South Boston Bridge, whose projectors counted as well on the rise in value of South Boston land. But these enterprises, though privately conceived and carried out, were built with an eye to the betterment of the city and contributed toward making it a handsomer and more spacious place to live in.[48]

This period saw the extension of the social boundaries of Boston far beyond the political limits of 1790 or even of 1845. During these fifty years six peripheral towns were gradually swept into the vortex of Boston life. In 1790, five — Brighton, Brookline, Cambridge, Dorchester, and Roxbury — were purely agricultural villages, no more connected with Boston than similar communities in Worcester and Berkshire counties. Even Charlestown, in parts of which the beginnings of town life existed, remained primarily rural. In the succeeding decades, however, urban Boston spread beyond the confines of its original narrow peninsula. Since even the reclamation of land from the Bay did not accommodate the city's needs, many Bostonians moved off to the outskirts where house rents were half those in Boston proper, abandoning their homes to the mounting number of hotels, offices, and blocks of stores. As transportation improved and commutation tickets became available at twenty to forty dollars a year, the number of those working in Boston but living elsewhere increased, and the tie between the city and suburbs grew closer.[44]

As a result, Boston absorbed sections of each town socially, whether or not they remained politically intact. South Boston was annexed, and East Boston and the South Cove were developed through the cupidity of real estate speculators.[45] Though attempts at political assimilation by Boston in 1834 failed, the urban portions of Charlestown were soon divorced from Somerville.[46] By 1845 the agricultural areas of Chelsea formed a new township, North Chelsea, leaving the urban districts to the metropolis. In the same way, East Cambridge became distinct from Cambridge, and Roxbury from West Roxbury. Within a decade, Washington Village was torn from Dorchester, and even distant Dedham felt the influence of Boston's proximity. By 1845, Boston had outgrown her charter limits, for its map expanded as rapidly as its face changed.[47]

A geographic redistribution of population accompanied the physical transformation. In 1790 Boston was a small, closely-knit town any part of which was easily reached by foot. The traders lived fairly close to their counting houses and could conveniently return home for the mid-day dinner. There was no great gap between classes, and therefore no desire for sectional distribution. But as the town grew, as the well-to-do became wealthy, and as the outlying districts became more accessible, the people spread out and at the same time were localized in distinctive areas. The filling in of the Mill Pond to form the West End and the levelling of Beacon Hill opened the first two new vicinities. Here and in "New or West Boston" were built the homes of the merchants who gradually abandoned the old North End in the decade or so after the turn of the century. The more numerous middle-class found its outlet in the developing suburbs, first in the South End, where they forced out a small, poorer population, then in South Boston, and finally, in Roxbury and Dorchester. The humbler inhabitants lived in "nigger hill" behind the State House and in the North End, but tended to concentrate particularly about Fort Hill, the cheapest part of the city. By 1845 residential areas were well fixed. The very wealthy either remained on Beacon Hill or moved to the rural suburbs, Roxbury or Cambridge. The middle classes scattered in the South Cove, in South Boston or in the outskirts. Finally, large districts were available at low rents in the North and West Ends.[48]

Accompanying the shift in neighborhoods was a change in

housing. The homes of the upper classes still bore traces of the great flourishing of federal architecture, but the wider use of Quincy granite in the 1830's encouraged a Gothicism imitated from Europe, expressed chiefly in public buildings and churches, but also in pretentious and elaborate residences.[49] The homes of the poor, however, remained unchanged. Small, generally of one story, and built of wood, with inflammable shingle roofs, they possessed few conveniences, but usually held not more than one or two families.[50] Multiple dwellings were slow to develop because of the cheapness of land in less desirable areas. The great tenement house, therefore, was unusual in Boston during this period. There were, of course, no sanitary provisions for the very poor. But, because of the avoidance of overcrowding and diligence in prevention of disease, living was not unhealthy.

Health protection, which enjoyed a tradition of long standing, dating back at least to Cotton Mather's fight for inoculation, acquired a permanent form at the end of the eighteenth century. As a great seaport dealing with many parts of the world, Boston's most immediate need was for a quarantine against the importation of infectious diseases. However, the Board of Health, organized in 1798, acquired not only this authority, but also broad powers for protecting the city internally.[51] And soon the second function absorbed an ever larger share of the Board's attention; throughout the thirty years of its existence, it continued to cope with a host of sanitary problems whose number and complexity increased with the growth of the city. In 1802 it helped spread the results of Jenner's work with smallpox vaccination. It regulated graveyards and the burial of the dead.[52] From rudimentary beginnings in which contractors were hired to cart away rubbish, the Board developed a comprehensive system of garbage collection that served its purpose quite efficiently.[53] It also encouraged the elimination of the old cesspool method of drainage by the substitution of private systems of sewers, though public sewers had to await the inauguration of a new city government.[54]

The problem of supplying the community with a permanent, dependable and pure supply of water was not solved until the new municipal government took charge. Various makeshifts having failed, the authorities finally undertook the ambitious task of connecting a reservoir in Brookline with the waters of Lake Cochituate in Middlesex County, a project which, when completed in 1848, assured the people of their water for the next half century.[55] These precautions reflected the desire of the citizens to make Boston a better and safer place to live in, and helped make it one of the healthiest of the nineteenth-century municipalities.

The expansion of functions necessitated the substitution in 1822 of a more efficient type of administration for the archaic town forms. Until that year, the town meeting determined public policy, theoretically at least. The Board of Selectmen, the only general administrative body, had comparatively little power, and no authority over other municipal agencies, which indeed often competed and quarrelled with one another.[56] Earlier attempts at revision had been defeated by the forces of tradition, by incumbent office-holders, and by fears, persistently expressed, that the cost would be ruinously high. Nevertheless in 1822 the General Court granted a city charter under which Boston's first mayor immediately took office.[57] Under Josiah Quincy, Jr., an efficient police force replaced the old system of watch and constable.[58] But the vested interests in the fire department delayed by several years the introduction of a modernized fire-fighting force. Although a series of disastrous fires, culminating in that of April 7, 1825, on Duane Street, made possible a reorganization, the reform was far from complete, and a volunteer element persisted in the companies until 1873.[59]

The solution of one urban problem — transportation — needed no external stimulation. The city always prided itself upon its well-built and lighted streets,[60] but until the 1820's people either walked or made use of private conveyances. By 1826 traffic had become so heavy that several omnibus lines were established.[61] The first ran every other hour to Roxbury and charged a fare of nine cents each way. Its success encouraged two others from Boston to Charlestown and South Boston, and by 1845 some twenty lines carried the Bostonian about his business quickly and expeditiously.[62] At the same time, railroads developed considerable local business, hackney coaches began to flourish, and a good ferry connected East Boston with the mainland. By 1847 more than 20,000 passengers were carried in and out of the city daily.[63]

Bostonians were also awake to their responsibilities in solving the social problems which beset the modern metropolis. Poverty and pauperism, later the most pressing of these disorders, were of no great importance during this period. Despite the limited opportunities for employment, few depended upon public or private benevolence. The population was small enough and the possibility of leaving broad enough for almost anyone to find work or depart. Consequently, pauperism was nearly unknown, and was declining relative to the total population.[64]

What necessity there was for relief was met generously and competently by the municipality and private agencies. Since the state reimbursed the city for the support of those without legal residence, the city was not anxious to stint on expenditures for much of which it did not pay.[65] The Board of Overseers — a survival of the old town government — administered partial outdoor relief while the city controlled a system of institutions including a House of Industry, a House of Juvenile Reformation (1826), and a municipal lunatic asylum (1839) that took care of those completely dependent. In addition, numerous religious and charitable societies whose objectives included not only the "improvement" of the "moral state of the poor and irreligious" but also the provision of aid and work for the unemployed, supplemented public assistance.[66] In either form relief was always ample enough to justify Miss Martineau's conclusion, "I know no large city where there is so much mutual helpfulness, so little neglect and ignorance of the concerns of other classes."[67]

Comparative freedom from poverty brought comparative freedom from lawlessness. The total number of crimes was small, and increased no faster than the population, a fact attested alike by casual travelers and the research of a trained penologist.[68] Proportionally fewer persons were accused of wrong-doing than in either London or Paris, and the number sentenced for serious transgressions was about half that of Berlin during the same period. Only one Bostonian in sixty-four was brought before a police court in each year, and only one of 107 was convicted.[69] Most of the crimes were not of a grave nature, more than half being misdemeanors arising out of drunkenness, a rather disturbing problem.[70] Bostonians, like other Americans, were not sparing in their use of hard liquors, and though many were able to hold their drinks, by the 1830's drunkenness was widespread enough to beget a thriving temperance movement and numerous abstinence societies.[71]

Prostitution was the only other social problem of any importance. Its frequency seems surprising in view of the relative absence of pauperism and the strict contemporary sexual code. But this was the period in which hundreds of New England farm girls were seeking work in the city. Many, failing to find places soon enough, drifted into the readiest alternative. Thus, a social worker pointed out "the State of Maine, in this manner, furnishes a large proportion of the abandoned females in our city." [72]

On the whole, however, social conditions were exceedingly favorable. Though its sons and daughters might leave it, though its commerce might languish and its industry remain at the handicraft level, Boston was a comfortable and well-to-do city in which the people managed to lead contented and healthy lives.[73] With the utmost confidence in himself, the Bostonian could look out upon the world with an unjaundiced and optimistic eye.

This optimism was the result of more than mere personal well-being. It derived from the fundamental ideas and basic assumptions permeating the social and economic structure of the society. The self-assurance of the merchant-prince in his world suffused the community, engendering a sublime faith in "the perfection of the creation" and of man's role in it. Essentially this confidence was grounded in a complete reliance upon the efficacy of the human will and its power to transform nature and the world. "Nature is thoroughly mediate . . . ," said Emerson, "It offers all its kingdom to man as the raw material which he may mould into what is useful. Man is never weary of working it up . . . until the world becomes at last only a realized will, — the double of man." [74]

In the world of nineteenth-century Bostonians one corollary followed automatically from this assumption: man not only could, but actually was, daily raising the world to an ever-loftier level. Where a few years before there had been only a series of mud flats, there was now a thriving, bustling city. By 1845, the docks sheltered steamers that had crossed the Atlantic, and news of far-flung investments began to arrive through the new medium of the telegraph. Every aspect of daily existence confirmed an already deep-rooted conviction of progress. And this conviction was not merely one of passive acceptance. Rather, it was intensely dynamic and aggressive, driving Bostonians into "the bright and beautiful sisterhood" of reform movements — temperance, prison discipline, women's rights, and other philanthropies, all rungs in the ladder leading to the ultimate, though imminent, perfectibility.[75] Bostonians heard "the Gospel of To-Day" sound "the . . . *assured hope* of Perfect Society" [76] and

lived to the glory of God, with the definite public spirit which belongs to such life. They had . . . absolute faith that God's Kingdom was to come, and . . . saw no reason why it should not come soon.[77]

Naturally, they were democrats.[78] They gloried in the Constitution, valued its blessings, and hoped its principles would spread to all the peoples of the earth. They sympathized with the revolutionary struggles of the French, Greeks, Poles, Magyars, Italians, and Irish and, when they could, aided materially and generously.[79] Nor did they find this attitude at all incompatible with the hegemony exercised by the propertied merchant class over politics within the city,[80] for they believed that "property . . . is the surface action of internal machinery, like the index on the face of a clock," [81] an external indication of worth and ability in a community where trade was "the pendulum" regulating "all the common and authorized machinery of the place." [82] Accordingly, while Bostonians were interested in politics, they were content to leave its actual management to those who had the leisure and ability to devote to it. Indeed, an observer found,

The people here are a little aristocratical but . . . they dont trouble thereselves much about politics as money & business is their aim.[83]

To this democracy, education was a vital necessity. No visitor failed to notice the free school system of Massachusetts and the zeal with which learning was pursued throughout life.[84] The popularity of lectures, evening schools, libraries, and, most striking of all, newspapers and periodicals, bore witness to this intellectual activity. In 1826 Boston boasted twenty-eight periodicals.[85] By 1848 the number had mounted to more than 120 with an aggregate circulation of more than a half-million.[86]

Currents from Europe perpetually expanded the educational process. An increasing number of Bostonians traveled abroad and brought back with them the new ideas that were upsetting the equilibrium of Metternich's continent. With

Ticknor and Bancroft came a wave of thrilling concepts from Germany, while French and English contacts of long standing exercised continuous influence, so that the young men who grew up in the thirties found themselves "married to *Europa*." [87] Few resented these imported ideas. Rather, they agreed with Ezra Gannett that,

Every packet ship . . . brings . . . the thought and feeling which prevail there, to be added to our stock of ideas and sentiments. We welcome each new contribution. We read and reprint foreign literature, we copy foreign manners, we adopt the . . . rules of judgment which obtain abroad. This is natural. It is foolish to complain about it. Imitation is the habit of youth; we are a young people. . . . Hence we shall . . . for a long time . . . receive from Europe a considerable part of our intellectual persuasions and our moral tastes. . . . If I thought it would be of any use, I might suggest the importance of forming a character of our own in spite of the influences . . . across the Atlantic. But it would be a vain undertaking, and perhaps it is not best. All that we can do is, to form a national character *with the help of these influences*.[88]

Indeed cosmopolitan currents had thoroughly transformed the puritan Bostonians whose chief prop, the old orthodoxy, had already been weakened by successive attacks from deism, unitarianism, universalism, and, finally, transcendentalism. Slowly, Bostonians became gentler and more gracious, and developed interests in a wide range of secular diversions. They had early evaded Hancock's interdiction of the theater, first under the guise of "moral lectures" and then openly.[89] The Handel and Haydn Society was formed in 1815, only five years after the Board of Selectmen had prohibited balls as "uncongenial to the habits and manners of the citizens of this place." [90] Through its agency and the aid of pioneer musicians, the taste for music was developed, leading to the flourishing concert life of the thirties.[91]

Bostonians of 1845 had outgrown breeches, satin waist-coats, buckled shoes, and many ideas; they more often drew dividends from Merrimac factories than from India ships. None the less, they were recognizable in their ancestors of 1790. For these changes had unfolded from the Boston of the past. There had been no disruption in the essential continuity of the city's history.

∽ II ∽

The Process of Arrival

1790–1865

Behold the duteous son, the sire decayed,
The modest matron, and the blushing maid,
Forced from their homes, a melancholy train,
To traverse climes beyond the western main,
Where wild Oswego spreads her swamps around,
And Niagara stuns with thundering sound.[1]

CERTAINLY, prospective settlers who could be at all selective would pass Boston by in favor of its younger and relatively more flourishing sisters. For in this community there
was no room for strangers; its atmosphere of cultural homo-
geneity, familiar and comforting to self-contained Bostonians,
seemed rigidly forbidding to aliens. And above all, space was
lacking. Boston offered few attractions in either agriculture
or industry. Its commercial ranks were not broad enough to
absorb the sons of its own merchant class, and the fields of retail trading and handicraft artisanry were limited. The constricted social and economic life of the city and the far greater
opportunities elsewhere, combined to sweep the currents of
migration in other directions.

From time to time isolated individuals did find their way

to Boston, became residents and, being few in number, were readily absorbed by its vigorous culture. Scattered French, English, Scotch, Irish, Scotch-Irish, German, and Italian families appeared throughout the eighteenth and early nineteenth centuries. One could find enough natives of Switzerland, the Azores, Armenia, Poland, Sweden, Spain, China, and Russia to credit the claim that twenty-seven different languages were spoken in Boston.[2] These foreigners, however, were just strays; and the reasons for their coming derived from personal contingencies rather than from great social causes for mass emigration. To their ranks were added, from time to time, deserters from foreign ships in port, for whom American wages and American freedom weighed more heavily than the obligations of contract or the claims of loyalty.[3] More respectable increments came from the merchants and consuls who form a foreign nucleus in any commercial community.[4] Occasionally, too, small groups arrived. Thus when 800 English veterans, out-pensioners of Chelsea Hospital, settled in the eastern United States, some came to Boston.[5] But the great waves of European migration, with one exception, caused scarcely a ripple in the placid stream of the city's life. Only one country directed a dislodged population to a city where no promise dwelled; elsewhere events promoted the departure of those only who could choose their destination more prudently.

Between 1815 and 1865 profound changes in the economic, social and political life of many communities uprooted some 5,000,000 people from the continent of Europe. The most direct cause of this migration from western and central Europe was the dissatisfaction of large groups of people with their political and legal status. Many abandoned their homes because they despaired of improving their circumstances where they were, while others were forced to flee precisely because they sought to alter conditions.

During the French revolutionary period, cautious noblemen, victims of the fighting in La Vendée, disillusioned Feuillant reformers, Girondins, Jacobins, Thermidorians, and, finally, Napoleonic exiles — in all between 150,000 and 200,000 — left their native country.[6] At about the same time, repressive English measures following the abortive insurrection of the Society of United Irishmen under Lord Edward Fitzgerald in 1798, the failure of the uprising of 1803, and the Act of Union which joined the two kingdoms, caused many to leave Ireland.[7] Thereafter, successive upheavals in many lands produced a host of expatriates — German Burschenschaft agitators, Polish and French exiles of the thirties, French-Canadians in 1837, and French, Hungarian, Italian, German, and Irish *émigrés* in 1848.[8]

Many thus became exiles; but few became immigrants. The right of political asylum was universally recognized in western Europe[9] and a revolutionary fugitive could easily find a base close at hand where he might participate in further plots. The first French *émigrés* went to Turin to raise a counter-revolutionary army, while most of their successors concentrated in the Rhineland, on the Austrian frontier, and in England, from which points almost three-quarters eventually returned to France.[10] Similarly the Irish *émigrés* from the beginning looked first to France for asylum. When the United Irishmen decided that "where freedom is, there should our country be," it was "the thoughts of lovely

France" that cheered them.[11] The German radicals tried always to stay as close to home as possible, using nearby territory as a base for attacks against the Metternich system; whole colonies developed in Alsace-Lorraine, Switzerland, and England.[12] And later French, Italian, and Hungarian refugees centered their activities in London where they plotted under Ledru-Rollin, Mazzini, and Kossuth.[13] Those only came to America who gave up active revolutionary projects to start life anew.[14] Nevertheless, enough entered the United States to justify the constant boast of Americans that "the downtrodden . . . Pole . . . the learned . . . German . . . the cultivated and ardent Italian . . . bends hitherward his expatriated steps, as towards a shrine of social and public safety, to contemplate institutions of which he has only read." [15]

Of the 10,000 to 25,000 early French refugees who fled to America, however, few chose to live in Boston.[16] Between 1794 and 1809 occasional groups did arrive from France and from the disturbed districts of the French West Indies. And isolated individuals appeared from time to time. Jean Baptiste Julien, for instance, opened a "Restorator" at the corner of Milk and Congress Streets where he concocted for the first time the *Consommé Julien* and received from Brillat-Savarin a recipe for eggs "brouillés au fromage" which "fit fureur." [17] But most French immigrants of that period either went to Philadelphia or thought of America as the land of the noble savage and went far from Boston in their search for primitivism. In 1848, later French revolutionaries appeared, but on the whole the town was only slightly affected by this emigration.[18]

Fugitives from other political upheavals of the mid-nineteenth century contributed more heavily to Boston's population. The cultural center of America attracted considerable numbers of intellectuals and professionals, though they were continually warned that there was no room for the educated classes in the United States.[19] Thus, the Germans, Karl Beck and Carl Follen, came to Harvard in 1825, and Francis Lieber arrived in Boston in 1827 to teach gymnastics.[20] The fiasco of 1848 drove several large contingents to the city, the most prominent individual being Karl Heinzen.[21] And while most Irish political refugees concentrated in New York — an early center of anti-British activity — many nevertheless settled in Boston. Walter Coxe, an old revolutionary, one of the first, was joined after 1848 by Phelim Lynch and by B. S. Treanor, who became leaders of the Boston Irish community.[22] Among others in this category who struck roots in the city were some Poles in 1831 and in 1834, some Italians, and some Hungarians who came with Kossuth and stayed on.[23]

Much more influential than the political reasons for emigration, however, were the social and economic factors that transformed Europe in the century after 1750. Most fundamental was the fabulous increase in population. Before 1750, years in which births exceeded deaths had alternated with years in which deaths exceeded births, while over long periods of time the number of people remained fairly stationary.[24] After 1750, primarily because of a decrease in mortality among children less than ten, the population mounted steadily, almost doubling in the next century. This expansion, even at the point of redundancy, was itself not enough to provoke emigration, but it was the catalytic agent which converted other economic developments into dynamic causes for mass exodus.[25]

Between 1750 and 1850 the Industrial Revolution destroyed the traditional handicraft industries by creating large-scale factory enterprises, and set loose countless artisans all over western Europe. The change became apparent first in England where a series of inventions after 1785 gradually converted the small-scale, individually-operated, domestic textile industries into large-scale undertakings manned by a proletariat. From England it spread to France and later to Germany. In both England and France the displaced found employment in factories as paid laborers, so that the shift in population was chiefly from rural to urban regions, with little effect upon external migration. The British government, furthermore, discouraged any tendency of skilled laborers to quit the country. The Act of 1782 and the Order in Council of April, 1795, forbade a large variety of workers to leave. Although these restrictions were sometimes circumvented by vessels which cleared for a British port but stopped at New York or Boston instead, they remained fairly effective until repealed in 1824.[26] Even after the removal of legal impediments, emigration was selective in nature and limited in quantity. Not the depressed miner or factory operative, but the independent craftsmen whose standards were steadily lowered by the new industrial system, sought out new lands beyond the sea. Thus, in the 1840's, the London Tailors' Union offered to assist the emigration of 7,000 unemployed tailors, and in Paisley 3,000 combined to secure aid for the same purpose.[27]

In Germany the exodus of displaced artisans was considerably more marked than in England. Throughout this period Germany was industrially dependent upon England and France, producing foodstuffs to supply their industrial cities, and taking in return their finished products. The influx of machine-made goods "when England poured her yarn . . . into the Hanse towns after Waterloo" destroyed German handicrafts and menaced the existence of many artisans.[28] In spite of a steadily increasing population the period between 1835 and 1860 saw a decline in the number of masters in all but a few trades.[29] Because the machines that discharged them were in England, these workers could find no new employment in Germany. They had little choice but to emigrate.[30]

English domination stifled the development of the factory system in Ireland and ruined the industries that had existed before the Union. During the eighteenth century independent craftsmen had, despite British hostility, developed flourishing trades in Cork, Dublin, Limerick, and other Irish cities. But the Act of Union was almost immediately disastrous. With the shift of the capital to London, most of the gentry left Ireland, taking with them the market for Irish manufactures.[31] Thereafter the English parliament persistently retarded the growth of native industry, already handicapped by the depression of the Napoleonic Wars. As a result the Industrial Revolution never reached Ireland, the number of artisans declined steadily, and many manufacturers who had "hitherto been the established employers of numerous workmen" were themselves impoverished "by the stagnation of trade."[32] Faced with pauperization or emigration, 600 of those "who compose the middle ranks of life, and who are the most useful members of society" left in 1797 alone, and the annual number of such emigrants mounted steadily thereafter.[33]

Coterminous with these industrial changes were a whole series of rural changes, generically termed the agricultural revolution, which transformed western European agriculture from a communal activity of peasants on small-scale holdings, to a large-scale capitalist enterprise with a paid proletariat as its labor force. First manifest in the midland and northern counties of England, this conversion derived from the development of new agricultural techniques and the expansion of urban markets. Successive enclosure acts after 1750 implemented the transition by breaking up open fields and replacing them with contiguous holdings. The immediate result was the displacement of innumerable agriculturists who held their land by customary rights but could display no legal title. Furthermore, the position of those who remained on the land was weakened. Large-scale scientific farming, now feasible, put small owners at a disadvantage, and eventually forced many to forfeit their farms.[34] The dispossessed could emigrate to the United States, Canada, or Australia, or they could go to the rapidly expanding cities. England's swelling population, however, set a limit to the number who found employment in urban industries. As early as 1826 a select committee complained that the country was burdened with too much labor, and that the range of industrial opportunities was quickly narrowing.[35] Under these circumstances, those who had managed to salvage anything from the collapse of the old agricultural system, those who still possessed the means for building a new life, chose to migrate. The paupers, the broken in spirit, drifted to the towns.[36]

In southwestern Germany and in Scandinavia similar innovations drove many from their native soil. Unlike the peasants of Prussia and Saxony who in 1800 still retained the servile status acquired after the collapse of the uprisings of the sixteenth century, those of Bavaria, Baden, Württemberg, and the Rhineland were free.[37] In both Norway and Sweden the *bøndar,* the predominant farmers, were also freeholders with extensive, almost aristocratic rights.[38] In all free areas, holdings had shrunk remorselessly through centuries of division and redivision, and tiny plots were a chronic source of discontent among those who found no opportunities at home in a rapidly growing population. Farms had become so small that further division among several heirs was economically impossible. Younger sons could either consent to a reduction in status by becoming day-laborers, or, unhampered by servile obligations, seek fresh opportunties elsewhere.[39]

Decreasing mortality and the consequent rising population between 1800 and 1865 further limited opportunities in the already circumscribed Scandinavian economy. But the situation became critical in the 1840's with the spread of enclosures and the displacement of countless *bøndar.* In that decade the movement advanced rapidly "until the greater part of Sweden south of Norrland and Dalarne had changed village communal ownership to individual farms." This transition inordinately stimulated the volume of emigration which had already started ten years earlier. Thousands of ousted farmers rushed to the seaports to get off to America. Everywhere in Norway and Sweden the fairly well-to-do peasants

33

surrendered their homes and sought elsewhere the opportunities denied them by the change in the system of cultivation.[40]

In Germany increasing pressure on the old agricultural system from new markets for grain and foodstuffs made the situation more acute. The extension of the market was particularly hard upon the southwestern peasant, for it created a tendency toward higher prices and higher rents, made small-scale farming comparatively unprofitable, and stimulated the application of large-scale techniques to agriculture. As a result the next fifty years witnessed a displacement of population similar to that in Sweden.[41] But in Germany as in Scandinavia there were no booming Manchesters or Birminghams into whose factories the peasants could go.[42] Emigration was the only, the inevitable, alternative. After the turn of the century restrictions upon leaving gradually slackened, the prohibition being relaxed as early as 1804 in Bavaria and, after the Wars of Liberation, elsewhere in the southwest. The removal of these restraints and the absence of servile shackles to the land, released a swelling tide, checked only temporarily by the Napoleonic Wars.[43]

Peace in 1815 brought rapid acceleration, and the agricultural depression of 1816–17 carried the movement to abnormally high levels.[44] It developed steadily in the next two decades. In 1846–47 and 1852–55 crop failures in Bavaria and Baden, inevitably accompanied by high prices, further stimulated peasant migration.[45] By that time the web of railroads over southwestern Germany had so increased peasant mobility that the volume of emigration remained consistently high.[46] As a result the number of emigrants, only 1,065 in

1820 and 2,174 in 1830, rose to 32,674 in 1840 and 83,169 in 1850. By 1854 it reached its highest mark, 239,246 and, though it declined thereafter, still numbered 31,360 at its lowest in 1862.[47] Throughout, the desire and ability to leave were confined almost exclusively to the discontented free peasants of southwestern Germany.[48]

Generally then, throughout this period, not the groups without opportunities migrated, but those whose opportunities were narrowing with changes in the economic system. And for a long time the physical difficulties involved in coming to America constituted an additional selective factor. Inland transportation and ocean passage were costly and irregular.[49] Prospective immigrants required more money and information than ordinary peasants or laborers possessed. Indeed, a cautious Scotsman in Boston advised his "countrymen to keep at home if they cannot bring from £500 to £1,000."[50] Above all, newcomers needed ambition and enterprise to carry them through the difficulties of changing worlds. As a result, both the causes and conditions of emigration restricted it to the most prosperous and the most venturesome.

These were not satisfied with what Boston had to offer, for new opportunities were not to be found there. The very conditions which created the impulse to leave directed the emigrants elsewhere. The guidebooks and travel accounts they read spoke clearly enough of what they looked forward to. It was the deep rich soil these books praised most enthusiastically. Cheap land and ideal climatic conditions waiting to be exploited by broad backs and strong arms were the most extolled attractions. For the city they had little but contempt.

35

Equally persistent was the advice to shun the seaboard, to push immediately westward, to settle beyond the Alleghenies at once. Every immigrant was warned, "Go farther west; not until you reach Koshkonong [Wisconsin] will you find America." [51] Hard-working, thrifty agriculturists, whether

Fig. 1. The fortunate pass through Boston to the West

German, English, Norwegian or Swedish, who felt an attachment to the soil and a dislike for confining themselves to the city, did not hesitate to follow this advice. Those able to come could generally well afford to get beyond the seaboard to the west, for they were by no means impoverished when they arrived. [52]

Nor were the artisans more likely to settle in Boston. They had been persons of standing, "not hopelessly and despairingly poor . . . not quite disinherited from the old village economy in which a man did not merely sell his labour but

had some kind of holding and independence of his own." [53]
Usually they managed to salvage a bit of capital to bring with
them, and, selective about their destination, sought new
towns from whose rapid growth and fresh opportunities
they might profit. Many landed in Boston, a fairly important
port of entry; but few remained. Some stayed to act as "run-
ners" or to supply the multitudinous needs of immigrants in
transit; others, because they were stranded. But they were not
numerous. Boston derived its immigrants from the ranks of
neither such artisans nor such peasants; they had sufficient
mobility to seek more fertile fields.

Two conditions were essential before a large immigrant
group would stay in Boston. First, the immigrants must be
more interested in escaping from Europe than in what faced
them in America. Secondly, they must have so little mobility
that, once in Boston, they could not go elsewhere because
poverty deprived them of the means, and despondence of the
desire. For a long time this combination of factors did not
apply to any migration that affected Boston. The indentured
servant, the imported contract laborer, and the conditionally
assisted emigrant who lacked mobility were unknown to Boston during this period.[54] Whatever assistance there was, was
directed away from the city. Aid to Germans was either discouraged entirely, as in Baden where only those who could
pay their own passage were permitted to emigrate, or
planned to create consistent, homogeneous groups, first in
eastern Europe, then in South America, and after the 1820's,
in the Balkans and in Texas.[55] Even when these projects
failed, the various *vereine* promoting immigration and ar-
ranging itineraries looked forward to the Germanization of

37

a single western state. Consequently their routes led directly to the west from New York or New Orleans.[56] Great Britain's assistance was just as persistently directed at strengthening her own colonies, Canada, Australia and New Zealand.[57]

But throughout the early part of the century, across the Irish Sea from England, relentless historic forces steadily neared a culmination which eventually swept thousands of immigrants into a startled and scarcely prepared Boston.

Ever since the treacherous King of Leinster, Dermot Mac-Murrough, fled beyond the sea to call to his aid Henry II, the "Sassenach" King of England, the "dear dark head" of Eire had bent beneath the weight of foreign rulers.[58] But until the seventeenth century the lack of independence had little influence upon the bulk of the people. Subjection began to affect the life of the common Irishman only with the changes in land tenure during the Cromwellian invasions. With Cromwell came a host of land-hungry retainers who had to be satisfied at the expense of the native Irish. The great confiscation created a landlord class of foreign birth and religion while the policy of surrender and regrant destroyed the communal basis of land ownership and concentrated what land was left to the Irish in the hands of a few, reducing the remainder to the position of rent-paying tenants.[59] Ruinous wars decimated the population from 1,300,-000 in 1650 to less than a million in 1660, and confiscations and anti-Catholic penal laws aimed at depriving "the majority of the Irish people of all wealth and ambition," — frankly, "to make them poor and keep them poor." Finally, changes in the land laws destroyed security of tenure, the only safeguard against rapacious absentee landlords.[60]

The dispossessed Irish, forced to rent as tenants at will, had neither fixed tenure nor reasonable freedom from their landlords. Expired leases went always to the highest bidder; the tenant in possession received no preference. The consequent competition for land encouraged a wasteful system of middlemen, and raised rents far above their true value.[61] Normal agriculture proved impossible. The farmers had to concentrate upon rent-paying crops since retention of their precarious hold on the land took precedence over every other consideration. Feeding themselves became a subsidiary matter, solved after a fashion by reliance on the potato. Irish agriculture therefore bore a twofold aspect. Cereal crops and cattle were raised for the market to bring money for rents, while potatoes were grown for food. For this reason grain exports mounted rapidly although very little was available for consumption at home.[62]

Even worse off than the farmers were the cottiers who throughout "remained the fixed substratum of the population."[63] Political changes and changes in land status affected them only remotely, for they had little interest in the former and none in the latter. They were completely landless, neither owning nor having any rights to the soil. From some more fortunate farmer they rented the *use* of enough ground for cabin and potato patch, paying for it by labor for the landlord and by the sale of the ubiquitous pig. The cottiers subsisted on potatoes, to which they occasionally added a bit of milk, these two staples constituting the whole of their diet.[64] Their standard of living was incredibly low. They live, remarked a contemporary, "in such cottages as themselves can make in 3 or 4 days; eat such food . . . as they buy not from others; wear such Cloths as the wool of their own sheep . . . doth make. . . . A hat costs 20d. a pair of stockings 6d. . . . In brief . . . the whole annual expence of such a family . . . of 6 . . . seems to be but about 52s. *per ann.* each head one with another." [65] Their miserable poverty

Fig. 2. Distributing clothing to the cottiers

apathetically perpetuated itself as population grew "disproportionate to the capital and extent of the country," the result "of cheap food and few wants." [66] By the end of the seventeenth century cottiers formed the great bulk of the population, embracing perhaps four-fifths of all families, and their number grew thereafter.

Meanwhile the condition of agriculture continued to degenerate. The growth of population to more than 4,000,000 and the attendant competition for land further raised rents and reduced the size of farms. Infinite subletting and subdivision of land continued until about 1820. Made feasible by the potato diet, it was intensified by the stimulus which Foster's Law of 1784 and the protection provided in the English market after 1806 gave to the production of grain.[67] By 1841, no less than 563,153 of the 691,114 holdings in Ireland consisted of less than fifteen acres.[68] Tiny plots, penal laws, uncertainty of tenure, and the utter hopelessness of deriving more than a bare subsistence, discouraged permanent improvements or replacements, even where the poverty of the farmer did not altogether prohibit them. Irish agriculture seemed doomed to inevitable decay.[69]

By the end of the eighteenth century the great masses of rural Irish accepted the situation as unavoidable. They became reconciled to, if not content with, their inferior status. Since "the labour of one man" could "feed forty," and opportunities for other work were wanting, habits of shiftlessness and laziness developed.[70] By the same token, drunkenness spread among the peasantry and the urban population, particularly when whiskey was cheaper than bread.[71] From time to time hopelessness begot a reckless despair expressed in violent outbreaks which brought swift and merciless reprisals.[72]

The impact of the agricultural revolution upon this economy was bound to differ from that in other countries. The problem facing the landlord — how to adjust the agricultural system to yield a maximum of profit — was immensely complicated by the fact that his land was occupied far beyond its capacity by numerous tenants holding tiny plots on a basis which precluded modernization. To oust the tenants would have undermined the foundations of Tory political power based on the voting rights of the forty-shilling freeholders.[73] And as long as Irish grains had a secure market in England under the provisions of the corn laws and Foster's Law, the landlords willingly suspended action. Relief, they theorized, might come from the extension of the amount of arable land or from the artificial reduction of population. The former they hoped to accomplish by introducing new agricultural techniques and by draining the bogs and swamps; the latter, by encouraging late marriages and continence.[74] Emigration they either resolutely opposed or regarded only as a last resort, an evil to be avoided at all costs.[75]

Nevertheless, there was always some peasant emigration from Ireland, to England at least. Early in the eighteenth century the spalpeen, the itinerant Irishman "going over to reap in harvest," was already a familiar figure there.[76] Every year, the families of hundreds of cottiers whose holdings could not support them "abandoned their dwellings" and went "out to beg through the country" while their men wandered across the Irish Sea, seeking employment as agricultural laborers.[77] By 1820 many walked annually to Dublin, crossed to Liverpool in the steerage at five shillings a head, and after tramping about for months, begging from parish to parish, brought back to Ireland some three pounds.[78] When economic changes created a demand for labor in England many gave up wandering and settled there as industrial proletarians. At the same time Irish farmhands played an increasingly prominent part in England as enclosures created large farms using day laborers. Areas like the West Riding of Yorkshire contained many of these immigrants.[79] By 1841, fully 419,256 persons born in Ireland were permanently domiciled in England and Scotland. London held not less "than one hundred thousand distressed Irish poor" in 1814 and Glasgow, Manchester, and Liverpool contained large colonies.[80] Stimulated by steam navigation across the Irish Channel and by the demand for cheap labor in the construction of the spreading chain of English railroads, the number of migrants continued to grow.[81] Meanwhile a steady movement from southern Ireland to Ulster pushed out many Scotch-Irish farmers who would not "sacrifice . . . comforts which for years they had been accustomed to . . . to pay . . . larger rents." [82] But few of these Irish wanderers reached America; the lack of money was an insuperable obstacle.

The slow siphoning off of Irish population to England brought no relief to those remaining. Throughout the early nineteenth century distress was common. "The country lived in a chronic state approaching famine, and . . . the particular years . . . mentioned . . . as famine years were simply the years in which the chronic symptoms became acute." [83] The slightest failure in any crop brought immediate disaster. A deficiency of potatoes, as in 1822, resulted inevitably in famine.[84]

However, not the impoverishment of the peasants, but the fact that landlords no longer found it politically or economically profitable to keep them on the land, finally caused hordes to flee to America. The precipitate fall in the price of grains after the Peace of 1815, and particularly after 1820, ruined the peasantry and made it difficult for landlords to collect rents.[85] The same drop in prices and competition with other, more efficient agricultural economies convinced the gentry that it would be more profitable to turn land into pasture — a process necessarily involving the consolidation of holdings and the wholesale eviction of tenantry.

Meanwhile, mounting English poor-rates presented an additional threat to Irish landlords. By the 1820's rates in England had reached unprecedented heights.[86] English ratepayers ascribed their difficulties to the Irish paupers in England, and demanded a poor law for Ireland.[87] An act of 1833, permitting English justices of the peace to return Irish dependents to their birthplace, and another, two years later, cutting off aid to nonresidents, aroused bitter resentment in Ireland, for they shifted a heavy burden from English to Irish landlords.[88] Finally, the Irish poor law of 1838 subjected Irish landowners to an incredibly high tax, and at once aroused their eagerness to stimulate emigration.[89] Moreover, they no longer had a political inducement for keeping small tenants on the land since the forty-shilling freeholders had been deprived of their votes in 1829.[90]

To evict prior to 1838 had been dangerous despite a compliant statute of 1816. The ejected had no place to go and, when desperate, constituted a menace to the lives and property of landowners. But the act of 1838 integrated emigration and eviction into a new economic policy. For, one of its leading proponents pointed out, "Emigration would prepare the way for consolidation of farms in Ireland, and for an amended administration of the poor laws in England." [91] The dispossessed could, thereafter, be conveniently and safely lodged in the new workhouses. And since the same law provided for assisted emigration, it was only a step from eviction to workhouse and from workhouse to emigrant ship.[92]

Evictions were inordinately stimulated in 1846 by the re-

44

peal of the Corn Laws which destroyed Ireland's protected position in the English market.[93] The climax came with the great famine which struck directly at the basis of the food supply. The potato rot, first appearing in 1845, dragged the hunger-ridden land for five terrible years through a succes-

Fig. 3. An evictment

sion of miseries and left it an economic ruin.[94] Complete chaos caused an upheaval in the system of land tenure, for the gentry were prepared to take advantage of the cottiers' disaster and drove the peasants, unable to pay rent and no longer politically useful, from their holdings. John Mitchel complained, "There is a very prevalent feeling amongst the landlord class . . . that the people of Ireland ought not to be fed . . . upon the grain produced in this country . . . and that it is desirable to get rid of a couple of millions of them . . . taking advantage of the *panic* which is driving the people away. . . ."[95] The number of judgments of eviction mounted from 2,510 in 1847 to 3,385 in 1848 and 3,782 in 1849. The total number of evictions grew from 90,000 in 1849 to 100,000 in 1850. In 1851 it declined to 70,000 with 40,000 in 1852 and 24,000 in 1853. The evictions of 1849, 1850, and 1851

Fig. 4. Searching for potatoes

Fig. 5. The hunger of women and children

alone involved some million persons, and the process of displacement continued until 1870. By 1861 the 491,300 one-room cabins of 1841 had diminished to 89,400.[96]

Those evicted had but one desire — to escape Ireland and English rule as quickly as possible. In the minds of the people the famine ingrained a dread of the hopeless future and a desire to get away at any cost. Even those who loved Ireland best felt there was no hope in remaining. Nothing could reveal the depth of this despair more eloquently than the panic-stricken letters of John O'Donovan, the antiquarian whose love for Ireland and things Irish was an essential part of his being. "I see no hope for Ireland yet," he said, "the potatoes produced too large a population. . . . I see no prospect of relief for two years or more. The number of poor is too great. . . ." "I am sick . . . of Ireland and the Irish and care very little what may happen; for whatever may take place things cannot be worse. . . . I would leave Ireland with a clear conscience!! I would leave it exultingly, retire among the Backwoods of America . . . move into the deserts of the western world there to learn a RUDE but STURDY civilization that knows not slavery or hunger." [97] The intensity of these ideas in the mind of the scholarly librarian threatened by neither hunger nor slavery, was multiplied a thousandfold in the hearts of millions of cottiers who "stood . . . begging for . . . soup which . . . would be refused by well bred pigs . . ." and daily faced the slavery of the workhouse. [98]

From 1835 to 1865 "the stream of emigration" continued to "flow with unabated rapidity," little affected by conditions in America. Though it fell off somewhat in the late fifties, new landlord troubles in the sixties and the reappearance of the potato rot in 1863 stimulated it again. [99] The movement was cumulative in effect. Those who left early did so with the intention of eventually sending for their families, relatives, and friends. Soon large sums of money streamed back to Ireland to aid others across, a course facilitated when Thayer and Warren started the sale of prepaid tickets to Boston. [100] Meanwhile even those only indirectly affected by the upheaval were drawn into the current of migration. Doctors, lawyers, trades people, and artisans moved from deserted villages where they could no longer find a livelihood.[101] To these were added many Irish who, after first emigrating to England or Scotland, decided to go to America.[102] Not until

Fig. 6. Towing out

late in 1864 did any real slackening in the tide occur. By that time some 2,500,000 Irishmen had abandoned their homes.[103]

Changes in ocean navigation after 1840 conditioned the immense volume of this movement and the route it took. The opening by the Cunard Line of regular transatlantic steam communication in 1842 kept rates so low that even the poor could cross. The Line itself did not engage in the immigrant trade until 1863; but by engrossing other passenger business almost at once, it forced the established packet lines to devote themselves to these least desirable customers.[104] By the fifties, one could travel from Liverpool to Boston on a respectable line such as Enoch Train and Company, Page, Richardson, or Wheeler & Armstrong for from $17 to $20, including provisions — rates which made profitable landlord-subsidized emigration.[105]

With the Cunarders came also a significant modification in the direction of traffic. In the old Black Ball days New York had monopolized the transatlantic packet trade.[106] But the Cunard Line was subsidized by the British government which desired, above all, to maintain swift, direct contact with its colonies.[107] When the Post Office Commission of Inquiry reported in 1841 that the best way to get mail from England to Canada was via Boston, the Line was directed in 1842 to establish its terminus there, and before long others regularly followed its route. Within a few years the Enoch Train Line and Harnden and Company, among others, had added considerably to Boston's importance as an immigrant port.[108]

Low as were the rates, the cost of transportation involved for most the expenditure of their last resources. Sailings occurred from Dublin, Cork, and other Irish ports, but the great packet lines, now specialists in the emigrant traffic, invariably started from Liverpool.[109] At the port of embarkation emigrant funds were inevitably depleted by weary weeks of waiting for passage, and any residue was used up during the long crossing.[110] In New York and in Boston the penniless newcomer landed with no alternative but to stay where he was.

Even less fortunate were those who, lacking the money for

passage to New York or Boston, were forced to go to Quebec, Nova Scotia, or the Maritime Provinces in the empty holds of returning timber ships. From Halifax and St. Johns "these debilitated, half starved human-beings" wandered down the coast, drifting aimlessly, sometimes riding on the cheap im-

Fig. 7. Emigrants at dinner

migrant trains of the Eastern Railroad, until they reached a large city — usually Boston — whose charitable institutions would shelter them.[111] As a result the Tenth General Report of the Colonial Land and Emigration Commissioners found that of 253,224 emigrants to Canada and New Brunswick, more than 73,000 went at once to the United States and an overwhelming majority eventually found their way to New England.[112]

That the Irish hegira was unique has been recognized by the more perspicacious students of population.[113] The nature of its distinctiveness may be gathered from the circumstances that produced it. This exodus was not a carefully planned movement from a less desirable to a more desirable home. This was flight, and precise destination mattered little. The *Cork Examiner* noted, "The emigrants of this year are not like those of former ones; they are now actually *running away* from fever and disease and hunger, with money scarcely sufficient to pay passage for and find food for the voyage." [114] No other contemporaneous migration partook so fully of this poverty-stricken helplessness. There was no foundation for the frequent complaints by Boston newspapers and politicians against the export of paupers from England and the continent; [115] even the German famine-scourged "flight from hunger" was "not characterized by the poverty and helplessness that the Irish exhibited. . . ." [116] And in this respect, the Irish migration also contrasted with earlier ones from that country. Until 1835 the north, Ulster and particularly Tyrone, had been the primary source of emigrants, chiefly displaced artisans and fairly well-to-do farmers — in general the wealthiest elements of the population.[117] The new movement concentrated in the south and in the west, especially in Cork, Kerry, Galway, and Clare, and comprised the poorest peasants, assisted in crossing by the bounty of others. From this group, above all, Boston got her immigrant population.

Imperfect as they are, the statistics of immigration by all groups into Boston reflect this situation.[118] Before 1830 the number landing there annually never exceeded 2,000; before 1840 it reached 4,000 only once (1837). Distributed among many nativities, most were transients, westward-bound. The few Irishmen who settled in Boston in this period came primarily from Ulster and Tyrone.[119] Thereafter arrivals increased rapidly from 3,936 in 1840 to 28,917 in 1849. These newcomers were overwhelmingly Irish. Even the large figures for England and the British North American Provinces represented, for the most part, Hibernians who had sojourned in other countries before finally coming to the United States. By 1850, about 35,000 Irish were domiciled in the city; five years later there were more than 50,000 — almost all natives of the southern and western counties. After 1855 the number of Irish in Boston remained fairly constant. For as the famine subsided, the influx declined, except for brief spurts in 1853 and 1854, to a low point in 1862.[120]

The other foreign groups in the city were exceedingly small. The number of Germans has always been exaggerated.[121] The 2,000 in the city proper in 1850 increased gradually to 3,790 in 1865; and not more than 6,500 dwelt in the entire metropolitan area.[122] The English and British North Americans, as has already been pointed out, were largely of Irish descent. The Scots totalled less than 2,000, while the French, Italians, and Scandinavians were even fewer.[123]

Two groups, the Negroes and the Jews, cannot be numbered by their nativity. For the latter one must rely upon guesses. As far back as the eighteenth century some Spanish and Portuguese Jews lived in Boston. These ceased immigrating after 1800, and by 1840 few remained.[124] A slow infiltration of German and even of Polish Jews in the next ten years brought some 200 families to the city, but they failed to increase noticeably thereafter.[125]

Although the colored man's status was probably better there than elsewhere in the Union, Boston attracted few Negroes. In 1790 there were only 767; in 1820 only 1,690; and in

1850 only 2,085. There were 2,216 in 1855 and 2,348 in 1865, but the census of 1860 disclosed no more than 1,615.[126] Obviously, these figures do not reveal the full number of Negroes because runaway slaves avoided enumeration. But in view of the many circumstances conducive to their settlement in the city, their failure to grow more considerably was surprising. Two conditions were primarily responsible. Boston was not an important station in the underground railway and played only a minor role in the surreptitiously organized scheme of aiding the fugitive slaves from the south to Canada. Furthermore its economic opportunities were so narrow that those who had the courage to risk their lives to escape slavery were hardly content to stay there. In 1830, for instance, a group of fifty already in Boston, led by their Methodist preacher, moved on to Canada.[127] Like all other non-Irish groups the Negroes chose to pass Boston by. Only among the Irish did the motives and circumstance of emigration necessitate settlement under the unfavorable conditions dictated by Boston's economic and social structure.

ꙮ III ꙮ

The Economic Adjustment

*It was sailing by dead reckoning to them, and they saw
not clearly how to make their port so; therefore I suppose they still take life bravely, after their fashion, face
to face, giving it tooth and nail, not having skill to
split its massive columns with any fine entering wedge.
. . . But they fight at an overwhelming disadvantage,
—living . . . alas! without arithmetic, and failing so.[1]*

THE elements conditioning the emigration of the foreigners, together with the social structure of Boston as they found
it, determined their position in the community. These factors
limited the whole orbit of the immigrants' lives in their new
homes. Their work, their health and longevity, their housing, their relations with the government, with their neighbors, and with one another, all were implicit in these two
forces. What drove the Europeans to Boston and what they
found there together produced a new society, far different
from its antecedents, yet unmistakably their heir.

The course of adjustment created a fundamental difference
between two categories of immigrants. Those who quickly
resumed familiar routines easily merged in interests and activities with native Americans. But those whose memories

held no trace of recognition for any feature of the new land, made room for themselves, if at all, only with the utmost difficulty. Many faltered, hesitated, were overwhelmed and lost, because in the whole span of their previous existence they found no parallel to guide them in their new life.

The most pressing concern of all newcomers on landing was to obtain employment. Those whose background had equipped them with an industrial skill or mercantile trade had little difficulty in adjusting to the economic conditions of their new world. Most, however, had escaped into a way of life completely foreign and completely unfavorable to them. Thousands of poverty-stricken peasants, rudely transposed to an urban commercial center, could not readily become merchants or clerks; they had neither the training nor the capital to set up as shopkeepers or artisans. The absence of other opportunities forced the vast majority into the ranks of an unemployed resourceless proletariat, whose cheap labor and abundant numbers ultimately created a new industrialism in Boston. But for a long time they were fated to remain a massive lump in the community, undigested, undigestible.

Since at the beginning, at least, the immigrants did not form an integral part of Boston's economy, it is difficult to know precisely how they managed to exist. They played no role in the usual accounts of her commercial and industrial life. Their contemporaries were aware that Europeans were there, of course, but completely neglected them in describing the business of the city. Save for occasional cursory notices of the number of arrivals, trade papers and journals throughout the forties and fifties consistently ignored the newcomers, and travelers' accounts which did mention them frequently misled, as they often do, by emphasizing the curious rather than the commonplace.[2]

For an accurate analysis of what happened to the immigrant in the maze of Boston's business life one must turn to the cold statistics of DeBow's federal census of 1850, the first to enumerate both nativity and occupations. In Boston it revealed a total of 136,881 inhabitants, of whom 37,465 were adult males; and it listed the vocations of 43,567 persons.[3] From the marshals' schedules of this census, the raw data have been classified in Tables XIII and XIV to determine the incidence of various employments in the city and their distribution within each nativity group.[4]

The 43,567 persons for whom material was available were engaged in over 992 distinct pursuits — an average of no more than forty-four persons per occupation in the entire city.[5] This widespread diversity emanated directly from Boston's complete orientation towards small-scale skilled enterprises and away from large-scale unskilled ones. As the nucleus of an important economic area, the town contained a multitude of retail trades. The center of a prosperous urban life, it encouraged the growth of highly skilled handicrafts to satisfy the demands for consumers' goods. Commercial rather than industrial in character, it possessed no large-scale establishments and therefore no great accumulations of labor in any industry or trade.[6] Broad occupational diversification was normal and inevitable in this society.

Viewed according to the nativity of those employed, this heterogeneity was particularly significant, for it reflected the economic health of any group within the city. A high degree of dispersion denoted the presence of considerable numbers of trained workmen, retailers, and merchants who conformed closely to the city's economic pattern. A low degree indicated a deficiency of such elements and presaged a period of difficulty in adjustment.

Table XIV, which gives the number of employed persons in 1850 with the number of occupations and the average number of persons per occupation of each nationality, proves that a general average for the entire city actually understates the extent of diversification. All nativities but one had far fewer persons per occupation than the city as a whole. The average varied almost directly with the number employed. Massachusetts with 13,553 had an average of 20.53; the rest of New England with 7,986 had an average of 14.16; British North America with 1,381 had an average of 7.31; and Germany with 929 had an average of 6.07. As the group grew smaller, its miscellaneous character progressively increased.[7]

The Irish formed the one exception. Their average, twice as high as any other group's, alone approached that of the entire city. While the 13,553 persons of Massachusetts birth worked at over 660 different occupations and New England's 7,986 at 564, Ireland's 14,595 were confined to only 362.[8]

The unusual degree of Irish concentration in an economic organization where dispersion was the rule arose from their convergence in two unskilled employments. A single occupation accounted for 48 per cent of the total Irish laboring force, another for almost 15 per cent more, and a third for 7 per cent.[9] In each of the other nativity groups represented in Charts A and B, no single vocation busied more than 20 per cent of the total working population. In each, the three most popular occupations employed between 24 and 50 per cent of

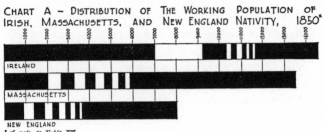

CHART A – DISTRIBUTION OF THE WORKING POPULATION OF IRISH, MASSACHUSETTS, AND NEW ENGLAND NATIVITY, 1850*

IRELAND

MASSACHUSETTS

NEW ENGLAND
* cf. note to Table XIII.

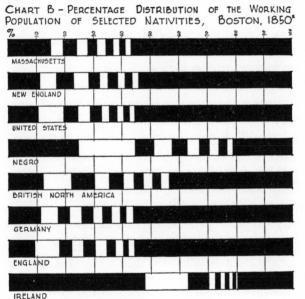

CHART B – PERCENTAGE DISTRIBUTION OF THE WORKING POPULATION OF SELECTED NATIVITIES, BOSTON, 1850*

%

MASSACHUSETTS

NEW ENGLAND

UNITED STATES

NEGRO

BRITISH NORTH AMERICA

GERMANY

ENGLAND

IRELAND
* cf. note to Table XIII; for legend, cf. Chart A.

the total, with the remainder of the workers engaged in from forty-three (in the case of the Negroes) to 657 (in the case of Massachusetts) different employments. By contrast, the three most popular occupations among the Irish included more than 70 per cent of the whole, and the ten most popular accounted for more than 80 per cent, leaving only 20 per cent divided among the residual 352.[10]

The concentration of nearly 65 per cent of the Irish working population in two occupations was an anomaly forced upon them by the conditions of their arrival. The vast majority left their ships in East Boston without the slightest conception of how they would earn a livelihood and with only enough money to keep them fed and sheltered for a week or two. "Unable to find employment or transportation elsewhere, . . . without one penny in store, the question, how they should live, was more easily put than solved."[11] Some had the way partly cleared by relatives or friends who assisted them; others managed to go west or to more prosperous eastern cities; and not a few, immediately discouraged by the "overstocked labor market," turned back to Ireland.[12] But most were completely immobilized; the circumstances that brought them to Boston compelled them to remain there, to struggle on as best they could.

They faced exhausting difficulties in making a place for themselves in the city's economic life. There was no one to help them; the hard-pressed Catholic priest and the overburdened benevolent and immigrant-aid societies could assist only a few.[13] Many fell into the clutches of the "Intelligence Bureaus" and the "Swindling Shops," traders in human misery which fleeced the guileless strangers.[14] More generally, the Irish relied upon their own simple ingenuity in finding employment. Tramping the crooked streets from shop to shop, they might, if they were fortunate, find someone to use their heavy labor. Frequenting the docks, watching the arrival of ships from across the water, they sometimes met a short-handed stevedore boss or wharfinger.[15] They procured casual employment on the streets or in the public works that were transforming the physical aspects of the city. But every element of selectivity was denied them. The pressing need for immediate earnings destroyed the possibility of choosing a job or preparing for a trade. Want swept them into the ranks of those 7,007 unskilled, insecure day laborers who informed the census takers that they were just laborers — a classification descriptive not of their function, but of their lack of function.[16] Well might the good Irish priest, Dr. Cahill, lament that "the emigrants from Ireland . . . to escape the horrors . . . of the emaciating poorhouse fly to this country with barely the passage money; and they have often landed . . . [without] a single penny! . . . It is a clear case that these poor friendless strangers, having no money, must have recourse to their only means of subsistence — namely, street or yard laborers or house servants." [17]

No other nationality depended so heavily upon unskilled work. There were 1,545 laborers in the city other than Irish, but in no group did they form a significant proportion. Among the natives no more than 5 per cent were so employed, and only the Negroes and the Germans had as much as 10 per cent. But even in these cases the actual number was small: 115 Negroes and 107 Germans.[18]

An employed laborer could not earn enough to maintain a

family of four. And as long as the head of the Irish household obtained nothing but sporadic employment, his dependents lived in jeopardy of exchanging poverty for starvation.[19] Supplementary earnings — no matter how small — became crucial for subsistence. The sons were first pressed into service, though youngsters had to compete with adults willing to work for boys' wages. To keep the family fed, clothed, and sheltered the women also were recruited. In Ireland they had occupied a clearly defined and important position in the cottiers' economy. That place being gone, they went off to serve at the table of strangers and bring home the bitter bread of banishment.

There was room in the comfortable households of Boston's middle classes for the Irish daughter or sister who wished to lighten her family's load by supporting herself and perhaps contributing a little something besides. There had long been an acute shortage of domestics in New England. Generation after generation of housewives had either done their own work or paid relatively high wages to natives who insisted on being "help," not servants. The supply of such labor had been extremely unsatisfactory and transitory in character. Most Americans "would rather want bread than *serve* to gain it," and farm girls in service for a few years while waiting to be married usually lacked the essential attributes of servility and loyalty.[20] Under these circumstances the "Irish help" were triply welcome for their good spirits, their loyalty, and their cheap wages. In all hotels and in thousands of native homes Bridget became a familiar, indispensable figure.[21] By 1850, at a conservative estimate, 2,227 Irish girls worked as domestic servants in Boston.[22]

For all other groups, the percentage in service was uniformly low.[23] None numbered more than 10 per cent, and of these, many were governesses and housekeepers rather than menial servants.[24] To some extent this preponderance of Irish domestics sprang from the greater percentage of females among the immigrants from Ireland; but above all, it derived from the pressing need to send women out to help support the family.

The tenuous character of their status drove the Irish into a constant search for better jobs and more secure employment. All aspired to skilled positions that would enable them to support their families alone. But the reluctance to employ Irishmen in any but the lowest capacities, added to their lack of capital and of training — itself an insuperable obstacle — rigorously excluded them from such occupations. Early attempts to ban foreigners from certain professions by law had failed,[25] but by 1845 the caption "None need apply but Americans" was familiar in Boston newspaper advertisements.[26] Prejudice became more intense as competition for jobs grew keener, though it proved no formidable barrier to those who had a trade to ply or a skill to offer. But while other groups filtered into the city and were accepted, the Irish remained unneeded and unabsorbed. The few who arrived with professions, or rose from the ranks of the unskilled by a gradual process of recruitment, did not leave the mass.

The degree of their penetration into any trade varied inversely with its desirability. Employments involving an element of personal service and therefore repugnant and degrading to Americans, quickly fell to the lot of the Irish. Many found work in the care and service of horses, the city's chief transport agent. As these trades called for menial labor of a rather low sort, few competed with the Irish for them. By 1850, more than 300 of the 877 smiths, more than those of any other nativity group, were Irish. The hostlers and stablers were also predominantly Irish, although the stablekeepers, who needed capital, were not.[27]

The same divergence prevailed in services to men as well as to beasts. Everywhere the waiters were Irish, while the skilled cooks were not.[28] Barbers, also skilled workers, were traditionally Negroes, and the elegant and fashionable hair-dressers and *coiffeurs* were Frenchmen or Italians.[29] With these exceptions the Irish had the service occupations almost entirely to themselves.

In the truly skilled employments, however, their percentage was low indeed. Only in the building trades did they have any opportunity at all, and that because Boston, like most American cities, was passing through a construction boom. The wealthy merchants were building grand residences down Beacon Hill and on toward the newer Back Bay. The middle classes, moving out to East and South Boston, were erecting hundreds of new dwellings. By their very presence even the Irish created a demand for more housing. They preëmpted the slums and the low rental sections of the city, pushing out the former inhabitants and stimulating the demand for new abodes. In 1843, more than 1,118 new structures were reared, and the annual number grew thereafter.[30] As a result labor was in demand. The various building trades embraced some 5 per cent (775) of the total Irish working population. This compared unfavorably with the 11 per cent (1,594) of Massachusetts birth and with that of the other nativities.[31] But it represented skilled employment for a significant section of the Irish community by which some actually acquired enough influence and capital to become contractors and construction bosses.[32]

In the other skilled occupations and handicrafts, most of which had been well developed before 1845 and did not expand thereafter, the Irish were, in the main, unimportant. They numbered only twenty-eight of the total of 450 employees in the maritime industries, and made no headway in furniture building or cabinet making, where highly trained workmen were needed. Nor did they progress very far in the crafts dealing with precious metals or with the manufacture of musical instruments.[33] Among the ordinary mechanics and machinists their proportion was smaller than any other group's, and relatively few became transport workers, truckmen, coachmen, or even sailors.[34]

They were more poorly represented in the commercial occupations than in the handicrafts. Though many fancied the dignity and independence of the traders' status, few attained it. Among the Irish immigrants were some shopkeepers and merchants who had followed their customers to the New World. A handful of others had accumulated a modicum of capital and longed to join the large and prosperous group of retail distributors of all sorts who supplied the necessities of life to Boston and its hinterland. In most branches of retailing, however, they competed directly against the superior skill and resources of other groups and were doomed to failure from the start.[35]

In some spheres immigrants had an advantage over their native competitors. Where they relied on the patronage of their compatriots they prospered. Food dealers — butchers, fruiterers, and, above all, grocers — dealt directly and intimately with immigrant women who preferred to purchase from those who spoke their own language, carried familiar foodstuffs, and served them as a friend, confidant, and adviser. Each national group, therefore, supported a comparatively large number of grocers and food dealers. With the exception of the Irish and Negroes, newcomers did not suffer by comparison with the native whites.[36] Among the Irish, as among the Negroes, deficiencies of capital and skill weighed more heavily in the balance, and their percentage of such retailers was lower than in any other group.[37]

For the humble immigrant the easiest ingress to commerce was through its least elegant form, peddling. Peddlers needed no permanent place of business. They required only a small capital investment and but passing acquaintance with trading methods. With their stock upon their backs they could move among their countrymen, deal with them on terms of confident familiarity, and earn a respectable livelihood. These inducements were attractive enough to draw approximately 2 per cent of the Irish, and even larger contingents from other groups into itinerant trading.[38]

In other forms of minor retailing involving close personal contacts, each nativity group created a demand for the services of its own members. Inevitably, a circle of saloons, restaurants, boarding houses, and a few hotels catered to foreigners. Germans would never think of residing or dining where they might have difficulty in securing their lager. It comforted the Irish to hear the old country brogue and feel the security of being with their own kind. Like the McGinnis in

Mrs. Dorsey's novel, most immigrants added to their income by keeping a few lodgers of their own nationality.[39] To meet the needs of the unmarried, of sailors, and of those who had either not yet settled down in the city or were on their way west, every group — particularly the Irish and Germans — provided a large number of boarding houses.[40] There were also German lunchrooms, restaurants, and *lager-bier* saloons, Irish bars and dance halls, and even some English coffee houses. From these enterprises many foreign-born saloon-keepers and bartenders earned their livings.[41]

The abundance of boarding houses and saloons was encouraged by, and in turn caused, a paucity of hotels. Hotel-keeping was a substantial business managed and owned by Americans, and none of the foreign establishments in Boston ever gained as high a reputation as the Revere or Tremont House. There were, no doubt, a few Frenchmen and Italians who became prominent as purveyors of food in the genteel tradition of Continental cookery. Although a place always remained for the puddings and *bombes* of the *confiseurs*, even the high esteem in which that tradition was held and memories of the great Julien did not sustain Nicholas Ouvre, Gallieni, and the other *pensionaires* and *restaurateurs* very long.[42] Only those supported by an adequate foreign clientele survived. By the forties the French and Italian places declined visibly. In 1846 Antoine Vigne gave up the Perkins House, a "tremendous establishment" in Pearl Street, and moved to New York where he opened the *Hotel de Paris* on Broadway.[43] No Irish hotel existed in the city until Henry Dooley, a jovial host from the British American Provinces, took over the Merchants Exchange on State Street.[44]

Prospering from the favor of the Irish societies which met there, it remained the only important foreign public house in the city.[45]

If the Irish progressed only slowly in the handicraft and retail trades, they made no impression at all on the financial occupations central to the city's commercial life. Merchants and bankers constituted the keystone of Boston's prosperity. Linked with them were the salesmen and agents, and at a yet lower level, the store clerks and bookkeepers, indispensable cogs in the functioning of the business machine. These classes, despite the differences among them, were all high in respectability and economic position. Theirs was the most favored place in Boston life. The foreigners such as the Frenchman, P. P. F. Degrand, and the Spanish Jew, Abraham Touro, who entered into these ranks, were conspicuous chiefly for their singularity.[46]

Generally, the only opportunity for aliens to figure in commerce or finance grew out of the patronage of their own communities. Foreign ship agents frequently saved enough from the profitable business of remitting funds to Ireland to engage in banking operations for their compatriots. The Tri-Mountain Insurance Company was directed by and at the Irish, and the Germania Life and Germania Fire Insurance Companies, by and at the Germans.[47] The New England Land Company united the prominent Irishman, Patrick Donahoe, with several well-known Bostonians (among them the Know-Nothing mayor, J. V. C. Smith), in a scheme to move the Irish to the west, and a number of other immigrant-controlled real estate agencies prospered.[48] But the commercial community was overwhelmingly American. Almost 90 per cent of all the merchants — 3.4 per cent of the total native working population — were native born. In no foreign group were the merchants proportionately or numerically significant. They ranged from .5 per cent of the group in the case of the Germans to 1.4 per cent in the case of the English. The Irish, as usual, lagged far behind, with only .1 per cent. In the lower categories the non-American groups played as small a role. More than 86 per cent of the agents and 88.2 per cent of the clerks were Americans, while only 4.2 per cent and 3.6 per cent, respectively, were Irish.[49]

The fact that Americans had somewhat recently entered the professions complicated the same basic pattern in that field. At one time Europeans had played a fairly prominent part in the city's professional life. In 1794 the number of qualified Americans was so limited that the builders of the Middlesex Canal advertised for a supervising engineer in French.[50] By 1850, however, the native professionals outnumbered the foreign born in every field, though in all but the government services, where Americans always predominated, the non-Irish immigrants were proportionately as important. These classes amounted to between 3 and 5 per cent of the total of each nativity group, except the Irish, which had only .2 per cent.[51]

In some spheres foreigners usually retained an advantage. They dominated the plastic arts and monopolized the dance, both as performers and teachers. Boston ladies insisted upon taking lessons from Mr. Williams of London, M. Duruissel of Paris or, most of all, from the glamorous Lorenzo Papanti of Leghorn.[52] They liked to study foreign languages either with Frenchmen or Italians, particularly when combined

The Economic Adjustment

with "tuition on the Piano Forte." [53] There were many prominent foreign musicians. The Englishman Hayter and the German Zeuner, the Frenchman Du Lang and the redoubtable Irishman, Patrick Gilmore, established firm reputations. But the rank and file of professional musicians and music teachers were American-born, as were instructors in most other branches of education.[54]

A small number of professionals served their own conationals. A few taught in evening and commercial schools, catering to the special needs of immigrants.[55] All groups demanded priests familiar with their ways and using their own language. Likewise, they preferred lawyers of their own kind, friends they could understand and trust when it was necessary to cope with the law or the government.[56] It comforted the Germans to learn that their doctor was a relative of the oculist to the King of Saxony, and the Irish to believe that their apothecary or physician had practiced for twenty-seven years in County Kerry.[57]

The exceptional Irishman who found satisfactory employment failed to mitigate the abject circumstances of the group as a whole. With no adequate outlets in the handicrafts, in commerce, or in the professions, the rank and file remained totally or partially unemployed. In this respect they differed from every other element. Unabsorbed laborers in other groups were more than counterbalanced by their skilled conationals already integrated in the scheme of Boston life. Even the Negroes, who stood closest to the Irish in occupational experience, fared better than they. Emancipation before 1790 did not wipe away the stigmata and disabilities of slave status. It was always difficult to acquire education, skill,

69

or capital, and the prejudices of the classes immediately above confined the Negroes to unpopular tasks.[58] Yet, though their employments were not particularly desirable or well paid, they had specific functions. Negroes were acquainted with the by-ways of Boston's economic organization, and, as time went on, adapted themselves to it. They did not remain simple unskilled laborers to the same extent as the Irish. Despite the risk of being sold as slaves on long voyages, many became seamen; others were barbers, chimney sweeps, and traders.[59] Some, like Robert Morris, a prominent lawyer, even rose to the professional ranks. By the time Walt Whitman visited Boston in 1860 the Negroes were better off there than elsewhere in the United States.[60] While their position shone chiefly by comparison with less fortunate members of their race, it was clearly closer to that of the natives than the Irish.[61] The latter unquestionably were lowest in the occupational hierarchy.

But unless it contained a reliable and constant productive element, no group could continue to subsist by employment in the service trades and by dealing with one another. As it was, the large body of casual, unskilled Irish labor created tremendous social problems and called for more adaptations than either the individual or his family could make for long. Though only a temporary escape was possible, the temptation to try it was great.

Paradoxically, the same immobility that rooted the Irish immigrants in Boston also drove them out to work in all parts of the United States. Surplus labor was an unthinkable anachronism in the body of American economic life. In so many places cheap labor was essential, yet lacking, that it was inevitable the Irish should be used for more productive purposes. In the west, in the south, and in Canada vitally important projects awaited the application of their brawn. From every part of the United States construction bosses in embankments and water projects, tunnels, canals, and railroads called on Boston for the cheap man-power they knew was always available there. Thus the city's role as labor reservoir assumed national proportions; often the Boston Irish newspapers, in single issues, printed advertisements for more than 2,000 men wanted in widely scattered places.[62]

Sooner or later the immigrant in search of employment discovered the labor contractor in search of men. In the columns of their weekly newspapers they saw, or heard read to them, the incredible, tempting advertisements detailing the blandishments of good wages, fine food, and excellent lodgings. The attractions of steady employment were hard to resist. True, railroading meant living a riotous camp life and the absence for a year from women, family and friends, and from the ministrations of the priest. But these partings were not novel to Irish life, for many sons and daughters had already left the family to earn a living. Moreover, before coming to America, the men had been accustomed to this type of migration; each fall the spalpeens had left their plots on the "ould sod" and crossed the Irish Sea to work for English landlords. In Boston as in Ireland, the wives and children remained behind to shift as best they could, sometimes assisted with occasional remittances, often becoming a burden upon the community. In any case, within a year the laborers were back, usually no better off than before.[63]

Unscrupulous exploitation was the theme of the construction camp; and dirt, disorder, and unremitting toil were its invariable accompaniments. Wages ranged from $1.00 to $1.25 a day, though skilled stonelayers and masons often got from $2.00 to $2.50.[64] The more prudent contracted for board as part of their pay, or for their upkeep at a flat weekly rate.[65] But most were victimized by rapacious sub-contractors who monopolized supplies in isolated construction camps and took back in exorbitant prices what they paid out in wages.[66] The railroads themselves frequently resorted to equally dishonest practices. The Irish, after traveling several hundred miles, had no recourse when the company decided to pay less than it had advertised. Many roads, by deliberately asking for more men than they needed, built up large labor reserves with which to bludgeon down the wages of those already working for them. With reason enough, the *Boston Pilot* advised "all laborers who can get employment elsewhere to avoid the railroads . . . to . . . do anything . . . in preference to 'railroading.' "[67] But the Irish were the guano of the American communications system. "Ferried over the Atlantic, and carted over America," despised and robbed, downtrodden and poor, they made the railroads grow.[68]

Back in Boston, the quondam railroaders, like those who stayed behind, still faced the problem of securing permanent employment. Some found openings of a sort as sweepers and janitors in the textile factories of neighboring cities. These were the most wearisome jobs in the mills, the least skilled and the lowest paid — the ones the native operatives would not take. Mill owners soon perceived the potentialities of this docile labor supply. The New England girls who had been working in the factories were independent, militant, and impermanent. "Amateur" rather than "professional" proletarians, they left abruptly when marriage set them free for their true careers. Their insistence upon decent working conditions proved burdensome and led to increasing costs, particularly after Sarah Bagley started the Lowell Female Labour Reform Association in 1845.[69] With men available at rates lower than those paid to women, the manufacturers turned to the Irish to run their machines, raising them from the meaner chores to higher ranks, and eventually using them for all tasks. And, as immigrants invaded the textile field, it lost status; native girls became more reluctant to enter it. By 1865, male employees outnumbered females in woolens and were gaining on them in cottons.[70] Foreign labor, for which Boston served as a convenient recruiting ground, manned both.[71]

Almost as important as textiles was the shoe industry. Before 1850 it had been loosely organized on a handicraft household basis as a supplement to fishing and farming.[72] When the first practical shoe machinery was invented, cheap labor in nearby Boston facilitated the transition to the factory system in towns like Quincy and Lynn. "Green hands," anxious to be exploited, replaced skilled artisans, enabling the "garret bosses" to reap tremendous profits and become large-scale manufacturers.[73] Throughout the fifties and the Civil War the presence of a labor surplus in Boston stimulated infant industries and accelerated the process of industrialization in New England.

This transformation of New England followed the general shift from craftsmanship towards mechanization in all phases of American economy. Emphasizing cheapness and mass production rather than skill, it required an abundant supply of labor. Wherever this essential condition existed, the trend left its impact; without it the change could not be effected. The process was particularly significant in Boston where a consistent deficiency af labor had seriously hampered the growth of industry until the forties. Between 1837, when the first business census was taken, and 1845, the total number of employees in the city's major industries (all those which at any time between 1837 and 1865 employed 100 persons) probably did not increase at all.[74] Few grew significantly, and many actually declined. The prospective manufacturer desiring a site for a new establishment, or the capitalist with an "abundance of money seeking an outlet," found little encouragement. And even those already established who wished to expand were inhibited by the apparently inflexible labor supply.[75]

But in the two decades after 1845 the Irish energized all aspects of industrial development in Boston by holding out to investors magnificent opportunities for profits from cheap labor costs. The total of industrial employees doubled between 1845 and 1855, and again between 1855 and 1865. Between 1837 and 1865, the number of workers in the older industries rose from 9,930 to 33,011, and, in addition, 6,272 appeared in new ones.[76] Meanwhile the stream of immigration through the early fifties replenished the supply of workers already drawn off into factories, and their presence guaranteed a continuance of low prices. Because it possessed this labor reserve after 1845 Boston could take advantage of every opportunity. Within little more than two decades it became the nation's fourth manufacturing city.

There was the ready-made clothing industry, for instance, which had grown appreciably in Boston since its inception by John Simmons in the early thirties. At first an adjunct to the trade in secondhand apparel, then a part of the ship store business which supplied "slops" to sailors on shore leave, it eventually turned to producing cheap garments for southern slaves, for western frontiersmen, and for California miners to whom considerations of style and fit meant little.[77] Until the mid-century, however, Boston was at a disadvantage with New York. Her rival on the Hudson was as accessible to supplies and, as a greater seaport, catered to more sailors and enjoyed more intimate connections with both the south and the west. Wages were also lower in New York, at least to 1845, and the cost of labor was the most important as well as the most variable factor in production, since the industry always "tended to concentrate at the points of cheapest labor."[78] As a result Boston remained behind, unable to compete on equal terms with New York.

Yet it was an exceedingly tempting industry promising high profits if only a way could be found of producing clothes good enough to command a wide market at a price lower than those made in New York. But cheap clothes depended upon cheap wages; and until 1845 the labor force consisted entirely of the ordinary journeyman tailors who worked primarily on custom clothes. The "ready-made" clothiers, unable to pay the same wages as the custom tailors, were compelled to produce only during the twenty-eight weeks or less each year when the journeymen were not busy at their usual work. On this basis the industry could never develop to significant proportions. No matter what degree of standardization the technical process of manufacturing reached, the absence of a cheap labor supply precluded conversion to factory methods. Machines alone could not create a factory system in Boston when only the 473 tailors employed in 1845 were available to man them.[79]

The situation changed, however, with the influx after 1845 of thousands of Irishmen ready to work for any wages. The manufacturers fully realized how important these immigrants were; and on the occasion of a journeymen's strike in 1849 they pointed out to Mayor John P. Bigelow that they had no need of his services as arbitrator, for an abundance of other labor sources was available to them.[80] Henceforth they expanded their business, firm in the assurance that profits would not be menaced by labor costs or strikes. Erstwhile peasants were unskilled, of course, and knew nothing of tailoring. But the simpler parts of the trade were not difficult to learn and it was profitable to press the raw immigrant into service at wages which no true tailor would consider. The invention of Howe's sewing machine in 1846 in Cambridge came just in time to facilitate the training of the Irish by mechanizing and simplifying the sewing operations.[81] By 1850 the 473 tailors of 1845 had grown to 1,547, of whom more than a thousand were Irish.[82] The Civil War brought rush orders for thousands of uniforms and capped the process of expansion.[83] By 1865, these circumstances had produced a distinctive method of factory production known in the trade as the "Boston System." Achieving an ultimate exploitation of cheap hands, it combined machinery with an infinite division of labor "which completely eliminated the skilled tailor." [84]

The factory failed to emerge during this period in New York primarily because of the absence of the labor surplus that made it possible in Boston. Instead, the pressure for cheaper costs led to the growth of the outside shop where the efforts of the entire family were utilized.[85] As a result Boston manufacturers gained an advantage, for the factory system permitted them to reduce wages while producing more *per capita*. The average value of the goods turned out there by a single worker in 1860 was $1,137 as compared with $788 in New York.[86] Moreover the New York employers paid from $8.00 to $10.00 a week for labor, and the Bostonians only from $4.50 to $5.50.[87] These differentials more than offset New York's other advantages. On this basis George Simmons' "Oak Hall," employing 3,000 tailors, became a national institution by 1860 and the whole industry in Boston quadrupled the value of its products between that year and 1870.[88] By then the city had become the center of the factory manufacture of ready-made clothing in the United States, a position it retained as long as cheap labor was available.

Precisely the same development revolutionized other industries. Because of the relative importance of transportation costs, Boston, like New York and Philadelphia, had early become a sugar refining center.[89] In the first four decades of the nineteenth century sugar boiling was a highly skilled but small occupation, carried on in Boston largely by German artisans. Before 1845 the industry employed only about a hundred persons.[90] In the forties, however, a series of mechanical inventions necessitated a complete change in plant and process. All over the country refineries, unable to make the adjustments, closed their doors.[91] In Boston, those surviving put more money into expanded factories, and hired additional hands. The number of employees, many of them Irish, tripled between 1845 and 1855; and the industry grew rapidly after 1858 when the Adams Sugar Refinery built the country's second largest plant in the city.[92] The manufacture of paper hangings experienced a similar transformation. When J. R. Bigelow entered the business in 1841, it was organized on an individual handicraft basis. By 1853 it became completely mechanized and Bigelow's factory itself employed 200 workers.[93]

Many old industries forced out of business by high costs before 1850 resumed on the basis of cheap immigrant labor, and many which suffered no radical change expanded because the surplus of wage-earners was available. In 1848, Jonas Chickering boasted that he employed one hundred men in his piano manufactory; when his sons opened a new plant in 1853 they required 400. Meanwhile the Mason & Hamlin Organ Company opened a mammoth factory in the West End and the total number of workers in the industry rose from 368 in 1845 to 1,248 in 1855. A shortage of hands would have thwarted growth indefinitely.[94]

The creation of new industries most clearly exemplified the importance of cheap labor. The expansion of Boston after 1845 was truly remarkable, particularly in the heavy industries where strong muscles counted most. Scores of new factories, drawing upon the services of hundreds of Irishmen, sprang up in East and South Boston. In 1837 only 776 persons were employed in casting furnaces, in copper and brass foundries, and in making machinery; by 1845 this number had grown to only 859. But in the next decade it almost tripled. By 1855 2,412 persons worked in these industries and an additional 1,097 in new rolling mills, forges, and rail factories.[95]

Fig. 8. Casting room, Alger's Iron Works, East Boston

In this decade, at least seven important iron works began operations in Boston. The Hinckley and Drury Locomotive Works, one of the earliest, expanded steadily after 1848 until it employed four hundred men regularly. Between 1846 and 1848, John Souther launched the Globe iron works, manufacturing locomotives, the first steam shovels, and dredging and sugar mill machinery, an enterprise which alone eventually employed four hundred laborers. In 1847, Harrison Loring built the City Point Iron Works to make engines, machinery, and iron ships. During the same year the Bay State Iron Company was founded in South Boston, and within the next few years, Hawes and Hersey, the Gray and Woods Machine Company, and Chubbuck and Sons established plants in Boston. Meanwhile the older Alger works broadened its own activities rapidly.[96]

In 1845 Donald McKay moved his shipyards to East Boston where he started the most active works in the country.[97] This marked the beginning of a resurgence of shipbuilding in the city. Only eighty-six persons worked in shipyards in 1837, and but fifty-five in 1845. But ten years later the number had increased to 922 and the business flourished thereafter.[98] And this growth characterized all types of industry. Felton and Sons developed their distilleries in South Boston; and James J. Walworth brought his steam fitting and foundry shops from New York, setting up plants in Boston and Cambridge. In these years, too, the Boston Rubber Shoe Company, Robert Bishop and Company, and the Shales and May Furniture Company opened important factories in the city. Upon the discovery of oil and the development of kerosene, the Downer Kerosene Oil Company and the Jenney Manufacturing Company established prominent refineries in Boston. The invention of the sewing machine created an industry which employed 168 persons in 1855 and 245 in 1865. The manufacture of glass found a place in the city in the fifties when machinery made possible the employment of unskilled labor, while the shoe industry and the cognate tanning business drifted in from suburban regions in response to cheap labor costs founded on the presence of the Irish.[99]

In the development of the new Boston the Irish woman was almost as important as the Irish man. When other forms of employment failed her, she turned to the ultimate expedient of women who needed money, sewing at home. The labor of women was used in the domestic manufacture of men's shirts, of women's dresses, and of millinery, where the "making" operations were simple enough to be carried on without supervision.[100] Wages were abysmally low; by constant toil a good seamstress might earn as much as $3.00 a week, but most received as little as $1.50 — just enough for a single woman to pay her rent.[101] For this pittance hundreds of women toiled under miserable conditions through all hours of the day

> Sewing at once with a double thread
> A shroud as well as a shirt.

Home sewing had always existed, but after 1845 an increasing number of women found it their only support.[102] By 1856 more were seeking such work than could find it, though a single large firm such as Whiting, Kehoe and Galouppe sent material out to more than 8,000 women in the city and through all parts of New England.[103] Many German, English, and native women participated, but most were Irish.

To find employment outside the home was a refreshing release from such conditions. After 1846 occurred a gradual but emphatic shift by Irish women to the factory manufacture of women's garments.[104] By 1860 there were at least ten large establishments in Boston, some of which employed as many as one hundred girls to produce cloaks, mantuas, and dresses.[105] After 1850 the number of immigrant women in all types of industry increased steadily until by the time the War broke out they were prepared to step into whatever places men left vacant. In 1865 fully 24,101 women of native and foreign birth were employed in Boston as compared with 19,025 men. Apart from the 19,268 women workers in the clothing trade, there was a significant number in other occupations, many even in heavy industry.[106] The majority of the workers were Irish who, like their men, were contributing an element of fluidity to Boston's economy.

Therein lay the significance of the Irish in the city's economic life. Before their arrival the rigid labor supply had made industrialization impossible. It was the vital function of the Irish to thaw out the rigidity of the system. Their labor achieved the transition from the earlier commercial to the later industrial organization of the city. Without it "the new and larger establishments could not have been operated." [107] Capitalists readily admitted that they could not "obtain good interest for their money, were they deprived of this constant influx of foreign labour." [108]

Those who benefited most from the transition were native Americans. Very few foreigners were manufacturers.[109] English merchants, like Boott and Lodge, did invest in industrial enterprises, and some Irish and Germans figured prominently in fields where they could readily exploit the labor of their own countrymen. Thus, the Irish firms of Carney and Sleeper and of Mahony and Kenna, and the German, Leopold Morse, were among the leading clothing makers.[110] Contrary to the rule, a few other businesses remained in the hands of the immigrants who founded them: John Donnelly, "city bill poster," who helped establish modern outdoor advertising, William S. Pendleton, an Englishman who introduced lithography into the United States, and two highly skilled German silversmiths maintained their positions.[111] But generally Americans gained control even of the piano industry, the manufacture of glass, brewing, and other industries established in Boston by alien newcomers.[112]

Immigration advanced other classes in the community as well as the manufacturers. Since the Irish could not satisfy their own needs, others had to. Irishmen needed doctors and teachers; they consumed dry goods and food, thereby quickening the city's commercial life. The demand for professional and commercial services directly aided the merchants and clerks, the traders and artisans, — the bulk of the American population of the city. A rise in the prevailing occupational level of the native Bostonians resulted from the general decline in labor costs and the increased value of their own services.

The only Americans who suffered permanently from the Irish invasion were the unskilled laborers and domestics, few in number, who competed directly with the newcomers. More important, although they eventually adjusted to the new conditions on favorable terms, was the injury to the artisans displaced by the combination of machinery and cheap labor.[113] They were a large group, eminently respectable, hitherto prosperous, and always influential in the community. Their protest against the use of green hands was one of the significant factors complicating the social orientation of the Irish in Boston.[114]

But though the industrial workers as a class lost ground throughout the period,[115] and though most of the individuals within that class suffered immediately by the transition, in the end they gained. The flexibility of the economic organization of the United States enabled the displaced artisans to set up as manufacturers, to enter other trades, or to move west. Edward Everett Hale pointed out:

We are here, well organized, and well trained, masters of the soil. . . . It must be, that when they come in among us, they come to lift us up. As sure as water and oil each finds its level they will find theirs. So far as they are mere hand-workers they must sustain the head-workers, or those who have any element of intellectual ability. Their inferiority . . . compels them to go to the bottom; and the consequence is that we are, all of us, the higher lifted because they are here. . . . If into the civilized community made up of hand-workers, and workers in higher grades, you pour in an infusion of a population competent at first only to the simplest hand-work, they take the lowest place, and lift the others into higher places. . . . Factory . . . and farm work comes into the hands of Irishmen. . . . Natives . . . are simply pushed up, into foremen . . . , superintendents . . . , railway agents, machinists, inventors, teachers, artists &c. . . .[116]

And the experience of all other groups, even of the Negroes, was similar to that of the native whites. With the minor exceptions occasionally noted above, there was little to distinguish them occupationally. Only the Irish stood apart.

The lads who left Skibbereen and Mallow and Macroom where daily wages ranged from sixpence for common laborers to one shilling sixpence for carpenters, the spalpeens who fled from Cork and the west where cash was scarce, received higher pay in Boston.[117] Of that there was no doubt. They came expecting better wages and got them. Those who once measured their income in terms of potatoes found dollars, no matter how few, a fair return indeed. But mercilessly linked

84

to these fine dollars was the price system, a ruthless monster which devoured the fruits of Irishmen's labor before they could gather them. The "pratties" and milk were gone from their garden; the garden itself was gone; and there was no room for the pig in Dock Square. Faced for the first time with the necessity of purchasing their own food and clothing, the peasants found costs high beyond anything they could have conceived, and rising rapidly throughout this period.[118] By contrast, the much more leisurely increase in

CHART C
WAGES AND COST OF LIVING. 1830-64[x]

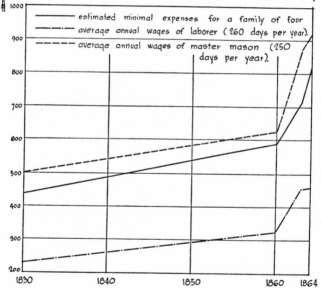

————— estimated minimal expenses for a family of four
—·—·— average annual wages of laborer (260 days per year).
— — — average annual wages of master mason (250 days per year).

[x] *Derived from Third Annual Report of the Bureau of Statistics of Labor...1872, pp. 517-520.*

wages counted for little.[119] The British consul noted that in spite of the rise in wages "it may be doubted if more food and raiment can be purchased by the workman than previously." [120] As a result, the Irish found the value of their labor low, often too low to support them and their families.[121]

The conditions of work were as bad as its price was low. The laborers and their employers spoke a different language. Their work week in Ireland had not included Sundays, but in Boston they must toil the full seven days.[122] Their day at home had not excluded time off to chat, to smoke, or just to rest; now they had to accept the rigid discipline of the factory or the contract boss. The leisurely independent peasant life was ended — replaced in a fifteen-hour working day by a feverish struggle for bread under the commands of an alien master.

But no matter — if only that struggle were consistently successful. It never was. From the day they landed, the immigrants competed for jobs that were fewer than men. Through all these years unemployment was endemic to the economic system. Even the Civil War brought no surcease; the condition of labor deteriorated steadily. The depression of the first year threw great masses of men out of work, particularly in industrial South Boston, where they starved in their hideous slums.[123] Not until the war had drawn thousands of men into the army and stimulated new manufacturing developments did the demand for labor approximate the supply. By that time employers were making hurried efforts to attract new immigrants — new workers to restore the labor surplus.[124]

Tossed in the swell of impersonal economic currents, the

Irish remained but shabbily equipped to meet the multifarious problems imposed upon them by urban life. Rising prices, ruthless factory exploitation, and unemployment caused "the wreck and ruin that came upon the Irish race in the foreign land!" In the new society "one in a hundred may live and prosper, and stand to be looked at as a living monument of . . . prosperity, but ninety-nine in a hundred are lost, never to be heard of." [125]

✐ IV ✐

The Physical Adjustment

How shall your houseless heads and unfed sides,
Your loop'd and window'd raggedness, defend you
From seasons such as these?

BOSTON'S economic transformation set apart one whole
section of society — the unskilled, resourceless, perennially
unemployed Irish proletariat, whose only prospect was absorption into industry at starvation wages. In every phase
of their reaction to the new environment, economic maladjustment complicated a process relatively simple for other
groups. This factor far overshadowed other aspects of Boston's ecological development. By their immobility the Irish
crammed the city, recasting its boundaries and disfiguring its
physical appearance; by their poverty they introduced new
problems of disease, vice, and crime, with which neither they
nor the community were ready to cope.

Up to 1840 Boston had easily accommodated the gradual
increase in residents, of whatever nationality, for it was well
on the way toward a solution of its urban problems. Slowly
and often laboriously it had surmounted the original limitations constricting its area. By 1845 the peninsula on which it
perched was no longer isolated from the mainland. The Mill

Dam obviated complete reliance on the sandy neck, at one time subject to frequent floods; and bridges tied the city to Cambridgeport, Charlestown, and South Boston, while a ferry linked it to East Boston. With the extension of transit facilities, it was no longer necessary for those who worked in the metropolis to live within walking distance of " 'change." Filling operations in the flats created new land and precluded the possibility of an acute shortage of space. Widespread building prevented overcrowding and led to a notable scarcity of slums. The rise in the number of persons per dwelling was probably "more than overcome by a larger and better class of houses," for facilities kept pace with the demand.[1]

After 1840, however, growth by immigration — completely unexpected and at a rate higher than ever before — violently upset the process of physical adjustment.[2] In 1845 the foremost authority on demography in Boston confidently asserted that there could be no further increase in inhabitants.[3] Yet the next decade witnessed the injection from abroad of more than 230,000 souls, of whom enough remained to raise the population more than a third and to convert a densely-settled into an overcrowded city.[4]

Those who were able to break away from the most congested portions of the town's center continued to have no difficulty in securing adequate and comfortable lodgings in many neighborhoods. The rustic villages surrounding Boston eagerly awaited the realtor who might turn abundant farm lands into metropolitan avenues, and welcomed alike foreigners and natives, financially able to escape from the teeming peninsula.

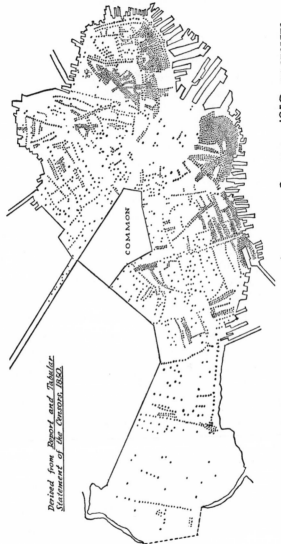

Derived from *Report and Tabular Statement of the Censors, 1850*

MAP I. DISTRIBUTION OF THE IRISH IN BOSTON. 1850. BY STREETS

COMMON

Primarily, this centrifugal movement winnowed the well-to-do from the impoverished, and consequently segregated the great mass of Irish within the narrow limits of old Boston. There was no such isolation in the distribution of other newcomers throughout the city. Once having secured employment, which their backgrounds enabled them to do more readily than the Irish, they easily adjusted the routines of their old lives to new homes. In some instances, several German, French, or English families resided on the same street, but generally there were no French, German, or English districts.[5] For heterogeneous pursuits scattered these aliens everywhere and limited numbers permitted them to slip at will into almost any section without altering its essential characteristics.

Although some Irish joined the exodus, the overwhelming number remained where they were. Their poverty, combined with Boston's geography, assured that. Unlike every other American city, Boston was completely waterlocked, with no direction in which its people could move without the payment of tolls or fares. Those who could not afford to pay twenty cents per day to go back and forth to the environs, necessarily sought accommodations within short walking distance of their daily fifteen-hour drudgery in the mill or at the wharf.[6] Even those who occasionally worked elsewhere felt compelled to keep close to the source of new assignments.[7] The peaceful suburbs of Roxbury and Dorchester, the quiet streets and roomy houses, were not for them.

Instead, they clustered about the commercial heart of Boston — the narrow peripheral strip of piers and the small area on the peninsula proper pivoting about State Street and ex-

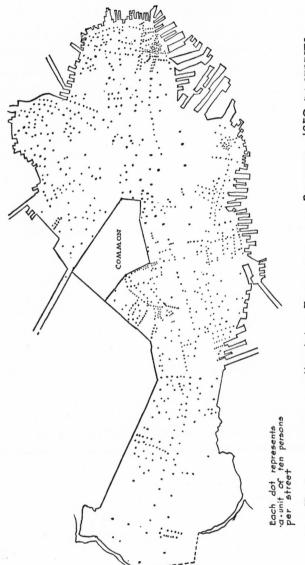

COMMON

Each dot represents
·a·unit of ten persons
per street

MAP II. DISTRIBUTION OF NON-IRISH FOREIGNERS IN BOSTON, 1850, BY STREETS

tending from the water front westward to Washington Street and from Water Street north to Ann. Here were the city's most important enterprises, its docks and markets, offices and counting houses, stores and work-shops. Intertwined with this section, in a long line down Washington Street and its extension, Ann Street, was the garment district, for the merchant was still the manufacturer and his shop the factory.[8] In this region tailors and unskilled laborers were most apt to find work.

Within easy reach of these crucial districts were two centers whose development made them the logical receiving points for the Irish proletariat. Above Ann Street, stretching from Commercial to Causeway Streets, was the North End, always the most congested part of the city. South of Water Street was a similar neighborhood encompassing Fort Hill and Pearl Street and extending to include the South Cove, made land created by filling operations in the 1830's.[9] Both the North End, which in its more prosperous days had contained many fine mansions, and the less elegant but eminently respectable Fort Hill, had once been purely residential, but the encroachment of trade impaired their fashionableness, draining off many old dwellers.[10] Nevertheless, the very proximity of business gave real estate a highly speculative value. Because it was unprofitable to make or maintain improvements where there was a "marked discrepancy between the value placed on the property by the owner and its value for any uses" to which it could immediately be put, landlords permitted their buildings to deteriorate.[11] Their prime object was to avoid expense and to rent at a price sufficient for mere upkeep while waiting to sell.

In this transition originated the Boston slums — precisely the housing the Irish needed. Near the wharves and cheap in rent, these localities became the first home of such immigrants in Boston. Newcoming Irishmen, nostalgic for the Emerald Isle, gravitated towards these vicinities, augmenting the number of Irish already there, and making their countrymen reluctant to leave the home-like community even when they could. As a result, there were few natives in the North End and Fort Hill and even fewer non-Irish aliens, for these groups fled, sacrificing other interests in order to avoid the decline in social status that resulted from remaining.[12]

Several towns convenient to these two primary Irish settlements received those who, "leaving the low and reclaimed land to foreign laborers, plant themselves in the suburbs . . . availing of the frequent omnibuses, or of special trains" to reach the city.[13] Each of these districts experienced approximately the same evolution. At first penetrated only by the very rich, and then by other natives, and English, Scots, and Germans, they gradually attracted some of the more affluent Irishmen after 1845. When industries existed in these places the employees sought homes nearby; but as long as the cost of transportation continued high, the Irish poor who worked in Boston were prevented from commuting. They surmounted this last obstacle only in the 1850's when the horse-railroad stretched from Scollay Square throughout the whole metropolitan region and threw open sections which theretofore had preserved their exclusiveness by steep rates. The laws which chartered these lines limited fares to five cents and provided for round-trip tickets at six and eight cents,

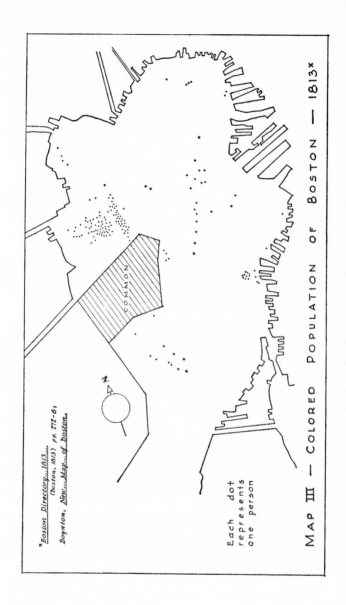

Boston Directory... 1813...
(Boston, 1813) pp. 272-6.
Boynton, *New... Map... of Boston.*

COMMON

N

Each dot
represents
one person

MAP III — COLORED POPULATION OF BOSTON — 1813*

loosing a floodgate and, by the 1860's, inundating the out-skirts of Boston with Irish immigrants.[14]

The West End, Charlestown, the South End, and even the remotest environs, felt the shift in population. As the Irish preëmpted the North End and South Cove, the original in-habitants of every class abandoned their homes to move into the West End, which then included some of the choicest resi-dences in the city, particularly on the south side of Beacon Hill. Though only the wealthiest lived there at first, those of more modest means entered early and increased in number when the former began to drift into the newly filled Back Bay after 1857.[15] The West End became a stronghold of mid-dle-class homes with luxurious fringes of moneyed elegance and shadier ones of poverty and vice. The more sordid quar-ters centered in "Nigger Hill" on the north side of Beacon Hill. Although more than half the city's Negroes concen-trated there, they took up only a small part of it, primarily in Belknap (now Joy) and Southac (now Phillips) Streets, where they had lived in their highly combustible houses since the turn of the century.[16] In addition, there was a cos-mopolitan mixture of bars, sailor dance halls, and low board-ing houses that were of special concern to the police, and that had early earned a disagreeable reputation as a "horrid sink of pollution." [17]

Most of the West End was respectably American, however. Until well in the 1850's, Irishmen and, indeed, other foreign-ers were few in number.[18] But soon, the trend which was to transform the area after the Civil War, began. The small in-dustries in the upper West End attracted many Irish; and the horsecar line to Watertown and Cambridge, passing through

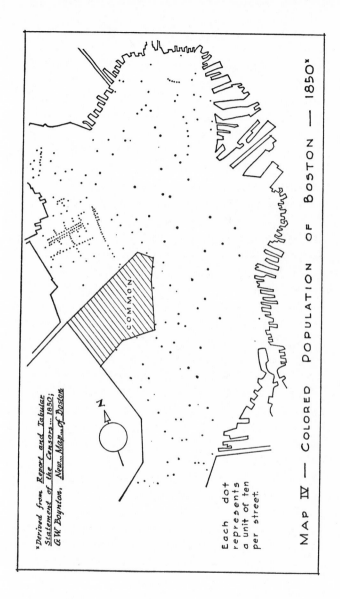

*Derived from Report and Tabular Statement of the Censors...1850; G.W. Boynton, New...Map...of Boston.

Each dot represents a unit of ten per street.

MAP IV — COLORED POPULATION OF BOSTON — 1850*

the heart of the district in 1858, enabled many workers to live there and commute at a nominal rate, so that the proportion of Irish grew constantly thereafter.[19] Following the route of the street railroads, they also crossed into East Cambridge, joining the nucleus of their countrymen already established around the glass works and other factories. Stimulated by the cheap five-cent fare of the Boston and Lowell Railroad, and by the opening of rapid transit service in 1856, they pushed the natives ever further into the dim reaches of Old Cambridge, Watertown, and Arlington.[20]

Other outlying suburbs paralleled this movement. In the 1830's Charlestown, linked to the North End by the Warren and Charles River Bridges, was still "a place almost wholly occupied by people of English descent." [21] But the Irish advance along the Middlesex Railroad (chartered 1854 to Somerville), added to those already employed in the Navy Yard, drove the earlier settlers into the rural wastes of Anglo-Saxon Somerville. By 1860 approximately 10,000 of Charlestown's 25,000 inhabitants were Catholics — almost all Irish.[22]

South Boston, once the seat of many opulent country homes, experienced a similar transition. Although in 1847 its residents still boasted that it contained "not a single colored family" and only immigrants "of that better class who will not live in cellars," changes were already impending.[23] The erection of the South Boston docks created a demand for common wharf labor, satisfied, at the beginning, by the influx of Irish hands; and the remarkable development of manufacturing there after 1840 accelerated this process. The neighborhood did not become thoroughly working-class until after the Civil War, but many poor Irish drifted in throughout the period, particularly after the Dorchester Railroad in 1857 and the Broadway Railroad a few years later made it accessible to those employed elsewhere.[24]

The newcomers edged the natives and even some Irish just beyond South Boston into Dorchester. This town was still thoroughly rural in 1855. But by then the Irish had already so far penetrated into Washington Village, the sector nearest Boston, that it seceded and joined South Boston.[25]

Somewhat more gradual, but ultimately as conclusive, was the development of the Neck or the South End. Its settlement had proceeded slowly, for, as an investigating committee discovered in 1845, none would live there unless they worked there.[26] After the extension of Washington, Harrison, and Suffolk (later Shawmut) Streets, and the introduction of horsecars (1856) through the South End to Roxbury, the Irish trickled into the area.[27] Their representation nevertheless was limited, composed largely of intelligent tradespeople and mechanics, and confined north of Dover Street in a minority among their neighbors. For throughout this period the South End, still a desolate marsh and less desirable than other suburbs, was yet too expensive and inconvenient for the slum dwellers of the North End and Fort Hill.[28]

Its extension, Roxbury, was even more isolated by high fares. Although by 1850, fully 40 per cent of Roxbury's population were foreigners or children of foreigners, these were primarily prosperous groups and included many non-Irish.[29] Only the opening of the street railroads in 1858 exposed Roxbury to the masses who thereafter moved in, forcing their predecessors back into West Roxbury and Dedham.[30]

Noodle's Island, East Boston, eventually the most important outskirt, lay across a narrow arm of Boston Bay. The East Boston Company, founded in 1833 to exploit its real estate, met with slight success until 1840, when the Cunard Line assured the future of the Island by fixing its western terminus there. The construction of piers and the subsequent necessity for stevedores attracted many Irish. In 1850 the introduction of Cochituate water ended the dependence upon wells and increased the capacity of the island. By then, a steam ferry shuttled across the Bay every five minutes transporting as many as 14,000 passengers each day for a two-cent fare and facilitating the migration of many North-Enders.[31] The isolation of Chelsea, the town beyond East Boston, persisted until the Winnisemet Ferry, closed before 1830, was replaced. But after the establishment of the Boston and Chelsea Railroad through Charlestown and the Winthrop Railroad through East Boston, even this remote community added to its population from the continuous drift out of peninsular Boston, and only such towns as Malden, Brighton, and Brookline, without direct connections, were unaffected.[32]

This process consolidated the lines drawn between the Irish and other groups by the city's economic evolution. Almost all the non-Irish, free to take advantage of the rise of contiguous towns, dispersed everywhere, never concentrating in a single section. But although rapid transit permitted some Irish to move out of the densest areas, most remained in the hideous slums of Fort Hill and the North End, subject to all their rotting evils.

Wherever the Irish proletariat resided, distinctive accommodations appeared to meet their extensive demands and limited ability to pay. Upon their arrival they could not hope to find truly permanent homes, for few had any notion of where to live or work. Coming without funds, they shifted about until they found a situation and earned enough to pay the initial costs of establishment. But even employment did not solve their problem, for their jobs were invariably low-paid and transitory. Their every-day expenses, subtracted from their wages, left only privation in the balance. It took years to accumulate even meager reserves, and many never managed to save enough to furnish a flat, much less to buy a home. Unable to afford domiciles of their own, they lodged awhile with friends, relatives, or countrymen; no matter how cramped the quarters of those already settled, there was always more room for the sake of rent, charity, or kinship. Such makeshifts were unsatisfactory, however, and a durable solution awaited the development of the only quarters thousands of Irishmen could afford.

The ultimate housing of the Irish required an extensive process of adaptation on the part of Boston real estate. The simplest form was conversion of old mansions and disused warehouses into tenements. In many cases, boardinghouse keepers, wishing to profit by the new demand, took over properties which, after a few alterations, emerged as multiple dwellings. In other cases, a sub-lease system developed, whereby a contractor, usually Irish himself and frequently a neighborhood tradesman, leased an old building at an annual rental, subdivided it into immigrant flats, and sub-rented it at weekly rates. Sometimes the structure passed through the hands of several agents, completely severing control from ownership.[33] Solely interested in immediate income, having the welfare of neither the building nor the tenants at heart, sub-landlords encouraged a host of evils, while the occupants suffered from their "merciless inflictions." [34] By this metamorphosis "houses . . . long inhabited by the well-to-do class of people, are vacated by them for others in more fashionable quarters . . . and then a less fortunate class of folk occupy for a while, — they, in their turn,

Fig. 9. View of tenements in Stillman Street

to make room for another class on the descending scale . . . till houses, once fashionable . . . become neglected, dreary tenement houses into which the families of the low-paid and poverty smitten . . . crowd by the dozens. . . ." [35]

Despite its lack of conveniences or sanitation, and its general inflammability, the remodeled type was far superior to any other available to the Irish. While those adapted from factories, as was Chickering's old Franklin Square plant, were unrivaled in their perniciousness, even the barracks in Stillman Street in the North End had some benefits of light, air, and privacy (Fig. 9).[36] Whatever the intention of proprietor or lessee, transformed buildings could not utilize space as carefully as those created specifically for immigrants.

New dwellings, completely free of restrictions, displayed every stratagem for economy at the expense of the most hum-

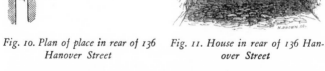

Fig. 10. Plan of place in rear of 136 Hanover Street   *Fig. 11. House in rear of 136 Hanover Street*

ble amenities. The prevailing architecture on hitherto unused space in the peripheral Irish areas such as the West End, South Boston, and East Boston, was characterized by many flats along a narrow passageway. In 1857, for instance, Samuel Hooper reared two four-story wooden edifices with brick ends in Friends Street Court, each holding thirty-two one-room apartments to which the sun never penetrated. A narrow path, fourteen feet wide, half obstructed by a row of privies and water hydrants, separated the two blocks. In Institute Avenue a similar development centering in an alley of only ten feet, exploited the available plot even more thoroughly.[37]

Within the focal points of Irish concentration, however,

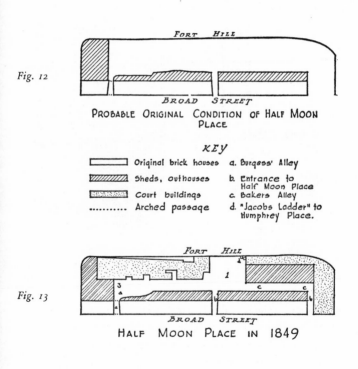

Fig. 12

FORT HILL

BROAD STREET

PROBABLE ORIGINAL CONDITION OF HALF MOON PLACE

KEY

▭ Original brick houses	a.	Burgess' Alley
▨ Sheds, outhouses	b.	Entrance to Half Moon Place
▦ Court buildings	c.	Bakers Alley
·········· Arched passage	d.	"Jacobs Ladder" to Humphrey Place.

Fig. 13

FORT HILL

BROAD STREET

HALF MOON PLACE IN 1849

the price of real estate was too high to permit like constructions. Instead, enterprising landowners utilized unremunerative yards, gardens, and courts to yield the maximum number of hovels that might pass as homes. The abundant

Fig. 14. View of Half Moon Place

grounds surrounding well-built early Boston residences, and the hitherto unusable sites created by the city's irregular streets, once guarantees of commodious living, now fostered the most vicious Boston slums. Every vacant spot, behind, beside, or within an old structure, yielded room for still another.[38] And eventually, to correct the oversight of the first

Fig. 15. Burgess' Alley. North view.

builders who had failed to exhaust the ultimate inch, their more perspicacious successors squeezed house within house, exploiting the last iota of space. This resulted in so tangled a swarm that the compiler of the first Boston atlas gave up the attempt to map such areas, simply dismissing them as "full of sheds and shanties." [39]

106

Fig. 16. Burgess' Alley. South view.

The whole brood of evils typical of this development materialized in Half Moon Place (represented by no. 1 in Fig. 13 and pictured in Fig. 14) and the two alleys leading off it. This pest hole consisted of a very limited tract, originally vacant, between the rear of the Broad Street tenements and Fort Hill (Fig. 4). A rise in the value of land led to the excavation of additional portions of the hill, and the erection of tottering rookeries with their backs flush upon it.[40] Not one of these melancholy warrens, moldering at their very conception, opened directly upon a street. The inhabitants of the central court (no. 1, Fig. 13; Fig. 14) and Bakers Alley (c in Fig. 13) emerged to the main thoroughfare through two gaps between the Broad Street buildings (b, Fig. 13), but the less fortunate denizens of Burgess Alley (a, Fig. 13, Figs. 15, 16) made their way through an arched crevice in the house in front of them (Figs. 13, 17). From Half Moon Place there was, as well, a battered staircase, "Jacob's Ladder," which led to the comparative heaven of Humphrey Place above.[41]

Fig. 17. Entrance to Burgess' Alley

Remodeled or new, these dwellings promoted a steady succession of evils, constant factors in the deterioration of the physical aspects of Irish life in Boston. No standards of decency and comfort were too low for erstwhile occupants in Ireland of crammed "hovels . . . without floors, without furniture and with patches of dirty straw." [42] The one evil of which Boston houses were free was excessive height, for most had only two or three stories — a blessing not to be underestimated.[43]

Immigrant rents were everywhere high beyond all reason because of the system whereby middlemen demanded dual and sometimes triple profits, and secured returns greater than on any other real estate in the city. In the Fort Hill district in 1845, the meanest accommodations commanded

$1.00 or $1.50 per week per room; an attic could not be gotten for less than $1.50, and a cellar, for $2.00, all paid weekly in advance.[44]

The failure of building to keep up with the increase of population and the steep cost of apartments bred overcrowding. In 1845 Shattuck warned that the area north of Beach Street could never hold more than 80,000 people with safety.[45] Yet ten years later more than 90,000 resided there.[46]

The Irish sections were the most congested in the city and immigrant homes felt a consequent strain upon living resources.[47] They were "not occupied by a single family or even by two or three families; but each room, from garret to cellar [was] . . . filled with a family . . . of several persons, and sometimes with two or more. . . ."[48] Every nook was in demand. Attics, often no more than three feet high, were popular. And basements were even more coveted, particularly in the Fort Hill area; by 1850 the 586 inhabited in Boston contained from five to fifteen persons in each, with at least one holding thirty-nine every night.[49]

Underground dwellings enjoyed refreshing coolness in the hot summer months and coal-saving warmth in the winter — important advantages in resisting the vicissitudes of Boston's climate. But with these benefits went many drawbacks. Built entirely beneath the street level, they enjoyed no light or air save that which dribbled in through the door leading down, by rickety steps, from the sidewalk above. Innocent of the most rudimentary plumbing, some normally held two or three feet of water, and all were subject to periodic floods and frequent inundations by the backwater of drains at high tide. Above all, there was little space. Some windowless vaults no more than eighteen feet square and five feet high held fourteen humans. That marked "A" in Figure 18, for instance, was no more than six feet in any dimension, with no ventilation except through bedroom "B" (Fig. 19). In some, two or more bedrooms huddled next to a parlor-

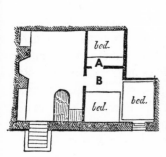

Fig. 18. Plan of Cellar in Bread Street

Fig. 19. Subterranean bedroom in Bread Street

kitchen which often served as bar or grocery as well. These were by no means exceptional. A committee of philanthropists reported in 1849 that cellars generally contained a "grocery and vegetable shop; and not infrequently, a groggery and dancing hall . . . ," and mournfully concluded, "As might be expected, intemperance, lewdness, riot . . . enter in and dwell there." [50] Despite a suggestion in the following year that such holes be outlawed, their number increased and they continued to draw high prices.[51] Indeed, the Irish population could not have been housed without them.

The most serious danger inherent in immigrant quarters

was the complete neglect of sewerage equipment and sanitation of any kind. In many cases, especially in houses "originally designed for warehouses and . . . converted . . . as economically as possible," the absolute lack of facilities obliged the occupants "to supply their necessities as best they" could.[52] Where drainage systems existed, they were inefficient and insufficient. The roads near Fort Hill were ungraded and in vicinities such as the South Cove and the Mill Pond the marshy ground had settled so that "the imperfect sewerage . . . originally provided" had become "altogether useless."[53] Usually residents relied on yard hydrants and water-closets "exposed to the transient custom of tenants or outsiders" alike.[54] Many houses had "but one sink, opening into a contracted and ill-constructed drain, or . . . into a passageway or street, and but one privy, usually a mass of pollution, for all the inhabitants, sometimes amounting to a hundred."[55] No one was responsible for the care of these communal instruments, and as a result they were normally out of repair. Abominably foul and feculent, perpetually gushing over into the surrounding yards, they were mighty carriers of disease. To make matters worse, lack of direct access to the streets in court dwellings made the disposal of rubbish a burdensome problem, most easily solved by permitting it to decay at its leisure in the tiny yards, a process which converted the few feet between adjoining buildings into storehouses of accumulated filth.[56]

The description of Half Moon Place by the Cholera Committee (1849) shows the result such conditions produced. "A large part of the area is occupied by . . . twelve or fourteen privies, constantly overflowing, and by ill constructed and worn out sinks and drains, into which are hourly thrown solid substances, of all sorts, which choke them up and cause the liquid . . . to run over. Into the area . . . a steep . . . staircase affords a passage to Humphrey place, some fifty feet above. Side by side with the staircase, and fully exposed, a large, square, plank drain makes a precipitous descent, conducting, half hidden, half revealed, not only the waste waters of the houses in Humphrey place, but also, the contents of its privies to the area below; which, as may be supposed, is redolent of the fact." [57]

Tenants relied on their own resources in securing heat, and therefore few succeeded in warming their rooms to any degree of comfort. Coal and wood were expensive, particularly since, "being too poor to be economical" and "obliged to buy in small quantities" they had to "pay . . . at least double . . . for wood and coal . . . [by] the bundle and the basket . . . there being neither money . . . , nor place for storage of articles bought in larger bulk." [58] For many the only means of outwitting the cold was to remain in bed throughout the day.[59] Under the circumstances small rooms were an advantage. But rooms were not only small; they were also low, dingy, and suffocating. In the Fort Hill buildings, air and light were complete strangers; either the hill behind or the Broad Street houses in front excluded them. Ventilation shafts were often no more than two feet square. Windows, where they existed, were always closed to keep out the stench of the yards in summer, and the bitterness of the wind in winter. In passage structures, of course, only the top floor saw the sun at all.[60]

In the absence of care and of proper facilities remarkable exertions were required to maintain a minimal standard of tidiness. Rooms were unpainted; closets were rare; furniture, inadequate. Want of any equipment beyond the rudimentary bed and table, a few chairs, and the ubiquitous washtub, necessitated scattering clothing and other articles wherever they might fall or, at best, hanging them on pegs. Baths were unheard of; inside water was uncommon, and the apartments with their own water supply few indeed. Walls were damp, roofs leaked. Stairs were generally dilapidated, windows were often broken, and many buildings had not felt the hand of the repair man in ten or more years. Decay and slothfulness led directly to the prevalence of fires which involved great loss of life and much suffering.[61]

Slovenliness and disorder were inevitable in the squalor of such conditions. "In such a state of things, there can be no cleanliness, privacy, or proper ventilation . . . ; and, with the ignorance, carelessness, and generally loose and dirty habits which prevail among the occupants, the necessary evils are greatly increased both in amount and intensity. In Broad Street and all the surrounding neighborhood . . . the situation of the Irish . . . is particularly wretched. . . . This whole district is a perfect hive of human beings, without comforts and mostly without common necessaries; in many cases, huddled together like brutes, without regard to sex, or age, or sense of decency; grown men and women sleeping together in the same apartment, and sometimes wife and husband, brothers and sisters, in the same bed. Under such circumstances, self-respect, forethought, all high and noble virtues soon die out, and sullen indifference and despair, or disorder, intemperance and utter degradation reign supreme." [62]

Inadequate housing, debarment from the healing sun, and inescapable filth took their toll in sickness and lives. Boston had been a healthy city before the 1840's, a city in which the life-span was long and disease rare. Smallpox, for instance, no longer existed by 1845. Although an unusually large number of cases had cropped up in 1839 and 1840 because of the relaxation of regulations in 1838, there had been no major epidemic since 1792. [63] But after 1845 the pestilence flourished, particularly among the Irish. [64] Nor was this the only scourge miserable living conditions bred to plague the city. Year after year endemic or contagious maladies returned to haunt the depressed areas. [65] In 1849 the cholera spread from Philadelphia and New York to Boston. Despite feverish efforts to halt it, the epidemic swept through the congested courts in the hot summer months, reaping a full harvest of victims with a severity "fully accounted for by the deplorable conditions of the emigrants from Europe." [66] It thrived best in places "least perfect in drainage, the worst ventilated and the most crowded," that is, in Irish districts. [67] The distribution of 611 fatal cases and ninety-six other identifiable ones coincided to a remarkable degree with Irish slum sections. The worst outbreaks occurred in the rear of 136 Hanover Street, Burgess Alley (200 cases), Mechanics Court, and the rear of Batterymarch Street, especially prominent points of Irish concentration. [68] Most of the patients in East Boston likewise resided in neighborhoods like Liverpool Street and "in every instance . . . the houses were without proper *drains*. . . ." In all, more than 500 of the 700 fatalities were Irish, or the children of Irishmen.[69]

More vicious in the long run than the spectacular ills were those which, conceived in squalor, quietly ate away resistance before delivering their final blow. Most important was tuberculosis. This disease had declined in Boston until 1845, but thereafter revived in the hovels of the Irish on whom it fattened year after year, reaching the unprecedented peak of 4.57 deaths per thousand living in 1855.[70] The impact of miserable environment was even more pernicious upon the children of the slums than upon their parents. This period witnessed a rise in infant mortality, attributable primarily to three products of foul surroundings — intestinal disorders, pneumonia, and bronchitis.[71] All three appeared overwhelmingly among the Irish, and, in the opinion of Dr. Howard Damon, superintendent of the Boston Dispensary, the first, including "diarrhœa, cholera infantum, and dysentery," certainly depended "upon two very distinct causes of insalubrity, — overcrowding and imperfect drainage."[72]

Irish longevity, low enough in the homeland, dwindled because of the debilitating crossing and the disheartening conditions in America. So many died soon after arrival that it was said the Irish lived an average of only fourteen years after reaching Boston.[73] Their coming consequently raised the death rate unexpectedly after 1845. Before then it had increased from 2.04 per cent for the ten year period ending 1830 to 2.20 per cent for the decade ending 1840, and to 2.53 per cent for the five years ending 1845, a rise due almost exclusively to the ever larger proportion of elderly people.[74] Far from lowering the mortality, as the injection of a young and medium-aged group should have, the immediate effect of immigration and of the diseases and hardships attending settlement in Boston, was to boost it even further to 2.94 per cent for the five-year period ending 1850. This was twice as high as for the rest of Massachusetts, and higher even than the English slums. After 1850 when the initial shock of transplantation wore off, the rate tended to revert to the level of 1845, with 2.74 per cent for 1850–55, 2.39 per cent for 1855–60, and 2.42 per cent for 1860–65. But though immigration had decreased the proportion of aged people in the city, the death rate still remained above that of most comparable communities.[75]

Mortality was actually not uniform in all groups. In sections inhabited by Americans and other non-Irish it was as low as outside the city, particularly before 1850 when the Irish had not yet spread, carrying disease with them. In that year the death rate was only 1.3 per cent in the Beacon Hill district, where there were but 561 foreigners, chiefly servants, in a total population of 2,615, and only 1.92 per cent in the Back Bay area, where there were 1,348 aliens in a population of 5,121, and these chiefly German; but in Broad Street and Fort Hill where 2,738 out of 2,813 were not natives, and almost all Irish, it was fully 5.65 per cent.[76] One out of every seventeen Broad Street Irishmen died in 1850. As the population scattered, the proportion of deaths in the various regions evened out somewhat; the disparity in 1855 was not as radical as in 1850, and in 1865, even less so. But distinctions did not completely disappear. In 1865 there was still a differential of 1.39 per cent between the North End and Beacon Hill.[77] On the basis of nativity, disregarding geographical variations, this inequality was almost as pronounced. While the rate for the whole city was 2.64 per cent in 1850, that for native Americans was 2.23, for non-Irish foreigners, 2.66, for Germans only 1.31, and for the Irish, fully 3.29.[78] From either perspective, Irishmen, although "not possessing, and scarcely thinking of the luxuries of life" and devoid of "the more debilitating and fatal effects of mental anxiety and luxurious enjoyment," hastened in the midst of life to death.[79]

Nevertheless, the city's foreign population multiplied, partly from continued immigration, but essentially from the fertility of immigrants — a particularly fortunate phenomenon because it came just in time to compensate for decreasing native births. In 1845, when the rate was 1:30 for Boston, it was twice as high (1:15) for the Broad Street section. By 1850 the native ratio was one birth for every forty living, but for the Irish it was one for every nineteen and for the Germans, a very youthful group, slightly larger — one for every seventeen. Although the incidence of births was high among the Germans, their meager number had little effect upon the general trend. Only 2.80 per cent of the total births were German, 35.27 per cent were native, and fully 52.87 per cent were Irish in 1850. The frequency of births among immigrants reflected a high proportion of marriages. One Irishman in fifty and one German in twenty-seven wed in 1850 — a rate higher than the native one in sixty-five, and attributable to the large number of young and middle-aged people.[80]

Fecundity was the only contribution of the Irish toward a solution of the community's social problems. Otherwise, their abject status spawned a brood of evils that burdened civic progress for many decades. Of these misfortunes, pauperism was the most important and the most pervasive, for thousands of Irish were constantly "idle and inactive, when there was an earnest craving for occupation. . . ." [81] Living on the brink of starvation even when at work, they necessarily called upon charity when discarded by the overstocked labor market, joining the ranks of the unemployables who could under no circumstances support themselves and of the aged for whom there was no security in an improvident economy.

Feeding idle mouths, particularly idle foreign mouths, was a difficulty complicated by the wasteful division of functions between Massachusetts' central government and its subdivisions. Although the care of the poor was essentially a municipal matter, the Commonwealth had early assumed the obligation of maintaining those without legal residence. The towns felt no incentive to economize where others paid the bill; instead, they rather welcomed, or at least did not vigorously oppose, the incursion of impoverished strangers who merely lowered the per-capita cost of assisting residents and provided free work-house labor as well.[82] Between 1845 and 1854, therefore, local officials did little to halt the hundreds of beggars who made their way to the Massachusetts almshouses. In that period Irish transient paupers outnumbered the sum of all others, of whatever status or nationality.[83]

But soon enough, Boston, like other municipalities, succumbed to the process which naturally and quietly transferred many to its care. Inevitably, state dependents acquired legal residence, and looked to the city for support. Accentuating the increasing burden even further was "the great influx of Foreign Diseased Paupers" requiring immediate medical attention, who forced Boston in 1847 to establish, at considerable cost, two hospitals on Deer Island, almost all of whose inmates were Irish.[84]

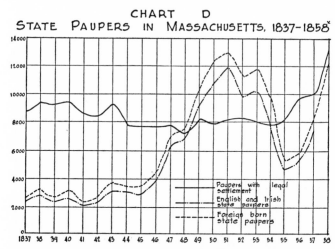

CHART D
STATE PAUPERS IN MASSACHUSETTS, 1837–1858*

Derived from "Report of the Special Joint Committee Appointed to Investigate Public Charitable Institutions of Massachusetts....1858," Massachusetts Senate, Documents, 1858, no. 2, pp. 131, 143.

Meanwhile, attempts to reduce the state's expense both by excluding unbonded aliens and by devolving part of the financial responsibility upon localities, failed.[85] Successive committees of the legislature only suggested minor reforms and palliatives to deal with the added load to the budget. The Commonwealth finally cut the Gordian knot by taking the administration into its own hands. In accordance with the recommendation of the Committee of 1851, it provided four workhouses where its wards could be at least partially self-sustaining, and, in addition, it imposed a commutation tax by which immigrants paid for the support of their unfortunate countrymen who became public charges.[86]

However, the crux of the matter lay not in the question of the agency to bear the expense, but in the fact that the number of indigents necessarily increased despite efforts to exclude or disown them. For poverty was an essential attribute of the city's economy. The system that begot a numerous proletariat perpetually on the verge of destitution, produced impoverishment as a matter of course upon the slightest slackening of the human or industrial machine. Mayor Quincy in 1848 and Mayor Bigelow in 1850 both expressed concern over the problem; but neither could do anything to cope with it. Under pressure of the exploited Irish, the cost of poor relief expanded monstrously year after year.[87]

The impact of Irish pauperism on the city was slight in comparison with the effects upon the immigrants themselves; for degradation by poverty was almost inevitable under the circumstances of Irish life in Boston. New conditions dissolved the old ties, habits, and traditions with which they were incompatible. The mores of the peasant farm could not readily be adapted to the tenement and the old adjustments that for many years had limited the social consequences of destitution in Ireland were inadequate in urban Boston. In this society want became a malignant and resourceful adversary; it insinuated itself into personal habits, perverting human relations and warping conceptions of right and wrong. Wherever it appeared, it encouraged intemperance, crime, and prostitution.[88]

Nothing the Irish found in Boston altered their tradition of alcoholic indulgence. Instead, crowded conditions drove men out of their homes into bars where they could meet friends, relax, and forget their anguish in the promised land. In 1846 there were 850 liquor dealers in the city, but by 1849 fully 1,200 groggeries were open for the flourishing trade. A survey by the city marshal in November, 1851, showed the great majority of these to be Irish, and almost half to be concentrated in the North End and Fort Hill.[89] In addition, numerous Irish families sold gin as a sideline, without license, to cater to the demands of their countrymen. Frequently drunk and often jailed for inebriety, the Irish "arrested and turned back" the short-lived temperance movement which had made promising progress up to their arrival.[90] Other nationalities, particularly the Germans, were also fond of the glass, but neither their habits nor environment encouraged or even tolerated excessive drinking.

Frequent intoxication led to the Irish reputation for criminality.[91] This impression actually derived from minor misdemeanors generally committed under the influence of drink, — misdemeanors which in many cases might have earned for more affluent offenders only a tolerant reprimand. Comparatively few Irishmen were guilty of more serious felonies. Negroes, whose transgressions frequently consisted of thefts of coal or wood, suffered from the same prejudice.[92] There were, of course, a few notorious cases involving crimes of violence, such as the trial for murder of the Negro, William Roby, but they were no more typical than Dr. Webster was of Harvard professors.[93] In no group was there an inherent predilection for crime, but among the Irish the combination of poverty and intemperance created a maladjustment expressed by petty infractions of the rules of a society strange to them.

Standing "in false relations to nearly everything about them . . . strangers in a strange land [,] surrounded by circumstances novel to them, met by customs to which they [could] . . . not adapt themselves, influenced by motives often extravagant and wild," the Irish necessarily became "involved in harassing doubt and perplexity." Their bewildered position in the city, together with overdrinking and the ill health of the slums, contributed to the rapid increase of insanity among them.[94] In 1764 the Selectmen had rejected Thomas Hancock's bequest for the relief of idiots because they were too few to justify special attention; and although, in the next eighty years, both state and municipality found it necessary to make provisions for the care of the mentally sick, before the coming of the Irish the problem was neither financially nor medically serious. Thereafter the number of patients and the cost of attending them rose rapidly. Massachusetts expanded its facilities by building two new hospitals and Boston erected an asylum of its own, largely to care for Irish laborers, for among other groups the incidence of lunacy was much lower.[95]

Finally, there was some prostitution among Irish immigrant women whose wages from ordinary employment did not "supply them with the necessities . . . of life."[96] Irish girls at one time enjoyed the reputation of comparative freedom from this vice, and indeed very few were guilty of it; but by 1860 illegitimate births were probably more frequent among them than among any other nationality.[97] The exigencies of the new society had driven many into a course completely alien to their background and training.

Indeed, in adjusting to the relentless drive of harsh, uncontrollable forces, the immigrants changed in many ways; and, in the changing, transformed the old Boston. The gap between the quiet suburban life of early South Boston and the bustling industrialism pervading it after 1850 was no greater than that between the Irishmen who turned their backs upon the placid fields of Kerry and those who tended the clamorous Bay State forges. Green meadows and heavy orchards gave way to dark rolling mills, and bronzed peasants turned into pallid hands whose sun shone from out the roaring hearth of the furnace. City and newcomer both felt the workings of the same force, the inevitable adaptation of new tenants to an old society. Each suffered a thoroughgoing physical metamorphosis, eventually reflected in an equally complete change in character and thought, and leaving in its wake the necessity for a radically different cultural orientation.

Conflict of Ideas

*As long . . . as the traditions of one's national and lo-
cal group remain unbroken, one remains so attached to
its customary ways of thinking that the ways of thinking which are perceived in other groups are regarded
as curiosities, errors, ambiguities, or heresies. At this
stage one does not doubt either the correctness of one's
own traditions of thought or the unity and uniformity
of thought in general.*[1]

BY 1845 Boston's cultural development had reached a
point of close contact with the highest aspects of European
civilization. Native Bostonians regarded England as the
"mother country." They were proud of their British ancestry
and remained "solidly and steadily English, settled down
into an English mold and hardened into it."[2] But they had
also learned to "expect an importation of the opinions and
manners of the old countries" and to "receive from Europe a
considerable part of [their] intellectual persuasions and
moral tastes. . . ."[3] Newcomers, be they English, French or
German, originating from similar backgrounds, and facing
few problems of physical or economic adjustment, could participate in a cosmopolitan society on terms of direct and simple equality. For these came prepared to share the world of

the Boston merchants — their music and literature, their ideas and politics, their rationalism and their all-pervading optimism. Whatever differences exsited were in degree and pace, easily reconcilable.

The Irish who settled in Boston, however, were products of a milieu completely isolated from the intellectual influences of London, Paris, or even Dublin. And every phase of their experience in America heightened the disparity between their heritage and that of their neighbors. The physical barriers segregating them from the dominant cultural currents of the day disappeared in the New World; but the spiritual ones crossed the Atlantic in the hold of every immigrant ship. Reaffirmed and strengthened by the difficulties of the new environment, these restraints ruled Irish thoughts as vigorously in Boston as in Cork.

In Ireland, a circumscribed agrarian economy gave form to their ideas, to the "implicit . . . *assumptions,* or . . . *unconscious mental habits*" dominating their thoughts.[4] In the bitter atmosphere of poverty and persecution, the Irish had found little in life that was not dark and nothing that was hopeful. Their utter helplessness before the most elemental forces fostered an immense sadness, a deep-rooted pessimism about the world and man's role in it, manifested even "on occasions of great joy and merriment . . . in grief and melancholy. . . ."[5]

Nor was this feeling modified in the transit to the New World. Irishmen fled with no hope in their hearts — degraded, humiliated, mourning reluctantly-abandoned and dearly-loved homes. From the rotting immigrant hulks, they nostalgically joined the local poet in plaintive farewell:

> Farewell to thee, Erin mavourneen,
>   Thy valleys I'll tread never more;
> This heart that now bleeds for thy sorrows,
>   Will waste on a far distant shore.
> Thy green sods lie cold on my parents,
>   A cross marks the place of their rest, —
> The wind that moans sadly above them,
>   Will waft their poor child to the West.[6]

The old homeland grew lush in their memories when compared with the miseries of constricted tenement districts and the hopelessness of the arbitrary factory economy. They found good cause to complain:

> I am tired, fatigued, weary,
>   Of this never ending strife —
> Of the journey, lone and dreary,
>   On the darksome path of life.[7]

Filthy homes, wretched working conditions, and constant hunger mocked the merchants' optimism, and bred, instead, the identical pessimism in Boston as in Ireland. On both sides of the Atlantic, Irish experience generated a brooding recognition that human relationships were transient, subject to the ever-threatening intervention of impersonal evils. The essential pessimism of these immigrants was reflected in the prominent role of the devil in their literature and even in the belief in retributive justice at the hands of a *deus ex machina* as compensation in a basically evil world. Both as peasants whose anxious livelihood derived from the capricious soil, and as cogs in an unpredictable industrial machine, they were victims of incalculable influences beyond their control. For those who met it so frequently in their own experience, untimely disaster, even death, was normal, a part of life accepted without complaint, indeed, without even the need for explanation.[8]

Buffeted about in a hostile universe by malevolent forces more powerful than themselves, Irish peasants could turn only to religion for consolation. The drama of salvation unfolded at every mass became a living reality from which emerged dogmas held with a tenacity beyond secular reason. Man's fall through original sin and his deliverance by grace were not theological abstractions but insistent realities reflected in all the features of their everyday existence.

When we luck at him there, we see our blissed Saviour, stripped a'most naked lake ourselves; whin we luck at the crown i'thorns on the head, we see the Jews mockin' him, jist the same as — some people mock ourselves for our religion; whin we luck at his eyes, we see they wor niver dry, like our own; whin we luck at the wound in his side, why we think less of our own wounds an' bruises, we get 'ithin and 'ithout, every day av our lives.[9]

To those who bore more than their share of hardships, religion's most valued assurance was its promise that "the world did not explain itself" and that man met his true destiny not in this constantly frustrating universe, but in the loftier sphere it preceded.[10] At the death of a child in a popular novel, the priest inwardly "rejoiced that another soul was about being housed from life's tempests"; for all earthly affairs, life itself, were insignificant and death was but a release for the tremendous process of redemption.[11] Preparation for that rebirth thoroughly eclipsed the affairs of the immediate present, engendering an attitude of complete acceptance toward mundane problems so long as salvation was unthreatened.[12]

Against the immense forces facing men, reason and science counted for nothing. The Irish scorned the independent rationalism basic to the religious feelings of other Bostonians, and discouraged "reading the bible and putting one's own construction upon it" or allowing "every tinker and ploughboy to interpret scripture as he thought proper." [13] The approval of the hierarchy reinforced this attitude. The pastoral letter of the American bishops in 1843 pointed out that "without faith it is impossible to please God" and warned against "preferring in the least point the dictates of your erring reason." [14]

The true guardian of the faith essential to salvation was the Catholic Church. Two centuries of violent attack in Ireland had strengthened and confirmed its position; for national and economic issues had fused with the religious in opposition to landlords who were at once masters, aliens, and representatives of a hostile faith.[15] Beliefs maintained at great personal sacrifice were not lightly held, and among those who came to America the Church gained particular prestige, for it was one of the few familiar institutions that followed them across the Atlantic.

In the New World as in the Old, Catholicism assumed a distinctive cast from the background of its adherents. Universal rather than national in organization, and catholic in essential dogma, it nevertheless partook of the quality of the men who professed it; for the nature of the milieu modified even religious doctrines, particularly in their application to the problems of secular life. Irish priests and theologians rose from the ranks of the people, surrounded by popular influences which inevitably affected their later work. The continuous process of clerical adjustment to the ideas of those they served intensified Irish devoutness in America, because the conclusions Catholicism derived from its theology coincided with the ideas emanating from the inner circumstances of the peasant-laborer's life.

The confidence of the Irish confirmed the Church's paramount position in their own affairs; church doctrine extended this ascendancy over all man-made institutions, including the state, and urged that

Religious liberty means, not religious slavery, not simply the liberty of infidelity, the liberty to deny and blaspheme, but . . . that religion herself is free . . . to be herself, and to discharge her functions in her own way, without let or hindrance from the State. . . . Who asserts the freedom of religion asserts the subjection of the State. Religion represents the Divine Sovereignty . . . in the affairs of men; the State . . . merely . . . human sovereignty. Is the Divine Sovereignty higher than the human . . . ? Then is religion . . . higher than the State . . . . Religion overrides all other sovereigns, and has the supreme authority over all the affairs of the world. . . . This is a terrible doctrine to atheistical politicians, infidels, and anarchists; and hence . . . they are the enemies . . . of religious liberty. . . .[16]

Since the "freedom of religion" was "its sovereignty" and since "to assert its independence of the State" was "to assert its supremacy over the State," secular government had merely to choose between particular measures within the limits of religious precepts, to which it must conform, and in conforming, compel its subjects to conform.[17]

In defense of this position Catholics argued that

Christianity is "part and parcel of the law of the land." . . . We are professedly a *Christian* State, and acknowledge ourselves bound by the law of nature as interpreted and re-enacted by Christianity.[18]

There could be no true tolerance, for, no matter what their professed beliefs, all citizens must ultimately comply with the basic tenets of the "true religion" through its temporal agency, the state. This opinion forced a denial of

the liberty of each man to be of what religion he pleases, or of none . . . a low and an altogether inadequate view . . . merely a political . . . not a religious right at all; for no religion that has any self-respect can acknowledge that one has the right to be of any religion he chooses. No man has or can have a *religious* or a *moral* right to be of any religion but the true religion. . . . Every religion by its very nature is intolerant of every other, and condemns itself, if it is not.[19]

Any deviation from this concept of "religious freedom" earned bitter condemnation as "latitudinarianism of the very worst sort." [20]

The belief that non-Christians were "free to profess no portion of their religion which contravenes Christian morality" certainly contrasted with the native conviction, as set forth by Channing, that formal sectarian boundaries had little significance. While most Bostonians felt, with John Adams, that "every honest, well-disposed, moral man, even if he were an atheist, should be accounted a Christian," Brownson insisted that "a *Christian* Protestant, is to the Catholic mind simply a contradiction in terms." [21] That disparity reflected a broad difference between the basic attitudes and unconscious presumptions of the rational, progressive optimist and of the religious, conservative pessimist.

This dichotomy was most marked when expressed in terms of concrete attitudes toward the pressing social problems of the period. The mental set of tenement or seminary scarcely harmonized with the rational Bostonian's concept of reform as an infallible guide along the straight path of progress to ultimate perfectibility. Indeed the Irish were completely alien to the idea of progress and necessarily antagonistic "to the spirit of the age."[22] Reform was a delusion inflating men's sense of importance, distorting the relative significance of earthly values, and obscuring the true goals of their endeavor — salvation of the eternal soul. Such movements were suspect because they exaggerated the province of reason, exalting it above faith, futile because they relied upon temporal rather than spiritual agencies, and dangerous because they undermined respect for established institutions.[23]

The failure of the Irish to comprehend fully the democratic feeling basic to reform intensified their hostility. Generations of enforced obedience bred a deep respect for class distinctions. Irishmen could scarcely have a firm appreciation of the equality of man when their very school books taught them

Q. If the poor will not try to be good, what will follow?
A. That the rich will not help them.[24]

At best, this acquiescence developed into the feudal loyalty of retainer for master, but more frequently it became the complete servility described by Arthur Young:

A landlord . . . can scarcely invent an order which a servant, laborer or cottar dares to refuse to execute. Nothing satisfies him but unlimited submission. . . . A poor man would have his bones broken, if he offered to lift his hand in his own defense.[25]

In America, too, the Irish agreed that everyone should "mate with their equals, high as well as low," and the *Pilot* pointed out that the poor Irish family was "much more happy and contented in its place in life" than the American.[26] But Judith O'Rourke expressed this acceptance of class most clearly when, scoffing at the possibility of educating her children, she hoped that her sons would "grow up honest good men, like them that's gone afore them, not ashamed of their station, or honest toil," while her daughter " 'll be the same lady her mother is . . . an' that's good enough. . . . She'd look purty I'm thinkin' wid her music in one corner an' I wid my wash tub in another." [27]

Thus, the whole galaxy of reforms that absorbed New England in the thirty years after 1835 met the determined opposition of the Irish Catholic population in Boston. Fundamental patterns of thought combined with group interests to turn them against their neighbors who "devoutly believe in any Woolly horse, any Kossuth, any Montes that may chance to come," and among whom "Freesoilerism, Millerism, Spiritual rappings, Mainea all are current." To follow such doctrines which had already "infected our whole society and turned a large portion of our citizens into madmen" was to become "a philanthropist . . . a person who loves everybody generally and hates everybody particularly." [28]

"Leading in majesty and peerless fidelity, the beautiful constellation of reforms," was abolition. Against slavery the finest spirits in Boston united in a movement which, after 1830, gained steadily in adherents until it dominated the city.[29] Yet the Irish concertedly opposed the spread of "Niggerology." They sometimes recognized that slavery was abstractly bad, and sometimes denied it; but in any case, humanitarianism was as powerless to eradicate the institution as to deal with the other evils in which the world abounded.[30] A number of practical objections reinforced the theory that only the influence of the Church could counteract social maladies.[31] The disruption of the Repeal Movement by O'Connell's anti-slavery speech revealed the danger of the issue; Catholic leaders hesitated to antagonize their powerful and influential communicants in Maryland, Louisiana, and throughout the south, dreading a controversy that might divide the Church as it had other religious groups.[32] And beyond immediate interests and ideology lay a deep horror of endangering the social fabric, or disturbing the Union as it existed.[33]

Even more concrete reasons tied the mass of unskilled Irish laborers to the Church in the belief that

> . . . when the negroes shall be free
> To cut the throats of all they see,
> Then this dear land will come to be
> The den of foul rascality.[34]

They feared the competition of the hordes of freed slaves who might invade the North; and valued the security that came from the existence in the country of at least one social class below them.[35] Rivalry for the same jobs as Negroes, elsewhere bondsmen, but in Boston economically and socially more secure than the Irish, strengthened this feeling and led the latter to object to Negro suffrage which aimed at "setting the Niggers high," to complain that colored people did not know their place, and to resent their "impertinence."[36]

Irish Catholics also turned against the other humanitarian reforms; for these used the state as an instrument for strengthening secular as against religious forces. On these grounds the immigrants fought the current temperance movement, although drunkenness was particularly prominent among them. Inspired by Father Mathew's efforts, the Church itself had attempted to cope with the problem. But it actively challenged the right of the state to legislate on the matter; and therein enjoyed the support of laborers who jealously guarded their only form of relaxation.[37]

Even the preponderance of Irish among the city's lawbreakers did not weaken the conviction that society was powerless to effect reforms attainable only through grace. Because Catholics felt that criminals were born evil, they objected to treating them "with maternal kindness," "merely as afflicted patients." "A superabundance of humanity in the public sentiment" and particularly in the Prisoners' Friend Society pampered wrongdoers by permitting them to work, to receive occasional visitors and to hear church services on Sunday. These "sickly sentimentalists," "worse . . . than the prisoners they whine over," were doomed to failure because most prisoners were

deliberate wrongdoers, intentionally at war with society; men who prefer to obtain a precarious livelihood by robbing . . . to the comforts resulting from the unexciting routine of honest industry . . . *men* who have thus become perverted. . . .[38]

Two current crusades seemed to strike at the roots of family life, and thus at Christian society. To those reared within the grooves of a patriarchal society the "domestic reformers" appeared to "have revived pagan orgies in the pitiful farce of 'Women's Rights,' and Bloomerism." [39] But more menacing to public morality were the common schools and the laws for compulsory education:

The general principle upon which these laws are based is radically unsound, untrue, Atheistical. . . . It is, that the education of children is *not* the work of the Church, or of the Family, but that it is the work of the State. . . . Two consequences flow from this principle. . . . In the matter of education, the State is supreme over the Church and the Family. *Hence,* the State can and does exclude from the schools religious instruction. . . . The inevitable consequence is, that . . . the greater number of scholars must turn out to be Atheists, and accordingly the majority of non-Catholics are people of no religion. . . . The other consequence . . . leads the State to *adopt* the child, to weaken the ties which bind it to the parent. So laws are made compelling children to attend the state schools, and forbidding the parents, if they be poor, to withdraw their little ones from the school. . . . The consequence of this policy is . . . universal disobedience on the part of children. . . . Our little boys scoff at their parents, call their fathers by the name of Old Man, Boss, or Governor. The mother is the Old Woman. The little boys smoke, drink, blaspheme, talk about fornication, and so far as they are physically able, commit it. Our little girls read novels . . . quarrel about their beaux, uphold Woman's Rights, and — . . . . We were a Boston school boy, and we speak of what we know.

When "second rate or tenth rate school masters . . . like Horace Mann . . ." were allowed "by the patient people to tinker over the schools until they . . . nearly ruined them," Irish parents hesitated to entrust their children to the common schools, and fought the laws that required them to do so. Persistent and unequivocal hostility to the "kidnapping" system generated sharp conflicts with other Bostonians who regarded Massachusetts public education as the keystone of its liberty and culture.[40]

In the conflict of ideas the Irish found all other foreign groups in the city ranged with the native Bostonians against them. The Germans could be as optimistic, rational and romantic as the natives, for their emigration rested on hope rather than on bare necessity. Unlike the Irish, they went off singing,

> Leb' wohl geliebtes Mädchen,
> Jetzt reis' ich aus den städtchen
> Muss nun, Feinsliebchen, fort
> An einem fremden Ort.[41]

And in America their economic and physical adjustment was relatively simple, so that within a short time they shared the ideas of the natives. Although divisions existed within the German groups, the predominant sentiment held the spirit of free enquiry and intellectual radicalism essential to human progress, measurable in terms of the development of the individual's personality as " a free man." [42] Consequently, they took the same position as the natives on all social questions save temperance, and were far more extreme on the specific issue of slavery.[43] Being few in number, the French did not always assume a position as a group. When they did, they were moderately liberal in politics and on the question of slavery, as were the English, Negroes, Italians, and smaller groups.[44]

About one point only — the revolutions of 1848 — was adjustment in the conflicting position of the Irish and other Bostonians at all possible. Coming when the immigrants had scarcely settled in their new homes, while the instruments of social control were still weak from the effects of transition, the exciting news from the Fatherland sent a tremendous wave of emotion among the Irish. Mobilized in the Repeal Movement, Irish national sentiment in America had grown steadily for several years. It had captured the *Boston Pilot,* originally a clerical paper founded by Bishop Fenwick, and turned it to support the revolutions against the conservative powers of Europe led by Austria.[45] Through the *Boston Catholic Observer,* the clergy at first resisted this metamorphosis. But they capitulated in 1848 when the Young Irelanders, impatient with O'Connellite conservatism, raised the banners of rebellion from Cork to Belfast, enlisting the loyalty of the great majority of Irish Americans. Enthusiasm was so great the hierarchy dared not stand in the way. By August Archbishop Hughes of New York gave his approval, proclaiming that the rush to arms had transformed the revolution from "plot" to "fact," and sanctioned a Directory collecting funds in New York. Bishop Fitzpatrick did not weaken to the extent of backing the insurrection, but did not openly oppose it. His organ, the *Boston Catholic Observer,* edited by Brownson, cautiously reprinted the Archbishop's statement without comment.[46]

The Bishop hesitated because of the uncertainty of Vatican policy. Pius IX had been regarded as a progressive from his accession.[47] His early liberal efforts promised so much that the future editor of the *Boston Pilot,* Father John T. Roddan, a brilliant young American priest educated at the Propaganda, had returned to Boston "almost a Mazzinian . . . quite enamored of the European revolutionary movements." [48] While the Pope was undecided, Catholic conservatives vacillated on the subject of revolution and permitted the radicals to dominate Irish opinion. [49]

A common stake in revolutionary success drew the Irish closer to other groups. Young Ireland, influenced by continental ideas, was not far different from Young Italy. Though it lacked the broad humanitarianism of the Boston reformers and was openly sympathetic toward slavery, nationalism nevertheless provided a point of contact with other Bostonians. [50] Collaboration with abolitionists like Quincy and Phillips was a potential wedge that might have split the Irish from their conservatism and opened their minds to the liberal position. Even the collapse of the insurrection did not discredit it, for many of its leaders eventually found their way to the United States. They were still popular; their opinions still carried weight; and for a time they exerted a positive liberalizing influence over their countrymen through lectures and through their newspapers, the *Irish-American* and the *Citizen*. [51]

The rapprochement did not last long, however; it finally gave way before the revived and unified opposition of the clergy. The insurgency of the Roman republic alienated the papacy from the cause of revolution; and the victory of Radetsky's Austrian legions facilitated the adoption of a clear-cut, conservative policy. As a result, Archbishop Hughes and the *Freeman's Journal* disowned Young Ireland, and Catholic policy in Boston as elsewhere resolutely opposed the policies of red republicanism which, in retrospect, it linked with an atheistic plot of Protestants to undermine Catholic civilization. These, it charged:

saw the Church gathering America to her bosom. . . . They saw themselves losing ground everywhere, and, as they gnashed their teeth with rage and pined away, the ministers in white choackers formed in England and in America an Alliance, and, resolved to carry the war into Italy, — to revolutionize that country. It would be a great triumph to them, and to their father, the devil, if they could match Catholic progress in Protestant countries with Protestant progress in Catholic countries. . . . They fermented the revolutions of 1848

by forming

a grand conspiracy, with its central government . . . in London, and its ramifications extending even to this country . . . armed not merely against monarchy, but against all legitimate authority, against all religion except an idolatrous worship of . . . the GOD–PEOPLE . . . , against all morality, . . . law, . . . order, and . . . society itself.[52]

The Church conducted a persistent campaign against the "spirit of radical Protestantism" which had "crept into every class of society, into every . . . political order" and which "nought can destroy . . . but the *true Catholic spirit.*" [53] Time after time it inveighed against the "political atheism" growing out of the belief that "the State, if not the sovereign, is at least not the subject of Religion," a belief that gave rise to "the revolutions, crimes, civil wars which have recently been and are coming again. . . ." [54] Led by Brownson, the Catholic press attacked the uprisings in Europe and their supporters in Boston, urging upon a restless people "the necessity of subordination and obedience to lawful rulers." [55] "Good Catholics," they argued, "must accept . . . the constitution of the State, when once established, whatever its form, yet . . . have no right to conspire to change the con-

stitution, or to effect a revolution in the State. Consequently
. . . our sympathies can never be with those who conspire
against the law, or with the mad revolutionists and radicals,
on the Continent of Europe, who are unsettling every
thing." [56]

In the face of this overwhelming propaganda, the influence of the Young Irelanders waned steadily. The success of
the revolution might have furnished a concrete rallying point
for progressive influences against the conservative tendencies
in Irish life. As it was, the movement dissolved in endless
talk. The conservatives easily recaptured the *Boston Pilot*
when its owner, Patrick Donohoe, ignominiously capitulated
to the Bishop and allowed his paper to be edited by an American priest, John T. Roddan, by now a disciple of Brownson. [57] Continual quarrels divided the ranks of the radicals
and desertion further depleted them. T. D. McGee withdrew
first to the clerical party and then to the hated English from
whom he accepted a cabinet post in Canada. Mitchel, disgusted, retired to the rusticity of Tennessee, and Meagher to
a law practice in New York and the career of a Democratic
politician. [58] Although Fenianism revived Irish nationalism in
1859, it had none of the liberal ideas of 1848. By then the opposition to conservatism had disappeared, lingering only in
the minds of a few die-hards.

Flirtation with revolution was a passing interlude with no
effect upon the normal Irish respect for authority. Always,
conservatism segregated them from other Bostonians, who
believed that all revolutions signified the dawn of a new era
that would spread the light of American liberty over a renais-
sant Europe. Natives, and for that matter, non-Irish foreign-

ers, had taken an active interest in the Polish struggle for liberty, and had hailed the French revolution of 1830 with delight, though Catholics dubbed it the work of "an irreligious and profligate minority." Americans approved of the uprisings of 1848 set off by the abdication of "that great swindle," Louis Philippe, as unanimously as the Irish eventually disapproved. Henry Adams was an ardent admirer of Garibaldi, and Margaret Fuller, among many, adored Mazzini whom the Irish hated. Almost all Bostonians liked the Hungarians and welcomed Kossuth, but Catholics branded him a disappointed manufacturer of humbugs. The Irish attacked the Swiss for sheltering rebels, and condemned the Fenian Brotherhoods in America; while in the Crimean War, which they called a struggle of "Civilized Society against red republican barbarism," they supported Russia against Protestant England and against Turkey, which had protected Kossuth.[59]

Fighting radicalism everywhere, they consistently maintained the principles of conservatism by defending the Catholic powers of Europe — Spain, Austria, and Italy — the nations considered most backward, ignorant, and intolerant by Boston public opinion.[60] Every unfavorable comment on these countries by an American provoked a bitter defense in the Irish press.[61] In the Mediai matter, they upheld religious intolerance in Italy, and left themselves open to charges of having "a different set of principles to suit the market of every country." [62] In the *Black Warrior* affair they championed Spain and in the Koszta case, Austria against the United States.[63] They went to great lengths in vindicating Napoleon III although most Americans condemned the treachery of the coup d'état of 1851.[64] The Irish were equally firm in shielding Catholic Latin America against filibustering Yankees whose "manifest destiny" led to repeated aggressions. They assailed alike the Texan "brigands" who threatened Mexico and those who attacked Cuba, while they supported the established church in Brazil, in a long series of unfortunate disputations which created bitterness by their very heat and which transferred, in the minds of many Bostonians, the qualities defended in these conservative countries to the Irish themselves.[65]

These political differences testified to the strength of the barrier reared between Irish and non-Irish by diametrically opposed ideas, whose literary and cultural expressions reflected and perpetuated the distinction. Resting on basically different premises, developed in entirely different environments, two distinct cultures flourished in Boston with no more contact than if 3,000 miles of ocean rather than a wall of ideas stood between them.

Irish intellectual life had few contacts with that of their neighbors. Education, rare indeed in Ireland, was scarcely more widespread among the Irish in Boston. The ability to read was by no means commonplace,[66] and repeated warnings against secular works narrowed the nature of what little the Irish did read.[67] The few Irishmen conscious of Boston's contemporary literature were shocked and antagonized by its rational romanticism, regarding it as exclusively Protestant, overwhelmingly English, and suspect on both grounds. Completely alien to the city's literary tradition, they branded Shakespeare a barbaric poet whose "monstrous farces" "befoul the stage with every abomination." Milton became a heretic minion of the Drogheda monster Cromwell, and English literature — "the most pernicious" that ever existed — merely a degraded and degenerate justification of the reformation, typified by "that liar and infidel, Hume" and "that hideous atheist, Hobbs." [68] Because this literature was basic to their thinking, the work of men like Emerson was necessarily rejected. C. M. O'Keefe spoke for many in gratitude that "We Irishmen are not yet reduced to that moral nakedness which startles and appals us in Mr. Emerson," whose "historical . . . is only . . . equalled by his philosophical ignorance." [69]

In place of Emerson's "puerilities" the most popular Irish writing of the day was that which glorified Ireland, its historic tradition, and its Catholic past. The dateless conflict with England, in all its phases, furnished an endless source of romantic themes, at once reflecting and stimulating an Anglophobia out of place amidst the Boston veneration of things English.[70] Stories of the Reformation — the root of all Irish misery — were always popular. A life of Mary, Queen of Scots, sold a thousand copies the day it was published in Boston, and the *Pilot* frequently printed romances and articles based upon the struggles of that period justifying the Catholic position.[71] That conflict continued in a long series of literary arguments, forgetting the injunction of a great German controversialist that disputes should be treated "with the utmost charity, conciliation and mildness." [72] On the contrary these theological battles, waged *fortiter in modo* as well as *in re,* wounded susceptibilities and stored up rancorous bitterness on all sides. Whatever the ultimate justice of the matter, defense of the inquisition and Saint Bartholomew's massacre, and continued attacks upon Luther, Calvin, and Henry VIII, the "infernal triumvirate" of Protestantism, and upon other propagators of "monstrous doctrines," scarcely drew the Irish closer to their neighbors who held completely different views.[73]

The sporadic clashes that marked the early years of Irish settlement in Boston stimulated this antagonism. Fitted into a familiar pattern, these conflicts became mere extensions of the old battle against English Protestantism. The Charlestown Convent fire left a heritage of bitterness, never eradicated. Years later Irishmen resented it and declaimed

> Foul midnight deed! I mark with pain
> Yon ruins tapering o'er the plain;
> Contrast them with your Bunker's height,
> And shame will sicken at the sight!
>
> Already thou hast learnt the rule,
> Of Cromwell's bloody English school;
> And far and wide the fame has flown,
> Of crimes which thou must ever own.[74]

Nor did the novels in which the Irish delighted most — tales of ancient Irish grandeur, glorifying Celtic culture at the expense of Saxon England — improve relations with other Bostonians. The common core of all was the inevitable contrast between Gael and Sassenach, decidedly to the disadvantage of the latter.[75] A series of violent articles by Dr. John McElheran furnished a philosophical and pseudo-ethnological basis for this contrast. "The divine spark of genius radiates from the Celtic centre of the world. . . . The Egyptians . . . the pure Pelasgi of Athens . . . the Romans by themselves — and the ancient Irish . . . show us . . . the natural tendency of the pure Celtic race, uncontaminated by Gothic bestiality, or eastern sensuality." The Gothic race, including the Germans, Scandinavians, Russians, Turks and Anglo-Saxons, were completely different, "essentially stupid . . . false, cruel, treacherous, base and bloody . . ." with "little or no faculty for poetry, music, or abstract science." By every criterion of civilization, the latter were far inferior to the former. And the lowest of all were the Saxons, "the very dregs and offal of the white population in America. . . . These flaxen-haired German men and women . . . are lower than the race with black wool. . . . Even when they are well to do they send their children out to beg." [76] Immensely popular, the publication of these articles elicited a steady stream of letters from readers asking for more of the same from the "Saxon-hating Dr." [77]

As opposed to these discordant tendencies only one strain — pride in their contributions to the making of America — drew the Irish nearer their neighbors. Although "the great current of American history" was "overwhelmingly heretic," and Catholic students could "receive no support" for their "faith from reading it," they cherished its Irish episodes.[78] The early Catholic explorers from St. Brandan to Marquette, and Charles Carroll, the Catholic signer, were important figures whose biographies appeared frequently in their reading. Though they distrusted live Orangemen, the Irish made the dead Scotch-Irish their own; they were fond of tales of John Barry and other Celtic military heroes.[79] But even this was pushed to a dangerous extreme when McElheran claimed all great Americans were "Celtic Normans, and French, and Spaniards, and Celtic Britons . . . and Gaels from Wales and Ireland and the north and west of Scotland. Look to the pedigree of your heroes . . . look at their physique, and say, Is it the type of Gothic nations? . . . Is it fat, lumpish, gross Anglo-Saxon?" [80]

While the chasm between Irish and native ideas deepened, cultural contacts furthered the assimilation of other immigrants. The Irish alone diverged from the Boston norm. All others participated readily in the intellectual life of the community. Englishmen were obviously at home there; and Germans were soon familiar in many phases of the city's activities. Admiring its school system and respecting Harvard, they sent their children to common schools as a matter of course. Germans were widely acquainted with western European literature. Their magazines contained sections on "Anglo-Amerikanischer," English, and French as well as German and German-American literature, while their own writing frequently used American themes and expressed the American spirit.[81] The thought and culture of Frenchmen was also broadly cosmopolitan; English and German works found a secure place in their reading.[82] Meanwhile these groups enriched the natives with a new heritage accepted gratefully. Follen and Beck, together with the Americans, Bancroft, Longfellow, and Ticknor, popularized the German language until more than seventy Harvard men were studying it in the fifties.[83] At the same time, the French press helped make the works of Balzac, Lamartine, and other authors and painters accessible to Bostonians.[84]

Ease of adjustment did not reflect a flat uniformity in the non-Irish groups. Each brought with it an intellectual tradition of which it was proud, and which it was anxious to preserve. But though different in detail, all had the same roots, and eventually coalesced without serious conflict. Thus the clash of two vigorous musical cultures that grew out of German immigration actually enriched both. At the beginning of the nineteenth century, Boston enjoyed a living, fruitful, musical tradition based upon the Anglo-Italianate musical life of eighteenth-century London. It first took concrete form in the Philo-harmonic Society (1810), an amateur group predominantly American in nativity, but including some Englishmen and a Russian, and led by an Anglo-German, Gottlieb Graupner, once oboist in Haydn's London Orchestra. From this nucleus grew the Handel and Haydn Society, an organization of some hundred amateurs formed in 1815 to interpret the oratorios of these composers. Later critics belittled its achievements, but its influence upon the mechanics and artisans who formed its rank and file was deep, and was perpetuated for many years in the rural "singing skewls" of all New England. Throughout at least the first thirty years of its existence, it vigorously sustained the music of those after whom it was named.[85]

Nourished by the fruit of Beethoven's revolt, and steeped in romanticism, German music by 1840 had evolved a tradition that was quite different. At first contact native Bostonians rejected it. Centered in a group of music masters who gave periodic concerts, but whose chief income derived from teaching culturally ambitious Bostonians, their normal musical life had little room for strangers. Traveling professionals might stop for an occasional concert; but isolated performances left little impression and there was no incentive for teachers without pupils to remain in the city. Heinrich, for instance, preferred to live there, but was forced by the financial failure of his concert to go to New York, and Charles Zeuner, who did remain, felt he was misunderstood.[86] With no one to play the new music, Bostonians could not become familiar with or like it.[87] Englishmen and a few Italians closely related to them remained the most popular foreign musicians. Such unfamiliar soil doomed the most valiant attempts at playing Beethoven to failure. Even Woodbridge and Mason confessed defeat after an unsuccessful series of concerts in the Boston Academy of Music, a product of their travels in Germany.[88]

The coming of the Germans who wanted German music teachers for their children made room for the new music. As soon as there was a resident basis of such musicians, Bostonians found opportunities to hear and to like it. Very quickly they learned it was not really strange for it synchronized with the romantic tendencies already woven into their culture. In the spread of the new music, Germans like Dresel, Kreissmann, Leonhard, and Heinrich, the Germania Society which came to Boston in 1849, the Mendelssohn Quintet Club, and the itinerant foreign opera companies were influential, but hardly more so than native teachers like Lowell Mason, or *Dwight's Journal of Music,* which voiced the cause of German romanticism consistently after 1852. Once the two cultures met, they found a common basis, fused, and under the vigorous leadership of Carl Zerrahn produced an ever more fruitful growth thereafter. Germans and Americans, they were the same kind of people, their ideas and feelings were rooted in the same social background; there was no occasion for serious conflict.[89]

The common store of ideas that made this adjustment possible was lacking in the intellectual relations of the Irish and non-Irish. The development of the fundamental aspects of their ideas left them so far apart there was no room for compromise. Contact bred conflict rather than conciliation. Irish Catholics could not think like their neighbors without a complete change in way of life.[90] And natives could adopt no aspect of Catholic ideas without passing through a radical intellectual revolution.

One outstanding personality attempted to adapt Irish Catholicism to American thought and failed signally in the attempt. By 1842 Orestes A. Brownson's intellectual development had itself carried him to the acceptance of many Catholic concepts. In philosophy he felt the need for tradition and revelation; in theology, for grace to counteract original sin and man's innate corruptness. In politics he was a conservative Democrat, opposed to abolition and reform, trying to temper the rule of the people by placing "Justice" above the popular will.[91] But the eminently Irish Bishop Fitzpatrick — "the hierarchical exponent of all that was traditional . . . in Catholic public life" — distrusted Brownson's philosophic background though it had brought him to the Church, and insisted upon complete renunciation before conversion.[92] Brownson yielded, and for ten years loyally submitted to the dictates of his Irish religious superiors, handing over every line he wrote to the censorship of the Bishop. Until 1854 Brownson and the *Review* thoroughly expressed the ideas of Irish Catholicism.[93]

In that year, stimulated by the criticisms of the Know-Nothing movement, Brownson reluctantly concluded that the Church in America must be American rather than Irish and thereby provoked a galling conflict with the Irish clergy that painfully grieved him and eventually drove him to New York where he hoped to profit from the less rigorous supervision of Archbishop Hughes.[94] Thereafter, Brownson evolved a new social philosophy based on Gioberti's theology, which enabled him to attack slavery, support the Republican party, and attempt to reconcile the Church with American ideas by liberalizing it.[95]

This endeavor met vigorous, relentless Irish disapproval. The *Pilot,* hitherto his cordial friend and follower, became his bitter foe, attacking his new position in a long series of sharp articles.[96] His influence among the Irish vanished. Too late he recognized what Father Hecker had always known, that "The R. C. Church is not national with us, hence it does not meet our wants, nor does it fully understand and sympathize with the experience and dispositions of our people. It is principally made up of adopted and foreign individuals." Without a common basis of ideas there could be no conciliation.[97]

The compromise too difficult for the acute mind of an intellectual aristocrat was never even attempted by the great mass of laboring Irishmen, completely preoccupied with the far more pressing problems of earning a bare livelihood. Hedged about by economic and physical as well as cultural barriers, they were strangers to the other society beside them. The development of Irish ideas created a further range of differences between themselves and all others in the city that stimulated and developed consciousness of group identity.

∽ VI ∽

The Development of Group Consciousness

Thinking to live by some derivative old country mode in this primitive new country, — to catch perch with shiners. . . . with his horizon all his own, yet he a poor man, born to be poor, with his inherited Irish poverty or poor life . . . not to rise in this world, he nor his posterity, till their wading webbed bog-trotting feet get talaria to their heels.[1]

ALL immigrants to Boston brought with them an awareness of group identity already sharpened by cultural contact with other peoples. Years of conflict with the English had strengthened this feeling among the Irish. The Germans emigrated during a turbulent period of patriotic awakening; and the English, French, and Italians had felt impassioned currents stirred up by the Napoleonic disorganization of Europe. Nationalists to begin with, all retained their ties with the homeland.

As long as it derived from sources external to Boston society, awareness of nationality expressed merely a sentimental attachment. Thus, Englishmen observed the birthdays of the royal family; the Swiss collected funds for the village of Travers, destroyed by fire in 1865; the French celebrated mass at the Cathedral upon the death of Princess Adelaide;

151

while German, Polish, and Hungarian emigrés sympathized with, organized for, and assisted the insurrections at home.[2]

Continuous demands from abroad likewise reaffirmed Irish devotion to the "bright gem of the sea." [3] Her needs were so pressing, so apparent, none could refuse assistance. Meager earnings somehow yielded a steady stream of drafts to friends and relatives who remained behind, and great disasters elicited even more remarkable contributions. Stimulated by Bishop Fitzpatrick's pastoral letter, Boston Irishmen remitted more than $200,000 during the scourge of 1847.[4] The less serious famine of 1863 drew £149 from the Montgomery Union Association of Boston alone, while a committee of Irishmen collected $18,000.[5] And Irish parish priests could always rely upon aid from former parishioners when calamity struck their districts.[6]

Love of Ireland enlisted a host of organizations in the perennial struggle against English oppression. These cropped up sporadically through the twenties and thirties, but until the Repeal Movement of the forties, accomplished little.[7] After 1840, however, agitation against Britain absorbed immigrants' attention for almost a decade, although it proved ultimately only a transitory influence upon Irish life in Boston. "The Friends of Ireland Society," founded October 6, 1840, by J. W. James and John C. Tucker, affiliated in 1841 with O'Connell's Dublin Loyal Association, and established agencies in South Boston, Charlestown, East Boston, Roxbury, and West Cambridge. At regular meetings in each locality it collected large sums of money, and its zeal inspired similar societies throughout the United States, which met in 1842 in convention in Philadelphia. A central directory in New

York, formed in 1843, coördinated their activities and established a national fund for Ireland.[8]

Interest waned, however, as Repealers limited their activities to exacting dues. Collections in 1845 were about half those in 1843; and sparsely attended meetings reflected rising dissatisfaction.[9] The Boston Irish had been intensely loyal to O'Connell; [10] but reckless tugging at the lion's tail by Smith O'Brien, Mitchel, and the more active Young Ireland Party, weaned many away, particularly after the old leader's death.[11] Finally, the purge of radicals from the Repeal Society in 1847 alienated many prominent members, and transferred to Young Ireland complete control of Irish opinion in Boston, already inflamed by revolutionary hopes.[12] Implicit approval by the Church in 1848, however, united conservative Repealers and radicals in the Confederation of the United Friends of Ireland, which resumed collections so vigorously as to provoke strenuous protests from the British ambassador at Washington.[13] But failure took the heart out of the movement, and renewed conservative opposition ended it. Nationalist activity thereafter showed life only in sporadic flurries in the radical press, and in momentary excitement over the exile of O'Brien and his followers.[14] In 1857, the last serious hope vanished with the redistribution of the funds collected in 1848 and saved for a new insurrection.[15]

Although residual loyalties rendered immigrants particularly sensitive, appeals from abroad evoked a response from all Bostonians and frequently presented a common denominator for coöperation. Non-Irishmen promptly and generously aided Ireland, loading the *Jamestown* with supplies for the famine stricken land in 1848, and actively participating in relief work in 1863.[16] Political sympathy, although more intense within each group, also existed outside it. Germans, Frenchmen, Italians, and, for a time, the Irish combined for common revolutionary objectives, thinking in terms of a

Fig. 20. Political discontent — arrest of William Smith O'Brien, 1848

general struggle of western peoples against tyranny — national in form, but liberal in substance.[17]

Thus the recollection of common origin was not a conclusive segregative factor. The group discovered its coherent identity, tested its cohesiveness, and apperceived its distinguishing characteristics only by rubbing against the ineluctable realities of existence in Boston. When experience diluted initial differences, newcomers entered smoothly into the flow of life about them. Otherwise, they remained a discordant element in the closely-knit society; reluctant or unable to participate in the normal associational activities of the community, they strove to reweave on alien looms the sundered fabric of familiar social patterns. Since new soil and new homes called for new forms of behavior, they created a wide range of autonomous organizations to care for their needy, provide economic and political protection for their helpless, and minister spiritual comfort and friendship to those who found it nowhere else.

The yearning for familiar pleasures, for the company of understanding men, and the simple sensation of being not alone among strangers, drew immigrants together in tippling shop and *bierhaus,* and in a wide variety of more formally organized social activities. Of these the most prominent was the Charitable Irish Society. By 1845 it had completely lost its original character and had settled down to the business of commemorating St. Patrick's day with a grand dinner which annually grew more magnificent until it attained the dignity of a Parker House setting in 1856.[18] Few Irishmen could join this venerable association, however. The "bone and sinew" concentrated in the Shamrock Society founded in 1844, and celebrated more modestly, but no less enthusiastically, at Dooley's, the Mansion House, or Jameson's.[19] In addition, informal neighborhood groups sprang up wherever the Irish settled.[20]

Canadians gathered in the British Colonial Society while Scotsmen preserved old customs, sported their kilts, danced to the bagpipe, and played familiar games, either in the ancient Scots Charitable Society, the Boston Scottish Society, or the Caledonian Club (1853).[21] Germans, who felt that Americans lacked *Gemüthlichkeit,* established independent fraternal organizations which often affiliated with native ones. Thus Herman Lodge was Branch 133 of the Independent Order of Odd Fellows, and Branch 71 of the Independent Order of Redmen was known as the Independent Order of Rothmänner.[22] Jews, however, formed none of their own, at first participating in American and later in German groups.[23]

No society considered its activities complete without a ball, annual, semiannual, or quarterly. At Hibernian Hall the Irish danced to the familiar music of Gilmore's band, while the Germans waltzed in Spring, Odd Fellow's, Phönix, or Turner halls to the rhythms of the Germania or Mainz's Orchestra.[24] Balls were so successful that Germans organized a *deutschen Ballgesellschaft,* and the Irish, the Erina Association, to sponsor them; and far-sighted entrepreneurs promoted them nightly to bring business to saloons and halls.[25]

Picnics were as popular; everyone arranged them. In Green Mountain Grove, Medford, Highland Grove, Melrose, or Bancroft's Grove, Reading, Germans enjoyed music and dancing, turning and games, absorbed mammoth lunches at ease, and set their children loose to roam in the woods (at half price).[26] For similar amusement, the Irish favored Waverly Grove or Beacon's Grove, Winchester, where even occasional fights and riots did not detract from the pleasure of escape from narrow streets and constricted homes.[27] For other relaxation the Germans turned to indoor gymnastics through the *Turnverein* founded by Heinzen and to shooting, climaxed by the annual *Turkey-schiessen* of the *Schutzenverein Germania.*[28] The Irish preferred rowing and several clubs engaged in vigorous boat-racing, modeled after regattas in Ireland. Run-of-the-mine matches took place in the harbor from Long Wharf to Castle Island, but major contests such as those of the *Maid of Erin* against the *T. F. Meagher,* or the *Superior* of New Brunswick, occurred in the Back Bay while hundreds of Irish spectators watched from along the Mill Dam.[29]

Militia companies were primarily social organizations, less attractive for their martial exploits than for the small bounty, the opportunity to parade in uniform, and the dinner and speeches that followed target practice and parade.[30] Though others joined American companies,[31] the Irish formed their own. Their earliest, the Montgomery Guards, had disbanded in 1839 after a dispute, but the Columbian Artillery, the Bay State Artillery, and the Sarsfield Guards took its place by 1852. Dissolved by the governor in 1853 as a result of Know-Nothing agitation, they continued their activities in new skins. The Columbian Artillery became the Columbian Literary Association, while the Sarsfield Guards became the Sarsfield Union Association, and their balls, picnics, and lectures suffered no loss in popularity.[32]

Saints' days furnished an annual social climax. The Scots Charitable Society celebrated St. Andrew's Day at a dinner at which "many a 'bannock' and dish of 'haggis' was eaten, and some whiskey punch was drank." [33] But the traditional St. Patrick's Day dinners of the Charitable Irish and the Shamrock Societies soon proved utterly inadequate for the Irish. No banquet room was broad enough to comprehend all the sons of Eire, even had they the price of the dinner. Only a spectacular parade could show their full ranks. Led by mu-

Fig. 21. An Irish militia company — Columbian Artillery

sic, 2,000 marched in 1841; and thereafter, the number of
loyal Irishmen and flamboyant bands grew. Mass usually followed, for the Church stressed the supranational, religious aspect of the holiday. But though German Catholics occasionally participated, St. Patrick remained essentially Irish.[34]

Immigrant fraternal activities often outlived the needs
which originally fostered them, becoming ancillary rather
than essential to the lives of the newcomers who did not differ basically from their neighbors. Among some, however,
economic status, geographical segregation, and alien culture
sustained and reinforced the initial feelings of strangeness,
and magnified the importance of organizations in absorbing
the shock of contact with foreign society. The Irish were al-

most alone in founding associations for material betterment, for only they were confined to a single economic class by industrial stratification. They unhappily realized their position in the city was distinct from that of any other group — exploited, indispensable, yet lowly and unwanted. Despairing of the prospects around them, persistently questioned,

> In the valleys of New England,
>> Are you happy, we would know?
> Are you welcome, are you trusted?
>> Are you not? — Then, RISE AND GO! [35]

some sought escape to the frontier. But desirous as they were of leaving, few had the funds to carry them to the freedom of cheap lands.[36] And those wealthy enough to subsidize emigration were unwilling to tamper with an adequate, tractable, and inexpensive supply of labor and votes. Bishop Fenwick's plan for a colony in Maine (1833), the New England Land Company's project for one in Iowa (1851), and the Buffalo Convention's day-dream of a new Ireland in Canada, all came to nought.[37]

Necessarily reconciled to remaining within Boston, the Irish turned to sporadic and largely futile efforts to improve their economic position there. In 1855 more than 200 East Cambridge Irishmen contributed $6.00 each and formed the first consumers' coöperative to avoid "the petty domineering of would-be tyrants. . . ."[38] They turned also to their own countrymen for advice on the protection of their savings, consulting first the Bishop and the English consuls, and ultimately establishing banks of their own.[39] After an unsuccessful strike in 1843, the tailors established a producers' co-operative under B. S. Treanor, the Young Irelander. That organization failed, but it evolved by 1853 into the Journeymen Tailors' Trade and Benevolent Association. Stimulated by the panic of 1857, the society reorganized (1858), and affiliated with a similar group in Philadelphia.[40] Another large sector of unskilled Irishmen formed the Boston Laborers Association (1846) in an attempt to control dock and warehouse employment. Though it lost a serious strike in 1856, it reorganized in 1862 and grew in strength and vitality through the Civil War, remaining distinctly Irish, as did similar societies of waiters and granite cutters.[41]

Among all groups, of course, there were those who lived from hand to mouth in the shadow of an involuntary and remorseless improvidence. When illness, fatigue, or unemployment cut short their labor, these turned not to the cold stranger, but each man to his countryman, each to his old neighbor. Resenting

> The organized charity scrimped and iced,
> In the name of a cautious, statistical Christ,

all were reluctant to rely upon Boston social agencies, even those set up for their special benefit.[42] Nor could they fall back upon the organizations of their precursory compatriots, for both the Scots Charitable Society (1657) and the Charitable Irish Society (1737) had early shed their original functions, becoming primarily wining and dining clubs.[43]

Numerous benevolent enterprises therefore marked the settlement of each new group in the city. But not all flourished. Many societies, hopefully launched, soon met disaster in seas of disinterestedness. The *Società Italiana di Benevolenza,* an early German Charitable Society, a Scandinavian Benevolent Relief Society, and a Swiss group, all failed to survive.[44] A British Charitable Society, founded in 1816, and a German Assistance Society, founded in July, 1847, with sixty members, struggled through the period, but always remained small.[45] The British organization almost disappeared during the Civil War, while apathy kept down the membership of the German Society, which only spent $300 to $400 annually for assistance. Intimate associations with limited functions, like the *Krankenunterstutzungsgesellschaft* — which provided death and illness benefits — were more successful; and religious institutions continued to extend charity. But on the whole the non-Irish immigrants failed to develop autonomous eleemosynary activities.[46]

The Irish, however, segregated in their murky slums, in their lowly occupations, and their dread of losing religion, never ceased to anticipate harsh treatment from strangers or to distrust unknown ways.[47] Centuries of struggles had engendered an acute wariness of Protestants, of Protestant friendship, and of Protestant assistance that too often masked proselytization with the guise of benevolence. "Talk to them of the Poorhouse and they associate with it all the disagreeable features of the prison-like Unions of their native land. Added to which is the horror, if placed there of being exiled, as they fear, from their priests; and *'they will sooner die in the streets'* (such is their language) than go to Deer Island or South Boston. . . ." [48] This misgiving was, of course, not without justification. Despite laws to restrict their influence, Protestant chaplains dominated the spiritual life of public institutions, controlling the inmates' reading material and religious services, while Catholic priests found great difficulty in securing access even after a resolve of the legislature in 1858 admitted them.[49]

The horror of dying in a hospital without the ministrations of a priest was not allayed until 1863 when Andrew Carney gave a South Boston estate to the Sisters of Charity for the institution named after him.[50] Destitute children, in danger of adoption by Protestants or the state, received earlier attention. In 1833, Sister Ann Alexis and the Sisters of Charity founded St. Vincent's Female Orphan Asylum. Accumulating funds from successive fairs and church collections, they finally purchased a building in 1842, and in April, 1858 opened new quarters, donated by Andrew Carney, to house the increasing number of children. The orphanage was exceedingly popular, but at most accommodated only 200.[51] Father Haskins' House of the Angel Guardian, established in 1851 for neglected boys, supplemented the activities of the Asylum.[52] But since the two combined could care for only a small fraction of those who looked to them for aid, the Irish organized a system of adoption by Catholic families.[53] However, when the Home for Destitute Catholic Children opened in 1864, more than one thousand gamins between the ages of eight and twelve were still prosecuted annually for vagrancy.[54]

Financial limitations necessarily relegated the immense problem of pauperism to the government. An early Hibernian Relief Society (c. 1827) was short-lived. The Irish could do little more for the poor than provide much needed clothing through parish societies, and occasional assistance through the Roman Catholic Mutual Relief Society, and, later, through the Society of St. Vincent de Paul.[55] The religious character of these associations drove the small group of Protestant Irish into a separate "Irish Protestant Mutual Relief Society." [56]

Except for the Negroes who in 1860 opened a home for aged women on Myrtle Street, Beacon Hill, the Irish alone established an independent institutional life. Their strength of numbers facilitated but did not cause separation. By 1865, the Germans, more numerous than the Irish in the year St. Vincent's Orphan Asylum opened, had failed to set up a single permanent agency. Social, economic and intellectual development gradually eliminated the necessity for autarchy in non-Irish groups, but ingrained in the Irish the insistence upon independent charities conducted according to Catholic principles.

Beyond the range of material needs, each group organized to preserve a precious cultural heritage, enlisting a wide variety of social instruments — churches, schools, newspapers, and clubs. Each cherished distinctive traditions whose chances of survival varied with the strength of the differences developed by experience in Boston. Language was the weakest barrier. Attempts to preserve German were futile. Pastors preached the necessity of learning English, and despite difficulties English words inevitably crept into German usage.[57] Thrown into continuous contact with neighbors who spoke no German, even purists inevitably "schäkt" hands, referred to "dem feinsten Köntry der Welt" and "unsere City," and used "no, sörri" and "ohl wreit" as liberally as any Yankee. Business taught them "aber Käsch daun," "Dammädsches," "engahdschd," and "indiht?." [58] Some used the two languages interchangeably, and all adapted the forms of one to the other.[59] French and German easily became second languages which could be acquired by the immigrants' children in the public schools. Separate organizations, founded on linguistic differences alone, proved superfluous.[60]

Similarly, the urge to maintain familiar forms of worship was most meaningful when it embodied a vital social difference. Thus although the Portuguese Jews had a synagogue as early as 1816, when Abraham Touro requested "that his religious profession might be recorded on the Town's books — & that he belonged to a Synagogue of the Jews," German Jews erected their own building in 1843 which in turn did not satisfy the Polish Jews who dedicated still another in 1849.[61] On the other hand, though German Protestants organized a congregation as early as 1839, constructing Zion Church (Shawmut Street, South End) in 1846–47, and a Methodist Church in Roxbury in 1852, they often accepted the facilities of natives. A number of German families, stopping in Roxbury for a few months in 1833, were content to attend St. James Episcopal Church and to send sixty children regularly to Sunday School, and the Reverend A. Rumpff, pastor of the Lutheran Church, worked as a missionary for the Unitarian Fraternity of Churches.[62]

Within the Catholic Church three nativity groups insisted upon national forms. When the Abbé de la Poterie read his first mass in 1788 to a congregation of between sixty and a hundred communicants, primarily French by nativity, but including some Irishmen, dispute arose as to the language to be used.[63] As soon as the English-speaking Reverend John Thayer appeared in Boston, the Irish seized the church by force, ousting the French priest whom the Bishop had delegated "to provide a Preacher for the most numerous part of the congregation." [64] Bishop Carroll finally ended the rift in the tiny Catholic community by retiring both Thayer and de Rousselet and installing the French Father Matignon. [65] Although the French had once preferred to be buried with Protestants rather than with Irish Catholics, and had felt bitter enough to remove their furniture from the church, the tact and kindly wisdom of Matignon and of the saintly Bishop Cheverus reconciled and reunited the two groups. Small in number, facing no serious problems until the forties, they remained harmonious in sentiment. [66]

But as immigration increased, the Church acquired a thoroughly Irish cast, marked by the accession to the episcopacy of John Bernard Fitzpatrick, the Boston-born son of Irish parents, who replaced the Maryland aristocrat Fenwick in 1846, and by an ever larger proportion of Irish-born clergymen, many from All-Hallows Missionary College near Dublin. [67] In its first four decades, the Church had scarcely grown at all. In 1816, Boston contained not more than 1,500 Catholics of all nativities, and Bishop Cheverus felt it could well be served as part of the New York diocese. [68] By 1830, only little St. Augustine's Chapel, South Boston (1819), had joined Holy Cross Cathedral, Franklin Square (1801–03). The three churches built in the thirties to provide for the inhabitants of the North End, the South End and Roxbury, and Charlestown could not serve those arriving in the forties. For in 1843, the absolute maximum capacity of all Catholic places of worship, including 2,000 seats reserved for Germans, was still less than 14,000 — clearly inadequate for the Irish. [69]

Active expansion, however, met the demands. In 1843, the Rev. J. B. M'Mahon opened the indispensable Moon Street Free Church in the heart of the North End slums, the first to accommodate the very poorest. In 1848, the Bishop bought the meeting house of the Purchase Street Unitarian Society for the use of the Irish in Fort Hill, naming it St. Vincent's. Finally, in 1855, the dedication of the Church of St. James, prepared to serve a congregation of 10,000, temporarily settled the problem within peninsular Boston, the Irish population of which did not increase sharply thereafter.[70]

As the Irish spread from the heart of the city, the Church followed, frequently purchasing the empty buildings of displaced Yankees. In 1842, they laid the cornerstone of St. John's Church in East Cambridge, and in 1848, opened St. Peter's, Cambridge. In 1844 the Meeting House of the Maverick Congregational Society in East Boston became the Church of St. Nicholas, joined before long by St. Mary's, the Star of the Sea, and Sacred Heart and Assumption. In 1845 a new church dedicated to SS. Peter and Paul replaced old St. Augustine's Chapel in South Boston, supplemented a few years later by the "Gate of Heaven" Church at City Point (1863). In 1855 a church was built in Brighton and in 1858 one in Brookline.[71]

Thoroughly Irish in character, the Church nevertheless profited by its early quarrels and made special provision for worship by each new national group. By 1840 the French element was thoroughly insignificant, but there were enough German Catholics to require attention. Served at first only by pastors who made occasional trips from New York, and by special masses in the Cathedral, the Germans soon demanded a church of their own. In 1841, they organized Trinity Church and erected a building (completed 1846) on Suffolk Street in the South End, which also served those in Roxbury and East Boston. Disturbed by a quarrel with Bishop Fenwick, however, they built their church slowly and with great difficulty, and remained in debt for many years, for Catholicism did not play the intimate role in German it did in Irish life.[72]

While immigrants might possibly transplant the familiar form of their churches as a matter of habit, they established successful independent educational organizations only in response to needs arising in America. Having no Old-World model — schools at home were either nonexistent or state-controlled — they created new institutions to protect a vital cultural difference. A German school system therefore remained a chimerical hope in the minds of isolated individuals. The ambition of intellectuals to establish a great German university in the New World led to fascinating speculations, but to nothing more. German Catholic priests may have given instruction throughout the period, but their attempt to found a formal academy failed; not until 1863 could they even buy a lot.[73] And the classes maintained by non-Catholic Germans in Roxbury and Boston had no more than ninety students by 1860.[74] Jews provided religious training for their children, but otherwise sent them to the public schools although a six-day teaching week made observance of their Sabbath difficult.

But a separate system was essential to the Irish, for compulsory education drew their children into the common schools, endangering their Catholic souls. Thus challenged, the Church attempted to cope with the problem even before the first Provincial Council of Bishops in 1829 urged the establishment of truly Catholic schools in each community.[75] Sunday Schools, the first line of defense, grew slowly; by 1829 not more than 500 Catholic children received instruction in the whole area. But after 1835 the Young Catholics Friend Society, overwhelmingly Irish by nativity, assumed the burden of these schools in Boston, organized branches in the Irish sections of the city, and educated more than a thousand pupils annually. By 1845 there were 4,100 children in Boston Catholic Sunday Schools. And thereafter societies of the same name exercised similar functions in South Boston and Roxbury.[76]

Parochial schools likewise started slowly, but expanded to meet the influx of Irish. The school Father Matignon is traditionally said to have kept in Holy Cross Church at the beginning of the century, probably offered only occasional haphazard instruction.[77] In 1820, the Ursuline nuns, with the aid of John Thayer and Bishop Cheverus, set up the first school for girls in their convent near the Cathedral. Although almost one hundred pupils attended at one time, it lost contact with the Boston Irish after moving in 1826 to Mt. Benedict, Charlestown.[78] There were classes of some sort in the Cathedral in 1826 and 1829, in Craigie's Point, Charlestown, in 1829, and in connection with St. Vincent's Orphan Asylum after 1830, but another permanent formally organized school was not founded until 1849, when the Sisters of Notre Dame de Namur from Cincinnati established one at St. Mary's, North End. The Sisters extended their activities by 1853 to the Church of SS. Peter and Paul, South Boston, opened academies by 1858 in Roxbury and on Lancaster Street, Boston, a convent on Berkeley Street, Back Bay, in 1864, and, after a quarrel over the use of the Bible in public schools, "Father Wiget's" in the North End in 1859.[79]

Higher education, less important to the mass of Irish laborers, came later. Holy Cross College in Worcester, established in 1843, attracted few Massachusetts residents, for its fees — more than $150 a year — were out of the reach of most.[80] But when the Jesuits opened Boston College on Harrison Street in the South End in 1863, the thirty-dollar annual charge and the possibility of living at home enabled more to attend.[81] Bishop Fenwick's hopes of founding a theological seminary were not realized, however, and in this period Boston Irishmen still found it necessary to send their children to France or to Canada for instruction leading to the priesthood.[82]

On all levels, of course, tuition charges limited attendance to those who could pay. Some, perforce, relied upon common schools. But many failed to attend at all, and the insistence upon parochial education often became a shield for truancy, creating a serious problem of child vagrancy.[83] But though the principle of Catholic instruction for every child remained an ideal rather than a reality, the Irish resisted the temptation of free public schools, and at considerable cost sponsored their own.

Among the Irish, educational efforts took special form in the total abstinence societies. Unable to deal with intemperance as other Bostonians did, they formed groups to provide nonalcoholic relaxation and entertainment. The earliest (1836) had been nonsectarian.[84] But after 1841, these organizations affiliated with the Church, their most active sponsor.

Stimulated by the visit of Father Mathew in 1849, these groups grew rapidly. In addition to the Hibernian and Father Mathew Total Abstinence Societies, clubs flourished in each parish and suburb, closely interrelated, but having no contact with non-Catholics. Thus, in 1865, at a procession after the death of President Lincoln, the nineteen non-Irish temperance groups marched together in Division 2, while the Irish paraded in Division 7.[85]

Their distinctive needs also shaped the less formally organized education of the Irish. Though some took advantage of such non-Catholic agencies as the adult evening school and the sewing school of the Benevolent Fraternity of Churches, most turned all their activities into Catholic channels.[86] Thus, the Young Catholics Friend Society early renounced its plan of inviting lecturers without regard to sect; and other groups adopted the same exclusive Catholic policy. The Hibernian Lyceum, the Tom Moore Club, literary institutes, debating societies, and Young Men's Sodalities all applied religious ideas to literature and current events, while the Boston Gregorian Society, formed in 1836 by young Irishmen, applied them to music.[87]

The French and Germans sponsored similar cultural activities. The *Gesangverein Orpheus* and the *Solo-Club* gave popular concerts for many years, and a society founded in 1847 offered numerous lectures and plays. Even earlier, German Jews founded a "Hebrew Literary Society" which met twice weekly for discussions and kept a file of Jewish, German, and English periodicals. In addition, enterprising saloonkeepers found it profitable to keep *Lesezimmer* where nostalgic countrymen could scan the pages of the *Berliner*

National-Zeitung, the *Leipziger Illustrierte,* and the good-natured *Kladderadatsch.*[88]

Periodicals from home were not enough. Each group at one time or another attempted to develop newspapers to express its own needs in the new world. However, though the press was the immigrants' most powerful educational instrument, it flourished in Boston only to the degree that it satisfied a significant social need. Since almost all these journals appeared weekly they competed with the superior resources of those in New York and failed unless supported by a group conscious of its identity. Thus, the French, first in the field with Joseph Nancrede's *Courrier de Boston* and de Rousselet's *Courier politique de l'univers* (1792–93), were unable to support one in Boston for any length of time because of competition from the splendid *Courrier des États-Unis* of New York.[89] Edited with great care, displaying an unusual regard for taste and accuracy, the latter was the outstanding immigrant newspaper of the period. In turn weekly, bi-weekly, and tri-weekly, it finally became a daily.[90] Vying with it, *Le Littérateur français* (1836), the *Petit Courrier des familles et des pensions* (1846), *Le Bostonien,* the *Gazette Française,* all of Boston, and the *Phare de New York,* could last only a short time.[91] Newspapers in other groups started hopefully, but faded rapidly. Short-lived Spanish and Italian sheets had little influence.[92] After the quick failure of the first British paper, *Old Countryman,* the English depended upon the *New York Albion* until one of its editors moved to Boston in 1855, and started the *Anglo-Saxon.* In the same year the *European* and in 1857 the *Scottish-American* were established in New York. But none succeeded.[93]

The only non-Irish immigrant paper that flourished in Boston was founded upon the personality of a brilliant editor. The *Boston Merkur* (1846–48), and *Der Neu England Demokrat* (a semi-weekly) had already disappeared when Karl Heinzen transplanted *Der Pionier* from Louisville and New York to Boston. A fiery radical, of deep culture and acute intelligence, extreme on every social issue, Heinzen, exiled from Prussia, had participated in the 1848 revolution in Baden, and had led a stormy career on several German-American papers. His personal organ thrived in Boston's friendly atmosphere, scarcely affected by the founding of the somewhat more popular *Bostoner Zeitung* in 1865, and exercised a deep influence both on Germans and on the Americans like Wendell Phillips and Garrison who read it.[94]

The strongest organs naturally developed among the Irish, who turned to them for news of home, for accounts of their own activities and organizations, and, above all, for sympathetic advice, derived from their own ideas, on the strange issues they faced as residents and citizens of a new world. But until the forties, even the Irish had no stable newspapers in Boston and relied on the New York *Shamrock,* the *Western Star and Harp of Erin,* and their successors.[95] Starting with Bishop Fenwick's short-lived children's paper, the *Expostulator,* a succession of very Catholic papers ingloriously collapsed.[96] The first, edited by the Bishop and Father O'Flaherty, and known variously as the *Jesuit or Catholic Sentinel* (1829–31), and the *United States Catholic Intelligencer* (1831–33), failed completely. Its successor, the *Literary and Catholic Sentinel,* edited by the popular poet, George Pepper, and by Dr. J. S. Bartlett, appeared at the opening of 1835. By the end of the year, to strengthen its appeal to the Irish, it became the *Boston Pilot* "in honor of one of the most popular and patriotic Journals in Dublin." [97] Subsisting from appeals to the generosity of its subscribers, it lasted through a second year, and gave up. Pepper then attempted to issue a secular paper, *The O'Connellite and Irish Representative,* but neither that nor his other ventures survived.[98]

The second *Boston Pilot,* founded after his death in 1838 to express the interests of the Irish-Catholic population of New England, like its less permanent predecessors, did not pay its way; by the end of the year, it had only 600 subscribers. It staggered on, however, although a meeting of its friends to raise funds was only partially successful. At the end of 1839, it was still in serious difficulties. But the immigration of the forties brought security.[99]

Prosperity completely reoriented the *Pilot's* policy. In 1842, Thomas D'Arcy McGee, a green Irishman of seventeen, electrified a Boston audience with a patriotic oration that won him an editorial position on the *Pilot,* and made him editor-in-chief in 1844. Set by him on a radical course, the *Pilot* preached Irish nationalism, even after he returned to Dublin to edit the *Nation.* Once drawn into the Repeal Movement, the paper became dependent less upon the support of the Church than upon that of popular opinion. And with the aid of that support it could outlive occasional rivals such as the *New England Reporter and Catholic Diary.*[100]

Repeal under the respectable auspices of O'Connell was safe, but after 1845, the *Pilot* espoused the program of Young Ireland and became intolerable to the Church. To counteract the *Pilot's* influence, the Bishop, through Brownson, sponsored the *Boston Catholic Observer,* a religious rival. At the same time a political newspaper, the *Boston Vindicator,* appeared and was hailed as an ally by the *Observer.*[101] Neither the *Vindicator* nor J. R. Fitzgerald's *Nation* which replaced it, lasted long; but for two years the *Observer* and *Pilot* bitterly fought out the issues of Irish conservatism and radicalism.[102] In 1848, however, the *Pilot* acquired still another competitor. In that year, McGee returned from Ireland, established the New York *Nation,* and by the glamor of actual participation in the revolution drew many readers away from the *Pilot.* Weakened further by continued opposition from the clergy, the *Pilot* recanted in 1849 and turned conservative. The cross and dove replaced the red cap of liberty in its masthead, and Father John T. Roddan, an American priest, became its editor. Although many felt that "Donahoe will have a jolly grill in Purgatory for the evil he has done," his paper remained religiously dependable thereafter.[103]

Meanwhile, McGee's radicalism had antagonized Archbishop Hughes of New York, who forced the *Nation* out of business by a vigorous destructive campaign in 1850. Left without a journal, the Massachusetts radicals invited the still unrepentant rebel to come to Boston where he established the *American Celt* in 1850. But McGee failed to prosper. The *Pilot* and the clergy attacked him and he faced the serious competition of Phelim Lynch's *Irish-American,* which had taken his place in New York by 1849. After two years he finally shed his radicalism and made peace with the Church. But since there was no room in Boston for two conservative papers, he left for Buffalo and eventually for Montreal.[104]

No longer strong enough to support a newspaper, the radicals thereafter confined their reading to the New York *Irish-American*. As the former revolutionaries splintered into cliques, each established an organ: John Mitchel's *Citizen,* Doheny's *Honest Truth* and, *Meagher's Irish News.* But neither these nor occasional fugitive papers like William Jackson's *Irish Pictorial Miscellany* or Patrick X. Keating's *Illustrated Irish Nation* menaced the secure hold of the *Pilot* upon the Irish reading public.[105]

Only the Negroes developed a group consciousness comparable to that of the Irish. Although accepted as equals in some sects,[106] sharp color prejudice compelled colored Methodists and Baptists to organize their own churches in the West End.[107] Discrimination kept them out of the common schools and made necessary the organization of a distinct system with the aid of the town and of the Abiel Smith legacy.[108] The refusal of the white Masons to admit Negroes caused the formation of autonomous lodges affiliated not with other Massachusetts lodges, but with the Grand Lodge of England.[109] Similar motives provoked the attempt to organize a Negro military company, while the struggle for equality for themselves and for freedom for their enslaved kinsmen fostered Russworm's *Freedom's Journal* and the New York *Colored American,* and the organization of vigilantes that helped save Shadrach and attempted to rescue Burns.[110] But Negro awareness of race derived not from differences they desired to cherish, but rather from a single difference — color — which they desired to discard. Thus, as soon as a change in law in 1855 admitted Negroes to the common schools, their own closed.[111] Their consciousness was a factor of the prejudice of others, and declined as that subsided. They lacked the cohesiveness and coherence generated in the Irish by their economic, physical, and intellectual development in Boston.

The flourishing growth of Irish institutions was an accurate reflection of their consciousness of group identity. These autonomous activities had no counterpart in the Old World where the community was a unified whole, adequately satisfying all the social desires of its members. Independent societies developed among immigrants only in Boston in response to the inadequacy of the city as it was to fill their needs. Since the non-Irish foreigners felt differences only at occasional particular points, they diverged from native social organizations infrequently, in localized activities of diminishing vitality. But the development of the Irish had broadened original differences so widely that the *Pilot* concluded, "cooperation for any length of time in important matters between *true* Catholics and *real* Protestants is morally impossible." [112] Unable to participate in the normal associational affairs of the community, the Irish felt obliged to erect a society within a society, to act together in their own way. In every contact therefore the group, acting apart from other sections of the community, became intensely aware of its peculiar and exclusive identity.

The degree of intermarriage at once reflected and buttressed the distinction between the Irish and all others. Among the Irish, religious and social considerations reënforced the natural tendency to mate with their own kind. As Catholics, they were repeatedly warned that union with Protestants was tantamount to loss of faith; while the great majority of non-Irish in the city considered marriage with them degrading.[113] As a result, the percentage of Irish intermarriage was lower than that of any other group including the Negroes, 12 per cent of whose marriages were with whites.[114]

Group consciousness in the newcomers provoked a secondary reaction in native Bostonians, almost nonexistent in the eighteenth and early nineteenth centuries, when French Huguenots, Jews, Scots, Scotch-Irish and Irishmen had had no difficulty in assimilating with the older stock.[115] Americans now became more conscious of their own identity. They began to distinguish themselves, the Anglo-Saxons, from the Irish "Kelts." [116] The old society felt a sense of *malaise* because newcomers did not fit into its categories, and resentment, because they threatened its stability. Uneasy, it attempted to avoid contact by withdrawing ever farther into a solid, coherent, and circumscribed group of its own, until in the fifties it evolved the true Brahmin who believed, with Holmes, that a man of family required "four or five generations of gentlemen and gentlewomen" behind him.[117]

∾ VII ∾

Group Conflict

We still drive out of Society the Ishmaels and Esaus. This we do not so much from ill-will as want of thought, but thereby we lose the strength of these outcasts. So much water runs over the dam — wasted and wasting! [1]

CONSCIOUSNESS of identity particularized groups; but mere pluralism evoked no conflict in Boston society. Those coherently welded by circumstances of origin, economic status, cultural variations, or color differences often moved in distinct orbits, but were part of a harmonious system. In some instances, native Bostonians adopted newcomers; in others, they adapted themselves to the existence of aliens in their community. But whatever friction arose out of the necessity for making adjustments produced no conflict, until the old social order and the values upon which it rested were endangered.

Thus, while prejudice against color and servile economic origin confined the Negroes to restricted residential areas, distinct churches, special jobs, separate schools, and undesirable places in theaters until the 1850's, the relationships between Negroes and other Bostonians were stable and peaceful.[2] Social and legal discriminations still limited Negro privileges in the Park Street Church in 1830, and incited protests when Alcott included a Negro child in his infant school.[3] But the stigmata and penalties for being different were slowly vanishing. Those who urged equality for the South were perforce obliged to apply their convictions at home. An attempt in 1822 to restrict the immigration of Negro paupers failed and repeated petitions after 1839 finally secured the repeal of laws against intermarriage, thus legalizing a process already in existence.[4] In 1855 separate schools were abolished and colored children unconditionally admitted to the public schools, so that by 1866 some 150 Negroes attended the primary, 103 the grammar, and five the high schools of Boston — in all, a high percentage of the Negro children of the city.[5] The state actively defended and protected Negroes' rights, even establishing missions for that purpose in Charleston and New Orleans where Boston colored seamen were often seized as fugitive slaves.[6] Public pressure forced the Eastern and New Bedford Railroads to admit colored people to their cars in the forties; and former slaves began to move to the same streets as whites.[7] In 1863, they were permitted to fight in the Union Army when Governor Andrew, with the aid of Lewis Hayden, recruited the Fifty-fourth Massachusetts Regiment, which included 300 fugitive slaves. In the same year, the militia was opened to them, and a colored company in Ward Six received a grant from the city. Negro regiments were segregated, but many prominent Bostonians "taking life and honor in their hands cast in their lot with" them.[8] By 1865, the Negroes, though still a separate part of Boston society, participated in its advantages without conflict. And most Bostonians agreed that "the theory of a natural antagonism and insuperable prejudice on the part of the white man against the black is a pure fiction. Ignorant men are always full of prejudices and antagonisms; and color has nothing to do with it." [9]

Group consciousness based upon religious differences was likewise not conducive to conflict. The Puritan dislike of Catholics had subsided during the eighteenth century,[10] and had disappeared in the early nineteenth as a result of the good feelings produced by revolutionary collaboration with the French and the growth of the latitudinarian belief that "inside of Christianity reason was free." [11] Governor Hancock had early abolished Pope's Day, and the Constitution of 1780 had eliminated the legal restrictions against Catholics. Catholics established a church in the city in 1789 "without the smallest opposition, for persecution in Boston had wholly ceased," and "all violent prejudices against the good bishop of Rome and the Church . . . he governs" had vanished, along with hostility towards hierarchical institutions in general.[12] Bishop Carroll, visiting Boston in 1791, preached before the Governor, pronounced the blessing at the annual election of the Ancient and Honorables, and was amazed at the good treatment accorded him. Bishop Cheverus commanded the respect and affection of all Protestants.

Thereafter the government was no longer hostile. The City Council frequently gave Catholics special privileges to insure freedom of worship, closing the streets near Holy Cross Church to exclude the noise of passing trucks.[13] It never took advantage of the laws that permitted it to tax all residents for sectarian purposes; on the contrary, Boston Protestants often contributed to Catholic churches and institutions. After 1799 no tithes were collected, by 1820 religious tests were abolished, and in 1833 Church and State completely separated.[14] The anti-Catholic activities of the *New York Protestant* and of the New York Protestant Association in the early thirties had no counterpart in Boston where an attempt to found an anti-Catholic paper (*Anti-Jesuit*) in 1829 failed.[15] Accepted as loyal members of the community, Catholics could easily partake of its opportunities.[16] Their right to be different was consistently defended by natives who urged that the particular sect each person chose was a private matter. "In individual instances where our friends and acquaintances join the Romish Church, there may be reason either to be glad of it or to grieve. If they join the Church . . . because they need its peculiar influence for their own good, if never having found peace in Christ elsewhere they do find it there, ought we not to rejoice in such a result? Why should we doubt that some minds are better fitted to find a personal union with God by the methods of the Catholic Church than by any other?"[17]

There were of course differences between the sects, expressed in theological disputations. As early as 1791 Thayer offered to debate any Protestant in a "controversial lecture."[18] Beecher and Bishop Fenwick, assisted by Father O'Flaherty, engaged in a series of debates in 1830–34, the most prominent of the period. And the religious press and sermons occasionally attacked Catholicism, sometimes violently, in the spirit of all contemporary disputes, while Protestant denominations urged their ministers to resist the spread of "Popery." [19]

But the expression of theological differences did not imply intolerance. Thus the Congregationalists urged their ministers to labor "in the spirit of prayer and Christian love . . . ," and even the *Christian Alliance and Family Visitor,* founded "to promote the union of Christians against Popery," failed to print "a single article or paragraph of any description against . . . Catholics." [20] Arguments were aimed against Catholicism, not against Catholics, just as they were against Methodism, or by the Orthodox against Unitarianism and by "Christians" against transcendentalists. [21] When Beecher became too violent, the *Boston Courier* and the Boston Debating Society, both non-Catholic, denounced him. For though some preferred one sect to another, the predominant feeling among Bostonians of this period was that "wherever holiness reigns, whether in the Protestant or Catholic communion . . . wherever there is a pious heart . . . there is a member of the true church." [22] Indeed, such men as Channing cared little for the particular sect in which they ministered. Their "whole concern was with religion, not even with Christianity otherwise than as it was, in . . . [their] estimation, the highest form of religion. . . ." [23]

Those who recognized distinctions between the sects generally felt that more important were "the grand facts of Christianity, which *Calvinists* and *Arminians, Trinitarians* and *Unitarians, Papists* and *Protestants, Churchmen* and *Dissenters* all equally believe. . . . We all equally hold that he came . . . to save us from sin and death, and to publish a covenant of grace, by which all sincere penitents and good men are assured of favour and complete happiness in his future everlasting kingdom." [24] In that vein, Holmes' "Cheerful Parson" affirmed,

> Not damning a man for a different opinion,
> I'd mix with the Calvinist, Baptist, Arminian,
> Greet each like a man, like a Christian and brother,
> Preach love to our Maker, ourselves and each other.[25]

And even the more conservative Baptists granted that "the various erring sects which constitute the body of Antichrist, have among them those who are beloved of God. . . ." "Wherein we think others err, they claim our pity; wherein they are right, our affection and concurrence." [26] In this roseate scheme of salvation there was room even for Jews, and from Bunker Hill, a poet proclaimed:

> Christian and Jew, they carry out one plan,
> For though of different faith, each in heart a man.[27]

Government action reflected the community's attitude towards immigrants. They were still welcome. The state had no desire to exclude foreigners or to limit their civic rights; on the contrary, during this period it relaxed some surviving restrictions.[28] Since the care of aliens was charged to the Commonwealth, the problem of poor relief aroused less hostility within Boston than outside it.[29] Yet nowhere was pauperism transmuted into a pretext for discrimination against the Irish. Legislation aimed only at barring the dependent, the insane, and the unfit, and shifted to newcomers part of the cost of those who could not support themselves. The function of the municipal Superintendent of Alien Passengers, under the act of 1837, was merely to prevent the landing of persons incompetent to maintain themselves, unless a bond be given that no such individual become a public charge within ten years, and to collect the sum of two dollars each from all other alien passengers as a commutation for such a bond.[30] All the subsequent changes in the law only modified it to conform with a decision of the Supreme Court.[31] Attempts to extend these restrictive provisions failed, partly because of the pressure of shipping firms which profited by the immigrant traffic, but primarily because successive administrations recognized that, "The evils of foreign pauperism we cannot avoid," and it is "wise to avail ourselves of the advantages of direct emigration which increases the business of the State." [32]

In the two decades after 1830, however, the differences so tolerantly accepted impinged ever more prominently upon the Bostonians' consciousness. The economic, physical, and intellectual development of the town accentuated the division between the Irish and the rest of the population and engendered fear of a foreign group whose appalling slums had already destroyed the beauty of a fine city and whose appalling ideas threatened the fondest conceptions of universal progress, of grand reform, and a regenerated mankind. The vague discomforts and the latent distrusts produced by the problems of these strangers festered in the unconscious mind of the community for many years. Though its overt manifestations were comparatively rare, the social uneasiness was none the less real.

Thus pauperism aroused some resentment among those who saw Massachusetts overwhelmed by a rising tax bill; [33] and indigent artisans continually complained that Irishmen displaced "the honest and respectable laborers of the State; and . . . from their manner of living . . . work for much less per day . . . being satisfied with food to support the animal existence alone . . . while the latter not only labor for the body but for the mind, the soul, and the State." [34] Above all, as the newcomers developed consciousness of group identity and sponsored institutions that were its concrete expression, they drove home upon other Bostonians a mounting awareness of their differences, and provoked complaints that "instead of assimilating at once with the customs of the country of their adoption, our foreign population are too much in the habit of retaining their own national usages, of *associating too exclusively with each other,* and living in groups together. These practices serve no good purpose, and tend merely to alienate those among whom they have chosen to reside. *It would be the part of wisdom, to* ABANDON AT ONCE ALL USAGES AND ASSOCIATIONS WHICH MARK THEM AS FOREIGNERS, *and to become in feeling and custom, as well as in privileges and rights, citizens of the United States."* [35] The inability of the native-born to understand the ideas of their new neighbors perpetuated this gap between them, rousing the vivid fear that the Irish were "a race that will never be infused into our own, but on the contrary will always remain distinct and hostile." [36]

That fear was the more pronounced because the Catholic Church in these years was a church militant, conscious of its mission in the United States, vigorous and active in proselytization and the search for converts. In the strategy of the hierarchy, and in their own minds, immigrants played a clear role in this process of redemption: they had been carried across the waters by a Divine Providence to present an irrefutable example of fortitude and faith to their unbelieving neighbors, to leaven the dull mass of Protestant America and ultimately to bring the United States into the ranks of Catholic powers.[37] No figure was more insistently, clearly, and admiringly drawn in immigrant literature than that of the humble Irishman in every walk of life who succeeded in converting his employer, friend, or patron.[38] Though Bostonians could not do without the Irish servant girl, distrust of her mounted steadily; natives began to regard her as a spy of the Pope who revealed their secrets regularly to priests at confession.[39] The growth of Catholicism in England warned them that a staunchly Protestant country might be subverted. Meanwhile, close at home, the mounting power of the Oxford movement in the Episcopal Church, reflected in the estrangement of Bishop Eastburn and the Church of the Advent (1844 ff.), and a growing list of widely publicized conversions lent reality to the warning of Beecher and Morse that Catholics plotted to assume control of the West.[40]

Before 1850, the potential friction inherent in these fears broke out only infrequently and sporadically. Incepted by irresponsible elements, these spontaneous brawls were always severely criticized by the community. Indeed, they were only occasionally directed against aliens, more often involving neighborhoods or fire companies. The rowdies singled out no special group. In 1814 West Enders rioted against Spanish sailors, in 1829 aganist Negroes and Irishmen, and in 1846 against some drunken Irishmen in Roxbury; but these were no more significant than the countless feuds between North

Enders and South Enders, or between truckmen and sailors, details of which enlivened many a police dossier.[41]

The Broad Street riot was exceptional only in size. On June 11, 1837, a collision between a volunteer fire company and an Irish funeral procession led to an outbreak, quelled after an hour or so by the militia. Caused by hot-headed, unruly firemen, proverbially a disruptive factor, it in no way reflected the feeling of the community. The firemen were immediately repudiated, and partly as a result of the affair, Mayor Lyman took the first steps towards replacing the volunteer system with a paid fire department.[42] A less permanent result was the establishment by the disbanded firemen of the *American,* the first anti-Catholic paper in Boston which for somewhat less than a year attacked alternately the Irish and the *"paid patriots"* who replaced them.[43]

Because it served for many years as an argument throughout the country in the propaganda for and against Catholics, the Charlestown Convent fire received a greater degree of notoriety than any other riot.[44] This disturbance grew primarily out of the failure of the school and the rural community in which it was located to adjust themselves to each other. To the laborers who lived nearby, the convent was a strange and unfamiliar institution, with which it was difficult to be neighborly or to follow the customary social forms. In addition, Catholicism meant Irishmen and for non-Irish laborers the convent was a symbol of the new competition they daily encountered. Rebecca Reed's lurid stories of life in the convent and the bickering of the Bishop and the Charlestown Selectman over a cemetery on Bunker Hill, provoked a sense of irritation that came to a head with the appearance and disappearance of Elizabeth Harrison, a demented nun.[45] The refusal of the Mother Superior to admit the Charlestown Selectmen to investigate the purported existence of dungeons and torture chambers until the very day of the fire inflamed

Fig. 22. Reminder of intolerance — ruins of the Ursuline Convent

the forty or fifty Charlestown truckmen and New Hampshire Scotch-Irish brickmakers who led the curious mob; and her threat that, unless they withdrew, she would call upon the Bishop for a defense contingent of 20,000 Irishmen precipitated the holocaust.[46]

After the initial excitement, every section of public opinion in Boston greeted the fire with horror and surprise. Bostonians had not disliked the school; many had actually sent their children there. There is no evidence that the residents of the city had any connection with the plot; not a voice was raised in its support. The press condemned the absence of adequate protection, and deplored the "high-handed outrage." Bostonians asserted that "The Catholics . . . are as . . . loyal citizens as their brethren of any other denomination." A mass meeting at Faneuil Hall expressed sympathy with the unfortunate victims of mob action and, resolving "to unite with our Catholic brethren in protecting their persons, their property, and their civil and religious rights," recommended a reward for the capture of the criminals and compensation to the convent, as did similar meetings under John Cotton in Ward Eight, under Everett at Charlestown, and under Story at Cambridge.[47] A reward of $500 offered by Governor Davis resulted in the arrest of thirteen men, the trial of eight, and the conviction of one. The life imprisonment sentence for the one of whose guilt there seemed to be no doubt was far more significant than failure to convict those who might have been innocent.[48]

The convent, reëstablished in Roxbury, failed "because of lack of harmony among the Sisters." [49] But the legislature was petitioned for compensation repeatedly in the next twenty years. Despite persistent reluctance to grant public funds for religious purposes, $10,000 was voted in 1846, but rejected by the Ursulines.[50] The rise of Know-Nothing sentiments thwarted further overtures, while anti-Catholic activities of city rowdies and the circulation of *Six Months in a Convent* somewhat balanced expressions of sympathy. But these antagonisms were more marked outside than within the city. None of the anti-Catholic papers founded after the publication of that scurrilous book were published in Boston.[51]

Occasional manifestations of hostility in the next few years were restricted in scope. The Montgomery Guards, the first Irish military company, were attacked in 1837 by the rank and file of the Boston City Guards who refused to parade with an Irish company to uphold "the broad principle . . . that *in all institutions springing from our own laws, we all mingle in the same undisguised mass, whether native or naturalized.*" Although the native militiamen complained that "the press . . . condemned our conduct with . . . open-mouthed language of wholesale reprehension . . . ," the very next year the same newspapers severely criticized the Irish soldiers who were finally disbanded in 1839.[52] In 1844 the reaction to the school quarrels in New York, to the riots in Philadelphia, and to the defeat of the national Whig ticket by the Irish vote, produced a short-lived nativist branch of the Whig Party. Although the American Republicans under T. A. Davis gained the mayoralty in 1845, it was only on the eighth ballot, in an election fought primarily on the issue of the local water supply.[53] Nativism declined steadily thereafter. An attempt to revive it in 1847 failed so disastrously, that the *Boston Catholic Observer* could triumphantly proclaim nativism dying.[54]

Nativist fears failed to develop more significantly because the Irish before 1845 presented no danger to the stability of the old society. They were in a distinct minority and, above all, were politically impotent. In 1834 the Irish claimed no more than 200 voters in all Suffolk County, and in 1839, no more than 500, while in 1845 less than one-sixth of the adult male foreigners in Boston were citizens.[55] Only a few had secured the right to vote, or took an interest in politics; their opinions were still a matter of private judgment, with no influence upon the policies of the community. The old inhabitants, as individuals, might look down upon their new neighbors as unabsorbable incubi, but the still powerful tradition of tolerance stifled their accumulated resentments. The dominant group took no step to limit social and political rights or privileges until the ideals of the newcomers threatened to replace those of the old society. At that moment the tradition of tolerance was breached and long repressed hostilities found highly inflammable expression.

The crisis came when, after a decade of efforts in that direction, the Irish acquired a position of political importance. After 1840 their press insisted upon the duty "to themselves as well as to their families" of naturalization and a role in the government. Politicians sponsored societies which aided the unknowing and stimulated the indifferent to become citizens, and professional agents drew up papers, filled out forms, and rapidly turned out new voters for the sake of fees and political power.[56] Between 1841 and 1845, the number of qualified voters increased by 50 per cent, then remained stable until 1852, when it grew by almost 15 per cent in two years, while in the five years after 1850, the number of naturalized voters increased from 1,549 to 4,564. In the same period, the number of native voters grew only 14 per cent.[57] Perennial political organizations flourished with every campaign and further mobilized the Irish vote.[58]

The coherence and isolation of Irish ideas facilitated political organization. And Irish leaders, consciously or unconsciously, encouraged group solidarity and the maintenance of a virtual Irish party. Though the Irish vote was not yet used to serve corrupt personal interests,[59] both those who aspired to gain public office in America through the support of a large bloc of voters, and those who hoped to return as liberators to the Emerald Isle, directed their energies toward activizing their countrymen. These efforts were so widespread that one of the most far-sighted Irish leaders complained that Irish political influence was being "fatally misused" and warned that "keeping up an Irish party in America is a fatal mistake, and . . . I will seek to induce them rather to blend and fuse their interests with American parties, than cause jealousy and distrust by acting as an exclusive and independent faction . . . a man has no right to interfere in American politics unless he thinks as an American. . . ."[60] But such views were rare.

With the political mobilization of the Irish in Boston, tolerance finally disappeared. The possibilities of Irish domination were the more startling because the political situation in Massachusetts, 1845–55, permitted a coherent, independent group to exercise inordinate influence. The unity of the old parties was crumbling as dissatisfied elements demanded new policies to meet the problems of reform, particularly those posed by slavery.[61] Although all, including the most conservative Abbott Lawrence, agreed on the ultimate desirability of reform, they were divided as to the methods of attaining it. Within each political party a restless group contended that the forces of good must prevail immediately, even at the expense of failure in national politics. Their insistence upon immediate, unequivocal action destroyed the coherence of the old alignments and yielded to the unified Irish the balance of power. For four years the reformers found these foreigners square in their path, defeating their most valued measures. In the critical year of 1854 this opposition drove them into a violent xenophobic movement that embodied all the hatreds stored up in the previous two decades.

Rantoul and Morton had blasted the stability of the Democrats, but the Whig party was the first torn asunder by the anti-slavery men. In the early forties, some members had already deserted to the Liberty party, but until 1846 most anti-slavery Whigs continued to believe in "reform within the Party." Even in that year the magic personality of Webster nullified the damage done by Southern aggressions and the turbulent Texas and Mexico questions, and held in rein such conscientious rebels as Stephen C. Phillips, Charles Allen, and Sumner. But the Whig nomination of a slaveholder to the presidency and the rejection of the Wilmot Proviso by their National Convention in 1848 opened an unbridgeable gap between the two factions, though the Whigs remained strong enough to win the gubernatorial election that year and again in 1849.[62]

A similar development among the Democrats led a few to support Van Buren, the Free-Soil nominee in 1848, but the party quickly united to profit from the more serious division of its rivals. In addition, hoping for a coalition, it offered the Whig dissidents an anti-slavery plank in 1849. But these overtures failed; Free-Soilers still preferred coöperation with the Whigs to alliance with the Democrats who, nationally, were the most prominent supporters of the South's peculiar institution. But while Webster squinted at the federal scene and dreamed of the White House, the Whigs would have no meddling with reform. Though controlling the legislature of 1849, they failed to pass a single Free-Soil measure. Finally, their support of the Fugitive Slave Law, and particularly Webster's role in its enactment, completed the cleavage and consolidated the Free-Soil party in Massachusetts.[63]

When the gubernatorial election of 1850 gave no candidate a majority, Democratic ambitions, after seven years of famine, approached fulfillment. The constitution provided for the choice of a governor by an absolute majority, in the absence of which the election was thrown into the legislature — a situation susceptible to a great deal of political maneuvering. In this election the Democratic state platform had endorsed the Free-Soil program, though without a formal coalition. A trade between the two parties, which together had a majority in the legislature that convened in January, 1851, was inevitable. The Free-Soilers, anxious to be heard in Washington, were impatient with the Whig demand that the designation of a senator wait eleven months for a new legislature, and threw their votes for a Democratic governor. In return, the Democrats supported a radical policy and handed the United States senatorship and the organization of the legislature to the Free-Soilers. Banks became speaker of the House, and Henry Wilson, president of the Senate; although the former was nominally a Democrat, both were actually Free-Soilers. The reformers got the better of the bargain, passing a series of radical measures, including a general incorporation law to break the power of monopolies, a law for more democratic control of Harvard College, a homestead and mechanics' lien law, and measures ensuring the secret ballot and plurality voting in national elections.[64]

The coalition held through the election of 1851. But though the Free-Soilers managed to push through the Maine Law over Governor Boutwell's veto, they were dissatisfied. They disliked the governor, who had obstructed many reform measures, and they distrusted their Democratic allies, who had bolted in considerable numbers on Sumner's election to the United States Senate and had contrived to defeat a personal liberty law, acts to liberalize divorce, to protect the property rights of women, and to extend the powers of juries. Whittier voiced the apprehension of the Free-Soilers when he wrote, after seeing the governor's first message, "It is . . . monstrous and insulting. May God forgive us for permitting his election." [65]

The Free-Soilers now recognized the need of a reform in government to gain complete control of the State — a reform impossible under the existing conditions of amending the constitution which called for a two-thirds vote in the House of Representatives of two successive legislatures on each clause.[66] With parties divided as they were, a simple majority was difficult enough, two-thirds almost impossible and two-thirds in two successive legislatures, out of the question. One solution was to change the basis of representation to reduce the influence of the conservative elements opposing them in Boston. But an attempt to do so in 1851 failed, leaving the reformers no alternative but a complete revamping of the constitution by a convention.[67]

In 1851 the Free-Soilers forced through the legislature a resolution for a constitutional convention. But when the question was presented to the voters, Democratic support was weak. The Irish, theretofore consistently Democrats, failed to follow their representatives who had indorsed revision. In the election several thousand who had voted for coalition candidates, turned against the constitutional convention.[68] Of these, more than 1,100 were in Boston, and they were predominantly Irish Democrats bolting the party.[69]

When the Democratic State Convention again supported coalition and revision the following year, the Irish, under J. W. James, the Repeal leader, finally seceded from the party. Though opposing the Democrats in the state election of 1852, they supported the national Democratic party which had repudiated Rantoul and coalition and whose presidential candidate, Pierce, was most acceptable as a conservative. Following the advice of Brownson and the *Pilot,* the Boston Irish became national Democrats and state Whigs. As a result of the confusion, the coalition ticket lost, but the project for a convention won.[70]

Impressed with the opportunity the convention presented for strengthening the party and consolidating its position, the Free-Soilers made special exertions in the March election and gained control. Their imprint upon the constitution that resulted was unmistakable. Single unit senatorial districts and plurality elections by secret ballots were proposed. To decrease the power of the executive, many appointive offices, including the Council, became elective; the judiciary was controlled by limiting the term of office and extending the powers of jurors; and the use of public funds for religious education was prohibited. While these measures would render government more responsive to the voice of the people, the proposed constitution was undemocratic in its most important provision. By changing the system of representation to favor country towns at the expense of large cities, bailiwicks of conservatism, the reformers unquestionably compromised their principles.[71]

With one important exception party lines held in the vote on the adoption of the constitution. The opposition of the few conscientious Free-Soilers who would not support the unfair system of representation was trivial compared with the force of conservative Irish Catholic opinion clamoring for defeat.[72] At the Democratic Convention which indorsed the constitution, James again led a seceding group of Boston Irishmen who formed a party of their own. Pressure for recruitment and organization of voters increased. In September the Calvert Naturalization Society in the South End joined the Ward Three Association of the North End. The *Pilot* repeatedly warned that "No Catholic . . . can possibly vote for this . . . Constitution without giving up rights for which he has been all along contending," and Brownson pointed out its revolutionary implications.[73]

In their campaign, the Irish joined the die-hard Whigs under Abbott Lawrence, who led "hundreds of honest men gulled by their sophistry," in opposing a constitution which seriously curtailed the influences of State Street in politics. Lawrence conferred with Bishop Fitzpatrick on the problem, and Whig newspapers appealed particularly to the Irish. Against this alliance the reformers' contention that the *Boston Pilot* was "trying to lead Irishmen into the jaws of a Boston aristocracy as remorseless as the one they had left Ireland to get rid of" counted little. The combination of Irish votes and cotton money in Boston defeated the constitution and elected a Whig ticket.[74]

In this crisis the reformers inveighed against the lords of the counting house and bemoaned the slowness of rank-and-file Whigs to recognize their true interests, but concluded that while the former could never be redeemed, and the latter would have to be educated, the main obstacle to reform was Catholic opposition. And by this time they had learned that differences with the Irish were too deep to be easily eradicated; they could only be fought. Butler, sensitive to every shift in popular opinion, realized that the "performance, which struck down the Constitution, invoked a bitterness among the people against the Catholic religion, such as had never before been, to any considerable degree, either felt or foreshadowed in the State of Massachusetts." [75]

Through the early months of 1854 a series of unconnected events heightened resentment against Catholics and evoked many antipathies developed since 1830. In December, 1853, Father Gavazzi, a rebellious priest, lectured in Boston on the reactionary role of the Church.[76] A few months later, the visit of the papal nuncio Bedini, who had been connected with the massacre of revolutionaries in Bologna, though not provoking the expected riot, did refresh memories of Irish opposition to liberalism.[77] Meanwhile, events at home confirmed that impression. Failure of the enforcement of the prohibition laws was laid at the door of the Irish, and the State Temperance Committee announced it would fight Catholicism as part of its struggle for human freedom.[78] The Burns case clearly linked the immigrants to pro-slavery forces and man-hunters. The *Pilot* supported the rendition of the fugitive slave; and the selection of the Columbian Artillery and Sarsfield Guards to protect him against indignant mobs seeking his freedom, incited an inflammatory handbill:

AMERICANS TO THE RESCUE!
AMERICANS! SONS OF THE REVOLUTION!!
A body of seventy-five Irishmen, known as the
"Columbian Artillery"
have volunteered their services to shoot down the
citizens of Boston! and are now under arms to defend
Virginia in kidnapping a Citizen of Massachusetts!
Americans! These Irishmen have called us
"Cowards and Sons of Cowards!"
Shall we submit to have our Citizens shot
down by a set of Vagabond Irishmen?

that turned many reformers against the Irish.[79] Finally, their defense of the Kansas-Nebraska Act connected them with the slave power, and drew criticism from such respectable sources as the *Commonwealth,* the *Worcester Spy* and Theodore Parker.[80]

Distrust of the Irish at once encouraged and was stimulated by attacks upon Catholics. Hatred and violence marched arm in arm, sustaining and strengthening each other. Early in 1853, the purported kidnapping of Hannah Corcoran, a Baptist convert, almost led to a riot. In the same year the city government entered into a long-drawn-out controversy with the Catholics over their right to build a church on the "Jail lands." In May, 1854, John S. Orr, the Angel Gabriel, led a mob that carried away a cross from the Catholic Church in Chelsea, and in July a church was blown up in Dorchester. *The Wide Awake: and the Spirit of Washington,* a vituperative sheet, appeared in October, 1854 to combat the "swarms of lazaroni from abroad;" and a venomous stream of anti-Papist literature reached Boston, particularly in the form of Frothingham's convent novels (1854).[81]

Meanwhile, as slavery absorbed the attention of Congress and the country, excited Free-Soilers found "every indication that the people are awakening from their unaccountable stupor on the . . . question." [82] The Kansas-Nebraska Bill infuriated even Everett and the conservative Webster Whigs. Sumner's correspondents informed him that "all parties seem to be approaching that happy state of . . . dissolution, for which we have sighed so long." [83] A Freedom Party tentatively formed in Boston, a "Republican" convention adopted a radical program, and a host of excited energies eagerly sought an outlet. Precisely where the immense anti-slavery impulse would be exerted was uncertain, however.[84]

But the Boston municipal elections of December, 1853 had already revealed the ultimate outlet. Only one month after their decisive defeat on the constitution, the reformers rallied to resist the reëlection of Nathaniel Seaver, a Whig supported by the liquor interests. As the "Citizens Union Party," they appealed to nativist feelings and drew 2,000 Whig votes, the entire Free-Soil vote, and 500 voters who had not troubled to go to the polls a month earlier.[85] These 500 voters came from a tremendous fund of nonvoting citizens, many of them Whigs disgusted with their party's vacillation.[86] The lesson to the reformers was obvious and was confirmed by simultaneous elections in Charlestown and Roxbury: [87] the Irish stood in the way of reform; reform forces could best be augmented and galvanized on an anti-Irish basis; the dormant voters must be awakened by an anti-alien alarm.

By 1853 the Order of the Star-Spangled Banner, a nativist secret organization popularly known as the Know-Nothings, had emerged in New York State.[88] Early in 1854 it spread into Massachusetts, swiftly, though quietly and unobtrusively, drawing "into its lodges tens of thousand of . . . anti-Nebraska men, ripe for Republicanism. . . ."[89] These recruits, inwardly ashamed of adopting means incompatible with the principles they professed, wrapped themselves in mantles of secrecy which served as a "spiritual fist-law" for gaining ascendancy without the use of force, and pursued their "purposes with the same disregard of the purposes of the structure external to . . . [themselves] which in the case of the individual is called egoism."[90]

In July, Henry Wilson, already a member, began to harness Know-Nothingism to the anti-slavery cause, and Seth Webb, Jr. decided, "Know-Nothingism is to be an important, perhaps the controlling, element in our state election; it will probably take us out of the hands of the Whigs. Into whose hands it will put us, nobody can tell."[91] The Know-Nothings presented the clearest platform in the next election. Without the support of the intellectual fronts of reform — Adams, Phillips and Sumner — who felt no ends justified nativist methods, they elected Henry J. Gardner, formerly president of the Boston Common Council, to the governorship by the unprecedented majority of 33,000, and gained complete control of the legislature in November. Until 1857, they ruled the state.[92]

Everywhere the success of the party rested upon thousands of new men drawn into politics by nativism.[93] The complexion of the new legislators reflected the ranks from which they rose. Among them were no politicians, and few lawyers. They were true representatives of those for whom they spoke. They included a few rascals and self-seekers; but by and large they were honest men, convinced that they were acting in the best interests of the community. Even the Democratic editor of the *Post* had to admit later that "the moral tone of the party was unquestioned. . . ." [94] Many did not even feel a personal antagonism to the Irish; J. V. C. Smith, an amateur sculptor, and Know-Nothing Mayor in 1854, associated with them in business and executed a fine bust of Bishop Fitzpatrick.[95]

Although the Know-Nothings made numerous mistakes, their administration was progressive and fruitful. They relaid the basis for the school system, abolished imprisonment for debt, established the first insurance commission, took the first steps to eliminate danger from railroad crossings, extended the power of juries, strengthened the temperance, homestead and women's rights laws, made vaccination compulsory, and assumed a firm anti-slavery position by passing a personal liberty law and petitioning for the removal of Judge Loring who had presided at the fugitive slave cases. In general, they embodied in their legislation the program of the party of reform. By 1855, they had sent Wilson to the United States Senate, amended the constitution so that a plurality sufficed in the gubernatorial election, and introduced many other innovations vetoed by the more conservative governor.[96]

The party's anti-foreign accomplishments were quite insignificant. To begin with, they disclaimed any intention of excluding immigrants, but stressed the necessity of making them "be as we are." [97] The most prominent achievement was the disbanding of the Irish military companies which annoyed natives particularly because they carried off prizes at drills. They served no useful purpose and in 1853 the *Boston Pilot* had itself suggested their dissolution. A breach of military discipline provided the pretext for the abolition of the Bay State Artillery in September, followed early the next year by the elimination of the remaining companies. Foreigners on the police force and in State agencies were discharged, and a number of cruel deportations displayed an ugly animus against helpless aliens. Finally, the misdeeds of individual members, notably of the Hiss Nunnery Committee, were exploited by the opposition and did much to discredit the party and obscure its constructive achievements.[98]

Ostensibly the party had acquired power to restrict the influence of immigrants in politics. Yet, though it had absolute control of the government, it failed to pass a single measure to that effect. In 1854, a bill to exclude paupers was not considered until the end of the session, and then referred to committee where it died. A literacy amendment to the constitution was rejected, and an amendment requiring a twenty-one year residence for citizenship which passed, was defeated at the second vote by the next Know-Nothing legislature.[99] Once reform, the essential feature of Know-Nothingism in Massachusetts, was assured, the party leaders attempted to jettison the anti-Catholic program. But the intolerance they had evoked could not readily be dispelled. Its influence persisted long after the death of the party it had served.

The Know-Nothings dissolved over the question of slavery, for the national party drew its strength from incompatible sources. In Massachusetts it was anti-slavery; elsewhere in the North it was unionist; in Virginia and throughout the South, it was pro-slavery.[100] Lack of a unified program inevitably split the party. Despite their strategic position in Congress, they could unite on few measures. Finally, when the national convention adopted a pro-slavery plank in June, 1855, the northerners under Henry Wilson bolted and the Massachusetts Council on August 7 adopted an uncompromising liberal position. At the same time a section of the party broke away and met at Worcester in June, called itself the Know-Somethings or American Freemen, and advocated an abolition platform and an end to secrecy.

The nomination of Fillmore, a pro-slavery man in 1856, completed the break between the state and national parties and a *de facto* coalition with the rising Republican party spontaneously formed. The latter nominated no candidate to oppose Gardner for the governorship, and most Know-Nothings voted for Frémont.[101] Thereafter the Know-Nothings in the state were absorbed in the tremendous growth of the new party, and Banks led the remnants to the Republicans in 1857–58 on his election to the governorship.[102]

Produced by the same reform impulse that fathered Know-Nothingism, the Republican party continued to express animosity toward the Irish, "their declared and uncompromising foe." The defeat of Frémont in 1856 was laid at the door of the Irish-Catholics, and confirmed the party's hostility to them. In retaliation, it helped pass an amendment in 1857 making ability to read the state constitution in English and to write, prerequisites to the right to vote; and in 1859, another, preventing foreigners from voting for two years after naturalization.[103]

Though the restrictive legislation affected all foreigners, the venom of intolerance was directed primarily against the Irish. Waning group consciousness among the non-Irish gave promise of quick acculturation, and similarities in economic condition, physical settlement and intellectual outlook had left little room for disagreement. In fact, the Irish found all others united with the natives against them. A Negro was as reluctant to have an Irishman move into his street as any Yankee,[104] and though the Germans distrusted the Know-Nothings and resented the two-year amendment, liberal principles led them into the Republican party.[105]

Indirectly, the Know-Nothing movement revived Irish nationalism. In Boston, nationalist activities first assumed the guise of the Irish Emigrant Aid Society, whose innocuous title concealed a secret revolutionary club, ostensibly aimed at organizing a liberating invasion of Ireland. Though some hotheads spoke of chartering ships to transport an army of Irish-Americans across the Atlantic, most recognized the obvious futility of such efforts. By and large, they hoped to organize politically, to support anti-English parties in America, to prepare for the Anglo-American war that would free Ireland, and to mobilize support against Know-Nothingism.[106] That the last motive, presumably incidental, was in fact primary, was clear from the movement's exclusively American character: it had no counterpart in Ireland. While expanding rapidly throughout 1855, the organization had little ultimate success. The clergy opposed it, cautious prosecution of would-be liberators in Cincinnati checked its growth, and internal quarrels finally dissipated its strength.[107]

But failure did not end the quest for a fatherland. So long

as the Irish were unaccepted in Boston, they looked back across the ocean. There was "always . . . some . . . machination to draw money from the pockets of the deluded lower order of Irish. . . ."[108] The Fenian Brotherhood emerged after 1859 and despite ecclesiastical disapproval grew in secret until it held its first national convention in Chicago in 1863. Its "centres" in Boston were numerous and active.[109]

Moreover, the Irish persisted in their opposition to reform. With Brownson, they believed Know-Nothingism "an imported combination of Irish Orangism, German radicalism, French Socialism and Italian . . . hate" and regarded Republicanism as its pernicious successor.[110] After 1856 they consistently supported the conservative Democratic party, voting for Buchanan and Douglas.[111] Although the violent phase had passed, the bitterness of conflict and antagonism remained. Out of it had grown a confirmed definition of racial particularism: the Irish were a different group, Celtic by origin, as distinguished from the "true" Americans, who were Anglo-Saxon, of course.[112] Once aroused, hatred could not be turned off at the will of those who had provoked it. The *Springfield Republican* sanely pointed out that "the American party, starting upon a basis of truth . . . has gone on, until [it] . . . denies to an Irishman . . . any position but that of a nuisance. . . ."[113] Group conflict left a permanent scar that disfigured the complexion of Boston social life even after the malignant growth producing it had disappeared.

∾ VIII ∾

An Appearance of Stability

The energy of Irish, Germans, Swedes, Poles, and Cossacks, and all the European tribes . . . will construct a new race, a new religion, a new state, a new literature, which will be as vigorous as the new Europe which came out of the smelting-pot of the Dark Ages. . . .[1]

THE crucible of civil war defined and clarified the position of all elements in Boston society. Republicans and Democrats, Free-Soilers and Whigs, all approved of the objectives of the struggle for union and, after the firing on Fort Sumter, turned their energies towards achieving them. Bostonians now wakened to a realization of the importance of foreigners. The demand for men was enormous. Particularly after the three-month volunteers trickled home, the community leaders faced the necessity of utilizing the most fertile source of new recruits — the immigrant groups. Soon after the fighting began, Governor John A. Andrew wrote to the Secretary of War:

Will you authorize the enlistment here . . . of Irish, Germans and other tough men . . . ? We have men of such description, eager to be employed, sufficient to make three regiments.[2]

That Germans supported the war and eagerly flocked to the colors was not surprising in view of their attitude towards abolition and their membership in the Republican party.[3] Indeed, by 1861 distinctions of national origin had little influence upon the reactions of Germans, Englishmen, Scots, Frenchmen, and Jews. These participated in the community's effort as a matter of course. The four years of struggle merely reaffirmed their secure position in the city; and whatever new problems they faced were not burdened with memories of old conflicts or with unforgotten resentments of social and economic segregation.

But aid from the Irish was less expected. They had opposed Lincoln, favored slavery, fought reform, and upheld the Democratic party and the South. Moreover those who now called for their help were the very men who, for the preceding six years, had sponsored restriction of Irish rights and privileges. "We hear on all sides the sound of disunion . . . ," John C. Tucker had openly warned, "Supposing it should come, and that Massachusetts stood alone, can she . . . expect that these men, who she is now about to proscribe, will rush to her assistance?"[4]

Yet stronger ties bound the Irish to the Union. The guns that roared across Charleston Harbor roused an echo of contradiction in the Church's social policy. Complete acceptance of lawfully established government was basic to the thinking of all Irish Catholics; that was at the root of their complaint that abolitionists were revolutionaries, and helped to account for their complete conservatism after 1848. But in April, 1861, there was no doubt as to which section was revolutionary. The issue was not slavery, but unity, and the Church in

Boston agreed with Archbishop Hughes that "It is one country and must and shall be one." [5] The very logic of its political theory ensured obedience to the government in power and transferred loyalty to Washington.

As the war unfolded, more practical reasons drew the ranks of common Irishmen along the same path as the Church in

> The grandest cause the human
> Race on earth can ever know. [6]

Lack of sectional feelings among the immigrants focused their devotion upon the national government; and the bounties that surpassed the average annual earnings of the common laborer rendered patriotism exceedingly profitable. In addition, Great Britain's southern sympathies, clear from the start, encouraged Irish hopes of a war with England in which the United States together with a resurgent Ireland would humble both Saxon and slaveholder. To some extent, therefore, enlistment became a Fenian tactic. "Centres" flourished in every Irish regiment and optimistic liberators sought to acquire in action against the Confederacy, skill for a further struggle. A common Anglophobia thus allied Irish nationalists and American unionists. [7]

The government was quick to take advantage of Irish feeling. [8] Group consciousness now proved no barrier, but actually an aid to united action. An Irish brigade was organized and Meagher was advanced to the generalcy on the basis of dubious military qualifications but of undoubted popularity among his countrymen. Boston alone mustered two regiments. The Columbian Artillery, banned by the Know-Nothings seven years earlier, emerged from its disguise as a fraternal organization, and under its old commander Thomas Cass furnished the nucleus of the Ninth Massachusetts Regiment. The Twenty-Eighth Regiment, also almost exclusively Irish, was formed later. In addition, Irish units joined other regiments and Irish leaders like P. Rafferty and B. S. Treanor became agents to recruit their compatriots.[9]

The war quickened understanding and sympathy. Serving with their own kinsmen and their own chaplain under their own green flag, assured of complete religious equality, the Irish lost the sense of inferiority and acquired the sense of belonging.[10] They were no longer unwanted aliens. In the armies of the field, men of all nativities fought a common battle. Living together, they came, for the first time, to know one another, and knowing each other, they insensibly drew closer together. A Boston volunteer noted in 1863 the strange celebration of St. Patrick's Day by Meagher's Brigade, but the following year found him joining the festivities.[11] And a visiting Englishman noted, "You cannot go through the camp and say — 'There is the sedate Yankee — there the rollicking Irishman' — all seem subdued together into the same good behaviour." [12]

At home, too, antagonisms became less bitter. The community needed the Irish and therefore cultivated their favor. The government relaxed its discriminations against them. On the recommendation of the governor, the two-year amendment was repealed and the foreign-born regained their full civic rights, with the result that Irish politicians advanced to municipal office in ever larger numbers.[13] At the same time other institutions became more tolerant. In 1861 Harvard University conferred the degree of Doctor of Divinity upon Bishop Fitzpatrick, the first time a Catholic divine was so honored.[14] By 1862 Bible reading had paled as an issue. The legislature revoked the law making it compulsory, and the Boston School Board declared its "public schools . . . unexceptional to all denominations and to all of every creed, by the liberality, equality, and just regard for the religious faith of all our citizens." [15] It was not long before the City Hospital decided that "Patients may be visited by clergymen of their own selection, and where there is a wish for the performance of any particular religious rite, it shall be indulged when practicable." [16]

Furthermore, the loyalty of the Irish in the crisis drew them more closely into the city's life. Colonel Corcoran was enthusiastically received by the city governments of Boston and Roxbury, while Patrick Gilmore, whose "When Johnny Comes Marching Home" was sung everywhere, became the most prominent parade-leader in the city.[17] The war had provided an issue on which the Irish did not menace, indeed supported, the existing social order and its ideals. Somewhat unexpectedly, therefore, the bitter sectional conflict created an appearance of harmony within the city.

In the next fifteen years the optimistic assumptions of 1865 seemed on the way to fulfillment. The city entered upon a period of relative stability, by grace of which each element of the population seemed able to locate itself quietly. The lines that divided the Yankees from the Irish were as clearly marked as ever; but there were grounds for hope that a complete rapprochement between the contending groups was imminent.

The tide of immigration had definitely slackened in the

1860's; and it mounted only moderately the first few years of the next decade. After the panic of 1873 it fell into a precipitous decline.[18] Boston did not, therefore, face a recurrence of the crisis of the 1850's after the Civil War.

Between 1865 and 1880 the city was most directly affected by movements that originated in the Western Hemisphere rather than in Europe. British America produced a substantial flow of newcomers to the United States. In Nova Scotia and in Prince Edward Island limited opportunities generated discontent; and the revival of the fisheries and of trade with New England gave some of the people of those provinces the opportunity to move south of the border. In 1880 there were well over 25,000 of them in Boston and Cambridge.[19]

Another sizable contingent of newcomers came from the South. When emancipation gave the freed slaves some mobility, Boston, the old center of abolitionism, proved a magnet for some Negroes of the upper South. Although the total numbers involved were not large, that movement was enough to double the colored population of the city between 1865 and 1880.[20]

Supported by friendly public opinion, the colored men continued to improve their status in the city. A law of 1865 forbade discrimination against them in public places; and, despite adverse judicial decisions, the barriers of prejudice were steadily lowered. In 1866, two Negroes were elected to the state legislature; and thereafter there were frequently colored officeholders, often from wards that were overwhelmingly white. While almost all of them engaged in some form of manual labor, a few individuals rose to affluence and many more advanced to the state of moderate competence that enabled them to move out to thriving suburban communities in Cambridge and in the South End.[21] Meanwhile their churches and other institutions flourished.

Finally, there continued a significant drift to the city from the rural countryside of New England. Farm boys from Maine, New Hampshire, Vermont, and New York State still looked to the Hub for their fortunes; they constituted 14.3 per cent of its population in 1880. A trickle of Chinese — 121 of them by 1880 — added an exotic element to the city's population.[22]

But the great migration of Europeans for the moment seemed over. And of the remnants who came few found Boston attractive. The immigrants of these years had far greater resources than the fugitives of the 1850's and could more readily choose their destinations. Boston stood decisively below New York as a port of arrival; and it failed to hold even those who landed there. Only a tiny fraction of the great English and Scandinavian immigration waves of these years passed through this port, so that those movements contributed but slightly to the city's population. Just about a thousand Italian immigrants in 1880 formed the vanguard of a movement that would become more important later in the century.[23]

The Irish supplied the bulk of the new European arrivals in the city; and they were just numerous enough to take the places of the immigrants of an earlier generation who died. Consequently, although the number of foreign-born in Boston rose slowly, their percentage of the total population remained about the same. Those already established therefore had the opportunity to adjust more thoroughly to the life about them.[24]

With the stimulus of foreign immigration gone, the total population grew largely through natural increase. It thus reflected the composition of the population in the 1850's, with the significant exception that among the native-born of 1880 were a substantial number of the children and grandchildren of immigrants. The spread of the city's residents to neighboring communities proceeded at an accelerated pace and the surrounding villages were quickly engulfed as an ever larger number of Bostonians sought living space in the suburbs. Political boundaries were altered to adjust to the shift of population. Roxbury was swallowed up in 1867, Dorchester two years later, and Charlestown, Brighton, and West Roxbury in 1873.[25]

Some of the old problems were more easily resolved than earlier. In these years the advances of the earlier period were consolidated. The city showed its economic health in the ability to survive two great economic crises. The great fire of 1872 leveled 65 acres and wiped out large parts of the business district.[26] The panic of 1873 struck the city a blow from which it had hardly recovered by the end of the decade. Nevertheless, its industrial growth continued, although at a slower pace. By 1880 Boston stood between third and fifth in manufacturing among the cities of the nation, depending upon the method of computation; it now lived by producing clothing, sugar, iron, candy, and meat and printing products — the industries that had appeared since the arrival of the immigrants.[27]

Local manufacturing and the growth of the mill towns in

the interior led to commercial stability as well. Boston marketed the shoes and cloth of its back country and imported the leather, wool, cotton, and sugar the factories needed. It also developed a flourishing export trade of corn, wheat, and meat that was sustained by improved railroad links to the West. The city, at the same time, was also able to establish profitable new contacts with Cuba, Puerto Rico, and the Caribbean through the import of sugar for its refineries.[28]

Other prewar social problems proved less amenable to the remedy of stability. The cost of government rose alarmingly; the municipal debt almost quadrupled in the 15 years after the war.[29] Yet it proved hard to carry forth desirable improvements. Plans for an impressive park system had been agitated since 1869, yet by 1880 nothing had been accomplished.[30] All available funds had to be reserved for essentials like sewerage improvement.[31]

Living conditions in the poor Irish districts remained harsh and, although the incidence of pauperism, insanity, intemperance, and crime declined, the burden of those disorders still evoked complaints. Then, too, the mortality and disease rates in the city remained high, particularly among the Irish.[32] Furthermore, almost 23,000 of the foreign-born were illiterate, most of them concentrated in the Irish wards.[33] The new times had thus not themselves removed the essential causes of the immigrants' difficulty of adjustment.

For, though the Irish acquired a secure place in the community, they remained distinct as a group. Prejudice against them lingered for many years.[34] Not until 1879, for instance, did Catholic chaplains secure the right to officiate in state institutions.[35] They never merged with the other elements in the city and consistently retained the characteristics originally segregating them from other Bostonians. Even while supporting the Union, their opposition to reform, their dislike of Lincoln, and their hatred of the Negroes, abolition, and the emancipation proclamation, shown in the draft riot of 1863, demonstrated that the basic divergence emanating from the nature of their adjustment to Boston society still existed.[36]

The mass of Irishmen continued to occupy the low places in society they had earlier held. Their wives and daughters performed most of the city's domestic service; and men and boys of Irish ancestry constituted the bulk of unskilled workers. The censuses of 1870 and 1880 still found them two-thirds of the laborers and the *Pilot* estimated that 60 per cent of the group in 1877 still occupied that rank.[37] The new immigrants from Ireland, like their predecessors of the 1850's, were bound down by their immobility. Once trapped in the round of unskilled toil, they could never accumulate the resources to escape. Their advisers, as earlier, preached the virtues of western settlement.[38] But such counsel was as futile as ever. "Some critic in next week's *Pilot* may tell me, why don't I 'go West'," complained a wharfman. "They say a man requires money to take him there and then requires something to start with." [39]

There was more mobility in the second generation, members of which found increased opportunities for apprenticeship and training. Many entered upon semiskilled occupations as longshoremen, teamsters, and draymen. Not a few also advanced to the skilled crafts in the building and furniture trades. But it remained difficult for the sons of Irishmen to move upward into clerical and professional occupations. In those spheres, they faced the barriers of prejudice and of lack of capital. They were also handicapped by their limited access to the facilities for education. At the end of the decade some 9,000 of the 43,000 children in Boston between the ages of 5 and 15 were not in school; and most of them were Irish.[40]

A few businessmen fared well. But the decline in real estate values and the failure of many savings banks after the fire and panic hit the Irish entrepreneurs hard. Most of them lacked the reserves of capital and credit that enabled their Yankee counterparts to survive; and they went to the wall. The fall of Patrick Donahoe in the aftermath of the depression was symbolic, for his countrymen had recognized his wealth through his philanthropies and public prominence.[41]

The dawning consciousness that their place in society was fixed led some Irishmen into union activity. The skilled workers had begun to form associations during the war; and by 1870 a Trades Assembly was active. But there was more marked stratification within the group now than earlier; and the strength of the fortunate few was no consolation to the great mass who remained helpless. When the laborers on a construction job in Newton struck, they were simply replaced by a gang of Italians.[42]

As earlier, the sense of exclusion from full participation in the society around them heightened Irish group consciousness. The newcomers by now had become thoroughly intrenched in their own organizations. The church, although still far from adequate to their needs, retained its central role in their lives.[43] It grew quietly under the moderate leadership of Archbishop Williams, who made no particular effort to develop the parochial school system and whose great achievements were the completion of the cathedral in 1875 and the establishment of a seminary under the Sulpicians, with whom he had himself studied in Paris.[44]

With the increase in the size of the group, internal divisions became more important than earlier. As some of the earlier associations acquired prestige and limited their membership selectively, new ones appeared at their side. Often, too, the fresh arrivals felt uncomfortable in existing organizations which seemed to them unfamiliar and almost alien. They therefore founded new ones, such as the county societies. But that did not diminish the sense of identity of the Irish group as a whole.

The Fenian movement was a distraction for a time. The wild national dream of Irish freedom had a special meaning for the immigrants, connected with their own desire for place in American society. "I am all the more American because of this old love — all Irishmen are," wrote John B. O'Reilly.[45] No more than earlier was nationalism itself divisive. The movement to liberate Ireland was regarded with favor even by old-stock Bostonians, particularly since relations with England remained strained after the Civil War.[46]

The failure of the effort to invade Canada from St. Albans in 1866 took the heart out of the Fenian movement. The organization collapsed soon thereafter and the Boston Irishmen turned with some relief from methods which involved the use of force to more peaceful agitation in support of Parnell's Land League. In one guise or another such activities were to remain important; they were a sign of the unity of the group and of the adjustment of its members to the life of the New World.[47]

The concern with status created by the presence of the Irish immigrants and their offspring affected every group in the city. No man now could think of his place in society simply in terms of occupation or income level. It was necessary also ever to consider ethnic affiliation.

Most of the non-Irish foreign-born groups tried with some success to adapt themselves to the ideals and patterns of action of the society around them.[48] They faced relatively little difficulty in doing so. The old Boston community offered them a ready model for emulation. Yet, at the same time, such people as the Germans and the Jews understood that their own separateness was the product of the recency of their arrival and compensated for it through creation of their own social institutions.[49]

But two segments of the city's population occupied a difficult and anomalous situation. They could not identify themselves completely with the old Boston community; nor yet could they afford to establish an identity completely separate from it.

The large group of unattached individuals and families that had drifted in from rural New England faced this problem with particular urgency. Such men indeed as Isaac Rich the fish dealer, Jacob Sleeper the clothing maker, Lee Claflin the tanner, and H. O. Houghton the printer, earned fortunes as wholesalers or manufacturers. But their wealth did not command the esteem attached to that inherited from overseas trade.[50] In any case, most of these people filled more modest roles as shopkeepers, salesmen, clerks, and skilled artisans; and they were ever haunted by the fear of the loss of status that might send them plunging headlong into the ranks of the proletariat. Therefore they were concerned with education to advance their children, with decent behavior to show their quality, and, above all, with maintaining their distance from the Irish below them. The effort to keep the gulf between themselves and the Irish as wide as possible called for continual emphasis upon their Protestantism and their Yankee heritage.[51]

Paradoxically, the Yankees often found themselves associated with the British-Americans. The latter were recent immigrants and poor; but they too wished to avoid identification with the Irish with whom they competed for places as servants, tailors and laborers. That rivalry, enflamed by differences in religion and in attitudes toward England, steadily generated tension and occasionally, as in 1871, led to riots.[52]

Some of the British-Americans clung to their Presbyterian affiliations after their immigration and they occasionally formed their own societies and Orange lodges. But common language and common Protestantism drew them close to the Yankees.[53] Together the two groups helped to swell the ranks of the Baptist and Methodist churches, the evangelical and revivalistic character of which expressed their desire for self-improvement and spiritual as well as material regeneration.[54]

These people looked for leadership to the descendants of the old Boston families who were still economically and socially dominant in the city. Sometimes the Yankees and

British-Americans resented the aloofness and the religious indifference of the Brahmins. But mingled with the distrust was an element of admiration, as for an aristocracy. Above all, the recent arrivals depended upon the old families, association with which established their superiority over the Irish. Therefore, they followed along as loyal members of the Republican party and were partisans of the old traditions. But though their support was useful they did not find among the Brahmins the leadership they sought.[55]

The Brahmins, and especially the generation that matured after 1860, had recoiled in despair from what their nation and their city had become. Surrendering or softening the ideals of their parents, they did not hope to exercise effective leadership.[56] Indeed, disillusioned by the failure of Civil War idealism, which seemed only to lead to the corruption of Reconstruction and of the Grant administration, they now began to question the validity of democracy. Depressed by the ugliness of industrialization and by the vulgarity of its new wealth, the proper Bostonians wished to think of themselves as an aristocratic elite rooted in the country, after the English model. They moved out to the rural suburbs of Brookline and Milton and resisted proposals to annex those towns to Boston. They sent their children to private schools and found self-contained satisfaction in their gentlemen's clubs.[57]

In the reaction, Brahmin Society became more highly organized and more difficult to penetrate than ever before. A few outsiders managed slowly to find acceptance. But, generally, those who took pride in their descent from old families were more concerned with defining their own exclusive position than with identifying with the mass of Yankees who seemed bogged down in mercantile materialism and evangelical superstition. In the Brahmin's strategy for attaining social esteem, the Yankee Silas Lapham was almost as much an outsider as the most recent Denis or Bridget from Ireland.[58]

Since midcentury a significant number of them had become adherents of the Episcopal Church. That communion grew in size through English immigration. But it acquired social strength from a much smaller group of Bostonians who deserted the congregationalism of their ancestors not so much out of doctrinal differences as out of the desire for an affiliation that gave greater emphasis to authority, order, ritual, and to ties with England.[59]

The lack of adequate leadership that left the Yankees adrift also troubled the Irish, who felt altogether alien to the Brahmins and yet could not readily find within their own group men of sufficient distinction to sustain "the duty of guardianship" and to elicit their support. "No people," complained the *Pilot,* have been "more neglectful of its poor than the rich and educated Irish of America. What schools and colleges have they endowed? What efforts for the establishment of industrial schools have been made to take their poor countrymen from the overcrowded unskilled labor class and distribute them among the different remunerative industries. What reading rooms have they established to keep men from liquor stores and for their mental improvement? None whatever. They shun their countrymen except at election time." [60]

Such complaints expressed the discontent of the Irish with

their leadership, but they did not take account of the significant reasons for its slow development. The communal life of other American groups was largely dominated by the businessmen who supplied the funds for their voluntary activities. The inability of all but a few Irishmen in Boston to rise above the laborers' level deprived them of this source of support and guidance; and no other element in the population took their place. The Catholic clergy were busy with immense parochial tasks and, in any case, since Know-Nothing days had been on the defensive and reluctant to intervene in secular affairs. The Irish immigrants could therefore look for leadership only to occasional individuals who attained political or intellectual prominence in the nationalist movement.[61]

The career of Patrick Collins illustrated the limitations of political leadership in this period. As an upholsterer he had become active in his craft union and in the Trades Assembly. As a gregarious young man he had also been a member of such Irish philanthropic and social organizations as the Columbian Association, the Catholic Union, and the Charitable Irish Society; and in addition he had acquired a local following as a Fenian.

These activities prepared him for politics. Naturally he was a Democrat and became involved in his neighborhood party organization. In 1867 he was chosen secretary of the Ward 7 Democratic Club, and later he served on the city and state committees. In 1867, also, and again a year later, he was elected to the legislature. In 1869, he became state senator for the Sixth District, the first Irishman to penetrate into the upper house.

This measure of success revealed that the possibility of still wider achievements lay not in the quest for other offices, but in the quest for fortune. Collins had already been attracted to law as a career and now entered upon its active practice. In 1871 he attended the Harvard Law School and was admitted to the Massachusetts bar. For the next decade, he concentrated mostly on his own affairs. While his following among the Irish retained its importance to him, he had thereafter also always to consider his standing in the general community.[62]

The problems of the intellectual as a communal leader emerged frequently in the career of young John Boyle O'Reilly, who assumed the editorship of the *Pilot* in 1876, at the age of thirty. O'Reilly had earlier been a fiery Fenian nationalist and still retained a violent dislike for England and a fierce pride in his race and his church. Thus far he was representative of his group. He also vigorously opposed attacks upon Negroes, Jews, and immigrants in general. And like other Irishmen he saw a threat in the Chinese and called for their exclusion.[63]

However, O'Reilly was also attracted by the culture of the Brahmin society around him, in some circles of which he came to be accepted. Before long the necessity of taking account of what his Yankee friends might think softened many of his attitudes.[64] He sometimes wrote as if he were in favor of socialism as an abstract ideal. But more generally he expressed ideas that came close to the point of view of the world of Beacon Hill and Cambridge with which he had contact. Like the liberals of that world whom he admired, he read J. S. Mill with approval and espoused a weak government.[65] Originally a believer in free trade, he soon came around to a moderate protectionist position.[66]

These attachments drew him away from his Irish following. Although the editor of the *Pilot* knew that 80 per cent of its readers were "honest horny-fisted sons of toil" and although he realized that laborers were sometimes obliged to strike or "go to the wall," his advice was to "Give up your trade unions to coerce Capital. You can't do it; every strike has proved it in the long run and the wild attempt earns for you the distrust of the lawful." [67] O'Reilly was suspicious of unions and of strikes, especially when they led to violence, as among the Molly Maguires of Pennsylvania or the followers of Denis Kearney in California.[68] On the whole he felt co-operation, colonization, compulsory arbitration, and political agitation were more useful modes of action.[69] These positions reflected a general timidity when it came to American affairs. He was vigorous enough in sustaining the rights of the Irish against England; but he was fearful of the consequences when one of his countrymen, W. R. Grace, ventured to run for mayor in New York City.[70]

Among the leaders, both Brahmin and Irish, the edge of bitterness was gone. They were willing to accept the fact that the two communities would stand at arm's length of one another. They had learned to tolerate each other and to live together. In politics they recognized a stalemate within which divisive issues were evaded or suppressed. Prohibition thus gave way to local licensing; and both the ten-hour law and the greenback movements were defeated. Although most of the Irish were Democrats, that party also had prominent old-stock adherents like Abbott, Gaston, Adams, Prince, and

Woodbury; and the Republicans still had hopes of winning the immigrant voters over.[71]

Above all there was a resolute effort to pretend that the genuine divisions in the city's life did not exist. Thus, in 1876, Collins, explaining why he supported Charles Francis Adams for the governorship, declared, "I . . . denounce any man or any body of men who seek to perpetuate divisions of races or religions in our midst. . . . I love the land of my birth but in American politics I know neither race, color nor creed. Let me say now that there are no Irish voters among us. There are Irish-born citizens like myself and there will be many more of us, but the moment the seal of the court was impressed upon our papers we ceased to be foreigners and became Americans. Americans we are and Americans we will remain." [72]

For motives similar to those which moved Collins, Henry Cabot Lodge, representative of a new generation of native Bostonians, would one day rise in the Senate and declaim: "The Irish spoke the same language as the people of the United States; they had the same traditions of government, and they had for centuries associated and intermarried with the people of Great Britain. . . . They presented no difficulties of assimilation." [73]

That Collins and Lodge were both inaccurate was less significant than that, though they knew it, they nevertheless felt the necessity of speaking as they did. Their generation had grown up in a city which had already outlived its vigorous commercial youth and the leisurely life attending it. These new Bostonians had not experienced the terrific shock produced by an unexpected influx of swarms of impoverished peasants. They had not witnessed the transformation of a neat, well-managed city into a slum- and disease-ridden metropolis. Even the bitterness of the desperate, violent, Know-Nothing assault upon alien ideas and attitudes was outside their ken. Instead, their most formative years witnessed a great social conflict that tried the loyalty of the Irish and found them not wanting. For them, mutual interests overshadowed the old differences and furnished a basis for cooperation, if not for social equality.

But in this regard the leadership could not altogether count on its following. The Yankees and British-Americans remained fearful and insecure. They were not so willing as the Brahmin was to recognize a place in America for Catholicism; nor did they enjoy the defense of aloofness and distance that protected the Brahmin from contact with the immigrants.[74] These anxious people worried often lest their leaders betray them by relaxing standards; and they therefore resented any measure that treated the Irish as their equals. When Mayor Prince, in 1877, appointed a few Irishmen to the police force, he lost his opportunity for reëlection. After 1880, the Yankees would be swept away by a fresh wave of hatred against the foreigners who seemed to threaten their place in society.

Nor were the Boston Irish soothed by the calm assurance that their interests were identical with those of the rest of the community. In 1876 they did not vote for Adams as Collins asked them to.[75] On the ward level and among the aldermen, Jim O'Donovan and Hugh O'Brien — who would soon be Boston's first Irish mayor — were acting as if there was an Irish vote; and General B. F. Butler was preparing to capi-

talize on it. And over in the West End, young Martin Lo-
masney had quit his job as a metal spinner. Convinced that
politics was the better way to rise, he was developing a type
of organization that would be increasingly important in the
city's future.[76]

Depressed to the status of helpless proletarians by the conditions of their flight from Ireland and by the city's constricted economic structure, driven into debilitating slums by
their position as unskilled laborers, and isolated intellectually
by their cultural background and physical seclusion, the Irish
saw insuperable barriers between themselves and their neighbors. As social circumstances dictated, these differences lent
themselves to either coöperation or conflict; but so long as
they persisted, they stimulated and perpetuated group consciousness in both immigrants and natives and left the community divided within itself.

Boston thus moved uneasily into the last two decades of
the century. It was divided within itself. But it had learned
it could survive through tolerance. Despite all the difficulties
of the four decades since 1840, there was still no demand for
an end to immigration, although concern was often expressed about the added burdens of pauperism and criminality and the decline of the birth rate of the Yankees due to
their "higher civilization or to a more artificial mode of life
and the unwholesome state of society." [77]

But it was still uncertain that the adjustment would en-
dure. A great new tide of immigration was soon to open a
new period of rapid expansion. Then both the Yankees and
the Irish would recoil from the tolerance of the post-Civil
War years. The underlying differences between the two

groups would come openly to the surface and the community would enter once more upon a long period of bitterness.

Yet in the longer perspective, it is clear, the possibility of coexistence never vanished entirely. There were always some men in every group who recognized the community of interests which transcended the particular divisions in Boston's population. If they were not much heeded in the trying years after 1880, they nevertheless carried forward into the new century the constructive ideals, the roots of which extended back to an older Boston that had not yet been disrupted by immigration.

APPENDIX

Appendix

NOTE ON THE STATISTICS OF IMMIGRATION INTO BOSTON

Both the federal and state governments kept some statements of immigration into Boston. The state records were kept by the successive Commissioners of Alien Immigration. This material, drawn up at first merely according to port of origin, and only for a short time by nativity, is in general less reliable and less complete than the federal records.[1] The latter, drawn up by the Customs House and transmitted annually to Congress by the Secretary of State, have been completely tabulated for each year 1820–65 in Table VII, Dissertation Copy, 421, and are summarized by five year periods in Table V, *supra.*

There were obstacles to the use of even these data. The annual summaries in each statement referred to different yearly periods, at various times including the calendar year, the fiscal year, and the year ending August 31. This difficulty was avoided by referring back to the original quarterly returns and retabulating them all on the basis of the calendar year. A more serious difficulty was the lack of consistency in the listings. Thus "Great Britain" sometimes included England, Ireland, Scotland, and Wales, sometimes excluded Ireland, and sometimes excluded both Ireland and Scotland, a situation which rendered accurate enumeration of the Irish impossi-

[1] Cf. Tables VII a, VII b, Dissertation Copy, 426 ff.

ble. Several attempts were made to find a compensating statistical device, but since the difference originated in the caprice of the individual customs official it was deemed best to accept the data as it was given. The listings of minor localities, wherever possible, were combined into larger geographical units, however.[2] A tabulation by the "Joint Special Committee appointed to investigate the Public Charitable Institutions of . . . Massachusetts . . . 1858" offered different figures for 1831, 1833, 1837 and 1841,[3] but those offered in Table V were more accurate.

All these statistics refer of course only to immigration by sea and must be raised from 30 per cent to 50 per cent to account for those who entered by land.

NOTE TO TABLE XIII

Table XIII was derived from the manuscript schedules of the federal marshals who collected the material for the Census of 1850. These were deposited, when used in this study, in the Division of Old Records of the Bureau of the Census, Commerce Building, Washington, D. C. They have since been transferred to the National Archives.

The Census of 1850 was the first to inquire into both the nativity and occupation of the population. Lacking precedent, its directors faced the complex problems it involved without a consistent formula and without a definite conception of objectives. DeBow and his collaborators apparently made no attempt to coördinate or reclassify the results on the

[2] For the details, cf. Dissertation Copy, 424.
[3] Cf. "Report . . . ," *Massachusetts Senate Documents, 1859,* no. 2, pp. 142, 143.

basis of any consistent principle; and the enumerators exercised a wide degree of latitude in recording occupations which resulted in an amazing variety of listings and occupational descriptions. The absence of standardized method and procedure and the failure to define a clear set of occupational categories enormously complicated the task of tabulating the results.

The tabulations in Tables XIII–XVI were made under a procedure designed to eliminate errors arising from the lack of uniformity in occupational description. The enumerators noted 1,466 different occupations. Each of these was tabulated separately by nativity and by ward. From this primary tabulation, 474 listings were eliminated as representing nominal differences only. The remaining 992 distinct occupations were again tabulated and then combined in Table XIII into sixty-four categories, drawn up after a careful historical consideration of the precise nature of the work involved in each occupation.

The basis of this classification was necessarily original. Modern classifications are not applicable to the pre-Civil War period and no previous attempt has been made to classify such occupations scientifically. The compilers of the census themselves used extremely arbitrary groupings that frequently destroyed the value of the figures. DeBow was not at all discriminating. He lumped together in one category "commerce, trade, manufactures, mechanic arts, and mining," while his others were as general as "agriculture," "labor not agriculture," "army," "sea and river navigation," "law, medicine and divinity," "other pursuits requiring education," "government civil service," "domestic servants," and "others." [1] These groupings were extremely unsatisfactory. In Boston almost every employed person could be included in the first classification. Emphasizing the type of product rather than the nature of the work performed, such classifications lacked a valid base.

The same fault marred Shattuck's compilation of the local census of 1845. Having specific reference to Boston, this was in some degree more satisfactory than the federal efforts. Shattuck divided the working population into fourteen groups, those contributing to building, clothing, education, food, furniture, health, justice, literature and arts, locomotion, machinery, navigation, religion, unclassified mechanics, and others (which included 40 per cent of the total). [2] Again the nature of the product rather than the type of work was stressed.

The classifications of the State Census of 1855 and of the Federal Census of 1840 and 1860 followed essentially the same principles and therefore had little value. As a result it was necessary to evolve a complete classification of all 992 occupations, based on the actual character of the work involved in each. Careful precautions were taken to ensure uniformity and to make the tables valid for absolute and comparative purposes.

The enumerators cited more than seventy different localities as the place of birth, but these were combined in the original table into twenty simple nativity groups. In Table XIII "Other United States" includes New England (other than

[1] J. D. B. DeBow, *Seventh Census of the United States 1850 . . .* (Washington, 1853), lxxx.

[2] Lemuel Shattuck, *Report to the Committee of the City Council . . . Census of Boston . . . 1845 . . .* (Boston, 1846), 83.

Massachusetts); "Other British" includes British North America, England, Scotland, and Wales; and "Others" includes Latin America, Switzerland, the Netherlands, France, Italy, Spain and Portugal, Scandinavia, Russia and Poland, and Miscellaneous, all of which are listed separately in Dissertation Copy, 436 ff. "Negroes" includes all colored people regardless of nativity.

TABLE I
Boston Industries, 1845 *

Average No. of Employees per Establishment	No. of Industries	No. of Establishments	No. of Employees	Value of Products
1–10	98	837	4,764	$ 7,994,356
11–25	21	79	1,453	1,768,197
26–50	10	35	1,228	1,267,475
51 and over	4	11	807	1,741,400
Unclassifiable	11	?	1,866	1,085,954
TOTAL	144	962	10,118	$13,857,382

* This table is derived from statistics in John G. Palfrey, *Statistics of the Condition of Certain Branches of Industry in Massachusetts for the Year Ending April 1, 1845* . . . (Boston, 1846), 1–8, 43–48, 243, 248, 258–261. These statistics give the total number of employees and the total number of establishments in each industry. From this the average number of employees per establishment in each industry was computed. The column headed "No. of Industries" gives the number of industries in Boston, Charlestown, Brighton, Chelsea, Cambridge, Brookline, and Roxbury, in which the average number of employees per establishment falls within the range indicated in the first column. The third and fourth columns give, respectively, the total number of establishments and the total number of employees comprised in these industries, while the last column gives the value of the products they produced. Unclassifiable industries are those in which the number of establishments is not given because, like the shoe industry, they operated by homework.

TABLE II

Population of Boston and Its Environs *

	1790	1810	1820	1830	1840	1845	1850	1855	1860	1865
Boston (proper) ...	18,038	32,896	43,298	61,392 §	85,475	99,036	113,721	126,296	133,563	141,083
Islands	282	519	...	...	277	292	325	530	1,000	1,300
East Boston	...	18	...	...	1,455	5,018	9,526	15,433	18,356	20,572
South Boston †	...	354	...	...	6,176	10,020	13,309	16,912	24,921	29,363
Roxbury	2,226	3,669	4,135	5,259	9,089	...	18,364	18,469	25,137	28,426
Dorchester	1,722	2,930	3,684	4,074	4,875	...	7,969	8,340	9,769	10,717
Brighton ‡	...	608	702	972	1,425	...	2,356	2,895	3,375	3,854
Charlestown	1,583	4,954	6,591	8,783	11,484	...	17,216	21,700	25,065	26,399
Brookline	484	784	900	1,041	1,365	...	2,516	3,737	5,164	5,262
Chelsea	472	594	642	770	2,390	...	6,701	10,151	13,395	14,403
Cambridge	2,115	2,323	3,295	6,073	8,409	...	15,215	20,473	26,060	29,112
West Cambridge ‡ ..	...	...	1,064	1,230	1,363	...	2,202	2,670	2,681	2,760

* Derived from Carroll D. Wright, *Analysis of the Population of the City of Boston as Shown in the ... Census of May, 1885* (Boston, 1885), 8 ff.; *Massachusetts House Documents, 1837*, no. 19, pp. 9, 10; United States. *Census, Aggregate Amount of ... Persons ... According to the Census of 1820* (s.l., n.d. [Washington, 1820?]), 7; *Massachusetts House Documents, 1842*, no. 48, pp. 1, 3, 5; *Massachusetts House Documents, 1811*, no. 10, pp. 1-6; *Report and Tabular Statement of the Censors ... May 1, 1850*, Boston City Documents, no. 42, 59; Joseph C. G. Kennedy, *Population of the United States in 1860; Compiled from the Original Returns of the Eighth Census ...* (Washington, 1864), xxxi; Francis DeWitt, *Abstract of the Census of ... Massachusetts ... 1855 ...*

† Part of Dorchester until 1804.
‡ Part of Cambridge until 1807.
§ This figure includes Boston proper, and the Islands.

TABLE III
EXPENDITURES FOR POOR RELIEF, CITY OF BOSTON, 1815–1866 *

Year Ending April	Board of Overseers	House of Industry	House of Reformation for Juvenile Offenders †	Total
1815–22 §	$28,400	...	...	$ 28,400
1823	25,859	$ 8,475	...	34,334
1825	20,709	8,398	...	29,107
1826	9,500	12,000	...	21,500
1827	12,256	23,500	$ 4,793	40,849
1828	11,386	16,190	5,500	33,076
1829	12,848	17,996	5,966	36,810
1830	12,803	17,977	6,342	37,122
1831	13,685	19,476	6,223	39,384
1832	14,000	19,999	6,498	40,497
1833	14,542	23,048	6,203	43,793
1834	8,929	18,527	6,645	34,101
1835	12,606	17,521	7,444	37,571
1836	12,916	19,495	6,999	39,410
1837	9,708	23,084	10,299	43,091
1838	11,746	21,509	8,668	41,923
1839	10,257	22,321	10,883	43,461
1840	11,831	21,995	9,490	43,316
1841	12,000	23,483	8,993	44,476
1842	13,000	28,007	4,954	45,961
1843	15,000	31,547	...	46,547
1844	15,000	30,752	...	45,752
1845	15,000	29,151	...	43,151
1846	15,700	28,000	...	43,700
1847	16,500	35,748	...	52,248
1848	21,000	41,314	...	62,314
1849	24,500	55,477	...	79,977
1850	24,500	90,955	...	115,455
1851	30,200	89,334	...	119,534
1852	28,200	111,017	...	139,217
1853	27,700	84,338	...	111,038
1854	30,000	102,610	...	132,610
1855	40,000	77,279	...	117,279
1856	45,000	69,104	...	114,104
1857	49,300	69,462	...	118,762
1858	62,800	97,852	...	160,652
1859	58,000	84,624	...	142,624
1860	60,000	108,389	...	168,389
1861	69,400	76,917	...	146,317
1862	70,200	68,905	...	139,105
1863	90,140	57,869	...	148,009
1864	39,000 ‡	85,792	...	124,792
1865	41,000	91,304	...	132,304
1866	44,500	87,202	...	131,702

* Derived from Boston Committee of Finance, *Auditor's Reports, 1815–1867* (for page references, cf. Dissertation Copy, 419). The figures given refer to current expenditures only.
† After 1843, the House of Industry bore the expense of the House of Reformation for Juvenile Offenders and the Deer Island Almshouse.
‡ The drop after 1863 was due to the shift of persons without settlement to state institutions.
§ Annual average.

TABLE IV
PRISON COMMITMENTS §

Year	MASSACHUSETTS STATE PRISON Total *	From Boston	BOSTON JAIL Debtors	Criminals ‡	BOSTON HOUSE OF CORRECTION †	BOSTON JUVENILE REFORMATORY
1821	... ...	..	1,652		...	...
1822	... ...	..	1,257		...	...
1823	... ...	..	1,166		250	...
1824	... ...	49	1,257		572	...
1825	... ...	37	878		589	...
1826	... ...	35	...		567	...
1827	... ...	43	...		504	...
1828	106	31	...		551	...
1829	79	37	...		290	...
1830	115	50	...		334	...
1831	71	22	...		348	...
1832	76	51	...		228	...
1833	119	59	678	1,044	182	...
1834	... ...	..	...	...	562	...
1835	116	..	...	...	530	...
1836	97	28	322	739	570	113
1837	99	..	543	1,263	887	118
1838	114	..	526	1,606	1,327	279
1839	105	..	555	1,245	1,280	236
1840	103	35	...	...	...	...
1841	131	32	439	1,341	648	...
1842	85	29	...	...	...	...
1843	97	28	...	...	...	...
1844	105	44	...	...	...	...
1845	96	40	480	1,676	680	...

* The total commitments between 1805 when the institution was founded and 1827, when the reports begin, numbered 2,070 or an average of ninety per year.

† This column refers to the year ending June 30; the others to the year ending December 31.

‡ These included witnesses and those held for examination before trial.

§ Derived from the annual "Reports of the Inspectors of the State Prison . . . , 1830–1846" in the *Massachusetts Senate Documents*, and from the "Abstract of the Returns of Persons Confined in Jails and Houses of Correction . . . ," 1826 ff. (for page references, cf. Dissertation Copy, 420). Cf. also N. H. Julius, *Nordamerikas sittliche Zustände nach eigenen Anschauungen in den Jahren 1834, 1835, und 1836* (Leipzig, 1839), II, Tables 10, 11, 12.

Blanks denote incomplete or unavailable data.

TABLE V

Passengers Entering Boston by Sea, 1821–1865

Place of Origin †	Five-Year Period ‖ Beginning								
	1821	1826	1831	1836	1841	1846	1851	1856	1861
Great Britain and Ireland	…	…	…	6,996	7,010	3,603	…	…	…
Great Britain	164	3,030	581	58	4,545	12,513	990	19	1,324
England	286	506	1,712	172	24	316	10,264	9,654	3,931
Wales	16	…	7	6	…	…	354	748	23
Scotland	90	55	102	24	389	2,249	2,469	1,870	682
Ireland	827	549	2,361	443	10,157	65,556	63,831	22,681	6,973
British North America	525	648	3,943	3,537	5,654	16,816	21,233	18,240	14,542
Germany	58	311	253	449	301	1,385	2,653	1,198	1,287
France	66	167	57	212	239	381	605	529	362
Italy	14	23	40	42	59	137	186	247	89
Spain and Portugal ‡	48	41	48	80	147	176	540	943	1,017
Holland	27	27	80	182	30	484	399	298	292
Switzerland	3	163	137	7	10	45	25	200	63
Scandinavia	9	38	62	244	110	723	4,120	1,317	708
Latin America §	80	83	147	264	172	429	772	300	226
Russia	4	12	23	4	5	66	40	28	28
Asia Minor	7	18	11	21	20	32	58	45	19
Asia and Pacific Islands	1	1	8	9	8	34	17	85	69
Africa	6	1	16	3	13	15	21	112	92
Unknown and Miscellaneous	2	54	31	228	671	18	1,018	1,013	760
United States	1,564	1,727	2,149	3,921	7,177	7,686	7,910	10,396	10,234
TOTAL	3,797	7,454	11,768	16,902	36,741	112,664	117,505	69,923	42,721

† Cf. Dissertation Copy, 424.
‡ Includes Azores.
§ Includes Mexico, West Indies, Central America, South America.
‖ 1833 and 1834 are for nine months only; 1842 includes figures for England and Ireland only.

TABLE VI

NATIVITY OF BOSTONIANS, 1850 *

Country of Birth	Number
United States	88,948
England and Wales	3,213
Ireland	35,287
Scotland	897
Germany	1,777
Prussia	39
France	225
Spain	67
Italy	134
Others	5,038
Unknown	1,256
TOTAL	136,881

* Ephraim M. Wright, *Twelfth Registration Report, 1853* (*Documents Prepared and Submitted to the General Court by the Secretary of State*, Boston, 1854), 110. City of Boston only.

TABLE VII

NATIVITY OF BOSTONIANS, 1855 *

Town	United States	British America	Ireland	England, Scotland and Wales	Germany †	France	Italy	Other Foreign	Unknown	Total
Brighton	2,097	21	697	47	22	2	··	9	··	2,895
Cambridge	13,903	832	4,574	733	251	80	8	66	26	20,473
Charlestown	16,530	557	3,833	467	176	23	7	105	2	21,700
Somerville	4,171	160	1,305	128	27	8	2	5	··	5,806
West Cambridge	1,996	56	511	87	20	··	··	··	··	2,670
Brookline	2,411	68	1,142	66	31	5	1	7	6	3,737
Dorchester	6,198	178	1,542	252	141	12	··	17	··	8,340
Roxbury	11,282	298	5,002	705	1,063	59	7	53	··	18,469
West Roxbury	3,189	103	1,275	157	44	9	3	32	··	4,812
Boston	98,018	5,850	46,237	5,241	3,376	372	245	1,032	119	160,400
Chelsea	7,340	536	1,740	429	42	11	3	49	··	10,150
North Chelsea	595	26	155	17	··	··	··	··	··	793
Winthrop	301	11	87	8	··	··	··	··	··	407
TOTAL	168,031	8,696	68,100	8,337	5,193	581	276	1,375	153	260,742

* [Nathaniel B. Shurtleff], *Abstract of the Census of the Commonwealth of Massachusetts Taken with Reference to Facts Existing on the First Day of June, 1855, with Remarks on the Same Prepared under the Direction of Francis DeWitt, Secretary of the Commonwealth* (Boston, 1857), 98–132.
† Includes Holland.

TABLE VIII

NATIVITY OF RESIDENTS OF THE BOSTON AREA, 1860 *

Country of Birth	Middlesex County	Norfolk County	Suffolk County
United States	166,126	83,693	125,439
England	4,273	2,494	4,472
Ireland	38,098	19,138	48,095
Scotland	1,272	607	1,440
Wales	28	34	61
Germany	629	1,159	1,290
France	187	133	397
Spain	39	9	59
Portugal	19	62	38
Belgium	5	6	19
Holland	67	17	177
Turkey	4	1	6
Italy	29	26	258
Austria	24	21	44
Switzerland	28	55	125
Russia	4	4	38
Norway	28	11	68
Denmark	26	18	97
Sweden	98	41	259
Prussia	150	103	744
Sardinia	1	1	64
Greece	3	3	10
China	9	5	4
Asia	19	13	29
Africa	..	2	20
British America	4,784	1,563	7,503
Mexico	6	1	2
South America	24	18	44
West Indies	59	27	149
Sandwich Islands	15	9	10
Atlantic Islands	39	5	260
Bavaria	33	246	250
Baden	73	331	663
Europe †	133	6	165
Hesse	14	32	107
Nassau	..	4	18
Poland	..	2	78
Württemberg	16	38	142
Australia	1	..	10
Pacific Islands	1	7	8
Other Countries	..	5	38
Total Foreign	50,238	26,257	67,261
Total Population	216,354	109,950	192,700

* George Wingate Chase, *Abstract of the Census of Massachusetts 1860 from the Eighth U.S. Census, with Remarks on the Same Prepared under the Direction of Oliver Warner, Secretary of the Commonwealth* (Boston, 1863), Table IV.

† Not specified.

TABLE IX

NATIVITY OF BOSTONIANS, 1865 *

Town	United States	British America	Ireland	England, Scotland and Wales	Germany †	France	Italy	Other Foreign	Unknown	Total
Brighton	2,840	61	820	86	43	..	..	4	..	3,854
Cambridge	21,063	972	5,588	987	347	73	3	79	..	29,112
Charlestown	20,423	619	4,443	522	242	13	4	133	..	26,399
Somerville	7,050	221	1,729	258	41	8	1	32	13	9,353
West Cambridge	2,039	53	551	98	13	..	..	3	1	2,758
Brookline	3,542	106	1,457	85	33	6	3	5	25	5,262
Dorchester	8,393	233	1,647	262	125	11	13	33	..	10,717
Roxbury	18,762	612	6,294	1,056	1,511	79	5	107	..	28,426
West Roxbury	5,029	132	1,426	154	133	10	1	27	..	6,912
Boston	126,432	8,060	46,225	5,480	3,790	367	366	1,533	65	192,318
Chelsea	11,551	531	1,655	512	71	6	5	59	13	14,403
North Chelsea	720	26	101	11	..	..	..	..	..	858
Winthrop	465	25	129	10	4	..	..	..	..	633
TOTAL	228,309	11,651	72,065	9,521	6,353	573	401	2,015	117	331,005

* Oliver Warner, Abstract of the Census of Massachusetts, 1865: with Remarks on the Same and Supplementary Tables . . . (Boston, 1867), 70–77.
† Includes Holland.

TABLE X

County	Boston	Roxbury	East Cambridge	South Boston	Charlestown
Antrim	5	4	..	..	6
Armagh	4	..	1	2	3
Carlow	17	..	..	3	..
Cavan	28	8	3	4	3
Clare	10	1	1	5	..
Cork	121	11	3	19	28
Donegal	35	4	2	5	7
Down	5	1	..	..	4
Dublin	10	..	2	2	1
Fermanagh	52	1	2	2	10
Galway	21	5	..	6	..
Kerry	23	3	..	5	3
Kildare	21	2	3	5	1
Kilkenny	40	2	7	12	7
Kings	1	..	..	..	..
Leitrim	13	1	..	..	..
Limerick	16	..	..	..	1
Londonderry	26	1	4	..	..
Longford	25	1	15	18	12
Louth	2	1	..	..	2
Mayo	..	..	..	..	1
Meath	20	9	3	3	..
Monaghan	25	1	4	2	1
Queens	12	1	1	3	2
Roscommon	10	47	1	1	2
Sligo	14	6	1	..	1
Tipperary	15	6	5	11	3
Tyrone	39	8	34	5	22
Waterford	15	3	6	2	6
Westmeath	6	1	3	4	..
Wexford	33	..	..	21	4
Wicklow	7	..	..	1	..
Unknown	30	9	25	11	..
Total	701	137	126	152	130

* Derived from *Boston Pilot*, 1841–1843. For citations, cf. Dissertation Copy, 435.

TABLE XI

Advertisements by Bostonians for Information in the *Boston Pilot*, 1841–1864 *

County †	1841	1843	1845	1847	1849	1851 ‡	1853	1855	1857	1859	1861	1863
Antrim	..	1	1	1	..	..	..	2	..	..	..	1
Armagh ...	1	1	1	1	2	1	5	1	4	2	1	..
Carlow	1	2	..	2	..	3	3	2	2	..	1	..
Cavan	2	1	5	11	14	7	4	11	3	7	9	3
Clare	1	..	4	8	13	16	11	10	9	1	6	8
Cork	19	11	58	94	112	106	117	97	67	65	29	56
Donegal ...	2	3	7	4	10	6	6	7	2	4	2	5
Down	..	..	1	1	5	2	..	4	3	3	..	..
Dublin	1	..	..	4	6	7	6	4	1	7	..	2
Fermanagh .	3	..	1	2	5	2	1	6	2	1	2	2
Galway ...	2	2	10	33	40	26	33	26	19	21	12	16
Kerry	2	2	9	16	42	37	41	38	23	29	11	21
Kildare	1	..	3	4	6	3	7	3	1	..	1	..
Kilkenny ..	1	3	5	8	17	14	12	12	3	7	5	4
Kings	1	..	3	1	1	3	..	2	1	1	..	..
Leitrim	1	1	4	8	14	8	13	6	4	4	2	6
Limerick ..	3	3	5	5	24	14	19	13	13	7	4	13
Londonderry	..	..	..	3	4	4	2	3	3	2	2	..
Longford ..	5	1	1	4	7	4	4	1	4	5	6	3
Louth	..	1	1	1	3	6	4	3	..	2	2	3
Mayo	2	1	7	20	16	17	9	11	11	5	1	6
Meath	1	..	8	8	13	6	8	5	6	2	1	..
Monaghan ..	..	..	6	3	4	6	6	3	2	2	4	6
Queens	2	..	2	5	4	2	5	3	2	2	3	4
Roscommon .	7	8	17	14	19	16	15	18	11	16	3	6
Sligo	2	..	8	12	9	7	7	6	2	2	5	3
Tipperary .	1	3	4	7	20	26	17	7	10	10	10	11
Tyrone	2	2	3	11	2	4	7	4	4	4	6	3
Waterford .	5	4	5	8	18	14	17	11	8	4	6	10
Westmeath .	1	..	..	3	2	1	3	8	1	..	1	3
Wexford ...	..	1	..	2	4	2	6	3	2	4	..	2
Wicklow ..	..	1	1	1	1	..	..	3	1	..	1	..
Unknown ..	..	..	..	..	..	3	7	..	..	..	..	..

* This table was derived from the requests for information of the whereabouts of friends and relatives, inserted regularly in the *Boston Pilot* by immigrants newly arrived in Boston. The *Pilot* was the leading vehicle for such advertisements in the United States (cf. Alexander Marjoribanks, *Travels* . . . [London, 1853], 126). This is the only criterion that has been found to measure the distribution of immigration into Boston from the various sections of Ireland. It is weighted, if at all, in favor of the "old" emigrants from north Ireland, more likely to have friends in America. Nevertheless, it shows a clear preponderance of immigrants from the southern and western counties. Annual figures are given, Dissertation Copy, 430.

† Doubtful locations were decided from John Bartholomew, *Philip's Handy Atlas of the Counties of Ireland* . . . (London, 1881).

‡ Twenty-one months only.

248

TABLE XII

NEGRO POPULATION OF THE BOSTON AREA, 1754–1865 *

Town	1754	1765	1790	1800	1810	1820	1830	1840	1850	1855	1860	1865
Brighton	..	..	..	..	2	1	2	1	5	12	4	..
Cambridge	56	90	60	25	38	53	79	77	141	292	354	371
Charlestown	..	136	25	38	61	38	96	129	206	133	202	109
Somerville	..	..	..	..	..	..	..	..	20	19	28	15
West Cambridge	..	..	..	..	5	3	2	2	2	4	2	6
Brookline	17	18	13	15	6	3	1	3	5	..	3	5
Dorchester	31	37	30	35	26	15	13	16	6	11	10	29
Roxbury	53	80	40	71	76	43	27	26	107	50	60	54
West Roxbury	..	..	..	..	..	..	..	..	..	14	24	47
Boston	989	848	766	1,174	1,468	1,690	1,875	2,427	1,999	2,160	2,284	2,348
Chelsea	35	43	21	20	16	36	8	11	37	70	136	151
North Chelsea	..	..	..	..	..	..	..	..	2	..	1	2
Winthrop	..	..	..	..	..	..	..	..	..	..	..	3
TOTAL	1,181	1,252	955	1,378	1,698	1,882	2,103	2,692	2,530	2,765	3,108	3,141

* Oliver Warner, Abstract of the Census of Massachusetts, 1865; with Remarks on the Same, and Supplementary Tables (Boston, 1867), 228–231.

TABLE XIII

DISTRIBUTION OF OCCUPATIONS BY NATIVITY, BOSTON, 1850 *

Occupational Category	Massachusetts	Other U.S.	Unknown	Negro	Ireland	Other British	Germany	Others	Total
Government employees	111	47	..	..	6	5	..	3	172
Police and watchmen	107	115	12	..	12	11	1	1	259
Clergymen	57	73	4	4	9	8	5	..	160
Teachers	108	45	2	..	4	9	13	16	197
Physicians	349	178	14	2	32	46	13	13	647
Actors, musicians	69	42	2	3	24	34	33	42	249
Other professions	271	124	16	..	25	30	4	4	474
Financiers	37	17	..	..	1	1	..	..	56
Merchants	668	227	36	..	18	37	5	14	1,005
Agents, salesmen	340	174	13	..	25	27	9	4	592
Clerks	2,170	1,071	108	3	132	151	19	22	3,676
Food dealers	441	361	7	1	184	53	9	5	1,061
Dry goods dealers	87	55	1	..	10	7	6	..	166
Pedlars, traders	462	354	27	25	211	40	41	23	1,183
Other retailers	604	321	24	11	117	46	17	6	1,146
Shop assistants	20	10	..	36	12	7	2	..	87
Manufacturers	164	88	5	..	48	52	11	10	378
Printers	317	199	11	1	81	80	5	1	695
Confectioners, bakers	124	81	5	17	98	59	55	10	449
Workers in heavy industry	203	156	2	..	247	123	79	9	819
Smiths	234	171	6	3	307	112	36	8	877
Builders, contractors	79	46	..	2	22	26	..	3	178
Carpenters	701	634	24	5	356	302	18	13	2,053
Masons	271	234	11	1	203	37	5	2	764
Painters	461	234	15	3	119	114	10	14	970
Plumbers	36	15	2	..	18	23	2	..	96
Sawyers, carvers	111	47	5	..	40	28	4	2	237
Roofers	14	5	..	..	39	12	..	..	70
Maritime industries	131	69	1	..	22	45	8	28	304
Chandlers, caulkers	110	14	2	..	6	6	..	2	140
Cabinet makers, upholsterers	131	84	3	..	56	62	18	15	369
Polishers, varnishers	44	21	2	..	7	17	3	1	95
Musical instrument makers	108	76	6	..	4	40	20	..	254
Coopers	111	44	..	..	79	32	16	7	289

								Total
Workers in precious metals	227	81	6		13	47	29	8	411
Machinists, mechanics	406	297	2		68	120	22	15	930
Undertakers	32	4			1				37
Wharfingers	23	9			1			1	34
Leather workers	67	47	7		105	46	11	3	286
Shoemakers	145	71	1	4	206	80	49	14	570
Hatters	107	47	4		38	16	8	2	222
Tailors	166	127	9	9	1,045	119	41	31	1,547
Miscellaneous apprentices	97	33	3		29	7			169
Other artisans	401	238	11	5	172	130	80	12	1,049
Miscellaneous sup'ts	12	24	1		3	4			44
Express business	24	43			10	3			80
Transportation, railroads	55	57	3		13	6	1	1	136
Drivers and teamsters	67	124	9		37	31	2	1	271
Truckmen and cabmen	244	616	12	4	169	46	2	1	1,094
Stevedores	30	43		5	41	11	3	7	140
Master mariners	82	31	3	1	5	13	7	3	145
Boatmen	45	26			37	10	2	7	127
Seamen	328	293	544	142	190	215	23	154	1,889
Hotel keepers	52	56		5	10	15	11	15	164
Restaurant keepers	112	118	5	5	18	10	4	7	279
Stable keepers	9	17			4	1			31
Stablers	30	53	2		70	9			164
Waiters	34	68	2	21	222	8	3	3	361
Barbers	59	40	1	48	6	6	3	23	186
Domestic servants	227	369	26	48	2,292	237	31	19	3,249
Laborers	538	466	19	115	7,007	264	107	36	8,552
Farmers	12	15			21	4			52
None	629	122	15	25	177	59	17	18	1,062
Unknown	42	16	13	21	11	7	6	3	119
TOTAL	13,553	8,983	1,064	575	14,595	3,206	929	662	43,567

* Supra, 234.

TABLE XIV

AVERAGE NUMBER OF PERSONS PER OCCUPATION OF EACH NATIVITY
GROUP IN BOSTON, 1850 *

Nativity	Total in Boston	Total of Employed Persons	Number of Occupations	Average Number per Occupation
Massachusetts	68,687	13,553	660	20.53
New England	17,220	7,986	564	14.16
United States	3,037	997	203	4.91
Unknown	†	1,064	136	7.82
Negro	1,999	575	46	12.50
British North America	†	1,381	189	7.31
Latin America	†	60	23	2.61
England	3,213 ‡	1,369	255	5.37
Ireland	35,287	14,595	362	40.32
Scotland	897	433	117	3.70
Wales	‡	23	16	1.44
Germany	1,816 ‖	929	153	6.07
Switzerland	†	10	9	1.11
Netherlands	†	36	19	1.89
France	225	143	68	2.10
Italy	134	105	33	3.18
Spain & Portugal	67 §	67	26	2.58
Scandinavia	†	172	46	3.74
Russia and Poland	†	46	19	2.42
Miscellaneous	5,038 †	23	15	1.53
All nativities	136,881	43,567	993	43.87

* Derived from the manuscript schedules of the Seventh Census of the United States (B.C.),
with the exception of the first column which is given in J. D. B. DeBow, *Statistical View of
the United States* . . . (Washington, 1854), 395, 399.
† Included in miscellaneous. Miscellaneous in the first column includes Unknown, British
North America, Latin America, Switzerland, the Netherlands, Scandinavia, Portugal, Russia and
Poland as well as the other nativities elsewhere included in this category.
‡ In the first column Wales is included in England.
§ In the first column the figure is for Spain alone; Portugal is included in Miscellaneous in
this column.
‖ Includes Prussia.

TABLE XV
LABORERS IN BOSTON, BY NATIVITY, 1850 *

Nativity	Total Working Population	Laborers	Percentage of Working Population
Ireland	14,595	7,007	48.01
Negro	575	115	20.00
Germany	929	107	11.52
England	1,369	119	8.70
British No. Amer.	1,381	115	8.33
New England	7,986	419	5.25
United States	997	47	4.71
Massachusetts	13,553	538	3.97
Others	2,182	85	3.90
TOTAL	43,567	8,552	19.63

* Derived from the marshal's schedules of the Seventh Census, cf. *infra*, note to Table XIII.

TABLE XVI
DOMESTIC SERVANTS IN BOSTON, BY NATIVITY, 1850 *

Nativity	Working Population	GENERAL HOUSE SERVANTS		Other Domestics †
		Number	Percentage of Working Population	
Ireland	14,595	2,227	15.3	65
British No. Amer.	1,381	138	10.0	3
Negro	575	39	6.8	9
England	1,369	62	4.5	6
United States	997	41	4.1	4
New England	7,986	304	3.8	20
Germany	929	30	3.2	1
Others	2,182	60	2.6	13
Massachusetts	13,553	206	1.5	21
TOTAL	43,567	3,107	7.1	142

* Derived from the marshal's schedules of the Seventh Census, 1850 (cf. note to Table XIII). The instructions for this census asked the enumerators to list the occupations of all males above the age of sixteen and thus excluded the female domestic servants. Some enumerators went beyond the letter of their instructions and noted such persons in their schedules. By and large they did not. Only 1,375 servants were listed in the entire state in the official tabulation (cf. J. D. B. DeBow, *Seventh Census of the United States 1850* . . . [Washington, 1853], lxxx), an absurdly low figure in view of the fact that a more careful study in 1845 had found 5,706 in Boston alone (Lemuel Shattuck, *Report to the Committee of the City Council . . . Census of Boston . . . 1845* . . . [Boston, 1846], 84). In many cases however, it was possible to distinguish the servants from the rest of the family, and where there could be no doubt as to status, they were tabulated whether the enumerator listed them or not. The figures given above are therefore minimal and are probably far below the true numbers. But since the same criteria were used in each nativity group, the table is valid for approximate comparisons between groups.
† Includes butlers, cooks, gardeners, housekeepers, and laundresses. These were specifically listed in the schedules.

TABLE XVII

NUMBER OF EMPLOYEES IN BOSTON INDUSTRIES EMPLOYING ONE HUNDRED OR MORE WORKERS IN ANY YEAR BETWEEN 1837 AND 1865 *

Total Industries Existing in	NUMBER OF EMPLOYEES			
	1837	1845 †	1855 †	1865
1837	9,930	4,928	9,084	33,011
1845	....	6,010	11,364	35,095
1855	....	....	13,147	37,268
1865	....	....	....	39,283

* Summarized from Table XIX, Dissertation Copy, 447, which itemizes 46 individual industries and which was derived from the industrial censuses of Massachusetts, 1837–1865.
† The clothing industries were not included in 1845 and 1855.

TABLE XVIII

CORRELATION OF TUBERCULOSIS WITH HOUSING AND NATIVITY, BY WARDS, BOSTON, 1865 *

Ward	Irish per Hundred	Persons per Dwelling	Death Rate per Thousand by Phthisis	Death Rate per Thousand, All Diseases
5	15.0	8.90	4.61	19.8
6	15.2	7.70	1.82	15.5
11	15.6	7.65	3.21	18.5
9	16.9	8.57	2.91	17.8
2	17.5	8.12	3.31	21.7
4	23.6	11.07	2.13	14.6
10	23.7	11.94	3.22	19.6
12	25.6	7.84	4.94	22.5
8	29.7	11.12	3.65	20.4
1	32.8	16.50	4.80	28.5
3	34.2	12.28	4.34	27.9
7	42.9	16.50	6.09	26.3

* Derived from Charles E. Buckingham, et al., *Sanitary Condition of Boston* . . . (Boston, 1875), 159, 126.

TABLE XIX

DISTRIBUTION OF THE POPULATION OF BOSTON BY AGE PERIODS, 1800–1855 *
Number in Every 10,000

Age Period	1800 to 1820 1800	1810	1820
Under 10	2,584.8	2,750	2,574
10–15	1,223.4	1,240	1,297
16–25	2,304.4	2,381	1,951
26–45	2,571.0	2,612	3,199
Over 45	1,318.4	1,017	979

Age Period	1830 to 1855 1830	1840	1855
Under 5	1,329	1,270	1,258
5–10	1,170	1,103	971
10–15	1,127	1,026	878
15–20	1,117	1,063	954
20–30	1,972	2,065	2,465
30–40	1,221	1,394	1,680
40–50	835	868	962
50–60	555	575	472
60–70	385	358	230
Over 70	289	278	104

* Derived from Lemuel Shattuck, *Letter to the Secretary of State on the Registration of Births, Marriages and Deaths* . . . (s.l., n.d. [Boston. 1845]), 6; Francis DeWitt, *Abstract of the Census of . . . Massachusetts . . . 1855* . . . (Boston, 1857), 90 ff.; Lemuel Shattuck, *Essay on the Vital Statistics of Boston* . . . (Boston, 1893), xvi, xviii, xx.

TABLE XX

NATIVITY OF THE PARENTS OF CHILDREN BORN IN BOSTON, 1863–1865 *

	1863	1865
Both American	1,207	1,306
Both English	69	67
Both Irish	2,375	2,287
Both Scots	27	18
Both British North Americans	122	147
Both Germans	184	197
Unmixed Foreign	93	61
Mixed Foreign	498	463
Mixed	634	698
Unknown	46	31
TOTAL	5,255	5,275

* Derived from the reports of the City Registrar, 1864, 1866, *Boston City Documents, 1864*, no. 47, p. 8; *ibid.*, *1866*, no. 88, p. 6.

TABLE XXI

PAUPERS IN THE METROPOLITAN AREA, 1848–1860 *

Year †	Total	Having Local Settlement	State Paupers	Foreign State Paupers	Irish and English State Paupers
1845	4,810	1,334	3,188	2,154	1,860
1846	5,640	1,375	4,205	2,947	2,543
1847	7,004	1,371	5,619	4,427	4,010
1848	6,664	1,270	5,374	4,339	3,974
1849	10,245	1,438	8,716	6,218	5,574
1850	11,294	1,026	10,200	7,924	7,130
1851	11,899	1,064	10,610	8,223	7,334
1853	12,068	1,117	10,233	8,080	6,951
1858	11,032	1,889	5,678	5,190	4,711
1859	12,346	2,129	6,092	6,247	5,988
1860	12,617	2,192	....	8,414	6,062

* Derived from material on Boston, Roxbury, Charlestown, Cambridge, Chelsea, Dorchester, West Roxbury, Somerville, Brighton, West Cambridge, Brookline, and North Chelsea in Dissertation Copy, Table XXII, 451 ff. Not all towns are complete in all categories each year.
† Year ending September.

TABLE XXII

NATIVITY OF INMATES OF THE DEER ISLAND HOUSE OF INDUSTRY *
REMAINING ON DECEMBER 31 OF EACH YEAR †

	1855 ‡	1856 ‡	1857 ‡	1858	1859	1860
Boston — native parentage ...	65	47	47			
Boston — Irish parentage	24	30	30	64	51	30
Massachusetts	29	32	32			
New England	29	29	29			
Ireland	128	154	154	266	219	179
England and British Provinces	..	..	..	58	34	28
Italy	..	..	..	..	1	1
Other foreigners	40	39	39	4	..	..
TOTAL	315	331	331	392	305	238

* Contained some paupers as well as criminals.
† Boston Committee of Finance, *Auditor's Reports, 1855*, no. 43, p. 174; *ibid., 1856*, no. 44, p. 210; *ibid., 1857*, no. 45, pp. 208–209; *ibid., 1859*, no. 47, p. 219; *ibid., 1860*, no. 48, p. 242; *ibid., 1861*, no. 49, p. 249.
‡ March 31.

TABLE XXIII

NATIVITY OF ALL THE INMATES IN THE HOUSE OF CORRECTION DURING THE YEAR ENDING DECEMBER 31 *

	1858	1859	1860	1861	1862	1863
Massachusetts	235	218	287	177	98	147
Other United States	158	143	104	107	70	103
England	75	54	39	45	30	33
Ireland	574	457	340	472	336	318
Scotland	24	†	18	12	75	10
British Provinces	88	50	48	44	29	22
Italy	..	..	..	2	..	1
Germany	..	..	..	5	..	..
France	..	..	..	1	..	1
Others	29	34	11	5	6	1
Colored	59	45	39	51	39	?
White	1124	911	808	819	543	?
TOTAL	1183	956	847	870	582 ‡	636

* Derived from Boston Finance Committee, *Auditor's Reports*, *1859*, no. 47, p. 218; *ibid.*, *1860*, no. 48, p. 239; *ibid.*, *1861*, no. 49, p. 262; *ibid.*, *1862*, no. 50, p. 275; *ibid.*, *1863*, no. 51, p. 290.
† Included in Others.
‡ Discrepancy, as given, in the figures.

TABLE XXIV

NATIVITY OF ARRESTS AND DETENTIONS BY THE BOSTON POLICE DEPARTMENT, YEAR ENDING DECEMBER 31, 1864 *

Nativity	Arrests	Lodgers
United States	2,143	4,580
Ireland	9,791	17,293
England	426	1,011
Africa	160	40
Germany	138	198
France	61	143
Scotland	61	203
Italy	30	25
Sweden	30	36
Portugal	25	7
Canada	15	12
Nova Scotia	9	..
Norway	6	51
Spain	4	12
Others	15	27

* "Annual Report of Chief of Police, 1865," *Boston City Documents*, *1865*, no. 8, pp. 8, 9.

TABLE XXV

AMOUNT PAID BY THE STATE FOR THE SUPPORT OF LUNATIC STATE PAUPERS IN SUFFOLK COUNTY,* 1838–1859 †

Year	Amount
1838	$ 1,573
1839	2,192
1840	2,793
1841	6,263
1842	6,820
1843	8,357
1844	9,511
1845	9,384
1846	10,170
1847	9,738
1848	9,940
1849	12,954
1850	15,906
1851	15,830
1852	17,295
1853	19,569
1854	19,805
1855	21,059
1856	18,538
1857	17,465
1858	20,183 ‡
1859	‡

* All in Boston.
† Derived from *Massachusetts Senate Documents, 1848*, no. 47; and from the annual reports of the City Auditor and of the Alien Passenger Commissioners (for page references, cf. Dissertation Copy, 468).
‡ The figures for 1858 also include 1859 until November, when all such insane were transferred to State institutions.

TABLE XXVI

ORPHANS SUPPORTED AT ST. VINCENT'S ORPHAN ASYLUM, BOSTON *

1843	18
1846	38
1848	38
1849	47
1851	50
1854	79
1855	81
1856	80
1857	79
1858	159 †
1859	191

* Derived from materials in the *Boston Pilot* and *Boston Catholic Observer*. For citations cf. Dissertation Copy, 471.
† New building opened.

TABLE XXVII

BOSTON MARRIAGES BY NATIVITY, THREE-YEAR PERIOD, 1863–1865 *

BIRTHPLACE OF GROOM	BIRTHPLACE OF BRIDE									TOTAL
	Boston	Massachusetts	United States	Great Britain	Ireland	British America	Germany †	Others	Unknown	
Boston	395	142	193	24	87	52	3	5	·	901
Massachusetts	258	319	320	32	50	57	1	5	4	1,046
United States	381	307	818	58	96	148	10	3	6	1,827
Great Britain	52	27	45	78	126	59	2	2	1	392
Ireland	170	37	47	42	1,997	78	2	5	·	2,378
British America	71	30	64	17	114	164	·	1	3	464
Germany †	51	13	31	11	78	15	247	12	1	459
Others	23	9	25	14	48	19	21	119	·	278
Unknown	1	2	1	·	·	1	·	·	35	40
TOTAL	1,402	886	1,544	276	2,596	593	286	152	50	7,785

* Derived from "Report of the City Registrar, 1863–1865," *Boston City Documents, 1866*, II, no. 88, p. 12; *ibid., 1865*, no. 42, p. 8; *ibid., 1864*, no. 47, p. 9. Cf. also Dissertation Copy, Table XXXII, 472.
† Includes Scandinavia.

TABLE XXVIII

Boston Voters, 1840–1858 *

Year	Legal Voters	Actual Vote Cast †
1840	14,474	11,573
1844	?	13,502
1845	20,351	10,191
1850	21,220	8,952
1851	?	12,314
1852	21,203	11,956
1853	23,792	12,409
1853	23,792	12,948 ‡
1854	24,157	13,410
1855	24,272	14,340
1856	?	16,865
1857	?	13,525
1858	?	14,466

* Derived from Lemuel Shattuck, *Report to . . . the City Council . . . Census of Boston . . . 1845 . . .* (Boston, 1846), 81; Josiah Curtis, *Report . . . Census of Boston . . . 1855* (Boston, 1856), 11; *Boston Semi-Weekly Advertiser*, November 12, 1851; *ibid.*, November 10, 1852; *ibid.*, November 16, 1853; *ibid.*, December 14, 1853; *ibid.*, November 5, 1856; *ibid.*, November 4, 1857; *Boston Atlas*, November 14, 1854; *Boston Daily Courier*, November 3, 1858; "Report and Tabular Statement," *Boston City Documents, 1850*, no. 42, p. 12.

† In the November gubernatorial election unless otherwise indicated.

‡ December mayoralty election.

TABLE XXIX

POPULATION OF THE BOSTON REGION
1865–1880 *

	1865	1870	1880
Native white.........	225,168	249,179	325,551
Foreign white.........	102,696	122,912	143,844
Total white..........	327,864	372,091	469,395
Colored.............	3,141	4,914	8,287
Total.............	331,005	377,005	477,682

* Towns included in Table IX, except for parts of West Cambridge, Dorchester, and Belmont transferred to Belmont, Hyde Park, and Cambridge. *See* Tables IX, XII; U.S. Ninth Census, *Population* (Washington, 1872), I, 166, 167; U.S. Tenth Census, *Population* (Washington, 1883), I, 208 ff., 416 ff., 450, 451.

TABLE XXX

FOREIGN-BORN POPULATION OF BOSTON AND CAMBRIDGE
BY SELECTED NATIVITIES, 1880 *

	Boston	Cambridge
Irish......................	64,793	8,366
British-American............	23,156	3,981
English....................	8,998	1,396
German....................	7,396	636
Swedish...................	1,450	169
Italian....................	1,277	36
Other Foreign-Born	7,726	1,084
Total Foreign-Born........	114,796	15,668

* U.S. Tenth Census, *Population* (Washington, 1883), I.

TABLE XXXI

Selected Occupations in Boston by Selected Nativities, 1880 *

	Total	U.S.	Ire.	Ger.	G. Br.	Norway, Sweden	Br. Am.	Others
All....................	149,194	88,244	34,745	3,990	6,650	1,121	11,237	3,207
Agriculture............	1,042	518	358	33	52	4	56	21
Servants..............	17,156	6,042	7,172	194	912	258	2,358	220
Laborers..............	15,854	4,037	10,066	280	436	83	623	329
Shop clerks...........	13,636	11,796	535	128	414	9	630	124
Tailors...............	11,246	6,833	1,866	298	504	64	1,384	297
Traders and Dealers....	9,187	6,599	1,407	324	328	24	280	225
Physicians............	882	758	28	20	29	..	34	13
Lawyers..............	648	604	18	6	8	1	7	4

* U.S. Tenth Census, *Population* (Washington, 1883), I, 864.

262

TABLE XXXII

Churches in Boston, 1870 *

	Number	Sittings
Baptist	25	21,500
Christian	1	500
Congregational	30	23,200
Episcopal	24	12,000
Methodist	28	15,925
Catholic	28	34,500
Unitarian	28	20,500
Universalist	11	5,500
Presbyterian	7	3,425
German Reformed	1	600
Jewish	6	1,800
Lutheran	2	400
German Lutheran	2	600
Swedish Lutheran	1	500
Colored Methodist	3	2,075
Others	10	2,775

* U.S. Tenth Census, *Social Statistics of Cities* (Washington, 1886), I, 112; Ninth Census, *Population*, I, 542.

TABLE XXXIII

ENTRIES AT THE PORT OF BOSTON, 1871–1880 *

Origin	Year Ending June 30									
	1871	1872	1873	1874	1875	1876	1877	1878	1879	1880 **
England.........	7,073	7,425	8,898	6,087	4,637	2,159	1,596	1,164	1,591	3,529
Ireland.........	9,693	9,378	11,981	9,395	6,615	3,072	2,021	2,212	2,610	9,099
Scotland........	732	936	1,140	784	541	351	177	135	203	764
Germany........	2,783	2,304	2,709	1,392	876	531	378	151	233	804
Sweden.........	398	1,030	1,094	798	476	543	363	461	1,091	3,539
British America..	4,461	4,184	3,958	3,507	2,367	1,672	2,380	3,685	3,748	8,641
Others..........	1,884	1,652	1,896	2,262	2,133	1,383	972	948	888	2,441
Total...........	27,024	26,909	31,676	24,225	17,645	9,711	7,887	8,756	10,364	28,817

* U.S. Tenth Census, *Social Statistics of Cities*, I, 115.
** Eleven months.

264

NOTE ON SOURCES

ABBREVIATIONS

B.C.	Bureau of the Census, Division of Old Records, Commerce Building, Constitution Avenue, Washington, D. C.
Bi.A.V	Bibliotheca Apostolica Vaticana, Vatican City
B.M.	British Museum Reading Room, Bloomsbury, London, W.C.1
B.P.L.	Boston Public Library, Boston, Massachusetts
H.C.L.	Harvard College Library, Cambridge, Massachusetts
I.A.H.S.	Irish American Historical Society, New York City
Li.C.	Library of Congress, Washington, D. C.
L.U.N.D.	Library of the University of Notre Dame, South Bend, Indiana
M.S.L.	Massachusetts State Library, State House, Boston
N.L.I.	National Library of Ireland, Kildare Street, Dublin
N.N.L.	National Newspaper Library, British Museum, Colindale Road, Colindale (Hendon), London, N.W.9
N.E.H.G.S.	New England Historical and Genealogical Society, 99 Ashburton Street, Boston
N.Y.P.L.	New York Public Library, Fifth Avenue, New York
P.R.O.	Public Record Office, Chancery Lane, London
R.A.d.S.	Reale Archivio di Stato — Napoli, Piazza del Grande Archivio, Naples, Italy
R.I.A.	Royal Irish Academy, Dawson Street, Dublin
S.J.E.S.	Saint John's Boston Ecclesiastical Seminary, Brighton, Massachusetts
T.C.D.	Trinity College, Dublin, Library, College Green, Dublin

NOTE ON SOURCES

THE materials for the understanding of a community are infinite. To limit sources is impossible, for, in a sense, everything that was written, read, said, or thought, in or about Boston between 1790 and 1880, is germane to the subject of this study. And beyond the purely literary materials lies an endless mine of physical survivals — the relics of the old city, and the descendants of those who lived in it — which offers rich perceptions to those willing to see. Yet this very prodigality bars completeness; the historian can only sample the wide variety before him and compensate by the judiciousness of his choices for the inevitable omissions.

The list which follows is thus in no sense an exhaustive bibliography; it does not even include all the works cited in the footnotes.[1] It only attempts to outline the *types* of material used in this study and to criticize the more important of them.

I. NEWSPAPERS AND PERIODICALS

THE IMMIGRANT PRESS [2] most consciously expressed the varied impulses of immigrant society and forms the most important single source for this study. Newspapers play a threefold part in illuminating the story of aliens. They are the most important source of information on the life of the immigrant community; nowhere else is there as complete a chronicle of arrivals and departures, of the meetings of its societies, and of the doings of its prominent men. Furthermore, the newspaper at once reflected and influenced the views of the immigrants on the problems they faced personally and in relation to the society about them. And because the press was not yet a big business, every significant shade of opinion could afford an organ of expression. Most important of all, the newspapers were the most comprehensive repositories of immigrant literature. The Germans had a few literary monthlies (e.g., *Atlantis. Eine Monatschrift für Wissenschaft . . . herausgegeben und redigiert von Christian Esselen* [Buffalo]; *Meyer's Monatshefte* [New York]), but these were restricted in scope, circulation, and influence. And among other groups formal literary journals found no place at all. The newspapers furnished the foreigners' only reading material and the fiction, the poetry, and the history that attracted their readers are the most sensitive mirrors of what went on in immigrant minds.

THE NEWSPAPERS OF IRELAND were disappointing for the purposes of this study. They threw some light on the famine and on the process of emigration but few were really interested in the condition of the peasantry. The most valuable was the *Cork Examiner* (N.N.L.) (1841 ff.), which retained its interest in Corkonians even in their new homes. Its columns contained occasional news of Boston Irishmen and sometimes letters of considerable importance to friends in the old country. Its rival, the *Cork Constitution* (N.N.L.) (1834 ff.), was less valuable; Tory in sympathy, it was impatient with the emigrants and glad to be rid of them. Dublin papers had little room for anything but politics and the pages of journals like the *Armagh Guardian* (N.N.L.) (1844) and the *Leinster Express* (N.N.L.) were devoted to sensational crimes and to similar news of interest to the gentry who read them.

OTHER PERIODICALS were of secondary importance. Boston's press was, on the whole, well above the average of its contemporaries. In the early period the *Massachusetts Centinel* (continued as the *Columbian Centinel*) (N.Y.P.L.) and the *Independent Chronicle* (H.C.L.) were temperate well-balanced sheets, the one Federalist, the other Republican. After 1830, the *Daily Evening Transcript* (H.C.L.) furnished accurate and generally unbiased news, while the tri-weekly *American Traveller* (H.C.L.) catered to a wider range of interests. Later in the period the *Boston Daily Courier* (H.C.L.) and the Whig *Boston Daily Atlas* (H.C.L.) were reliable, while the *Boston Semi-Weekly Advertiser* (H.C.L.), like its daily counterpart, reflected the interests and opinions of State Street and the business community. In addition, the city was the home of innumerable weeklies that spoke for special causes. The most helpful were the precursors of the Know-Nothing papers, the *American* (B.P.L.) and *Wide Awake: And the Spirit of Washington* (B.P.L.). But in general it was necessary only to sample these in periods of special interest since the most significant articles were liberally quoted in the immigrant papers.

II. PUBLIC DOCUMENTS

This period was intensely interested in the preservation of its records. The abundance of documentary materials published by all branches of government facilitated the solution of many problems; while their general reliability compensated for the lack of vision on the part of their compilers who could not always foresee the uses to which historians would put them.

The quality of the statistical material is especially gratifying. The municipal, state and federal governments all compiled CENSUS RECORDS, which after 1845 included a vast amount of social data of considerable significance. Until then, the federal census had followed fairly traditional forms concentrating primarily upon enumeration of the population for purposes of representation. But Lemuel Shattuck's *Report to the Commitee of the City Council . . . Census of Boston for . . . 1845 . . .* (Boston, 1846) broke new ground in pointing out the potential social usefulness of the census. His report included a mass of well-digested material on all phases of the life of Boston and its people and furnished a model for all subsequent censuses.

The most significant enumeration for the purposes of this study was that of 1850, taken at the height of the immigration, while the process of adjustment was most critical. Fortunately, the federal census of that year was directed by the far-sighted J. D. B. DeBow who published its results in *The Seventh Census of the United States: 1850 . . .* (Washington, 1853) and summarized them in his *Statistical View of the United States . . .* (Washington, 1854). DeBow attempted, with some success, to follow the model set by Shattuck. His was the first federal census, for example, to inquire into both the nativity and occupation of the population; and Vols. XXIII–XXVI of the Original Returns of that census formed the basis for much of the discussion in Chapter III of this work (cf. also *supra,* 234).

The same year also witnessed a municipal census, reported in the "Report and Tabular Statement of the Censors Appointed . . . to Obtain the State Census of Boston, May 1, 1850 . . . ," *Boston City Documents, 1850,* no. 42, and discussed in Jesse Chickering's "Report of the Committee . . . and also a Comparative View of the Population of Boston in 1850 . . . ," *ibid., 1851,* no. 60. This census was unusual and valuable for a street by street tabulation of the nativity of the residents.

Thereafter federal and state censuses alternated every five years in providing an enlightening statistical account of the city's development. Nathaniel B. Shurtleff prepared an *Abstract of the Census of . . . Massachusetts Taken . . . the First Day of June, 1855, with Remarks on the Same Prepared under the Direction of Francis DeWitt . . .* (Boston, 1857), that supplemented the more detailed *Report of the Joint Special Committee of the Census of Boston, May, 1855 . . .* (Boston, 1856) by Josiah Curtis. The federal census of 1860 was summarized by Joseph C. G. Kennedy in the *Population of the United States in 1860; Compiled from the Original Returns of the Eighth Census . . .* (Washington, 1864); but the data on Massachusetts may be found in greater detail in George Wingate Chase's *Abstract of the Census of Massachusetts 1860 from the Eighth U. S. Census . . . Prepared under . . . Oliver Warner . . .* (Boston, 1863). The last two decades are ably covered on both the state and the federal levels in Oliver Warner's *Abstract of the Census of Massachusetts, 1865 . . .* (Boston, 1867); Carroll D. Wright's *Census of Massachusetts, 1875* (Boston, 1876); the U.S. Ninth Census (Washington, 1872); and the U. S. Tenth Census (Washington, 1883–1888), the two last named prepared under the direction of Francis A. Walker.

The economic history of Massachusetts is remarkably clarified by a series of four INDUSTRIAL CENSUSES, 1837–1865. These were compiled carefully from data collected by the Secretaries of State. John P. Bigelow's *Statistical Tables: Exhibiting the Condition . . . of Industry in Massachusetts . . . 1837 . . .* (Boston, 1838), John G. Palfrey's *Statistics of the Condition of . . . Industry in Massachusetts . . . 1845 . . .* (Boston, 1846), Francis DeWitt's *Statistical Information Relating to . . . Industry in Massachusetts . . . 1855 . . .* (Boston, 1856), and Oliver Warner's *Statistical Information Relating to . . . Industry in Massachusetts . . . 1865 . . .* (Boston, 1866) furnish a sturdy framework for the story of the evolution of Massachusetts' economy through its most important phase. Additional material may be found in McLane's *Documents Relative to the Manufactures in the United States* (22 Congress, 1 Session, *House Executive Documents,* no. 308), in the volumes on manufactures of the Eighth, Ninth, and Tenth Censuses, and in the historical introductions of the *Ninth Census, 1870* (Washington, 1872) and the *Twelfth Census, 1900, Manufactures,* IX (Washington, 1902).

Beyond the bare statistics there is a rich store of records of all the agencies which had contact with immigrants in Boston. The MUNICIPAL DOCUMENTS vary in value. The records of the Town of Boston and the minutes of the Selectmen's Meetings down to 1822, published in seven volumes by the Boston Registry Department between 1896 and 1908, cover a period when the immigrant was not yet prominent enough to warrant more than passing attention. Thereafter there is no complete record of the city government, except between 1826 and 1828, when *Bowen's Boston News-Letter and City Record,* edited by J. V. C. Smith, chronicled its affairs. The *Auditor's Reports* (1813–67) contain the financial details of all the municipal institutions, the *Inaugural Addresses of the Mayors of Boston . . . Published by the City Registrar* (Boston, 1894) give a cross section of the city's problems, and the changes in its laws may be traced in Peleg W. Chandler's *Charter and Ordinances of the City of Boston together with the Acts of the Legislature Relating to the City . . .* (Boston, 1850) and in the City Council's compilation of ordinances in 1856 and 1865. The manuscript records of the town Board of Health (1799–1824) are preserved in the Boston Public Library, but the reports of other city departments are scattered and fragmentary until 1839 when they began to be issued serially in the *Boston City Documents.* The annual reports of the agencies there collected became progressively more important as the aliens assumed greater prominence in the city's life.

It was the STATE, however, that was most prominently concerned with immigrants in this period. Its public DOCUMENTS throw welcome light upon the process of settlement, and in addition possess a wealth of data on all aspects of Boston life. The reports of the State departments were thrown haphazardly into either the *Massachusetts House Documents* or the *Massachusetts Senate Documents* between 1826 and 1856 but thereafter were collected in the *Massachusetts Public Documents* while the two older series were confined to purely legislative concerns. The reports of the State Board of Education, of the Alien Passenger Commissioners, of the State charitable institutions, and of the keepers of jails, included in these documents, were of prime importance.

Although the *Acts and Resolves* of the General Court are available in full throughout the period, the proceedings were printed only under special circumstances as in 1856 when interest in the Know-Nothing legislature induced the *Daily Advertiser* to issue a volume of *Debates and Proceedings. . . .* (Boston, 1856).

The only FEDERAL DOCUMENTS directly relevant to the first half of the nineteenth century are the annual *Letter from the Secretary of State Transmitting a Statement of Passengers Arriving in the United States . . .* (1820 ff.) in the Congressional documents (cf. *supra,* 233). The reports of the national Commissioner of Immigration begin in 1865.

In a somewhat special category is the BRITISH CONSULAR CORRESPONDENCE (P.R.O.) in two series (F.O. 4, F.O. 5). The letters of the English consuls in Boston to their government and to the Embassy in Washington (British Embassy Archives [P.R.O., F.O. 115]) are of considerable value particularly after the 1830's when the early placemen were supplanted by Consuls Manners, Grattan, and Lousada. Their reports touched regularly not only upon the condition of the Irishmen, still theoretically British subjects, but also upon the whole range of social conditions in Boston, and offer intelligent and well-informed comments upon them. The reports of Consul Buchanan, at New York, are also worth consulting. He was intensely interested in the problems of emigration and persistently showered his complaining but helpless superiors in London with long, detailed reports which they found irrelevant, but which are mines of serviceable information.

Outside the run of normal government documents are a number of REPORTS OF INVESTIGATIONS into some of the more pressing problems of the period. Perhaps the earliest was Theodore Lyman, Jr.'s brief report to the House of Representatives on *Free Negroes and Mulattoes . . . January 16, 1822 . . .* (s.l.,n.d.). As immigration grew such inquiries became more frequent. In 1846 public spirited citizens, disturbed by the possibilities of a shortage in housing, prepared the *Report of the Committee on the Expediency of Providing Better Tenements for the Poor* (Boston, 1846). Interest in the causes of cholera provoked the exhaustive analysis by Buckingham's Committee of 1849 into all phases of the city's health and the factors conditioning it (detailed in *Report of the Committee of Internal Health on the Asiatic Cholera . . . , Boston City Documents, 1849,* no. 66, and discussed in William Read's "Communication . . . on the Asiatic Cholera . . . 1866," *Boston City Documents, 1866,* no. 21). Although these reports and Dr. Howard F. Damon's *Localities of One Thousand Cases of . . . Diseases . . .* (Boston, 1866), contain some illuminating material, the most accurate descriptions of housing conditions are found in the early *Annual Reports* (1870–1880) of the Massachusetts State Labor Statistics Bureau, based on investigations made in 1866–67, but valid for the whole period after 1850. The Massachusetts Sanitary Commissioners under Shattuck issued a *Report of a General Plan for the Promotion of Public and Personal Health. . . .* (Boston, 1850), summarized in "Sanitary Reform," *North American Review,* July, 1851, LXXIII, which contained an excellent statistical section on the health of the city. The *Sanitary Condition of Boston, the Report of a Medical Commission . . . Appointed by the Board of Health of the City of Boston. . . .* (Boston, 1875) by Chas. E. Buckingham and others, had some useful historical data. Finally, the *Annual Reports* of the Executive Committee of the Benevolent Fraternity of Churches (1835–1866) and of the Children's Mission to the Children of the Destitute (1850–1863) described the findings of two organizations in close contact with the immigrants.

III. OTHER CONTEMPORARY MATERIAL

The well-known ACCOUNTS OF VISITORS to Boston were of value in dealing with the background of the city, but threw little light on the condition of the immigrants. Few travelers ventured off the beaten track that led inevitably from the State House to Bunker Hill and Mount Auburn. La Rochefoucauld-Liancourt's *Voyage dans les États-Unis d'Amérique . . .* (Paris, An VII) gives an early description of the town; "Boston as It Appeared to a Foreigner at the Beginning of the Nineteenth Century . . ." (*Bostonian Society Publications,* Series I, IV) pictures it ten years before and W. Faux's *Memorable Days in America . . .* (London, 1823) ten years after the War of 1812. Harriet Martineau's *Society in America* (New York, 1837) has overshadowed other accounts of the 1830's quite unjustly, for that decade also saw the publication of *A Journal of a Residence . . . in the United States of North America . . .* (London, 1835) by the English abolitionist, Edward S. Abdy, of George Combe's *Notes on the United States of North America during a Phrenological Visit in 1838–40* (Philadelphia, 1841), and of a significant criminological study by Nikolaus Heinrich Julius. *Nordamerikas sittliche Zustände nach eigenen Anschauungen in den Jahren 1834, 1835, und 1836* (Leipzig, 1839). Boston welcomed Sir Charles Lyell, the geologist, ten years later and in return was sympathetically described in *A Second Visit to the United States of North America* (London, 1849). *L'Aristocratie en Amérique* (Paris, 1883) by Frederic Gaillardet, editor of the *Courrier des États-Unis* in this period, is disappointingly superficial; but Thomas C. Grattan's *Civilized America* (London, 1859) embodies the results of his intelligent observations as consul in Boston, and Edward Dicey's *Six Months in the Federal States* (London, 1863) is adequate for the Civil War years.

IMMIGRANT GUIDES fall into a special category. Their most eloquent evidence was negative in so far as they failed to mention Boston at all. *America and Her Resources . . .* (London, 1818) by John Bristed, and Martin Doyle's *Hints on Emigration . . .* (Dublin, 1831) were typical of the English and L. von Baumbach's *Neue Briefe aus den Vereinigten Staaten . . .* (Cassel, 1856), of the German. *The German in America, or Advice and Instruction for German Emigrants in the United States . . .* (Boston, 1851) was worth noting because it was written by Frederick W. Bogen, pastor of the Lutheran church in Boston. The discussion of industrial developments and opportunities in *Erwerbszweige, Fabrikwesen und Handel von Nordamerika . . .* (Stuttgart, 1850) by C. L. Fleischmann, an American consul in Germany, is informative, and Franz Löher's *Geschichte und Zustände der Deutschen in Amerika . . .* (Cincinnati, 1847) contains one of the few good accounts of the German community in Boston.

PAMPHLETS proved useful in many phases of this study. They were one of the most important sources of information on the background of emigration from Ireland. This fugitive literature came from the presses of Dublin and the provincial towns with bewildering frequency; everyone who had an opinion expressed it through this medium. The poor-law issue provoked a particularly valuable succession of controversial publications and the famines of 1814 and 1823 were described in considerable detail by investigating committees. Few of these pamphlets were outstanding; rather their value lay in the cumulative weight of their evidence. Several thousand are admirably arranged in the Haliday Collection of the Royal Irish Academy, catalogued by J. T. Gilbert (MS., R.I.A.).

Similar material for Boston is also plentiful. The Harvard College Library has a complete file of *Directories* from 1789 and of *Almanacs* and *Registers* from 1830. There is no lack of guide books and an abundance of pamphlets on all the important issues of the day. In addition low printing costs and prolific preachers combined to produce an outpouring of sermons that dealt with all phases of the city's intellectual life, and sometimes, as in Parker's case, with many broader aspects of its social and economic structure.

IV. Immigration and Its Background

There is no satisfactory GENERAL ACCOUNT of American immigration. The *Immigrant in American History* . . . (Cambridge, 1940) contains a series of provocative essays by Marcus Lee Hansen which display insight as well as scholarship. Carl Wittke's *We Who Built America . . .* (New York, 1939) summarizes the results of recent investigations but is marred by a lack of proportion in emphasis. Probably the best general approach to the problem is through the documents collected in Edith Abbott's *Immigration Select Documents . . .* (Chicago, 1924) and *Historical Aspects of the Immigration Problem . . .* (Chicago, 1926), although in both, the legal aspects are given too much weight. Oscar Handlin, *The Uprooted* (Boston, 1951) examines the effects of migration upon the immigrant.

There are a number of worth-while studies of the causes of emigration both in individual countries and for EUROPE AS A WHOLE. The broader trends in population may be traced in A. M. Carr-Saunders, *Population Problem . . .* (Oxford, 1922) and *World Population . . .* (Oxford, 1936). Maurice R. Davie's *World Immigration . . .* (New York, 1936) contains a more comprehensive general account than René Gonnard's *L'Émigration européènne au XIXe siècle . . .* (Paris, 1906). Far more detailed than either, but in some ways less useful, is *International Migrations* (New York, 1929, 1932) edited by Imre Ferenczi and Walter F. Willcox; lack of consistency among the contributors, and the failure to integrate the discussion with the statistics detract seriously from its value. All of these have been superseded, within the field it covers, by Marcus Lee Hansen's *Atlantic Migration, 1607–1860 . . .* (Cambridge, 1940), a careful study of all phases of the movement, particularly valuable for its light on emigration from central Europe. In comparison Edwin C. Guillet's *Great Migration . . .* (New York, 1937), which deals primarily with Great Britain, is superficial. In the last decade or so, interest in the subject of economic development has elicited the following studies by economists which, in general, sustain the argument advanced in this book: Julius Isaac, *Economics of Migration* (New York, 1947); Brinley Thomas, *Migration and Economic Growth* (Cambridge, 1954); and Brinley Thomas, ed., *Economics of International Migration* (London, 1958).

The literature for the background of BRITISH emigration is ample. Élie Halévy's *History of the English People in 1815* (Harmondsworth, 1937) gives a sympathetic account of the social structure of the island while J. H. Clapham describes its economic institutions in *Economic History of Modern Britain* . . . (Cambridge, 1932). Industrial and agricultural changes may be followed in the works of J. L. and Barbara Hammond while the *Population Problems of the Age of Malthus* (Cambridge, 1926) are dealt with in a competent but uninspired fashion by G. Talbot Griffith. Sidney and Beatrice Webb have adequately discussed the problems of poor relief in *English Poor Law Policy* (London, 1910) and *English Poor Law History* . . . (London, 1927–29). Clapham's study of "Irish Immigration into Great Britain in the Nineteenth Century" (*Bulletin of the International Committee of Historical Sciences,* V) draws attention to an important subject. On the problem of population movements to the United States, the older works, Stanley C. Johnson's *History of Emigration from the United Kingdom* . . . (London, 1913) and William A. Carrothers' *Emigration from the British Isles with Special Reference to the* . . . *Overseas Dominions* (London, 1929), have now been supplanted by Rowland T. Berthoff, *British Immigrants in Industrial America 1790–1950* (Cambridge, 1953).

Carl Wittke, *The Irish in America* (Baton Rouge, 1956) is a general survey. The number of scholarly studies of this group remains small. *Ireland and Irish Emigration to the New World from 1815 to the Famine* . . . (New Haven, 1932) have been dealt with in detail by William Forbes Adams in a scholarly study which, however, passes lightly over the poor law issue, and, in addition, is unsympathetic to the peasantry. George O'Brien's *Economic History of Ireland in the Eighteenth Century* (Dublin, 1918) and his *Economic History of Ireland from the Union to the Famine* (London, 1921) are useful and may now be supplemented by R. D. Edwards and T. D. Williams, *The Great Famine* (New York, 1957).

Constantina Maxwell's *Country and Town in Ireland under the Georges* (London, 1940) and *Dublin under the Georges, 1714–1830* (London, 1936) deal primarily with the gentry with only occasional reference to the peasantry. There is considerable material on emigration in the Letters and Papers of William Smith O'Brien (MSS., N.L.I.), and Robert Bennet Forbes' *Voyage of the Jamestown on Her Errand of Mercy* (Boston, 1847) contains a graphic account of the famine. Much undigested information on Irish politics at the turn of the nineteenth century is scattered through R. R. Madden's *United Irishmen* . . . (New York, 1916) and the collection of his papers on the subject in Trinity College, Dublin. *Rossa's Recollections, 1858 to 1898.* . . . (Mariner's Harbor, N. Y., 1898) and *Irish Rebels in English Prisons* . . . (New York, 1880) are autobiographies of Jeremiah

Note on Sources

O'Donovan-Rossa, a Fenian, with general reflections on the life of the Irish in the United States; and Thomas D'Arcy McGee's *History of the Irish Settlers . . .* (Boston, 1852) and Edward Everett Hale's *Letters on Irish Emigration . . .* (Boston, 1852) are contemporary accounts worth consulting because of the familiarity of their authors with their subjects.

The GERMAN background is compactly discussed in John Harold Clapham's *Economic Development of France and Germany . . .* (Cambridge, 1936); and Marcus Lee Hansen carefully describes the economic causes of the migrations of the Fifties in "Revolutions of 1848 and German Emigration" (*Journal of Economic and Business History,* II). René Le-Conte summarizes the legal aspects of the movement in *La Politique de l'Allemagne en matière d'émigration* (Paris, 1921) but for a more detailed treatment one must still consult the essays in *Auswanderung und Auswanderungspolitik in Deutschland . . .* (Leipzig, 1892) edited by Eugen von Phi-lippovich. Albert B. Faust's *German Element in the United States, with Special Reference to Its Political, Moral, Social and Educational Influence* (New York, 1927) is a reliable though sometimes intemperate account of the Germans in America, with emphasis on the leading personalities. The discussion of politics in Ernest Bruncken's *German Political Refugees in the United States . . .* (s.l., 1904) is valuable; and Franz Löher's *Geschichte und Zustände der Deutschen in Amerika* (Cincinnati, 1847) is a contemporary history of high order. A. E. Zucker, ed., *The Forty-Eighters* (New York, 1950) and Carl Wittke, *Refugees of Revolution* (Philadelphia, 1952) deal with the movement after the failure of the revolutions of 1848.

Although Howard Mumford Jones' excellent *America and French Culture, 1750–1848* (Chapel Hill, 1927) has a broader scope, most studies of the FRENCH have dealt with political refugees of the revolutionary period. The story of later French immigrants is still largely untold. On the eighteenth-century migrations, Frances S. Childs' *French Refugee Life in the United States, 1790–1800* . . . (Baltimore, 1940) supplements J. G. Rosengarten's *French Colonists and Exiles in the United States* (Philadelphia, 1907), but deals primarily with Philadelphia. Leo F. Ruskowski's *French Emigré Priests in the United States (1791–1815)* . . . (Washington, 1940) adds little to earlier works. The best account of this movement, on the whole, is in the relevant sections of Fernand Baldensperger's *Mouvement des idées dans l'émigration française* . . . (Paris, 1924).

The material on ITALIAN immigration is scarce. Robert F. Foerster's *Italian Emigration of Our Times* (Cambridge, 1919) and Lawrence Frank Pisani's *Italian in America* (New York, 1957) hardly deal with the period before 1880. Paulo G. Brenna's *Storia dell'emigrazione italiana* . . . (Roma, 1928) is brief and superficial. Giovanni Schiavo's *Italians in America before the Civil War* . . . (New York, 1934) is an exhaustive compilation but deals primarily with personalities. Details on the movement can be found only in the ill-organized volumes of Leone Carpi's *Delle colonie e dell'emigrazione d'Italiani all'estero* . . . (Milano, 1874).

Florence Edith Janson's *Background of Swedish Immigration, 1840–1930* . . . (Chicago, 1931) is excellent and Theodore C. Blegen's *Norwegian Migration to America, 1825–1860* (Northfield, 1931) is adequate. Marcus Lee Hansen deals with some phases of the movement from Canada in *Mingling of the Canadian and American Peoples* . . . (New Haven, 1940) and in "Second Colonization of New England" (*New England Quarterly,* II); but the *Report of the Select Committee of the Legislative Assembly Appointed to Inquire into the Causes* . . . *of the Emigration* . . . *from Lower Canada to the United States* . . . (Montreal, 1849), though essential, has been too often overlooked.

V. OTHER HISTORIES

The *Memorial History of Boston* . . . *1630–1880* . . . (Boston, 1880) edited by Justin Winsor is the most valuable of the numerous GENERAL HISTORIES. The articles are uneven in quality and sometimes do not hang together well, but most are competently written and are not yet outdated. By and large, other works in this category deal with social history in the limited sense. Mary Caroline Crawford's *Romantic Days in Old Boston* . . . (Boston, 1910) is more sober than its title. Samuel Adams Drake's *Old Landmarks and Historic Personages of Boston* . . . (Boston, 1873) is almost purely antiquarian as is the *Town of Roxbury* . . . (Boston, 1905) by Francis S. Drake; but both are accurate and interesting. The similar works of Gillespie and Simonds on South Boston and of Hunnewell on Charlestown can also be used with profit.

The evolution of the municipal GOVERNMENT and of its DEPARTMENTS in their first thirty years may be traced in the *Municipal History of . . . Boston* . . . (Boston, 1852) by Josiah Quincy, the first mayor. The municipal institutions are conventionally described in James M. Bugbee's *City Govern-*

ment of Boston . . . (Baltimore, 1887). The history of the police receives sprightly treatment in *Police Records and Recollections; or, Boston by Daylight and Gaslight* . . . (Boston, 1873) by Edward H. Savage, himself a constable at one time. The annals of other city departments are given by Arthur Wellington Brayley in *The Complete History of the Boston Fire Department* . . . (Boston, 1889) and *Schools and Schoolboys of Old Boston* . . . (Boston, 1894). The relationships of the metropolis to the communities around it are analyzed in George Herbert McCaffrey's Political Disintegration and Reintegration of Metropolitan Boston (MS., H.C.L.), a carefully prepared doctoral dissertation.

The COMMERCIAL HISTORY of Boston has been ably treated in Samuel Eliot Morison's *Maritime History of Massachusetts, 1783–1860* (Boston, 1921). Contemporary analyses by E. H. Derby (1850) and James H. Lanman (1844) may be found in *Hunt's Merchants' Magazine and Commercial Review,* X, XXIII. E. S. Chesbrough, the City Engineer, prepared a useful *Tabular Representation of the Present Condition of Boston* . . . (Boston, 1851) which covers a wide variety of topics; and John Macgregor's *Progress of America . . . to the Year 1846* (London, 1847) contains a mass of miscellaneous statistics.

There is no satisfactory INDUSTRIAL HISTORY of Boston, Massachusetts, or New England. Victor S. Clark's *History of Manufactures in the United States* (Washington, 1916–1929) and Emerson D. Fite's *Social and Industrial Conditions in the North during the Civil War* (New York, 1910) contain some references to the city's industries, but their generalizations are not always valid for Boston. Edward C. Kirkland's

Men, Cities and Transportation (Cambridge, 1948) is an outstanding study of New England development; and Oscar and Mary F. Handlin, *Commonwealth* (New York, 1947) examines the role of government in the economy of Massachusetts. *The History of Labour in the United States* (New York, 1918–26), edited by John R. Commons, Norman Ware's *Industrial Worker, 1840–1860* . . . (Boston, 1924), Isaac A. Hourwich's *Immigration and Labor* . . . (New York, 1922), and Edith Abbott's *Women in Industry* . . . (New York, 1913) are excellent studies dealing with aspects of industrial labor in this period and have some data relevant to the problems of Boston. Scattered material may also be found in Albert Aftalion's study of the clothing industries, in Raymond McFarland's study of the fisheries, in Blanche E. Hazard on shoes, Caroline F. Ware on cottons, Paul T. Cherrington and Arthur Harrison Cole on woolens, Lura Woodside Watkins on glass, Jesse Eliphalet Pope on clothing, and Paul L. Vogt on sugar. But the most important source of information on the history of individual companies was a series of industrial compendia; C. L. Fleischmann's *Erwerbszweige* . . . (Stuttgart, 1850), Edwin T. Freedley, *United States Mercantile Guide. Leading Pursuits and Leading Men* . . . (Philadelphia, 1856), volume III of J. Leander Bishop's *History of American Manufactures* . . . (Philadelphia, 1868), *Eighty Years Progress of the United States: a Family Record of American Industry* . . . (Hartford, 1869), *Great Industries of the United States* . . . (Hartford, 1872) edited by Horace Greeley, and C. M. Depew's *One Hundred Years of American Commerce* . . . (New York, 1895) contain descriptions of numerous concerns available nowhere else. One can find hostile comments on Boston's wealthy in *"Our First Men:" a Calendar of Wealth* . . . (Boston, 1846), and friendly ones in A. Forbes and J. W. Greene, *Rich Men of Massachusetts* . . . (Boston, 1851) or in *Aristocracy of Boston* . . . (Boston, 1848).

The materials on the INTELLECTUAL DEVELOPMENT of the city are abundant and familiar. The Bostonians who participated in the "flowering" were extremely self-conscious, wrote a good deal about themselves and their ideas, and, in addition, found frequent biographers. Toward the end of the last century when interest in this group reached a peak, it received friendly and sympathetic, if often uncritical, treatment at the hands of the generation which had been its students. Octavius Brooks Frothingham and others produced a succession of biographies which breathed a pious veneration for a bygone golden age, but which often embodied the results of sound scholarship and patient research. More recent biographers have been more detached and have brought broader perspectives to their work. Henry Steele Commager's *Theodore Parker* . . . (Boston, 1936), for example, contains little that is "new" but paints a vivid and appealing portrait through an understanding examination of its subject's social background. Among the useful biographies of the last decade are also: Arthur S. Bolster, Jr., *James Freeman Clarke* (Boston, 1954); Harold Schwartz, *Samuel Gridley Howe* (Cambridge, 1956); and Oscar Sherwin, *Prophet of Liberty: the Life and Times of Wendell Phillips* (New York, 1958). Other phases of Boston's cultural history are touched on in William B. Whiteside, *The Boston Y.M.C.A.* . . . (New York, 1951), Arthur Mann, *Yankee Reformers in the Urban*

Age (Cambridge, 1954), Barbara M. Solomon, *Ancestors and Immigrants* (Cambridge, 1956), and Barbara M. Solomon, *Pioneers in Service* . . . (Boston, 1956).

The POLITICAL history of the city can hardly be separated from that of the state of which it was capital. *The Commonwealth History of Massachusetts* (New York, 1930), edited by A. B. Hart, contains some articles of value and Samuel Eliot Morison's brief *History of the Constitution of Massachusetts* . . . (Boston, 1917) is useful. Two thorough works cover the specific issues of this period. Arthur B. Darling's *Political Changes in Massachusetts, 1824–1848* . . . (New Haven, 1925), and William G. Bean's Party Transformation in Massachusetts with Special Reference to the Antecedents of Republicanism 1848–1860 (MS. doctoral dissertation, H.C.L., summarized in "Puritan versus Celt 1850–1860," *New England Quarterly,* VII, 70 ff.) trace the impact of new issues upon party structure in scholarly detail. Both, however, labor under the handicap of an untenable thesis. Their attempt to impose a sectional pattern upon Massachusetts politics is hardly successful, and is contradicted by much of their own material; other lines of division were much more important than those between east and west. Edith E. Ware's *Political Opinion in Massachusetts during the Civil War and Reconstruction* . . . (New York, 1916) is a conventional work which fails to prove that the State was never antislavery, and contributes little of value.

Three newspapermen have left valuable comments on the political scene in Massachusetts. William S. Robinson's *"Warrington" Pen-Portraits* . . . (Boston, 1877) contains the penetrating observations of one familiar with all the complexities of state politics in the fifties. George S. Merriam's *Life and Times of Samuel Bowles* (New York, 1885) is a biography with copious extracts from the correspondence of the editor of the *Springfield Republican;* and Benjamin P. Shillaber of the Democratic *Post* has recalled his "Experiences During Many Years" for the *New England Magazine,* VIII, IX.

Bostonians of the period left ample stores of papers and memoirs which were turned into biographies. Josiah Quincy's *Figures of the Past from the Leaves of Old Journals* (Boston, 1883) contains a series of charming vignettes in which his most prominent contemporaries are etched with real understanding; it would be difficult, for instance, to find a shrewder appraisal of Edward Everett than that which appears in the story of his meeting with a French prince. *The Life and Letters of Harrison Gray Otis . . .* (Boston, 1913) is a careful study of one mayor of the city by Samuel Eliot Morison; and the Papers and Correspondence of another, John Prescott Bigelow, are in H.C.L. Also in the H.C.L. is the correspondence of Charles Sumner whose pre-war career is most sympathetically treated in Archibald H. Grimké's *Life . . .* (New York, 1892). The campaign *Life of Henry Wilson . . .* (Boston, 1872) by Jonathan B. Mann is the only formal account; but there are large elements of the autobiographical in Wilson's *History of the Rise and Fall of the Slave Power in America* (Boston, 1872). Fred H. Harrington gives a very unsympathetic, though probably not unjust, account of "Nathaniel Prentiss Banks . . ." in the *New England Quarterly,* IX. Ben Butler has received no adequate discussion; one must still consult his *Autobiography . . .* (Boston, 1892). Henry Greenleaf Pearson's *Life of John A.*

Andrew . . . (Boston, 1904) is a thorough account of the Civil War governor.

BOSTON'S IMMIGRANTS have received occasional treatment and some of their prominent men have found biographers. James Bernard Cullen's *Story of the Irish in Boston* . . . (Boston, 1890) is a compilation of ill-assorted data on Irish institutions and personalities, but is the only work of its kind. The best studies refer to a later period. *Americans in Process* . . . (Boston, 1902) and *City Wilderness* . . . (Boston, 1898) are coöperative investigations of the South and West Ends of Boston at the opening of the Twentieth Century, edited by Robert A. Woods. They contain some material on the historical background but are permeated with a settlement house attitude toward their subjects. Frederick A. Bushee's *Ethnic Factors in the Population of Boston* . . . (New York, 1903) deals with the same period but is almost purely statistical and shows remarkably little insight. The life of Thomas D'Arcy McGee is narrated exhaustively but dully by Isabel Skelton (Gardenvale, 1924), and rapturously by Mrs. J. Sadlier in a "Biographical Sketch" that prefaces his *Poems* . . . (New York, 1869). Michael P. Curran's *Life of Patrick A. Collins* (Norwood, 1906) and James J. Roche's *Life of John Boyle O'Reilly* (Boston, 1891, with collected poems and speeches) deal with later immigrants of prominence. Andrew Carney, the only other Irishman to receive formal treatment, is the subject of a sketch by the Rev. G. C. Treacy in the *Historical Records and Studies* of the American Catholic Historical Society, XIII. Among the Germans, Karl Heinzen has written his own biography, *Erlebtes* . . . (Boston, 1874) and has been written about by Carl Wittke (Chicago, 1945).

Solomon Schindler is the subject of an article by Arthur Mann in the *New England Quarterly,* XXIII (1950), 457 ff.; and the physician Maria Zakrzewska gives the story of her life in *A Practical Illustration of "Woman's Right to Labor"* . . . , ed. by C. H. Dall (Boston, 1860). Lorenzo Papanti, the Italian dancing master, is described by Charles F. Reed in the *Proceedings of the Bostonian Society . . . 1928;* and the Negress, Mrs. Chloe Spear, is the subject of a *Memoir . . .* (Boston, 1832) by a "Lady of Boston."

Additional material on the Negroes may be found in George W. Crawford's monograph on *Prince Hall and His Followers . . .* (New York, 1914) and in the publications on Negro Masonry by Lewis Hayden. There is some data on Boston in W. H. Siebert's *Underground Railroad . . .* (New York, 1898), in Volumes Thirteen and Fourteen of the collection of his manuscripts in H.C.L., and in Charles H. Wesley's *Negro Labor in the United States . . .* (New York, 1927). Material on legal status may be found in Volume IV of Helen T. Catterall's *Judicial Cases Concerning American Slavery and the Negro . . .* (Washington, 1936).

For the story of the CATHOLIC CHURCH we now can turn to the splendid *History of the Archdiocese of Boston* (New York, 1944) by Robert H. Lord, John E. Sexton, and Edward T. Harrington. Earlier Catholic histories had been concerned primarily with specific institutions and with personalities, but within those limits had made a good deal of material available. The Rev. James Fitton's *Sketches of the Establishment of the Church in New England* (Boston, 1872) and the more ambitious *History of the Catholic Church in the New England States* (Boston, 1899), edited by the Very Rev.

William Byrne and others, supplement John Gilmary Shea's detailed chronicle of the *History of the Catholic Church within the . . . United States . . .* (New York, 1886). Thomas D'Arcy McGee's *Catholic History of North America . . .* (Boston, 1855) has more value for light on its author than for its contributions to serious history. Within a narrower field, the Rev. Arthur J. Riley's temperate and scholarly *Catholicism in New England to 1788 . . .* (Washington, 1936) is one of the best works on any phase of the subject. There is material on the early history of the Church in Boston in the "Catholic Recollections" of Samuel Breck, *American Catholic Historical Researches,* XII; but the most careful account is given in E. Percival Merritt's "Sketches of the Three Earliest Roman Catholic Priests in Boston," *Publications of the Colonial Society of Massachusetts,* XXV. Bishop Fenwick is discussed in an article by Robert H. Lord in the *Catholic Historical Review,* XXII; and Bishop Fitzpatrick in one by Isaac T. Hecker in the *Catholic World,* XLV. Father Hecker himself is the subject of a penetrating biography by Vincent F. Holden (Washington, 1939) which gives a good account of the process of conversion. Arthur M. Schlesinger, Jr.'s *Orestes A. Brownson . . .* (Boston, 1939) is excellent for the early years but does not deal adequately with the issues of the Catholic period. For the latter it is still necessary to consult the pious biography by Brownson's son (Detroit, 1898) and the voluminous edition of the *Works of Orestes A. Brownson* (Detroit, 1882).

Few studies of the ANTI-CATHOLIC movement have dealt with it dispassionately. Most have regarded it as an inherent feature of American Protestant society and have zealously chronicled every reference to "Papists" without examining its true characteristics or causes. Sister Mary Augustina (Ray) in *American Opinion of Roman Catholicism in the Eighteenth Century* (New York, 1936), for instance, has patiently compiled a long list of such references without discriminating between those in which there was a real animus, those which were just thoughtless, and those in which the word was used with no more derogatory sense than "Methodist" or "Quaker."

Undoubtedly the best account of all phases of this movement is Ray Allen Billington's *Protestant Crusade, 1800– 1860* . . . (New York, 1938), a conscientious and thorough work, although its conclusions are not always applicable to Boston. Billington unfortunately views the Know-Nothing movement purely from its anti-alien aspect and misses the significance of the reform issue which is hinted at in William G. Bean, "An Aspect of Know-Nothingism — the Immigrant and Slavery," *South Atlantic Quarterly,* XXIII, and Harry J. Carman and R. H. Luthin, "Some Aspects of the Know-Nothing Movement Reconsidered," *ibid.,* XXXIX. The material in Humphrey J. Desmond's study of the party (Washington, 1904) and in the four articles of George H. Haynes (*American Historical Review,* III, *New England Magazine,* XV, XVI, *Annual Report of the American Historical Association, 1896,* I) is distorted by the failure to understand the character of the movement in Massachusetts. Later aspects of nativism are treated in John Higham, *Strangers in the Land* (New Brunswick, 1955), and Charlotte Erickson, *American Industry and the European Immigrant* . . . (Cambridge, 1957).

NOTES

Notes

Foreword

[1] From the introduction to a projected epic, *The Emigrants*, by Thomas D'Arcy McGee (cf. *Poems* . . . [New York, 1869], 130).

[2] Charles Elmer Gehlke, *Émil Durkheim's Contributions to Sociological Theory* (Columbia University Studies in History, Economics and Public Law, LXIII, New York, 1915), 70.

Chapter I. Social Boston, 1790–1845

[1] Bronson Alcott in 1828 (Odell Shepard, *Journals of Bronson Alcott* [Boston, 1938], 15).

[2] In 1641. Quoted by Samuel Eliot Morison, *Maritime History of Massachusetts, 1783–1860* (Boston, 1921), 12. On this trade, cf. Arthur Meier Schlesinger, *Colonial Merchants and the American Revolution, 1763–1776* (New York, 1918), 22 ff.

[3] Cf. Robert Noxon Toppan, *Edward Randolph . . . a Memoir* (Publications of the Prince Society, Boston, 1898–1909), I, 78, 134 ff., III, 79; cf. also George Louis Beer, *Old Colonial System, 1660–1754* . . . (New York, 1912), II, 269, 284, 285; Schlesinger, *op. cit.*, 40 ff.

[4] Cf. George Louis Beer, *British Colonial Policy, 1754–1765* (New York, 1907), 220 ff., 277 ff.; Schlesinger, *op. cit.*, 57 ff.

[5] Beer, *British Colonial Policy*, 228 ff.; Schlesinger, *op. cit.*, 592 ff.

[6] For the revolutionary period and the years following, cf. Robert A. East, *Business Enterprise in the American Revolutionary Era* (New York, 1938), 49 ff.; Samuel Flagg Bemis, *Jay's Treaty, a Study in Commerce and Diplomacy* (New York, 1923), 23, 258; Theodore Lyman, Jr., *Diplomacy of the United States* . . . (Boston, 1828), II, 2, 12, 59 ff., 310 ff.; Morison, *op. cit.*, 174, n. 1; John D. Forbes, "Port of Boston, 1783–1815" (Harvard University Dissertation, 1937).

[7] *Dublin Chronicle*, January 12, 1792; cf. also *Brief Examination into the Increase of the Revenue, Commerce, and Navigation of Great Britain since the Conclusion of the Peace in 1783* (Dublin, 1792), 50; Bemis, *op. cit.*, 22, 24, 25; Justin Winsor, *Memorial History of Boston, Including Suffolk County, Massachusetts, 1630–1880* (Boston, 1881), IV, 202.

Notes to Chapter 1

8 Cf. Morison, *op. cit.*, 30 ff.

9 *Ibid.*, 43 ff., 50–71; Edward G. Porter, "Ship Columbia and the Discovery of Oregon," *New England Magazine*, June, 1892, VI, 472 ff.; Winsor, *op. cit.*, IV, 204 ff.; La Rochefoucauld-Liancourt, *Voyage dans les États-Unis d'Amérique fait en 1795, 1796, et 1797* (Paris, An VII [1799]), III, 17.

10 *Independent Chronicle* (Boston), April 4, May 27, 1811; Morison, *op. cit.*, 154, 155; Winsor, *op. cit.*, IV, 223.

11 Morison, *op. cit.*, 275; R. B. Forbes, *Remarks on China and the China Trade* (Boston, 1844), 27.

12 Forbes, *op. cit.*, 28; Morison, *op. cit.*, 280 ff.; Winsor, *op. cit.*, IV, 221 ff.

13 La Rochefoucauld-Liancourt, *op. cit.*, V, 167.

14 Winsor, *op. cit.*, IV, 121 ff. For the canal and its effects, cf. Robert Greenhalgh Albion, *Rise of New York Port*, [1815–1860] . . . (New York, 1939), 76–94.

15 Winsor, *op. cit.*, IV, 111.

16 Henry Bradshaw Fearon, *Sketches of America, a Narrative of a Journey* . . . (London, 1818), 109; John Robert Godely, *Letters from America* (London, 1844), I, 17; Oscar Handlin, Ph.D. dissertation, 1940, Harvard College Library, Cambridge, Massachusetts, 10, n. 37, hereafter referred to as Dissertation Copy. Albion stresses the importance of geographical position and the establishment of the packet lines in explaining the preëminence of New York (Albion, *op. cit.*, 16–54). But Boston's position was fully as advantageous as that of New York (cf. *ibid.*, 24–37; Edwin J. Clapp, *Port of Boston* . . . [New Haven, 1916], 21 ff.), and the failure of the packets to develop in Boston was itself the result of the lack of hinterland (cf. Albion, *op. cit.*, 46; *infra*, 299, n. 21).

17 Cf. Edward Everett, "The Western Railroad" (1835), *Orations and Speeches on Various Occasions* (Boston, 1850), II, 144 ff.; Edward Everett, "Opening of the Railroad to Springfield" (1839), *ibid.*, II, 367 ff.; Christopher Roberts, *Middlesex Canal, 1793–1860* (Cambridge, 1938), 19 ff.; Winsor, *op. cit.*, IV, 112–116.

18 "Report of the Select Committee of the House of Representatives . . . on the . . . Expediency of Constructing a Railway . . . to . . . Albany," *Massachusetts House Documents, 1826–27*, no. 13, p. 28.

19 Winsor, *op. cit.*, IV, 126, 129, 138 ff.; Morison, *op. cit.*, 230. Hopes that Boston might share in the great western trade when the completion of the Vermont Central Railroad gave her a direct connection with Canada were never realized; Canadian rail traffic failed to grow significantly in this period ([E. S. Chesbrough], *Tabular Representation of the Present Condition of Boston, in Relation to Railroad Facilities* . . . [Boston, 1851], 25, 26; Grattan to Clarendon, July 10, 1853, British Consular Correspond-

Social Boston

ence, F.O. 5/568; [Otis Clapp], *Letter to the Hon. Abbott Lawrence . . . on the Present Condition and Future Growth of Boston* [Boston, 1853], 4). On the development of transportation, *see also* Edward C. Kirkland, *Men, Cities and Transportation* (Cambridge, 1948); Oscar and Mary F. Handlin, *Commonwealth: A Study of the Role of Government in the American Economy, Massachusetts 1774–1861* (New York, 1947), 108 ff., 115 ff., 185 ff.

[20] For the growth of the coastwide trade, cf. Dissertation Copy, 12, n. 45; also E. H. Derby, "Commercial Cities and Towns of the United States — no. XXII — . . . Boston," *Hunt's Merchants' Magazine and Commercial Review,* November, 1850, XXIII, 490.

[21] Morison, *op. cit.,* 299. Transatlantic trade gravitated towards New York, however, particularly after the establishment of the Black Ball Line in 1816. Similar lines failed in Boston in 1818, 1822, and 1827 because of "the difficulty in obtaining return freights of sufficient amounts" (Consul Grattan, enclosure, May 15, 1844, British Consular Correspondence, F.O. 5/411, no. 12; Morison, *op. cit.,* 232 ff.; Albion, *op. cit.,* 46; H. A. Hill, "Boston and Liverpool Packet Lines . . . ," *New England Magazine,* January, 1894, IX, 549 ff.). Only in the Mediterranean trade did Boston hold a commanding position (Morison, *op. cit.,* 287, 292; statistics in Neapolitan Consular Correspondence, Reale Archivio di Stato, Politica, fasc. 2415, package 63).

[22] John Macgregor, *Progress of America . . .* (London, 1847), II, 176; Winsor, *op. cit.,* IV, 229; Morison, *op. cit.,* 228; Albion, *op. cit.,* 63, 241 ff.; Robert G. Albion, "Yankee Domination of New York Port, 1820–1865," *New England Quarterly,* October, 1932, V. 665 ff.

[23] For statements of tonnage, cf. Dissertation Copy, 15, 414; Morison, *op. cit.,* 378; Macgregor, *op. cit.,* II, 170 ff.; Chesbrough, *op. cit.,* 16.

[24] Consul Manners to Lord Palmerston, June 10, 1832, British Consular Correspondence (F.O. America, II Series), F.O. 5/276, no. 10, p. 2.

[25] Winsor, *op. cit.,* IV, 96, 153.

[26] Cf. *Boston Directory, 1789,* 50; *Boston Directory, 1800,* 7; Margaret H. Foulds, "Massachusetts Bank, 1784–1865," *Journal of Economic and Business History,* February, 1930, II, 256 ff.; Albert Bushnell Hart, *Commonwealth History of Massachusetts* (New York, 1929), III, 363 ff.

[27] Cf. "Report of the List of Incorporations . . . Granted by the Legislature of Massachusetts . . . ," *Massachusetts Senate Documents, 1836,* no. 90, pp. 47–54; *Massachusetts House Documents, 1840,* no. 60, pp. 13–16; and Dissertation Copy, Table II, 415; Macgregor, *op. cit.,* II, 154; Winsor, *op. cit.,* IV, 164; *Massachusetts Senate Documents, 1838,* no. 38, pp. 5 ff.; *Daily Evening Transcript* (Boston), March 2, 1830.

[28] *Massachusetts House Documents, 1840,* no. 60, p. 29; cf. also Winsor,

op. cit., IV, 104 ff., 190 ff.; Derby, *loc. cit.,* 488. For complaints by manufacturers against this financial control, cf. E. B. Bigelow, *Remarks on the
Depressed Condition of Manufactures in Massachusetts . . .* (Boston,
1858), 18, 19.

[29] Chesbrough, *op. cit.,* 6 ff.

[30] This is indicated by the professional composition of the population of
Boston in 1789, an approximate, though of course, not exact conception of
which may be derived from the number of listings in the directory
of 1789 classifiable into each of the following groups:

Merchants	183	Marine industries	89
Brokers	31	Mariners	49
Professionals	142	Unskilled laborers	16
Shopkeepers, skilled craftsmen	331	Innkeepers	68
Artisans	501	Unknown	66
		TOTAL	1,476

Total number of families in Boston 3,343

(Tabulated from *Boston Directory . . .* [Boston, 1789], passim. For the
number of families cf. S. N. D. North, *Heads of Families at the First
Census . . . 1790, Massachusetts* [Washington, 1908], 10.) Contemporary
evidence (analyzed in Dissertation Copy, 20 ff., n. 61) supports this point
of view; and the occupational distribution of the city's population seems
not to have changed substantially in the next half century. The federal
census of 1820 showed 2,905 engaged in manufactures, 2,499 in commerce
and 192 in agriculture in Suffolk County in a total population of 43,940
(United States Census, *Aggregate Amount of . . . Persons in the United
States . . . 1820* [s.l.,n.d. (Washington, 1820)], 7) while that of 1840
showed, in the city of Boston alone, 5,333 employed in manufactures and
trade, 2,040 in commerce, 586 in the learned professions and 10,831 in
navigation (the last figure undoubtedly too high, cf. *Massachusetts House
Documents, 1842,* no. 48, p. 1; *Massachusetts House Documents, 1849,* no.
127, pp. 6 ff.).

[31] Cf. Morison, *op. cit.,* 101, 103, 330.

[32] See Table I, *supra,* 238.

[33] Total of the towns included in this table, *see supra,* Table II, 239.
This has always been true.

[34] C. Bancroft Gillespie, *Illustrated History of South Boston . . .*
(South Boston, 1900), 110–112; Lura Woodside Watkins, *Cambridge Glass,
1818 to 1888, The Story of the New England Glass Company* (Boston,
[1930], 4, 7, 182; [Anne Royall], *Sketches of History . . .* (New Haven,
1826), 341.

[35] Harriet Martineau, *Society in America* (New York, 1837), II, 59.

[36] *Eighty Years Progress of the United States: a Family Record of American Industry* . . . (Hartford, 1869), 324; Winsor, *op. cit.,* IV, 99.

[37] Cf. *Daily Evening Transcript,* September 25, 30, 1830; *Boston Pilot,* August 30, 1856; Benevolent Fraternity of Churches, *Twenty-Second Annual Report of the Executive Committee* . . . (Boston, 1856), 26.

[38] *Address of the American Society for the Encouragement of Domestic Manufactures to the People of the United States* (New York, 1817), 11, 14. Cf. also Arthur Harrison Cole, *American Wool Manufacture* (Cambridge, 1926), I, 86 ff.

[39] Raymond McFarland, *History of the New England Fisheries* . . . (New York, 1911), 129 ff., 187; Morison, *op. cit.,* 31, 150, 375.

[40] Derby, *loc. cit.,* 496.

[41] This by no means implies that the wealth of Boston was declining. On the contrary, the assessed value of its property rose steadily from $42,140,200 in 1822 to $135,948,700 in 1845, while the valuation of its suburbs in 1840 totalled some $15,000,000 (Nathan Matthews, *City Government of Boston* [Boston, 1895], 190, 191; Derby, *loc. cit.,* 485; Chesbrough, *op. cit.,* 20, 21).

[42] Cf. Jesse Chickering, "Report of the Committee . . . 1850," *Boston City Documents, 1851,* no. 60, pp. 24 ff.; *Historical Review and Directory of North America . . . by a Gentleman Immediately Returned from a Tour* . . . (Cork, 1801), II, 63; *infra,* Table II. For the movement away from rural New England, cf. Percy Wells Bidwell, "Rural Economy in New England at the Beginning of the Nineteenth Century," *Transactions of the Connecticut Academy of Arts and Sciences,* April, 1916, XX, 383–391; for the absence of foreign immigration, cf. Josiah Quincy, *Figures of the Past from the Leaves of Old Journals* (Boston, 1883), 112; [James W. Hale], *Old Boston Town . . . by an 1801-er* . . . (New York, 1880), 34; John Stetson Barry, *History of Massachusetts* . . . (Boston, 1857), III, 372; [William Tudor], *Letters on the Eastern States* (New York, 1820), 315; Timothy Dwight, *Travels in New England* . . . (New Haven, 1821), I, 506.

[43] Cf. Francis S. Drake, *Town of Roxbury . . . Its History and Antiquities* . . . (Boston, 1905), 345; Robert A. Woods, *City Wilderness* . . . (Boston, 1898), 23 ff.; State Street Trust Company, *Boston, England and Boston, New England* . . . (Boston, 1930), 12 ff.; Dissertation Copy, 26, 177; George H. McCaffrey, *Political Disintegration and Reintegration of Metropolitan Boston* (MS., H. C. L.), 189 ff.; Winsor, *op. cit.,* IV, 25–33, 46. For a perspective of the extent of these operations, cf. the maps for 1789, 1800, 1820, and 1848, cited in Boston, Engineering Department, *List*

Notes to Chapter 1

of Maps of Boston . . . (Annual Report of the City Engineer, February 1, 1903, Appendix I, Boston, 1903), 79, 84, 95, 125.

[44] Derby, *loc. cit.,* 484 ff.; "Report and Tabular Statement of the Censors . . . ," *Boston City Documents, 1850,* no. 42, pp. 13, 39; Josiah Curtis, *Report of the Joint Special Committee . . .* (Boston, 1856), 4; *Courrier des États-Unis* (New York), June 28, 1850. For the difference in rents, cf. Consul Manners to the Undersecretary of State, March 10, 1832, British Consular Correspondence (F.O. America, II Series), F.O. 5/276, no. 6.

[45] Edward H. Savage, *Boston Events . . . from 1630 to 1880 . . .* (Boston, 1884), 7; Thomas C. Simonds, *History of South Boston . . .* (Boston, 1857), 72 ff.; Boston Common Council, "South Boston Memorial . . . April 22, 1847," *Boston City Documents, 1847,* no. 18, p. 5; Samuel Eliot Morison, *Life and Letters of Harrison Gray Otis . . .* (Boston, 1913), I, 243; Dissertation Copy, 28, n. 89; McCaffrey, *op. cit.,* 182 ff.; Winsor, *op. cit.,* IV, 30, 38–40.

[46] McCaffrey, *op. cit.,* 53 ff., 196 ff.; Winsor, *op. cit.,* III, 284, IV, 25; Hon. Ellis W. Morton, *Annexation of Charlestown . . . a Condensed Report of the Argument . . . February 27, 1871* (Boston, 1871), 5.

[47] For Boston's relationship to these towns, cf. McCaffrey, *op. cit.,* 147 ff., 170 ff.; "Report of Standing Committee on Towns . . . ," *Massachusetts Senate Documents, 1851,* no. 82, pp. 2, 3, 9 ff.; Winsor, *op. cit.,* III, 275, IV, 26, 41; D. Hamilton Hurd, *History of Norfolk County . . .* (Philadelphia, 1884), 72, 73; John Hayward, *Gazeteer of Massachusetts . . . with a Great Variety of Other Useful Information (Revised Edition)* (Boston, 1849), 41; P. Tocque, *Peep at Uncle Sam's Farm, Workshop, Fisheries, &c.* (Boston, 1851), 20. For the population of all these towns, cf. *infra,* Table II.

[48] [Hale], *op. cit.,* 29; E. Mackenzie, *Historical . . . View of the United States . . .* (Newcastle upon Tyne, 1819), 103; Van Wyck Brooks, *Flowering of New England, 1815–1865* (New York, 1936), 11, n.; *Wide Awake: and the Spirit of Washington* (Boston), October 7, 1854; Benevolent Fraternity of Churches, *Eleventh Annual Report of the Executive Committee . . .* (Boston, 1845), 27; and *Tenth Annual Report of the Executive Committee . . .* (Boston, 1844), 25.

[49] Cf. Sándor Farkas, *Útazás Észak Amerikában* (KOLOZSVAR, 1834), 91.

[50] William Priest, *Travels in the United States . . .* (Boston, 1802), 168.

[51] Boston Board of Health, Records, 1799–1824 (MSS., B. P. L.), I.

[52] *Rules, Regulations and Orders of the Boston Board of Health Relative to the Police of the Town . . .* (s.l., 1821), 5, 6, 8–16; Boston Board of Health, Records, II.

[53] Cf. Robert A. Woods, ed., *Americans in Process . . .* (Boston, 1902), 74.

[54] *Rules, Regulations and Orders* . . . , 2, 5, 6; and Board of Health Records, IV; also Joseph B. Egan, *Citizenship in Boston* . . . (Philadelphia, n.d. [1925]), 264; Woods, *Americans in Process,* 73.

[55] Cf. [Theodore Lyman, Jr.], *Communication to the City Council on the Subject of Introducing Water into the City* . . . (Boston, 1834), passim; Winsor, *op. cit.,* III, 252.

[56] Cf., e.g., Boston City Council, *Report of the Committee* . . . *on the Powers* . . . *of the Overseers* . . . (Boston, 1825), 3 ff.; Winsor, *op. cit.,* III, 221.

[57] Winsor, *op. cit.,* III, 218 ff.; James M. Bugbee, *City Government of Boston* (Baltimore, 1887), 19 ff.

[58] Edward H. Savage, *Police Records and Recollections; or Boston by Daylight and Gaslight* . . . (Boston, 1873), 84, 94 ff.

[59] Cf. Josiah Quincy, *Municipal History of* . . . *Boston* . . . (Boston, 1852), 160; Arthur Wellington Brayley, *Complete History of the Boston Fire Department* . . . (Boston, 1889), 144 ff., 149, 150 ff.; *Boston City Documents, 1873,* no. 97.

[60] In this period, expenditures on streets rose from $30,000 in 1829 to $180,000 in 1847, on the fire department from $14,000 to $57,000, on constables from $1,500 to $55,000, and on lighting from nothing to $31,000 (Boston Common Council, "Annual Appropriations, 1846–47," *Boston City Documents, 1846,* no. 15, pp. 8 ff.; Josiah Quincy, *Report of the Committee of Appropriations, Boston* [Boston, 1828], 4, 5).

[61] For an estimate of the number of vehicles entering and leaving Boston, cf. Dissertation Copy, 36, n. 120; *Bowen's Boston News-Letter and City Record,* October 14, 1826.

[62] For a list of these lines cf. Peleg W. Chandler, *Charter and Ordinances of* . . . *Boston* . . . *with the Acts of the Legislature Relating to the City* . . . (Boston, 1850), 68 ff.; cf. also Francis S. Drake, *Town of Roxbury* . . . *Its History and Antiquities* . . . (Boston, 1905), 51; *Bowen's Boston News-Letter and City Record,* February 25, April 29, 1826.

[63] Cf. the timetables in George Adams, *Brighton and Brookline Business Directory* . . . (Boston, 1850), 20, 22, 24, 28; Chandler, *op. cit.,* 64 ff.; Tocque, *op. cit.,* 14; Nathaniel Dearborn, *Boston Notions* . . . (Boston, 1848), 221.

[64] Lemuel Shattuck, *Report to the Committee of the City Council* . . . *Census of Boston for* . . . *1845* . . . (Boston, 1846), 113. Cf. also Sir Charles Lyell, *A Second Visit to the United States of North America* (London, 1849), I, 186; and the remarkable failure of expenditures on paupers to rise in Boston over a period of a quarter-century (cf. *infra,* Table III).

[65] Dissertation Copy, 39 ff.

[66] Cf. e.g., [John Gallison], *Explanation of the Views of the Society*

... (Cambridge, 1825), 3; Leah Hannah Feder, *Unemployment Relief in Periods of Depression* ... (New York, 1936), 20; Benevolent Fraternity of Churches, *Act of Incorporation and By-Laws* ... (Boston, 1859), 4.

[67] Martineau, *op. cit.*, II, 290; also the letter of Father Ambrose Manahan, *Boston Pilot*, April 19, 1851; Winsor, *op. cit.*, IV, 647–649, 672 ff.; *infra*, Table III; Dissertation Copy, 39.

[68] Cf. Table IV, *infra*; D. B. Warden, *Statistical, Political, and Historical Account of the United States* ... (Edinburgh, 1819), I, 304; "Report of the Attorney-General, 1834," *Massachusetts House Documents, 1834*, no. 4, p. 11.

[69] N. H. Julius, *Nordamerikas sittliche Zustände nach eigenen Anschauungen in den Jahren 1834, 1835 und 1836* (Leipzig, 1839), II, 66, and Tables 2, 3, 9, 12.

[70] Cf. Capt. Marryatt, *A Diary in America with Remarks on Its Institutions* (New York, 1839), 168; also Julius, *op. cit.*, II, Table 11.

[71] Cf. "Report of the City Marshal," quoted in Benevolent Fraternity of Churches, *Twelfth Annual Report of the Executive Committee* ... (Boston, 1846), 15.

[72] Benevolent Fraternity of Churches, *Twelfth Annual Report of the Executive Committee* ... (Boston, 1846), 30. Cf. also Savage, *Police Records and Recollections*, 182; Boston Female Society for Missionary Purposes, *A Brief Account ... with Extracts from the Reports* ... (Boston, n.d.), 15, 16 ff.

[73] Disease and epidemics were rare. Between 1811 and 1820 there were only six cases of smallpox, between 1821 and 1830, only seven. Thereafter the number increased but was unusually large only in 1840 (cf. *supra*, 114).

[74] Ralph Waldo Emerson, "Nature," *Complete Works* ... (Boston, 1903), I, 40. Cf. also Handlin, *Commonwealth*, 202 ff.

[75] W. H. Channing, *Gospel of Today, a Discourse ... at the Ordination of T. W. Higginson* ... (Boston, 1847), 11. For reforms, cf. Arthur B. Darling, *Political Changes in Massachusetts, 1824–1848* ... (New Haven, 1925), 157 ff.; *Daily Evening Transcript*, October 2, 1830; A. B. Hart, *Commonwealth History of Massachusetts* (New York, 1929), III, 518, IV, 273 ff.

[76] Channing, *op. cit.*, 26.

[77] Edward Everett Hale, quoted in M. A. DeWolfe Howe, *Holmes of the Breakfast Table* (New York, 1939), 42.

[78] Cf. Farkas, *op. cit.*, 90, 102, 127.

[79] Cf. *Independent Chronicle*, September 6, 1810; Elizabeth Brett White, *American Opinion of France from Lafayette to Poincaré* (New York, 1927), 86, 119; *supra*, 140, 141, 153, 154; Hart, *op. cit.*, IV, 116.

[80] Cf. Morison, *Maritime History,* 24; Nathan Matthews, *City Government of Boston* (Boston, 1895), 171.

[81] Emerson, *op. cit.,* I, 37.

[82] Theodore Parker, *Sermon of the Moral Condition of Boston . . .* (Boston, 1849), 4.

[83] D. R. Burden to Thomas Russell, July 5, 1796, Russell Correspondence (MSS., T. C. D.), II. Cf. also Consul Manners to Lord Palmerston, June 10, 1832, British Consular Correspondence, F.O. 5/276, no. 10, p. 2.

[84] Cf., e.g., Farkas, *op. cit.,* 122.

[85] *Bowen's Boston News-Letter and City Record,* April 15, 1826.

[86] Dearborn, *Boston Notions,* 200, 201.

[87] Archibald H. Grimké, *Life of Charles Sumner . . .* (New York, 1892), 58 ff. Cf. also, Frank Luther Mott, *History of American Magazines, 1850–1865* (Cambridge, 1938), 228, 229; *supra,* 124. For German influences cf. Brooks, *op. cit.,* 191, 192; Darling, *op. cit.,* 31; Henry Steele Commager, *Theodore Parker* (Boston, 1936), 45, 95 ff.; for French, Howe, *op. cit.,* 36; and for English, *Independent Chronicle,* August 29, 1811; Lieut. Col. A. M. Maxwell, *Run Through the United States . . . 1840* (London, 1841), I, 46.

[88] Ezra S. Gannett, *Arrival of the Britannia, a Sermon . . . Federal Street Meeting-House . . . July 19, 1840 . . .* (Boston, 1840), 16, 17.

[89] John Lambert, *Travels through Lower Canada and the United States . . . 1806 . . .* (London, 1810), III, 118 ff.; Priest, *op. cit.,* 157; Morison, *Harrison Gray Otis,* I, 37, 218 ff.

[90] Cf. *Independent Chronicle,* January 4, 1810.

[91] Cf. Winsor, *op. cit.,* IV, 415 ff.; *supra,* 147; and the advertisements in *Daily Evening Transcript,* 1831, and *Boston Musical Gazette . . . ,* May 2, 1838.

Chapter II. The Process of Arrival

[1] "Native Poet [Oliver Goldsmith]," in "Traveller," as quoted in Hibernicus, *Practical Views and Suggestions on the Present Condition . . . of Ireland . . .* (Dublin, 1823), 117.

[2] Benevolent Fraternity of Churches (Boston), *Twenty-Sixth Annual Report of the Executive Committee . . . 1860* (Boston, 1860), 8. For examples of each of the nationalities cited, cf. Dissertation Copy, 51–53, and the references there cited.

[3] Cf. a bundle of correspondence on this subject in Reale Archivio di Stato, Naples, Politica, Fasc. I, package 17. For Norwegian deserters, cf. Theodore C. Blegen, *Norwegian Migration to America, 1825–1860* (Northfield, Minnesota, 1931), 331.

4 For a list of merchants, cf., "British Mercantile Houses Established in Boston," Grattan to Bidwell, November 30, 1848, British Consular Correspondence, F.O. 5/488, no. 6, enclosures; also La Rochefoucauld-Liancourt, *Voyage dans les États-Unis d'Amérique* . . . (Paris, An VII [1799]), III, 139. For some Scotch merchants, cf. Ethel S. Bolton, ed., *Topliff's Travels, Letters from Abroad in the Years 1828 and 1829* . . . (Boston, 1906), 15, 16. For the Marquis Niccolo Reggio and other Italian merchants, cf. *Boston Pilot,* July 11, 1846; Giovanni Schiavo, *Italians in America before the Civil War* . . . (New York, 1934), 226; Reale Archivio di Stato, Naples, Politica, Fasc. I, package 15; Leone Carpi, *Delle Colonie e dell' emigrazione d'Italiani all'estero* . . . (Milano, 1874), II, 230 ff.

5 Baker to Consul Skinner, January 14, 1817, British Embassy Archives, F.O. 115/27, f. 185; Joseph Jennings to Chargé d'Affaires, August 18, 1832, British Consular Correspondence, F.O. 5/277.

6 Cf. Fernand Baldensperger, *Mouvement des idées dans l'émigration française* . . . (Paris, 1924), I, iii; Leo Gershoy, *French Revolution and Napoleon* (New York, 1933), 131; Emmanuel Vingtrinier, *La Contre-Révolution* . . . (Paris, 1924), I, 36, 37, II, 269; Dissertation Copy, 55, 56.

7 Cf. R. R. Madden, *United Irishmen, Their Lives and Times, Newly Edited* (New York, 1916), II, 30 ff., 101, 261, III, 10; R. R. Madden, *Connexion between . . . Ireland and England* . . . (Dublin, 1845), 116, 132; Marcus Lee Hansen, *Atlantic Migration, 1607–1860* . . . (Cambridge, 1940), 65, 66; R. R. Madden, *Life and Times of Robert Emmet* (New York, 1856), 59 ff.

8 Cf. Ernest Bruncken, *German Political Refugees in the United States* . . . (s.l., 1904), 11, 12; *Report of the Select Committee of the Legislative Assembly Appointed to Inquire into the Causes . . . of the Emigration . . . from Lower Canada to the United States* . . . (Montreal, 1849), 5; Marcus Lee Hansen, *Mingling of the Canadian and American Peoples* . . . (New Haven, 1940), 115 ff.; Hansen, *Atlantic Migration,* 122 ff.

9 Cf. Max J. Kohler, "Right of Asylum with Particular Reference to the Alien," *American Law Review,* LI (May, June, 1917), 384, 399–401.

10 Vingtrinier, *op. cit.,* I, 69; M. F. de Montrol, *Histoire de l'émigration* . . . (Paris, 1827), 45, 104, 273, 283, 305; Le Comte de Sainte-Colombe, *Catalogue des émigrés français à Fribourg* . . . (Lyon, 1884), passim; Charles Robert, "Les Émigrés Bretons . . . ," *Revue de Bretagne, de Vendée & d'Anjou* . . . , Juin, 1898, XIX, 427 ff.

11 Thomas Atkinson, *Hibernian Eclogues* . . . (Dublin, 1791), 14; Madden, *United Irishmen,* III, 295, IV, 151; Thomas Addis Emmet, *Memoir of Thomas Addis and Robert Emmet* (New York, 1915), II, 61–80.

12 Otto Wiltberger, *Die deutschen politischen Flüchtlinge in Strassburg,*

The Process of Arrival

1830–1849 (Berlin, 1909), 8 ff.; Karl Heinzen, *Erlebtes. zweiter Theil: nach meiner Exilirung (Gesammelte Schriften, vierter Band)* (Boston, 1874), 54, 326, 328, 356.

[13] Alvin R. Calman, *Ledru-Rollin après 1848 et les proscrits français en Angleterre* (Paris, 1921), 35, 93, 105.

[14] Cf. e.g., Heinzen, *op. cit.,* 455.

[15] George Ticknor Curtis, *Rights of Conscience* . . . (Boston, 1842), 18.

[16] Baldensperger, *op. cit.,* I, 105, n. 1; Frances S. Childs, *French Refugee Life in the United States* . . . (Baltimore, 1940), passim.

[17] F. B., "Le Séjour de Brillat-Savarin aux États-Unis," *Revue de Littérature Comparée,* II (1922), 95; Howard Mumford Jones, *America and French Culture, 1750–1848* (Chapel Hill, 1927), 304; J. G. Rosengarten, *French Colonists and Exiles in the United States* (Philadelphia, 1907), 103; Samuel Adams Drake, *Old Landmarks . . . of Boston* . . . (Boston, 1873), 270, 271.

[18] Cf. *Boston Selectmen Minutes from 1787 through 1798 (Report of Record Commissioners of the City of Boston, XXVII), Boston City Documents, 1896,* no. 81, pp. 271, 272; Jackson to Canning, November 19, 1809, British Consular Correspondence, F.O. 5/64, no. 20; MacDonough to Grenville, July 24, 1794, *ibid.,* F.O. 5/6; Francis S. Drake, *Town of Roxbury . . . Its History and Antiquities* . . . (Boston, 1905), 123, 124; Baldensperger, *op. cit.,* I, 107 ff.; Edmund Patten, *Glimpse at the United States* . . . (London, 1853), 14; Jones, *op. cit.,* 135, 167.

[19] Cf., e.g., letters to the Mayor of Boston asking for aid from A. A. Dieffenbach, "stud. theolog." of Berlin, September 18, 1850, and from F. Guillerez, December 13, 1849 (John Prescott Bigelow Papers, 1723–1865 [MSS., H. C. L.], Box VI); Henry Steele Commager, *Theodore Parker* (Boston, 1936), 111 ff.

[20] Bruncken, *op. cit.,* 13; A. B. Faust, *German Element in the United States* . . . (New York, 1927), II, 214 ff.

[21] Heinzen, *op. cit.,* 503; Carl Wittke, *Against the Current* (Chicago, 1945).

[22] Walter Coxe to Thomas Finn, December 14, 1816 in Dr. R. Robert Madden, "Collection of Papers on the History of the United Irishmen, 1790–1832" (MSS., T. C. D.), I; *Irish-American* (New York), May 30, 1857, June 11, 1853.

[23] *Daily Evening Transcript,* November 11, 12, 1831; Samuel A. Drake, *op. cit.,* 264; *Boston Pilot,* February 2, 1856, June 12, 1852, December 10, 1853.

[24] Robert R. Kuczynski, *Population Movements* (Oxford, 1936), 23.

[25] A. M. Carr-Saunders, *World Population* . . . (Oxford, 1936), 30; Walter F. Willcox, ed., *International Migrations,* II (New York, 1931),

49, 78; Donald H. Taft, *Human Migration* . . . (New York, 1936), 86; A. M. Carr-Saunders, *Population Problem, a Study in Human Evolution* (Oxford, 1922), 298–300, 308; Oscar Handlin, *The Uprooted* (Boston, 1951).

²⁶ Cf. Robert Holditch, *Emigrant's Guide to the United States of America* . . . (London, 1818), 40; Grenville to Hammond, April 15, 1795, British Embassy Archives, F.O. 115/4; Manners to Castlereagh, November 27, 1818, British Consular Correspondence, F.O. 5/135; Hansen, *Atlantic Migration,* 97; [John Talbot], *History of North America* . . . *Including* . . . *Information on* . . . *Emigrating to That Country* (Leeds, 1820), II, 316; Carr-Saunders, *World Population,* 182.

²⁷ *Boston Merkur,* December 26, 1846; A. H. Simpson to W. S. O'Brien, July 17, 1840 (W. S. O'Brien Papers and Letters, 1819–1854, MSS., N. L. I.), VI, no. 749); also letters from Scotch weavers in 1840 and 1841 (*ibid.,* VI, nos. 737, 739, 777); Edwin C. Guillet, *The Great Migration* . . . (New York, 1937), 29.

²⁸ John Harold Clapham, *Economic Development of France and Germany* . . . (Cambridge, 1928), 87; Gustav Schmoller, *Zur Geschichte der deutschen Kleingewerbe im 19. Jahrhundert* (Halle, 1870), 661, 671; Eugen von Philippovich, ed., *Auswanderung und Auswanderungspolitik in Deutschland* . . . (Liepzig, 1892), 110.

²⁹ Schmoller, *op. cit.,* 105, 110.

³⁰ Cf. Marcus L. Hansen, "Revolutions of 1848 and German Emigration," *Journal of Economic and Business History,* II (1930), 656.

³¹ Cf. George O'Brien, *Economic History of Ireland in the Seventeenth Century* (Dublin, 1919), 118, 119, 221; George O'Brien, *Economic History of Ireland in the Eighteenth Century* (Dublin, 1918), 269 ff.; George O'Brien, *Economic History of Ireland from the Union to the Famine* (London, 1921), 297 ff., 415 ff.; William Forbes Adams, *Ireland and Irish Emigration to the New World from 1815 to the Famine* . . . (New Haven, 1932), 57; J. Dunsmore Clarkson, *Labour and Nationalism in Ireland* (New York, 1925), 23.

³² [Rev. Gilbert Austin], *Charity Sermon for the Sick and Indigent Roomkeepers Preached at St. Peter's, Dublin* . . . *February 19, 1797* . . . (Dublin, 1797), 29; cf. also (Rev. William Hickey), *State of the Poor of Ireland* . . . (Carlow, 1820), 20; Clarkson, *op. cit.,* 58, 59, 101, 106. For a list of industries in the neighborhood of Dublin which were ruined and whose "protestant inhabitants fled to America," cf., *A Freeman's Letter to the Right Hon. Robert Peel on the Present State of the City of Dublin* . . . (Dublin, n.d.), 8, 9.

³³ William Warren, *Political and Moral Pamphlet* . . . *Addressed to the* . . . *Lord Lieutenant* . . . (Cork, 1797), 6; *The Causes of Discon-*

tents in Ireland, and Remedies Proposed . . . (s.l., n.d. [Dublin, 1823]), 46; *Statement of the Proceedings of the Western Committee for the Relief of the Irish Poor* . . . (London, 1831), 37.

[34] For the whole problem, cf. Elie Halévy, *History of the English People* . . . (Harmondsworth, 1937), I, Bk. II, 31 ff., 37 ff., 58 ff., 70 ff.; J. L. and Barbara Hammond, *Village Labourer, 1760–1832* . . . (London, 1912), 71.

[35] Stanley C. Johnson, *History of Emigration from the United Kingdom to North America* . . . (London, 1913), 16; A. M. Carr-Saunders, *Population* (London, 1925), 8.

[36] Cf. Paul Mantoux, *Industrial Revolution of the Eighteenth Century* (New York, 1928), 186.

[37] Cf. Max Sering, *Deutsche Agrarpolitik* . . . (Leipzig, 1934), 26; also Clapham, *op. cit.,* 30 and the end map, "German Empire — Agrarian."

[38] Cf. Florence Edith Janson, *Background of Swedish Immigration, 1840–1930* (Chicago, 1931), 43 ff.

[39] Cf. Willcox, *op. cit.,* II, 315, 341; Hansen, *Atlantic Migration,* 211 ff.; Blegen, *op. cit.,* 82, 123, 168 ff.; Janson, *op. cit.,* 40, 55 56; Robert R. Kuczynski, *Balance of Births and Deaths* (New York, 1928), I, 98, 99.

[40] Janson, *op. cit.,* 49 ff., 14; Blegen, *op. cit.,* 19.

[41] Imre Ferenczi, *International Migrations,* I (New York, 1929), 116; Willcox, *op. cit.,* II, 342, 347.

[42] For the slow growth of German industry, cf. Clapham, *op. cit.,* 86 ff.

[43] Cf. Philippovich, *op. cit.,* 6, 111; René Le Conte, *La Politique de l'Allemagne en matière d'émigration* (Paris, 1921), 7, 9 ff.

[44] Ferenczi, *op. cit.,* I, 114 ff.; Marcus Lee Hansen, Emigration from Continental Europe, 1815–1850 . . . (MS., H. C. L.), Chapter I, part 2; Hansen, *Atlantic Migration,* 79 ff.

[45] For the status of agriculture in these years, cf. Sigmund Fleischmann, *Die Agrarkrisis von 1845–1855* . . . (Heidelberg, 1902), passim; Philippovich, *op. cit.,* 77; Willcox, *op. cit.,* II, 316; Hansen, *Atlantic Migration,* 252 ff.

[46] Maurice R. Davie, *World Immigration* . . . (New York, 1936), 69; for the development of German railways, cf. Clapham, *op. cit.,* 150 ff.

[47] Willcox, *op. cit.,* II, 333; E. Tonnelat, *L'Expansion allemande hors d'Europe* . . . (Paris, 1908), 88.

[48] René Gonnard, *L'Emigration européène au XIXe siècle* . . . (Paris, 1906), 99; Hansen, *loc. cit.,* 632.

[49] D. F. Donnant, *Statistical Account of the United States of America* (transl. . . . by William Playfair . . . , London, 1805), 21; O'Brien, *Union to the Famine,* 213; Guillet, *op. cit.,* 43 ff.; Hansen, *Atlantic Migration,* 83, 89.

[50] W. Faux, *Memorable Days in America . . . a Journal of a Tour to the United States . . .* (London, 1823), 29.

[51] Blegen, *op. cit.,* 97, 147, 344; cf. also Whitely Stokes, *Projects for Reestablishing the Internal Peace . . . of Ireland . . .* (Dublin, 1799), 12; Charles Norton, *Der treue Führer des Auswanderers nach den Vereinigten Staaten von Nord-Amerika . . .* (Regensburg, 1848), 4, 5; Walter Cox, *Advice to Emigrants or Observations . . . of the American Union* (Dublin, 1802), 6; *Boston Pilot,* October 23, 1841, September 8, 1848; [Johan Ulrich Buechler], *Land und Seereisen eines St. Gallischen Kantonburgers nach Nordamerika . . . 1816, 1817 und 1818 . . .* (St. Gallen, 1820), 212 ff.; Ole Rynning, *True Account of America* (translated by T. C. Blegen, Minneapolis, 1926), 79 ff.

[52] Thus, emigrants from Bavaria, who numbered 256,336 between 1835 and 1865, took out with them 70,450,198 fl. or an average of 275 fl. per individual (computed from tables in Philippovich, *op. cit.,* 76, 90, 91). Emigrants from Germany as a whole took an average of £29-10-0 with them in 1848-52 and £35-0-0 in 1853-54 (Michael G. Mulhall, *Dictionary of Statistics* [London, 1892], 246).

[53] J. L. and Barbara Hammond, *Skilled Labourer, 1760-1832* (London, 1919), 3.

[54] Young immigrants, among them Joseph Pulitzer, imported on contract to be enlisted for the sake of bounty money, formed an exception during the Civil War. Cf. *Boston Pilot,* March 19, 1864; *Cork Examiner,* April 16, 1864; Don C. Seitz, *Joseph Pulitzer . . .* (New York, 1924), 42; *Bostoner Zeitung,* December 23, 1865. The only earlier exceptions were the *catenoni,* Sardinians imported by Italians in America to act as professional beggars. Surprisingly large numbers of them were brought over and exploited for several years before being freed (cf. account in *L'Eco d'Italia* [New York], May 10, 17, 1851).

[55] Philippovich, *op. cit.,* 112; Marcus L. Hansen, "German Schemes of Colonization . . . ," *Smith College Studies in History,* October, 1923, IX, 9, 11 ff., 17, 33, 37 ff.; Hansen, *Atlantic Migration,* 108 ff., 228 ff.

[56] Hansen, *Atlantic Migration,* 123 ff., 166 ff., 188 ff., 238 ff. For the desire to perpetuate Germanism, cf. Tonnelat, *L'Expansion allemande hors d'Europe,* 31.

[57] Cf. *Daily Evening Transcript,* May 4, 1832; Johnson, *op. cit.,* 16, 344; W. A. Carrothers, *Emigration from the British Isles . . .* (London, 1929), 305; Willcox, *op. cit.,* II, 244 ff.; Guillet, *op. cit.,* 20 ff.; Hansen, *Atlantic Migration,* 115 ff., 227. The English consuls in New York and Boston actually had a fund to assist British subjects in Boston to go to Canada (Buchanan, "Report," October 2, 1816, British Consular Correspondence, F.O. 5/119; Manners to Bidwell, January 2, 1834, British Consular Cor-

respondence, F.O. 5/295, no. 1; Hansen, *Mingling of the Canadian and American Peoples,* 100).

[58] Cf. Helen Landreth, *Dear Dark Head, an Intimate Story of Ireland* (New York, 1936), 142 ff.

[59] Cf. O'Brien, *Seventeenth Century,* 2 ff., 15 ff., 101 ff.

[60] *Ibid.,* 12, 122, 123, 135, 215 ff.; John O'Donovan, *Economic History of Livestock in Ireland* (Dublin, 1940), 73 ff.; O'Brien, *Eighteenth Century,* 52 ff.

[61] Cf. *Lachrymae Hibernicae; or the Grievances of the Peasantry of Ireland . . . by a Resident Native . . .* (Dublin, 1822), 8, 10 ff.; John Revans, *Evils, of the State of Ireland . . .* (London, 1837), 10 ff., 23; O'Brien, *Eighteenth Century,* 66 ff.; O'Brien, *Union to the Famine,* 91.

[62] Robert Bell, LL.B., *Description of the Conditions . . . of the Peasantry of Ireland . . . between the Years 1780 & 1790 . . .* (London, 1804), 4; O'Brien, *Eighteenth Century,* 78 ff., 112, 122 ff.; O'Brien, *Union to the Famine,* 25 ff.; *Statement of the Proceedings of the Western Committee . . .* (London, 1831), 3; Frederick Merk, "The British Corn Crisis of 1845–46 . . . ," *Agricultural History,* VIII (1934), 97.

[63] O'Brien, *Seventeenth Century,* 117, 136 ff.; O'Brien, *Eighteenth Century,* 86 ff.; O'Brien, *Union to the Famine,* 10 ff.; Halévy, *op. cit.,* I, Bk. 2, 25 ff.

[64] O'Brien, *Seventeenth Century,* 140; O'Brien, *Union to the Famine,* 21.

[65] Sir William Petty, *Tracts Chiefly Relating to Ireland Containing . . . the Political Anatomy of Ireland* (Dublin, 1799), 351, 352; O'Brien, *Seventeenth Century,* 138; also *Thoughts on the Present State of the Cottiers . . .* (Dublin, 1796), 6; *Right Honorable Henry Grattan's Answer to the Rev. Michael Sandys* (Dublin, 1796), 8–21.

[66] W. Parker, Esq., *A Plea for the Poor and Industrious, Part the First . . .* (Cork, 1819), 54. Robert Bellew, *Thoughts and Suggestions on . . . the Condition of the Irish Peasantry . . . Second Edition* (London, 1808), 8.

[67] Cf. O'Brien, *Eighteenth Century,* 10–12; O'Brien, *Union to the Famine,* 43.

[68] Cf. Petty, *op. cit.,* 305; O'Brien, *Seventeenth Century,* 175; *Irish National Almanack for 1852 . . .* (Dublin, 1851), 31.

[69] For the effect of these factors on agricultural improvements cf. O'Brien, *Eighteenth Century,* 58, 69, 125; Parker, *op. cit.,* 57, 58; O'Brien, *Union to the Famine,* 27 ff., 99 ff.; Revans, *op. cit.,* 73, 75; and in general, R. Dudley Edwards and T. Desmond Williams, *The Great Famine* (Dublin, 1956), 3 ff.

[70] Petty, *op. cit.,* 366, 367; O'Brien, *Seventeenth Century,* 125; Edward

MacLysaght, *Irish Life in the Seventeenth Century* . . . (London, 1939), 38; O'Brien, *Eighteenth Century*, 31 ff.

71 Cf. O'Brien, *Eighteenth Century*, 39 ff.; MacLysaght, *op. cit.*, 72; *Address to the Public on Behalf of the Poor* . . . (Dublin, 1815), 48; *Annual Report of the Managing Committee of the House of Recovery . . . in Cork Street, Dublin . . . 1813* (Dublin, 1813), 5.

72 O'Brien, *Eighteenth Century*, 81 ff.

73 Cf. *Lachrymae Hibernicae* . . . , 4 ff.; O'Brien, *Union to the Famine*, 45; Adams, *op. cit.*, 13.

74 Cf., e.g., Parker, *op. cit.*, 59; Rev. William Hickey, *State of the Poor of Ireland Briefly Considered* . . . (Carlow, 1820), 23. For Irish publications on agricultural improvements, cf. Dissertation Copy, 86, 87; J. T. Gilbert, Catalogue of Haliday 8vo Pamphlets, 1750–1848 (MS., R. I. A.), I, 378, 409, 436, 460, 498, II, 536, 553, 560, 561, 575, 589, 602, 612, 632, 653; also O'Brien, *Union to the Famine*, 129 ff.

75 For contemporary opinion opposed to emigration, cf. Dissertation Copy, 87–89.

76 G. C. Duggan, *Stage Irishman* . . . (London, 1937), 156. The only systematic account of this movement is a short article by J. H. Clapham, "Irish Immigration into Great Britain in the Nineteenth Century," *Bulletin of the International Committee of Historical Sciences*, July, 1933, V, 596 ff.

77 *Report of the Committee for the Relief of the Distressed Districts in Ireland* . . . (London, 1823), 41; O'Brien, *Eighteenth Century*, 98 ff.; Revans, *op. cit.*, 7, 8.

78 *A Letter to a British Member of Parliament on the State of Ireland in . . . 1825* . . . (Dublin, 1825), 35; *Poor Rates the Panacea for Ireland* (London, 1831), 9; O'Brien, *Union to the Famine*, 15; Sidney and Beatrice Webb, *English Local Government: English Poor Law History: Part I. The Old Poor Law* (London, 1927), 393.

79 Cf. J. L. and Barbara Hammond, *Town Labourer, 1760–1832* (London, 1920), 13; George Strickland, *Discourse on the Poor Laws of England. . . . Second Edition* . . . (London, 1830), 68, 22; George A. Grierson, *Circumstance of Ireland Considered* . . . (London, 1830), 59; Ralph Waldo Emerson, "English Traits," *Collected Works* (Boston, 1903), V, 17.

80 Cf. *An Account of the Calmel Building Charity . . . the Institution for Ameliorating the Situation of the Irish Poor in the Metropolis . . .* (London, 1814), 5; O'Brien, *Union to the Famine*, 209; Clapham, *loc. cit.*, 598; *Cork Examiner*, September 16, 1844; Frederick Engels, *Condition of the Working Class in England in 1844* . . . (Transl. by F. K. Wischnewetzky) (London, [1926]), 90 ff.

81 Sir John Walsh, *Poor Laws in Ireland* . . . (London, 1830), 99; *Thoughts on the Poor of Ireland and Means of their Amelioration By a*

Barrister . . . (Dublin, 1831), 23; W. Neilson Hancock, *On the Condition of the Irish Labourer . . . a Paper Read Before the Dublin Statistical Society* . . . (Dublin, 1848), 7.

[82] *The Causes of Discontents in Ireland, and Remedies Proposed* (s.l., n.d. [Dublin, 1823]?), 45, 46.

[83] O'Brien, *Eighteenth Century*, 102.

[84] Cf. *Report of the Committee for the Relief of the Distressed Districts in Ireland* . . . (London, 1823), 47, 70; O'Brien, *Union to the Famine*, 224 ff.; *Statement of the Proceedings of the Western Committee for the Relief of the Irish Poor* . . . (London, 1831), 4, 7; *Daily Evening Transcript*, September 3, 1830, June 15, 1831; *Boston Pilot*, July 9, 1842.

[85] Cf. O'Brien, *Eighteenth Century*, 121; O'Brien, *Union to the Famine*, 52; Adams, *op. cit.*, 10.

[86] Cf. Sidney and Beatrice Webb, *English Poor Law History: Part II: The Last Hundred Years* (London, 1929), I, 1, 2.

[87] George A. Grierson, *The Circumstance of Ireland Considered with Reference to the Question of Poor Laws* (London, 1830), 1; cf. also the works cited in Dissertation Copy, 92.

[88] Cf. Sidney and Beatrice Webb, *English Poor Law Policy* (London, 1910), 53; *Cork Examiner*, March 27, 1844.

[89] O'Brien, *Union to the Famine*, 186; S. and B. Webb, *English Poor Law History:* Part II, II, 1025–1030.

[90] O'Brien, *Union to the Famine*, 55, 161 ff.; Hansen, *Atlantic Migration*, 132 ff.

[91] R. Torrens, *Letter to the Right Honorable Lord John Russell on the Ministerial Measure for Establishing Poor Laws in Ireland* . . . (London, 1838).

[92] Cf. O'Brien, *Union to the Famine*, 53, 190 ff., 216; William Stewart, *Comments on the Civil Bill Ejectments Act* . . . (Dublin, 1825), 1, 71; William Stewart, *Comments on the Act 1, George IV, cap. 67* . . . (London, 1826).

[93] O'Brien, *Union to the Famine*, 59, 201 ff.

[94] *Ibid.*, 237 ff.; Hansen, *Atlantic Migration*, 242 ff.; Edwards and Williams, *Great Famine*, 263 ff.; *Courrier des États-Unis*, February 23, 1847.

[95] To W. S. O'Brien, April 24, 1847, William Smith O'Brien Papers and Letters (MSS., N. L. I.), XIV, no. 1882. Cf. also G. H. Kerin to W. S. O'Brien, February 6, 1846, *ibid.*, XI, no. 1501.

[96] *Irish National Almanack for 1852*, 26; Gonnard, *op. cit.*, 23; Michael G. Mulhall, *Fifty Years of National Progress, 1837–1887* (London, 1887), 115; Mulhall, *Dictionary of Statistics*, 190. The change in the number of holdings of various sizes shows the extent of consolidation:

Number	1841	1849
Less than 1 acre	134,314	31,989
1–5 acres	310,436	98,179
5–15 acres	252,799	213,897
15–30 acres	79,342	150,120
Over 30 acres	48,625	156,960

(*Irish National Almanack for 1852,* 31, 33; O'Brien, *Union to the Famine,* 59).

[97] O'Donovan to Daniel McCarthy, February 6, 1848, February 14, 1848, and April 1, 1848 (John O'Donovan, Correspondence, 1845–1861 [MSS., N. L. I.], no. 17, p. 4; no. 18, p. 3; no. 19, p. 3).

[98] Robert Bennet Forbes, *Voyage of the Jamestown . . .* (Boston, 1847), 22; Edwards and Williams, *Great Famine,* 391 ff.

[99] Cf. references to *Cork Examiner* and *Boston Pilot,* cited Dissertation Copy, 96, 97, ns. 212–214.

[100] Cf. *Massachusetts House Documents, 1859,* no. 243, p. 6; Edward E. Hale, *Letters on Irish Emigration . . .* (Boston, 1852), 6; *Cork Examiner,* April 2, 1847. For approximate figures, cf. Johnson, *op. cit.,* 352; Willcox, *op. cit.,* II, 250. For an estimate of the total ($78,000,000), cf. *Boston Pilot,* September 22, 1855.

[101] Cf. references to *Boston Pilot,* cited Dissertation Copy, 97.

[102] Cf. references to *Boston Pilot,* cited in Dissertation Copy, 98.

[103] *Cork Examiner,* June 13, 17, 1864; Mulhall, *Fifty Years,* 115.

[104] Cf. *Cork Examiner,* May 21, 1863.

[105] Cf. e.g., *Boston Pilot,* January 12, 1856, December 4, 1858; Hale, *op. cit.,* 7. At the same time passage from the continent in the Nordeutschen Lloyd or the Vanderbilt Line still cost $35–$40 (cf. e.g., *Der Pionier,* September 26, 1861; *Der Neu England Demokrat,* December 23, 1857).

[106] Cf. *supra,* 7, 8; Frank C. Bowen, *Century of Atlantic Travel, 1830-1930* (Boston, 1930), 7 ff.; Dissertation Copy, 100.

[107] Cf. British Consular Correspondence, America I Series, F.O. 4/14, fol. 421; Bidwell to Manners, September 27, 1827, British Consular Correspondence, F.O. 5/229.

[108] British Consular Correspondence, F.O. 5/350; F. Lawrence Babcock, *Spanning the Atlantic* (New York, 1931), 79 ff. For Boston's proximity to Canada, cf. "Extract from the Report of the Post Office Commission of Inquiry . . ." (British Embassy Archives, F.O. 115/78, fol. 18).

[109] Hansen, *Atlantic Migration,* 183 ff. For unsuccessful attempts to establish regular direct communications with Ireland, cf. *Boston Pilot,* September 18, 1858; *Cork Examiner,* February 23, 1842; *Cork Constitution,* May 23, 1835.

[110] Cf. Buchanan to Palmerston, January 9, 1837, British Consular Correspondence, F.O. 5/315; Adams, *op. cit.,* 83; John R. Commons, et al., eds., *Documentary History of American Industrial Society* (Cleveland, 1910), VII, 81 ff.; Guillet, *op. cit.,* 66 ff.; "First Report of the Commissioner of Immigration . . . 1866," Thirty-Ninth Congress, First Session, *House Executive Documents,* VIII, no. 65, pp. 3 ff.; Patten, *op. cit.,* 17 ff.; Hale, *op. cit.,* 11 ff.; *Cork Examiner,* April 5, 1847, October 30, 1848; *Courrier des États-Unis* (New York), March 28, April 13, 1848.

[111] *Massachusetts Senate Documents, 1848,* no. 46, p. 5; *ibid., 1847,* no. 109, p. 5.

[112] Cf. "Report and Tabular Statement of the Censors . . . ," *loc. cit.,* 44; *Massachusetts Senate Documents, 1848,* no. 89, p. 2. This movement has been treated only in brief discussions by Marcus L. Hansen in "Second Colonization of New England," *New England Quarterly,* October, 1929, II, 539 ff., and *Atlantic Migration,* 180 ff. There is a contemporary description in the *Irish-American* (New York), January 20, 1850. For individual cases of such migrations, cf. references to *Jesuit or Catholic Sentinel* (Boston), *United States Catholic Intelligencer* (Boston), and *Boston Pilot,* cited Dissertation Copy, 103, n. 234.

[113] Cf., e.g., Hansen, *Atlantic Migration,* 249.

[114] *Cork Examiner,* March 10, 1847.

[115] Cf. Benevolent Fraternity of Churches, *Fourteenth Annual Report of the Executive Committee . . .* (Boston, 1848), 23, 24; Dissertation Copy, 103, 104.

[116] Marcus Lee Hansen, "Revolutions of 1848," *loc. cit.,* 649.

[117] Cf. A. C. Buchanan, Esq., *Emigration Practically Considered: with Detailed Directions to Emigrants . . .* (London, 1828), 36; O'Brien, *Union to the Famine,* 208, 218; Elizabeth Fry and J. J. Gurney, *Report . . . to the Marquess Wellesley . . .* (Dublin, 1827), 74; Hansen, *Atlantic Migration,* 97, 121; Adams, *op. cit.,* I, 158; *supra,* 31.

[118] The statistics of immigration into Boston are given *infra,* Table V and are discussed in the note thereto. These include temporary visitors and passengers in transit, and are therefore not altogether satisfactory as a measure of the growth of Boston's immigrant population. More reliable in this respect are the census figures (cf. *infra,* Tables VI–IX).

[119] Cf. the nativity of the members of the Boston Repeal Association, the most representative group of Boston Irishmen in 1840 (*infra,* Table X), and the requests for information in the *Literary and Catholic Sentinel* (Boston), 1835–1836, I, II (cf. note to Table XI, *infra*).

[120] Cf. Jesse Chickering, *Report of the Committee . . . Population of Boston in 1850 . . .* (Boston, 1851), 9; *infra,* Table XI. Figures for arrivals should be raised from 30 per cent to 50 per cent to account for immigra-

tion by land. For the available statistics of this type of immigration cf. *Dissertation Copy*, 428, 429; "Report and Tabular Statement of the Censors . . . ," *loc. cit.*, 47; Josiah Curtis, *Report of the Joint Special Committee . . . 1855 . . .* (Boston, 1856), 19.

[121] Thus they were supposed to number 10,000 in 1849 (*Boston Pilot*, January 13, 1849) although the census of 1850 found only 4,400 in the entire state ("Annual Registration Report, 1852," *Massachusetts Public Documents, 1854*, 95).

[122] Chickering, *op. cit.*, 9; Edward Dicey, *Six Months in the Federal States* (London, 1863), II, 179.

[123] Cf. *infra*, Tables VI–IX; *Dissertation Copy*, 51–53.

[124] Cf. Lee M. Friedman, *Early American Jews* (Cambridge, 1934), 18 ff.

[125] Cf. *Boston Pilot*, September 22, 1849, October 18, 1851.

[126] Cf. *Boston Pilot*, February 9, 1861; *infra*, Table XII; Chickering, "Report," *loc. cit.*, 15; La Rochefoucauld-Liancourt, *op. cit.*, V, 178.

[127] Only one route, and that by sea, passed through the city (Wilbur H. Siebert, "Underground Railroad," *New England Magazine*, XXVII [1903], 566; Wilbur H. Siebert, *Underground Railroad from Slavery to Freedom* [New York, 1898], map opposite 113; Wilbur H. Siebert, "Underground Railroad in Massachusetts," *New England Quarterly*, IX [1936], 447 ff.). Cf. also *Daily Evening Transcript*, September 28, 1830.

Chapter III. The Economic Adjustment

[1] Henry David Thoreau, *Walden or, Life in the Woods* (*Writings of Henry David Thoreau*, II, Boston, 1894), 322.

[2] Cf., e.g., *Hunt's Merchants' Magazine and Commercial Review* (New York) and *Niles' Weekly Register* (Baltimore, New York and Philadelphia), and travelers' accounts listed in *Dissertation Copy*, 500 ff.

[3] Cf. *infra*, Table XIII; Francis A. Walker, *The Statistics of the Population of the United States . . . Compiled from the Original Returns of the Ninth Census . . . 1870 . . .* (Washington, 1872), I, 167. A municipal tabulation at another date found a total of 138,788 ("Report and Tabular Statement of the Censors . . . ," *Boston City Documents, 1850*, no. 42, p. 30).

[4] Cf. *infra*, Tables XIII, XIV.

[5] Cf. *infra*, Table XIV.

[6] Cf. *supra*, 10 ff.

[7] Cf. *infra*, Table XIV.

[8] *Idem*.

[9] Cf. *infra*, Chart B.

[10] Cf. *infra*, Charts A and B. The comparison would be even more striking if the Negroes were excluded. The maximum for the three leading occupations in any other group was 30 per cent. The reasons why the Negroes come near the Irish in this respect are discussed *supra*, 69, 70.

[11] Benevolent Fraternity of Churches, *Fourteenth Annual Report . . .* (Boston, 1848), 23, 24.

[12] Cf. e.g., *Irish American*, October 21, 1849; *Cork Examiner*, July 11, 1861.

[13] Cf. Edward E[verett] Hale, *Letters on Irish Emigration . . .* (Boston, 1852), 33.

[14] Cf. *Boston Merkur*, June 5, 1847; *Boston Pilot*, September 25, 1841, February 7, 1857.

[15] There is no way of estimating the actual number of dock laborers in the city. The term "stevedore" generally applied to the contractor who hired the labor in behalf of the merchant. Most laborers were recruited as they were needed. They were predominantly foreign by nativity, and their numbers were quite large (cf. Boston Board of Trade, *Third Annual Report of the Government . . . January, 1857 . . .* [Boston, 1857], 7; *Third Annual Report of the Bureau of Statistics of Labor, Massachusetts . . . 1872, Massachusetts Senate Documents, 1872*, no. 180, p. 56).

[16] The total number of laborers in the city in 1850 was 8,552, which represented a significant increase over the 3,240 of 1845. The number continued to rise until 1855 when it equaled 10,402, and thereafter it declined to 9,745 in 1860 and to 9,103 in 1865. Since almost all these laborers were Irish, it is apparent that the number increased steadily with the growth of Irish immigration from 1845 to the early fifties and declined thereafter as the laborers were absorbed in industry (cf. *infra*, Tables XIII, XV; Lemuel Shattuck, *Report to the Committee of the City Council . . . Census of Boston . . . 1845 . . .* [Boston, 1846], Appendix Y, 43; Oliver Warner, *Abstract of the Census of Massachusetts, 1860* [Boston, 1863], 183, 283; Oliver Warner, *Abstract of the Census of Massachusetts, 1865 . . .* [Boston, 1867], 133).

[17] Dr. Cahill, "Seventh Letter from America . . ." (*Boston Pilot*, March 3, 1860).

[18] Cf. *infra*, Table XV.

[19] *Third Annual Report of the Bureau of Statistics of Labor . . . 1872, Massachusetts Senate Documents, 1872*, no. 180, pp. 516 ff.; Chart C.

[20] Alfred Bunn, *Old England and New England in a Series of Views . . .* (London, 1853), I, 61.

[21] Cf. *Boston Pilot*, August 19, 1854.

[22] Cf. *infra*, Tables XIII, XVI. It was impossible to enumerate accurately

the number of domestics employed in Boston because of deficiencies in the census (cf. *infra*, note to Table XVI). The figures given above and in Tables XIII and XVI are approximate and minimal, intended merely to show the relative proportion in each nativity group. An accurate count of domestics in this period appears to have been made only in the state censuses of 1845 and 1865. The former found 5,706 (Shattuck, *op. cit.*, 84); the latter, 11,204 (Warner, *Abstract of the Census of Massachusetts, 1865*, 142). The figure for 1850 is probably closer to that of 1865 than to that of 1845, so that Table XVI should be scaled radically upward.

23 Cf. *infra*, Table XVI.

24 Cf. references to *Courrier des États-Unis* (New York), cited Dissertation Copy, 123.

25 Cf., e.g., *Minutes of the Selectmen's Meetings 1799 to . . . 1810 (Volume of Records Relating to the Early History of Boston, XXXIII), Boston City Documents, 1904*, no. 93, p. 122.

26 Cf. *Boston Pilot*, June 16, 1838, June 8, 1839, February 17, 1855, September 30, 1854.

27 Cf. *infra*, Table XIII.

28 *Idem;* Bunn, *op. cit.*, I, 61, 62; Alexander Marjoribanks, *Travels in South and North America* (London, 1853), 177.

29 Cf. *infra*, Table XIII; Dissertation Copy, 126.

30 Cf. "Report and Tabular Statement of the Censors . . . 1850," *Boston City Documents, 1850*, no. 42, p. 49; James H. Lanman, "Commerce of Boston," *Hunt's Merchants' Magazine and Commercial Review*, May, 1844, X, 431, 432.

31 Dissertation Copy, 445. The 4,190 persons employed in these occupations were fairly equally distributed among the various nativity groups, with the exception of the British North Americans who were abnormally concentrated in carpentry. The explanation for their unusually high percentage may be that the emigrants from Canada and New Brunswick, coming as a result of the decline of the lumber industry there, were accustomed to working with wood and therefore made better carpenters (cf. *Report of the Select Committee of the Legislative Assembly Appointed to Inquire into the Causes . . . of the Emigration . . . from Lower Canada to the United States . . .* [Montreal, 1849], 6, 11; Marcus Lee Hansen, *Mingling of the Canadian and American Peoples . . .* [New Haven, 1940], 121).

32 Cf., e.g., Patrick Gargan (Conrad Reno, *Memoirs of the Judiciary and the Bar of New England . . .* [Boston, 1900], I, 66); also *infra*, Table XIII.

33 For all these, cf. *infra*, Table XIII. There were a few exceptions, for which cf. *Boston Pilot*, June 19, 1858.

[34] For coachmen, cf. *infra,* Table XIII. The seafaring community, though vital to Boston's prosperity, has not been more fully discussed because it was not an integral part of the city's population. Sailors on the Boston ships after the forties were no longer the New England boys who had formerly come down to wrest a career from the sea. Instead, Boston's merchant marine was manned by "an international proletariat of the sea." Transient foreigners of many races made up the crews of most ships that sailed out of Boston in these years, with only a slight addition of natives (Samuel Eliot Morison, *Maritime History of Massachusetts . . .* [Boston, 1921], 353, 354; Boston Board of Trade, *Report . . . and a Memorial to Congress on the Subject of Seamen and Marine Disasters* [Boston, 1855], 5; *infra,* Table XIII). The only group permanently domiciled in the city that went to sea were the Negroes (cf. *supra,* 69 ff.).

[35] Cf. the "dry goods dealers" and "other retailers," *infra,* Table XIII. The Irish dry goods and clothing stores catered chiefly to their own group (for immigrant stores cf. references to *Jesuit or Catholic Sentinel* [Boston], *Boston Pilot,* and *Gazette Française* in Dissertation Copy, 129).

[36] In all, food dealers came to between 3 and 4 per cent of the total working population, cf. *infra,* Table XIII.

[37] The Irish had only about 1 per cent (*idem*) though there were some prominent grocers among them (cf. references to the *Boston Pilot* cited in Dissertation Copy, 130, n. 53).

[38] Cf. *infra,* Table XIII.

[39] Anna H. Dorsey, "Nora Brady's Vow," *Boston Pilot,* February 21, 1857.

[40] For Irish boarding houses, cf. references to *United States Catholic Intelligencer, Jesuit or Catholic Sentinel,* and *Boston Pilot* cited Dissertation Copy, 131; for German boarding houses, cf., references to *Der Pionier, Boston Merkur, Bostoner Zeitung,* and *Neu England Demokrat* cited Dissertation Copy, 132.

[41] Cf. *infra,* Table XIII; also references to *Der Pionier, Bostoner Zeitung, Neu England Demokrat, Boston Pilot,* and *Old Countryman . . .* (Boston), cited Dissertation Copy, 132.

[42] Cf., e.g., *Gazette Française,* April 15, 1851.

[43] *Courrier des États-Unis,* April 9, 1846, March 3, 1844, October 31, 1843.

[44] Cf. *Courrier des États-Unis,* March 3, 1846, October 30, November 6, 1847.

[45] For a list of hotels and boarding houses, cf. *Chase's Pocket Almanac . . . 1850* (Boston, n.d. [1850]), 15, 17.

[46] For Degrand, cf. *Boston Pilot,* January 5, 1856; Justin Winsor, *Memorial History of Boston . . .* (Boston, 1880), IV, 135–137. For Touro,

cf. Christopher Roberts, *Middlesex Canal, 1793–1860* (Cambridge, 1938), 131, 200, 227; Lee M. Friedman, *Early American Jews* (Cambridge, 1934), 21. For a few other exceptional cases, cf. Dissertation Copy, 54.

[47] For these companies cf. *Boston Pilot*, October 5, 19, 1861, March 3, 1860; *Der Pionier*, October 26, 1864.

[48] For the New England Company, cf. *Massachusetts Senate Documents, 1852*, no. 112, p. 2; *supra*, 159. For others, cf. *Boston Pilot*, March 24, 1860.

[49] For these occupations, cf. Dissertation Copy, 446.

[50] Roberts, *op. cit.*, 48.

[51] Cf. *infra*, Table XIII. These figures are for clergymen, teachers, physicians, actors, musicians, and "other professions."

[52] Charles F. Read, "Lorenzo Papanti . . . ," *Proceedings of the Bostonian Society* (Boston, 1928), 41 ff.

[53] *Independent Chronicle* (Boston), January 3, 1811.

[54] For totals cf. *infra*, Table XIII. For other prominent foreigners, cf. Dissertation Copy, 137, 138.

[55] Cf. references to *Boston Pilot* cited in Dissertation Copy, 139.

[56] For Irish lawyers cf. references to *Boston Pilot* and *Irish American* (New York), cited in Dissertation Copy, 139, n. 94.

[57] *Boston Pilot*, September 4, 1852. For similar references to *Boston Pilot, United States Catholic Intelligencer, Jesuit or Catholic Sentinel* (Boston), and *Irish American*, cf. Dissertation Copy, 140, n. 96. For French doctors, cf. *Gazette Française*, April 12, 19, 1851.

[58] Cf., e.g., the *Boston Pilot*, April 18, 1863; also John M. Duncan, *Travels through . . . the United States . . . in 1818 . . .* (Glasgow, 1823), I, 67.

[59] Cf. *infra*, Tables XIII, XV; also La Rochefoucauld-Liancourt, *Voyage dans les États-Unis . . .* (Paris, An VII [1799]), V, 178; E. S. Abdy, *Journal of a Residence . . . in the United States . . .* (London, 1835), I, 121; *Minutes of the Selectmen's Meetings . . . 1818 to . . . 1822 (Volume of Records . . . Early History of Boston, XXXIX), Boston City Documents*, 1909, no. 61, p. 12.

[60] Cf. Archibald H. Grimké, *Life of Charles Sumner . . .* (New York, 1892), 220; also *Columbian Centinel* (Boston), June 18, 1791; *Boston Pilot*, September 25, 1858; *Der Pionier* (Boston), July 2, 1862; C. J. Furness, "Walt Whitman Looks at Boston," *New England Quarterly*, July, 1928, I, 356.

[61] Cf. also Charles H. Wesley, *Negro Labor in the United States . . .* (New York, 1927), 43 ff.

[62] Cf., e.g., *Boston Pilot*, April 22, 1854. For other advertisements, cf. the citations in Dissertation Copy, 143, n. 110.

[63] Cf., e.g., Benevolent Fraternity of Churches, *Twenty-First Annual Report of the Executive Committee* . . . (Boston, 1855), 12; Consul Grattan to Lord Aberdeen, January 28, 1843, British Consular Correspondence, F.O. 5/394.

[64] Cf. the advertisements in the *Boston Pilot*, cited Dissertation Copy, 144.

[65] Cf., e.g., *Boston Pilot*, November 6, 1852, February 19, 1853.

[66] For these evils cf. *Irish American*, November 1, 1851; for the truck system cf. John R. Commons, et al., eds., *Documentary History of American Industrial Society* (Cleveland, 1910), VII, 50, 51.

[67] Cf. *Boston Pilot*, July 31, September 11, 1852.

[68] Emerson, quoted in *Boston Pilot*, March 2, 1861; Hale, *op. cit.*, 53. Cf. also Thoreau, *Walden*, 146.

[69] Cf. John R. Commons, *History of Labour in the United States* (New York, 1926), I, 539; B. M. Stearns, "Early Factory Magazines in New England," *Journal of Economic and Business History*, II (1930), 693 ff.; Norman Ware, *Industrial Worker, 1840–1860* . . . (Boston, 1924), 149; Allan Macdonald, "Lowell: a Commercial Utopia," *New England Quarterly*, X (1937), 57; Caroline F. Ware, *Early New England Cotton Manufacture* . . . (Boston, 1931), 12, 64 ff., 198 ff.

[70] Arthur Harrison Cole, *American Wool Manufacture* (Cambridge, 1926), I, 274, 369 ff.; United States Census Office, *Eighth Census, 1860, Manufactures* (Washington, n.d. [1864]), xxxv; M. T. Copeland, *Cotton Manufacturing Industry of the United States* (Cambridge, 1917), 13 ff.; Edith Abbott, *Women in Industry* . . . (New York, 1910), 102, 103.

[71] Cf. Emerson David Fite, *Social and Industrial Conditions in the North during the Civil War* (New York, 1910), 187, n. 1; Susan M. Kingsbury, ed., *Labor Laws and Their Enforcement* . . . (New York, 1911), 56 ff.; C. F. Ware, *Early New England Cotton Manufacture*, 228 ff.

[72] Cf. *supra*, 10; Albert Aftalion, *Le Développement de la fabrique* . . . *dans les industries de l'habillement* (Paris, 1906), 21 ff.; Blanche E. Hazard, *Organization of the Boot and Shoe Industry in Massachusetts before 1875* (Cambridge, 1921), 24 ff., 93, 94.

[73] Cf. Fite, *op. cit.*, 90, 91; George C. Houghton, "Boots and Shoes" (United States Census Bureau, *Twelfth Census, 1900, Manufactures*, IX, 755; Aftalion, *op. cit.*, 61 ff.; *Eighty Years Progress of the United States: a Family Record of American Industry* . . . (Hartford, 1869), 324; Commons, *History of Labour*, II, 76–78; Ware, *Industrial Worker*, 38 ff.; John R. Commons, "American Shoemakers," *Quarterly Journal of Economics*, XXIV (1909), 73 ff.

[74] The actual number cited *infra* in Table XVII fell from 9,930 to

6,010, but this excludes approximately 2,900 in the building and clothing trades not listed in 1845. If these were added the figures for both years become roughly equal.

75 Cf. Lousada to Russell, February 29, 1864, British Consular Correspondence, F.O. 5/973; *Third Annual Report of the Bureau of Statistics of Labor*, 535.

76 Cf. *infra*, Table XVII.

77 Cf. Winsor, *op. cit.*, IV, 98; Jesse Eliphalet Pope, *Clothing Industry in New York* (Columbia, Missouri, 1905), 7; Horace Greeley, et al., *Great Industries of the United States* . . . (Hartford, 1872), 588, 589; *Eighth Census, 1860, Manufactures*, lxiii; Edwin T. Freedley, *United States Mercantile Guide* . . . (Philadelphia, 1856), 125; Cole, *op. cit.*, I, 293.

78 Cf. *Documents Relative to the Manufactures in the United States* . . . , United States Congress, 22 Congress, 1 Session, *House Executive Documents*, no. 308, I, 465; Victor S. Clark, *History of Manufactures* . . . (Washington, 1928), II, 447; Martin E. Popkin, *Organization, Management, and Technology in the Manufacture of Men's Clothing* (New York, n.d. [1929]), 36.

79 Cf. Pope, *op. cit.*, 11; J. M. Budish and George Soule, *New Unionism in the Clothing Industry* (New York, 1920), 17; Axel Josephsson, "Clothing," United States Census Bureau, *Twelfth Census, 1900, Report, Manufactures*, IX, 296 ff.; for the number of tailors, cf. Shattuck, *op. cit.*, Appendix Y, 40.

80 Cf. the MS. letter of thirteen master tailors to Mayor Bigelow, August 13, 1849 (John Prescott Bigelow Papers, Box VI [MSS., H. C. L.]).

81 Cf. J. Leander Bishop, *History of American Manufactures from 1608 to 1860* . . . (Philadelphia, 1864), II, 474, 475.

82 Cf. *infra*, Table XIII.

83 Cf. Pope, *op. cit.*, 9; Fite, *op. cit.*, 89; Clark, *op. cit.*, II, 32.

84 Cf. Josephsson, *loc. cit.*, 297; Pope, *op. cit.*, 69 ff. Pope's claim that the Boston System originated among English tailors settled in Boston is accepted by Clark (*op. cit.*, II, 448). The only ground for this hypothesis is the similarity of conditions in the English clothing industry, particularly in Leeds, to those in Boston. This similarity is, however, merely the result of the fact that the factory in England grew out of the same cause that produced it in Boston, a cheap labor surplus (cf. J. H. Clapham, *Economic History of Modern Britain* . . . [Cambridge, 1932], II, 92 ff.; Aftalion, *op. cit.*, 88 ff.; Karl Marx, *Capital, a Critique of Political Economy* . . . *Translated* . . . *by Samuel Moore and Edward Aveling* . . . [Chicago, 1909], I, 514 ff.).

85 Pope, *op. cit.*, 70, 15 ff., 23 ff.

[86] Men's Clothing Industry in New York and Boston:

		Value of Product	Number of Employees	Average value per Employee
1860	New York	$17,011,370	21,568	$ 788
	Boston	4,567,749	4,017	1,137
1870	New York	34,456,884	17,084	2,017
	Boston	17,578,057	7,033	2,322

(Derived from material in Pope, *op. cit.,* 303.)

[87] Cf. *ibid.,* 31, 32; *Hunt's Merchants' Magazine,* August, 1853, XXIX, 253; Paul T. Cherington, *Wool Industry* . . . (Chicago, n.d. [1916]), 194.

[88] Cf. Pope, *op. cit.,* 303; C. L. Fleischmann, *Erwerbszweige, Fabrikwesen und Handel der Vereinigten Staaten* . . . (*Stuttgart,* 1850), 333; Freedley, *op. cit.,* 135.

[89] Cf. Paul L. Vogt, *Sugar Refining Industry in the United States* (Philadelphia, 1908), 11, 14.

[90] Cf. Marshals' Schedules of the Seventh Census (MSS., B. C.); also *Boston Pilot,* May 17, 1845, January 29, 1853; Franz Löher, *Geschichte und Zustände der Deutschen in Amerika* (Cincinnati, 1847), 297.

[91] Vogt, *op. cit.,* 16; Victor S. Clark, *History of Manufactures in the United States* . . . (Washington, 1916), I, 491. For some of these inventions, cf. *Scientific American* (New York), October 18, 1851, VII, 36.

[92] Bishop, *op. cit.,* III, 303, 305; Dissertation Copy, 448.

[93] Bishop, *op. cit.,* III, 305.

[94] Cf. *Massachusetts House Documents, 1848,* no. 110; Bishop, *op. cit.,* III, 285, 287; Freeman Hunt, *Lives of American Merchants* (New York, 1856), I, 516; Greeley, *op. cit.,* 115; Dissertation Copy, 447.

[95] Cf. Dissertation Copy, 447.

[96] Cf. Dissertation Copy, 447, 470; *Eighty Years Progress,* 246; Freedley, *op. cit.,* 265, 292, 296, 305, 306; Bishop, *op. cit.,* III, 281, 282, 284 ff., 297 ff., 301, 302, 566; Clark, *op. cit.,* II, 93; Chauncey M. Depew, *One Hundred Years of American Commerce* . . . (New York, 1895), II, 339; Gillespie, *op. cit.,* 37, 45, 110–112, 168.

[97] Bishop, *op. cit.,* III, 295; A. B. Hart, *Commonwealth History of Massachusetts* . . . (New York, 1930), IV, 442 ff.

[98] Cf. Dissertation Copy, 470; Boston Board of Trade, *Third Annual Report* . . . *1857,* 84; Boston Board of Trade, *Seventh Annual Report* . . . *1861,* 175.

[99] For all these companies, cf. Gillespie, *op. cit.,* 44, 162, 173, 175 ff., 186; Bishop, *op. cit.,* III, 148, 288 ff., 307, 310 ff.; Depew, *op. cit.,* I, xxvi, II, 367, 541; Edwin M. Bacon, *Book of Boston* . . . (Boston, 1916), 383; *Third*

Annual Report of the Bureau of Statistics of Labor, 147; Alfred Pairpoint, *Uncle Sam and His Country* . . . (London, 1857), 154 ff., 156. For the number of employees, cf. Table XIII, *infra;* Dissertation Copy, 447.

[100] *Boston Pilot,* November 5, 1853; Fleischmann, *Erwerbszweige,* 336 ff.; Virginia Penny, *Employments of Women* . . . (Boston, 1863), 350, 351.

[101] *Hunt's Merchants' Magazine,* August, 1853, XXIX, 253; Isaac A. Hourwich, *Immigration and Labour, the Economic Aspects of European Immigration to the United States* (New York, 1912), 364.

[102] Cf. Ware, *Industrial Worker,* 48 ff.; Abbott, *op. cit.,* 237.

[103] *Boston Pilot,* August 30, 1856; Benevolent Fraternity of Churches, *Twenty-Second Annual Report . . . 1856,* 26.

[104] L. L. Lorwin, *Women's Garment Workers* . . . (New York, 1924), 5.

[105] *Ibid.,* 10; *Eighth Census, 1860, Manufactures* (Washington, 1861), lxxxiii ff.

[106] Warner, *Abstract of the Census of Massachusetts, 1865,* 164 ff.

[107] *Report of the Bureau of Statistics of Labor . . . , Massachusetts Senate Documents, 1870,* no. 120, p. 91.

[108] Sir Charles Lyell, *Second Visit to the United States* . . . (London, 1849), I, 187; Jesse Chickering, "Report of the Committee . . . Boston in 1850 . . . ," *Boston City Documents, 1851,* no. 60, p. 50.

[109] Cf. *infra,* Table XIII.

[110] *Our First Men* . . . (Boston, 1846), 14, 17, 31; Rev. G. C. Treacy, "Andrew Carney, Philanthropist," United States Catholic Historical Society, *Historical Records and Studies,* XIII, 101 ff.; *Irish American,* February 28, 1852; *Boston Pilot,* September 17, 1853; Dissertation Copy, 166; Reno, *op. cit.,* I, 100.

[111] Cf. advertisements in *Irish American,* October 15, 1859; *Boston Pilot,* August 30, 1862; Bishop, *op. cit.,* II, 318, 319; Freedley, *op. cit.,* 236, 395–398.

[112] Cf. Dissertation Copy, 22, 167–169.

[113] Cf. Lyell, *op. cit.,* I, 186; "Report and Tabular Statement," *loc. cit.,* 49.

[114] Cf. *supra,* 184 ff.

[115] Cf. Ware, *Industrial Worker,* xii, 6 ff., 26 ff., 110 ff.

[116] E. E. Hale, *Letters on Irish Emigration,* 54, 55; Isaac A. Hourwich, "Economic Aspects of Immigration," United States Congress, 62 Congress, 2 Session, *Senate Documents,* no. 696, pp. 10 ff.; Hourwich, *Immigration and Labour,* 367; Depew, *op. cit.,* I, 12, 13.

[117] Cf. *First Report of the General Board of Health in the City of Dublin* . . . (Dublin, 1822), 56, 57.

[118] *Boston Pilot,* November 28, 1863; also Walter B. Smith and Arthur H. Cole, *Fluctuations in American Business, 1790–1860* (Cambridge, 1935), xxvii, 94; Ware, *Industrial Worker,* 31. For the period 1860–1865, cf. *Tenth Annual Report of the Bureau of the Statistics of Labor, January, 1879, Massachusetts Public Documents, 1879,* no. 31, pp. 81 ff.

[119] Cf. Clark, *op. cit.,* II, 143; *Tenth Annual Report of the Bureau of Statistics of Labor,* 67 ff., 78, 87; Edith Abbott, "Wages of Unskilled Labor in the United States, 1850–1900," *Journal of Political Economy,* June, 1905, XIII, 321 ff.; Chart C, *infra.*

[120] Lousada to Russell, May 7, 1863, British Consular Correspondence, F.O. 5/910.

[121] The complaints against high costs are most clearly and most poignantly stated in letters from Irish laborers to friends in Ireland, occasionally reprinted in the Irish press. Cf. particularly the letter to his father from James O'Leary, a Killarney immigrant, dated Boston, December 27, 1863 (*Cork Examiner,* January 23, 1864), and the letter from a Cambridgeport immigrant to his former parish priest (*ibid.,* August 19, 1864).

[122] Cf. *Cork Examiner,* August 19, 1864.

[123] Cf. *Cork Examiner,* July 11, 1861; *Boston Pilot,* October 5, September 28, 1861; also Commons, *op. cit.,* II, 13; Fite, *op. cit.,* 199 ff., 212. For prices and wages, cf. Wesley Clair Mitchell, *History of the Greenbacks . . .* (Chicago, 1903), 239 ff., 280 ff.

[124] Cf. *Boston Pilot,* October 18, 1862, January 16, 1864.

[125] Jeremiah O'Donovan-Rossa, *Rossa's Recollections 1838 to 1898 . . .* (Mariner's Harbor, New York, 1898), 154.

Chapter IV. The Physical Adjustment

[1] Lemuel Shattuck, *Report to the Committee of the City Council . . . Census of Boston . . . 1845 . . .* (Boston, 1846), 55.

[2] The conventionally accepted figures show an increase of 52.11 per cent for the decade 1830–40 and only 46.58 per cent for 1840–50 and 29.92 per cent for 1850–60 (cf., e.g., Adna F. Weber, *Growth of Cities in the Nineteenth Century . . .* [New York, 1899], 37). This is due to an error of almost 10,000 in the federal census of 1840, which raised the rate of increase for the preceding decade and lowered it for the succeeding one (Shattuck, *op. cit.,* 7 ff.). Cf. also Josiah Curtis, *Report of the Joint Special Committee on the Census of Boston . . . 1855 . . .* (Boston, 1856), 3, 23.

[3] Lemuel Shattuck, *Letter . . . in Relation to the Introduction of Water into . . . Boston* (Boston, 1845), 13 ff.

[4] Cf. *infra,* Tables II, V; for the density of population in peninsular

Notes to Chapter 4

Boston in 1845, cf. *Report of the Committee on the Expediency of Providing Better Tenements for the Poor* (Boston, 1846), 4.

5 Cf., e.g., *infra*, Map II.

6 For communications, cf. Dissertation Copy, 180.

7 Cf., e.g., *Report of the Bureau of Statistics of Labor . . . 1870 . . . , Massachusetts Senate Documents, 1870,* no. 120, pp. 175, 176.

8 Dissertation Copy, Map IV; also Horace Greeley, et al., *Great Industries of the United States . . .* (Hartford, 1872), 592.

9 Robert A. Woods, ed., *City Wilderness . . .* (Boston, 1898), 21 ff.; Justin Winsor, ed., *Memorial History of Boston . . .* (Boston, 1880), IV, 40.

10 Cf. Albert B. Wolfe, *Lodging House Problem in Boston . . .* (Boston, 1906), 11; Henry F. Jenks, "Old School Street," *New England Magazine,* November, 1895, XIII, 259; Robert A. Woods, ed., *Americans in Process . . .* (Boston, 1902), 16 ff.; Freeman Hunt, *Lives of American Merchants* (New York, 1856), I, 143 ff.; *Wide Awake: and the Spirit of Washington* (Boston), October 7, 1854.

11 Cf. Mabel L. Walker, *Urban Blight and Slums . . .* (Cambridge, 1938), 6, 3 ff.; cf. also James Ford, *Slums and Housing . . .* (Cambridge, 1936), I, 5, 6.

12 Cf. *supra*, Maps I, II. An analysis of the Broad, Cove, and Sea Street district in 1850 found only 75 Americans in a population of 2,813 (Amasa Walker, *Tenth Report to the Legislature . . . Births, Marriages and Deaths . . . 1851, Massachusetts Public Documents, 1853,* 111; "Report and Tabular Statement of the Censors, . . . 1850," *Boston City Documents, 1850,* no. 42, p. 39).

13 E. H. Derby, "Commercial Cities . . . Boston," *Hunt's Merchants' Magazine,* November, 1850, XXIII, 484 ff.

14 For statutory fare provisions, cf. *Charter and Ordinances of the City of Boston . . .* (Boston, 1856), 422, 424, 433; *Ordinances of the City of Boston . . .* (Boston, 1865), 65; for routes, cf. H. A. Brown, *Guide-Book for the City and Vicinity of Boston, 1869* (Boston, 1869), 23; *Irish-American,* May 8, 1858.

15 Cf. Woods, *Americans in Process . . . ,* 33 ff.; Winsor, *op. cit.,* IV, 35–37.

16 For the distribution of Negro population, 1813–1850, cf. *infra,* Maps III, IV. Throughout the period the concentration persisted in the same streets of the West End, with a scattering in other parts of the city. Cf. also [James W. Hale], *Old Boston Town . . .* (New York, 1880), 29; *Daily Evening Transcript,* December 22, 1831; and, in general, Alexander Marjoribanks, *Travels in South and North America* (London, 1853), 177.

[17] Boston Female Society for Missionary Purposes, *A . . . Brief Account . . . with Extracts from the Reports of their Missionaries . . .* (Boston, n.d.), 15 ff. Cf. also *Minutes of the Selectmen's Meetings 1811 . . . 1818 (Volume of Records . . . , XXXVIII), Boston City Documents, 1908, no. 60, pp. 107, 113, 116.*

[18] Cf. Dissertation Copy, Map IX; Woods, *Americans in Process,* 36, 37, 42; Walker, *Tenth Report . . . 1851, Massachusetts Public Documents, 1853,* 110.

[19] Cf. Edwin M. Bacon, *Book of Boston . . .* (Boston, 1916), 110.

[20] Cf. Dissertation Copy, Maps X, XI; George Adams, *Brighton and Brookline Business Directory . . .* (Boston, 1850), 20 ff.; Chauncey M. Depew, *1795–1895 — One Hundred Years of American Commerce . . .* (New York, 1895), I, xxvii.

[21] James F. Hunnewell, *Century of Town Life . . .* (Boston, 1888), 36.

[22] Cf. *Charter and Ordinances of the City of Boston . . .* (Boston, 1856), 436; Dissertation Copy, Maps X, XI; *Boston Pilot,* August 25, 1860.

[23] Boston Common Council, *South Boston Memorial, Boston City Documents, 1847,* no. 18, p. 11.

[24] *Ordinances of the City of Boston . . .* (Boston, 1865), 76; State Street Trust Company, *Boston, England and Boston, New England . . .* (Boston, 1930), 10; Dissertation Copy, Map X.

[25] Cf. Alfred Pairpoint, *Uncle Sam and His Country . . .* (London, 1857), 196–201; Dissertation Copy, Map XI; *Boston Pilot,* June 2, 1855; Edward H. Savage, *Boston Events . . .* (Boston, 1884), 7, 8; George H. McCaffrey, Political Disintegration and Reintegration of Metropolitan Boston (MS., H. C. L.), 194.

[26] *Report of the Committee on Expediency,* 14.

[27] Woods, *City Wilderness,* 26, 27; *Charter and Ordinances of the City of Boston . . .* (Boston, 1856), 408 ff.; *Ordinances of the City of Boston* (Boston, 1865), 78, 79; Francis S. Drake, *Town of Roxbury . . .* (Boston, 1905), 51.

[28] Walker, *Tenth Report . . . 1851, Massachusetts Public Documents, 1853,* 111; cf. also Dissertation Copy, Map XI; Woods, *City Wilderness,* 53, 28–30; *Tenth Annual Report of the Benevolent Fraternity of Churches . . .* (Boston, 1844), 25.

[29] Particularly a large representation of Germans (cf. Dissertation Copy, Map XI). Cf. also "Report and Tabular Statement of the Censors . . . 1850," *Boston City Documents, 1850,* no. 42, p. 34; "Report of the Standing Committee on Towns . . . ," *Massachusetts Senate Documents, 1851,* no. 82, passim.

30 Cf. D. Hamilton Hurd, *History of Norfolk County* . . . (Philadelphia, 1884), 72, 73; Dissertation Copy, Maps IX, XI.

31 Winsor, *op. cit.,* IV, 39; Dissertation Copy, Map X; "Report . . . on the East Boston Ferry, 1864," *Boston City Documents, 1864,* no. 44, pp. 4 and passim; *Boston Pilot,* June 8, 1850.

32 *Ordinances of the City of Boston* . . . (Boston, 1865), 75, 82; Dissertation Copy, 192–194.

33 For instance, a building in Kingston Court, owned by L. M. Sargeant was leased to T. Thompson whose agent was James Connors, who subleased it to a neighborhood grocer, P. Collins (*Report of the Bureau of Statistics of Labor* . . . *1871, Massachusetts Senate Documents, 1871,* no. 150, pp. 524, 526).

34 John H. Griscom, *Sanitary Condition of the Laboring Population of New York* . . . (New York, 1845), 6; Ford, *op. cit.,* I, 105, 134.

35 *Third Annual Report of the Bureau of Statistics of Labor* . . . *1872, Massachusetts Senate Documents, 1872,* no. 180, p. 437.

36 *Boston Pilot,* June 2, 1855.

37 *Report of the Bureau of Statistics of Labor, 1870,* 169 ff.; 176; Edward H. Savage, *Police Records and Recollections* . . . (Boston, 1873), 268.

38 Cf., e.g., the plan and the picture of the house in the rear of 136 Hanover Street, Figs. 10 and 11. For others, cf. Woods, *City Wilderness,* 62 ff.

39 Cf. C. Pinney, *Atlas of the City of Boston* . . . (Boston, 1861), Plate 17, 23; *Report of the Bureau of Statistics of Labor, 1870,* 166.

40 Represented by the shaded areas in Fig. 13.

41 Cf. Fig. 14; also Norman J. Ware, *Industrial Worker, 1840–1860* . . . (Boston, 1924), 13.

42 Cf. Robert B. Forbes, *Voyage of the Jamestown* . . . (Boston, 1847), 22.

43 A few in Broad Street were six floors high, but these were exceptional (*Report of the Committee of Internal Health on the Asiatic Cholera* . . . [Boston, 1849], 14).

44 Cf. *Twelfth Report Benevolent Fraternity of Churches* (Boston, 1846), 17; *Report of the Committee on Expediency,* 12, 13; *Report of the Bureau of Statistics of Labor, 1870,* 165 ff., 175; *Report of the Committee of Internal Health,* 14; *Report of the Bureau of Statistics of Labor, 1871,* 521, 526; *Boston Pilot,* November 8, 1856.

45 Shattuck, *Letter,* 15. In that year the number of persons per house was already at its maximum, and did not decline appreciably in the next ten years.

Year	Persons per House in Boston	Year	Persons per House in Boston
1790	7.97	1845	10.57
1800	8.31	1850	9.16
1810	8.51	1855	10.16
1820	9.84	1860	8.92
1830	9.99	1870	8.46
1840	10.04		

("Report and Tabular Statement of the Censors . . . 1850," *loc. cit.,* 32; Curtis, *op. cit.,* 11; Carroll D. Wright, *Social, Commercial, and Manufacturing Statistics of the City of Boston . . .* [Boston, 1882], 10; Shattuck, *Report . . . Census of Boston . . . 1845,* 54).

[46] Curtis, *op. cit.,* 7.

[47] Compare Wards 6, 9, 11, with 1, 3, 7, 8 in Map IX, Dissertation Copy.

[48] *Report of the Committee of Internal Health,* 12; *Report of the Bureau of Statistics of Labor, 1870,* 167.

[49] *Report of the Bureau of Statistics of Labor, 1870,* 166–168; *Report of the Committee of Internal Health,* 173; *Courrier des États-Unis,* May 6, 1851.

[50] *Report of the Committee of Internal Health,* 15; also Fig. 10.

[51] "Report and Tabular Statement of the Censors . . . 1850," *loc. cit.,* 15; *Report of the Committee of Internal Health,* 172, 173.

[52] *Report of the Committee of Internal Health,* 13, 14.

[53] *Ibid.,* 11.

[54] *Report of the Massachusetts Bureau of Statistics of Labor, 1870,* 176.

[55] *Report of the Committee of Internal Health,* 13.

[56] *Report of the Bureau of Statistics of Labor, 1870,* 165; *Report of the Committee of Internal Health,* 169, 174; *Report of the Bureau of Statistics of Labor, 1871,* 521, 524; Figs. 18, 19.

[57] *Report of the Committee of Internal Health,* 14.

[58] *Report of the Bureau of Statistics of Labor, 1870,* 164.

[59] Benevolent Fraternity of Churches, *Fourth Annual Report of the Executive Committee . . .* (Boston, 1838), 18.

[60] *Report of the Committee of Internal Health,* 14; *Report of the Bureau of Statistics of Labor, 1870,* 176.

[61] *Report of the Bureau of Statistics of Labor, 1870,* 164 ff., 175 ff.; *Report of the Bureau of Statistics of Labor, 1871,* 521, 522, 525; *Boston Pilot,* August 9, 1856.

[62] *Report of the Committee of Internal Health,* 13.

[63] Cf. Lemuel Shattuck, *Letter to the Secretary of State on the Registra-*

Notes to Chapter 4

tion of Births, Marriages, and Deaths . . . (s.l., n.d. [Boston, 1845]), 23; Massachusetts Sanitary Commissioners, *Report of a General Plan for the Promotion of Public* . . . *Health* . . . (Boston, 1850), 69 ff.; "Memorial of the Boston Sanitary Association," *Massachusetts House Documents, 1861,* no. 153, p. 13; Shattuck, *Report,* 144.

[64] Deaths from Smallpox in Boston — five year periods, 1811–65:

Years	Deaths	Years	Deaths
1811–15	6	1841–45	185
1816–20	0	1846–50	349
1821–25	2	1851–55	331
1826–30	5	1856–60	401
1831–35	17	1861–65	250
1836–40	197		

(Derived from data in Charles E. Buckingham, et al., *Sanitary Condition of Boston* . . . [Boston, 1875], 84; "Memorial of the Boston Sanitary Association," *loc. cit.,* 5, 15).

[65] Cf. Massachusetts Sanitary Commissioners, *Report,* 90, 92.

[66] Jesse Chickering, *Report of the Committee* . . . *1850, Boston City Documents, 1851,* no. 60, p. 29.

[67] *Report of the Committee of Internal Health,* 8, 165.

[68] Cf. *ibid.,* Map, 163–169; Dissertation Copy, Map XII.

[69] Cf. *Report of the Committee of Internal Health,* 9, 57–160, 180.

[70] Shattuck, *Report,* 146; Massachusetts Sanitary Commissioners, *Report,* 91; Buckingham, *op. cit.,* 122 ff.; "Report by the City Registrar . . . 1864," *Boston City Documents, 1865,* no. 42, p. 27. The close correlation of deaths by consumption with the poor housing conditions of the Irish may be seen *infra,* Table XVIII.

[71] Percentage of Total Deaths Due to Infant Mortality:

Ten Year Period	Percentage Deaths Under One Year Old of Total Deaths	Percentage Deaths Under Five Years Old of Total Deaths
1820–29	8.73	25.69
1830–39	12.66	35.17
1840–49	12.76	37.52
1850–59	23.84	46.49

(Buckingham, *op. cit.,* 53; also Shattuck, *Letter on Registration,* 19).

[72] [William Read], *Communication* . . . *on Asiatic Cholera* . . . *1866, Boston City Documents, 1866,* no. 21, p. 37. One thousand cases of children's intestinal diseases, located Dissertation Copy, Map XII, coincide almost exactly with the Irish areas. Cf. also Buckingham, *op. cit.,* 64–69.

[73] Ware, *op. cit.*, 14.

[74] Massachusetts Sanitary Commissioners, *Report*, 82. For the increase in elderly people, cf. *infra*, Table XIX.

[75] Cf. "Sanitary Reform," *North American Review*, July, 1851, LXXIII, 120; Buckingham, *op. cit.*, 47; Chickering, *op. cit.*, 28.

[76] "Sanitary Reform," *loc. cit.*, 121, 122; *Tenth Report to the Legislature . . . Relating to the Registry and Return of Births, Marriages, and Deaths . . . 1851* (Boston, 1852), 110, 111.

[77] Cf. Curtis, *op. cit.*, 56–58; *infra*, Table XVIII.

[78] Chickering, *op. cit.*, 28.

[79] Chickering, *op. cit.*, 53. Their youth as a group kept the Irish death rate from increasing in the following years and led to Chickering's opinion that the American rate was higher than the foreign (*ibid.*, 32). Chickering was also misled by the large and rapidly growing number of deaths among the Boston-born infants of Irish parents (Curtis, *op. cit.*, 44, 46 ff.).

[80] Cf. *infra*, Table XX; Chickering, *op. cit.*, 17, 19, 23, 52; *Report of the Committee on Expediency*, 7; Dissertation Copy, 450.

[81] Benevolent Fraternity of Churches, *Twelfth Annual Report of the Executive Committee . . .* (Boston, 1846), 11.

[82] Cf. *supra*, 18 ff.; *Massachusetts Senate Documents, 1839*, no. 47, pp. 6 ff.

[83] Cf. *Massachusetts House Documents, 1851*, no. 152, pp. 1, 2; Chart D. After 1854 the number of foreign state paupers declined as they acquired legal residence. Cf. also Table XXI, *infra*.

[84] Boston Finance Committee, *Auditor's Report, 1848*, no. 36, p. 3; Massachusetts Sanitary Commissioners, *Report*, 203.

[85] Cf. Massachusetts Commissioners of Alien Passengers and Foreign Paupers, *Report, 1854* (Boston, 1855), 22 ff.; *Massachusetts House Documents, 1851*, no. 152, pp. 4, 5. Cf. also *Massachusetts Senate Documents, 1859*, no. 2; *Massachusetts Senate Documents, 1839*, no. 47, pp. 10, 13 ff.; *Massachusetts Senate Documents, 1844*, no. 44.

[86] Robert W. Kelso, *History of Public Poor Relief in Massachusetts, 1620–1920* (Boston, 1922), 136; *Massachusetts Senate Documents, 1852*, no. 127; Massachusetts Commissioners of Alien Passengers and Foreign Paupers, *Report, 1851* (Boston, 1852), 3, 6. For the nativities of admissions to the workhouses, cf. Dissertation Copy, 467.

[87] Cf. *Inaugural Addresses of the Mayors of Boston . . .* (Boston, 1894), I, 363, 385. Table III, *infra*, shows the rapid increase of the cost of poor relief after 1847 and particularly after 1850 when the city began to take up the burden of the support of former state paupers. Until then the cost had scarcely risen (cf. also, *supra*, 18 ff.). All available indices point to the Irish as the cause of this growth. Outdoor relief was concentrated in

Irish wards. The Irish were the largest components of the state poorhouse population and a great majority of all paupers in the city and its suburbs after 1845 were Irish (cf. *infra*, Table XXI).

88 Cf. Theodore Parker, *Sermon of the Moral Condition of Boston* . . . (Boston, 1849), 15, 18, 19.

89 Cf. Benevolent Fraternity of Churches, *Twelfth Annual Report*, 15; Parker, *op. cit.*, 15; Massachusetts Sanitary Commission, *Report*, 203; *Fifteenth Annual Report of the Executive Committee, Benevolent Fraternity of Churches* . . . (Boston, 1849), 6, 33; *Harbor Excursion and Intemperance in Boston* (Boston, 1853), 8.

90 Benevolent Fraternity of Churches, *Twelfth Annual Report*, 11, 15; Shattuck, *Report . . . Census of Boston . . . 1845*, 126.

91 For relative statistics of criminality, cf. *infra*, Tables XXII–XXIV.

92 Cf. *Boston Pilot*, February 2, 1856, March 3, 1855; *Irish American*, September 12, 1857; *African Repository*, July, 1826, II, 152 ff.

93 For Roby, cf. Dissertation Copy, 224; for Doctor Webster, cf. Marjoribanks, *op. cit.*, 179 ff.; A. B. Hart, *Commonwealth History of Massachusetts* (New York, 1930), IV, 56.

94 *Twenty-Sixth Annual Report of the Trustees of the State Lunatic Hospital at Worcester, October, 1858, Massachusetts Public Documents, 1858*, no. 27, p. 20.

95 Cf. William I. Cole, "Boston's Insane Hospital," *New England Magazine*, February, 1899, XIX, 753; Boston Finance Committee, *Report of the City Auditor, 1864*, no. 52, p. 263; "Abstract of the Returns from Overseers of the Poor," *Massachusetts Public Documents, 1848*, 1; Boston Finance Committee, *Auditor's Report, 1856*, no. 44, p. 219; *infra*, Table XXV; Dissertation Copy, 460.

96 Cf. *Report of the Bureau of Statistics of Labor, 1871*, 207.

97 Cf. *Daily Evening Transcript*, August 9, 1831; Massachusetts Secretary of State, "Registry and Return of Births, Marriages and Deaths . . . 1858," no. 16, *Massachusetts Public Documents, 1858*, no. 1, pp. 177 ff.; *ibid., 1859*, no. 17, *Massachusetts Public Documents, 1859*, no. 1, p. 23; *ibid., 1860*, no. 18, *Massachusetts Public Documents, 1860*, no. 1, p. 25.

Chapter V. Conflict of Ideas

1 Karl Mannheim, *Ideology and Utopia* . . . (London, 1936), 6.

2 Cf. Grattan to Palmerston, June 15, 1850, British Consular Correspondence, F.O. 5/350; *Cork Examiner*, November 7, 1856; Ralph Waldo Emerson, "English Traits," *Collected Works* (Boston, 1903), V; Edward Everett, *Orations and Speeches* . . . (Boston, 1850), II, 429 ff., 462 ff.; Edward Dicey, *Six Months in the Federal States* (London, 1863), II, 180.

Conflict of Ideas

[3] Cf. Ezra S. Gannett, *Arrival of the Britannia, a Sermon . . . Federal Street Meeting-House . . . July 19, 1840 . . .* (Boston, 1840), 16, 17; cf. also, *supra,* 22 ff.

[4] For a definition of ideas in this sense, cf. Arthur O. Lovejoy, *Great Chain of Being, a Study of the History of an Idea . . .* (Cambridge, 1936), 7 and Chapter I.

[5] Robert Bell, *Description of the Conditions and Manners . . . of the Peasantry of Ireland . . .* (London, 1804), 17.

[6] "Izzie," "The Emigrant's Farewell," *Boston Pilot,* August 16, 1862.

[7] P.L., "I Am Tired," *Boston Pilot,* March 26, 1864.

[8] Cf. the analysis of Irish newspaper literature, Dissertation Copy, 231–233.

[9] Kathleen Kennedy in "Cross and Beads," *Boston Catholic Observer,* November 8, 15, 1848.

[10] *Boston Pilot,* August 12, 1854. Compare the English industrial background of Methodism in J. L. and Barbara Hammond, *Town Labourer, 1760–1832 . . .* (London, 1920), 276.

[11] Mrs. Anna H. Dorsey, "Nora Brady's Vow," *Boston Pilot,* March 7, 1857.

[12] Cf. Arthur M. Schlesinger, Jr., *Orestes A. Brownson, a Pilgrim's Progress* (Boston, 1939), 205.

[13] Cf. *Boston Pilot,* September 9, 1854; *United States Catholic Intelligencer,* February 24, 1832; *Jesuit or Catholic Sentinel,* July 19, 1834.

[14] *Boston Pilot,* June 10, 1843.

[15] Cf. Edward MacLysaght, *Irish Life in the Seventeenth Century . . .* (London, 1939), 283–285, 288 ff.

[16] *Boston Catholic Observer,* March 29, 1848; cf. also *Boston Pilot,* January 22, 1853.

[17] *Boston Catholic Observer,* April 5, 1848; cf. also Brownson's description of Charlemagne as an ideal Catholic ruler (*Boston Pilot,* December 4, 1852), and the peasant conception of the priest who ruled the Irish village both as priest and lawgiver (Allen H. Clington, "Frank O'Donnell. A Tale of Irish Life," *ibid.,* January 24, 1863).

[18] *Boston Catholic Observer,* March 22, 1848.

[19] *Ibid.,* March 29, 1848.

[20] Cf., e.g., Brownson's criticism of the works of Cardinal Newman and of Bishop John England (Brownson to Father J. W. Cummings, Boston, September 5, 1849 [Brownson Papers, MSS., L.U.N.D.]; Henry F. Brownson, *Orestes A. Brownson's Middle Life: from 1845 to 1855* [Detroit, 1899], 105; Schlesinger, *op. cit.,* 199–201).

[21] Cf. *Boston Catholic Observer,* March 28, 1848; Brownson, *Works of Brownson,* I, 254; Schlesinger, *op. cit.,* 28; James F. Clarke, *The Church*

... *as It Was* ... (Boston, 1848), 20; Josiah Quincy, *Figures of the Past from the Leaves of Old Journals* (Boston, 1883), 71; *supra,* 181 ff.

22 Cf., e.g., *Boston Pilot,* September 9, July 29, 1854.

23 Cf. J. W. Cummings, D. D., *Social Reform, a Lecture* ... (Boston, 1853), 18.

24 *Questions and Answers Adapted to the Reading Lessons and the Stories in Mrs. Trimmer's Charity School Spelling Book, Part 1* ... (Dublin, 1814), Lesson fifth, 11.

25 Quoted in F. Spencer Baldwin, "What Ireland Has Done for America," *New England Magazine,* XXIV (1901), 73. Cf. also the character of Nora Brady, Mrs. Anna H. Dorsey, "Nora Brady's Vow," *Boston Pilot,* January 3, 1857; also Constantia Maxwell, *Country and Town in Ireland under the Georges* (London, 1940), 55.

26 *Boston Pilot,* January 10, 1857, July 15, 1854.

27 Cf. Mrs. Anna H. Dorsey, "Old Landlord's Daughter," *Boston Pilot,* January 21, 1854.

28 Cf. *Boston Pilot,* April 24, October 16, 1852; Brownson, *Brownson's Middle Life,* 296.

29 Cf. *Voice of Industry,* January 7, 1848; Henry Steele Commager, *Theodore Parker* ... (Boston, 1936), 151 ff.; A. B. Darling, *Political Changes in Massachusetts* ... (New Haven, 1925), 153 ff.; A. B. Hart, *Commonwealth History of Massachusetts* ... (New York, 1930), IV, 324 ff.; Arthur S. Bolster, Jr., *James Freeman Clarke* (Boston, 1954), 229 ff.

30 Cf. E. S. Abdy, *Journal of a Residence* ... *in the United States* ... (London, 1835), I, 159; Dissertation Copy, 242; *Boston Pilot,* January 22, 1853, February 3, March 3, 1855.

31 Cf. *Boston Pilot,* February 18, 1854, March 3, 1855; Brownson, *Brownson's Middle Life,* 295 ff.

32 On this score the *Pilot* objected to Brownson's hostility to slavery after the opening of the Civil War (cf. *Boston Pilot,* April 12, 1862). Cf. also *ibid.,* July 8, 1843; *Cork Examiner,* July 21, 1843; British Consular Correspondence, F.O. 5/426, no. 59.

33 Cf. *United States Catholic Intelligencer,* October 1, 1831; Brownson, *Brownson's Middle Life,* II, 280 ff.

34 *Boston Pilot,* December 31, 1859.

35 Cf. John R. Commons et al., eds., *A Documentary History of American Industrial Society* (Cleveland, 1910), VII, 60; John Robert Godely, *Letters from America* (London, 1844), II, 70; William S. Robinson, *"Warrington" Pen-Portraits* ... *1848 to 1876* ... (Boston, 1877), 298.

36 Cf. *Boston Pilot,* October 18, 1856. Cf. also, the treatment of the Negro characters, Dolly in Agnes E. St. John's "Ellie Moore" (*ibid.,* June 30–September 1, 1860), Phillis in Mrs. Anna H. Dorsey, "Nora Brady's

Conflict of Ideas

Vow" (*ibid.*, February 21, 1857), and the butler in Mrs. Anna H. Dorsey, "The Heiress of Carrigmona" (*ibid.*, March 3, 1860).

[37] Cf. *Boston Catholic Observer*, April 12, 1848; *Boston Pilot*, April 24, July 24, 1852, November 9, 1839; *Irish-American*, November 4, 1854.

[38] Cf. *Boston Pilot*, March 29, 1851, January 10, 1857.

[39] Cf. Cummings, *Social Reform*, 7; *Jesuit or Catholic Sentinel*, July 19, 1834.

[40] Cf. *Boston Pilot*, April 24, October 9, 1852; *Boston Catholic Observer*, November 15, 1848; *United States Catholic Intelligencer*, May 18, 1832. For the attitude of other Bostonians, cf. "Report of the Board of Education, 1849," *Massachusetts House Documents, 1849*, no. 1, pp. 105 ff.; Everett, *op. cit.*, II, 235 ff., 313 ff.

[41] *Meyer's Monatshefte*, February, 1855, V, 128.

[42] Cf. Karl Heinzen, *Teutscher Radikalismus in Amerika* . . . [s.l., 1867], 5–27, 237–260; *Atlantis*, August, 1857, VII, 81 ff.; A. Siemering, "Die Prinzipien . . . der modernen Erziehung," *Der Pionier*, January 26–February 2, 1860; *ibid.*, January 5, 1860.

[43] Cf., e.g., Address of the "German Republican Association" of Boston (*European* [New York], December 6, 1856; *Der Pionier*, March 30, 1856). A short-lived Democratic paper took a compromising attitude based on the constitutionality of slavery (*Der Neu England Demokrat*, November 21, 1857), but quickly failed. Germans opposed the temperance movement not because they objected to reform, but because they felt drinking was a legitimate pleasure needing no reform (cf. *Meyer's Monatshefte*, February, 1855, V, 128, 147).

[44] Cf. *Courrier des États-Unis*, September 2, 1835, December 5, 1850, September 23, 1847; *Gazette Française* [Boston], June 28, July 5, 1851; *Colored American* [New York], March 4, 1837; *L'Eco d'Italia* [New York], December 6, April 26, 1851.

[45] Cf., e.g., *Boston Pilot*, January 1, 8, July 19, 1848.

[46] Cf. *Boston Catholic Observer*, August 23, 1848.

[47] Cf., e.g., *Voice of Industry* (Boston), November 26, 1847; *Boston Merkur*, October 2, December 25, 1847, January 1, 1848.

[48] Brownson to Montalembert, June 30, 1851 (Brownson, *Brownson's Middle Life*, 326, 327). For Father Roddan, cf. *Boston Pilot*, December 11, 1858.

[49] Thus Brownson's *Boston Catholic Observer* was occasionally hostile to reactionary Austria (cf., e.g., *Boston Catholic Observer*, December 4, 11, 18, 1847, January 8, 1848).

[50] For the attitude of Irish-American radicals towards slavery, cf. *European* [New York], December 6, 1856; *Irish-American*, January 18, 1851.

335

Notes to Chapter 5

⁵¹ Cf. Alfred Bunn, *Old England and New England . . .* (London, 1853), II, 12, 13.

⁵² Cf. *Boston Pilot,* January 22, 1853; Brownson, *Brownson's Middle Life,* 418 ff.; *Boston Catholic Observer,* September 20, October 11, November 1, 1848.

⁵³ *Boston Catholic Observer,* February 16, 1848; cf. also O. A. Brownson, "Liberalism and Catholicity," *Works of Brownson,* V, 476 ff.

⁵⁴ *Boston Catholic Observer,* March 29, 1848.

⁵⁵ *Boston Catholic Observer,* August 2, 1848. Cf. also the attacks on the *Pilot* by the *New York Freeman's Journal* and the *Propagateur Catholique* (quoted *Boston Pilot,* August 18, 1849).

⁵⁶ *Boston Catholic Observer,* December 6, 1848; Brownson, *Brownson's Middle Life,* 358.

⁵⁷ Cf. *Boston Pilot,* September 14, 28, June 22, 1850.

⁵⁸ Cf. Frederick Driscoll, *Sketch of the Canadian Ministry* (Montreal, 1866), 81; E. M. Coulter, *William Brownlow . . .* (Chapel Hill, 1937), 48, 49, 65.

⁵⁹ For the native attitude, cf. George Sumner, *Oration . . . before the Municipal Authorities of . . . Boston, July 4, 1859 . . .* (Boston, 1882), 24–34; *Daily Evening Transcript,* June 10, 13, 1831; Samuel Adams Drake, *Old Landmarks and Historic Personages of Boston* (Boston, 1873), 264; *Massachusetts House Documents, 1848,* no. 147; Elizabeth Brett White, *American Opinion of France, from Lafayette to Poincaré* (New York, 1927), 119–122; *Voice of Industry,* March 31, 1848; *New Era of Industry,* June 2, 1848; Mason Wade, *Margaret Fuller, Whetstone of Genius* (New York, 1940), 185, 243; Giovanni Mori, "Una Mazziniana d'America . . . ," *Rivista d'Italia e d'America,* September, 1924, II, 478 ff.; George S. Boutwell, "Kossuth in New England," *New England Magazine,* X (1894), 525 ff. For the Irish attitude, cf. *Jesuit or Catholic Sentinel,* November 13, October 30, 1830; *United States Catholic Intelligencer,* October 8, 1831; *Boston Pilot,* June 15, 22, August 31, 1850, April 24, 1852; Brownson, *Brownson's Middle Life,* 418 ff.; Schlesinger, *op. cit.,* 207; *Boston Pilot,* February 8, 1851; *Boston Catholic Observer,* February 23, 1848; *Acta Sanctae Sedis* (Romae, 1865), I, 290 ff.; Dissertation Copy, 259.

⁶⁰ Cf., e.g., *Daily Evening Transcript,* January 6, 1832; Wade, *op. cit.,* 225.

⁶¹ *Boston Pilot,* February 11, 1854, March 17, 1855; *Jesuit or Catholic Sentinel,* May 28, 1831, October 23, 1830.

⁶² Cf. *Boston Pilot,* February 12, 19, January 22, 29, 1853, November 27, December 11, 1858; *Massachusetts House Documents, 1853,* no. 62.

⁶³ Cf. *Boston Pilot,* May 27, 1854, August 27, September 17, 1853. Brownson was directed to write articles in defense of Spain by Mme.

Conflict of Ideas

Calderon, wife of the Spanish ambassador (cf. Brownson, *Brownson's Middle Life*, 311 ff.), and received from her financial aid through Nicholas Reggio, consul of the Papal States in Boston (cf. Nicholas Reggio to Brownson, Boston, April 1, 1852, Brownson Papers [MS., L.U.N.D.]).

[64] Cf. Ralph Waldo Emerson, "English Traits," *Collected Works* (Boston, 1903), V, 350; *Boston Pilot*, March 17–November 10, 1855, November 20, 1852; Brownson, *Brownson's Middle Life*, 359. Catholics turned against him only in 1854 when he showed hostility to Austria and allied with England (*Boston Pilot*, March 4, 1854).

[65] Cf. Schlesinger, *op. cit.*, 207; *Boston Pilot*, April 16, 1842, May 23, 1846, January 29, 1853; *United States Catholic Intelligencer*, June 8, 1832.

[66] *Boston Pilot*, March 10, 1860.

[67] Cf., e.g., the fate of Ellen Harcourt in "Neglect of Prayer" (*Boston Catholic Observer*, July 10, 1847); also, that of Margaret in Mrs. J. Sadlier, "Alice Riordan — The Blind Man's Daughter" (*Boston Pilot*, July 4–September 27, 1851); cf. also *Boston Catholic Observer*, September 6, 1848; *Boston Pilot*, June 9, 1860.

[68] Cf. *Boston Pilot*, September 2, August 26, 1854, March 21, January 10, 1857; *Boston Catholic Observer*, June 5, 1847.

[69] *Boston Pilot*, January 10, 1857, March 2, 1861.

[70] Cf. Dissertation Copy, 263, 264; Thomas Colley Grattan, *Civilized America* (London, 1859), II, 40 ff.

[71] Cf. *United States Catholic Intelligencer*, October 1, 1831; *Boston Pilot*, November 8, 1856. Cf. also Elizabeth H. Stewart, "Rising in the North," *ibid.*, September 4, 1858 ff.; Walsh, "Jerpoint Abbey," *ibid.*, June 4, 1859.

[72] John Adam Moehler, *Symbolism . . .* (New York, 1844), xi.

[73] Cf. Brownson, *Works of Brownson*, I, xix; *United States Catholic Intelligencer*, February 24, July 13, 1832; *Boston Catholic Observer*, January 10, 1847, January 26, 1848; *Jesuit or Catholic Sentinel*, July 2, 1831; *Boston Pilot*, October 5, 1839. For the contemporary Boston view of Luther, cf. Camillo von Klenze, "German Literature in the Boston Transcript," *Philological Quarterly*, XI (1932), 11.

[74] J. Tighe, "To Massachusetts," *Boston Pilot*, July 4, 1846; cf. also "Lines on the Ruins of a Nunnery," *Literary and Catholic Sentinel*, August 29, 1835.

[75] Cf., e.g., the "historical romances" of C. M. O'Keefe, *Boston Pilot*, May 8, 1858; Mrs. Anna H. Dorsey, "Mona: — The Vestal," *ibid.*, January 5, 1856–March 22, 1856; *United States Catholic Intelligencer*, October 1, 1831.

[76] John McElheran, "The Condition of Women," *Boston Pilot*, April 5–July 12, 1856.

77 Cf., e.g., *Boston Pilot*, July 26, 1856, and the issues following.

78 Cf. *Boston Pilot*, October 16, 1858; *Literary and Catholic Sentinel* (Boston), August 22, 1835.

79 Cf., e.g., *Boston Pilot*, November 24, 1855–March 8, 1856, November 15, 1856, January 21, 1854–January 20, 1855; Thomas D. McGee, *History of the Irish Settlers in North America* . . . (Boston, 1852), passim.

80 *Boston Pilot*, March 22, 1856.

81 Cf., e.g., *Meyer's Monatshefte*, March, 1855, V, 223; *ibid.*, April, 1855, V, 298, 302, 309, 312; also "Die schöne Literatur Nordamerika's" (*Amerika, wie es ist . . . Serie III der Volkschriften des deutsch-amerikanischen Vereins* . . . [Hamburg, 1854], 20–28); Franz Kielblock's opera, "Miles Standisch" (*Der Pionier*, April 5, 12, 1860).

82 Cf., e.g., *Courrier des États-Unis*, March 3, October 17, 1832, October 18, 1834.

83 Cf. A. B. Faust, *German Element* . . . (New York, 1927), II, 215; Karl Quentin, *Reisebilder und Studien aus dem Norden der Vereinigten Staaten von Amerika* (Arnsberg, 1851), I, 80; von Klenze, *loc. cit.*, 1–25.

84 Cf. *Courrier des États-Unis*, March 19, May 21, 1836, November 24, 1832.

85 Cf. William Treat Upton, *Anthony Phillip Heinrich* . . . (New York, 1939), 71, 87; O. G. Sonneck, *Early Opera in America* (New York, n.d. [1915]), 144, 145, 197, 217; John Tasker Howard, *Our American Music, Three Hundred Years of It* (New York, 1939), 135–138; Justin Winsor, *Memorial History of Boston* . . . (Boston, 1880), IV, 415–419; John Sullivan Dwight, "Handel and Haydn Society," *New England Magazine*, I (1889), 382 ff.; Henry C. Lahee, "Century of Choral Singing in New England," *ibid.*, XXVI (1902), 102, 103.

86 Cf. Winsor, *op. cit.*, IV, 421; *Upton, Heinrich*, 76, 199; Howard, *op. cit.*, 155; Francis H. Jenks, "Boston Musical Composers," *New England Magazine*, II (1890), 476.

87 Cf., e.g., the confused criticism which greeted Hermann & Co.'s musical soirées in 1832 (*Daily Evening Transcript*, June 22, 1832).

88 Cf. Dissertation Copy, 272, 273; Winsor, *op. cit.*, IV, 423, 426.

89 Cf. Winsor, *op. cit.*, IV, 429, 433 ff., 437, 441, 442; Howard, *op. cit.*, 217 ff., 220–225, 244; Upton, *Art Song*, 31, 38, 70; Upton, *Heinrich*, 202 ff.; Elson, *loc. cit.*, 236, 237; Faust, *op. cit.*, II, 269; Christine Merrick Ayars, *Contributions to the Art of Music in America* . . . (New York, 1937), 79.

90 Cf. a long article on this subject in *Boston Pilot*, May 31, 1851.

91 For the early phases of Brownson's thought, cf. Schlesinger, *op. cit.*, especially 75–88, 117–120, 136–137, 140–141, 149, 151, 159, 169, 241; Brownson, "The Convert," *Works of Brownson*, V, 120, 121.

The Development of Group Consciousness

[92] Isaac T. Hecker, "Dr. Brownson and Bishop Fitzpatrick," *Catholic World*, XLV (1887), 7; Schlesinger, *op. cit.*, 193, 194; Brownson, *Brownson's Middle Life*, 4, 8; Henry F. Brownson, *Orestes A. Brownson's Early Life: from 1803 to 1844* (Detroit, 1898), 476 ff.

[93] As such, his works in this period have been used in this chapter. Cf. also Brownson, *Brownson's Middle Life*, 98; Schlesinger, *op. cit.*, 195, 210.

[94] Schlesinger, *op. cit.*, 213, 209 ff., 218, 219.

[95] Schlesinger, *op. cit.*, 219, 248 ff. For the difference in his attitude towards Gioberti's liberalism before and after he left Boston, compare the articles written in 1850 and in 1864 (Brownson, *Works*, II, 102, 106, 110 ff., and *ibid.*, II, 211-270).

[96] *Ibid.*, II, 142, 143; references to *Boston Pilot*, 1857-1864, Dissertation Copy, 277.

[97] Rev. Vincent F. Holden, *Early Years of Issaac Thomas Hecker* . . . (Washington, 1939), 202.

Chapter VI. The Development of Group Consciousness

[1] Henry David Thoreau, *Walden or, Life in the Woods* (*Writings of Henry David Thoreau*, II, Boston, 1894), 325, 326.

[2] Cf., e.g., *Boston Pilot*, November 15, 1862; *Bostoner Zeitung*, November 11, 18, 1865; *Courrier des États-Unis*, March 4, 1848.

[3] "The Irish Emigrant's Lament," *Boston Pilot*, March 2, 1839; T. D. McGee, "A Vow and Prayer," *Poems* . . . (New York, 1869), 123.

[4] Cf. *Boston Catholic Observer*, February 13, March 13, 1847; Robert Bennet Forbes, *Voyage of the Jamestown* . . . (Boston, 1847), xxxix, 8.

[5] Cf. *Cork Examiner*, September 2, 1863; *Boston Pilot*, April 11, May 9, 1863.

[6] Cf., e.g., *Boston Pilot*, June 28, 1862; Thomas D'Arcy McGee, *Catholic History of North America* . . . (Boston, 1855), 148.

[7] Cf. Thomas D'Arcy McGee, *History of the Irish Settlers in North America* . . . (Boston, 1852), 131; *Literary and Catholic Sentinel* (Boston), March 21, 1835, March 26, 1836.

[8] Cf. Grattan to Fox, February 17, 1841, British Consular Correspondence, F.O. 5/360, fol. 59; *Boston Pilot*, January 2, 23, 1841, February 26, 1842, July 15, September 30, December 9, 1843; *Cork Examiner*, March 28, 1842; Dissertation Copy, 282.

[9] Cf. *Boston Pilot*, September 30, 1843, January 3, April 25, May 2, 1846.

[10] *Boston Pilot*, May 28, 1842; *Cork Examiner*, December 24, 1841, July 17, 1844; *Boston Catholic Observer*, July 10, 1847.

[11] *Boston Pilot*, June 26, 1847.

[12] Cf. *Boston Pilot*, July 31, 1847.

13 *Boston Catholic Observer,* August 23, 1848; *supra,* 137. For English protests, cf. Palmerston to Crampton, July 7, 1848, British Consular Correspondence, F.O. 5/483, no. 37; Palmerston to Crampton, August 4, 1848, *ibid.,* F.O. 5/483, no. 43; Crampton to Palmerston, August 28, 1848, *ibid.,* F.O. 5/486.

14 Cf. Crampton to Palmerston, October 9, 1848, *ibid.,* F.O. 5/487, no. 122; Bulwer to Palmerston, May 5, 1851, *ibid.,* F.O. 5/528; Crampton to Granville, January 25, 1852, *ibid.,* F.O. 5/544, 112–113; *Cork Examiner,* February 11, 1852.

15 *Boston Pilot,* November 14, 1857.

16 Cf. *Bowen's Boston News-Letter and City Record,* February 25, 1826; McGee, *Catholic History,* 147; Forbes, *op. cit.,* passim; Freeman Hunt, *Lives of American Merchants* (New York, 1858), II, 279; Edward Everett, *Orations and Speeches . . .* (Boston, 1850), II, 533 ff.; *Boston Pilot,* April 11, 1863; *Measures Adopted in Boston, Massachusetts for the Relief of the Suffering Scotch and Irish* (Boston, 1847).

17 Cf., e.g., the annual "democratic banquets" at the International Salon on the anniversary of the February Revolution of 1848 (*Der Pionier,* February 21, 1861). Cf. also Dissertation Copy, 286; McGee, *Irish Settlers,* 133; and Grattan to Fox, February 17, 1841, British Consular Correspondence, F.O. 5/360, f. 59.

18 Cf. Dissertation Copy, 287; Very Rev. Wm. Byrne et al., *History of the Catholic Church in the New England States* (Boston, 1899), I, 11.

19 Cf. Dissertation Copy, 288.

20 Cf., e.g., *Boston Pilot,* May 25, 1861.

21 Cf. *Boston Directory, 1853,* 379 ff.; *Boston City Documents, 1865,* no. 59, p. 74. For the Scots Charitable, cf. George Combe, *Notes on the United States . . .* (Philadelphia, 1841), II, 199; James Bernard Cullen, *Story of the Irish in Boston . . .* (Boston, 1889), 37.

22 Cf. L. von Baumbach, *Neue Briefe aus den Vereinigten Staaten . . . mit besonderer Rücksicht auf deutsche Auswanderer* (Cassel, 1856), 183; *Der Neu England Demokrat,* December 30, 1857, February 3, 1858; *Bostoner Zeitung,* December 9, 16, 1865.

23 Moses Hays had been Grand Master of Masons at the turn of the century (cf. *Columbian Centinel* [Boston], June 4, 1791; Lee M. Friedman, *Early American Jews* [Cambridge, 1934], 18, 19; Carl Wittke, *We Who Built America . . .* [New York, 1939], 41).

24 Cf. *Literary and Catholic Sentinel,* January 16, October 8, 1836; *Boston Pilot,* March 8, 1862, May 25, 1861; *Bostoner Zeitung,* December 9, 16, 1865.

25 Cf. *Boston Merkur,* January 16, 1847; Dissertation Copy, 289, 290.

26 Cf. references to *Der Pionier,* Dissertation Copy, 290, n. 50.

The Development of Group Consciousness

[27] Cf. references to *Boston Pilot* and *Boston Catholic Observer*, Dissertation Copy, 290, ns. 51, 52.

[28] Wittke, *op. cit.*, 217–219; *Bostoner Zeitung*, November 11, 1865; *Der Pionier*, March 11, 1863, September 14, 1864, June 28, 1865.

[29] Cf., e.g., *Cork Examiner*, August 12, 1844; Dissertation Copy, 291.

[30] Cf. L. von Baumbach, *Neue Briefe*, 75; *Boston Pilot*, October 21, 1854; Wittke, *op. cit.*, 174.

[31] Cf., e.g., *Der Pionier*, March 12, 1862; Zachariah G. Whitman, *History of the Ancient and Honorable Artillery Company . . .* (Boston, 1842), 345 ff. 351, 371.

[32] Cf. *supra*, 203; *Boston Pilot*, July 22, 1854, February 24, April 7, 1855; *Irish-American*, February 24, 1855.

[33] *Boston Pilot*, December 22, 1855; cf. Combe, *op. cit.*, II, 199.

[34] Cf. *Boston Pilot*, March 20, 1841, March 6, 1858; *Der Pionier*, March 29, 1865.

[35] McGee, *Poems*, 155; Isabel Skelton, *Life of Thomas D'Arcy McGee* (Gardenvale, Canada, 1925), 261. For interest in the frontier, cf. advertisements of western land agents in *Boston Pilot*, April 24, May 1, 1852, April 2, 1853.

[36] Cf. Sister Mary Gilbert Kelly, *Catholic Immigrant Colonization Projects in the United States, 1815–1860* (New York, 1939), 40.

[37] Kelly, *op. cit.*, 37–47, 208, 209, 223–237, 241; Robert H. Lord, "Organizer of the Church in New England . . . ," *Catholic Historical Review*, XXII (1936), 184; John Gilmary Shea, *History of the Catholic Church within the . . . United States . . .* (New York, 1890), III, 472; *Boston Pilot*, June 22, 1852; Mrs. J. Sadlier, *Biographical Sketch . . .* (in McGee, *Poems*), 28; Skelton, *op. cit.*, 270 ff.

[38] Cf. *Boston Pilot*, September 13, 1856.

[39] Cf. *One Hundred Years of Savings Bank Service . . .* (Boston, 1916), 11; British Consular Correspondence, F.O. 5/397, no. 5; the Columbian Mutual in "Fourth Annual Report on Loan Fund Associations . . . ," *Massachusetts Public Documents, 1859*, no. 9, p. 11.

[40] *Boston Pilot*, April 24, 1847, July 3, 1858; Norman J. Ware, *Industrial Worker 1840–1860 . . .* (Boston, 1924), 195; John R. Commons et al., eds., *Documentary History of American Industrial Society* (Cleveland, 1910), VIII, 275–285; *Eighth Annual Report of the Bureau of Statistics of Labor . . . 1877, Massachusetts Public Documents, 1877*, no. 31, pp. 85–86; Dissertation Copy, 295. For the strikes, cf. *Third Annual Report of the Commissioner of Labor, 1887 . . .* (Washington, 1888), 1038; John R. Commons, *History of Labour in the United States* (New York, 1918), I, 566, 576; *Irish-American*, July 31, September 4, 1858.

[41] Cf. "Procession," *Boston City Documents, 1865*, no. 59, pp. 71, 72. Cf.

Notes to Chapter 6

also *Third Annual Report of the Commissioner of Labor, 1887* . . . , 1044; Boston Board of Trade, *Third Annual Report of the Government* . . . *1857* (Boston, 1857), 6–13; *Eleventh Annual Report of the Bureau of Statistics of Labor* . . . *1880*, *Massachusetts Public Documents, 1880*, no. 15, p. 15; *Boston Pilot*, October 24, 1863, February 6, October 22, 1864; *Third Annual Report of the Bureau of Statistics of Labor* . . . *1872*, *Massachusetts Senate Documents, 1872*, no. 180, p. 57.

42 Cf. Dissertation Copy, 297.

43 Cf. *supra*, 155 ff.; *Boston Pilot*, April 3, 1841. In 1857, a suggestion that the Scots Charitable Society organize an office to aid immigrant Scots came to nothing (cf. Scots Charitable Society, Records and Minutes . . . [MSS., N.E.H.G.S.], October 15, 1857, 25).

44 Cf. *Constituzione della società italiana di benevolenza, residente in Boston, Massacciussets, Stati Uniti di America* (Boston, 1842), passim; *Verfassung des deutschen Wohlthätigkeit-Vereins, in Boston* . . . (Cambridge, 1835), passim; Albert B. Faust, *Guide to the Materials for American History in Swiss and Austrian Archives* (Washington, 1916), 27; *Boston City Documents, 1865*, no. 59, p. 74.

45 *British Charitable Society for the Years 1849 to 1855. Report* . . . (Boston, 1855), 2, 3; *Boston Merkur*, July 10, 24, 31, August 7, 1847; *Der Pionier*, January 16, 1862.

46 Cf. *British Charitable Society for the Years 1849 to 1855*, 3; *Der Neu England Demokrat*, January 23, 1858; Dissertation Copy, 300; *Boston Merkur*, December 5, 1846, May 9, July 24, 1847; *Constitution, By-Laws and Rules of Order of the Hebrew Congregation Ohabei Shalom* . . . (Boston, 1855), 8; *Der Pionier*, January 5, 1860.

47 Cf., e.g., *Boston Pilot*, May 15, 1841.

48 Benevolent Fraternity of Churches, *Annual Report of the Executive Committee* . . . *1851*, no. 17 (Boston, 1851), 21; cf. also *Fifth Annual Report* . . . *Children's Mission to the Children of the Destitute* . . . (Boston, 1854), 3; "Cross and Beads . . . ," *Boston Catholic Observer*, November 8–15, 1848.

49 Cf. *Massachusetts Senate Documents, 1844*, no. 15, 2–4; *ibid.*, no. 79; *Boston Pilot*, December 4, 1858; Bishop John B. Fitzpatrick to J. P. Bigelow, May 29, 1850, Bigelow Papers (MSS., H. C. L.), Box VI.

50 *Boston Pilot*, March 21, 1863; William H. Mahoney, "Benevolent Hospitals in Metropolitan Boston," *Quarterly Publications of the American Statistical Association*, XIII (1913), 420; Rev. G. C. Treacy, "Andrew Carney . . . ," United States Catholic Historical Society, *Historical Records and Studies*, XIII (1919), 103; Shea, *op. cit.*, IV, 516.

51 Cf. Dissertation Copy, 302, 303, Table XXVI; Lord, *loc. cit.*, 183.

52 Cf. Shea, *op. cit.*, IV, 511.

The Development of Group Consciousness

[53] Cf., e.g., *Boston Pilot*, June 3, 1855.

[54] Cullen, *op. cit.*, 156; *Boston Pilot*, June 4, 1864.

[55] Cf. T. A. Emmet, *Memoir of Thomas Addis and Robert Emmet* . . . (New York, 1915), I, 501; *Jesuit or Catholic Sentinel*, January 29, 1831; *Boston Catholic Observer*, April 17, 1847, October 4, 1848; *Constitution of the Boston Roman Catholic Mutual Relief Society . . . 1832 . . .* (Boston, 1837); Dissertation Copy, 304.

[56] Cf. *Boston Pilot*, June 25, 1842.

[57] Cf. F. W. Bogen, *German in America* . . . (Boston, 1851), 11, 13.

[58] For the use of such words, cf. Karl Heinzen, *Luftspiele* (*Zweite Auflage, Gesammelte Schriften*, II, Boston, 1872), 172, 176, 177, 179, 181, 195, 212 and passim; A. Douai, "Der Ueberfall," *Meyer's Monatshefte*, April, 1855, V, 241; *Der Pionier*, January 31, 1861.

[59] Thus the Germans adapted the past prefix "Ge" to English words, viz., "hab' ich denn gesuppos't," "gekillt," "getschähnscht" (cf. Heinzen, *Luftspiele*, 170, 191). For English words in American French, cf. references to *Courrier des États-Unis*, Dissertation Copy, 306.

[60] Cf. "Annual Report of the Boston School Committee, 1864," *Boston City Documents, 1865,* no. 39, p. 164.

[61] Cf. *Minutes of the Selectmen's Meetings, 1811 to 1817 . . .* (*Volume of Records Relating to the Early History of Boston . . . ,* XXXVIII), *Boston City Documents, 1908,* no. 60, p. 171; Abraham G. Daniels, *Memories of Ohabei Shalom, 1843 to 1918 . . .* (s.l., n.d. [Boston, 1918]); *Constitution, By-Laws and Rules of Order of the Hebrew Congregation Ohabei Shalom . . .* (Boston, 1855); *Boston Pilot*, September 23, 1849.

[62] Cf. Lemuel Shattuck, *Report . . . Census of Boston . . . 1845 . . .* (Boston, 1846), 123; *Boston Merkur*, December 19, 1846; Justin Winsor, *Memorial History of Boston . . .* (Boston, 1880), III, 444; cf. *Journal of the Proceedings of the Annual Convention of the Protestant Episcopal Church in . . . Massachusetts . . . 1833* (Boston, 1833), 30; *Journal of the Proceedings . . . 1834* (Boston, 1834), 17; Benevolent Fraternity of Churches, *Twenty-Third Annual Report of the Executive Committee* (Boston, 1857), 3.

[63] E. Percival Merritt, "Sketches of the Three Earliest Roman Catholic Priests in Boston" (*Publications of the Colonial Society of Massachusetts,* XXV), 173 ff. Cf. also Shea, *op. cit.*, II, 315 ff., 387 ff.

[64] Cf. Merritt, *loc. cit.*, 185, 191 ff., 212 ff.

[65] Cullen, *op. cit.*, 125; *Boston Catholic Observer*, April 3, 1847; Leo F. Ruskowski, *French Émigré Priests in the United States . . .* (Washington, 1940), 11 ff.

[66] Cf. Merritt, *loc. cit.*, 198–201; Shea, *op. cit.*, II, 435 ff., 617, 621, III, 107 ff.; *Boston Catholic Observer*, May 29, 1847; McGee, *Catholic History,*

97 ff.; Ruskowski, *op. cit.*, 121; Frances S. Childs, *French Refugee Life in the United States* . . . (Baltimore, 1940), 40, 41.

67 Cf., e.g., *Annales de la propagation de la foi* . . . *1865*, XXXVII, 485. For Fitzpatrick, cf. Cullen, *op. cit.*, 131, 132. For Fenwick, cf. Lord, *loc. cit.*

68 Bishop Cheverus to Archbishop Neale, December 19, 1816, quoted in *Boston Pilot*, February 16, 1856.

69 Cf. *Boston Pilot*, January 28, February 25, 1843; Shattuck, *op. cit.*, 123; *Boston Catholic Observer*, April 17, 1847; *United States Catholic Almanac, 1833*, 46, 47.

70 Cf. *Boston Catholic Observer*, May 10, 17, 1848; *Boston Pilot*, January 21, 1843, September 29, 1855.

71 *Boston Pilot*, May 21, 1842, November 10, December 8, 1855, December 13, 1862, March 28, 1863; *Boston Catholic Observer*, July 5, September 13, 1848; *Cambridge Directory, 1865-6*, 185; Cullen *op. cit.*, 136; C. Bancroft Gillespie, *Illustrated History of South Boston* . . . (South Boston, 1900), 67, 73.

72 Cf. Rev. James Fitton, *Sketches of the Establishment of the Church in New England* (Boston, 1872), 146, 147; Shea, *op. cit.*, III, 486, 488, IV, 145; *Boston Pilot*, June 25, 1842, January 14, February 25, 1843, May 30, 1846.

73 Cf. *Boston Pilot*, October 31, 1863; *Boston Merkur*, June 12, 1847; *Boston Catholic Observer*, June 5, 1847; Richard J. Quinlan, "Growth and Development of Catholic Education in the Archdiocese of Boston," *Catholic Historical Review*, April, 1936, XXII, 32.

74 Cf. *Bostoner Zeitung*, September 1, 1865; *Der Pionier*, March 5, 1862.

75 Cf. *Official Catholic Year Book, 1928*, 407.

76 Cf. Fitton, *op. cit.*, 134, 135; Dissertation Copy, 316; *Boston Catholic Observer*, October 25, 1848; *Boston Pilot*, November 18, 1854, November 24, 1855; Shattuck, *op. cit.*, 124.

77 Cf. Quinlan, *loc. cit.*, 28.

78 Cf. *Boston Catholic Observer*, June 5, 1847; Quinlan, *loc. cit.*, 29; Winsor, *op. cit.*, III, 519; [Charles Greely Loring], *Report of the Committee Relating to the Destruction of the Ursuline Convent* . . . (Boston, 1834), 5.

79 Cf. Quinlan, *loc. cit.*, 30, 34; Gillespie, *op. cit.*, 67; *Boston Pilot*, July 24, 1858; Cullen, *op. cit.*, 134, 136; Moses King, *Back Bay District* . . . (Boston, 1880), 18.

80 Cf. *Massachusetts House Documents, 1849*, no. 130, p. 2; Lord, *loc. cit.*, 183.

81 Cullen, *op. cit.*, 135; Shea, *op. cit.*, IV, 515; *Boston Pilot*, December 24, 1864.

The Development of Group Consciousness

82 For examples, cf. *Boston Pilot,* January 18, 1862, June 4, 1864; Cullen, *op. cit.,* 132. Cf. also [Report on Dioceses Subject to the College of the Propaganda] (MS., B. A. Vat. no. 9565), fol. 132; Quinlan, *loc. cit.,* 30.

83 Cf. *Boston City Documents, 1864,* no. 30, p. 42; *Massachusetts Senate Documents, 1850,* no. 55, pp. 1 ff. For fees, cf. *Boston Pilot,* August 28, 1858.

84 Cf. *Literary and Catholic Sentinel,* April 16, 1836.

85 Cf. "Proceedings at the Memorial to Abraham Lincoln . . . ," *Boston City Documents, 1865,* no. 59, pp. 69, 73; also Dissertation Copy, 320.

86 Benevolent Fraternity of Churches, *Twenty-second Annual Report of the Executive Committee . . .* (Boston, 1856), 7, 8; Benevolent Fraternity of Churches, *Twenty-third Annual Report . . .* (Boston, 1857), 13; Benevolent Fraternity of Churches, *Twenty-fifth Annual Report . . .* (Boston, 1859), 23.

87 Cf. Dissertation Copy, 320–321; *Literary and Catholic Sentinel,* November 26, 1836.

88 Cf. *Boston Directory, 1853,* 382; *Der Neu England Demokrat,* November 21, 1857; *Bostoner Zeitung,* January 6, 1866; *Boston Merkur,* December 12, 1846, April 24, 1847; *Der Pionier,* March 14, 28, 1861.

89 Cf. *Courrier de Boston, affiches, annonces et avis . . . ,* April 23–October 15, 1789; Merritt, *loc. cit.,* 210; Howard Mumford Jones, *America and French Culture* (Chapel Hill, 1927), 136; George Parker Winship, "Two or Three Boston Papers," *Papers of the Bibliographical Society of America,* XIV, 57 ff., 76 ff.; Childs, *op. cit.,* 129.

90 Cf. *Courrier des États-Unis, journal politique et littéraire,* March 1, 1828, November 14, 1829, November 12, 1839, June 10, April 24, 1851.

91 Cf. *Literary and Catholic Sentinel,* December 10, 1836; *Courrier des États-Unis,* April 16, 1837; *Boston Almanac, 1846,* 145; *Le Bostonien, journal des salons* (Boston), May 12, 1849 ff.; *Gazette Française* (Boston), September 14, 1850–July 19, 1851; *Le Phare de New York, echo . . . des deux mondes,* February 24, 1851 ff.; also Henri Herz, *Mes Voyages en Amérique . . .* (Paris, 1866), 192 ff.

92 *El Redactor* (New York), March 10, 1828 ff. (apparently founded in 1827); *L'Eco d'Italia, giornale politico populare letterario* (New York), Februray 8, 1850 ff.; *Il Proscritto, giornale politico, artistico e litterario* (New York), August 7, 1851 ff. For others, cf. *Courrier des États-Unis,* August 2, 1849.

93 Cf. *Old Countryman: and English, Irish, . . . Colonial Mirror,* October 10, 1829; *Anglo-Saxon, European and Colonial Gazette* (Boston), December 22, 1855 ff., September 12, 1856; *Boston Pilot,* December 29, 1855; *European* (New York), November 15, 1856 ff.; *Scottish-American Journal,* January 30, 1864.

345

Notes to Chapter 6

⁹⁴ Cf. *Boston Merkur, ein Volksblatt für Stadt und Land*, November 21, 1846 ff.; *Der Neu England Demokrat*, October 17, 1857 ff.; Karl Heinzen, *Erlebtes, zweite Theil: nach meiner Exilirung (Gesammelte Schriften*, IV, Boston, 1874); *Gedenkbuch, Erinnerung an Karl Heinzen . . .* (Milwaukee, 1887), 8, 32; *Der Pionier*, April 29, 1863, February 28, 1861; *Bostoner Zeitung, ein Organ für die Neu England Staaten . . .* , September 1, 1865 ff.

⁹⁵ Cf. *Western Star and Harp of Erin* (New York), May 16, 1812–May 1, 1813; Louis Dow Scisco, *Political Nativism in New York State* (New York, 1901), 19.

⁹⁶ Lord, *loc. cit.*, 177. Another children's newspaper, *Young Catholics Friend*, edited by H. B. C. Greene, appeared for a short time in March, 1840.

⁹⁷ *Literary and Catholic Sentinel*, January 3, December 19, 1835, January 2, 1836. To avoid confusion with a later paper of the same name, it is referred to throughout this work by its original title.

⁹⁸ *Ibid.*, June 11, October 22, November 12, 19, 1836; McGee, *History of the Irish Settlers*, 132.

⁹⁹ *Boston Pilot*, December 22, 29, 1838, November 16, 1839.

¹⁰⁰ Cf. Mrs. J. Sadlier, *Biographical Sketch*, 17, 18; Robert D. McGibbon, *Thomas D'Arcy McGee . . .* (Montreal, 1884), 7; Skelton, *op. cit.*, 11 ff.; *Boston Pilot*, July 23, 1842, October 11, 1845.

¹⁰¹ Cf. Shea, *op. cit.*, IV, 154; *Boston Catholic Observer*, January 23, 1847, June 21, 1848. The break was not open at first, the *Observer* being printed by P. Donahoe, owner of the *Pilot* (*ibid.*, January 16, 1847).

¹⁰² The *Pilot* was at a tremendous disadvantage, since it could not openly attack the priest who edited the *Observer*. Its criticisms were guarded and apologetic. But its rival had no scruples, attacking it as "avowedly anti-Catholic," "guilty of uttering *heresy*" cf. *Boston Catholic Observer*, June 7, 14, May 24, and especially June 28, 1848).

¹⁰³ Cf. Henry F. Brownson, *Orestes A. Brownson's Middle Life . . .* (Detroit, 1899), 441; Skelton, *op. cit.*, 162 ff.; *Boston Pilot*, January 1, 1848, January 4, 1851.

¹⁰⁴ Cf. Sadlier, *loc. cit.*, 22, 23, 27–30; Skelton, *op. cit.*, 163 ff., 183 ff., 194 ff., 199, 281 ff.; *Irish-American*, August 12, 1849, May 30, 1857.

¹⁰⁵ Cf. *Citizen* (New York), January 7, 1854; *Boston Pilot*, March 24, 1855, April 24, March 27, 1858, April 2, 1859; *European*, December 6, 1856.

¹⁰⁶ Cf., e.g., *Memoir of Mrs. Chloe Spear, a Native of Africa . . . by a Lady of Boston* (Boston, 1832), 41, 49, 71 ff.

¹⁰⁷ John Hayward, *Gazetteer of Massachusetts . . .* (Boston, 1849), 88, 90, 97; *Massachusetts House Documents, 1840,* no. 60, p. 22; Winsor, *op.*

The Development of Group Consciousness

cit., III, 424, 425, 441; *Bowen's Picture of Boston* . . . (Boston, 1829), 149, 151, 152; *Boston Directory, 1830,* 31; W. H. Siebert, *Underground Railroad from Slavery to Freedom* (New York, 1898), facing 235.

[108] Cf. Dissertation Copy, 333 ff.; George W. Crawford, *Prince Hall and His Followers* . . . (New York, n.d. [1914]), 13 ff.; *Minutes of the Selectmen's Meetings . . . 1818 . . . 1822 (Volume of Records Relating to the Early History of Boston,* XXXIX), *Boston City Documents, 1909,* no. 61, p. 192; *African Repository and Colonial Journal,* May, 1830, VI, 89; *ibid.,* November, 1827, III, 271; Helen T. Catterall, *Judicial Cases Concerning American Slavery and the Negro* . . . (Washington, 1936), IV, 512 ff.

[109] Lewis Hayden, *Grand Lodge Jurisdictional Claim* . . . (Boston, 1868), 30 ff., 84; Charles H. Wesley, *Richard Allen* . . . (Washington, n.d. [1935]), 93; *Boston Almanac, 1866,* 166, 167.

[110] Cf. *Boston Pilot,* September 8, 1855, June 12, 1852, October 5, 1850, February 22, 1851; Catterall, *op. cit.,* IV, 502 ff.; *Colored American* (New York), January 7, 1837 ff.; Vernon Loggins, *Negro Author* . . . (New York, 1931), 53 ff.; William S. Robinson, *"Warrington" Pen-Portraits . . . 1848 to 1876* . . . (Boston, 1877), 71 ff., 191; Siebert, *Underground Railroad,* 72, 251.

[111] "Report of the State Board of Education," *Massachusetts Public Documents, 1860,* no. 2, p. 134; *Boston Pilot,* September 15, 1855.

[112] *Boston Pilot,* July 29, 1854.

[113] Cf., e.g., *Courrier des États-Unis,* May 15, 1851; Edward Dicey, *Six Months in the Federal States* (London, 1863), II, 179.

[114] "Annual Report by the City Registrar . . . 1865," *Boston City Documents, 1866,* no. 88, p. 15; *Der Pionier,* January 26, 1860. Table XXVII gives figures of intermarriage in 1863–65 when the degree of assimilation should have been at its height. Only German women married more closely into their own group than the Irish, and that because they were so far outnumbered by German men. However, German male intermarriages more than counterbalanced this.

[115] Cf., e.g., Winsor, *op. cit.,* II, 553 ff.; Wittke, *op. cit.,* 24 ff.; Cullen, *op. cit.,* 194, 195.

[116] Cf., e.g., "The Anglo-Saxon Race," *North American Review,* July, 1851, LXXIII, 53, 34 ff.; and Emerson's use of the term in "English Traits," *Collected Works* (Boston, 1903), V.

[117] Cf. M. A. DeWolfe Howe, *Holmes of the Breakfast Table* (New York, 1939), 7, 12.

347

Chapter VII. Group Conflict

1 Theodore Parker, *A Sermon of the Dangerous Classes in Society* . . . (Boston, 1847), 12.

2 Cf., e.g., the sober editorial on Negro problems in *Daily Evening Transcript,* September 28, 1830; cf. also Mary Caroline Crawford, *Romantic Days in Old Boston* . . . (Boston, 1910), 249; Helen T. Catterall, *Judicial Cases Concerning American Slavery and the Negro* . . . (Washington, 1936), IV, 524.

3 Cf. E. S. Abdy, *Journal of a Residence and Tour in the United States* . . . (London, 1835), I, 133 ff.; Odell Shepard, *Journals of Bronson Alcott* (Boston, 1938), 110.

4 Cf. [Theodore Lyman, Jr.], *Free Negroes and Mulattoes, House of Representatives, January 16, 1822* . . . *Report* . . . (Boston, n.d.); Henry Wilson, *History of the Rise and Fall of the Slave Power in America* (Boston, 1872), I, 489–492.

5 316 between the ages of 10 and 15 ("Report of the School Committee, 1866," *Boston City Documents, 1866,* no. 137, p. 188). Cf. also *Boston Pilot,* September 15, October 6, 1855.

6 Cf. the letters of Edward Everett to John P. Bigelow, dated July 23, 1839, September 30, 1839 (Bigelow Papers [MSS., H. C. L.], Box V, VI); Arthur B. Darling, *Political Changes in Massachusetts* . . . (New Haven, 1925), 320; Catterall, *op. cit.,* IV, 511, 524; Edward Channing, *History of the United States* (New York, 1925), VI, 93 ff.

7 Cf. Wilson, *op. cit.,* I, 492–495; Lady Emmeline S. Wortley, *Travels in the United States* . . . (New York, 1851), 60; Edward Dicey, *Six Months in the Federal States* (London, 1863), II, 215.

8 *Exercises at the Dedication of the Monument to Colonel Robert Gould Shaw* . . . *May 31, 1897* . . . (Boston, 1897), 10; Henry Greenleaf Pearson, *Life of John A. Andrew* . . . (Boston, 1904), II, 70 ff.; William S. Robinson, *"Warrington" Pen-Portraits* . . . (Boston, 1877), 107, 274, 406; A. B. Hart, *Commonwealth History of Massachusetts* . . . (New York, 1930), IV, 535; *Boston City Documents, 1863,* no. 100, pp. 11, 18.

9 Robinson, *op. cit.,* 298; cf. also Dicey, *op. cit.,* I, 70, 74; *Massachusetts Senate Documents, 1841,* no. 51; *Massachusetts House Documents, 1841,* no. 17.

10 Thus with few exceptions there was a "general absence of anti-Catholic references" in eighteenth-century textbooks, and the Dudleian lectures were founded to counteract "the rapid rise of liberalism" (Rev. Arthur J. Riley, *Catholicism in New England* . . . [Washington, 1936], 307, 23, 31, 225). The only exception was the hostility, primarily political, to Jesuit activities in Maine (*ibid.,* 6, 193 ff.; Channing, *op. cit.,* II, 131 ff.,

531, 545 ff.). Puritan intolerance sprang from the desire to found a "bible commonwealth" and was therefore directed against Baptists, Quakers and Arminians as well (cf. Channing, *op. cit.*, II, 68; Ray Allen Billington, *Protestant Crusade, 1800–1860, A Study of the Origins of American Nativism* [New York, 1938], 7, 15, 18; Riley, *op. cit.*, 45 ff., 217 ff. When priests visited Boston under circumstances that did not endanger the "Standing Order" they "received a cordial welcome befitting the social amenities exchanged between educated persons" (Riley, *op. cit.*, 190, 184 ff., 206, 207).

[11] Octavius B. Frothingham, *Boston Unitarianism, 1820–1850 . . .* (New York, 1890), 23; Archibald H. Grimké, *Life of Charles Sumner . . .* (New York, 1892), 38. For the popularity of the French in Boston, cf. H. M. Jones, *America and French Culture . . .* (Chapel Hill, 1927), 126; for the effect of the revolution, cf. John G. Shea, "Catholic Church in American History," *American Catholic Quarterly Review,* January, 1876, I, 155; Billington, *op. cit.*, 19.

Those who regard anti-Catholicism as inherent in the nature of Protestant society, and define "the Protestant milieu" as "nothing else than opposition to Catholicism" (Riley, *op. cit.*, vii, 1; "Anti-Catholic Movements in the United States," *Catholic World,* XXII [1876], 810; Billington, *op. cit.*, 1) have been hard put to explain the tolerance of the early nineteenth century. The simplest escape has been to mark it a period of subsidence arising from absorption in other problems (cf. Billington, *op. cit.*, 32; Humphrey J. Desmond, *Know-Nothing Party* [Washington, 1904], 12), with the anti-Catholicism of the forties and fifties simply a recrudescence of forces always present, thus missing completely the significance of the special factors that produced it in those two decades.

[12] Samuel Breck, "Catholic Recollections," *American Catholic Historical Researches,* XII (1895), 146, 148; E. Percival Merritt, "Sketches of the Three Earliest Roman Catholic Priests in Boston," *Publications of the Colonial Society of Massachusetts,* XXV, 218 ff.; William Wilson Manross, *Episcopal Church in the United States, 1800–1840, A Study in Church Life* (New York, 1938), 59; Samuel Eliot Morison, *History of the Constitution of Massachusetts . . .* (Boston, 1917), 24.

[13] Cf. Merritt, *loc. cit.*, 205–207; Billington, *op. cit.*, 20; Josiah Quincy, *Figures of the Past from the Leaves of Old Journals* (Boston, 1883), 311, 312; *Minutes of the Selectmen's Meetings, 1811 to 1817 . . .* (*Volume of Records Relating to the Early History of Boston,* XXXVIII), *Boston City Documents, 1908,* no. 60, p. 69; James Bernard Cullen, *Story of the Irish in Boston . . .* (Boston, 1890), 125; Leo F. Ruskowski, *French Emigré Priests in the United States . . .* (Washington, 1940), 85.

[14] Cf. Morison, *op. cit.*, 24, 32; *Boston Catholic Observer,* April 17, 1847;

Notes to Chapter 7

Rev. James Fitton, *Sketches of the Establishment of the Church in New England* (Boston, 1872), 141; Darling, *op. cit.*, 23; Hart, *op. cit.*, IV, 12.

15 Cf. Billington, *op. cit.*, 53 ff., 76. The Boston Irish Protestant Association which Billington claimed was anti-Catholic (*ibid.*, 78, n. 48) specifically disavowed such activities (cf. the correspondence in *Boston Pilot*, June 25, July 2, 1842; also *Boston Catholic Observer*, August 2, 1848).

16 Cf., e.g., *Jesuit or Catholic Sentinel*, July 23, 1831; Marcus Lee Hansen, *Immigrant in American History* . . . (Cambridge, 1940), 107.

17 James Freeman Clarke, *The Church . . . as It Was, as It Is, as It Ought to Be, a Discourse at the . . . Chapel . . . Church of the Disciples . . . 1848* (Boston, 1848), 13; Arthur M. Schlesinger, Jr., *Orestes A. Brownson* . . . (Boston, 1939), 175.

18 Cf. *Columbian Centinel* (Boston), January 26, 1791; *ibid.*, February 2, 1791; *American Catholic Historical Researches*, V (1888), 51.

19 Cf. Dissertation Copy, 347, 348; Billington, *op. cit.*, 43 ff., 69 ff., 79. For the religious press in general, cf. Frank Luther Mott, *History of American Magazines* . . . (Cambridge, 1938), II, 60.

20 Cf. the complaints on this score in *Boston Catholic Observer*, March 1, 1848; also Billington, *op. cit.*, 177, 86.

21 Cf., e.g., Darling, *op. cit.*, 29; Clarence Hotson, "Christian Critics and Mr. Emerson," *New England Quarterly*, March, 1938, XI, 29 ff.

22 R. C. Waterston, *"The Keys of the Kingdom of Heaven," a Sermon* . . . (Boston, 1844), 13; cf. also Frothingham, *op. cit.*, 48; *Jesuit or Catholic Sentinel*, December 29, 1830, *ibid.*, February 26, 1831.

23 Frothingham, *op. cit.*, 6.

24 Richard Price, *Sermons on the Christian Doctrine as Received by the Different Denominations of Christians* . . . (Boston, 1815), 8.

25 Cf. M. A. DeWolfe Howe, *Holmes of the Breakfast Table* . . . (New York, 1939), 17.

26 *Minutes of the Boston Baptist Association . . . 1821* (Boston, n.d.), 13.

27 Cf. Morris A. Gutstein, *Aaron Lopez and Judah Touro* . . . (New York, 1939), 98.

28 Cf. Massachusetts Commissioners of Alien Passengers and Foreign Paupers, *Report . . . 1851* (Boston, 1852), 14; also Edith Abbott, *Historical Aspects of the Immigration Problem* . . . (Chicago, 1926), 622, 739 ff.; *Cork Examiner*, July 6, 1853; *Massachusetts House Documents, 1828-29*, no. 25; *ibid.*, *1829-30*, no. 8; *Massachusetts Senate Documents, 1852*, no. 11.

29 Cf. the source of petitions for repeal of the State pauper laws, *Massachusetts Senate Documents, 1847*, no. 109.

[30] *Ordinances of the City of Boston Passed since the Year 1834 . . .* (Boston, 1843), 3, 4; Hart, *op. cit.*, IV, 143 ff.; Edith Abbott, *Immigration. Select Documents . . .* (Chicago, 1924), 105 ff., 148.

[31] Cf. Norris v. City of Boston (7 *Howard's U. S. Reports*, 283, XVII, 139 ff.); *Massachusetts Senate Documents, 1847,* no. 109; *ibid., 1848,* no. 46; Peleg W. Chandler, *Charter and Ordinances of the City of Boston together with Acts of the Legislature Relating to the City . . .* (Boston, 1850), 25 ff.; *Charter and Ordinances of the City of Boston together with the Acts of the Legislature . . .* (Boston, 1856), 34 ff.

[32] *Massachusetts Senate Documents, 1852,* no. 7, p. 7. For the influence of shipping firms, cf. *Massachusetts Senate Documents, 1847,* no. 109, p. 5; Boston Board of Trade, *Second Annual Report of the Government . . . 1856* (Boston, 1856), 3.

[33] For evidence of this complaint, cf. *American Traveller* (Boston), August 5, 1834; *American,* October 21, 1837; Abbott, *Immigration,* 112 ff.; Edith Abbott, *Historical Aspects of the Immigration Problem . . .* (Chicago, 1926), 572 ff., 758 ff.; *Massachusetts House Documents, 1836,* no. 30, pp. 9 ff.

[34] Cf. *Massachusetts Senate Documents, 1847,* no. 109, p. 4.

[35] *American* (Boston), October 21, 1837.

[36] Mayor Lyman (*Inaugural Addresses of the Mayors of Boston . . .* [Boston, 1894], I, 195).

[37] Cf., e.g., *Boston Catholic Observer,* February 16, 1848; Thomas D'Arcy McGee, *History of the Irish Settlers in North America . . .* (Boston, 1852), 71; Billington, *op. cit.,* 291.

[38] Cf., e.g., Ellie in Agnes E. St. John, "Ellie Moore or the Pilgrim's Crown," *Boston Pilot,* June 30–September 1, 1860.

[39] Cf. James O'Connor, "Anti-Catholic Prejudice," *American Catholic Quarterly Review,* I (1876), 13.

[40] Cf. Billington, *op. cit.,* 118 ff., 263; William Wilson Manross, *History of the American Episcopal Church* (New York, 1935), 283 ff.; *Boston Catholic Observer,* July 24, 1847; S. F. B. Morse, *Foreign Conspiracy against the United States* (s.l., n.d. [186–], 26, 3, 29; S. F. B. Morse, *Imminent Dangers to the Free Institutions of the United States . . .* (New York, 1854), passim; Louis Dow Scisco, *Political Nativism in New York State* (New York, 1901), 21.

[41] Cf. "Boston as it Appeared to a Foreigner at the Beginning of the Nineteenth Century," *Bostonian Society Publications,* Series I, IV, 117, 118; Joseph E. Chamberlin, *Boston Transcript . . .* (Boston, 1930), 37 ff.; *Minutes of the Selectmen's Meetings, 1811 to 1817 . . .* (*Volume of Records . . . ,* XXXVIII), *Boston City Documents, 1908,* no. 60, p. 113;

Notes to Chapter 7

Boston Pilot, September 12, 1846; Arthur Wellington Brayley, *Complete History of the Boston Fire Department* . . . (Boston, 1889), 185, 186; Edward H. Savage, *Police Records and Recollections* . . . (Boston, 1873), 65, 66, 110, 257.

⁴² Chamberlin, *op. cit.,* 48 ff.; Brayley, *Complete History,* 197 ff.; State Street Trust Company, *Mayors of Boston* . . . (Boston, [1914]), 15.

⁴³ Cf. *American,* October 21, 1837, March 17, 1838.

⁴⁴ There are numerous short accounts of this affair; but the best, though differing in interpretation from that offered here, is in Billington, *op. cit.,* 68 ff.

⁴⁵ Billington, *op. cit.,* 71 ff.; Shea, *op. cit.,* III, 462, 463; Charles Greely Loring, *Report of the Committee Relating to the Destruction of the Ursuline Convent* . . . (Boston, 1834), 8. Miss Harrison's disappearance was probably not important. In 1830 a rumor spread by the *New England Herald* (Vol. I, no. 28) that "a young lady, an orphan has lately been inveigled into the Ursuline Convent . . . after having been cajoled to transfer a large fortune to the Popish massmen" was ridiculed and had no repercussions (cf. *United States Catholic Intelligencer,* April 24, 1830).

⁴⁶ Billington, *op. cit.,* 81, n. 85; Benj. F. Butler, *Autobiography and Personal Reminiscences* . . . (Boston, 1892), 111; Darling, *op. cit.,* 165, n. 79.

⁴⁷ Cf. Billington, *op. cit.,* 69, 81–85, 86, 108; Loring, *op. cit.,* 2, 6, 16; *American Traveller,* August 15, 19, 1834; [H. Ware, Jr.], *An Account of the Conflagration of the Ursuline Convent . . . by a Friend of Religious Toleration* (Boston, 1834), 3; Chamberlin, *op. cit.,* 44 ff.; *Jesuit or Catholic Sentinel,* August 16, 1834; *ibid.,* August 23, 1834; Crawford, *Romantic Days,* 22.

⁴⁸ Cf. Ware, *op. cit.,* 10; *Jesuit or Catholic Sentinel,* August 23, 1834; Billington, *op. cit.,* 86, 87; Loring, *op. cit.,* 4.

⁴⁹ Robert H. Lord, "Organizer of the Church in New England," *Catholic Historical Review,* XXII (1936), 182.

⁵⁰ Cf. Billington, *op. cit.,* 89, 110, n. 27; *Documents Relating to the Ursuline Convent in Charlestown* (Boston, 1842), 21, 22, 31; "Anti-Catholic Movements in the United States," *Catholic World,* XXII (1876), 814; *Boston Pilot,* February 18, 1854.

⁵¹ Cf. *Boston Pilot,* April 16, 1853; Billington, *op. cit.,* 92 ff.

⁵² Cf. *American,* October 21, 1837; *Boston Pilot,* February 3, 17, 1838, October 12, 1839.

⁵³ Cf. State Street Trust Company, *Mayors of Boston,* 17; Darling, *op. cit.,* 327–329; William G. Bean, Party Transformation in Massachusetts . . . (MS. H. C. L.), 228 ff.

[54] *Boston Catholic Observer*, August 28, June 19, July 24, 1847; Bean, *op. cit.*, 232 ff.

[55] Cf. *Jesuit or Catholic Sentinel*, January 18, 1834; *Boston Pilot*, November 9, 1839; George H. Haynes, "Causes of Know-Nothing Success in Massachusetts," *American Historical Review*, III (1897), 74, n. 1.

[56] Cf. *Boston Pilot*, February 19, 1853; Dissertation Copy, 367.

[57] Cf. Josiah Curtis, *Report of the Joint Special Committee . . . 1855 . . .* (Boston, 1856), 11; "Report and Tabular Statement of the Censors," *Boston City Documents, 1850*, no. 42, p. 12; Billington, *op. cit.*, 325, 326.

[58] Cf., e.g., *Boston Pilot*, July 8, 1860.

[59] The only instance of devious Irish politics in this period came in the election of John C. Tucker to the legislature in 1860 (cf. E. P. Loring and C. T. Russell, Jr., *Reports of Controverted Elections . . . 1853 to 1885 . . .* [Boston, 1886], 89 ff.).

[60] Richard O'Gorman to W. S. O'Brien, May 24, 1849, W. S. O'Brien Papers and Letters, 1819–1854 (MSS., N. L. I.), XVIII, no. 2, 547.

[61] Cf. Darling, *op. cit.*, 312 ff.

[62] Cf. Robinson, *op. cit.*, 28–38, 416, 513; Bean, *op. cit.*, 8–38; Darling, *op. cit.*, 245 ff., 317, 334, 290, n. 67, 326; Wilson, *op. cit.*, I, 545 ff., II, 145 ff.; George S. Merriam, *Life and Times of Samuel Bowles* (New York, 1885), I, 45 ff.; *Reunion of the Free-Soilers of 1848–1852 . . . June 28, 1888* (Cambridge, 1888), 15, 17; Hart, *op cit.*, IV, 97; Grimké, *op. cit.*, 182 ff., 190 ff.

[63] Bean, *op. cit.*, 17, 28, 35 ff., 53 ff.; Darling, *op. cit.*, 340, 349–354; Grimké, *op. cit.*, 205; Haynes, *loc. cit.*, 80; Wilson, *op. cit.*, II, 247 ff.

[64] Cf. Bean, *op. cit.*, 54, 57, 64–87; Wilson, *op. cit.*, II, 347 ff.; *Address to the People of Massachusetts* (s.l., n.d., [Boston, 1852]), 3, 6, 7, 10 ff.; Robinson, *op. cit.*, 47, 433; Hart, *op. cit.*, IV, 99, 475.

[65] Alfred S. Roe, "Governors of Massachusetts . . . ," *New England Magazine*, XXV (1902), 547; Bean, *op. cit.*, 90–92, 113–120; Robinson, *op. cit*, 433; *Address*, 5 ff.; Grimké, *op. cit.*, 209.

[66] A simple majority sufficed in the Senate (Bean, *op. cit.*, 116; Morison, *op. cit.*, 38).

[67] Bean, *op. cit.*, 88, 89. Legislators from Boston were elected on a general ticket which usually denied representation to minorities and gave the whole delegation to the Whigs (cf. Morison, *op. cit.*, 41).

[68] The election of 1851:

	GOVERNOR			CONVENTION	
	State	Boston		State	Boston
Winthrop (W)	64,611	7,388	no	65,846	7,135
Boutwell (D)	43,992	3,632			
Palfrey (FS)	28,599	1,294	yes	60,972	3,813

Notes to Chapter 7

(*Boston Semi-Weekly Advertiser*, November 12, 1851; Bean, *op. cit.*, 109, 111). Cf. also Morison, *op. cit.*, 42.

69 Bean's claim that the Free-Soilers bolted (*op. cit.*, 111) is wholly illogical since they wanted the convention and the Irish did not (for the Free-Soiler's attitude on constitutional change, cf. Robinson, *op. cit.*, 401 ff.

70 Cf. in general, Bean, *op. cit.*, 127 ff., 217– 220. For the new attempt to revise the constitution, cf. *Massachusetts Senate Documents, 1852*, no. 36, pp. 6 ff.

71 Cf. J. B. Mann, *Life of Henry Wilson . . .* (Boston, 1872), 36 ff.; Hon. Charles Allen, *Speech . . . at Worcester, Nov. 5, 1853* (s.l., n.d.), 1–3; Bean, *op. cit.*, 147–166; Morison, *op. cit.*, 49–60; Henry F. Brownson, *Orestes A. Brownson's Middle Life . . .* (Detroit, 1899), II, 465, 466; Mann, *op. cit.*, 43.

72 For Free-Soil opposition, cf. Bean, *op. cit.*, 168, 177.

73 Cf. Brownson, *Brownson's Middle Life*, II, 455 ff.; Dissertation Copy, 377–378; Bean, *op. cit.*, 221.

74 Robinson, *op. cit.*, 204; Bean, *op. cit.*, 162, 166, 174–179; Butler, *op. cit.*, 119. The analysis of the vote from which Morison concludes that "the wards where most of the Irish-born population then lived did not poll so heavy a negative vote as the fashionable residential districts" (*op. cit.*, 63) is not valid because the wards were gerrymandered in the redistricting of 1850 to split the Irish vote (cf. Dissertation Copy, 383). Even in 1854 votes against the Know-Nothings showed no special concentration in any area (cf. *Boston Atlas*, November 14, 1854). Bean has shown that votes to defeat the constitution came from Boston: the 5,915 negative balance of Suffolk County more than offset the 997 positive balance elsewhere in the state (*op. cit.*, 173).

75 Butler, *op. cit.*, 120.

76 Cf. *Boston Semi-Weekly Advertiser*, November 30, December 3, 1853; Billington, *op. cit.*, 301.

77 *Boston Pilot*, October 8, 1853, February 11, 1854; Billington, *op. cit.*, 300–302; Desmond, *op. cit.*, 72; Shea, *op. cit.*, IV, 360 ff.

78 *Massachusetts Life Boat*, September 19, 1854; *cf. also Address of the State Temperance Committee to the Citzens of Massachusetts on the Operation of the Anti-Liquor Law* (Boston, 1853), 2; Billington, *op. cit.*, 323.

79 Cf. *Boston Pilot*, June 3, 1854; *Irish-American*, September 23, 1854; Billington, *op. cit.*, 435, n. 81; Bean, *op. cit.*, 187, 239, 241.

80 Cf. Bean, *loc. cit.*, 239 ff.; Carl Wittke, *We Who Built America . . .* (New York, 1939), 168.

[81] *Boston Pilot*, April 9, December 10, 1853, May 13, 1854, January 20, 1855; *Wide Awake: and the Spirit of Washington* (Boston), October 7, 1854; Billington, *op. cit.*, 305–313, 348 ff., 368; Bean, *op. cit.*, 207, 209; Shea, *op. cit.*, IV, 509; Charles W. Frothingham, *Six Hours in a Convent: — or — The Stolen Nuns! . . .* (Boston, 1855).

[82] Albert G. Browne to Sumner, July 28, 1854, Sumner Correspondence (MSS., H. C. L.), XXV, no. 109.

[83] Seth Webb, Jr., July 14, 1854, *ibid.*, XXV, no. 72; also Bean, *op. cit.*, 188 ff.

[84] Cf. Amasa Walker to Sumner, Sumner Correspondence, July 2, 1854, XXV, no. 15; Bean, *op. cit.*, 193; Merriam, *op. cit.*, I, 122.

[85] Cf. *Boston Semi-Weekly Advertiser*, December 10, 1853.

BOSTON ELECTIONS, 1853

Governor	(November)	Mayor	(December)
Whig	7,730	Whig	5,651
Free-Soil	1,403	Citizen's Union	4,691
Coalition Democrat	2,455	Young Men's League	2,010
Hunker Democrat	821	Democrat	596
Total	12,409	Total	12,948

(*Boston Semi-Weekly Advertiser*, November 16, December 14, 1853).

[86] Cf. Darling, *op. cit.*, 290; *infra*, Table XXVIII.

[87] Cf. Bean, *op. cit.*, 246.

[88] Cf. Billington, *op. cit.*, 380; Bean, *op. cit.*, 226; Desmond, *op. cit.*, 60; Scisco, *op. cit.*, 63 ff., 71 ff.

[89] Pearson, *op. cit.*, I, 65.

[90] Cf. Georg Simmel, "Sociology of Secrecy and of Secret Societies," *American Journal of Sociology*, XI (1906), 446 ff., 489.

[91] Webb to Sumner, July 14, 1854, Sumner Correspondence, XXV, no. 72; cf. also Wilson to Sumner, July 2, 1854, *ibid.*, XXV, no. 12; Bean, *op. cit.*, 192; Harry J. Carman and R. H. Luthin, "Some Aspects of the Know-Nothing Movement Reconsidered," *South Atlantic Quarterly*, XXXIX (1940), 221.

[92] Roe, *loc. cit.*, 653; Haynes, *loc. cit.*, 68; Bean, *op. cit.*, 259 ff.; George H. Haynes, "Know-Nothing Legislature," *New England Magazine*, XVI (1897), 21, 22.

[93] Robinson, *op. cit.*, 219. In Boston, 1,101 voters who had not gone to the polls in 1853 cast their ballots for the Know-Nothings together with the whole coalition reform vote, and almost half the Whig vote.

Notes to Chapter 7

GUBERNATORIAL VOTES IN BOSTON

	1853	1854
Whig	7,730	4,196
Know-Nothing	. . .	7,661
Free-Soil	1,403	401
Democrat	2,455	1,252
Hunker Democrat	821	. . .
	12,409	13,510

(*Boston Atlas, November* 14, 1854; *Boston Semi-Weekly Advertiser,* November 16, 1853).

[94] Benjamin P. Shillaber, "Experiences during Many Years," *New England Magazine,* VIII (1893), 722; George H. Haynes, "Know-Nothing Legislature," *Annual Report of the American Historical Association . . . 1896* (Washington, 1897), I, 178 ff.; Roe, *loc. cit.,* 654.

[95] State Street Trust Company, *Mayors of Boston,* 23.

[96] Cf. Billington, *op. cit.,* 425; Robinson, *op. cit.,* 62, 209, 210; Bean, *op. cit.,* 166, 268, 272–277, 284, 286–288; Merriam, *op. cit.,* I, 126, 132 ff., 164; Haynes, "Know-Nothing Legislature," *Annual Report of the American Historical Association . . . 1896,* I, 180–184; Bean, *loc. cit.,* 322.

[97] Bean, *op. cit.,* 261.

[98] Cf. Dissertation Copy, 389; Desmond, *op. cit.,* 77; *Boston Pilot,* May 13, 1854, April 7. May 12, 1855; Abbott, *Immigration,* 160, 161; Billington, *op. cit.,* 414 ff.; Bean, *op. cit.,* 291 ff.; Shea, *op. cit.,* IV, 510.

[99] Cf. *Debates and Proceedings in the Massachusetts Legislature . . . 1856, Reported for the Boston Daily Advertiser* (Boston, 1856), 141, 343, 348; Bean, *loc. cit.,* 322; Billington, *op. cit.,* 413. Most of these measures were sponsored by the purely nativist branch of the party, which declined in importance after 1854 and left the reformers in complete control (cf. Bean, *op. cit.,* 248). To those overlooking the concrete accomplishments of the 1854 legislature, the Free-Soilers under Wilson seemed to have "captured" the Know-Nothing organization in 1855 (cf., e.g., Haynes, "Causes of Know-Nothing Success," *loc. cit.,* III, 81). In fact, true nativists like Morse had so little sympathy for Massachusetts Know-Nothingism that they charged it was "a Jesuitical ruse, gotten up for the purpose of creating a sympathy in favor of the church" (Morse, *Foreign Conspiracy,* 31).

[100] Cf. Bean, *loc. cit.,* 324 ff.; E. Merton Coulter, *William Brownlow . . .* (Chapel Hill, 1937), 124 ff.; Scisco, *op. cit.,* 137; Carman and Luthin, *loc cit.,* 223.

[101] Cf. Billington, *op. cit.,* 407 ff., 426; James Ford Rhodes, *History of the United States . . .* (New York, 1893), II, 89 ff.; Bean, *op. cit.,* 295–

Group Conflict

322, 339 ff.; Mann, *op. cit.*, 50; Scisco, *op. cit.*, 146 ff.; Wilson, *op. cit.*, II, 423 ff.; Merriam, *op. cit.*, I, 165, 173 ff.; cf. also Fred H. Harrington, "Frémont and the North Americans," *American Historical Review*, XLIV (1939), 842 ff.

VOTE IN BOSTON, 1856

Presidential			Gubernatorial		
Frémont (R)		7,646	Gardner (KN)		7,513
Fillmore (KN)		4,320	Gordon (Fillmore KN)		7,511
Buchanan (D)		5,458	Bell (Whig)		1,449
		17,424	Beach (D)		5,392
					16,865

(*Boston Semi-Weekly Advertiser*, November 5, 1856).

[102] Cf. Fred H. Harrington, "Nathaniel Prentiss Banks . . . ," *New England Quarterly*, IX (1936), 645 ff. The "straight" American party nominated candidates in 1857 and 1858 but received a meager vote and then expired (Bean, *op. cit.*, 362–365). Gardner's personal popularity helped them in the former year but in the latter they received less than 2,000 votes.

VOTES FOR GOVERNOR IN BOSTON

	1857	1858
Republicans	4,224	6,298
Know-Nothings	4,130	1,899
Democrats	5,171	6,369
	13,525	14,566

(*Boston Semi-Weekly Advertiser*, November 4, 1857; *Boston Daily Courier*, November 3, 1858).

[103] Cf. Bean, *op. cit.*, 367–372; Bean, *loc. cit.*, 323; Charles Theo. Russell, *Disfranchisement of Paupers . . .* (Boston, 1878), 8; *Massachusetts House Documents, 1857*, no. 114; *ibid., 1859*, no. 34.

[104] Cf., e.g., the petition of the residents of Elm Street (Bean, *op. cit.*, 206).

[105] Cf. Ernest Bruncken, *German Political Refugees in the United States . . .* (s.l., 1904), 45 ff.

[106] Cf. the illuminating report of Consul Grattan to Crampton, Boston, November 23, 1855, British Embassy Archives, F.O. 115/160; also Rowcroft to Crampton, November 12, 1855, *ibid.*, F.O. 115/160.

[107] Cf. Grattan to Crampton, January 21, 1856, *ibid.*, F.O. 115/172; Grattan to Crampton, March 4, 1856, *ibid.*, F.O. 115/172; Abbott, *Historical Aspects*, 475, 476; *Citizen* (New York), August 25, 1855, February 9, 1856.

108 Lousada to Russell, September 8, 1864, British Consular Correspondence, F. O. 5/973.

109 Cf. Jeremiah O'Donovan-Rossa, *Rossa's Recollections* . . . (Mariner's Harbor, N. Y., 1898), 271, 272, 381; "Proceedings . . . ," British Consular Correspondence, F.O. 5/973; E. Wells to Lousada, *ibid.*, F.O. 5/973; *Boston Pilot*, November 21, 1863.

110 Cf. Bean, *op. cit.*, 257.

111 Cf. references to *Irish-American* and *Boston Pilot*, 1856–1860, Dissertation Copy, 397, ns. 301–303; *Boston Pilot*, November 3, 1860; *Boston Post*, November 7, 1860.

112 Cf., e.g., "The Anglo-Saxon Race," *North American Review*, LXXIII (1851), 53, 34 ff.

113 *Springfield Daily Republican*, July 10, 1857.

Chapter VIII. An Appearance of Stability

1 Quoted from Ralph Waldo Emerson by Ralph Henry Gabriel, *Course of American Democratic Thought* . . . (New York, 1940), 45.

2 Henry Greenleaf Pearson, *Life of John A. Andrew Governor of Massachusetts 1861–1865* (Boston, 1904), I, 205.

3 Cf. Dissertation Copy, 400.

4 Cf. William G. Bean, Party Transformation in Massachusetts with Special Reference to the Antecedents of Republicanism . . . (MS., H. C. L.), 370.

5 Cf. *Der Pionier*, August 13, 1862.

6 James Donnelly, "Song to Colonel Corcoran," *Boston Pilot*, July 20, 1861.

7 Cf. Marcus Lee Hansen, *Immigrant in American History* . . . (Cambridge, 1940), 143.

8 Cf. Edward Dicey, *Six Months in the Federal States* (London, 1863), II, 280 ff.

9 Cf. James Bernard Cullen, *Story of the Irish in Boston* . . . (Boston, 1890), 105–107; Daniel George Macnamara, *History of the Ninth Regiment* . . . (Boston, 1899), 4, 5; *Massachusetts Soldiers, Sailors, and Marines in the Civil War, Compiled* . . . *by the Adjutant General* (Norwood, 1931), I, 616; Dissertation Copy, 403, 404.

10 Cf. William Schouler, *History of Massachusetts in the Civil War* (Boston, 1868), I, 230; *Massachusetts Soldiers, Sailors, and Marines* . . . , I, 616, 617; F. Spencer Baldwin, "What Ireland . . . ," *New England Magazine*, XXIV (1901), 80, 82.

11 Cf. Charles William Folsom, Diary, 1861–1864 (MS., B. P. L.), III, March 17, 1863; *ibid.*, IV, March 17, 1864.

[12] Robert Ferguson, *America during and after the War* (London, 1866), 109, 110.

[13] Cf. the lists in *Municipal Register Containing the City Charter . . . 1866* (Boston, 1866), 58 ff., 105 ff., 173–184; also, *Massachusetts Senate Documents, 1861,* no. 2, p. 23; *ibid.,* no. 102; *Der Pionier,* May 23, 1861.

[14] *Boston Pilot,* July 27, 1861.

[15] *Boston Pilot,* February 1, 1862; "Report of the School Committee, 1863," *Boston City Documents, 1864,* no. 50, p. 42.

[16] "Proceedings at the Dedication of the City Hospital," *Boston City Documents, 1865,* no. 55, p. 95.

[17] Cf. *Boston Pilot,* September 6, 1862; John Tasker Howard, *Our American Music . . .* (New York, 1939), 583.

[18] Table XXXIII; Hamilton A. Hill, *Immigration* (Boston, 1875), 3 ff.; Hamilton A. Hill, *The Present Condition and Character of the Immigration Movement* (Boston, 1876), 4 ff.

[19] Table XXX; Carroll D. Wright, *Census of Massachusetts, 1875* (Boston, 1876), I, 302–303; U. S. Tenth Census, *Population* (Washington, 1883), I, 471; Rowland T. Berthoff, *British Immigrants in Industrial America 1790–1950* (Cambridge, 1953), 83.

[20] Table XXIX; U. S. Tenth Census, *Population,* I, 419, 420; John Daniels, *In Freedom's Birthplace* (Boston, 1914), 85 ff., 140 ff., 458.

[21] Daniels, *op. cit.,* 94, 99 ff., 103, 145.

[22] Wright, *Census of Massachusetts, 1875,* I, 279–282; U. S. Tenth Census, *Population,* I, 477–479, 536–537.

[23] Hamilton A. Hill, *An Inquiry into the Relation of Immigration to Pauperism* (Boston, 1876), 12, 13; Hill, *Immigration,* 8 ff.; Table XXXIII; Wright, *Census of Massachusetts, 1875,* I, 293–294.

[24] Table XXIX; Wright, *Census of Massachusetts, 1875,* I, 279–282; U. S. Tenth Census, *Population,* I, 419, 420, 450 ff., 477–479.

[25] Wright, *Census of Massachusetts, 1875,* I, XXIX, XXX; U. S. Tenth Census, *Social Statistics of Cities* (Washington, 1886), I, 113 ff.; Frederick A. Bushee, "Growth of the Population of Boston," American Statistical Association, *Publications,* XLVI (1898–99), 260 ff.

[26] *Boston City Documents, 1879,* no. 73; U.S. Tenth Census, *Social Statistics of Cities,* I, 106–107; Harold Murdock, ed., *Letters from a Gentleman in Boston to His Friend in Paris Describing the Great Fire* (Boston, 1909).

[27] U. S. Ninth Census, *Wealth and Industry* (Washington, 1872), III, 528, 677, 678; Wright, *Census of Massachusetts, 1875,* I, 551–555, II, 85 ff., 136 ff., 142, 350–352, 768, 857; U. S. Tenth Census, *Manufactures* (Washington, 1883), II, xxiv ff., 259–263, 379, 385–386, 390, 438; U. S. Tenth Census, *Social Statistics of Cities,* I, 159 ff.

Notes to Chapter 8

[28] Wright, *Census of Massachusetts, 1875*, II, 843, 901; U. S. Tenth Census, *Social Statistics of Cities*, I, 150 ff.; E. C. Kirkland, *Men, Cities, and Transportation* (Cambridge, 1948), I, 362 ff.

[29] U. S. Tenth Census, *Social Statistics of Cities*, I, 115.

[30] U. S. Tenth Census, *Social Statistics of Cities*, I, 111.

[31] U. S. Tenth Census, *Social Statistics of Cities*, I, 131 ff.

[32] U. S. Ninth Census, *Population* (Washington, 1872), I, 599; U. S. Ninth Census, *Vital Statistics* (Washington, 1872), II, 483, 502; Wright, *Census of Massachusetts, 1875*, I, xliii, xliv; U. S. Tenth Census, *Mortality and Vital Statistics* (Washington, 1885), XI, xxi, 501 ff., XII, 442–443, 444–445; U. S. Tenth Census, *Social Statistics of Cities*, I, 119; J. S. Potter, *Past, Present and Future of Boston* (Boston, 1873), 42 ff.; Carroll D. Wright, *An Analysis of the Population of the City of Boston* (Boston, 1885), 14, 15; Hill, *Present Condition of Immigration*, 12 ff.; Hill, *Inquiry*, 14 ff.

[33] U. S. Ninth Census, *Population*, I, 415, 440; Wright, *Census of Massachusetts, 1875*, I, liii; U. S. Tenth Census, *Social Statistics of Cities*, I, 137–139.

[34] Cf., for example, *Boston Pilot*, August 10, 1861, June 21, 1862.

[35] Barbara M. Solomon, *Ancestors and Immigrants* (Cambridge, 1956), 46.

[36] Cf. Lewis Hayden, *Grand Lodge Jurisdictional Claim . . .* (Boston, 1868), 50; Dissertation Copy, 408; *Boston City Documents, 1863*, no. 75; *ibid., 1864*, no. 6, pp. 31–34; Edith E. Ware, *Political Opinion in Massachusetts during the Civil War and Reconstruction* (New York, 1916), 103.

[37] Table XXX; U. S. Ninth Census, *Population* (Washington, 1872), I, 778; *Boston Pilot*, October 13, 1877.

[38] *Boston Pilot*, March 23, 1878, September 20, 1879.

[39] *Boston Pilot*, November 29, 1873. Cf. also Wright, *Census of Massachusetts, 1875*, II, 358, 825.

[40] *Boston Pilot*, May 1, 1876, June 23, 1877.

[41] James B. Cullen, *Story of the Irish in Boston* (Boston, 1890), 229 ff.; Joseph V. Donahoe and Michael J. Jordan, "Patrick Donahoe," American Irish Historical Society, *Journal*, XXIII (1924), 127 ff.

[42] *Boston Pilot*, April 28, 1876.

[43] Table XXXII.

[44] Robert H. Lord, John E. Sexton, and Edward T. Harrington, *History of the Archdiocese of Boston* (New York, 1944), III, 6 ff., 53 ff.; John E. Sexton and Arthur J. Riley, *History of Saint John's Seminary Brighton* (Boston, 1945), 51 ff.

[45] O'Reilly to Edward Whipple, March 20, 1878.

[46] *Boston Herald*, June 2, 6, 1866; *Boston Transcript*, June 6, 1866. Cf. in general, *supra*, 209; Henri Le Caron (pseud. of Thomas M. Beach),

Twenty-Five Years in the Secret Service (London, 1892); William D'Arcy, *The Fenian Movement in the United States: 1858–1886* (Washington, 1947).

[47] James Jeffrey Roche, *Life of John Boyle O'Reilly* (New York, 1891), 115 ff., 143; Carl Wittke, *The Irish in America* (Baton Rouge, 1956), 150 ff.

[48] Cf., for example, Arthur Mann, "Solomon Schindler," *New England Quarterly*, XXIII (1950), 457.

[49] Barbara M. Solomon, *Pioneers in Service. The History of the Associated Jewish Philanthropies of Boston* (Boston, 1956), 6 ff.

[50] Daniel L. Marsh, *Founders of Boston University* (Boston, 1932), 9 ff.; H. E. Scudder, *Henry Oscar Houghton* (Cambridge, 1897).

[51] Cf. *infra*, n. 74.

[52] Table XXX; U. S. Tenth Census, *Social Statistics of Cities*, I, 115.

[53] Berthoff, *op. cit.*, 158, 178, 191, 193.

[54] Table XXXII; William B. Whiteside, *The Boston Y.M.C.A. and Community Need; A Century's Evolution, 1851–1951* (New York, 1951), 63 ff.

[55] Cf., for example, Mary B. Claflin, *Under the Old Elms* (New York, 1895), 33–34; Scudder, *op. cit.*, 89–90.

[56] Arthur Mann, *Yankee Reformers in the Urban Age* (Cambridge, 1954), 7 ff.

[57] Solomon, *Ancestors and Immigrants*, 11, 13, 15, 21, 25 ff.; Alfred D. Chandler, *Annexation of Brookline* (Brookline, 1880).

[58] Julia Ward Howe, *Is Polite Society Polite* (Boston, 1895), 12–14; John T. Morse, Jr., *Life and Letters of Oliver Wendell Holmes* (Boston, 1896), II, 169.

[59] Table XXXII. Cf. also Alexander V. G. Allen, *Life and Letters of Phillips Brooks* (New York, 1900), I, 621 ff., II, 9, 26, 92; Morse, *Holmes*, I, 281; Solomon, *Ancestors and Immigrants*, 45; Timothy L. Smith, *Revivalism and Social Reform* (New York, 1957), 100 ff.

[60] *Boston Pilot*, July 7, 1877.

[61] Lord, Sexton, and Harrington, *op. cit.*, II, 719 ff.

[62] M. P. Curran, *Life of Patrick A. Collins* (Norwood, 1906).

[63] *Boston Pilot*, May 20, 1876, June 30, 1877, March 8, 1879; Roche, *op. cit.*, 142.

[64] Roche, *op. cit.*, 101 ff.

[65] Mann, *Yankee Reformers*, 24 ff.

[66] *Boston Pilot*, November 24, 1877, October 26, 1878.

[67] *Boston Pilot*, August 11, 1877, August 17, 1878, February 28, 1880.

[68] *Boston Pilot*, May 3, 1876, February 17, 24, 1877, January 19, 1878, June 29, July 6, 13, August 17, 1878, March 29, 1880; Roche, *op. cit.*, 185.

Notes to Chapter 8

[69] *Boston Pilot,* August 4, 11, 25, 1877.

[70] *Boston Pilot,* November 7, 1880.

[71] Curran, *Collins,* 37.

[72] Patrick A. Collins, *Speech in support of Charles Francis Adams for Governor of Massachusetts, Delivered at Marlboro, Massachusetts on September 14, 1876* (Boston, 1876); Roche, *op. cit.,* 128, 129.

[73] "Speech of Henry Cabot Lodge on Immigration," 60 Cong., Sess., *Sen. Doc. No. 423,* p. 3.

[74] James Parton, "Our Roman Catholic Brethren," *Atlantic Monthly,* XXI (1868), 433 ff. Rejoinder in *Zion's Herald,* May 28, August 13, September 10, 24, 1868. Lord, *et. al., op. cit.,* III, 66.

[75] *Boston Pilot,* October 7, 1876.

[76] *Boston Herald,* December 5, 6, 1925; Benjamin F. Butler, *Butler's Book* (Boston, 1892), 967 ff.; Cullen, *op. cit.,* 216 ff.; Solomon, *op. cit.,* 47 ff.; Oscar Sherwin, *Prophet of Liberty the Life and Times of Wendell Phillips* (New York, 1958), 586 ff.

[77] Hamilton A. Hill, *et. al., Arguments in Favor of the Freedom of Immigration* (Boston, 1871); Dr. Nathan Allen, "Statement," Massachusetts Board of State Charities, *Third Annual Report* (Boston, 1867), 31; Hamilton A. Hill, "Immigration," National Conference of Charities and Correction, *Proceedings 1875* (Boston, 1875), 92–96; "Report of the Committee on Immigration," National Conference of Charities and Correction, *Proceedings 1881* (Boston, 1881), 218–227; Solomon, *op. cit.,* 43. For differential fertility data, cf. Wright, *Census of Massachusetts, 1875,* I, xlii, xliii, 408–422.

Index

Index

Balls, 23, 156
Balzac, Honoré de, 146
Bancroft, George, 13, 23, 146
Bancroft's Grove, 156
Bank of the United States, 8
Bankers, 67
Banking, 8, 9
Banks, N. P., 194, 204
Banquets, 155, 157, 340
Baptists, 175, 183, 199, 220, 349
Barbers, 63, 70
Barry, John, 145
Bars, 66, 96, 121
Bartenders, 66
Bartlett, J. S., 172–73
Basements. *See* Cellars
Batterymarch Street, 114
Bavaria: emigration from, 34, 310;
  peasants of, 33
Bay State Artillery, 157, 203
Bay State Iron Company, 80
Beach, E. D., 357
Beach Street, 109
Beacon Hill, 13, 15, 96, 116
Beacon Hill Light, 13
Beacon's Grove, 156
Bean, W. G., 354
Beck, Karl, 29, 146
Bedini, Gaetano, 198
Beecher, Lyman, 181, 182, 186
Beethoven, L. van, 148
Beggars, 118, 310
Belknap Street, 96
Bell, 357
Benevolent Fraternity of Churches, 164,
  170
Benevolent societies, 59, 160, 161
Berkeley Street, 169
Berliner National-Zeitung, 170–171
Bible, 128, 169, 211
Bierhaus, 155
Bigelow, J. R., 78
Bigelow, John P., 76, 120
Billington, R. A., 350
Birth rate, 117, 228
Bishop, Robert, and Company, 80
Black Ball Line, 49, 299

Black Warrior case, 141
Blighted areas. *See* Slums
Bloomerism, 135. *See also* Women's
  rights
Board of Health, 16
Board of Overseers, 19
Board of Selectmen, 17, 23, 122
Boarding houses, 71, 96, 101
Bologna, 198
Bøndar. *See* Peasants
Bookkeepers, 67
Boott, Kirk, 82
Boston Academy of Music, 148
Boston and Chelsea Railroad, 100
Boston and Lowell Railroad, 98
Boston Catholic Observer, 137, 173,
  190
Boston City Guards, 190
Boston City Hospital, 211
Boston College, 169
Boston Courier, 182
Boston Debating Society, 182
Boston Dispensary, 115
Boston Gregorian Society, 170
Boston Irish Protestant Association, 350
Boston Laborers Association, 160
Boston Merkur, 172
Boston Pilot, 72, 143, 150, 176, 198,
  203; after *1865,* 216, 222, 224, 225;
  history of, 173, 174, 175; on con-
  stitutional reform, 196, 197; on revo-
  lution, 137, 140, 141
Boston Post, 202
Boston Repeal Association, 315. *See
  also* Repeal movement
Boston Rubber Shoe Company, 80
Boston School Board, 211
Boston Scottish Society, 155
"Boston System," 76
Boston Vindicator, 174
Bostoner Zeitung, 172
Bostonien, 171
Bounties, 209, 310
Boutwell, G. S., 195, 353
Brahmins, 177, 220, 221, 222, 224,
  227
Brass foundries, 79

364

Index

Brazil, 142
Bread Street, 110
Bread trade, 2
Brewing industry, 83
Brickmakers, 187
Bridges, 13, 89, 98
Brighton, 14, 100, 166; annexed, 214
Brillat-Savarin, J. A., 28
British Charitable Society, 161
British Colonial Society, 155
British North Americans, 52, 57, 155, 212, 220, 227, 318. *See also* Canada; and by province
Broad Street, 107, 108, 112, 113, 116, 117
Broad Street Riot, 187
Broadway Railroad, 99
Brookline, 14, 100, 166, 221
Brownson, O. A., 130, 173, 206, 333, 334, 336, 337; and the Irish, 149, 150; on constitutional revision, 196, 197; on revolution, 137, 139
Brownson's Quarterly Review, 149
Buchanan, James, 206, 357
Buffalo, 174
Buffalo Convention, 159
Building trades, 63, 318, 322
Bulfinch's Pillar, 13
Bunker Hill, 183, 187
Burgess Alley, 108, 114
Burns, Anthony, 175, 198
Burschenschaft, 27
Business district, 91
Butchers, 65
Butler, Benjamin F., 198, 227

Cabinet making, 64
Cahill, Dr. W., 60
Calderon de la Barca, Mme., 336, 337
Caledonian Club, 156
California, 4, 225
Calvert Naturalization Society, 197
Calvin, John, 144
Cambridge, 14, 15, 80, 96, 98, 166, 189; immigrants in, 212; Negroes in, 213
Cambridgeport, 89

Canada, 38, 159, 169, 212, 218, 298. *See also* British North Americans; Emigration
Canadian fraternal societies, 155–156
Canals, 6
Canton, 4
Carney, Andrew, 162
Carney and Sleeper, 82
Carpentry. *See* Building trades
Carroll, Charles, 145
Carroll, John, 165, 180
Cass, Thomas, 210
Casting furnaces, 79
Castle Island, 157
Catenoni, 310
Cathedral, 218
Catholic Church, abstinence societies, 169–170; activities against, 144, 187, 188, 199, 200; and abolition, 133; and Civil War, 208, 209; and common schools, 135, 136; and Irish ideas, 128, 129, 130; and Irish nationalism, 205, 206; and prison reform, 134; and reform, 133, 134, 135; and revolution, 137–141; and temperance, 134; and women's rights, 135; attitude to, in Boston, 180, 181, 182, 185, 186, 199, 215; charities, 161–163; churches in Boston, 164–167, 199, 217, 218, 227; conservatism, 133, 139, 141, 142; colleges, 169; French in, 164, 165, 166; Germans in, 158, 166, 167; in England, 186; Irish in, 128, 129, 130, 164, 165, 166, 223; laws against, 38; literature against, 189, 199, 200; newspapers, 172, 173, 174, 175; newspapers against, 181, 187, 189; on intermarriage, 176; prejudice against, 180–182, 190, 198, 203; schools, 167, 168, 169. *See also* Irish immigrants; Know-Nothing Party
Catholic Union, 223
Causeway Street, 93
Cellars, 109, 110
Cemetery, 187

365

Index

366

Index

367

Index

DuLang, 69
Duruissel, 68
Dwight's Journal of Music, 148
Dysentery, 115

East Boston, 10, 13, 14, 18, 99, 100, 114, 152; churches, 166, 167; ferry, 13, 18, 89, 100; industries, 10, 78–80
East Boston Company, 100
East Cambridge, 14, 98, 159, 166
Eastburn, Manton, 186
Eastern Railroad, 50, 179
Education, 22, 135, 136, 142, 167, 168, 169, 175, 196. *See also* Schools
Elections, 196; constitutional convention, 196; gubernatorial, 193, 196, 200–204, 355, 356, 357; municipal, 190, 200; presidential, 204
Ellie, 351
Ellie Moore, 334
Elm Street, 357
Emancipation Proclamation, 216
Emerson, R. W., 21, 22, 143, 207, 358
Emigrants. *See* by nativity
Emigration: assisted, 30, 37, 44, 51; economic, 29 ff.; from Baden, 34, 37; from Bavaria, 34, 310; from Boston, 12, 53; from Canada, 27; from England, 30, 32, 51; from Europe, 26 ff., 51; from France, 27, 28; from Germany, 27, 28, 30, 34, 35–38, 51; from Hungary, 27, 28; from Ireland, 27, 28, 31, 32, 42, 43, 46–51; from Italy, 27, 28; from Poland, 27; from Scandinavia, 33, 34; from West Indies, 28; Negro, 53, 212; of artisans, 30, 31, 32; peasant, 32–36, 46–51; political, 27 ff.; Scotch-Irish, 43; sporadic, 26
Employment, search for, 55, 59, 60
Enclosures, 32
Engineers, 68
England, John, 333
England: agriculture in, 32; and Civil War, 209; Boston attitude to, 124, 220, 222, 224, 225; Catholicism in,
186; clothing industry in, 322; consuls of, in Boston, 159; immigration to, 27, 28, 42, 43; industry in, 30; influence of, 23, 124; Irish hatred of, 143, 152, 153, 205, 209; oppression by, 38, 39, 152; trade laws, 2, 3; trade with, 3, 7. *See also* Emigration
English immigrants, 26, 213; and Civil War, 208; benevolent societies, 161; coffee houses, 66; dancers, 68; distribution of, 91; ideas, 136, 146; merchants, 68, 82; musicians, 69, 147, 148; nationalism, 151; newspapers, 171; number of, 52; seamstresses, 81; tailors, 322
English words, 163, 164
Enoch Train and Company, 49
Episcopal Church, 186, 222
Erie Canal, 6
Erina Association, 156
Europe: influence of, 22, 23; population of, 29. *See also* Emigration
European, 171
Everett, Edward, 189, 200
Evictions, 44, 46
Exclusion laws, 119. *See also* Restrictions
Expostulator, 172

Factory system, 10, 11. *See also* Mechanization of industry
Faith, 128, 131
Fall River, 7, 9
Famine, 43, 45, 152, 153
Faneuil Hall, 189
Farmers, 39. *See also* Peasants
Farmhands, 42. *See also* Peasants
Father Mathew Total Abstinence Society, 170
Father Wiget's, 169
Felton and Sons, 80
Fenian Brotherhood, 140, 141, 206, 209, 218, 223, 224
Fenwick, B. J., 137, 159, 165, 167, 169, 172, 181, 187
Ferguson, Robert, 359

368

Index

Ferries, 13, 18, 89, 100
Fertility, 117
Feuillants, 27
Fifty-Fourth Massachusetts Regiment, 179
Filibusters, 142
Fillmore, Millard, 204
Finance. *See* Banking
Fire, Charlestown Convent, 187, 188, 189; Duane Street, 18; of 1872, 214
Fire companies, 187
Fire Department, 18
Fishing, 2, 11
Fitzgerald, Edward, 27
Fitzgerald, J. R., 174
Fitzpatrick, J. B., and *Boston Catholic Observer*, 173, 174; and *Boston Pilot*, 140; and Brownson, 149; and Catholic churches, 165, 166; bust of, 202; Harvard degree to, 210, 211; letter on Irish famine, 152; on constitutional revision, 197; on revolution, 137
Follen, Carl, 29, 146
Food Dealers, 65
Forges, 79
Fort Hill, 13, 15; churches, 166; death rate, 116; Irish in, 93, 94, 100; saloons, 121; sewerage, 111; tenements, 107, 108, 109, 112
Fort Sumter, 207
Forty-shilling freeholders, 42, 44
Foster's Law, 41, 42
Foundries, 79
France, 22, 23, 27, 169. *See also* Emigration
Franklin Square, 102
Fraternal societies, 155, 156
Fraternity of Churches. *See* Benevolent Fraternity of Churches
Free Soil Party, 193–197, 200, 207, 355, 356
Free Trade, 225
Freedom of religion, 129
Freedom Party, 200
Freedom's Journal, 175
Freeman's Journal, 138

Frémont, J. C., 204
French immigrants, 26, 28; and Civil War, 208; Catholics, 164, 165, 166; cooks, 28, 66; cultural groups, 170; dancers, 68; distribution of, 91; hairdressers, 63; hotels, 66; Huguenots, 177; ideas, 136, 146; merchants, 67; musicians, 69; nationalism, 151; newspapers, 146, 171; number, 52
French language, 164
French Revolution, 22, 27, 141
Friends of Ireland Society, 152
Friends Street Court, 104
Frothingham, C. W., 200
Fruiterers, 65
Fugitive Slave Law, 194
Fugitive slaves, 53, 175, 179, 198, 199, 202
Fuller, Margaret, 141
Funerals, 187
Fur trade. *See* China trade
Furniture building, 64

Gabriel, Angel, 199
Gallieni, 66
Galway, 51
Gannett, Ezra, 23
Garbage collection, 17, 111
Gardner, H. J., 201, 204
Garibaldi, Giuseppe, 141
Garment district, 93
Garret bosses, 73
Garrison, W. L., 172
Gaston, William, 225
Gate of Heaven Church, 166
Gavazzi, Alessandro, 198
Gazette Française, 171
General Court. *See* Legislature
Geography of Boston, 91
German Assistance Society, 161
German Charitable Society, 161
German immigrants, 26, 28; and Civil War, 207, 208; and Irish, 145; and reform, 136; after *1865*, 219; balls, 156; benevolent societies, 161; birth rate, 117; boarding houses, 65, 66;

369

Index

Catholics, 158, 166, 167; charitable societies, 161; churches, 164, 165, 166, 167; cultural groups, 170; death rate, 117; distribution, 91; doctors, 69; fraternal societies, 156; gymnastics, 156; ideas, 136, 146; insurance companies, 67; intemperance, 121; intermarriage, 347; Jews, 52, 164; laborers, 60; lunchrooms, 66; manufacturers, 82; marriage rate, 117; merchants, 68; musicians, 69, 148; nationalism, 151; newspapers, 172, 335; number, 52; occupational dispersion, 57; picnics, 156; Republicanism, 205, 208; restaurants, 65, 66; schools, 167; seamstresses, 81; silversmiths, 83; sugar boilers, 77

German language, 146, 163, 164
German music, 147, 148
German Republican Association, 335
Germania Fire Insurance Company, 67
Germania Life Insurance Company, 67
Germania Society, 148, 156
Germany, agriculture in, 33, 34; industry in, 31; influence of, 23. *See also* Emigration
Gesangverein Orpheus, 170
Gilmore, Patrick, 69, 156, 211
Gioberti, V., 150
Girondins, 27
Glasgow, 43
Glass industry, 80, 300
Globe Iron Works, 79
Goldsmith, Oliver, quoted, 25
Gordon, 357
Gothic architecture, 16
Governesses, 62
Government, 215
Governor, Massachusetts, 194, 202. *See also* Elections; and by name
Grand Lodge of England, 175
Granite cutters, 160
Grant, U. S., 221
Graupner, Gottlieb, 147
Gray, Robert, 4
Gray and Woods Machine Company, 80

Great Britain. *See* England
Greece, revolutions in, 22
"Green hands," 73, 83
Green Mountain Grove, 156
Greenback movement, 225
Greene, H. B. C., 346
Grocers, 65, 328
Guillerez, F., 307
Gymnastics, 156

Hairdressers, 63, 70
Hale, E. E., 84
Half Moon Place, 107, 108, 111, 112
Halifax, 50
Halls, 156
Hancock, John, 12, 23, 180
Hancock, Thomas, 122
Handbills, 199
Handel and Haydn Society, 23, 147
Hanover Street, 114, 328
Harcourt, Ellen, 337
Harnden and Company, 49
Harrison, Elizabeth, 188
Harrison Street, 99
Harvard Law School, 224
Harvard University, 29, 146, 194, 210, 211
Haskins, G. F., 162
Haverhill, 9
Hawaii, 4
Hawes and Hersey, 80
Hayden, Lewis, 179
Hays, M. M., 340
Hayter, A. U., 69
Health, 16, 114. *See also* Disease; Vaccination
Heating, 112
Hebrew Literary Society, 170
Hecker, I. T., 150
Heinrich, A. P., 147, 148
Heinzen, Karl, 29, 156, 172
Heiress of Carrigmona, 335
Henry VIII, 144
Herman Lodge, 156
Hermann & Co., 338
Hibernian Hall, 156
Hibernian Lyceum, 170

Index

Index

Index

Index

Mechanization of industry, 73–80
Medford, 156
Mediai case, 141
Mediterranean trade, 299
Melrose, 156
Mendelssohn Quintet Club, 148
Merchants, 1, 2, 5, 7, 11, 12, 20, 22; and immigration, 82, 83; foreign, 26, 64, 67, 68; ideas, 20 ff., 125; nativity of, 64–68; Negro, 70. *See also* Manufacturers
Merchants Exchange Hotel, 66, 155
Methodist Episcopal Church, 164, 175, 220, 333
Metternich system, 28
Mexico, 142, 193
Middlesex Canal, 68
Middlesex Railroad, 98
Militia, 157, 175, 179, 190, 203. *See also* companies by name
Mill, J. S., 224
Mill Dam, 11, 13, 88, 89, 157
Mill Pond, 13, 15, 111
Milton, 221
Milton, John, 142, 143
Miscegenation. *See* Intermarriage
Mitchel, John, 45, 140, 153, 175
Mobility, economic, 70, 84
Moehler, J. A., 143
Molly Maguires, 225
Montgomery Guards, 157, 190
Montgomery Union Association, 152
Montreal, 174
Moon Street Free Church, 166
"Moral lectures," 23
Morison, S. E., 354
Morris, Robert, 70
Morse, Leopold, 82
Morse, S. F. B., 186, 356
Mortality. *See* Death rate; Infant mortality
Morton, Marcus, 193
Mother Superior, 188
Mt. Benedict, 168. *See also* Charlestown Convent fire
Municipal government, 17, 18
Music, 24, 147–148

Musical instruments, manufacture of, 64. *See also* Piano industry
Musicians, 69, 147, 148

Nancrede, Joseph, 171
Napoleon III, 141
Napoleonic exiles, 27
Nation (Boston), 174
Nation (New York), 174
National convention, Know-Nothing party, 204
Nationalism, 151–153, 205, 206, 223
Nativism, 190, 191, 199–204
Naturalization, 191
Nature, 21
Neck. *See* South End
Negelect of Prayer, 337
Negroes in Boston: and Irish, 133, 205, 216; after *1865,* 212, 213; barbers, 63; charities, 163; children, 179; churches, 175; crime, 121; distribution of, 96, 98; education, 175; emigration, 53; food dealers, 65; group consciousness, 175, 176; housing, 96; ideas, 136; immigration, 53, 179; in army, 179; in South Boston, 98; intermarriage, 176, 179; laborers, 60; Masons, 175; militia, 175, 179; newspapers, 175; number, 52; occupational distribution, 59, 69; on railroads, 179; prejudice, 205; prejudice against, 178, 179, 180, 224; riots, 186; sailors, 319; schools, 175, 178, 179. *See also* Fugitive slaves
Neu England Demokrat, 172, 335
New Bedford Railroad, 179
New Brunswick, 50. *See also* British North Americans
"New colonial system," 2
New England, 12, 57, 213
New England Herald, 335
New England Land Company, 67, 159
New England Reporter and Catholic Diary, 173
New Hampshire, 188, 213
New Orleans, 38,
New York, 172; cholera, 114; clothing

375

Index

377

Index

Quincy, Josiah, Jr., 18, 120
Quincy, Mass., 73
Quincy granite, 16

Racialism, 144–146, 177, 206
Radetsky, J. J. W., 138
Rafferty, P., 210
Rail factories, 79
Railroad crossings, 202
Railroading, 71, 72
Railroads, 6, 9, 215; horse, 94; Negroes on, 179. *See also* by name; Transportation in Boston
Randolph, John, 2
Rantoul, Robert, 193, 196
Reading, Mass., 156
Reading, 142, 170, 171
Real estate agencies, 67
Reason, 128, 131
Reconstruction, 221
Recruiting, 210
Reed, Rebecca, 187
Reform, 21, 131–135, 138, 192, 202–206, 216
Reformation, 143, 144
Reggio, Niccolo, 306, 337
Religion, 127, 128, 164–167
Religious education, 196. *See also* Schools
Religious liberty, 129, 130. *See also* Freedom of religion
Religious prejudice, 180–182
Remittances, 152. *See also* Prepaid tickets
Rents, 109, 301; in Ireland, 39, 40, 43
Repeal Movement, 133, 137, 152, 153, 173, 196
Republican Convention, 200
Republican Party, 150, 204, 205, 206, 207, 221, 226
Restaurants, 66
Restrictions, immigration, 118, 119, 179, 183, 184, 202, 203
Retributive justice, 126
Revere House, 66
Revolutions, 22, 27, 136–141, 349
Rhineland, 27; peasants, 33

Rich, Isaac, 219
Riots, 186–190, 220
Robert Bishop and Company, 80
Roby, William, 121
Roddan, John T., 137, 140, 174
Rolling mills, 79
Roman Catholic Mutual Relief Society, 162
Roman Republic, 138
Rousselet, Louis de, 165, 171
Rowing, 156, 157
Roxbury, 14, 15, 99; annexed, 214; churches, 164, 165, 167; Colonel Corcoran in, 211; elections in, 200; repeal movement in, 152; riots in, 186; schools, 169; Ursuline convent, 189
Rumpff, Rev. A., 164
Russia, 4, 5
Russian immigrants, 26, 147
Russworm, J. B., 175

Sacred Heart and Assumption Church, 166
Sailors, 64, 70, 186
St. Andrew's Day, 157
St. Augustine's Chapel, 165
St. Bartholomew's Massacre, 143, 144
St. Brandon, 145
St. James Church (R. C.), 166
St. James Episcopal Church, 164
St. John, Agnes E., 334
St. John, N. B., 50
St. John's Church, 166
St. John's Seminary, 218
St. Mary's Church, E. B., 166
St. Mary's Church, N. E., 168
St. Nicholas Church, 166
St. Patrick's Day, 155, 157, 158, 210
St. Peter's Church, 166
St. Vincent's Female Orphan Asylum, 162, 168
Saints' days, 157
SS. Peter and Paul Church, 166, 168
Salesmen, 67
Saloon keepers, 66
Saloons, 65, 66, 121. *See also* Bars

378

Index

379

Index

Index

Oscar Handlin

Oscar Handlin is Charles Warren Professor of American History at Harvard University. *Boston's Immigrants* was first published in 1941, when it won the Dunning Prize of the American Historical Association. In 1951 Professor Handlin won the Pulitzer Prize for his book *The Uprooted*.

Praise for Jasper Fforde and *First Among Sequels*

'Clever, funny and pacey, this is cult reading for the beach.'
Daily Mail

'Fforde describes a melange of the mundane and the
phantasmagorical that reads like a well-edited Harry Potter; *First
Among Sequels* is for adults who want sophisticated wit
with their fantasy, but who still possess an appreciation for the
intricate world-building of a well-imagined children's novel.'
New Statesman

'Fforde is highly inventive' *The Sunday Times*

'[Jasper Fforde] is the wittiest novelist around' *Sunday Telegraph*

'Jasper Fforde has gone where no other fictioneer has gone
before. Millions of readers now follow. Thank you, Jasper'
Guardian

'Jasper Fforde's imagination is a literary volcano in full spate'
Independent

'Ingenious – I'll watch Jasper Fforde nervously' Terry Pratchett

'Don't ask. Just read it. Fforde is a true original' *Sunday Express*

'I kicked the door open, dislodging the Danverclone, who seemed to hang in the air for a moment before a large wave caught her and she was left behind the rapidly moving taxi.'

FIRST AMONG SEQUELS

A BookWorld Novel

JASPER FFORDE

HODDER

First published in Great Britain in 2007 by Hodder & Stoughton
An Hachette Livre UK company

First published in paperback in 2008

I

Copyright © Jasper Fforde 2007

The right of Jasper Fforde to be identified as the Author
of the Work has been asserted by him in accordance with the
Copyright, Designs and Patents Act 1988.

A CIP catalogue record for this title is
available from the British Library

A format ISBN 978 0 340 839843
B format ISBN 978 0 340 75202 9

Typeset in Bembo by Palimpsest Book Production,
Grangemouth, Stirlingshire

Printed and bound by
Clays Ltd, St Ives plc

Hodder & Stoughton policy is to use papers that are natural, renewable
and recyclable products and made from wood grown in sustainable
forests. The logging and manufacturing processes are expected to
conform to the environmental regulations of the country of origin.

Hodder and Stoughton Ltd
338 Euston Road
London NW1 3BH

www.hodder.co.uk

For Cressida,
the bestest sister in the world.

The year is 2002. It is fourteen years since Thursday almost pegged out at the 1988 Croquet SuperHoop, and life is beginning to get back to normal . . .

Author's Note:

This book has been bundled with **Special Features** including:
The Making of . . . wordamentary, deleted scenes,
alternative endings and much more.

To access all these free bonus features,
log on to: **www.jasperfforde.com/features.html**
and follow the onscreen instructions.

Contents

I

Breakfast

'The Swindon I knew in 2002 had a lot going for it. A
busy financial centre coupled with excellent infrastructure and
surrounded by green and peaceful countryside had made the city
about as popular a place as you might find anywhere in the
nation. We had our own 40,000-seater croquet stadium, the newly
finished Cathedral of St Zvlkx, a concert hall, two local TV
networks and the only radio station in England dedicated solely
to mariachi music. Our central position in southern England also
made us the hub for hi-speed overland travel from the newly
appointed Clary-LaMarr travelport. It was little wonder that we
called Swindon "The Jewel on the M4".'

The dangerously high level of the Stupidity Surplus was once again
the lead story in *The Owl* that morning. The reason for the crisis
was clear: Prime Minister Redmond Van de Poste and his ruling
Commonsense Party had been discharging their duties with a reckless degree of responsibility that bordered on inspired sagacity. Instead
of drifting from one crisis to the next and appeasing the nation
with a steady stream of knee-jerk legislation and headline-grabbing
but arguably pointless initiatives, they had been resolutely building
a raft of considered long-term plans that concentrated on unity,
fairness and tolerance. It was a state of affairs deplored by Mr Alfredo
Traficcone, leader of the opposition 'Prevailing Wind' party, who
wanted to lead the nation back on to the safer grounds of unin-
formed stupidity.

'How could they let it get this bad?' asked Landen as he walked
into the kitchen, having just dispatched our daughters off to school.

They walked themselves, naturally; Tuesday was thirteen and took great pride in looking after Jenny, who was now ten.

'Sorry?' I said, my mind full of other matters, foremost among them the worrying possibility that Pickwick's plumage might *never* grow back, and that she would have to spend the rest of her life looking like a Tesco's oven-ready chicken.

'The Stupidity Surplus,' repeated Landen as he sat down at the kitchen table. 'I'm all for responsible government, but storing it up like this is bound to cause problems sooner or later – even by acting sensibly, the government has shown itself to be a bunch of idiots.'

'There are a lot of idiots in this country,' I replied absently, 'and they deserve representation as much as the next man.'

But he was right. Unlike previous governments, which had skil-fully managed to eke out our collective stupidity all year round, the current administration had decided to store it all up and then blow it on something *unbelievably* dopey, arguing that one major balls-up every ten years or so was less damaging than a weekly helping of mild political asininity. The problem was, the surplus had reached absurdly high levels where it had even surpassed the 'monu-mentally dumb' mark. Only a blunder of staggering proportions would remove the surplus, and the nature of this mind-numbing act of idiocy was a matter of considerable media speculation.

'It says here,' he said, getting into full rant mode by adjusting his spectacles and tapping at the newspaper with his index finger, 'that even the government is having to admit that the Stupidity Surplus is a far, far bigger problem than they had first imagined.'

I held the striped dodo-cosy I was knitting for Pickwick against her pink and blotchy body to check the size and she puffed herself up to look more alluring, but to no avail. She then made an indig-nant plocking noise which was the only sound she ever uttered.

'Do you think I should knit her a party one as well? Y'know, black, off the shoulder and with sparkly bits in it?'

'But,' Landen went on in a lather of outrage, 'the prime minister has poured scorn on Traficcone's suggestion to offload our unwanted stupidity on Third World nations, who would be only too happy to have it in exchange for several sacks of cash and a Mercedes or two.'

'He's right,' I replied with a sigh, 'Idiocy Offsets are bullshit; stupidity is our own problem and has to be dealt with on an individual "stupidity footprint" basis – and landfill *certainly* doesn't work.'

I was thinking of the debacle in Cornwall, where 40,000 tons of half-wittedness was buried in the sixties, only for it to percolate to the surface two decades later, when the residents started to do inexplicably dumb things, such as using an electric hand whisk in the bath, and parting their hair in the centre.

'What if,' Landen continued thoughtfully, 'the thirty million or so inhabitants of the British Archipelago were to all simultaneously fall for one of those e-mail "tell us all your bank details" phishing scams or – I don't know – fall down a manhole or something?'

'They tried the mass "walking-into-lamp-post" experiment in France to try and alleviate *La Dette Idiote*,' I pointed out, 'but the seriousness under which the plan was undertaken made it de facto sensible, and all that was damaged was the proud Gallic forehead.'

Landen took a sip of coffee, unfolded the paper and scanned the rest of the front page before remarking absently:

'I took up your idea and sent my publisher a few outlines for self-help books last week.'

'Who do they think you should be helping?'

'Well . . . *me* . . . and them, I suppose – isn't that how it's meant to work? It looks really easy. How about this for a title: *Men Are from Earth, Women Are from Earth – Just Deal with It.*'

He looked at me and smiled, and I smiled back. I didn't just love him because he had a nice knee, was tall and made me laugh, but because we were two parts of one whole, and neither of us could imagine life without the other. I wish I had a better way to describe it, but I'm not a poet. Privately he was a husband and father to our three mostly wonderful kids, but professionally he was a writer. Unfortunately, despite winning the 1988 Armitage Shanks fiction award for *Bad Sofa*, a string of flops had left the relationship with his publisher a bit strained. So strained, in fact, that he was reduced to penning point-of-sale non-fiction classics such as: *The Little Book of Cute Pets that You Really Like to Hug* and *The Darnedest Things Kids Say*. When he wasn't working on these he was looking after our children and attempting to rekindle his career with a seriously good blockbuster – his Magnum Opus. It wasn't easy, but it was what he loved and I loved *him*, so we lived off my salary, which was about the size of Pickwick's brain – not that big, and unlikely to become so.

'This is for you,' said Landen, pushing a small parcel wrapped in pink paper across the table.

'Sweetheart,' I said, *really* annoyed and *really* pleased all at the same time, 'I don't do birthdays.'

'I know,' he said without looking up, 'so you'll just have to humour me.'

I unwrapped the package to find a small silver locket and chain. I'm not a jewellery person but I am a *Landen* person, so held my hair out of the way while he fitted the clasp, then thanked him and gave him a kiss, which he returned. And then, since he knew all about my abhorrence of birthdays, he dropped the matter entirely.

'Is Friday up?'

'At this hour?'

Friday, it should be noted, was the eldest of our three children and the only boy. He was now sixteen and instead of gearing himself up for a successful career with the Time Industry's elite operatives known as the ChronoGuard, he was instead a tedious teenage cliché – grunting, sighing at any request no matter how small and staying

4

in bed until past midday, then mooching around the house in a state of semi-consciousness that would do credit to a career zombie. We might not have known he was living with us if it wasn't for the grubby cereal bowls that mysteriously appeared in the vague vicinity of the sink, a muffled heavy-metal beat from his bedroom that Landen was convinced kept the slugs from the garden, and a succession of equally languid no-hopers who called at the door to mumble: 'Is Friday at home?', something that I couldn't resist answering with: 'It's a matter of some conjecture.'

'When does he go back to school?' asked Landen, who did most of the day-to-day kid work but, like many men, had trouble remembering specific dates.

'Next Monday,' I replied, having gone to retrieve the mail that had just fallen through the door. 'Exclusion from school was better than he deserved – it's a good job the cops didn't get involved.'

'All he did was throw Barney Plotz's cap in a muddy puddle,' said Landen reflectively, 'and then stomp on it.'

'Yes, but Barney Plotz was *wearing* it at the time,' I pointed out, thinking privately that the entire Plotz family stomped on in a muddy puddle might be a very good idea indeed. 'Friday shouldn't have done what he did. Violence never solved anything.'

Landen raised an eyebrow and looked at me.

'Okay, *sometimes* it solves things – but not for him, at least not yet.'

'I wonder,' mused Landen, 'if we could get the nation's teenagers to go on a serious binge of alcohol-inspired dopiness to use up the excess stupidity?'

'It's a surplus of stupidity we have, not stereotypical dreariness,' I replied, picking up an envelope at random and staring at the postmark. I still received at least half a dozen fan letters every day, even though the march of time had thankfully reduced my celebrity to what the Entertainments Facilitation Department termed 'Z-4',

5

which is the kind who appear in 'Whatever happened to . . . ?' articles and only ever get column inches if arrested, divorced, in rehab or, if the editor's luck is really in, all three at the same time – and with some tenuous connection to Miss Corby Starlet, or whoever else happens to be the *célébrité du jour*.

The fan mail was mostly from diehard fans who didn't care I was Z-4, bless them. They usually asked obscure questions about my many adventures that were now in print, or something about how crap the movie was, or why I'd given up professional croquet. But for the most part it was from fans of *Jane Eyre* who wanted to know how Mrs Fairfax could have been a ninja assassin, whether I *had* to shoot Bertha Rochester and if it was true I had slept with Edward Rochester – three of the more persistent and untrue rumours surrounding the factually dubious first novel of my adventures, *The Eyre Affair*.

'What's it about?' Landen grinned. 'Someone wanting to know whether Lola Vavoom will play you in the next Thursday film?'

'There won't be one. Not after the disaster of the first. No, it's from the World Croquet Federation. They want me to present a video entitled *The Fifty Greatest Croquet Sporting Moments*.'

'Is your Superhoop fifty-yard peg-out in the top ten?'

I scanned the list.

'They have me at twenty-six.'

'Tell them bollocks.'

'They'll pay me five hundred guineas.'

'Cancel the bollocks thing – tell them you'll be honoured and overjoyed.'

'It's a sell-out. I don't do sell-outs. Not for *that* price, anyway.'

I opened a small parcel that contained a copy of the third book in my series: *The Well of Lost Plots*. I showed it to Landen, who pulled a face.

'Are they still selling?'

'Unfortunately.'

'Am I in that one?'

'No, sweetheart – you're only in number five.'

I looked at the covering letter.

'They want me to sign it.'

I had a stack of standard letters in the office that explained why I *wouldn't* sign it – the first four Thursday Next books were about as true to real life as a donkey is to a turnip, and my signature somehow gave a credibility that I didn't want to encourage. The only book I *would* sign was the fifth in the series, *The Great Samuel Pepys Fiasco*, which unlike the first four had my seal of approval. The Thursday Next in *The Great Samuel Pepys Fiasco* was much more of a caring and diplomatic heroine – unlike the Thursday in the previous four, who blasted away at everything in sight, drank, swore, slept around and generally kicked butt all over the BookWorld. I wanted the series to be a thought-provoking romp around literature; books for people who like stories or stories for people who like books. It wasn't to be. The first four in the series had been less light-hearted chroniclings of my adventures and more 'Dirty Harry meets Fanny Hill', but with a good deal more sex and violence. The publishers not only managed to be factually inaccurate but dangerously slanderous as well. By the time I had regained control of the series for *The Great Samuel Pepys Fiasco*, the damage to my reputation had been done.

'Oh-ho!' said Landen, reading a letter. 'A rejection from my publishers. They didn't think *Fatal Parachuting Mistakes and How to Avoid Making Them Again* was what they had in mind for self-help.'

'I guess their target audience doesn't include dead people.'

'You could be right.'

I opened another letter.

'Hang on,' I said, scanning the lines thoughtfully, 'the Swindon Dodo Fanciers' Society are offering us thirty grand for Pickers.'

I looked across at Pickwick, who had started to do that 'almost falling over' thing she does when she goes to sleep standing up. I had built her myself when home-cloning kits were all the rage. At almost twenty-nine and with the serial number D-009 she was the oldest Dodo in existence. Because she was an early version 1.2 she didn't have any wings as the sequence wasn't complete at that time, but then she didn't have built-in cell redundancy either. It was likely she'd outlive . . . well, everything. In any event, her value had grown considerably as interest in the seventies home-cloning unextincting revolution had suddenly become fashionable. A 1978 V1.5.6 mammoth recently changed hands for sixty thousand, Great Auks in any condition could be worth up to five grand each and if you had a pre-1972 trilobite of any order you could pretty much name your price.

'Thirty grand?' echoed Landen. 'Do they know she's a bit challenged in the brain and plumage department?'

'I honestly don't think they care. It would pay off the mortgage.'

Pickwick was suddenly wide awake, and looked at us with the dodo equivalent of a raised eyebrow, which is indistinguishable from the dodo equivalent of sniffing a raw onion.

'. . . and buy one of those new diesel-molasses hybrid cars.'

'Or a holiday.'

'We could send Friday off to the Swindon Home for Dreary Teenagers,' added Landen.

'And Jenny could have a new piano.'

It was too much for Pickwick, who fainted dead away in the centre of the table.

'Doesn't have much of a sense of humour, does she?' said Landen with a smile, returning to his paper.

'Not really,' I replied, tearing up the letter from the Swindon Dodo Fanciers' Society, 'but you know, for a bird of Incalculably Little Brain, I'm sure she understands almost everything we say.'

Landen looked at Pickwick, who had recovered and was staring

8

suspiciously at her left foot, wondering whether it had *always* been there, and if not, what it might be doing creeping up on her.

'It's not likely.'

'How's the book going?' I asked, returning to my knitting.

'The self-help stuff?'

'The Magnum Opus.'

Landen looked thoughtful for a moment and then said:

'More Opus than Magnum. I'm trying to figure out whether the lack of progress is writer's block, procrastination, idleness or just plain incompetence.'

'Well now,' I said, feigning seriousness, 'with such an excellent choice, it's hard to put my finger on it – have you considered that it might be a mixture of all four?'

'By Gad!' he said, slapping his palm on his forehead. 'You could be right!'

'Seriously, though?'

He shrugged.

'It's so-so. Although the story is toodling along there's no real bite to it – I really need to inject a new plot twist or character.'

'Which book are you working on?'

'*Bananas for Edward.*'

'You'll think of something, sweetheart – you usually do.'

I dropped a stitch on my knitting, rehooked it, checked the wall clock and then said:

'Mum texted me earlier.'

'Has she got the hang of it yet?'

'She said: "L&Ks4DnRNXT-SNDY??"'

'Hmm,' said Landen, 'one of the most coherent yet. That's probably code for "I've forgotten how to text". Why does she even bother to try and use new technology at her age?'

'You know what she's like. I'll nip over and see what she wants on my way to work.'

'Don't forget about Friday and the ChronoGuard *If you've got time for us we've got time for you* careers presentation this evening.'

'How could I forget?' I replied, having cajoled Friday about this for weeks.

'He's behind with his homework,' added Landen, 'and since you're at least six times more scary than I am, would you do phase one of the teenager waking procedure? Sometimes I think he's actually glued to the bed.'

'Considering his current level of personal hygiene,' I mused, 'you're probably right.'

'If he doesn't get up,' added Landen with a smile, 'you could always threaten him with a bar of soap and some shampoo.'

'And traumatise the poor lad? Shame on *you*, Mr Parke-Laine.'

Landen laughed and I went up to Friday's room.

I knocked on his door, received no reply and opened it to a fetid smell of old socks and unwashed adolescence. Carefully bottled and distilled, it would do sterling work as a shark repellent, but I didn't say so. Teenage sons react badly to sarcasm. The room was liberally covered with posters of Jimi Hendrix, Che Guevara and Wayne Skunk, lead guitar and vocals of Strontium Goat. The floor was covered with discarded clothes, deadline-expired schoolwork and side plates with hardened toast crusts on them. I *think* the room was once carpeted, but I couldn't be sure any more.

'Hiya, Friday,' I said to an inert object wrapped up in a duvet. I sat on the bed and prodded a small patch of skin I could see.

'Grunt,' came a voice from somewhere deep within the bedclothes.

'Your father tells me that you're behind with your homework.'

'Grunt.'

'Well, *yes*, you might be excluded for two weeks, but you still need to do your coursework.'

'Grunt.'

'The time? It's nine right now and I need you to be sitting up with your eyes open before I leave the room.'

There was another grunt and a fart. I sighed, prodded him again and eventually something with unwashed dark hair sat up and stared at me with heavy lids.

'Grunt,' it said, 'grunt-grunt.'

I thought of making some sarcastic remark about how it helps to open your mouth when talking, but didn't, as I desperately needed his compliance, and although I couldn't actually speak teenage mumblegrunt, I could certainly understand it.

'How's the music going?' I asked, as there is a certain degree of consciousness that you have to bring teenagers towards before leaving them to get up on their own. Fall even a few degrees below the critical threshold and they would go back to sleep for eight hours – sometimes more.

'Mumble,' he said slowly, 'I've grunt-mumble formed a band grunty-mutter.'

'A band? What's it called?'

He took a deep breath and rubbed his face. He knew he wouldn't get rid of me until he'd answered at least three questions. He looked at me with his bright intelligent eyes and sniffed before announcing in a rebellious tone:

'It's called the Gobshites.'

'You can't call it that!'

Friday shrugged.

'All right,' he grumbled in a slovenly manner, 'we'll go back to the original name.'

'Which is?'

'The Wankers.'

'Actually, I think Gobshites is a terrific name for a band. Pithy and degenerate all at the same time. Now listen, I know you're not keen on this whole "Career in the Time Industry" stuff, but you did promise. I'll expect you to be all bright eyed, alert and bushy tailed, washed, showered, scrubbed and all homework finished by the time I get back.'

I stared at the picture of slovenly teenagerhood in front of me. I'd have settled for 'awake and/or coherent' – but I always aim high.

'Alrightmum,' he said in a long slur.

As soon as I had closed the door behind me I heard him flop back. It didn't matter. He was awake and his father could do the rest.

'I expect he's raring to go?' suggested Landen when I came downstairs. 'Had to lock him in his room to curb his enthusiasm?'

'Champing at the bit,' I replied wearily. 'We'd get a more dynamic response from a vapid slug on tranquillisers.'

'*I* wasn't so dreary when I was a kid,' said Landen thoughtfully, handing me my tea. 'I wonder where he gets it from?'

'Modern living, but don't worry. He's only sixteen – he'll snap out of it.'

'I hope so.'

And that was the problem. This wasn't just the usual worries of concerned parents with grunty and unintelligible teenagers; he *had* to snap out of it. I'd met the future Friday several times in the past and he'd risen to the lofty heights of ChronoGuard Director General with absolute power over the Standard History Eventline; a job of awesome responsibilities. He was instrumental in saving my life, his own and the planet from destruction no less than seven hundred and fifty-six times. By his fortieth birthday he would be known as 'Apocalypse Next'. But that hadn't happened yet. And with Friday's chief interest in life at present being Strontium Goat, sleeping, Che Guevara, Hendrix and more sleeping, we were beginning to wonder how it ever would.

Landen looked at his watch.

'Isn't it time you were off to work, Wifey-darling? The good folk of Swindon would be utterly lost and confused without you to take the burden of floor covering decision-making from them.'

He was right. I was already ten minutes late, and kissed him several times, just in case something unexpected occurred that might separate us for longer than planned. By 'unexpected' I was thinking of the time he was eradicated for two years by the Goliath Corporation. Although the vast multinational were back in business after many years in the financial and political doldrums, they had not yet attempted any of the monkey business that had marked out our relationship in the past. I hoped they'd learned their lesson, but I'd never quite freed myself of the idea that a further fracas with them might be just around the corner, so always made quite sure that I'd told Landen everything I needed to tell him.

'Busy day ahead?' he asked as he saw me to the garden gate.

'A large carpet to fit for a new company in the financial centre – bespoke executive pile, plus the usual quotes. I think Spike and I have a stair carpet to do in an old Tudor house with uneven treads, so one of those nightmare jobs.'

He paused and sucked his lower lip for a moment.

'Good, so . . . no . . . no . . . *SpecOps* stuff or anything?'

'Sweetheart!' I said, giving him a hug. 'That's all past history. I do carpets these days – it's a lot less stressful, believe me. Why?'

'No reason – it's just that what with Diatrymas being seen as far north as Salisbury, people are saying that the old SpecOps personnel might be recalled into service.'

'Six-foot-tall carnivorous birds from the late Palaeocene would be SO-13 business if they were real, which I doubt,' I pointed out. 'I was SO-27. The Literary Detectives. When copies of *Tristram Shandy* are threatening old ladies in dark alleys I just *might* be asked for my opinion. Besides, no one's reading books much any more so I'm fairly redundant.'

'That's true,' said Landen. 'Perhaps being an author isn't such a great move after all.'

'Then write your Magnum Opus for *me*,' I told him tenderly. 'I'll be your audience, wife, fan club, sex kitten and critic all rolled into one. It's me picking up Tuesday from school, right?'

'Right.'

'And you'll pick up Jenny?'

'I won't forget. What shall I do if Pickwick starts shivering in that hopelessly pathetic way that she does?'

'Pop her in the airing cupboard – I'll try and get her cosy finished at work.'

'Not *so* busy, then?'

I kissed him again, and departed.

2

Mum and Polly and Mycroft

———

'My mother's main aim in life was to get from the cradle to the grave with the minimum of fuss and bother, and the maximum of tea and Battenberg. Along the way she brought up three children, attended a lot of Women's Federation meetings and managed to squeeze a few severely burned meals somewhere in between. It wasn't until I was six that I realised that cake wasn't meant to be 87 per cent carbon, and that chicken actually tasted of something. Despite all this, or perhaps even *because* of it, we all loved her a great deal.'

My mother lived less than a mile away and actually on the route to work, so I often dropped in just to make sure she was okay and wasn't about to embark on a hare-brained scheme, as was her habit. A few years ago she had hoarded tinned pears on the principle that once she'd cornered the market she could 'name her price', a flagrant misunderstanding of the rules of supply and demand which did no damage to the tinned fruit producers of the world, but condemned her immediate family and friends to pears at every meal for almost three years.

She was the sort of parent you would want to have living close by, but only on the grounds that she would then never come to stay. I loved her dearly but in small doses. A cup of tea here, a dinner there – and as much childcare as I could squeeze out of her. The text excuse I gave Landen was actually something of a mild fib as the *real* reason for me popping round was to pick something up from Mycroft's workshop.

'Hello, darling!' said Mum as soon as she opened the door. 'Did you get my text?'

'Yes. But you must learn how to use the backspace and delete key – it all came out as nonsense.'

'L&Ks4DnRNXT-SNDY??' she repeated, showing me her mobile. 'What else *could* that mean but: "Landen and kids for dinner next Sunday?" Really, darling, how you even *begin* to communicate with your children I have no idea.'

'That wasn't *real* text shorthand,' I said, narrowing my eyes suspiciously, 'you just made it up.'

'I'm barely eighty-two,' she said indignantly, 'I'm not on the scrapheap yet. Made up the text indeed! Do you want to come back for lunch?' she added, without seeming to draw breath. 'I've got a few friends coming around, and after we've discussed who is the most unwell, we'll agree volubly with one another about the sorry state of the nation and then put it all to rights with poorly thought-out and totally impractical ideas. And if there's time after that, we might even play cribbage.'

'Hello, Auntie,' I said to Polly, who hobbled out of the front room with the aid of a stick. 'If I texted you "L&Ks4DnRNXT-SNDY??" what would you think I meant?'

Polly frowned and thought for a moment, her prune-like forehead rising in a folding ripple like a festoon curtain. She was over ninety and looked so unwell that she was often mistaken for dead when asleep on the bus. Despite this, she was totally sound upstairs, with only three or four fair-to-serious medical ailments, unlike my mother, who had the full dozen – or so she claimed.

'Well, do you know I'd be a bit confused—'

'Hah!' I said to Mum. 'You see?'

'—because,' Polly carried on, 'if *you* texted me asking for Landen and the kids to come over for Sunday dinner, I'd not know why you hadn't asked him yourself.'

'Ah – I see,' I mumbled, suspicious that the two of them had been colluding in some way – as they generally did. Still, I never

16

knew why they made me feel as though I were an eighteen-year-old when I was now fifty-two and myself in the sort of respectable time of life that I thought they should be. That's the thing about hitting fifty. All your life you think the half-century is death's adolescence, but actually it's really not that bad, as long as you can remember where you left your specs.

'Happy birthday, by the way,' said my mother. 'I got you something – look.'

She handed me the most hideous jumper you could possibly imagine.

'I don't know what to say, Mum, and I really mean that – a short-sleeved lime-green jumper with a hood and mock-antler buttons.'

'Do you like it?'

'One's attention is drawn to it instantly.'

'Good! Then you'll wear it straight away?'

'I wouldn't want to ruin it,' I replied hastily. 'I'm just off to work.'

'Ooh!' said Polly. 'I've just remembered.'

She handed me a CD in a plain slip.

'This is a pre-production copy of *Hosing the Dolly.*'

'It's what?'

'*Please* try and keep with the times, darling. *Hosing the Dolly.* The new album by Strontium Goat. It won't be out until November. I thought Friday might like it.'

'It's really totally out there, man,' put in my mother, 'whatever that means. There's a solo guitar riff on the second track that reminded me of Friday's playing and was so good it made my toes tingle – although that might just have been a trapped nerve. Wayne Skunk's granny is Mrs Arbuthnot – you know, the funny old lady with the large wart on her nose and the elbows that bend both ways. He sent it to her.'

I looked at the CD. Friday *would* like it, I was certain of that.

'And,' added Polly, leaning closer and with a conspiratorial wink, 'you don't have to tell him it was from us – I know what teenagers are like and a bit of parental kudos counts for a lot.'

'Thank you,' I said, and meant it. It was more than a CD – it was currency.

'Good!' said my mother. 'Have you got time for a cup of tea and a slice of Battenberg?'

'No thank you – I'm going to pick something up from Mycroft's workshop and then I'll be on my way.'

'How about some Battenberg to go, then?'

'I've just had breakfast.'

The doorbell rang.

'Ooooh!' said Polly, peering furtively out of the window. 'What fun. It looks like a market researcher!'

'Right,' said my mother in a very military tone, 'let's see how long we can keep him before he runs out screaming. I'll pretend to have mild dementia and you can complain about your sciatica in German. We'll try and beat our personal Market Researcher Containment record of two hours and twelve minutes.'

I shook my head sadly.

'I wish you two would grow up.'

'You are *so* judgemental, daughter dear,' scolded my mother. 'When you reach our age and level of physical decrepitude, you'll take your entertainment wherever you can find it. Now be off with you.'

And they shooed me into the kitchen while I mumbled something about how remedial basket weaving, whist drives or daytime soaps would probably suit them better. Mind you, inflicting mental torture on market researchers kept them busy, I suppose.

I walked out the back door, crossed the back garden and quietly entered the wooden outhouse that was my Uncle Mycroft's laboratory. I switched on the light and walked to my Porsche, which was looking a little forlorn under a dustsheet. It was still unrepaired from the accident five years before. The damage hadn't been that severe, but 356 parts were getting pricey these days, and we couldn't spare the cash. I reached into the cockpit, pulled the release and opened the bonnet. It was here that I kept a holdall containing twenty thousand Welsh Tocyns. On this side of the border pretty worthless, but enough to buy a three-bedroomed house in Merthyr. I wasn't planning to move to the Welsh Socialist Republic, of course – I needed the cash for a Welsh cheese deal I had cooking that evening. I checked the cash was all still there and was just replacing the sheet on the car when a noise made me turn. Standing at the workbench in the half-light was my Uncle Mycroft. An undeniable genius, his keen mind had pushed the frontiers in a range of disciplines that included genetics, fusion power, abstract geometry, perpetual motion and romantic fiction. It was he who had ushered in the home-cloning revolution, he who may have developed a memory erasure machine, and he who had invented the Prose Portal that had catapulted me into fiction. He was dressed in his trademark wool three-piece suit but without the jacket, his shirtsleeves were rolled up and he was in what we all called his 'inventing mode'. He seemed to be concentrating on a delicate mechanism the function of which it was impossible to guess. As I watched him in silence and with a growing sense of wonder, he suddenly noticed me.

'Ah!' he said with a smile. 'Thursday! Haven't seen you for a while – all well?'

'Yes,' I replied a bit uncertainly, 'I think so.'

'Splendid! I just had an idea for a cheap form of power: by bringing pasta and anti-pasta together we could be looking at the utter annihilation of ravioli and the liberation of vast quantities of energy. I safely predict an average-sized cannelloni would be able to power Swindon for over a year. Mind you, I could be wrong.'

'You're not often wrong,' I said quietly.

'I think I was wrong to start inventing in the first place,' he replied after a moment's reflection. 'Just because I *can* do it, it doesn't follow that I *should*. If scientists stopped to think about their creations more, the world might be a better—'

He broke off talking and looked at me in a quizzical manner.

'You're staring at me in a strange way,' he said, with uncharacteristic astuteness.

'Well, yes,' I replied, trying to frame my words carefully, 'you see – I think – that is to say – I'm *very* surprised to see you.'

'Really?' he said, putting down the device he was working on. 'Why?'

'Well,' I replied with greater firmness, 'I'm surprised to see you because . . . you died six years ago!'

'I did?' enquired Mycroft with genuine concern. 'Why does no one tell me these things?'

I shrugged as there was really no good answer to this.

'Are you sure?' he asked, patting himself on the chest and stomach and then taking his pulse to try to convince himself I might be mistaken. 'I know I'm a bit forgetful but I'm sure I would have remembered *that*.'

'Yes, quite sure,' I replied, 'I was there.'

'Well, goodness,' murmured Mycroft thoughtfully, 'if what you say is correct and I *am* dead, it's entirely possible that this isn't me at all, but a variable-response holographic recording of some sort – let's have a look for a projector.'

And so saying, he began to ferret through the piles of dusty machinery in his lab, and with nothing better to do and faintly curious, I joined in.

We searched for a good five minutes, but after finding nothing even vaguely resembling a holographic projector Mycroft and I sat down on a packing case and didn't speak for some moments.

'Dead,' muttered Mycroft with a resigned air, 'never been that before. Not even once. Are you quite sure?'

'Quite sure,' I replied. 'You were eighty-seven. It was expected.'

'Oh yes,' he said, as though some dim memory was stirring. 'And Polly?' he added, suddenly remembering his wife. 'How is she?'

'She's very well,' I told him. 'She and Mum are up to their old tricks as usual.'

'Annoying market researchers?'

'Among other things. But she's missing you dreadfully.'

'And I her.' He looked nervous for a moment. 'Has she got a boyfriend yet?'

'At ninety-two?'

'Damn good-looking woman – smart, too.'

'Well, she hasn't.'

'Hmm. Well, if you see someone suitable, oh favourite niece, push them her way, won't you? I don't want her to be lonely.'

'I'll do that, Uncle, I promise.'

We sat in silence for a few seconds more and I shivered.

'Mycroft,' I said, suddenly thinking that perhaps there wasn't a scientific explanation for his appearance after all, 'I'm going to try something.'

I put out my fingertips to touch him but where they should have met the firm resistance of his shirtsleeve there was none – my fingers just melted into him. He wasn't there; or if he was, he was something insubstantial – a phantom.

'Ooooh!' he said as I withdrew my hand. 'That felt odd.'

'Mycroft . . . you're a *ghost*.'

'Nonsense! Scientifically proven to be completely impossible.' He paused for thought. 'Why would I be one of those?'

I shrugged.

'I don't know – perhaps there's something you hadn't finished at your death and it's been bothering you.'

'Great Scott! You're right. I never did finish the final chapter of *Love among the Begonias*.'

In retirement Mycroft had spent his time writing romantic novels, all of which sold surprisingly well. So well, in fact, that he had attracted the lasting enmity of Daphne Farquitt, the indisputable leader in the field. She fired off an accusatory letter accusing him of 'wanton' plagiarism. A barrage of claims and counter-claims followed, which only ended when Mycroft died. It was so venomous, in fact, that conspiracy theorists claimed he was poisoned by crazed Farquitt fans. We had to publish his death certificate to quell the rumours.

'Polly finished *Love among the Begonias* for you,' I said.

'Ah,' he replied, 'maybe I've come back to haunt that loathsome cow Farquitt.'

'If that was the case you'd be over at her place doing the wooo wooo thing and clanking chains.'

'Hmm,' he said disdainfully, 'that doesn't sound very dignified.'

'How about some last-minute inventing? Some idea you never got round to researching?'

Mycroft thought long and hard, and pulled several bizarre faces as he did so.

'Fascinating!' he said at last, panting with the effort. 'I can't do original thought any more – as soon as my brain stopped functioning, that was the end of Mycroft the inventor. You're right: I must be dead. It's *most* depressing.'

'But no idea why you're here?'

'None,' he said despondently.

'Well,' I said as I got up, 'I'll make a few enquiries. Do you want Polly to know you've reappeared in spirit form?'

'I'll leave it to your judgement,' he said, 'but if you do tell her, you might mention something about how she was the finest partner any man could have. Two minds with but a single thought, two hearts that beat as one.'

22

I snapped my fingers. That was how I wanted to describe Landen and me.

'That was good — can I use it?'

'Of course. Have you any idea how much I miss Polly?'

I thought of the two years Landen had been eradicated.

'I do. And she misses you, Uncle, every second of every day.'

He looked up at me and I saw his eyes glisten.

I tried to put my hand on his arm but it went through his phantom limb and instead landed on the hard surface of the workbench.

'I'll have a think about why I might be here,' said Mycroft in a quiet voice. 'Will you look in on me from time to time?'

He smiled to himself and began to tinker with the device on the workbench again.

'Of course. Goodbye, Uncle.'

'Goodbye, Thursday.'

And he slowly began to fade. I noticed as he did so that the room grew warmer again, and within a few more seconds he had vanished entirely. I retrieved the bag of Welsh cash and walked thoughtfully to the door, turning to have one last look. The workshop was empty, dusty and forgotten. Abandoned as it was when Mycroft died, six years before.

3

Acme Carpets

'The Special Operations Network was instigated in 1928
to handle policing duties considered either too unusual
or too specialised to be tackled by the regular force.
Among the stranger departments were those that dealt with
vampires (SO-17), Time Travel (SO-12), literary crime (SO-27)
and the Cheese Enforcement Agency (SO-31). Notoriously secre-
tive and with increased accusations of unaccountability and heavy-
handedness, 90 per cent of the service was disbanded during the
winter of 1991/92. Of the thirty-two departments only five were
retained. My department, the Literary Detectives, was not among
them.'

The name Acme Carpets was a misnomer, to be honest. We didn't
just do carpets – we did tiles, linoleum and wooden floor coverings, too. Competitive, fast and reliable, we had been trading in
Swindon for ten years, ever since the SpecOps divisions were
disbanded in '92. In 1996 we moved to bigger premises on the
Oxford Road trading estate. If you needed any sort of floor covering
in the Swindon area, you could come to us for the most competitive quote.

I pushed open the front doors and was surprised that there was
no one around. Not that there was a lack of customers, as Mondays
before ten were generally pretty light, but that there were no staff
– not even in the office or skulking next to the spotlessly clean
complimentary tea area. I walked to the back of the store, past
quality rolls of carpet and a varied selection of samples piled high
on the light and spacious showroom floor. I opened the heavy

swing-doors that led to the storerooms and froze. Standing next to a pile of last year's sample books was a flightless bird about four foot high and with an unfeasibly large and rather nastily serrated beak. It stared at me suspiciously with two small black eyes. I looked around. The stockroom staff were all dutifully standing still, and behind the Diatryma was a stocky figure in an Acme Carpets uniform with a large brow-ridged head and deeply sunken brown eyes. He had a lot in common with the Palaeocene anomaly that faced me – he too had once been extinct and was here not courtesy of the meanderings of natural selection, but from the inconsiderate meddling of a scientist who never stopped to ask whether if a thing *could* be done, it *should*. His name was Stig and he was a re-engineered Neanderthal, ex-SO-13 and a valued colleague from the old days of SpecOps. He'd saved my butt on several occasions, and I'd helped him and his fellow extinctees to species self-determination.

'Don't move,' said Stig in a low rumble, 'we don't want to hurt it.'

He never did. Stig saw any renegade unextinctee as something akin to family, and always caught them alive, if possible. On the other hand, chimeras, a hotchpotch of the hobby sequencer's art, were another matter – he dispatched them without mercy, and without pain.

The Diatryma made a vicious jab towards me; I jumped to my left as the beak snapped shut with the sound of oversize castanets. Quick as a flash Stig leapt forward and covered the creature's head with an old flour sack, which seemed to subdue it enough for him to wrestle it to the floor. I joined in, as did the entire stockroom staff, and within a few moments we had wrapped some duct tape securely around its massive beak, rendering it harmless.

'Thanks,' said Stig, securing a leash around the bird's neck.

'Salisbury?' I asked as we walked past the rolls of Wilton shag and cushioned linoleum in a wide choice of colours.

26

'Devizes,' replied the Neanderthal. 'We had to run for eight miles across open farmland to catch it.'

'Did anyone see you?' I asked, mindful of any rumours getting out.

'Who'd believe them if they did?' he replied. 'But there's more Diatrymas – we'll be out again tonight.'

Acme Carpets, as you might have gathered, was just the cover story. In truth it was the old SpecOps under another name. The service hadn't really been disbanded in the early nineties – it just went underground, and freelance. All *strictly* unofficial, of course. Luckily, the Swindon Chief of Police was Braxton Hicks, my old divisional boss at SpecOps. Although he suspected what we got up to, he told me he would feign ignorance unless 'someone gets eaten or something'. Besides, if we didn't mop up all the bizarrer elements of modern living, his regular officers would have to, and Braxton might then face a demand for bonus payments for 'actions beyond the call of duty'. And Hicks loved his budget almost as much as he loved his golf. So the cops didn't bother us and we didn't bother them.

'We have a question,' asked Stig. 'Do we have to mention the possibility of being trampled by mammoths on our Health and Safety risk assessment form?'

'No – that's the part of Acme we don't want anyone to know about. The safety stuff only relates to carpet laying.'

'We understand,' said Stig. 'What about being shredded by a chimera?'

'Just carpets, Stig.'

'Okay. By the way,' he added, 'have you told Landen about all your SpecOps work yet? You said you were going to.'

'I'm . . . building up to it.'

'You should tell him, Thursday.'

'I know.'

27

'And have a good anniversary of your mother giving birth to you.'

'Thank you.'

I bade Stig good day and then walked to the store offices, which were situated in a raised position halfway between the storeroom and the showroom floor. From there you could see pretty much everything that went on in the building.

As I walked in a man looked up from where he was crouched under the desk.

'Have you captured it?' he asked in a quavering voice.

'Yes.'

He looked relieved and clambered out from his hiding place. He was in his early forties and his features were just beginning to show the shades of middle age. Around his eyes were fine lines, his dark hair now flecked with grey. Even though he was management he also wore an Acme Carpets uniform. Only his looked a lot better on him than mine did on me. In fact, he looked a lot better in his than *anyone* in the establishment, leading us to accuse him of having his professionally tailored, something he strenuously denied, but given his fastidious nature, not outside the bounds of possibility. Bowden Cable had been my partner at the Swindon branch of the Literary Detectives, and it seemed only natural that he would have the top admin job at Acme Carpets when we were all turfed out of SpecOps.

'Are we busy today?' I asked, pouring myself a cup of coffee.

Bowden pointed to the newspaper. 'Have you read this?'

'The Stupidity Surplus?'

'Part of it, I guess,' he replied despondently. 'Incredibly enough, reality TV has just got *worse*.'

'Is that possible?' I asked. 'Wasn't *Celebrity Trainee Pathologist* the pits?' I thought for a moment. 'Actually, *Whose Life Support Do We Switch Off*? was worse. Or maybe *Sell Your Granny*. Wow, the choice these days makes it all so tricky to decide.'

Bowden laughed.

'I'll agree that *Granny* lowered the bar for distasteful programme makers everywhere, but RTA-TV, never one to shirk from a challenge, have devised *Samaritan Kidney Swap*. Ten renal failure patients take it in turns to convince a tissue-typed donor – and the voting viewers – which one should have his spare kidney.'

I groaned. Reality TV was to me the worst form of entertainment – the modern equivalent of paying sixpence to watch lunatics howling at the walls down at the local madhouse. I shook my head sadly.

'What's wrong with a good book?' I asked.

Bowden shrugged. In these days of junk TV, short attention spans and easy-to-digest soundbites, it seemed that the book, the noble device to which both Bowden and I had devoted much of our lives, was being marginalised into just another human storytelling experience also-ran, along with the epic poem, Greek theatre, *Jackanory*, BETA and Tarzanagrams.

'How's the family?' asked Bowden, trying to elevate the mood.

'They're all good,' I replied, 'except Friday, who is still incapable of any human activity other than torpidity.'

'And Pickwick? Feathers growing back?'

'No – listen, can you knit?'

'No . . . Why?'

'No reason. What's on the books for us today?'

Bowden picked up a clipboard and thumbed through the pages.

'Spike's got a brace of undead to deal with and a possible pack of howlers in the Savernake. Stig's still on the path of those Diatrymas. The Taste Division have got an outbreak of stonecladding to deal with in Cirencester, and the Pampas squad will be busy on a slash'n'burn in Bristol. Oh yes – and we've an outbreak of doppel-gängers in Chippenham.'

'Any literary stuff?' I asked hopefully.

'Only Mrs Mattock and her stolen first editions – *again*. Face it, Thurs, books just don't light anyone's candle these days. It's good that they don't – add the sixteen or so carpets to be fitted and the twenty-eight quotes needed yesterday, and we're kind of stretched. Do we pull Spike off zombies to do stair carpets?'

'Can't we just drag in some freelance fitters?'

'And pay them with what? An illegal Diatryma each?'

'It's that bad, is it?'

'Thursday, it's *always* that bad. We're nuzzling up to the overdraft limit again.'

'No problem. I've got a seriously good cheese deal going down this evening.'

'I don't want to know about it. When you're arrested I need *deniability* – and besides, if you actually sold carpets instead of gallivanting around like a lunatic, you wouldn't need to buy and sell on the volatile cheese market.'

'That reminds me,' I said with a smile, 'I'll be out of my office today, so don't put any calls through.'

'Thursday!' he said in an exasperated tone. '*Please* don't vanish today of *all* days. I really need you to quote for the new lobby carpet in the Finis, I've got the Wilton rep popping in at four thirty to show us their new range and the Health and Safety Inspectorate are coming in to make sure we're up to speed.'

'On safety procedures?'

'Good Lord, no! On how to fill the forms in properly.'

'Listen,' I said, 'I've got to take Friday to the ChronoGuard careers evening at five thirty, so I'll try to get back a couple of hours before then and do some quotes. Have a list ready for me.'

'Already done,' he said, and before I could make up an excuse, he passed me a clipboard full of addresses and contact names.

'Good,' I muttered, 'very efficient – nice job.'

*

I took my coffee and walked to my own office, a small and window-less room next to the forklift recharging point. I sat at my desk and stared despondently at the list Bowden had given me, then rocked backwards and forwards on my chair in an absent mood. Stig had been right. I *should* tell Landen about what I got up to, but life was better with him thinking I was working at Acme. Besides, running several illegal SpecOps departments wasn't all I did. It was . . . well, the tip of a very large and misshapen iceberg.

I got up, took off my jacket and was about to change into more comfortable clothes when there was a tap at the door. I opened it to reveal a large and muscular man a few years younger than myself and looking even more incongruous in his Acme Carpets uniform than I looked in mine – although I doubted anyone would ever try to tell him so. He had long dreadlocks that almost reached to his waist and which were tied back in a loose hairband, and he was wearing a liberal amount of jewellery, similar to the sort that Goths like – skulls, bats, things like that. But it wasn't for decoration – it was for protection. This was ex-SO-17 operative 'Spike' Stoker, the most successful vampire staker and werewolf hunter in the South-West, and although no friend of the undead, he was a friend of mine.

'Happy birthday, bookworm,' he said genially. 'Got a second?'

I looked at my watch. I was late for work. Not work, of course, since I was already there, but *work*-work.

'Is it about Health and Safety?'

'No, this is important and relevant.'

He led the way to the other side of the storeroom, just next to where we kept the adhesive, tacks and grippers. We entered a door hidden behind a poster for Brinton's Carpets and took a small flight of steps down to the level below. Spike opened a sturdy door with a large brass key and we stepped into what I described as 'The Containment Suite' but Spike referred to as the 'Weirdshitorium'. His

31

appraisal was better. Our work took us to the very limits of credibility – to a place where even the most stalwart conspiracy theorists would shake their heads and remark sarcastically: 'Oh, yeah . . . right.' When we were SpecOps we had secrecy, manpower, budget and unaccountability to help us do the job. Now we had just secrecy, complimentary tea and biscuits and a big brass key. It was here that Stig kept his creatures until he decided what to do with them and where Spike incarcerated any of the captured undead for observation – in case they were thinking of becoming either *nearly* dead or *mostly* dead. Death, I had discovered long ago, was available in varying flavours, and none of them particularly palatable.

We passed a cell that was full of gallon-sized glass jars containing captured Supreme Evil Beings. They were small, wraith-like objects about the size and texture of well-used dishcloths, only less substantial, and they spent most of the time bickering over who was the *most* supreme Supreme Evil Being. But we weren't here to bother with SEBs; Spike led me on to a cell right at the end of the corridor and opened the door. Sitting on a chair in the middle of the room was a man in jeans and a plain leather jacket. He was staring at the floor with the light above him so I couldn't at first see his face, and his large and well-manicured hands were clenched tightly in front of him. I also noticed that his ankle was attached to the floor by a sturdy chain. I winced. Spike would have to be right about this one – imprisonment of something actually *human* was definitely illegal and could be seriously bad for business.

'Hey!' said Spike, and the figure slowly raised his head to look at me. I recognised him instantly, and not without a certain degree of alarm. It was Felix8, Acheron Hades' henchman from way back in the days of the *Jane Eyre* adventure. Hades had taken the face from the first Felix when he died and implanted it on a suitable stranger who had been bent to his evil will. Whenever a Felix died, which was quite often, he just swapped the face. Felix8's real name was Danny Chance, but his free will had been appropriated by Hades – he was merely an empty vessel, devoid of pity or morals. His life had no meaning other than to do his master's bidding. The point was, his master had died sixteen years ago and the last time I saw Felix8 was at the Penderyn Hotel in Merthyr, the capital of the Welsh Socialist Republic.

Felix8 looked at me with a slight sense of amusement and gave a subtle nod of greeting.

'Where did you find him?' I asked.

'Outside your place half an hour ago. He had this on him.' Spike showed me an ugly-looking machine pistol with a delicately carved stock. 'There was a single round in the chamber.'

I bent down to Felix8's level and stared at him for a moment.

'Who sent you?'

Felix8 smiled, said nothing and looked at the chain that was firmly clasped around his ankle.

'What do you want?'

Still Felix8 said nothing.

'Where have you been these past sixteen years?'

All my questions met with blank insolence, and after five minutes of this I walked back outside the cell block, Spike at my side.

'Who reported him?'

'Your stalker – what's his name again?'

'Millon.'

'Right. He thought Felix8 might have been *another* stalker and was going to warn him off, but when he noticed the absence of notebooks, cameras or even a duffel coat, he called me.'

I thought for a moment. If Felix8 was back on my trail, then somebody in the Hades family was looking for revenge – and they were big on revenge. I'd had run-ins with the Hades family before and I thought they'd learned their lesson by now. I had personally defeated Acheron, Aornis and Cocytus, which left only Lethe and

33

Phlgethon. Lethe was the 'white sheep' of the family and spent most of his time doing charity work, which left only Phlgethon, who had dropped off the radar in the mid-nineties, despite numerous manhunts by SO-5 and myself.

'What do you suggest?' I asked. 'He doesn't fall into any of the categories that might ethically give us a reason to keep him under lock and key without a trial of some sort. After all, he's only wearing the *face* of Felix – under there he's an erased Danny Chance, married father-of-two who went missing in 1985.'

'I agree we can't keep him,' replied Spike, 'but if we let him go he'll just try and kill you.'

'I live to be over a hundred,' I murmured. 'I know, I've met the future me.'

It was said without much conviction. I'd seen enough of time's paradoxical nature to know that meeting the future me wasn't any guarantee of a long life.

'We'll keep him for twenty-four hours,' I announced. 'I'll make a few enquiries and see if I can figure out which Hades is involved – if any. He might be simply trying to carry out the last order he was given. After all, he was under orders to kill me but no one said anything about *when*.'

'Thursday—?' began Spike in a tone that I recognised and didn't like.

'No,' I said quickly, 'out of the question.'

'The only reason he'd mind being killed,' said Spike in an annoyingly matter-of-fact way, 'is that it would mean he failed to carry out his mission – to kill you.'

'I hear you, Spike, but he's done nothing wrong. Give me a day and if I can't find anything we'll hand him over to Braxton.'

'Okay, then,' replied Spike with a sulky air of disappointment.

'Another thing,' I said as we returned to the carpet storeroom, 'my Uncle Mycroft has returned as a ghost.'

'It happens,' replied Spike with a shrug. 'Did he seem substantial?'

'As you or I.'

'How long was he materialised for?'

'Seven minutes, I guess.'

'Then you got him at first haunting. First-timers are always the most solid.'

'That might be so, but I'd like to know *why*.'

'I'm owed a few favours by the Realm of the Dead,' he said offhandedly, 'so I can find out. By the way, have you told Landen about all this crazy SpecOps shit?'

'I'm telling him this evening.'

'Sure you are.'

I walked back to my office, locked the door and changed out of the less-than-appealing Acme Carpet uniform and put on something more comfortable. I would have to speak to Aornis Hades about Felix8, but she would probably tell me to go and stick it in my ear – after all, she was seven years into a thirty-year enloopment based on my testimony, and yours truly was unlikely to fill her evil little soul with any sort of heart-warming benevolence.

I finished lacing my boots, refilled my water bottle and placed it in my shoulder bag. Acme Carpets may have been a cover for my clandestine work at SpecOps, but this itself was cover for *another* job that only Bowden knew about. If Landen found out about SpecOps he'd be annoyed – if he found out about Jurisfiction he'd go bonkers. Not long after the Minotaur's attack following the '88 Superhoop, Landen and I had a heart-to-heart during which I told him I was giving up Jurisfiction – my prime duty being wife and mother. And so it was agreed. Unfortunately, my *other* primary duty was to fiction – the make-believe. Unable to reconcile the two I did both and lied a bit – well, a lot, actually – to plaster over the gaping crack in my loyalties. It wasn't with an easy or light heart, but it had worked for the past fourteen years. The odd thing was, Jurisfiction didn't earn me a penny and was dangerous and wildly unpredictable. There was another reason I liked it, too – it brought me into close contact with *story*. It would have been easier to get a registered cheesehead off a five-times-a-day Limburger habit than to keep me away from fiction. But hey – I could handle it.

I sat down, took a deep breath and opened the TravelBook I kept in my bag. It had been given to me by Mrs Nakajima many years before and was my passport in and out of the world on the other side of the printed page. I lowered my head, emptied my mind as much as possible and read from the book. The words echoed about me with a resonance that sounded like wind chimes and looked like a thousand glow-worms. The room around me rippled and stretched, then returned with a *twang* to my office at Acme. Blast. This happened more and more often these days. I had once been a natural bookjumper but the skill had faded with the years. I took a deep breath and tried again. The wind chimes and glow-worms returned and once more the room distorted around me like a barrel, then faded from view to be replaced by a kaleidoscope of images, sounds and emotions as I jumped through the boundary that separates the real from the written, the actual from the fable. With a rushing sound like distant waterfalls and a warm sensation that felt like hot rain and kittens, I was transported from Acme Carpets in Swindon to the entrance hallway of a large Georgian country house.

4
Jurisfiction

'Jurisfiction is the name given to the policing agency
***within* books**. Working with the intelligence-gathering capabil-
ities of Text Grand Central, the Prose Resource Operatives at
Jurisfiction work tirelessly to maintain the continuity of the narrative within the pages of all the books ever written, a sometimes
thankless task. Jurisfiction agents live mostly on their wits as they
attempt to reconcile the author's original wishes and the reader's
expectations with a strict and largely pointless set of bureaucratic
guidelines laid down by the Council of Genres.'

It was a spacious hallway, with deep picture windows that afforded a
fine view of the extensive parklands beyond the gravel drive and
perfectly planted flower beds. Inside, the walls were hung with delicate silks, the woodwork shone brightly and the marble floor was so
polished I could see myself in it. I quickly drank a pint of water as
the bookjumping process could leave me dangerously dehydrated these
days, and dialled TransGenreTaxis on my mobile footnoterphone to
order a cab for a half-hour's time, as they were always busy and it
paid to book ahead. I then looked around cautiously. Not to check
for impending danger, as this was the peaceful backstory of Jane
Austen's *Sense and Sensibility*. No, I was making quite sure my current
Jurisfiction cadet wasn't anywhere in sight. My overriding wish at
present was not to have to deal with her until roll-call had finished.

'Good morning, ma'am!' she said, appearing in front of me so
abruptly I almost cried out. She spoke in the over-eager manner
of the terminally keen; a trait that had begun to annoy soon after
I'd agreed to assess her suitability, twenty-four hours before.

'Do you have to jump in so abruptly?' I asked her. 'You nearly gave me a heart attack!'

'Oh! I'm sorry. But I did bring you some breakfast.'

'Well, in that case . . .' I looked into the bag she handed me and frowned. 'Wait a minute – that doesn't look like a bacon sandwich.'

'It isn't. It's a crispy lentil cake made with soya milk and bean curd. It cleanses the bowels. Bacon definitely *will* give you a heart attack.'

'How thoughtful of you,' I remarked sarcastically. 'The body is a temple, right?'

'Right. And I didn't get you coffee because it raises blood pressure; I got you this beetroot and edelweiss energy drink.'

'What happened to the squid ink and hippopotamus milk?'

'They were out.'

'Look,' I said, handing back the lentil animal-feed thing and the drink, 'tomorrow is the third and last day of your assessment and I haven't yet made up my mind. Do you want to be a Jurisfiction agent?'

'More than anything.'

'Right. So if you want me to sign you out for advanced training, you're going to have to do as you're told. If that means killing a grammasite, recapturing an irregular verb, dressing Quasimodo or even something as simple as getting me coffee and a bacon roll, then that's what you'll do. Understand?'

'Sorry,' she said, adding as an afterthought: 'Then I suppose you don't want this?'

She showed me a small lump of quartz crystal.

'What do I do with it?'

'You wear it. It can help retune your vibrational energy system.'

'The only energy system I need right now is a bacon roll. You might be a veggie, but I'm not. I'm not *you* – you're a version of *me*. You might be into tarot and yogurt and vitamins and standing naked in the middle of crop circles with your eyes closed and your palms facing skywards, but don't think that I am as well, okay?'

She looked crestfallen, and I sighed. After all, I felt kind of responsible. Since I'd made it into print I'd been naturally curious about meeting the fictional me, but never entertained the possibility that they might want to join Jurisfiction. But here she was – the Thursday Next from *The Great Samuel Pepys Fiasco*. It was mildly spooky at first because she wasn't just similar in the way that identical twins are similar, but physically *indistinguishable* from me. Stranger still, despite *Pepys Fiasco* being set six years before, she looked as old as my fifty-two years. Every crag and wrinkle, and even the flecks of grey hair that I pretended I didn't care about. To all intents and purposes, she *was* me. But only, I was at pains to point out, in facial appearance. She didn't act or dress like me; her clothes were more earthy and sustainable. Instead of my usual jeans, shirt and jacket, she wore a naturally dyed cotton skirt and a home-spun crocheted pullover. She carried a shoulder bag of felt instead of my Billingham, and in place of the scarlet scrunchie holding my ponytail in place, hers was secured with a strip of hemp cloth tied in a neat bow. It wasn't by accident. After I had endured the wholly unwarranted aggression of the first four Thursday books I'd insisted the fifth reflect my more sensitive nature. Unfortunately, they took me a little too seriously and Thursday5 was the result. She was sensitive, caring, compassionate, kind, thoughtful – and unreadable. *The Great Samuel Pepys Fiasco* sold so badly it was remaindered within six months and never made it to paperback, something I was secretly glad of. Thursday5 might have remained in unreadable retirement, too, but for her sudden wish to join Jurisfiction and 'do her bit', as she called it. She'd passed her written tests and basic training and was now with me for a three-day assessment. It hadn't gone that well – she was going to have to do something pretty dramatic to redeem herself.

'By the way,' I said, as I had an unrelated thought, 'can you knit?'

'Is this part of my assessment?'

'A simple yes or no will suffice.'

'Yes.'

I handed her Pickwick's half-knitted jumper.

'You can finish this. The dimensions are on that piece of paper. It's a cosy for a pet,' I added, as Thursday5 stared at the oddly shaped stripy piece of knitting.

'You have a deformed jellyfish for a pet?'

'It's for Pickwick.'

'Oh!' said Thursday5. 'I'd be delighted. I have a dodo, too – she's called Pickwick5.'

'You don't say.'

'Yes – how did yours lose her plumage?'

'It's a long story that involves the cat next door.'

'I have a cat next door. It's called . . . now what *was* her name?'

'Cat next door5?' I suggested.

'That's right,' she said, astonished at my powers of detection. 'You've met her, then?'

I ignored her and pushed open the doors to the ballroom. We were just in time. The Bellman's daily briefing was about to begin.

Jurisfiction's offices were in the disused ballroom of Mr and Mrs John Dashwood's residence of Norland Park, safely hidden in the backstory of Jane Austen's *Sense and Sensibility*. Wagging and perhaps jealous tongues claimed that it was for 'special protection' but I'd never seen any particular favours shown myself. The room was painted pale blue and the walls, where not decorated with delicate plaster mouldings, were hung with lavish gold-framed mirrors. It was here that we ran the policing agency that functioned *within* books to keep order in the dangerously flexible narrative environment. We called it Jurisfiction.

The offices of Jurisfiction had long been settled at Norland. It had been many years since they had been used as a ballroom. The floor space was liberally covered with tables, chairs, filing cabinets and piles of paperwork. Each desk had its own brass-horned footnoterphone, typewriter and an in-tray that always seemed larger than the out. Although electronics were a daily part of life in the real world, here in fiction there was no machine that was too complicated it couldn't be described in a line or two. It was a different story over in non-fiction, where they had advanced technology coming out of their ears – it was a matter of some pride that we were about eight times more efficient with half the workforce. I paused for a moment. Even after sixteen years, walking into the Jurisfiction offices always gave me a bit of a buzz. Silly, really, but I couldn't help myself.

'Just in time!' barked Commander Bradshaw, who was standing on a table so as to be more easily seen. He was Jurisfiction's longest-serving member and one-time star of the 'Commander Bradshaw' colonial ripping adventure stories for boys. His jingoistic and anachronistic brand of British Empire fiction wasn't read at all these days, which he'd be the first to admit was no great loss, and freed him up to be the head of Jurisfiction or Bellman, a post he was unique in having held twice. He and Mrs Bradshaw were two of the best friends I possessed. His wife, Melanie, had been Friday and Tuesday's au pair, and even though Jenny was now ten and needed less looking after, Mel was still around. She loved our kids as if they were her own. She and Bradshaw had never had children. Not surprisingly, really, since Melanie was, and had always been, a gorilla.

'Is everyone here?' he asked, scanning the small group of Jurisfiction agents carefully.

'Hamlet's dealing with a potentially damaging outbreak of reasonable behaviour inside *Othello*,' said Mr Fainset, a middle-aged man dressed in worn merchant navy garb. 'He also said he needed to see Iago about something.'

'That'll be about their Shakespeare spin-off play *Iago V Hamlet*,' said the Red Queen, who was actually not a real queen at all but an anthropomorphised chess piece from *Through the Looking Glass*.

'Does he really think he's going to get the Council of Genres to agree to a thirty-ninth Shakespeare play?'

'Stranger things have happened.' Bradshaw sighed. 'Where are Peter and Jane?'

'The new feline in *The Tiger Who Came to Tea* got stage fright,' said Lady Cavendish, 'and after that they said they needed to deal with a troublesome brake van in *The Twin Engines*.'

'Very well,' said Bradshaw, tingling a small bell, 'Jurisfiction meeting number 43,369 is now in session. Item one: the number of fictioneers trying to escape into the real world has increased this month. We've had seven attempts, all of them rebuffed. The Council of Genres have made it abundantly clear that this will not be tolerated without a Letter of Transit, and anyone caught moving across or *attempting* to move across will be reduced to text on sight.'

There was silence. I was the only one who crossed over on a regular basis, but no one liked the idea of reducing anyone to text whether they deserved it or not. It was irreversible and the closest thing there was to death in the written world.

'I'm not saying that you *have* to do that,' continued Bradshaw, 'and I want you to pursue all other avenues before lethal force. But if it's the only way, then that's what you'll do. Item two: it's been six months and there's still no sign of the final two volumes of *The Good Soldier Švejk*. If we don't hear anything more, we'll just bundle up the four volumes into one and reluctantly call it a day. Thursday, have you seen anything around the Well that might indicate they were stolen to order to be broken up for scrap?'

'None at all,' I replied, 'but I spoke with our opposite number over at Jurisfiktiví and he said they'd lost it over there, too.'

'That's wonderful news!' breathed Bradshaw, much relieved.

'It is?'

'Yes – it's someone else's problem. Item three: the inexplicable

42

departure of comedy from the Thomas Hardy novels is still a cause for great concern.'

'I thought we'd put a stop to that?' said Emperor Zhark.

'Not at all,' replied Bradshaw. 'We tried to have the comedy that was being leached *out* replaced by fresh comedy coming *in*, but because misery has a greater natural affinity for the Wessex novels, it always seems to gain the ascendancy. Hard to believe *Jude the Obscure* was once one of the most rip-roaringly funny novels in the English language, eh?'

I put up my hand.

'Yes, Thursday?'

'Do you think the Comedy genre might be mining the books for laughs? You know how those guys will happily steal and modify from anything and everywhere for even the most perfunctory of chuckles.'

'It's possible, but we need hard evidence. Who wants to have a trawl around Comedy for a Thomas Hardy funnyism we can use to prove it one way or the other?'

'I will,' said the Red Queen, before I could volunteer.

'Better get busy. If they *are* sucking the comedy out of *Jude* we don't have much time. Now that the farce, rib-cracking one-liners and whimsical asides have all been removed, a continued drain on the novel's reserves of lightheartedness will place the book in a state of negative funniness. Insufferably gloomy – miserable, in fact.'

We thought about it for a moment. Even until as little as thirty years ago the whole Thomas Hardy series was actually very funny – pointlessly frivolous, in fact. As things stood at the moment, if you wanted a happy ending to anything in Hardy, you'd be well advised to read it backwards.

'Item four,' continued Bradshaw, 'a few genre realignments.'

There was an audible sigh in the air and a few agents lost interest. This was one of those boring-but-important items that while of

43

little consequence to the book in question subtly changed the way in which it was policed. We had to know what novel was in what genre – sometimes it wasn't altogether obvious, and when a book stretched across two genres or more, it could open a jurisdictional can of worms that might have us tied up for years. We all reached for our notepads and pencils as Bradshaw stared at the list.

'Eric Von Daniken's *Chariots of the Gods?* has been moved from non-fiction to fiction,' he began, leaving a pause so we could write it down, 'and Orwell's *1984* is no longer truly fiction, so has been reallocated to non-fiction. Vonnegut's *The Sirens of Titan* is no longer Sci-Fi, but Philosophy.'

This was actually good news; I'd thought the same for years.

'The sub-genre of Literary Smut has finally been disbanded with *Fanny Hill* and *Moll Flanders* being transferred to Racy Novel and *Lady Chatterley's Lover* to Human Drama.'

We diligently wrote it all down as Bradshaw continued:

'*The History of Tom Jones* is now in Romantic Comedy, and *The Story of O* is part of the Erotic Novel genre, as are *Lolita* and *The Autobiography of a Flea*. As part of a separate genre reappraisal, Orwell's *Animal Farm* belongs to not just the Allegorical and Political genres, but has expanded to be part of Animal Drama and Juvenilia as well.'

'Four genres bad, two genres good,' murmured Mr Fainset.

'I'm sorry?'

'Nothing.'

'Good,' said Bradshaw, stroking his large white moustache. 'Item five: the entire works of Jane Austen are down in the maintenance bay for a refit. We've diverted all the Outlander readings through a book club boxed set, and I want someone to patrol the series until the originals are back online. Volunteers?'

'I will,' I said.

'You're on cadet assessment, Thursday. Anyone else?'

Lady Margaret Cavendish put up her hand. Unusually for a

resident of fiction, she had once been real. Originally a flamboyant seventeenth-century aristocratic socialite much keen on poetry, women's issues and self-publicity, our Lady Cavendish hailed from an unfair biography. Annoyed by the slurs suffered so often by the defamed dead, she took flight to the bright lights of Jurisfiction, in which she seemed to excel, especially in the Poetry genre, which no one else much liked to handle.

'What would you have me do?' she asked.

'Nothing, really – just maintain a presence to make sure any mischievous character understudies think twice before they do their own dialogue or try to "improve" anything.'

Lady Cavendish shrugged and nodded her agreement.

'Item six,' said Bradshaw, consulting his clipboard again, 'falling Outlander read-rates.'

He looked at us all over his glasses. We all knew the problem but saw it more as a systemic difficulty rather than something we could deal with on a book-to-book policing basis.

'The Outlander Reading Index has dropped once again for the 1,782nd day running,' reported Bradshaw, 'and although there are certain books that will always be read, we are finding that more and more minor classics and a lot of general fiction are going for long periods without even being opened. Because of this, Text Grand Central are worried that bored characters in lesser books might try and move to more popular novels for work, which will doubtless cause friction.'

We were all silent. The inference wasn't lost on any of us – the fictional characters in the BookWorld could be a jittery bunch and it didn't take much to set off a riot.

'I can't say any more at this point,' concluded Bradshaw, 'as it's only a *potential* problem, but be aware of what's going on. The last thing we need right now is a band of disgruntled bookpeople besieging the Council of Genres, demanding the right to be read. Okay, item seven: the MAWk-15H virus has once again resurfaced in Dickens, particularly in the death of Little Nell, which is now so uncomfortably saccharine that even our own dear, gentle, patient, noble Nell complained. I need someone to liaise with the BookWorld Communicable Textual Diseases Unit to deal with this. Volunteers?'

Foyle reluctantly put up his hand. Working for the BCTD on bookviruses was never popular as it required a lengthy quarantine on completion; most of Victorian melodrama was to some degree infected with MAWk-15H, and it was often blamed on Jurisfiction agents with poor hygiene.

'Item eight: Jurisfiction recruitment. The percentage of recruits making it to full agent status is currently eight per cent, down from twenty-two per cent three years ago. I'm not saying that standards need to slip or anything, but Senator Jobsworth has threatened to force agents upon us if we can't recruit, and we don't want that.'

We all muttered our agreement. Just recently a few cadets had been making themselves conspicuous by their poor performance. None of us wanted to be understaffed, but then neither did we want the service swamped with knuckleheads.

'So,' continued Bradshaw, 'on the basis that poor training makes failed cadets, I want you all to think about giving them all a little more of your time.'

He put down his clipboard.

'That's it for now. Do the best you can, keep me informed as to progress, and as regards Health and Safety, we've had the welcome news that you can ignore safety practices to save time, but you *must* complete the paperwork. Good luck, and . . . let's be *careful* out there.'

Everyone started to talk among themselves, and after I had told Thursday5 to wait at my desk I threaded my way through the small gathering to speak to Bradshaw. I caught up with him as he was making his way back to his desk.

'You want me to report on the Jane Austen refit?' I asked him. 'Any particular reason?'

Bradshaw was dressed as you might expect a colonial white hunter to dress: in a safari suit with shorts, pith helmet and a revolver in a leather holster. He didn't need to dress like that any more, of course, but he was a man of habit.

'That was mostly misdirection,' he asserted. 'I *do* want you to take a gander but there's something else I'd like you to look at – something I don't want Senator Jobsworth to know about – or at least, not yet.'

Senator Jobsworth was the head of the Council of Genres and a powerful man. Politics within Jurisfiction could be tricky at times, and I had to be particularly diplomatic as far as Jobsworth was concerned – I often had to cross swords with him in the debating chamber. As the only real person in fiction, my advice was often called for – but rarely welcomed.

'What do you want me to do?'

Bradshaw rubbed his moustache thoughtfully.

'We've had a report of something that sounds transfictional.'

'Another one?'

It was the name given to something that had arrived from the real world – the Outland, as it was known. I was a transfictional, of course, but the term was more usually used to refer to something or somebody that had crossed over unexpectedly.

Bradshaw handed me a scrap of paper with the title of a book on it. 'I feel happier with you doing it because you're an Outlander. Appreciate a woman who's proper flesh and blood. By the way, how's Thursday5 doing?'

'She isn't,' I replied. 'Her timidity will end up getting her killed. We had a run-in with a grammasite inside *Lord of the Flies* while dealing with the spectacles problem, and she decided to give the Verbisoid the benefit of the doubt and a very large hug.'

'What type of Verbisoid? Intransitive?'

I shook my head sadly.

47

'Nope. *Ditransitive.*'

Bradshaw whistled low. He hadn't been kidding about recruit-ment troubles or Senator Jobsworth's involvement. Even I knew there were at least three totally unsuitable candidates Jobsworth was pressurising us to 'reappraise'.

'She's lucky to have a single verb left in her body,' said Bradshaw after a pause. 'Give her the full three days before firing her, yes? It has to be by the book in case she tries to sue us.'

I assured him I would and moved back to my desk, where Thursday5 was sitting on the floor in the lotus position. I had a quick rummage through my case notes, which were now stacked high on my desk. In a rash moment I'd volunteered to look at Jurisfiction 'cold cases', thinking that there would only be three or four. As it turned out there were over a hundred infractions of sorts, ranging from random plot fluctuations in the *Gormenghast* trilogy to the inexplicable and untimely death of Charles Dickens, who had once lived long enough to finish *Edwin Drood*. I did as much as I had time for, which wasn't a lot.

'Right,' I said, pulling on my jacket and grabbing my bag, 'we're off. Stick close to me and do *exactly* as I say – even if that means killing grammasites. It's them or us.'

'Them or us,' repeated Thursday5 half-heartedly, slinging her felt handbag over her shoulder in exactly the same way I did. I stopped for a moment and stared at my desk. It had been rearranged.

'Thursday?' I remarked testily. 'Have you been doing feng shui on my desk again?'

'Well, it was more of a *harmonisation*, really,' she replied some-what sheepishly.

'Well, don't.'

'Why not?'

'Just, just . . . *don't.*'

48

5
Training Day

'The BookWorld was a minefield for the unwary, so apprenticeships were essential. We'd lost more agents through poor training than were ever taken by grammasites. A foot wrong in the imaginatively confusing world of fiction could see the inexperienced Jurisfiction cadet mispelled, conjugated or reduced to text. My tutor had been the first Miss Havisham, and I like to think it was her wise counsel which had allowed me to survive as long as I did. Many cadets didn't. The average expectancy for a raw recruit in the BookWorld was about forty-seven chapters.'

We stepped outside the colonnaded entrance of Norland Park and basked in the warmth of the sunshine. The story had long ago departed with the Dashwood family to Devon, and this corner of *Sense and Sensibility* was quiet and unused. To one side a saddled horse was leaning languidly against a tree with a hound sitting on the ground quite near it. Birds sang in the trees, and clouds moved slowly across the heavens. Each cloud was identical, of course, and the sun didn't track across the sky as it did back home, and come to think of it the birdsong was on a twenty-second loop. It was what we called 'narrative economics', the bare amount of description necessary to create a scene. The BookWorld was like that – mostly ordered, and without the rich texture that nature's randomness brings to the real world.

We sat in silence for a few minutes to wait for my taxi. I was thinking about the mostly bald Pickwick, Friday's ChronoGuard presentation, Felix8's return and my perfidy to Landen. Thursday5 had no such worries – she was reading the astrology section of the BookWorld's premier newspaper, *The Word*. After a while she said:

'It's my birthday today.'

'I know.'

'You do? How?'

'Never mind.'

'Listen to what it says in the horoscopes: "If it is your birthday, there may be an increased amount of mail. Expect gifts, friendly salutations from people and the occasional surprise. Possibility of cake." That's so weird – I wonder if any of it will come true?'

'I've no idea. Have you noticed the number of Mrs Danvers you see wandering around these days?'

I mentioned this because a pair of them had been seen at Norland Park that morning. They were becoming a familiar sight around fiction, hanging around popular books out of sight of the reader, looking furtive and glaring malevolently at anyone who asked what they were up to. The excess of Mrs Danvers in the BookWorld was easily explained. Generics, or characters-in-waiting, are created blank without any personality or gender, and are then billeted in novels until called up for training in character schools. From there they are sent either to populate the books being built or to replace characters who are due for retirement or replacement. The problem is, generics have a chameleonic habit of assimilating themselves to a strong leading character, and when six thousand impressionable generics were lodged inside *Rebecca*, all but eight became Mrs Danvers, the creepy housekeeper of Manderley. Since creepy house-keepers are not much in demand these days, they were mostly used as expendable drones for the Mispeling Vyrus Farst Respons Groop or, more sinisterly, for riot control and any other civic disturbances. At Jurisfiction we were concerned that they were becoming another layer of policing, answerable only to the Council of Genres, something that was stridently denied.

'Mrs Danvers?' repeated Thursday, studying a pull-out guide to reading tea leaves. 'I've got one or two in my books but I think they're meant to be there.'

'Tell me,' I said by way of conversation, 'is there any aspect of the BookWorld that you'd like to learn about as part of your time with me?'

'Well,' she said after a pause, 'I'd like to have a go and see what it's like inside a story during a recitation in the Oral Tradition – I've heard it's really kind of *buzzing*.'

She was right. It was like sweaty live improv theatre – anything could happen.

'No way,' I said, 'and if I hear that you've been anywhere near OralTrad you'll be confined to the *Great Samuel Pepys Fiasco*. It's not like books where everything's laid out and orderly. The Oral Tradition is *dynamic* like you've no idea. Change anything in there and you will, quite literally, give the narrator an aneurism.'

'A *what*?'

'A brain haemorrhage. The same can be said of Poetry. You don't want to go hacking around in there without a clear head on your shoulders.'

'Why?'

'It's like a big emotion magnifier. All feelings are exacerbated to a dangerous level. You can find things out about yourself that you never knew – or ever wanted to know. We have a saying: "You can lose yourself in a book, but you find yourself in poetry." It's like being able to see yourself when drunk.'

'Ah-ha,' she said in a quiet voice.

There was a pause.

'You've never been drunk, have you?'

She shook her head.

'Do you think I should try it?'

'It's overrated.'

I had a thought. 'Have you ever been up to the Council of Genres?'

'No.'

'A lamentable omission. That's where we'll go first.'

I pulled out my mobile footnoterphone to call TransGenreTaxis to see where my cab had got to. The reason for a taxi was not altogether obvious to Thursday5, who, like most residents of the BookWorld, could bookjump to any novel previously visited with an ease I found annoying. My *inter*-fictional bookjumping was twenty times better than my *trans*-fictional jumps, but even then a bit ropy. I needed to read a full paragraph to get in, and if I didn't have the right section in my TravelBook, then I had to walk via the Great Library or get a taxi — as long as one was available.

'Wouldn't it be quicker to just bookjump?' asked Thursday with annoying directness.

'You young things are always in a hurry, aren't you?' I replied. 'Besides, it's more dignified to walk — and the view is generally better. However,' I added with a sense of deflated ego, 'in the absence of an available cab, we shall.'

I pulled out my TravelBook, turned to the correct page and jumped from *Sense and Sensibility* to the Great Library.

6

The Great Library and Council of Genres

'The textual sieve was designed and constructed by JurisTech, the technological arm of Jurisfiction. The textual sieve is a fantastically useful and mostly unexplained device that allows the user to "sieve" or "strain" text in order to isolate a specified search string. Infinitely variable, a well-tuned textual sieve on "full opaque" can rebuff an entire book, but set to "fine" can delicately remove a spider's web from a half-million-word novel.'

I found myself in a long, dark, wood-panelled corridor lined with bookshelves that reached from the richly carpeted floor to the vaulted ceiling. The carpet was elegantly patterned and the ceiling was decorated with rich mouldings that depicted scenes from the classics, each cornice supporting the marble bust of an author. High above me, spaced at regular intervals, were finely decorated circular apertures through which light gained entry and reflected off the polished wood, reinforcing the serious mood of the library. Running down the centre of the corridor was a long row of reading tables, each with a green-shaded brass lamp. In both directions the corridor vanished into darkness with no definable end.

I had first entered the Great Library sixteen years ago, and the description of it hadn't altered by so much as a word. Hundreds of miles of shelves containing not every single book, but every single *edition* of every book. Anything that had been published in the real world had a counterpart logged somewhere within its endless corridors.

Thursday5 was near by and joined me to walk along the corridor, making our way towards the crossover section right at the heart of the Library. But the thing to realise was that it wasn't in any sense of the word *real*, any more than the rest of the BookWorld was. The Library was as nebulous as the books it contained; its form was decided not only by the base description but my *interpretation* of what a Great Library might look like. Because of this, the library was as subtly changeable as my moods, at times dark and sombre, at others light and airy. Reading, I had learned, was as creative a process as writing, sometimes more so. When we read of the dying rays of the setting sun or the boom and swish of the incoming tide, we should reserve as much praise for ourselves as for the author. After all, the reader is doing all the work – the writer may have died long ago.

We approached another corridor perpendicular to the one we had just walked down. In the middle of the crossway was a large circular void with a wrought-iron rail and a spiral staircase bolted securely to one side. We walked over to the handrail and peered down. Not more than thirty feet below us I could see another floor, exactly like this one. In the middle of that floor was another circular void through which I could see another floor, and another and another and so on to the depths of the library. It was the same above us.

'Twenty-six floors for the published works,' replied Thursday5 as I caught her eye and raised an eyebrow quizzically, 'and twenty-six sub-basements where books are actually constructed – the Well of Lost Plots.'

I beckoned her to the ornate wrought-iron lift and pressed the 'call' button. We got into the lift, I drew the gates shut with a clatter and the electric motors whined as we headed upwards. Because there are very few authors whose names begin with Q, X and Z, floors seventeen, twenty-four and twenty-six were relatively empty and thus free for other purposes. The seventeenth floor housed the Mispelling Vyrus Farst Respons Groop, the twenty-fourth floor was used essentially for storage, and the twenty-sixth was where the legislative body that governs the BookWorld, the Council of Genres, had taken up residence.

This was a floor unlike any other in the Great Library. Gone was the dark wood, moulded plaster ceilings and busts of long-dead writers, and in their place was a light, airy working space with a roof of curved wrought iron covered in glass through which we could see the clouds and sky. I beckoned Thursday5 to a large picture window in an area to one side of the corridor. There were a few chairs scattered about and it was a restful spot, designed so that overworked CofG employees could relax for a moment. I had stood here with my own mentor, the first Miss Havisham, almost sixteen years previously.

'The Great Library looks smaller from the outside,' observed Thursday, staring out of the window at the rain-streaked exterior.

She was right. The corridors in the library below could be as long as two hundred miles in each direction, expandable upon requirements, but from the outside the library looked more akin to the Chrysler Building, liberally decorated with stainless-steel statuary and measuring less than 200 yards along each face. And even though we were only on the twenty-sixth floor it looked a great deal higher. I had once been to the top of the 120-storey Goliath tower at Goliathopolis, and this seemed easily as high as that.

'The other towers?' she asked, still staring out of the window. Far below us were the tops of a deep forest flecked with mist, and scattered around at varying distances were other towers just like ours.

'The nearest one is German,' I said, 'and behind those are French and Spanish. Arabic is just beyond them – and that one over there is Welsh.'

'Oh,' said Thursday5, staring at the green foliage far below.

'The Council of Genres look after fictional legislature,' I said, walking down the corridor to the main assembly chamber. It had become busier since we had arrived, with various clerks moving around holding files of papers, reports and so forth. I had thought red tape was bad in the real world, but in the paper world it was everything. I had come to realise over the years that anything created by mankind had error, mischief and bureaucratic officialdom hardwired at inception, and the fictional world was no different.

'The Council govern dramatic conventions, strictly control the use of irony, legislate on word use, and through the Book Inspectorate, decide which novels are to be published, and which ones are to be scrapped.'

We had arrived at a viewing gallery overlooking the main debating chamber, which was a spacious hall of white marble with an arched roof supported by riveted iron girders. There was a raised dais at the back with a central and ornately carved chair flanked by four smaller ones on either side. A lectern for the speaker was in front of that, and facing both the lectern and the dais was a horsehoe pattern of desks for the representatives of the various genres. The back wall of the chamber was decorated with a vast mosaic representing the theoretical positions of the genres as they hung in the Nothing. The only other item of note in the debating chamber was the Read-O-Meter, which gave us a continually updated figure of just how many books had been read over the previous twenty-four hours. This instrument was a constant reminder of the falling readrates that had troubled the BookWorld over the past five years, and every time the numbers flopped over – and they did every five seconds – the number went *down*. Sometimes in depressingly large amounts. There was someone speaking volubly at the lectern, and the debating chamber was less than a third full.

'The main genres are seated at the front,' I explained, 'and the sub-genres radiate out behind them, in order of importance and size. Although the CofG look after broad legislative issues, each

56

individual genre can make its own decision on a local level. They all field a senator to appear before the Council and look after their own interests – sometimes the debating chamber resembles something less like a seat of democracy, and more like plain old horse-trading.'

'Who's talking now?' she asked as a new member took the podium. He looked as though he hadn't brushed his hair that morning, was handsome if a bit dim looking, had no shoes and was wearing a shirt split open to the waist.

'That'll be Speedy Muffler, the senator from the Racy Novel genre, although I suspect that might not be his real name.'

'They have a senator?'

'Of course. Every genre has at least one, and depending on the popularity of sub-genres, they might have several. Thriller, which is sub-genred into Political, Spy and Adventure, has three. Comedy at the last count had six; Crime has twelve.'

'I see. So what's Racy Novel's problem?'

'It's a border dispute. Although each book exists on its own and is adrift in the inter-genre space known as the Nothing, the books belonging to the various genres clump together for mutual protection, free trade of ideas and easy movement of characters.'

'I get it. Books of a feather flock together, yes?'

'Pretty much. Sensibly, Thriller was placed next door to Crime, which itself is bordered by Human Drama – a fine demonstration of inspired genreography for the very best mutual improvement of both.'

'And Racy Novel?'

'Some idiot placed it somewhat recklessly between Ecclesiastical and Feminist, with the tiny principality of Erotica to the far north and a buffer zone with Comedy to the south comprising the crossover sub-genre Bedroom Farce/Bawdy Romp. Racy Novel get along with Comedy and Erotica fine, but Ecclesiastical and Feminist really don't think Racy Novel is worthy of a genre at all, and often fire salvos of long-winded intellectual dissent across the border, which might do more damage if anyone in Racy Novel could understand them. For their part Racy Novel send panty-raiding parties into their neighbours, which wasn't welcome in Feminist, and even less in Ecclesiastical – or was it the other way round? Anyway, the whole deal might have escalated into an all-out genre war without the Council of Genres stepping in and brokering a peace deal. The CofG would guarantee Racy Novel's independence as long as they agreed to certain . . . *sanctions.*'

'Which were?'

'An import ban on metaphor, characterisation and competent description. Speedy Muffler is a bit of a megalomaniac, and both Feminist and Ecclesiastical thought containment was better than out-and-out conflict. The problem is, Racy Novel claim that this is worse than a slow attritional war as these sanctions deny them the potential of literary advancement beyond the limited scope of their work.'

'I can't say I'm very sympathetic to their cause.'

'It's not important that you are – your role in Jurisfiction is only to defend the status—'

I had stopped talking as something seemed to be going on down in the debating chamber. In a well-orchestrated lapse of protocol, delegates were throwing their ballot papers around and among the jeering and catcalls, Muffler was struggling to make himself heard. I shook my head sadly.

'What is it?'

'Something that Racy Novel have been threatening for some time – they claim to have developed and tested a . . . *dirty bomb.*'

'A what?'

'It's a tightly packed mass of inappropriate plot devices, explicit suggestions and sexual scenes of an expressly gratuitous nature. The "dirty" elements of the bomb fly apart at a preset time and attach themselves to any unshielded prose. Given the target, it has the potential for untold damage. A well-placed dirty bomb could scatter poorly described fornication all across drab theological debate, or drop a wholly unwarranted scene of a sexually exploitative nature right into the middle of *Mrs Dalloway*.'

Even Thursday5 could see this was not a good thing.

'Would he do that?'

'He just might. Senator Muffler is as mad as a barrel of skunks, and the inclusion of Racy Novel in the Council of Genre's definition of the "Axis of Unreadable" along with Misery Memoirs and Pseudo-intellectual Drivel didn't help matters at all. It'll be all over the BookWorld by nightfall, mark my words – the papers love this kind of combative sabre-rattling crap.'

'Ms Next!' came an annoying high-pitched voice.

I turned to find a small weasel of a man with pinched features dressed in robes and with a goodly retinue of self-important assistants stacked up behind him.

'Good morning, Senator,' I said, bowing as protocol demanded. 'May I introduce my apprentice, Thursday5? Thursday5, this is Senator Jobsworth, Director General of the CofG and head of the Pan-Genre Treaty Organisation.'

'Sklub,' gulped Thursday5, trying to curtsy, bob and bow all at the same time. The senator nodded in her direction, then dismissed everyone before beckoning me to join him at the large picture window.

'Ms Next,' he said in a quiet voice, 'how are things down at Jurisfiction?'

'Underfunded as usual,' I replied, well used to Jobsworth's manipulative ways.

'It needn't be so,' he replied. 'If I can count on your support for policy direction in the near future, I am sure we can rectify the situation.'

'You are too kind,' I replied, 'but I will base my decisions on what is best for the BookWorld as a whole, rather than the department I work in.'

His eyes flashed angrily. Despite being the head of the Council, policy decisions still had to be made by consensus – and it annoyed the hell out of him.

'With Outlander read-rates almost in free-fall,' continued Jobsworth with a snarl, 'I'd have thought you'd be willing to compromise on those precious scruples of yours.'

'I don't compromise,' I told him resolutely. 'I base my decisions on what is best for the BookWorld.'

'Well,' said Jobsworth with an insincere smile, 'let's hope you don't regret any of your decisions. Good day.'

And he swept off with his entourage at his heels. He didn't frighten me with his threats; he'd been making them – and I'd been ignoring them – for almost as long as we'd known one another.

'I didn't realise you were so close to Senator Jobsworth,' said Thursday5 as soon as she had rejoined me.

'I have a seat at the upper-level policy directive meetings as the official LBOCS. Since I'm an Outlander I have powers of abstract and long-term thought that most fictioneers can only dream about. The thing is, I don't generally toe the line, and Jobsworth doesn't like that.'

'Can I ask a question?' asked Thursday5 as we took the lift back down into the Great Library.

'Of course.'

'I'm a little confused over how the whole ImaginoTransference technology works? I mean, how do books *here* get to be read out *there*?'

I sighed. Cadets were meant to come to me for assessment when they already knew the basics. This one was as green as *Brighton*

Rock. The lift stopped on the third floor and I pulled open the gates. We stepped out into one of the Great Library's endless corridors and I waved a hand in the direction of the bookshelves.

'Okay: ImaginoTransference. Did any of your tutors tell you even vaguely how the reader/writer thing actually *works?*'

'I think I might have been having a colonic that morning.'

I moved closer to the shelves and beckoned her to follow. As I came to within a yard of the books I could feel their influence warm me like a hot radiator. But it wasn't heat I was feeling, it was the warmth of a good story, well told – a potpourri of jumbled narrative, hovering just proud of the books like morning mist on a lake. I could actually feel the emotions, hear the whispered snatches of conversation and see the images that momentarily broke free of the gravity that bound them to the story.

'Can you feel that?' I whispered.

'Feel what?'

I sighed. Fictional people were less attuned to *story*; it was rare indeed that anyone in the BookWorld actually read a book – unless the narrative called for it.

'Place your hands gently against the spines.'

She did as I asked, and after a moment's puzzlement she smiled.

'I can hear voices,' she whispered back, trying not to break the moment, 'and a waterfall. And joy, betrayal, laughter – and a young man who has lost his hat.'

'What you're feeling is the raw ImaginoTransference energy, the method by which all books are dispersed into the reader's imagination. The books we have in the Outland are no more similar to these than a photograph is to the subject – these books are *alive*, each one a small universe unto itself – and by throughputting some of that energy from here to their counterparts in the real world, we can transmit the story direct to the reader.'

Thursday took her hand from the books and experimented to

see how far out she had to go before losing the energy. It was barely a few inches.

'Throughputting? Is that where textual sieves come into it?'

'No. I've got to go and look at something for Bradshaw so we'll check out core containment – it's at the heart of the ImaginoTransference technology.'

We walked a few yards up the corridor, and after carefully consulting the note Bradshaw had given me, I selected a book from the bewildering array of the same title in all its various incarnations. I opened the volume and looked at the stats page, which blinked up a real-time Outland read-rate, the total number of the edition still in existence and much else besides.

'Nineteen twenty-nine book club deluxe leather-bound edition with nine copies still in circulation from a total of two thousand five hundred,' I explained, 'and with no readers actually making their way through it. An ideal choice for a bit of tuition.'

I rummaged in my bag and brought out what looked like a large-calibre flare pistol.

Thursday5 looked at me nervously.

'Are you expecting trouble?'

'I *always* expect trouble.'

'Isn't that a textmarker?' she asked, her confusion understandable because this wasn't officially a weapon at all. They were generally used to mark the text of a book from within so an agent could be extracted in an emergency. Once an essential piece of kit, they were carried less and less as the mobile footnoterphone had made such devices redundant.

'It was,' I replied, breaking open the stubby weapon and taking a single brass cartridge from a small leather pouch, 'but I've modified it to take an eraserhead.'

I slipped the cartridge in, snapped the pistol shut and put it back in my bag. The eraserhead was just one of the many abstract technologies that JurisTech built for us. Designed to sever the bonds between letters in a word, it was a devastating weapon to anyone of textual origin – a single blast from one of these and the unlucky recipient would be nothing but a jumbled heap of letters and a bluish haze. Its use was strictly controlled – Jurisfiction agents only.

'Gosh,' said Thursday after I'd explained it to her, 'I don't carry any weapons at all.'

'I'd so love not to have to,' I told her, and with the taxi still nowhere in sight I passed the volume across to her.

'Here,' I said, 'let's see how you good you are at taking a passenger into a book.'

She took the novel without demur, opened it and started to read. She had a good speaking voice, fruity and expressive, and she quickly began to fade from view. I grabbed hold of her cuff so as not to be left behind and she instantly regained her solidity; it was the Library that was now faded and indistinct. Within a few more words we had travelled into our chosen book. The first thing I noticed as we arrived was that the chief protagonist's feet were on fire. Worse still, he hadn't noticed.

7

A Probe inside Pinocchio

**'The idea of using footnotes as a communication medium
was suggested by Dr Faustus as far back as 1622, it wasn't
until 1856 that the first practical footnoterphone was
demonstrated.** The first trans-genre trunk line between Human
Drama and Crime was opened in 1915, and the network has been
expanded and improved ever since. Although the system is far
from complete, with many books still having only a single foot-
noterpayphone; on the outer reaches of the known BookWorld,
many books are without coverage at all.'

It was Pinocchio, of course, I'd know that nose anywhere. As we
jumped into the toy workshop on page twenty-six, the wooden
puppet – Geppetto's or Collodi's creation, depending on which way
you looked at it – was asleep with his feet on a brazier. The workbench was clean and tidy. Half-finished wooden toys filled every
available space and all the woodworking tools were hung up neatly
on the wall. There was a cot in one corner, a sideboard in another
and the floor was covered with curly wood shavings, but no sawdust
or dirt. The fictional world was like that; a sort of narrative shorthand that precluded any of the shabby grottiness and *texture* that
gives the real world its richness.

Pinocchio was snoring loudly. Comically, almost. His feet were
smouldering and within a few lines it would be morning and he
would have nothing left but charred stumps. He wasn't the only
person in the room. On the sideboard were two crickets watching
the one-day international on a portable TV. One was wearing a
smoking jacket and a pillbox hat and held a cigarette in a silver

holder, and the other had a broken antenna, a black eye and one leg in a sling.

'The name's Thursday Next,' I announced to them both, holding up my Jurisfiction badge, 'and this is . . . Thursday Next.'

'Which is the real one?' asked the cricket in the pillbox hat — somewhat tactlessly, I thought.

'I am,' I replied through gritted teeth, 'can't you tell?'

'Frankly, no,' replied the cricket, looking at the pair of us in turn. 'So . . . which is the one that does naked yoga?'

'That would be me,' said Thursday5 brightly. I groaned audibly.

'What's the matter?' she asked, amused by my prudishness. 'You should try it some day. It's relaxing and very empowering.'

'I don't do yoga,' I told her.

'Take it up and drop the bacon sandwiches and it will put ten years on your life.'

The cricket, who spoke in a clipped accent reminiscent of Noël Coward, folded up his paper and said:

'We don't often get visitors, you know — the last lot to pass through this way was the Italian Translation Inspectorate making sure we were keeping to the spirit of the original.'

The cricket had a sudden thought and indicated the damaged cricket sitting next to him.

'How rude could I be? This is Jim "Bruises" McDowell, my stunt double.'

Bruises looked as though the stunt sequence with the mallet hadn't gone quite as planned.

'Hello,' said the stunt cricket with an embarrassed shrug, 'I had an accident during training. Some damn fool went and moved the crash mat.' As he said it he looked at the other cricket, who did nothing but puff on his cigarette and preen his antennae in a nonchalant fashion.

'I'm sorry to hear that,' I said by way of conversation — a good

66

relationship with the characters within the BookWorld was essential in our work. 'Have you been read recently?'

The cricket in the pillbox hat suddenly looked embarrassed.

'The truth is,' he said awkwardly, 'we've *never* been read. Not once in seventy-three years. Deluxe book club editions are like that – just for show. But if we *did* have a reading, we'd all be primed and set to go.'

'I can do a lot more than the "being hit with the mallet" stunt,' added Bruises excitedly. 'Would you like me to set myself on fire and fall out of a window? I can wave my arms very convincingly.'

'No thanks.'

'Shame,' replied Bruises wistfully. 'I'd like to broaden my skills to cover car-to-helicopter transfers and being dragged backwards by a horse – whatever that is.'

'When the last of the nine copies of this book have gone,' pointed out the cricket, 'we can finally come off duty and be reassigned. I'm studying for the lead in *Charlotte's Web*.'

'Do you know of any other books that require stunt crickets?' asked Bruises hopefully. 'I've been practising the very dangerous and not at all foolhardy leap over seventeen motorcycles in a double-decker bus.'

'Isn't it meant to be the other way round?'

'I told you it seemed a bit rum,' said the cricket as Bruises' shoulders sagged. 'But never mind all that,' he added, returning his attention to me. 'I suppose you're here about . . . the *thing*?'

'We are, sir. Where is it?'

The cricket pointed with three of his legs at a pile of half-finished toys in the corner and, thus rendered lopsided, fell over. His stunt double laughed until the cricket glared at him dangerously.

'It appeared unannounced three days ago – quite ruined my entrance.'

'I thought you'd never been read?'

'*Rehearsals*, dahling. I do like to keep the thespian juices fresh – and Bruises here likes to practise his celebrated "falling from the wall after being struck by a mallet" stunt – and then the leg-twitching and death throes which he does *so* well.'

Bruises said nothing and studied the tips of his antennae modestly.

I cautiously approached the area of the room the cricket had indicated. Half hidden behind a marionette with no head and a hobby horse in need of sanding was a dull metallic sphere about the size of a grapefruit. It had several aerials sticking out of the top and an array of lenses protruding from the front. I leaned closer and sniffed at it cautiously. I could smell the odour of corrosion and see the fine pits on the heat-streaked surface. This wasn't an errant space probe from the Sci-Fi canon; it was too well described for that. Bradshaw had been right – it was transfictional.

'Where do you think it's from?' asked the cricket. 'We get scraps of other books blowing in from time to time when there's a word-storm, but nothing serious. Bottom from *Midsummer Night's Dream* sheltered here for a while during the textphoon of '32 and picked up a thing or two from Lamp-Wick, but only the odd verb or two otherwise. Is it important?'

'Not really,' I replied. It was a lie, of course – but I didn't want a panic. This was anything *but* unimportant. I gently rotated the probe and read the engraved metal plate on the back. There was a serial number and a name that I recognised only too well – the Goliath Corporation. My least favourite multinational and a thorn in my side for many years. I was annoyed and heartened all at the same time. Annoyed that they had developed a machine for hurling probes inside fiction, but heartened that this was all they had managed to achieve. As I peered closer at the inert metallic ball there was a warning chirrup from my bag. I quickly dug out a small instrument and tossed it to Thursday5.

'A reader?' she said with surprise. 'In here?'

'So it seems. How far away are they?'

She flipped the device open and stared at the flickering needle blankly. Technology was another point she wasn't that strong on.

'We're clear. The reader is – er – two paragraphs ahead of us.'

'Are you sure?'

She looked at the instrument again. It was a Narrative Proximity Device, and was designed to ensure that our interfictional perambulations couldn't be seen by readers in the Outland. One of the odd things about the BookWorld was that when characters weren't being read they generally relaxed and talked, rehearsed, drank coffee, watched the cricket or played mah-jong. But as soon as a reading loomed they all leapt into place and did their thing. They could sense the reading approaching out of long experience, but we couldn't – hence the Narrative Proximity Device. Being caught up in a reading wasn't particularly desirable for a Jurisfiction agent as it generally caused a certain degree of confusion in the reader. I was spotted once myself – and once is once too often.

'I think so,' replied Thursday, staring at the meter again. 'No, wait – yes.'

'A positive echo means the reader is ahead of us, a negative means—'

'Bother,' she muttered. 'They're two paragraphs *behind* and coming this way – ma'am, I think we're about to be *read*.'

'Are they a fast reader?'

She consulted the meter once more. If they were fast – a fan on a reread or a bored student – then we'd be fine. A slow reader searching every word for hidden meaning and subtle nuance and we might have to jump out until they'd passed.

'Looks like a 41.3.'

This was faster than the maximum throughput of the book, which was pegged at about sixteen words per second. It was a speed-reader, as likely as not reading every fifth word, and skimming over the top of the prose like a stone skipping on water.

'They'll never see us. Press yourself against the wall until the reading moves through.'

'Are you sure?' asked Thursday5, who had done her basic training with the old Jurisfiction adage of 'Better dead than read' ringing in her ears.

'You should know what a reading looks like if you're to be an asset to Jurisfiction. Besides,' I added, 'overcaution is for losers.'

I was being unnecessarily strict – we could quite easily have jumped out or even hopped back a few pages and followed the narrative *behind* the reading, but cadets need to sail close to the wind a few times. Both the crickets were in something of a tizzy at the prospect of their first ever reading and tried to run in several directions at once before vanishing off to their places.

'Stand still,' I said as we pressed ourselves against the least well-described part of the wall and looked again at the NPD. The needle was rising rapidly and counting off the words to what we termed 'Read Zero', the actual time and place – the comprehension singularity – where the story was being *read*.

There was a distant hum and a rumble as the reading approached, a light buzz in the air like static and an increased heightening of the senses as the reader took up the descriptive power of the book, and translated it into his or her own unique interpretation of the events – channelled from here through the massive ImaginoTransference storycode engines back at Text Grand Central and into their imagination. It was a technology of almost incalculable complexity which I was yet to fully understand. But the beauty of the whole process was that the reader in the Outland never suspected there was any sort of process at all – the act of reading was to most people, myself included, as natural as breathing.

Geppetto's woodworking tools began to jiggle on the workbench and a few of the wood shavings started to drift across the floor, gaining more detail as they moved. I frowned. Something wasn't right. I had expected the room to gain a small amount of increased reality as the reader's imagination bathed it in the power of their own past experiences and interpretations, but as the trembling and warmth increased I noticed that this small section of Collodi's nineteenth-century allegorical tale was being raised to an unprecedented level of descriptive power. The walls, which up until then had been a blank wash of colour, suddenly gained texture, a myriad of subtle hues and even areas of damp. The window frames peeled and dusted up, the floor moved and undulated until it was covered in flagstones that even I, as an Outlander, would not be able to distinguish from reality. As Pinocchio slept on, the reading suddenly swelled like a breaking ocean roller and crossed the room in front of us, a crest of height-ened reality that moved through us and imparted a warm feeling of well-being. But more than that, a rare thing in fiction, a delicate potpourri of *smells*. Freshly cut wood, cooking, spice, damp – and Pinocchio's scorched legs, which I recognised were carved from cherry. There was more, too, a strange jumble of faces, a young girl laughing and a derelict castle in the moonlight. The smells grew stronger until I could taste them in my mouth, the dust and grime in the room seemingly accentuated until there was a faint hiss and a *ploof* sound and the enhanced feelings dropped away in an instant. Everything once more returned to the limited reality we had experienced when we arrived – the bare description necessary for the room to be Geppetto's workshop. I nudged Thursday5, who opened her eyes and looked around with relief.

'What was *that*?' she said, staring at me in alarm.

'We were *read*,' I said, a little rattled myself – whoever it was could not have failed to see us.

'I've been read many times,' murmured Thursday5, 'from perfunc-tory skim to critical analysis, and nothing ever felt like *that*.'

She was right. I'd stood in for GSD knows how many characters over the years, but even I'd never felt such an in-depth reading.

'Look,' she said, holding up the Narrative Proximity Device. The read-through rate had peaked at an unheard-of 68.5.

'That's not possible,' I muttered. 'The ImaginoTransference bandwidth doesn't support readings of that depth at such a speed.'

'Do you think they saw us?'

'I'm sure of it,' I replied, my ears still singing, and a strange woody taste still in my mouth. I consulted the NPD again. The reader was now well ahead of us and tearing through the prose towards the end of the book.

'Goodness!' exclaimed the cricket, who looked a little flushed and spacey when he reappeared along with his stunt double a few minutes later, 'that was every bit as exhilarating as I thought it would be – and I didn't dry. I was excellent, wasn't I?'

'You were just *wonderful*, darling,' said his stunt double. 'The whole of allegorical juvenilia will be talking about you – one for the envelope, I think.'

'And you, sir,' returned the cricket, 'that fall from the wall – *simply* divine.'

But self-congratulatory crickets didn't really concern me right now, and even the Goliath probe was momentarily forgotten.

'A *Superreader*,' I breathed. 'I'd heard the legends but thought they were nothing more than that; tall tales from burned-out text jockeys who'd been mainlining on irregular verbs.'

'Superreader?' echoed Thursday inquisitively, and even the crickets stopped congratulating each other on a perfect performance and leaned closer to listen.

'It's a reader with an unprecedented power of comprehension; someone who can pick up every subtle nuance, all the inferred narrative and deeply embedded subtext in one tenth the time of normal readers.'

'The reading suddenly swelled like a breaking ocean roller and crossed the room in front of us.'

'That's good, right?'

'Not really. A dozen or so Superreads could strip all the meaning out of a book, leaving the volume a tattered husk with little characterisation and only the thinnest of plots.'

'So . . . most Daphne Farquitt novels have been subjected to a Superreader?'

'No, they're just bad.'

I thought for a moment, made a few notes in my pocketbook and then picked up the Outlander probe. I tried to call Bradshaw to tell him but got only his answering machine. I placed the probe in my bag, recalled that I was also here to tell Thursday5 something about the ImaginoTransference technology, and turned to the crickets.

'Where's the Core Containment Chamber?'

'Cri-cri-cri,' muttered the cricket, thinking hard. 'I think it's one of the doors off the kitchen.'

'Right.'

I bade farewell to the crickets, who had begun to bicker when the one with the pillbox hat suggested it was high time he did his own stunts.

'I say, do you mind?' enquired Pinocchio indolently, neither opening his eyes nor removing his feet from the brazier, 'some of us are trying to get some shut-eye.'

8

Julian Sparkle

'Standard-issue equipment to all Jurisfiction agents, the dimensionally ambivalent TravelBook contains information, tips, maps, recipes and extracts from popular or troublesome novels to enable speedier interfiction travel. It also contains numerous JurisTech gadgets for more specialised tasks such as an MV mask, textmarker and Eject-O-Hat. The TravelBook's cover is read-locked to each individual operative and contains as standard an emergency alert and auto-destruct mechanism.'

We entered the kitchen of Geppetto's small house. It had a sort of worthy austerity about it but was clean and functional. A cat was asleep next to a log basket and a kettle sang merrily to itself on the range. But we weren't the only people in the kitchen. There were two other doors leading off, and in front of each was a bored-looking individual sitting on a three-legged stool. In the centre of the room was what appeared to be a quiz show compère dressed in a gold lamé suit. He had a fake tan that was almost orange, heavy jewellery and a perfectly sculpted hairstyle that looked as though it had been imported from the fifties.

'Ah!' he said as soon as he saw us. 'Contestants!'

He picked up his microphone.

'Welcome,' he said with faux bonhomie, showing acres of perfect white teeth, 'to *Puzzlemania*, the popular brain game – and I am your host, Julian Sparkle.'

He smiled at us and an imaginary audience and beckoned Thursday5 closer, but I indicated for her to stay where she was.

'I can do this—!' she exclaimed.

'No,' I whispered, 'Sparkle might *seem* like an innocuous game show host, but he's a potential killer.'

'I thought you said overcaution was for losers?' she returned, attempting to make up for the bacon-roll debacle. 'Besides, I can look after myself.'

'Then be my guest,' I said with a smile, 'or rather, you can be *his* guest.'

My namesake turned to Sparkle and walked up to a mark on the floor that he had indicated. As she did so, the lights in the room dimmed, apart from a spotlight on the two of them. There was a short blast of applause, seemingly from nowhere.

'So, contestant number one, what's your name, why are you in Geppetto's kitchen and where do you come from?'

'My name's Thursday Next-5, I want to visit the Core Containment Chamber as part of a training mission and I'm from *The Great Samuel Pepys Fiasco*.'

'Well then, if you can *contain* your excitement you could have a prize *visited* upon you – fail and it might well be a *fiasco*.'

Thursday5 blinked at him uncomprehendingly.

'*Contain* your excitement . . . prize *visited* . . . a *Fiasco*?' repeated Sparkle, trying to get her to understand his appalling attempts at humour.

She continued to stare at him blankly.

'Never mind. All righty, then. Ms Next, who wants to visit Core Containment, today we're going to play . . . "Liars & Tigers".'

He indicated the two doors leading off the kitchen, each with the bored-looking individual staring vacantly into space in front of it.

'The rules are very simple. You have two identical doors. Behind one is the Core Containment Chamber you seek, and behind the other . . . is a tiger.'

The confident expression dropped from Thursday5's face, and I hid a smile.

'A what?' she asked.

'A tiger.'

'A real one, or a written one?'

'It's the same thing. Guarding the door of each is an individual, one who always tells the truth, and the other who always lies. You can't know which is which, nor which door is guarded by whom – and you have one question, to one guard, to discover the correct door. Ms Next, are you ready to play "Liars & Tigers"?'

'A *tiger*? A real tiger?'

'All eight feet of it.' Julian, who was enjoying himself again, smiled. 'Teeth one end, tail the other, claws at all four corners. Are you ready?'

'If it's all the same to you,' she said politely, 'I'll be getting on my way.'

In a flash Sparkle had pulled out a shiny automatic and pressed it hard into her cheek.

'You're going to play the game, Next,' he growled. 'Get it right and you win today's super-duper prize. Get it wrong and you're tiger poo. Refuse and I play the "spread the dopey cow all over the kitchen" game.'

'Can't we form a circle of trust, have a herbal tea and then discuss our issues?'

'That,' said Sparkle softly, a maniacal glint in his eyes, 'was the *incorrect* answer.'

His finger tightened on the trigger and the two guards both covered their heads. This had gone far enough.

'Wait!'

Sparkle stopped and looked at me.

'What?'

'I'll take her place.'

'It's against the rules.'

'Not if we play the "double death tiger snack" game.'

Sparkle looked at Thursday5, then at me.

'I'm not fully conversant with that one,' he said slowly, eyes narrowed.

'It's easy,' I replied, 'I take her place and if I lose then you get to feed us *both* to the tiger. If I win we both go free.'

'Okay,' said Sparkle, and released Thursday5, who ran and hid behind me.

'Shoot him,' she said in hoarse whisper.

'What about the herbal tea?'

'*Shoot him.*'

'That's *not* how we do things,' I said in a quiet voice. 'Now just watch and listen and *learn.*'

The two guards donned steel helmets and Sparkle himself retreated to the other side of the room, from where he could escape if the tiger were released. I walked up to the two individuals, who looked at me with a quizzical air and started to rub some tiger repellent on themselves from a large tube. The doors were identical, and so were the guards. I scratched my head and thought hard, considering my answer. Two doors, two guards. One guard always told the truth, one always lied – and one question to one guard to find the correct door. I'd heard of this puzzle when a kid, but never thought my life might depend upon it. But hey, this was fiction. Strange, unpredictable – and *fun.*

9

Core Containment

'For thousands of years OralTrad was the only Story Operating System and indeed it is still in use today. The *recordable* Story Operating Systems began with ClayTablet V2.1 and went through several competing systems (WaxTablet, Papyrus, VellumPro) before merging into the award winning SCROLL, which was upgraded eight times before being swept aside by the all new and clearly superior BOOK V1. Stable, easy to store and transport, compact and with a workable index, BOOK has led the way for nearly eighteen hundred years.'

I turned to the guard on the left.

'If I asked the *other* guard,' I said with some trepidation, 'which was the door to the Core Containment Chamber, which one would he say?'

The guard thought for a moment and pointed to one of the doors, and I turned back to look at Sparkle and the somewhat concerned face of Thursday5, who was rapidly coming to terms with the idea that there was a lot of weird shit in the BookWorld that she'd no idea how to handle – such as potential tiger attacks inside *Pinocchio*.

'Have you chosen your door, Ms Next?' asked Julian Sparkle. 'Remember, if you win you get through to Core Containment – and if you lose, there is a high probability of being eaten. Choose your door . . . wisely.'

I gave a smile and grasped the handle – not on the door that had been indicated by the guard, but the *other* one. I pulled it open to reveal . . . a flight of steps leading downwards.

Sparkle's eyebrow twitched and he grimaced momentarily before breaking once more into an insincere grin. The two guards breathed a sigh of relief and removed their helmets to mop their brows; it was clear dealing with tigers wasn't something they much liked to do and the tiger, itself a bit miffed, growled from behind the other door.

'Congratulations,' muttered Sparkle, 'you have chosen ... correctly.'

I nodded to Thursday5, who joined me at the doorway, leaving Sparkle and the two guards arguing over what my super-duper prize should be.

'How did you know which guard was which?' she asked in a respectful tone.

'I didn't,' I replied, 'and still don't. But I assumed that the guards would know who told the truth and who didn't. Since my question would *always* show me the wrong door irrespective of who I asked, I just took the opposite to the one indicated.'

'Oh!' she said, trying to figure it out. 'What were they doing there anyway?'

'Sparkle and the others are what we call anecdotals. Brainteasers, puzzles, jokes, anecdotes and urban legends that are in the Oral Tradition but not big enough to exist on their own. They need to be instantly retrieved, so they have to be flexible and available at a moment's notice – so we billet them unseen around the various works of fiction.'

'I get it,' replied Thursday5. 'We had the joke about the centipede playing football with us at *Fiasco* for a while. Out of sight of the readers, of course. Total pest – we kept on tripping over his boots.'

We stopped at the foot of the stairs. The room was about the size of a double garage and seemed to be constructed of riveted brass that was green with oxidisation. The walls were gently curved, giving the impression that we were inside a huge barrel, and there was a hollow cathedral-like quality to our voices. In the centre of the room was a circular waist-high bronze plinth about the size and shape of a ship's capstan, upon which two electrodes sprouted upwards and then curved gently outwards until they were about six inches apart. At the end of each electrode was a carbon sphere no bigger than a ping-pong ball, and between the two of them a languid blue arc of electricity crackled quietly to itself.

'What's that?' asked Thursday5 in a deferential whisper.

'It's the spark, the notion, the *core* of the book, the central nub of energy that binds a novel together.'

We watched for a few moments as the arc of energy moved in a lazy wave between the poles. Every now and then it would fizzle as though somehow disturbed by something.

'It moves as the crickets talk to one another upstairs,' I explained. 'If the book were being read you'd really see the spark flicker and dance. I've been in the core of *Anna Karenina* when it was going full bore with fifty thousand simultaneous readings, and the effect was better than any fireworks display – a multi-stranded spark in a thousand different hues that curved and arced out into the room and twisted around one another. A book's reason for being is to be read; the spark reflects this in a shimmering light show of dynamic proportions.'

'You speak as though it were alive.'

'Sometimes I think it is,' I mused, staring at the spark. 'After all, a story is born, it can evolve, replicate and then die. I used to go down to Core Containment quite a lot, but I don't have so much time for it these days.'

I pointed at a pipe about the width of my arm that led out from the plinth and disappeared into the floor.

'That's the throughput pipe that takes all the readings to the Storycode Engine Floor at Text Grand Central and from there to the Outland, where they are channelled direct to the reader's imagination.'

'And . . . all books work this way?'

'I wish. Books that are *not* within the influence of Text Grand Central have their own on-board storycode engines, as do books being constructed in the Well of Lost Plots and most of the vanity publishing genre.'

Thursday5 looked thoughtful.

'The readers are everything, aren't they?'

'Now you've got it,' I replied, '*everything*.'

We stood in silence for a moment.

'I was just thinking about the awesome responsibility that comes with being a Jurisfiction agent,' I said pointedly. 'What were you thinking about?'

'Me?'

I looked around the empty room.

'Yes, you.'

'I was wondering if extracting aloe vera hurt the plant. What's that?'

She was pointing at a small round hatch that was partially hidden behind some copper tubing. It looked like something you might find in the watertight bulkhead of a submarine. Riveted and of robust construction, it had a large central lever and two locking devices farther than an arm span apart, so it could never be opened accidentally by one person.

'That leads to . . . *Nothing*,' I murmured.

'You mean a blank wall?'

'No, a blank wall would be something. This is not *a* nothing, but *the* Nothing, the Nothing by which all somethings are defined.'

She looked confused, so I beckoned her to a small porthole next to the hatch and told her to look out.

'I can't see anything,' she said after a while. 'It's completely black . . . no, wait, I can see small pinpoints of light – like stars.'

'Not stars,' I told her, '*books*. Each one adrift in the firmament and each one burning not just with the light that the author gave it upon creation, but the warm glow of being read, and appreciated. The brighter ones are the most popular.'

'I can see *millions* of them,' she murmured, cupping her hands around her face to help her eyes penetrate the inky blackness.

'Every book is a small world unto itself, reachable only by bookjumping. See how some points of light tend to group near others?'

'Yes?'

'They're clumped together in genres, attracted by the gravitational tug of their mutual plot lines.'

'And between them?'

'An abstraction where all the laws of literary theory and storytelling conventions break down – the Nothing. It doesn't support textual life and has no description, form or function.'

I tapped the innocuous-looking hatch.

'Out there you'd not last a second before the text that makes up your descriptive existence were stripped of all meaning and consequence. Before bookjumping was developed every character was marooned in his or her own novel. For many of the books outside the influence of the Council of Genres and Text Grand Central, it's still like that. *Pilgrim's Progress* and the Sherlock Holmes series are good examples. We know roughly where they are owing to the literary influence they exert on similar books, but we still haven't figured out a way in. And until someone does, a bookjump is impossible.'

I switched off the light and we returned to Geppetto's kitchen.

'Here you go,' said Julian Sparkle, handing me a cardboard box. Any sort of enmity he might have felt towards us had vanished.

'What's this?'

'Why, your prize, of course! A selection of Tupperware™

containers. Durable and with an ingenious spill-proof lid, they are the ideal way to keep food fresh.'

'Give them to the tiger.'

'He doesn't like Tupperware – the lids are tricky to get off with paws.'

'Then *you* have them.'

'I didn't win them,' replied Sparkle with a trace of annoyance, but then he added after a moment's thought: 'but if you would like to play our "Super Wizzo Double Jackpot" game we can double your prize the next time you play!'

'Good, fine – whatever,' I said as a phone on the kitchen table started jangling. They all went quiet as Julian picked it up.

'Hello? Two doors, one tiger, liar/non-liar puzzle speaking.'

He raised his eyebrows and picked up a handy pen to scribble a note.

'We'll be on to it right away.'

He replaced the phone and addressed the two guards, who were watching him expectantly. 'Scramble, lads – we're needed on a boring car journey on the M4 westbound near Lyneham.'

The room was suddenly a whirl of activity. Each guard removed his door, which seemed to be on quick-release hinges, and then held it under his arm. The first guard placed his hand on the shoulder of Sparkle, who had turned his back, and the second on the shoulder of his compatriot. The tiger, now free, stood behind the second guard and placed one paw on his shoulder, and with the other picked the telephone off the table.

'Ready?' called out Sparkle to the odd queue that had formed expertly behind him.

'Yes,' said the first guard.

'No,' said the second.

'Growl,' said the tiger, and turned to wink at us.

There was a mild concussion as they all jumped out. The fire blazed momentarily in the grate, the cat ran out of the room and loose papers were thrown into the air. Phone call to exit had taken less than eight seconds. These guys were professionals.

Thursday5 and I, suitably impressed and still without a taxi, jumped out of *Pinocchio* and were once again in the Great Library.

She replaced the book on the shelf and looked up at me.

'Even if I *had* played "Liars & Tigers",' she said with a mournful sigh, 'I wouldn't have been able to figure it out. I'd have been eaten.'

'Not necessarily,' I replied. 'Even by guessing your chances were still fifty-fifty, and that's considered favourable odds at Jurisfiction.'

'You mean I have a fifty per cent chance of being killed in the service?'

'Consider yourself lucky. Out in the real world, despite huge advances in medical science, the chance of death remains unchanged at one hundred per cent. Still, there's a bright side to the human mortality thing – at least, there is for the BookWorld.'

'Which is?'

'A never-ending supply of new readers. Come on, you can jump me back to the Jurisfiction offices.'

She stared at me for a moment, and then said:

'You're not so good at bookjumping any more, are you?'

'Not really – but that's between you and me, yes?'

'Do you want to talk about it?'

'No.'

10

The Well of Lost Plots

——

'Owing to the specialised tasks undertaken by Prose
Resource Operatives, JurisTech is permitted to build
gadgets deemed outside the usual laws of physics – the
only department (aside from the SF genre) licensed to
do so. The standard item in a PRO's manifest is the TravelBook
(q.v.), which itself contains other JurisTech devices such as the
Martin-Bacon Eject-O-Hat, MV Mask, textmarker, String™ and
Textual Sieves of various sizes and porosity, to name but a few.'

As soon as we were back at the Jurisfiction offices in Norland Park
I gave Thursday5 an hour off for lunch so I could get some work
done. I pulled all the files on potential transfictional probe appear-
ances and discovered I had the only solid piece of evidence – all
the rest had merely been sightings. It seemed that whenever a
Goliath probe appeared it was gone again in under a minute. The
phenomenon had begun seven years ago, reached a peak eight
months before and now seemed to be ebbing. Mind you, this was
based on only thirty-six sightings, so couldn't be considered conclusive.

I took the information to Bradshaw, who listened carefully to
my report and what I knew about Goliath, which was quite a lot,
and none of it good. He nodded soberly as I spoke, and when I
had finished paused for a moment before observing:

'Goliath are Outlander and well outside our jurisdiction. I'm
loath to take it to Senator Jobsworth as he'll instigate some daft
"initiative" or something with resources that we just don't have. Is
there any evidence that these probes do anything other than observe?

Throwing a metal ball into fiction is one thing; moving a person between the two is quite another.'

'None at all,' I replied, 'but it must be their intention, even if they haven't managed it yet.'

'Do you think they will?'

'My uncle could do it. And if he could, then it's possible.'

Bradshaw thought for a moment.

'We'll keep this to ourselves for now. With our plunging read-rates I don't want to needlessly panic the CofG into some insane knee-jerk response. Is there a chance you could find out something from the real world?'

'I could try,' I replied reflectively, 'but don't hold your breath – I'm not exactly on Goliath's Christmas card list.'

'On the contrary,' said Bradshaw, passing me the probe, 'I'm sure they'd be overjoyed to meet someone who can travel into fiction. Can you check up on the Jane Austen refits this afternoon? Isambard was keen to show us something.'

I told him I'd go down there straight away and he thanked me, wished me good luck and departed. I had a few minutes to spare before Thursday5 got back, so I checked the card-index databases for anything about Superreaders, of which there was frustratingly little. Most Superreader legends had their base in the Text Sea, emanating usually from word-fishermen home on leave from scrawl-trawlers. The issue was complicated by the fact that one Superread is technically identical to a large quantity of simultaneous reads, so only an examination of a book's maintenance log would identify whether it had been a victim or not.

Thursday5 returned exactly on time, having spent the lunch hour in a mud bath, the details of which she felt compelled to tell me, at length. Mind you, she was a lot more relaxed than I was, so something was working. We stepped outside and after I had argued with TransGenreTaxis dispatch for five minutes, we read ourselves to the Great Library, then took the elevator and descended in silence to the sub-basements, which had been known colloquially as the Well of Lost Plots for so long that no one could remember their proper name – if they'd ever had one. It was here that books were actually constructed. The 'laying of the spine' was the first act in the process, and after that a continuous series of work gangs would toil tirelessly on the novel, embedding plot and subtext within the fabric of the narrative. They carefully lowered in the settings and atmosphere before the characters, fresh from dialogue training and in the presence of a skilled imaginator, would record the book on to an ImaginoTransferoRecordingDevice ready for reading in the Outland. It was slow, manpower-intensive and costly – any Supervising Book Engineer who could construct a complex novel in the minimum of time and on budget was much in demand.

'I was thinking,' said Thursday5 as the lift plunged downwards, 'about being a bit more proactive. I would have been eaten by that tiger and it was, I must confess, the seventh time you've rescued me over the past day and a half.'

'Eighth,' I pointed out. 'Remember you were attacked by that adjectivore?'

'Oh, yes. It didn't really take to my suggestion of a discussion group to reappraise the passive role of grammasites within the BookWorld, now, did it?'

'No – all it wanted was to tear the adjectives from your still-breathing body.'

'Well, my point is that I think I need to be more aggressive.'

'Sounds like a good plan,' I replied. 'If a situation arises we'll see how you do.'

The lift stopped and we stepped out. Down here in the Well the sub-basements looked more like narrow Elizabethan streets than corridors. It was here that purveyors of book-construction-related merchandise could be found displaying their wares in a multitude of specialist shops that would appeal to any genre, style or setting. The corridors were alive with the bustling activity of artisans moving hither and thither in the gainful pursuit of book building. Plot-traders, backstoryists, holestitchers, journeymen and generics trotted purposefully in every direction, and cartloads of prefabricated sections for proto-books were being slowly pulled down the centre of the street by Pitman ponies, which are a sort of shorthand horse that doesn't take up so much room.

Most of it was salvage. In the very lowest sub-basement was the Text Sea, and it was on the shores of this ocean that scrapped books were pulled apart by work gangs using nothing more refined than hammers, chains and muscle. The chunks of battered narrative were then dismantled by cutters, who would remove and package any salvageable items to be resold. Any idea, setting or character that was too damaged or too dull to be reused was unceremoniously dumped in the Text Sea, where the bonds within the sentences were loosened until they were nothing but words, and then these too were reduced to letters and punctuation, the meaning burning off into a bluish mist that lingered near the foreshore before evaporating.

'Who are we going to see?' asked Thursday5 as we made our way through the crowded throng.

'Bradshaw wanted me to cast an eye over the Jane Austen refit,' I replied. 'The engineer in charge is Isambard Kingdom Buñuel, the finest and most surreal book engineer in the WOLP. When he constructed *War and Peace* no one thought anything of that scale and grandeur *could* be built, let alone launched. It was so large an entire sub-basement had to be constructed to take it. Even now, a permanent crew of twenty are needed to keep it going.'

Thursday5 looked curiously around as a gang of riveters walked past, laughing loudly and talking about a spine they had been working on.

'So once the book is built it's moved to the Great Library?' she asked.

'If only,' I replied. 'Once it's completed and the spark has been ignited, it undergoes a rigorous twelve-point narrative safety and compliance regime before being studiously and penetratively test-read on a special rig. After that the book is taken on a trial reading by the Council of Genres Book Inspectorate before being passed – or not – for publication.'

We walked on and presently saw the Book Maintenance Facility hangars in the distance, rising above the low roofs of the street like the airship hangars I knew so well back home. They were always full; book maintenance carried on 24/7. After another five minutes' walk and with the street expanding dramatically to be able to encompass the vast size of the complex, we arrived outside the Book Maintenance Facility.

11
The Refit

'Books suffer wear and tear, just the same as hip joints, cars and reputations. For this reason, all books have to go into the maintenance bay for a periodic refit, either every thirty years or a million readings, whichever is sooner. For those books which suffer a high initial readership but then lose them through boredom or insufficient reader intellect, a partial refit may be in order. Salmon Thrusty's intractable masterpiece *The Demonic Couplets* has had the first two chapters rebuilt six times, but the rest is relatively unscathed.'

Ever since the ProCaths had mounted a guerrilla-style attack on *Wuthering Heights* during routine maintenance, security had been increased, and tall cast-iron railings now separated the BookWorld Maintenance Facility from the rest of the Well. Heathcliff – possibly the most hated man inside fiction – had not been harmed, owing partly to the vigilance of the Jurisfiction agents who were on Heathcliff protection duty that day, but owing also to a misunderstanding of the word 'guerrilla', a woeful lexicological lapse that left five confused apes dead, and the facility littered with bananas. There was now a guardhouse, too, and it was impossible to get in unless on official business.

'Now here's an opportunity,' I whispered to Thursday5, 'to test your aggressiveness. These guys can be tricky so you need to be firm.'

'Firm?'

'Firm.'

She took a deep breath, steeled herself and marched up to the guardhouse in a meaningful manner.

'Next and Next,' she announced, passing our IDs to a guard who was sitting in a small wooden shed at the gates of the facility, 'and if you cause us any trouble we'll . . . not be happy. And then *you'll* not be happy because we can do unhappy things . . . to people . . . *sometimes.*'

'I'm sorry?' said the guard, who had a large white moustache and seemed to be a little deaf.

'I said — ah — how are you?'

'Oh, we're fine, thank you, missy,' replied the guard amiably. Thursday5 turned to me and gave me the thumbs-up sign and I smiled. I actually quite liked her, but there was a huge quantity of work to be done before she might be considered Jurisfiction material. At present, I was planning on rating her 'potential with retraining' and sending her back to cadet school.

I looked around as the guard stared at our identification and then at us. Above the hangars I could see tall chimneys that were belching forth clouds of smoke, while in the distance we could hear the ring of hammers and the rumble of machinery.

'Which one is Thursday Next?' asked the guard, staring at the almost identical IDs closely.

'Both of us,' said Thursday5. 'I'm Thursday5 and she's the Outlander.'

'An Outlander?' repeated the guard with great interest. I glared at Thursday5. My Outlander status wasn't something I liked to bandy about.

'Hey, Bert!' he said to the other guard, who seemed to be on a permanent tea break. 'We've got an Outlander here!'

'No!' he said, getting up from a chair that had its seat polished to a high shine. 'Get out of here!'

'What an honour!' said the first guard. 'Someone from the *real* world.' He thought for a moment. 'Tell me, if it rains on a really hot day, do sheep shrink?'

'Is that a security question?'

'No, no,' replied the guard quickly. 'Bert and I were just discussing it recently.'

This wasn't unusual. Characters in fiction had a very skewed view of the real world. To them, the extreme elements of human experience were commonplace as they were generally the sort of issues that made it into books, which left the mundanities of real life somewhat obscure and mysterious. Ask a resident of the BookWorld about terminal diseases, loss, gunshot trajectories, dramatic irony and problematic relatives and they'd be more expert than you or I – quiz them on paintbrushes and they'd spend the rest of the week trying to figure out how the paint stays on the bristles until it touches another surface.

'It's *woollens* that shrink,' I explained, 'and it has to be *very* hot.'

'I told you so,' said Bert triumphantly.

'Thank you,' I said, taking the security badges from the guard while I signed the ledger. He admitted us both to the facility and almost from nowhere a bright yellow jeep appeared with a young man dressed in blue overalls and a cap sporting the BMF logo.

'Can you take us to Isambard Kingdom Buñuel?' I said as we climbed in the back.

'Yes,' replied the driver without moving.

'Then would you?'

'I suppose.'

The jeep moved off. The hangars were, as previously stated, of gigantic proportions. Unlike in the real world where practical difficulties in civil engineering might be a defining factor in the scale of a facility, here it was not a consideration at all. Indeed, the size of the plant could expand and contract depending on need, a little like Mary Poppins' suitcase, which was hardly surprising as they were designed by the same person. We drove on for a time in silence.

'What's in Hangar One at the moment?' I asked the driver.

'*The Magus.*'

'Still?'

Even the biggest refit never took more than a week, and John Fowles' labyrinthine-plotted masterpiece had been in there nearly five.

'It's taking longer than we thought – they removed all the plot elements for cleaning and no one can remember how they go back together again.'

'I'm not sure it will make a difference,' I murmured as we pulled up outside Hangar 8. The driver said nothing, waited until we climbed out and then drove off without a word.

To say the interior of the hangar was vast would be pointless, as the Great Library, Text Grand Central and the CofG *also* had vast interiors, and continued descriptions of an increasingly hyperbolic nature would be insufferably repetitive. Suffice to say that there was room on the hangar floor for not only Darcy's country home of Pemberley, but also Rosings, Netherfield *and* Longbourn as well. They had all been hoisted from the book by a massive overhead crane so the empty husk of the novel could be checked for fatigue cracks before being fumigated for nesting grammasites and repainted. At the same time an army of technicians, plasterers, painters, chippies and so forth were crawling over the houses, locations, props, furnishings and costumes, all of which had been removed for checking and maintenance.

'If this is *Pride and Prejudice,*' said Thursday5 as we walked towards the Bennets' property of Longbourn, 'then what are people reading in the Outland?'

The house was resting incongruously on wooden blocks laid on the hangar floor but without its grounds – they were being tended to elsewhere by a happy buzz of gardeners.

'We divert the readings to a lesser copy on a stand-by storycode

96

engine and people read that,' I replied, nodding a greeting to the various technicians who were trying to make good the damage wrought by the last million readings or so. 'The book is never *quite* as good, but the only people who might see a difference are the Austen enthusiasts and scholars. They would notice the slight dulling and lack of vitality, but unable to come to a satisfactory answer as to why this might be so, they would simply blame themselves – a reading later in the week would once again renew their confidence in the magnificence of the novel.'

We stepped inside the main doorway of Longbourn, where a similar repair gang was working on the interior. They had only just got started and from here it was easier to see the extent of the corrosion. The paintwork was dull and lifeless, the wallpaper hung off the wall in long strips, and the marble fireplace was stained and darkened by smoke. Everything we looked at seemed tired and worn.

'Oh, mercy!' came a voice behind us, and we turned to find Mrs Bennet dressed in a threadbare poke bonnet and shawl. Following her was a construction manager, and behind him was Mr Bennet.

'This will *never* be ready in time,' she lamented, looking around the parlour of her house unhappily, 'and every second not spent looking for husbands is a second wasted.'

'My dear, you must come and have your wardrobe replaced,' implored Mr Bennet, 'you are *quite* in tatters and unsuited for being read, let alone receiving gentlemen – potential husbands or otherwise.'

'He's quite right,' urged the manager. 'It is only a refit, nothing more; we will have you back on the shelf in a few days.'

'On the shelf?' she shrieked. 'Like my daughters?'

And she was about to burst into tears when she suddenly caught sight of me.

'You there! Do you have a single brother in possession of a good fortune who is in want of a wife?'

'I'm afraid not,' I replied, thinking of Joffy, who failed on all three counts.

'Are you sure? I've a choice of five daughters; one of them *must* be suitable – although I have my doubts about Mary being acceptable to anyone. Ahhhhh!'

She had started to scream.

'Good lady, calm yourself!' cried Mr Bennet. 'Whatever is the matter?'

'My nerves are so bad I am now seeing double!'

'You are *not*, madam,' I told her hastily, 'this is my . . . twin sister.'

At that moment a small phalanx of seamstresses came in holding a replacement costume. Mrs Bennet made another sharp cry and ran off upstairs, quickly followed by the wardrobe department, who would doubtless have to hold her down and undress her – like the last time.

'I'll leave it in your capable hands,' said Mr Bennet to the wardrobe mistress. 'I am going to my library and don't wish to be disturbed.'

He opened the door and found to his dismay that it too was being rebuilt. Large portions of the wall were missing, and plasterers were attempting to fill the gaps to the room beyond. There was the flickering light of an arc welder and a shower of sparks. He harrumphed, shrugged, gave us a wan smile and walked out.

'Quite a lot of damage,' I said to the construction manager, whose name we learned was Sid.

'We get a lot of this in the classics,' he said with a shrug. 'This is the third P^2 refit I've done in the past fifteen years – but it's not as bad as the *Lord of the Rings* trilogy; those things are *always* in for maintenance – the *fantasy* readership really give it a hammering – and the fan fiction doesn't help, neither.'

'The name's Thursday Next,' I told him, 'from Jurisfiction. I need to speak to Isambard.'

He led us outside to where the five Bennet sisters were running through their lines with a wordsmith holding a script.

'But you are not entitled to know mine; nor will such behaviour ever induce me to be explicit,' said Elizabeth.

'Not *quite* right,' replied the wordsmith as she consulted the script. 'You dropped the "as this" from the middle of the sentence.'

'I did?' queried Lizzie, craning over to look at the script. 'Where?'

'It still sounded *perfect* to me,' said Jane good-naturedly.

'This is all just so *boring*,' muttered Lydia, tapping her foot impatiently and looking around. Wisely, the maintenance staff had separated the soldiers and especially Wickham from Kitty and Lydia – for their own protection, if not the soldiers'.

'Lydia dearest, do *please* concentrate,' said Mary, looking up from the book she was reading, 'it is for your own good.'

'Ms Next!' came an authoritarian voice that I knew I could ignore only at my peril.

'Your Ladyship,' I said, curtsying neatly to a tall woman bedecked in dark crinolines. She had strongly marked features, which might once have been handsome, but now appeared haughty and superior.

'May I present Cadet Next?' I said. 'Thursday5, this is the Right Honourable Lady Catherine de Bourgh, widow of Sir Lewis de Bourgh.'

Thursday5 was about to say something but I caught her eye and she curtsied instead, which Lady Catherine returned with a slight incline of her head.

'I must speak to you, Ms Next,' continued Her Ladyship, taking my arm to walk with me, 'upon a matter of considerable concern. As you know I have a daughter named Anne who is unfortunately of a sickly constitution, which has prevented her from making accomplishments which she otherwise could not have failed. If good health had been hers she would have joined Jurisfiction many years ago, and about now would begin to accrue the benefits of her age, wisdom and experience.'

'Doubtless, Your Ladyship.'

Lady Catherine gave a polite smile.

'Then we are agreed. Miss Anne should join Jurisfiction on the morrow at a rank, salary and with duties commensurate with the standing that her ill health has taken from her – shall we say five thousand guineas a year, and light work only with mornings off and three servants?'

'I will bring it to the attention of the relevant authorities,' I told her diplomatically. 'My good friend and colleague Commander Bradshaw will attend to your request personally.'

I sniggered inwardly. Bradshaw and I had spent many years attempting to drop each other in impossible situations for amusement, and he'd never top this.

'Indeed,' said Lady Catherine in an imperious tone, 'I spoke to Commander Bradshaw and he suggested I speak to *you*.'

'Ah.'

'Shall we say Monday?' continued Lady Catherine. 'Jurisfiction can send a carriage for my daughter, but be warned – if it is unfit for her use it shall be returned.'

'Monday would be admirable,' I told her, thinking quickly. 'Miss Anne's assumed skill will be much in demand. As you have no doubt heard, *Fanny Hill* has been moved from Literary Smut to the Racy Novel genre, and your daughter's considerable skills may be required for character retraining.'

Lady Catherine was silent for a moment.

'Quite impossible,' she said at last. 'Next week is the busiest in our calendar. I shall inform you as to when and where she will accept her duties – good day!'

And with a *harrumph* of a most haughty nature, she was gone.

I rejoined Thursday5, who was waiting for me near two carriages that were being rebuilt, and we then made our way towards the engineer's office. As we passed a moth-eaten horse I heard it say to another shabby old nag: 'So what's this *Pride and Prejudice* all about, then?'

'It's about a horse who pulls a carriage for the Bennets,' replied his friend, taking a mouthful from the feed bucket and munching thoughtfully.

'Please come in,' said the construction manager, and we entered the works hut. The interior was a neat and orderly drawing office with half a dozen octopuses seated at draughtsman's desks and dressed in tartan waistcoats that made them all look like oversized bagpipes – apart from one, who actually *was* an oversized set of bagpipes. They were all studying plans of the book, consulting damage reports and then sketching repair recommendations on eight different notepads simultaneously. The octopuses blinked at us curiously as we walked in, except for one who was asleep and muttering something about his 'garden being in the shade', and another who was playing a doleful tune on a bouzouki.

'How odd,' said Thursday5.

'You're right,' I agreed. 'Tim usually plays the lute.'

In the centre of the room was Isambard Kingdom Buñuel. He was standing in shirtsleeves over the blueprints of the book and was a man in healthy middle age who looked as if he had seen a lot of life and was much the better for it. His dark wool suit was spattered with mud, he wore a tall stovepipe hat and moving constantly in his mouth was an unlit cigar. He was engaged in animated conversation with his three trusty engineering assistants. The first could best be described as a mad monk, who was dressed in a coarse habit and had startling divergent eyes. The second was a daringly sparkly drag queen who it seemed had just hopped off a carnival float in Rio, and the third was more ethereal – he was simply a disembodied voice known only as Horace. They were all discussing the pros and cons of balancing essential work with budgetary constraints, then about Loretta's choice of sequins and the available restaurants for dinner.

'Thursday!' said Isambard as we walked in. 'What a very fortu-itous happenstance – I trust you are wellhealthy?'

'Wellhealthy indeedly,' I replied.

Buñuel's engineering skills were without peer – not just from a simple *mechanistic* point of view, but on account of his somewhat surreal method of problem solving that made lesser book engin-eers pale into insignificance. It was he who first thought of using custard as a transfer medium for speedier throughput from the books to the storycode engines, and he who pioneered the hydro-ponic growth of usable dramatic irony. When he wasn't working towards the decriminalisation of Class 'C' grammatical abuses such as starting a sentence with 'and', he was busy designing new and interesting plot devices. It was he who suggested the groundbreaking twist in *The Murder of Roger Ackroyd*, and also the 'Gally Threepwood memoirs' device in the *Blandings* series. Naturally, he'd had other, lesser ideas that didn't find favour, such as the discarded U-boat/Nautilus battle sequence in *Mysterious Island*, a new process for distilling quotation marks from boiled mice, a method of making books grammasite proof by marinading them in dew, and a whole host of farcical new words that only he used. But his hits were greater than the sum of his misses, and such is the way with great-ness.

'I hope we are not in any sort of troublesome with Jurisfiction?'

'Not at all,' I assured him. 'You spoke to Bradshaw about some-thing?'

'My memory is *so* stringbagness these days,' he said, slapping his forehead with his palm. 'Walk with me.'

We left the works hut at a brisk pace and walked towards the empty book, Thursday5 a few steps behind.

'We've got another seventeen clockchimes before we have to click it all back on-wise,' he said, mopping his brow.

'Will you manage it?'

'We should be dokey,' replied Isambard with a laugh, 'always supposeding that Mrs Bennet doesn't do anything sensible.'

We walked up a set of wooden stairs and stepped on to the novel. From our vantage point we could see the empty husk of the book laid out in front of us. Everything had been removed and it looked like an empty steel barge several hundred acres in size.

'What's happening over there?' asked Thursday5, pointing to a group of men working in an area where several girders joined in a delicate latticework of steel and rivets.

'We're checklooking for fatigue splitcracks near the irony expansion slot,' explained Isambard. 'The ceaseless flexiblations of a book as readers of varying skill make their way through it can set up a harmonic that exacts stresstications the book was never blueprinted to take. I expect you heard about the mid-read fractsplosion of *Hard Times* during the post-maintenance testification in 1932?'

Thursday5 nodded.

'We've had to be more uttercarefulness since then,' continued Isambard, 'which is why classics like this come in for rebuildificance every thirty years whether they require it or not.'

There was a crackle of bright blue light as the work gang effected a repair, and a sub-engineer supervising the workgang waved to Isambard, who waved back.

'Looks like we found a fatigue crevicette,' he said, 'which goes to show that one can never be too carefulphobic.'

'Commander Bradshaw said you had something you wanted to say?'

'That's true,' replied Buñuel. 'I've done enough rebuildificances to know when something's a bit squiddly. It's the Council of Genres. They've been slicediceing budgets for years and now they ask us to topgrade the ImaginoTransference conduits.'

He pointed at a large pipe that looked like a water main. A conduit that size would take a lot of readers – far more than we had at present. Although in itself a good move, with falling read-rates it seemed a little . . . well, *odd*.

'Did they give a reason?'

'They said *Pride and Prejudice* has been added to twenty-eight more teachcrammer syllabuses this year and there's another silver-flick out soon.'

'Sounds fair to me.'

'Posstruthful, but it makes nonsense. It's potentious *new* books we should be cashsquandering on, not the stalnovelwarts who will be read no matter what. Besides, the costcash of the extra conduits is verlittle compared to the amount of custard needed to fillup all.'

'I'll make some enquiries,' I told him.

We watched as the overhead crane gently lowered Darcy's stately home of Pemberley back into its position in the book. It was securely bolted into position by a group of men in overalls wielding spanners as big as they were.

'Spot-on-time-tastic,' murmured Isambard, consulting a large gold pocket watch. 'We might make the deadule after all.'

'Mr Buñuel?' murmured a disembodied voice that sounded as though it came from everywhere at once.

'Yes, Horace?'

'Sorry to trouble you, sir,' came the voice again, 'but Mrs Bennet and Lady de Bourgh have locked antlers in the living room and are threatening to kill one another. What do you want to do?'

'No time to lose!' exclaimed Buñuel, reaching into his pocket. 'I'll have five guineas on Mrs Bennet.'

Thursday5 and I walked out of the Maintenance Facility and back to the busy corridors of the Well of Lost Plots. I called TransGenreTaxis and was told my cab was 'stuck in a traffic jam in Mrs Beeton's' but would 'be with me shortly', so we walked towards the elevators. Buñuel had a point about the extra conduiting – but equally it could be just another of the bizarre accounting anomalies that abound at the Council – they once refused to allocate funds for maintenance on *Captain Corelli's Mandolin*, despite an almost unprecedented burst of popularity. By the time they agreed to some remedial construction work it was too late – the first few chapters suffered permanent damage. On the other side of the coin they had no problem issuing the Danvers with new black uniforms and designer dark glasses so 'they looked nice on parade'.

'Is it true you have a chair at the Council of Genres?' asked Thursday5 with a sense of wholly unwarranted awe in her voice.

'And a table, too. As an Outlander I don't have the strictures of the narrative to dictate my actions so I'm quite good at forward planning, and— Hang on a moment.'

Recalling Landen's writer's block I ducked into a bric-a-brac store full of plot devices, props, backstories and handy snatches of verbal banter for that oh-so-important exchange. I made my way past packing cases full of plot twists and false resolutions, and walked up to the counter.

'Hello, Murray.'

'Thursday!' replied the owner of the store, a retired gag-and-groan man who had worked the Comedy genre for years before giving it all up to run a used plot shop. 'What can I do you for?'

'A plot device,' I said somewhat vaguely. 'Something exciting that will change a story from the mundane to the fantastic in a paragraph.'

'Budget?'

'Depends on what you've got.'

'Hmm,' said the shopkeeper, thinking hard and staring at the wall of small drawers behind him, which made it look a little like an apothecary's shop. On each drawer there was a painted label denoting some exciting and improbable plot-turning device. 'Tincture of breathlessness,' said one, and 'Paternal root,' read another.

'How about a *Suddenly, a shot rang out*? That's always a safe bet for mysteries or to get you out of a scrape when you don't know what to do next.'

'I think I can afford something better than that. Got anything a bit more . . . complex?'

Murray looked at the labels on the drawers again.

'I've got a: *And that, said Mr Wimple, was when we discovered . . . the truth.*'

'Too vague.'

'Perhaps, but it's cheap. Okay. How about a *Mysterious stranger arriving during a thunderstorm*? We've got a special on this week. Take the stranger and you can have a corrupt local chief of police and an escaped homicidal lunatic at no extra charge.'

But I was still undecided.

'I was thinking of something more character than plot led.'

'I hope you've got deep pockets,' said the shopkeeper ominously, and with a trace of annoyance, as the queue behind me was becoming longer by the second.

'How about the arrival of a distant and *extremely* eccentric ex-military uncle upsetting the delicate balance of the ordered household?'

'That sounds like just the thing. How much?'

'He was pulled out complete and unused a few days ago; took a lot of skill to pluck him out of the narrative without damage, and with all ancillary props and walk-ons—'

'Yes, okay, okay, I get the picture – *how much*?'

'To you, a thousand guineas.'

'I get the uncle fully realised for that, yes?'

'He's over there.'

I turned to see a slender and very jovial-looking gentleman sitting on a packing case on the other side of the shop. He was dressed in a suit of outrageously loud green-and-yellow checks, and was resting his gloves on the top of a cane. He inclined his head in greeting when he saw us looking at him, and smiled impishly.

'Perfect. I get a full backstory as well, yes?'

'It's all here,' said Murray, placing on the counter a glass jar that seemed to be full of swirling coloured mist.

'Then it's a deal.'

We shook hands and I gave him my BookWorld charge card. I was just standing there in that blank sort of way you do while waiting for a shopkeeper to complete a transaction when the hair on the back of my neck suddenly rose. It was a sixth sense, if you like – something you acquire in the BookWorld where jeopardy is sometimes never more than a line away. I surreptitiously slipped my hand into my bag and clasped the butt of my pistol. I looked cautiously out of the corner of my eye at the customer to my left. It was a freelance imaginator buying powdered kabuki – no problem there. I looked to the right and perceived a tall figure dressed in a trenchcoat with a fedora pulled down to hide his face. I tensed as the faint odour of bovine reached my nostrils. It was the Minotaur, the half-man, half-bull son of Queen Pasiphaë of Crete. He'd killed one Jurisfiction agent and tried the same with me several times, so consequently had an 'erase on sight' order across sixteen genres – there were few these days who would dare harbour him. I stayed calm and turned towards Thursday5, who was looking at a pair of toucans that were a job lot from a scrapped bird identification handbook. I caught her eye and showed her three fingers, which was a prearranged signal of imminent danger, then gave an almost imperceptible nod in the Minotaur's direction. Thursday5 looked bewildered. I gave up and turned slowly back.

'Soon be done!' muttered Murray, filling out the credit form. I stole a look towards the Minotaur again. I could have erased him there and then but it was always possible that this wasn't the Minotaur we were hunting. After all, there were thousands of Minotaurs dotted around the BookWorld, and they all looked pretty much alike. Admittedly, not many wore trenchcoats and fedoras, but I wasn't going to dispatch anyone without being sure.

'Would you like that frying pan wrapped, Mr Johnson?' asked the lady serving the Minotaur. I required nothing more. He'd been using the 'Mr Johnson' pseudonym for many years, and the frying pan? Well, we'd darted him once with SlapStick as a tracking device, and it seemed to have crept into his modus operandi of assassination. Steamrollers, banana skins, falling pianos – he'd used them all. In the pantheon of slapstick the close-quarters hand weapon of choice was . . . a frying pan. Without waiting another second I drew my pistol. The Minotaur, with a speed out of all proportion to his bulk, flipped the frying pan to his other hand and swiped it in my direction, catching the pistol and sending it clattering to the other side of the room. We paused and stared at one another. The frying pan had a two-foot handle and he brandished it at me in a threatening manner. He removed his hat and, as the other customers realised who he was, there was a cry of fear and a mass exodus from the shop. He had the body of a man but the head of a bull, which had a kind of *humanness* about it that was truly disturbing. His yellow eyes gleamed at me with malevolence, and his horns, I noticed, had been sharpened to wickedly fine points.

'We can talk about this,' I said in a quiet tone, wondering whether Thursday5 had the nous to try to distract him.

'No talk,' said the Minotaur in a basso profundo voice. 'My job is to kill you, and yours . . . is to *die*.'

I tried to stall him.

'Let's talk for a minute about job descriptions.'

But the Minotaur wasn't in the talking vein. He took a pace forwards and made a swipe at me with the frying pan. I took a step backwards, but even so felt the breeze of the pan as it just missed my head. I grabbed the nearest object to hand, which was a golf club, and tried to hit him with it, but he was faster and the wooden shaft of the club was reduced to splinters and wood dust with the ferocity of his blow. He gave out a deep hearty laugh and took a further step towards me.

'I say,' came a voice that sounded like crumpets and tea at four o'clock sharp, 'you, sir – with the horns.'

The Minotaur looked to where the voice had come from but still kept me within his vision. The interloper, of course, was the eccentric relative I had just purchased for Landen's book. He had left his packing case and stood facing the beast armed with nothing more than his walking stick.

'Now run along, there's a good chap,' he said, as though he were talking to a child. The Minotaur curled a lip and breathed a threatening: '*Begone!*'

'Now look here,' replied the character in the yellow-and-green checks, 'I'm not sure I care for the tone of your voice.'

The Minotaur was suddenly a whirling mass of demonic destruction. He swung the frying pan towards the gentleman in an arc that could never have missed. But he *did* miss. There was a flash of silver, a blur of green and yellow and the frying pan clattered to the floor – with the Minotaur's hand still clutching it. The Minotaur looked at the frying pan and the severed hand, then at his stump. He grimaced, gave out a deafening yell that shattered the windows of the shop, and then evaporated into nothing as he jumped off and away.

'By Gad, what a to-do,' exclaimed the gentleman as he calmly cleaned his swordstick and returned it to his sheath. 'Anyone know who he was?'

'The Minotaur.'

'Was he, by George?' exclaimed the gentleman in surprise. 'Would have expected a better fight than that. Are you quite well?'

'Yes,' I replied, 'thanks to you. That was a nifty piece of swordwork.'

'My dear girl, think nothing of it,' he replied with the ghost of a smile. 'I was captain of the fencing team at Rugby.'

He was a handsome man in his mid-forties and everything he did and said was liberally iced with a heavy coating of stiff British reserve. I couldn't imagine what book he had come from, or even why he had been offered up as salvage.

'Thursday Next,' I said, putting out my hand.

'The pleasure is all mine, Ms Next,' he replied. 'Wing Commander Cornelius Scampton-Tappett at your service.'

The customers were warily looking back into the store, but Murray was already placing 'closed' signs on the doors.

'So,' said Scampton-Tappett, 'now that you've bought me, what would you have me do?'

'Oh – yes – right.'

I dug a calling card from my pocket, wrote down the title of Landen's latest novel – *Bananas for Edward* – and handed it to him.

'Do the best you can, would you? And if you need anything, you can contact me down at Jurisfiction.'

Scampton-Tappett raised an eyebrow, told me he would do the very best he could, tucked the jar containing his backstory under his arm, and vanished.

I breathed a sigh of relief and looked around. Thursday5 was looking at me with such a sense of abject loss and failure on her face that I thought at first she had been hurt.

'Are you all right?'

She nodded and looked down. I followed her gaze. Lying at her feet was my pistol.

'Is that where it ended up after it was knocked from my grasp?'

She nodded miserably, her eyes brimming with tears of self-anger.

I sighed. She and I both knew that this was the end of the road as regards her cadetship. If Scampton-Tappett hadn't intervened, I might well be dead – and she'd done nothing to prevent it.

'You don't have to say it,' she said, 'I'm manifestly not cut out for this work, and never shall be. I'd try and apologise but I can't think of words that could adequately express my shame.'

She took a deep breath, pulled the bow out of her hair, put it in her mouth and then gathered up her hair in a ponytail again before retying it. It was just the way I did it, and I suddenly felt a pang of guilt. After all, she acted in her morbidly peaceable way only because she was *written* that way as an antidote to the rest of the Thursday series. The thing was, the sex-and-violence nature of the first four books had been my fault too. I'd sold the character rights in order to fund Acme Carpets.

'I'd best be getting back to my book now,' she said, and turned to go.

'Did I say you could leave?' I asked in my stoniest voice.

'Well, that is to say . . . no.'

'Then until I *say* you can go, you stay with me. I'm still undecided as to your fate, and until that happens – Lord help me – you'll stay as my cadet.'

We returned to Jurisfiction and Thursday5 went and did some Pilates in the corner, much to the consternation of Mrs Dashwood, who happened to be passing. I reported the Minotaur's appearance and the state of the Austen refit to Bradshaw, who told me to have the Minotaur's details and current whereabouts texted to all agents.

After returning to my desk, filling in some paperwork and being consulted on a number of matters, I drew out Thursday5's assessment form, filled it in and then ticked the 'failed' box on the last page before I signed it. I folded it twice, placed it in the envelope and wavered for a moment before eventually placing it in the top drawer of my desk.

I looked at my watch. It was time to go home. I walked over

to Thursday5, who had her eyes closed and was standing on one leg.

'Same time tomorrow?'

She opened her eyes, and stared into mine. I got the same feeling when staring into the mirror at home. The touchy-feely New Age stuff was all immaterial. She was me, but me as I *might* have been if I'd never joined the police, army, SpecOps or Jurisfiction. Perhaps I wouldn't have been any happier if I'd connected with the side of me that was her, but I'd be a lot more relaxed, and a good deal healthier.

'Do you mean it?' she asked.

'Wouldn't say it if I didn't. But remember one thing: it's coffee and a bacon roll.'

She smiled.

'Right. Coffee and bacon roll it is.'

She handed me a paper bag.

'This is for you.'

I looked inside. It contained Pickwick's blue and white knitted cosy – finished.

'Good job,' I murmured, looking at the delicate knitting enviously. 'Thank—'

But she'd gone. I walked to the corridor outside and dug out my TravelBook, turned to the description of my office at Acme Carpets and read. After a few lines the air turned suddenly colder, there was the sound of crackling cellophane and I was back in my small office with a dry mouth and a thirst so strong I thought I would faint. I kept a pitcher of water close by for just such moments, so spent the next ten minutes drinking water and breathing deeply.

12

Kids

'Landen and I had often talked about it, but we never had a fourth. By the time Jenny came along I was forty-two, and that, I figured, was it. At the time of our last attempt to induct Friday into the Academy of Time he was the eldest at sixteen, Tuesday was thirteen and Jenny, the youngest, was ten. I resisted naming Jenny after a day of the week; I thought at least one of us should have the semblance of normality.'

I arrived at Tuesday's school at ten to four and waited patiently outside the maths room. She'd shown a peculiar flair for the subject all her life but had first achieved prominence when aged nine. She'd wandered into the sixth-form maths room and found an equation written on the board, thinking it was homework. But it wasn't. It was Fermat's Last Theorem, and the maths master had written it down to demonstrate how this simple equation could not be solved. The thing was, Tuesday had *found a solution*, thus rendering a proof of the unworkability of the equation both redundant and erroneous.

When the hunt was on for who had solved it, Tuesday thought they were angry with her for spoiling their fun, so she wasn't revealed as the culprit for almost a week. Even then, she had to be cajoled into explaining the answer. Professors of mathematics had tubed in from every corner of the globe to see how such a simple solution could have been staring them in the face without any of them noticing it.

At four on the button, Tuesday came out of the maths class looking drained and a bit cross.

'Hi, sweetheart,' I said, 'how was school?'

'S'okay,' she said with a shrug, handing me her Bagpuss schoolbag, pink raincoat and half-empty Winnie-the-Pooh lunch box. 'Do you have to pick me up in your Acme uniform? It's like soooooo embarrassing.'

'I certainly do,' I replied, giving her a big smoochy kiss to embarrass her further, something that didn't really work as the pupils in her maths class were all grown up and too obsessed with number sets and parametrised elliptic curves to be bothered by a daughter being embarrassed by her mother.

'They're all a bit *slow*,' she said as we walked to the van. 'Some of them can barely count.'

'Sweetheart, they are the finest minds in mathematics today; you should be happy that they are coming to you for tuition. It must have been a bit of a shock to the mathematics fraternity when you revealed that there were sixteen more odd numbers than even ones.'

'Seventeen,' she corrected me. 'I thought of another one on the bus this morning. The odd/even disparity is the easy bit,' she explained. 'The hard part is trying to explain that there actually *is* a highest number; a fact that tends to throw all work regarding infinite sets into a flat spin.'

Clearly the seriously smart genes that Mycroft had inherited from *his* father had bypassed my mother and me but appeared in Tuesday. It was odd to think that Mycroft's two sons were known collectively as 'The Stupids' – and it wasn't an ironic title, either.

Tuesday groaned again when she saw we were driving home in the Acme Carpets van, but agreed to get in when I pointed out that a long walk home was the only alternative. She scrunched down in her seat so as not to be spotted.

We didn't go straight home. I'd spoken to Spike before leaving work and he mentioned that he had some news about Mycroft's haunting,

114

and agreed to meet me at Mum's. When I arrived she and Polly were in the kitchen bickering about something pointless, such as the average size of an orange, so I left Tuesday with them: mother to burn her a cake, and Polly to discuss advanced Nextian geometry.

'Hiya,' I said to Spike, who had been waiting in his car.

'Yo. Thought about what to do with Felix8?'

'Not yet. I'll interview him again later this evening.'

'As you wish. I made a few enquiries on the other side. Remember my dead partner Chesney? He said Mycroft's spooking was what we call a "Non-recurring Informative Phantasm".'

'You have them categorised?'

'Sure. The A-list contains: "Pointless Screamer", "Crisis Warner", "Vengeful" and "Recurring ad nauseam dumb and dreary". From there it's all downhill: poltergeists, faceless orbs, quasi-religious visions and phantom smells – more usually associated with recently departed pet Labradors.'

We walked up the garden path to Mycroft's workshop.

'I get the picture. So what does it all mean?'

'It means that Mycroft had something he wanted to say before he died – but didn't manage to. It was obviously important enough for him to be given a licence to come back, if only for a few hours. Turn off your mobile.'

I reached into my pocket and did as he asked.

'Radio waves scramble their energy field,' he explained. 'Spooking's dropped big time since the mobile phone network kicked in. I'm amazed there are any ghosts left at all. Ready?'

'Ready.'

We had arrived at my uncle's workshop, and Spike grasped the handle and gently pushed the door open. If we were hoping to find Mycroft standing there in all his spectral glory, we were disappointed. The room was empty.

'He was just over there.'

Spike closed his eyes, sniffed the air and touched the workbench.

'Yeah,' he said, 'I can feel him.'

'Can you?'

'No, not really. Where was he again?'

'At the worktop. Spike, what exactly *is* a ghost?'

'A phantom,' said my Uncle Mycroft, who had just materialised, 'is essentially a heteromorphic wave pattern that gains solidity when the apparition converts thermal energy from the surroundings to visible light. It's a fascinating process and I'm amazed no one has thought of harnessing it – a holographic TV that could operate from the heat given off by an average-sized guinea pig.'

I shivered. Mycroft was right, the temperature *had* dropped, and there he was, but a lot less solid than the previous time. I could easily see the other side of the workshop through him.

'Hello again, Thursday,' he said. 'Good afternoon, Mr Stoker.'

'Good afternoon, sir,' replied Spike. 'Word in the Realm of the Dead says you've got something to tell us.'

'I have?' asked Mycroft, looking at me.

'Yes, Uncle,' I told him. 'You're a Non-recurring . . . um—'

'—Non-recurring Informative Phantasm,' put in Spike helpfully, 'a NIP, or what we call in the trade: "Speak Up and Shut Down".'

'It means, Uncle,' I said, 'that you've got something *really* important to tell us.'

Mycroft looked thoughtful for so long that I almost nudged him before I realised it would be useless.

'Like what?' he said at last.

'I don't know. Perhaps a . . . philosophy of life or something?'

Mycroft looked at me doubtfully and raised an eyebrow.

'The only thing that springs to mind is: "You can never have too many chairs".'

'That's it? You returned from the dead to give me advice on furniture distribution?'

'I know it's not much of a philosophy,' said Mycroft with a shrug, 'but it can pay dividends if someone unexpectedly pops round for dinner.'

'Uncle, *please* try and remember what it is you have to tell us!'

'Was I murdered or anything?' he asked in a dreamy fashion. 'Ghosts often come back if they've been killed or something – at least, Patrick Swayze did.'

'You definitely weren't murdered,' I told him, 'it was a long illness.'

'Then this is something of a puzzle,' murmured Mycroft, 'but I suppose I've got the greater part of eternity to figure it out.'

That's what I liked about my uncle – always optimistic. But that was it. In another moment, he had gone.

'Thirty-three seconds,' said Spike, who had put a stopwatch on him, 'and about fifty-five per cent opacity.'

Spike flicked through a small book of tables he had with him.

'Hmm,' he said at last, 'almost certainly a tri-visitation. You've got him one more time. He'll be down at fifteen to twenty per cent opacity and will only be around for about fifteen seconds.'

'Then I could miss him?'

'No,' said Spike with a smile, 'he appeared to you twice out of twice. The final appearance will be to you, too. Just have a proper question ready for him when you next come here – Mycroft's memory being what it is, you can't rely on him remembering what he came back for. It's up to you.'

'Thanks, Spike,' I said as I closed the door of the workshop, 'I owe you.'

Tuesday and I were home in a few minutes. The house felt warm and comfy and there was a smell of cooking that embraced me like an old friend.

'Hi, darling!' I called out. Landen stopped his typing, and came out of the office to give me a hug.

'How was work?' he asked.

I thought of what I'd been doing that day. Of firing and not firing my drippy alter ego, a Superreader loose somewhere in the BookWorld, Goliath's unwelcome intrusion and Mycroft as a ghost. Then there was the return of Felix8, the Minotaur and my bag of Welsh cash. The time for truth was now. I *had* to tell him.

'I had to do a stair carpet over in Baydon. Hell on earth; the treads were all squiffy, none of the stair rods would fit and Spike and I spent the whole afternoon on it – how's the book going?'

He kissed me and tousled Tuesday's hair affectionately, then took me by the hand and led me into the kitchen, where there was a stew on the stove.

'Kind of okay, I guess,' he replied, stirring the dinner, 'but nothing really spectacular.'

'No ideas?' I prompted. 'An odd *character* perhaps?'

'No – I was mostly working on pace and atmosphere.'

This was strange. I'd specifically told Scampton-Tappett to do his best work. I had a sudden thought.

'What book are you working on, sweetheart?'

'*The Mews of Doom.*'

Ah-ha.

'I thought you said you'd be rewriting *Bananas for Edward*?'

'I got bored with it. Why do you ask?'

'No reason. Where's Friday?'

'In his room. I made him have a shower so he's in a bit of a snot.'

'*Plock.*'

'A clean snot is better than a dirty snot I suppose. And Jenny?'

'Watching TV.'

I called out: 'Hey, Jenny!' but there was no answer.

'*Plock.*'

'She's upstairs in her room.'

I looked at the hall clock. We still had a half-hour until we had to go to the ChronoGuard's career advisory presentation.

'*PLOCK!*'

'Yes, yes, hello, Pickwick — how's this?'

I showed her the finished blue-and-white sweater and before she could even think of complaining I had slipped it over her featherless body. Landen and I stared at her this way and that, trying to figure out whether it was for the better or worse.

'It makes her look like something out of the Cornish Blue pottery catalogue,' said Landen at last.

'Or a very large liquorice allsort,' I added.

Pickwick looked at us sullenly, then realised she was a good deal warmer, and hopped off the kitchen table and trotted down the corridor to try to look in the mirror, which was unfortunately just too high, so she spent the next half-hour jumping up and down to try to catch a glimpse of herself.

'Hi, Mum,' said Friday, looking vaguely presentable as he walked down the stairs.

'Hello, Sweetpea,' I said, passing him the CD Polly had given me. 'I got this for you. It's an early release of *Hosing the Dolly*. Check out the guitar riff on the second track.'

'Cool,' replied Friday, visibly impressed in a 'nothing impresses me' sort of way. 'How did you get hold of it?'

'Oh, you know,' I said offhandedly, 'I have friends in the recording industry. I wasn't always just a boring mum, you know.'

'Polly gave it to you, didn't she?'

I sighed.

'Yes. Ready to go?'

Landen joined us and he and I moved towards the door. Friday stood where he was.

'Do I have to?'

'You promised. And there isn't another ChronoGuard career advisory meeting in Swindon for another six months.'

'I don't want to work in the time industry.'

'Listen,' I said, my voice rising as I finally lost patience, 'get your lazy butt out of the door – okay?'

He knew better than to argue with angry-determined Mum. Landen knocked on the partition wall and a minute later our neighbour, Mrs Berko-Boyler, was on the doorstep wearing a pink quilted dressing gown and hair in curlers.

'Good evening, Mrs Berko-Boyler,' I said.

'Is it?' she said with a snarl. 'Is it *really*?'

'We'll be about an hour,' explained Landen, who was more skilled at dealing with our volatile yet oddly helpful neighbour.

'Do you know the last time Mr Berko-Boyler took me out anywhere?' she asked, scowling at all three of us.

'I've no idea.'

'Saturday.'

'Well, that's not *that* long ago—'

'—Saturday, October sixth, 1983,' she said with a contemptuous sniff, and shuffled past us into the living room. 'Nineteen years ago. Makes me sick, I tell you. Hello, Tuesday,' she said in a more kindly tone, 'where's your sister?'

We walked down to the tram stop in silence. Friday's lack of interest in the ChronoGuard was a matter not only of annoyance, but *surprise*. The Standard History Eventline had him joining the industry three years ago on their 'Junior Time Scout' programme, something that he had failed to do, despite our efforts and those of the ChronoGuard, who were as concerned as we were. But we couldn't force him, either – time was the glue of the cosmos, and had to be *eased* apart. Push destiny too hard and it had an annoying habit of pushing back. He had to join the ChronoGuard, but it had to be his decision. Every way you looked at it, the time was out of joint.

14
The ChronoGuard

'SpecOps 12 are the ChronoGuard, the governmental department dealing with Temporal Stability. It is their job to maintain the integrity of the Standard History Eventline (SHE) and police the timestream against any unauthorised changes or usage. Their most brilliant work is never noticed, as changes in the past always seem to have been that way. Planet-destroying cataclysms generally happen twice a week but are carefully re-routed by skilled ChronoGuard operatives. The citizenry never notice a thing – which is just as well, really.'

The ChronoGuard had their regional offices in the old SpecOps building where I had worked at SO-27, the Literary Detectives. It was a large, no-nonsense Germanic design that had certainly seen better days. Landen and I walked into what had once been the main debriefing room, Friday shuffling in behind us, hands thrust deeply in pockets and head nodding to the beat of his Walkman. Of course, this being the ChronoGuard, they already had a list of attendees from the forms we had filled out at the end of the evening, which seemed to work quite well until a couple with a spotty kid in front of us found they weren't on the list.

'Oh dear,' said the woman at the registration desk in an apologetic tone. 'It seems that you don't stay until the end of the presentation so we've been unable to include you in the registration process. You're going to have to come to the next careers presentation in six months' time.'

The father of the group scratched his head for a moment, stopped to say something, thought better of it and then departed, arguing with his wife.

'Mr and Mrs Parke-Laine-Next and their son Friday,' I said to the woman, who blinked for a few seconds, looked at Friday, gave a shy smile and then stood and started to chatter and gush in a most unseemly manner.

'Mr Next — Friday — how do you do? I've wanted to meet you again for the first time. May I shake you by the hand and congratulate you on—'

She stopped, realised she was being a bit previous and making a fool of herself, so coughed in an embarrassed manner before smoothing her skirt absently and sitting down again.

'Sorry. Welcome to the presentation. Here is your badge and your information pack. If you would like to go in Mr Scintilla will join you soon.'

We dutifully took our seats, and Friday slouched in a very obvious don't-give-a-monkey's manner until I told him to sit up straight, which he didn't like, but he sat up nonetheless.

'What are we doing here?' he asked in a bored voice. 'And why the Time Industry? What about plumbing or something?'

'Because your grandfather was a time operative.'

'Yeah,' he grunted, 'and look what happened to him.'

Landen and I exchanged looks. Friday was right. Ending up not having existed was not a terrific end to a promising career.

'Well!' said a youthful-looking man in the pale blue uniform of the ChronoGuard, who up until now had been helping escort the previous group out of the room. 'My name is Captain Bendix Scintilla and I am head of ChronoGuard Recruitment. I'd like to welcome all of you to this ChronoGuard careers presentation, and hope that this short talk might go some way towards explaining what it is that we done. Did. *Do.* Anyhow, my aims are twofold: secondly, to try and demonstrate to the young people here that a career in the Time Industry is a very exciting prospect indeed, and firstly, to lift the lid on the temporal trade and explode a few common myths and misunderstandings. As I'm about to say, did say, or would say, my name is Bendix Scintilla, and I was died on the sixteenth of March 3291. I'm twenty-three years old in my own personal time, seven hundred and twenty-six in my elapsed work time, and you meet me twenty-seven per cent through my life.'

He smiled, unaware that he was making very little sense. I was used to it, but by the manner in which the rest of the audience were scratching their heads and looking at one other, they weren't. Bendix picked up a solid rod of yellow plastic that was about three feet long, two inches wide and domed at either end.

'Does anyone know what this is?' he asked. There was silence, so he passed it to the nearest family, and told them to pass it on. 'Anyone who can guess wins a prize.'

The first family shrugged and passed it to us. Friday gave it the most cursory of glances and I passed it on.

'Yes, sir?' asked Bendix, pointing to a man in the front row who was with his painfully thin wife and a pair of swotty-looking twins.

'Me?' said the man in a confused voice.

'Yes. I understand you have a question? Sorry, I should have explained. To save time I thought I'd ask you *before* you actually raised your hand.'

'Oh!' said the man, then shrugged and said: 'I was wondering, since we were told this was the only open day for six months, just who the previous party filing out of the door were – and why were they looking at us in that extremely inquisitive manner?'

'Why, that's all you good people, of course! In order not to keep you from your busy schedules this meeting actually takes no time at all. The moment you arrived was precisely the time you left, only out through the other entrance so you wouldn't meet yourselves.'

As soon as he said it a twitter of understanding and wonderment went through the small group. I'd experienced the ChronoGuard in the past so these sorts of cheap parlour tricks didn't impress me, but for many of the people present, to whom time was immutable, it was something new and exciting. Scintilla had been doing this show for many years, and knew how to get an audience's attention.

'Time is odd,' said Bendix, '*very* odd. It's odder than almost anything you can think of. What you *consider* the usual march of time – effect rather quaintly following cause, and so forth – is actually a useful illusion, impressed upon you by rules of physics so *very* benign that we consider them devised by Something Awfully Friendly indeed; if it wasn't for time everything would happen at the same instant, and existence would become tiresomely frenetic and be over very quickly. But before we get into all of that, let's have a show of hands to see who is actually considering a career in time?'

Quite a few hands went up, but Friday's was not among them. I noticed Scintilla staring in our direction as he asked the question, and he seemed put out by Friday's intransigence.

'Yes, miss, you have a question?'

He pointed to a young girl with expensive-looking parents who were sitting in the back row.

'How did you know I was going to ask a question?'

'That was your question, wasn't it?'

'Um . . . yes.'

'Because you've already asked it.'

'I haven't.'

'Actually, you *have*. Everything that makes up what you call the present is in reality the long distant past. The *actual* present is in what you regard as the far distant future. All of this happened a long time ago and is recorded in the Standard History Eventline, so we know what will happen, and can see when things happen that weren't *meant* to. You and I and everything in this room are actually ancient history – but if that seems a bit depressing let me assure you that these really *are* the good old days. Yes, madam?'

A woman just next to us hadn't put up her hand, of course, but was clearly thinking of it.

'So how is it possible to move through time?'

'The force that pushes the fabric of time along is the past attempting to catch up with the future in order to reach an equilibrium. Think of it as a wave – and where the past starts to break over the future in front of it, that's the present. At that moment of temporal instability is a vortex – a *tube*, in surfing parlance – that runs perpendicular to the arrow of time but leads to everything that has ever happened or ever will happen. Of course, that's greatly simplified, but with skill, training, a really good uniform and a bit of aptitude, you'll learn to ride the tube as it ripples through the fabric of space–time. Yes, sir?'

A young lad in the front row was the next to ask a question.

'How can you surf a time wave that is squillions of years in the future?'

'Because it isn't. It's everywhere, all at once. Time is like a river, with the source, body and mouth all existing at the same time.'

Friday turned to me and said in a very unsubtle whisper:

'Is this going to take long?'

'Keep quiet and pay attention.'

He looked heavenward, sighed audibly and slouched deeper in his chair. Scintilla carried on:

'The Time Industry is an equal opportunities employer, has its own union of Federated Timeworkers and a pay structure with overtime payments and bonuses. The working week is forty hours, but each hour is only fifty-two minutes long. Time-related holidays are a perk of the service, and can be undertaken after the first ten years' service. And also, to make it *really* attractive, we will give each new recruit a Walkman and vouchers to buy ten CDs of your—'

He had stopped talking because Friday had put up his hand. We noticed that the other members of the ChronoGuard were staring in dumb wonderment at Friday. The reason wasn't altogether clear until it suddenly struck me: *Scintilla hadn't known Friday was going to ask a question.*

'You . . . have a question?'

'I do. The question is: *Tell me the question I'm going to ask.*'

Scintilla gave a nervous laugh and looked around the audience in an uncomfortable manner. Eventually he hazarded a guess:

'You . . . want to know where the toilet is?'

'No. I wanted to know if everything we do is preordained.'

Scintilla gave out another shrill, nervous laugh. Friday was a natural and they all knew it. The thing was, I think Friday did too – but didn't care.

'A good point, and as you just demonstrated, not at all. Your question was what we call a "free radical", an anomalous event that exists independent of the Standard History Eventline, or SHE. Generally, SHE is the one that must be obeyed, but time also has an annoying propensity for random flexibility. Like rivers, time starts and finishes in generally the same place. Certain events – like gorges and rapids – tend to stay the same. However, on the flat temporal plain the timestream can meander quite considerably, and when it moves towards danger, it's up to us to change something in the event-past to swing the timestream back on course. It's like navigation on the open seas, really, only the ship stays still and you navigate the storm.'

He smiled again.

'But I'm getting ahead of myself. Apocalypse avoidance is but one area of our expertise. Patches of bad time that open spontaneously need to be stitched closed, ChronoTheft is very big in the seventh millennium, and the total eradication of the Dark Ages by a timephoon is requiring a considerable amount of effort to repair, and—'

He had stopped talking because Friday had inexplicably raised his hand once again.

'Why don't you tell us about the downside?' asked Friday in a sullen voice from beneath a curtain of hair. 'About time aggregations, and leaks in the gravity suits that leave cadets a molecule thick?'

'That's why we're here,' explained Scintilla, attempting to make light of the situation, 'to clear up any small matters of misrepresentation that you might have heard. I won't try and convince you that accidents haven't happened, but like all industries we take Health and Safety very seriously.'

'Son,' I said, laying a hand on his arm, 'hear what he has to say first.'

Friday turned and parted his long hair so I could see his eyes. They were intelligent, bright and *scared*.

'Mum, you told me about the accidents – about Dad's eradication and Filbert Snood. Why do you want me to work for an industry that seems to leave its workers dead, non-existent or old before their time?'

He got up and made for the exit, and we followed him as Scintilla attempted to carry on his talk, although firmly rattled. But as we tried to leave, a ChronoGuard operative stood in our way.

'I think you should stay and listen to the presentation,' he said, addressing Friday, who told him to get stuffed. The Chrono took exception to this and made a grab for him, but I was quicker and caught the guard's wrist, pulled him round and had him on the floor with his arm behind his back.

'*Muumm!*' growled Friday, more embarrassed than outraged. 'Do you have to? People are *watching!*'

'Sorry,' I said, letting go of the guard. Scintilla had excused himself from his talk and made his way over to see what was going on.

'If we want to leave, we leave,' growled Landen.

'Of course!' agreed Scintilla, motioning to the Chrono to move off with a flick of his head. 'You can go whenever you want.' He looked at me; he knew how important it was to get Friday inducted, and knew I knew it too.

'But before you go,' he said, 'Friday, I want you to know that we would be very happy to have you join the Time Industry. No minimum academic qualifications, no entrance exam. It's an unconditional offer – the first we've ever made.'

'And what makes you think I'd be any good at it?'

'You can ask questions that aren't already lodged in the SHE. Do you think *anyone* can do that?'

He shrugged

'I'm not interested.'

'I'm just asking for you to stay and hear what we have to say.'

'I'm . . . not . . . interested,' replied Friday more forcefully.

'Listen,' said Scintilla, after looking around furtively and lowering his voice, 'this is a bit unofficial, but I've had a word with Wayne Skunk and he's agreed to let you play a guitar riff on the second track of *Hosing the Dolly*.'

'It's too late,' said Friday, 'it's already been recorded.'

Bendix stared at him.

'Yes – and by *you*.'

'I never did anything of the sort!'

'No – but you *might*. And since *that* possibility exists, you did. Whether you *actually* do it is up to you but either way you can have that one on us. It's your solo either way. Your name is already on the sleeve notes.'

Friday looked at Scintilla, then at me. I knew how much he loved Strontium Goat, and Scintilla did too. He had Friday's complete

128

service record, after all. But Friday wasn't interested. He didn't like being pushed, cajoled, bullied or bribed. I couldn't blame him – I hated it too, and he was my son, after all.

'You think you can *buy* me?' he said finally, and left without another word.

'I'll catch you up,' I said as he walked out with Landen. While the swing-doors shut noisily behind them, Scintilla said to me:

'Do I need to emphasise how important it is that Friday joins the ChronoGuard as soon as possible? He should have signed up three years ago and be surfing the timestream by now.'

'You may have to wait a little longer, Bendix.'

'That's just it,' he replied, 'we don't have much time.'

'I thought you had all the time there was.'

He took me by the arm and we moved to a corner of the room.

'Thursday – can I call you Thursday? We're facing a serious crisis in the Time Industry, and as far as we know, Friday's leadership several trillion bang/crunch cycles from now is the only thing that we can depend on – his truculence this end of time means his desk is empty at the other.'

'But there's *always* a crisis in time, Bendix.'

'Not like this. This isn't a crisis *in* time – it's a crisis *of* time. We've been pushing the frontiers of time forward for trillions upon trillions of years and in a little over four days we'll have reached the . . . End of Time.'

'And that's bad, right?'

Bendix laughed.

'Of course not! Time has to end *somewhere*. But there's a problem with the very mechanism that controls the way we've been scooting around the here-and-now for most of eternity.'

'And that is?'

He looked left and right and lowered his voice.

'*Time travel has yet to be invented!* And with the entire multiverse one giant hot ball of superheated gas contracting at incalculable speed into a point one trillion trillionth the size of a neutron, it's not likely to be.'

'Wait, wait,' I said, trying to get this latest piece of information into my head, 'I know the whole time travel thing makes very little logical sense, but you must have machines to enable you to move through time, right?'

'Of course – but we've got no idea how they work, who built them or when. We've been running the entire industry on something we call "Retro-deficit-engineering". We use the technology *now*, safe in the assumption that it will be invented in the *future*. We did the same with the Gravitube in the fifties and the microchip ten years ago – neither of them actually get invented for over ten thousand years, but it helps us more to have them *now*.'

'Let me get this right,' I said slowly, 'you're using technology you don't have – like me overspending on my credit card.'

'Right. And we've searched every single moment in case it *was* invented and we hadn't noticed. Nothing. Zip. Nada. *Rien*.'

His shoulders slumped and he ran his fingers through his hair.

'Listen, if Friday doesn't retake his seat at the head of the ChronoGuard and use his astonishing skills to somehow save us, then everything that we've worked towards will be undone as soon as we hit Time Zero.'

'I think I get it. Then why is Friday not following his usual career?'

'I've no idea. We always had him as dynamic and aggressively inquisitive as a child – what happened?'

I shrugged.

'All kids are like that today. It's a modern thing caused by too much TV, video games and other instant-gratification bullshit. Either that – or kids are *exactly* the same and I'm getting crusty and intolerant in my old age. Listen, I'll do what I can.'

Scintilla thanked me and I joined Friday and Landen outside.

'I don't want to work in the Time Industry, Mum. I'd only break some dumb rule and end up eradicated.'

'My eradication was pretty painless,' reflected Landen. 'In fact, if your mother hadn't told me about it, I never would have known it happened.'

'That doesn't help, Dad,' grumbled Friday. 'You were reactualised – what about Grandad? No one can say whether he exists or not – not even him.'

I rested my hand on his shoulder. He didn't pull away this time.

'I know, Sweetpea. And if you don't want to join, no one's going to make you.'

He was quiet for a while, then said:

'Do you *have* to call me Sweetpea? I'm sixteen.'

Landen and I looked at one another and we took the tram back home. True to his word, Bendix had slipped us back a few minutes to just before we went in, and as we rattled home in silence we passed ourselves arriving.

'You know that yellow rod Bendix showed us?' said Friday, staring out of the window.

'Yes?'

'It was a half-second of snooker ball.'

15
Home Again

'Noting with dismay that most cross-religion bickering occurred only because all the major religions were convinced they had the *right* one, and every other religion was the *wrong* one, the founders of the Global Standard Deity based their fledgling "portmanteau" faith on the premise that most religions want the same thing once all the shameless manipulative power play had been subtracted: peace, stability, equality and justice – the same as the non-faiths. As soon as they found that centralising thread that unites all people, and made a dialogue of sorts with a Being of Supreme Moral Authority mostly optional, the GSD flourished.'

Friday went to his room in a huff as soon as we got in. Mrs Berko-Boyler told us that the girls were fine, and that she had folded all the washing, cleaned the kitchen, fed Pickwick and made us all cottage pie. This wasn't unusual for her and she scoffed at any sort of payment, then shuffled off home, muttering darkly about how if she'd killed her husband when she'd first thought of it, she'd be 'out of prison by now'.

'Where's Jenny?' I asked Landen, having just gone upstairs to check. 'She's not in her room.'

'She was just in the kitchen.'

The phone rang, and I picked it up.

'Hello?'

'It's Millon,' came a soft voice, 'and I'm sorry to call you at home.'

'Where are you?'

'Look out of the window.'

I did as he asked and saw him wave from his usual spot between the compost heap and the laurels. Millon de Floss, it should be explained, was my official stalker. Even though I had long ago dropped to the bottom of the Z-class celebrity list, he had insisted on maintaining his benign stalkership because, as he explained it, 'we all need a retirement hobby'. Since he had shown considerable fortitude during a sojourn into the Elan back in '88, I now counted him as a family friend, something which he always denied, when asked. 'Friendship,' he intoned soberly, 'always damages the pest factor that is the essence of the bond between stalker and stalkee.' None of the kids was bothered by him at all, and his early-warning capabilities were actually very helpful – he'd spotted Felix8, after all. Not that stalking was his sole job, of course. Aside from fencing cheese to the east of Swindon, he edited *Conspiracy Theorist* magazine and worked on my official biography, something that was taking longer than we had both thought.

'So what's the problem? You still up for the cheese buy this evening?'

'Of course – but you've got visitors. A car on the street with two men in it, and another man climbing over the back wall.'

I thanked him and put the phone down. I'd made a few enemies in the past so Landen and I had some prearranged contingency measures.

'Problems?' asked Landen.

'It's a code yellow.'

Landen understood and without a word dashed off towards the front of the house. I opened the back door and crept out into the garden, took the side passage next to the dustbins and slipped behind the summerhouse. I didn't have to wait long as a man wearing a black boilersuit and a balaclava helmet came tiptoeing up the path towards where I was hidden. He was carrying a sack and a packet of marshmallows. I didn't waste any time on pleasantries; I simply whacked him hard on the chin with my fist and when he staggered, momentarily stunned, I thumped him in the chest and he fell over backwards with a grunt. I pulled off the balaclava to reveal a man I recognised – it was Arthur Plunkett of the Swindon Dodo Fanciers' Society.

'For God's sake, Arthur,' I told him, 'how many times do I have to tell you that Pickwick's not for sale?'

'Uuuuh,' he said, groaning and wheezing as he tried to get his wind back.

'Come on, idiot,' I said as I heaved him up and rested him against the back of the summerhouse, 'you know better than to break into my house – I can be dangerously protective of my family. Why do you think I'm the only one in Swindon able to leave my car unlocked at night?'

'Ooooooh.'

'Wait here,' I said to him, and trotted back indoors. I could be dangerous, but then so could Landen, even with one leg. The front door was open and I could see him hiding behind the privet hedge. I ran low across the lawn and joined him.

'It's only dodo fanciers,' I hissed.

'Again?' he replied. 'After what happened last time?'

I nodded. Clearly Pickwick's Version 1.2 rarity was a prize worth risking a lot for. I looked across the road to where a Buick was parked by the kerb. The two men inside were wearing dark glasses and making a lot of effort to be inconspicuous.

'Shall we stop them?'

'No,' giggled Landen, 'they won't get far.'

'What have you done?' I asked in my serious voice.

'You'll see.'

As we watched, Arthur Plunkett decided to make a run for it – well, a hobble for it actually – and came out of the back garden and limped across the road. The driver of the car started up the engine, waited until Plunkett had thrown himself in the back, then pulled rapidly away from the kerb. They got about twenty feet before the cable that Landen had tied around their back axle whipped tight and, secured to a lamp-post at the other end and far too strong to snap, it tore the rear axle and most of the suspension clear from the back of the car, which then almost pitched up on to its nose before falling back with a crunch in the middle of the road. Momentarily stunned, the three men got out of the car and then legged it off down the street, Plunkett bringing up the rear.

'Was that *really* necessary?' I asked.

'Not at all,' admitted Landen through a series of childish giggles, 'but I'd always wanted to try it.'

'I wish you two would grow up.'

We looked up. My brother Joffy and his partner Miles were staring at us over the garden gate.

'I don't know what you mean,' I said, getting up from where we had been crouched behind the hedge and giving Landen a heave to get him on his feet, 'it's just a normal evening in Swindon.' I looked around as the neighbours had come out to look at the wreck of the Buick and motioned Joffy and Miles inside. 'Come on in for a cup of tea.'

'No tea,' said Joffy as we walked into the house, 'we've just had a tankerful at Mum's – can't you hear me slosh as I walk?'

'. . . and enough Battenberg cake to fill the Grand Canyon,' added Miles in a stuffed-with-cake sort of voice.

'How's the carpet business, Doofus?' asked Joffy as we stood in the hall.

'Couldn't be better – how's the faith unification business?'

'We've *nearly* got everyone,' said Joffy with a smile. 'The atheists came on board last week. Once we'd suggested that "God" could be a set of essentially beneficent physical rules of the cosmos, they were only too happy to join. In fact, apart from a few scattered remnants of faith leaders who can't quite come to terms with the loss of their power, influence and associated funny hat, it's all looking pretty good.'

Joffy's nominal leadership of the British Archipelago branch of the Global Standard Deity was a matter of considerable import within the Next family. The GSD was proposed by delegates of the 1978 Global Interfaith Symposium and had gathered momentum since then, garnering converts from all the faiths into one diverse religion that was flexible enough to offer something for everyone.

'I'm amazed you managed to convert them all,' I said.

'It wasn't a *conversion*,' he replied, 'it was a *unification*.'

'And you are here now ... because?'

'Landen said he'd videotape *Dr Who* for me, and the Daleks are my favourite.'

'I'm more into the Sontarans myself,' said Miles.

'Humph!' said Joffy. 'It's what I would expect from someone who thinks Jon Pertwee was the best Doctor.'

Landen and I stared at him, unsure of whether we should agree, postulate a different theory – or what.

'It was Tom Baker,' said Joffy, ending the embarrassed silence. Miles made a noise that sounded like 'conventionalist', and Landen went off to fetch the tape.

'Doofus?' whispered Joffy when Landen had gone.

'Yes?'

'Have you told him?'

'No,' I whispered back.

'You can't *not* tell him, Thursday – if you don't tell him the truth about the BookWorld and Acme Carpets it's like you're – I don't know – lying to him or something.'

'It's for his own good,' I hissed. 'It's not like I'm having an affair or something.'

'Are you?'

'No, of course not!'

'It's still a lie, sister dearest. How would you like it if he lied to you about what he did all day?'

'I dare say I'd not like it. Leave it to me, Joff – I'll be fine.'

'I hope so. Happy birthday – and in case you hadn't noticed, there's some Camembert on fire in the bonnet of your Acme Carpets van.'

'Some what?'

'Camembert. On fire.'

'Here it is,' said Landen, returning with a video. '*Remembrance of the Daleks*. Where did Thursday go?'

'Oh, she just nipped out for something. Well, must be off! People to educate, persuade and unify – hopefully in that order. Ha-ha-ha.'

'Sorry about that,' I said, coming back from outside. 'I thought I saw Pickwick make faces at the cat next door – you know how they hate one another.'

'But she's over there,' said Landen, pointing to where Pickwick was still struggling to look at herself and her blue-and-white stripy jumper in the mirror.

I shrugged.

'Must have been another dodo.'

'*Is* there another bald dodo in the neighbourhood with a blue stripy cardigan? And can you smell burning cheese?'

'No,' I said innocently. 'What about you, Joff?'

'I've got to go,' he said, staring at his watch. 'Remember what I said, sister dearest!'

And they both walked off towards the crowd that had started to gather around the wrecked car.

'I swear I can smell burning cheese,' said Landen as I shut the front door.

'Probably Mrs Berko-Boyler cooking next door.'

Outwardly I was worry free, but inside I was more nervous. A chunk of burning Camembert on your doorstep meant only one thing – a warning from the Swindon Old Town Cheese Mafia – or, as they liked to be known, the Stiltonistas.

138

16
Cheese

'The controversial Milk Levy from which the unpopular "Cheese Duty" is derived was instigated in 1970 by the then Whig government, which needed to raise funds for a potential escalation of war in the Crimea. With the duty now running at 1,530 per cent on hard and 1,290 per cent on smelly, illegal cheese-making and smuggling had become a very lucrative business indeed. The Cheese Enforcement Agency was formed not only to oversee the licensing of cheese but also to collect the tax levied on it by an overzealous government. Small wonder that there was a thriving underground cheese market.'

'Thanks for tipping us the wink about the dodo fanciers,' I said as we drove through the darkened streets of Swindon two hours later. A tow truck had removed the wreckage of the fanciers' car, and the police had been round to collect statements. Despite it being a busy neighbourhood, no one had seen anything. They had, of course, but the Parke-Laine-Nexts were quite popular in the area.

'Are you sure we weren't followed?' asked Millon as we pulled up outside an empty industrial unit not a stone's throw from the city's airshipfield.

'Positive,' I replied. 'Have you got buyers for it?'

'The usual cheeseheads are all champing at the bit, recipes at the ready. The evening air will be rich with the scent of Welsh rarebit tonight.'

A large seventy-seater airship rose slowly into the air behind the factory units. We watched as its silver flanks caught the colours of the late evening sun as it turned, and with its four propellers beating the still air with a rhythmic hum, it set course for Southampton.

'Ready?' I asked.

'Ready,' said Millon.

I beeped the horn twice and the steel shutters were slowly raised on the nearest industrial unit.

'Tell me,' said Millon, 'why do you think the Old Town Stiltonistas gave you the Flaming Camembert?'

'A warning, perhaps. But we've never bothered them and they've never bothered us.'

'Our two territories don't even overlap,' he observed. 'Do you think the Cheese Enforcement Agency are getting bolder?'

'Perhaps.'

'You don't seem very worried.'

'The CEA is underfunded and knows nothing. Besides, we have customers to attend to – and Acme needs the cash. Think you can liberate five grand by tomorrow morning?'

'Depends what they've got,' he said after a moment's reflection. 'If they're trying to peddle common-or-garden Cheddaresque or that processed crap then we could be in trouble. But if they've got something exotic, then no problem at all.'

The roller shutter was high enough to let us in by now and we drove inside, the shutter reversing direction to close behind us.

We climbed out of the van. The industrial unit was empty except for a large Welsh-registered Griffin V8 truck, a long table with leather sample cases lying on it and four men all wearing black suits with black ties and sunglasses, and looking vaguely menacing. It was all bravado, of course – Scorsese movies were big in the Welsh Republic. I tried to detect whether any of them were packing heat by the swing of their jackets and guessed that they weren't. I'd only carried a gun once in the real world since SpecOps was disbanded and hoped I never had to again. Cheese smuggling was still a polite undertaking. As soon as it turned ugly, I was out.

'Owen Pryce the Cheese,' I said in a genial manner, greeting the leader of the group with a smile and a firm handshake, 'good to see you again. I trust the trip across the border was uneventful?'

'It's getting a lot harder these days,' he replied in a sing-song Welsh accent that betrayed his roots in the south of the Republic, probably Abertawe. 'There are dutymen everywhere and the bribes I have to pay have a bearing on the price of the goods.'

'As long as it's fair price, Pryce,' I replied pleasantly. 'My clients love cheese but there's a limit to what they'll pay.'

We were both lying, but it was the game we played. My clients would pay good money for high-quality cheese, and as likely as not he didn't bribe anyone. The border with Wales was a hundred and seventy miles long, and had more holes than a hastily matured Emmental. There weren't enough dutymen to cover it all, and to be honest, although illegal, no one took cheese smuggling that seriously.

Pryce nodded to one of his compatriots and they opened the sample cases with a flourish. They were all there – every single make of cheese you could imagine, from pure white to dark amber. Crumbly, hard, soft, liquid, gas. The rich aroma of well-matured cheese escaped into the room and I felt my taste-buds tingle. This was top-quality shit – the best available.

'Smells good, Pryce.'

He said nothing and showed me a large slab of white cheese.

'Caerphilly,' he said, 'the best. We can—'

I put up a hand to stop him.

'The punks can deal with the mild stuff, Owen. We're interested in Level 3.8 and above.'

He shrugged, set the Caerphilly down and picked up a small chunk of creamy-coloured cheese.

'Quintuple Llanboidy,' he announced, 'a 5.2. It'll play on your taste-buds like the plucked strings of a harp.'

'We'll have the usual of that, Pryce,' I muttered, 'but my clients are into something a little stronger. What else you got?'

We always went through this charade. My speciality was the volatile cheese market, and when I said volatile, I didn't mean the market – I meant the cheese.

Pryce nodded and showed me a golden-yellow cheese that had veins of red running through it.

'Quadruple-strength Dolgellau Veinclotter,' he announced. 'It's a 9.5. Matured in Blaenafon for eighteen years and not for the faint-hearted. Good on crackers but can function equally well as an amorous skunk repellent.'

I took a daringly large amount and popped it on my tongue. The taste was extraordinary; I could almost *see* the Cambrian mountains just visible in the rain, low clouds, gushing water and lime-stone crags, frost-shattered scree and—

'Are you all right?' said Millon when I opened my eyes. 'You passed out for a moment there.'

'Kicks like a mule, doesn't it?' said Pryce kindly. 'Have a glass of water.'

'Thank you. We'll take all you have – what else you got?'

'Mynachlog-ddu Old Contemptible,' said Pryce, showing me a whitish crumbly cheese. 'It's kept in a glass jar because it will eat through cardboard or steel. Don't leave it in the air too long as it will start dogs howling.'

'We'll have thirty kilos. What about this one?' I asked, pointing at an innocuous-looking ivory-coloured soft cheese.

'Ystradgynlais Molecular Unstable Brie,' announced Pryce, 'a soft cheese we've cloned from an original supplied by our cheese-making brethren in France – but every bit as good. Useful as a contact anaesthetic or paint stripper. It can cure insomnia and ground to dust is very useful self-defence against muggers and wandering bears. It has a half-life of twenty-three days, glows in the dark and can be used as a source of X-rays.'

'We'll take the lot. Got anything *really* strong?'

Pryce raised an eyebrow and his minders looked at one another uneasily.

'Are you sure?'

'It's not for me,' I said hastily, 'but we've got a few serious cheese-heads who can take the hard stuff.'

'We've got some Machynlleth Wedi Marw.'

'What the hell's that?'

'*Really* strong cheese. It'll bring you up in a rash just by looking at it. Denser than enriched plutonium, two grams is enough to season a macaroni cheese for eight hundred men. The smell alone will corrode iron. A concentration in air of only seventeen parts per million will bring on nausea and unconsciousness within twenty seconds. Our chief taster ate a half-ounce by accident and was unconscious for six hours. Open only out of doors, and even then only with a doctor's certificate and well away from areas of population. It's not really a cheese for eating – it's more for encasing in concrete and dumping in the ocean a long way from civilisation.'

I looked at Millon, who nodded. There was *always* someone stupid enough to experiment. After all, no one had ever died from cheese ingestion.

'Let us have a half-pound and we'll see what we can do with it.'

'Very well,' said Pryce. He nodded to a colleague, who opened another suitcase and very gingerly took out a sealed lead box. He laid it very gently on the table and then took a hurried step backwards.

'You won't attempt to open it until we are at least thirty miles away, will you?'

143

'We'll do our best.'

'Actually, I'd advise you not to open it at all.'

'Thanks for the advice.'

The trading went on in this manner for another half-hour, and with our order book full and the cost totted up we transported the cheese from the back of their truck to the Acme van, whose springs groaned under the weight.

'What's that?' I asked, pointing at a wooden crate in the back of their truck. It was securely fixed to the floor with heavy chains.

'That's nothing,' Pryce said quickly, his henchmen moving together to try to block my view.

'Something you're not showing us?'

Pryce took me by the arm as they slammed the rear doors and threw the latch.

'You've always been a good customer, Ms Next, but we know what you will and won't do, and this cheese is not for you.'

'Strong?'

He wouldn't answer me.

'It's been good doing business with you, Ms Next. Same time next month?'

'Yes,' I said slowly, wondering just how strong a cheese has to be before you have to keep it chained down. More interestingly, the box was stencilled with the code: 'X-14'.

I handed over the Welsh cash. It was swiftly counted and before I knew it Owen Pryce and his marginally threatening henchmen had revved up the truck and vanished into the night, off to sell cheese to the Stiltonistas in the Old Town. I always got first dibs – that was probably what the Flaming Camembert was all about.

'Did you see that cheese chained up in the back?' I asked Millon as we got back into the van.

'No – what cheese?'

'Nothing.'

I started the van and we drove out of the industrial estate. This was the point at which the CEA would have pounced if they'd known what was going on, but they didn't. All was quiet in the town, and within a few minutes Millon had dropped me off at home, taking the Acme van himself to start peddling the cheese.

I had only just opened the garden gate when I noticed a figure standing in the shadows. I instinctively made to grab my pistol, before remembering that I didn't carry one in the Outland any more. I needn't have worried: it was Spike.

'You made me jump!'

'Sorry,' he replied soberly. 'I came to ask you if you wanted any help to dispose of the body.'

'I'm sorry?'

'The body. The ground can be hard this time of year.'

'*Whose* body?'

'Felix8. You did him in, right?'

'No.'

'Then how did he escape? You, me and Stig have the only keys.'

'Wait a moment,' I said nervously, 'Felix8 has *gone*?'

'Completely. Are you *sure* you didn't kill him?'

'I think I would have remembered.'

'Well,' said Spike, handing me a spade, 'you'd better give this back to Landen then.'

I must have looked horrified because he added:

'I told him it was to plant some garlic. Listen, you get inside and keep the doors and windows locked – I'll be in my car across the street if you need me.'

I went into the house and locked the door securely behind me. Felix8 was a worry, but not tonight – I had a complimentary block of Llangloffan and nothing was going to come between me and Landen's unbeatable macaroni cheese.

17
Breakfast Again

'**Commonsense Party leader Redmond Van de Poste MP
succeeded Chancellor Yorrick Kaine in the hastily called
elections of 1988, changed the job title back to "Prime
Minister" and announced a series of innovative policies.**
For a start, he insisted that democracy, while a good idea for a
good idea, was potentially vulnerable to predation by the greedy,
egotistical and insane, so his plan to *democratise* democracy was
ruthlessly implemented. There were initial issues regarding civil
liberties but now, fourteen years later, we were beginning to
accrue the benefits.'

The news on the radio that morning was devoted – once again –
to the ongoing crisis of the week: namely, where the nation's Stupidity
Surplus could be discharged safely. Some suggested a small war in
a distant country with a race of people we weren't generally ill
disposed towards, but others thought this too risky and favoured
crippling the efficiency of the public services by adding a new layer
of bureaucracy at huge expense and little benefit. Not all suggestions were sensible: fringe elements of the debate maintained that
the nation should revitalise the stupendously costly 'Anti-Smote
Shield' project. Designed to protect mankind – or at least England
– against the potential threat of an enraged deity eager to cleanse
a sinful race with a rain of fire, the shield project would have the
twin benefits of a profligate waste of good cash and the possibility
that other European nations could be persuaded to join, and thus
deal with Europe's combined stupidity excess at one fell swoop.

Prime Minister Redmond Van de Poste took the unusual step

of speaking on live radio to not only reject all the suggestions, but also make the inflammatory statement that despite the escalating surplus, they would continue the Commonsense approach to government. When asked how the Stupidity Surplus might be reduced, Van de Poste replied that he was certain something would come along that 'would be fantastically dim witted, but economic', and added that as a conciliatory dumb measure to appease his critics, they would be setting fire to a large quantity of rubber tyres for no very good purpose. This last remark was met with a cry of 'too little, too late' from Mr Alfredo Traficcone of the opposition 'Prevailing Wind' party, who were gradually gaining ground promoting policies of 'immediate gain', something that Mr Traficcone said was 'utterly preferable to the hideously long-sighted policies of cautious perceptiveness'.

'What a load of old poo,' said Landen, giving Tuesday a boiled egg for breakfast and putting one in front of Jenny's place, then yelling up the stairs to her that breakfast was on the table.

'What time did Friday get in last night?' I asked, since I had gone to bed first.

'Past midnight. He said he was making noise with his mates.'

'The Gobshites?'

'I think so, but they might as well be called the Feedbacks and working on the single "Static" from the *White Noise* album.'

'It's only because we're old and fuddy-duddy,' I said, resting an affectionate hand on his. 'I'm sure the music we listened to was as crap to our parents as his music is to us.'

But Landen was elsewhere. He was composing an outline for a self-help book for dogs called *Yes, You CAN Open the Door Yourself*, and was thus functionally deaf to everything.

'Land, I'm sleeping with the milkman.'

He didn't look up but said:

'That's nice, darling.'

Tuesday and I laughed, and I turned to look at her with an expression of faux shock and said:

'What are you laughing about? You shouldn't know anything about milkmen!'

'Mum,' she said with a mixture of precocity and matter-of-factness, 'I have an IQ of two hundred and eighty and know more about everything than you do.'

'I doubt it.'

'Then what does the ischiocavernosus muscle do?'

'Okay, you *do* know more than I do. Where is Jenny? She's *always* late for breakfast!'

I took the tram towards the old SpecOps building to do some investigating. The escape of Felix8 was fresh in my mind, and several times I saw someone who I thought was him, but on each occasion it was a harmless passer-by. I still had no idea how he had escaped, but one thing I *did* know was that the Hades family had some pretty demonic attributes, and they looked after their friends. Felix8, loathsome cur that he was, would have been considered a friend. If he was still in their pay, then I would have to speak to a member of the Hades family. It could only be Aornis: the only one in custody.

I got off the tram at the town hall and walked down the hill to the SpecOps building. It was eerily empty as I stepped in, a strong contrast to the hive of activity that I had known. I was issued with a visitor's badge and headed off down the empty corridors towards the ChronoGuard office. Not the briefing hall we had visited the previous evening, but a small room on the second floor. I'd been here on a number of occasions so knew what to expect – as I watched, the decor and furniture changed constantly, the ChronoGuard operatives themselves jumping in and out, their speed making them little more than smears of light. There was one piece of furniture that remained unchanged while all about raced, moved and blurred in a never-ending jumble. It was a small table with an old candlestick telephone upon it, and as I put out my hand, it rang. I picked up the phone and held the earpiece to my ear.

'Mrs Parke-Laine-Next?' came a voice.

'Yes?'

'He'll be right down.'

And in an instant, he was. The room stopped moving from one time to the next and froze with a decor that looked vaguely contemporary. There was a figure at the desk who smiled when he saw me. But it wasn't Bendix or my father – it was *Friday*. Not the mid-twenties Friday whom I had met at my wedding bash or the old Friday I had met during the Samuel Pepys Fiasco, but a young Friday – almost indistinguishable from the one who was still fast asleep at home, snoring loudly in the pit of despair we called his bedroom.

'Hi, Mum!'

'Hi, Sweetpea,' I said, deeply confused and also kind of relieved. This was the Friday I thought I was meant to have – clean cut, well presented, confident and with an infectious smile that reminded me of Landen. And he probably bathed more than once a fortnight, too.

'How old are you?' I asked, placing a hand on his chin to make sure he was real, and not a phantasm or something like Mycroft. He *was* real. Warm and still only needing to shave once a week.

'I'm sixteen, Mum, the same age as the lazy slob asleep at home. In a context that you'd understand, I'm a *potential* Friday. I started with the Time Scouts at thirteen and popped my first tube at fifteen – the youngest ever to do so. The Friday you know is Friday *Present*. The older me that will hopefully be the Director General is Friday *Last*, and because he's indisposed owing to a mild temporal ambiguity caused by the younger alternative me not joining the Time Scouts, Bendix reconstituted me from the echoes of the might-have-been. They asked me to see what I can do.'

'Nope,' I replied in some confusion, 'didn't understand a word.'

'It's a split timeline thing, Mum,' explained Friday, 'in which two versions of the same person can exist at the same time.'

'So can't *you* become the Director General at the other end of time?'

'Not that easy. The alternative timelines have to be in concurrence to go forward to a mutually compatible future.'

I understood – sort of.

'I guess this means you haven't invented time travel yet?'

'Nope. Any idea why the other me is such a slouch?'

'I asked you to join the Time Scouts three years ago but you couldn't be bothered,' I murmured by way of explanation. 'You were too busy playing computer games and watching TV.'

'I don't blame you or Dad. Something's seriously out of joint but I don't know what. Friday Present seems to have the intelligence but not the pizzazz to want to do anything.'

'Except play the guitar in Gobshite.'

'If you can call it playing,' said Friday with an unkind laugh.

'Don't be so—'

I checked myself. If this wasn't self-criticism, I didn't know what was.

All of a sudden there was *another* Friday standing next to potential Friday. He was identical, except he was carrying a buff folder. They looked at one another curiously. The newest Friday said 'Sorry' in an embarrassed fashion and walked a little way down the corridor, where he pretended to be interested in the carved wood around the door frame.

'This morning I only had one son,' I muttered despondently, 'now I've got three!'

Friday glanced over his shoulder at the second Friday, who was caught staring at us and quickly looked the other way.

'You've only got one, Mum. Don't worry about him.'

'So what's gone wrong?' I asked. 'Why is Friday Present so unlike potential Friday?'

'It's difficult to tell. This 2002 isn't like the one in the Standard History Eventline. Everyone seems introspective and lacking in any sort of charisma. It's as though a heavy sky is forcing lassitude on the population – in a word, a *greyness* seems to have spread across the land.'

'I know what you mean,' I said, shaking my head sadly. 'We've seen a sixty per cent drop in book readership; it seems no one can be bothered to invest their time in a good novel.'

'That would figure,' replied Friday thoughtfully. 'It's not meant to be like this, I assure you – the best minds have it as the beginning of the Great Unravelling. If what we suspect is true and time travel isn't invented in the next three and a half days, we might be heading towards a spontaneously accelerated inverse obliteration of the all-history.'

'Can you put that into a carpet metaphor I might understand?'

'If we can't secure our existence right at the beginning, time will start to roll up like a carpet, taking history with it.'

'How fast?'

'It will begin slowly at 22.03 on Friday with the obliteration of the earliest fossil record. Ten minutes after that all evidence of ancient hominids will vanish, swiftly followed by the sudden absence of everything from the middle Holocene. Five minutes later and all megalithic structures will vanish as if they had never been. The pyramids will go in another two minutes with ancient Greece vanishing soon after. In the course of another minute the Dark Ages will disappear, and in the next twenty seconds the Norman Conquest will never have happened. In the final twenty-seven seconds we will see modern history disappear with increased rapidity, until at 22.48 and nine seconds, the end of history will catch up with us and there will be nothing left at all, nor any evidence that there ever was – to all intents and purposes, we won't ever have existed.'

'So what's the cause?'

'I've no idea, but I'm going to have a good look around. Did you want something?'

'Oh – yes. I need to speak to Aornis. One of her family's old henchmen is on the prowl – or was.'

'Wait a moment.'

And in an instant he was gone.

'Ah!' said the other Friday, returning from just up the corridor. 'Sorry about that; enloopment records are kept in the twelfth millennium and being accurate to the second on a ten-thousand-year jump is still a bit beyond me.'

He opened the buff file and flicked through the contents.

'She's done seven years of a thirty-year looping for unlawful memory distortion,' he murmured. 'We had to hold her trial in the thirty-seventh century, where it actually *is* a crime. The dubious legality of being tried outside one's own time zone would have been cause for an appeal but she never lodged one.'

'Perhaps she forgot.'

'It's possible. Shall we go?'

We stepped outside the SpecOps building, turned left and walked the short distance to the Brunel Shopping Centre.

'Have you seen anything of my father?' I asked. I hadn't seen him for over a year; not since the last potential life-extinguishing Armageddon, anyway.

'I see him flash past from time to time,' replied Friday, 'but he's a bit of an enigma. Sometimes we're told to hunt him down, and the next moment we're working under him. Sometimes he's even *leading* the hunt for himself. Listen, I'm ChronoGuard and even I can't figure it out. Ah! We're here.'

I looked up and frowned. 'Here' didn't seem to be anywhere particular – we were outside TK-Maxx, the discount clothes store.

18

Aornis Hades

'They called it being "in the loop", but the official name was "Closed Loop Temporal Field Containment". It was only used for criminals where there was little hope of rehabilitation, or even contrition. It was run by the ChronoGuard and was frighteningly simple. They popped the convict in an eight-minute repetitive time loop for five, ten, twenty years. The prisoner's body aged but never needed sustenance. It was cruel and unnatural – yet cheap and required no bars, guards or food.'

We walked into the Swindon TK-Maxx, threaded our way through the busy morning bargain-hunters and found the manager, a well-dressed woman with a kindly manner who had been in my class at school but whose name I had forgotten – we always gave polite nods to one another, but nothing more than that. Friday showed her his ID. She smiled and led us to a keypad mounted on the wall. The manager punched in a long series of numbers, and then Friday punched an even *longer* series of numbers. There was a shift in the light to a greeny-blue, the manager and all the customers stopped dead in their tracks as time ground to a halt, and a faint buzz replaced the happy murmur of shoppers.

Friday looked at the buff folder he was carrying and then around the store. The illumination was similar to the cool glow you get from underwater lights in a swimming pool, with reflections that danced on the ceiling. Within the gloomy greeny-blueness of the store's interior I could see spheres of warm light, and within these there seemed to be some life. We walked past several of these spheres, and I noted that while most of the people inside were dark and indistinct, at least one was more vivid than the rest and looking very much alive – the prisoner.

'She should be at Checkout Six,' said Friday, leading the way past a ten-foot-wide translucent yellow sphere that was centred around the chair outside the changing rooms. 'That's Oswold Danforth,' murmured Friday. 'He assassinated Mahatma Winston Smith al Wazeed during his historic speech to the citizens of the World State in 3419. Looped for seven hundred and ninety-eight years in an eight-minute sliver of time where he's waiting for his girlfriend Trudi to try on a camisole.'

'Does he know he's looped?'

'Of course.'

I looked at Danforth, who was staring at the floor and clenching and unclenching his fists in frustration.

'How long's he been in?'

'Thirty-four years. If he tells us who his co-conspirator was we'll enlarge his loop from eight minutes to fifteen.'

'Do you just loop people in stores?'

'We used to use dentists' waiting rooms, bus stops and cinemas during Merchant Ivory films as these tended to be natural occurrences of slow time, but there were too many prisoners so we had to design our own. Temporal-K, Maximum security – why, what did you think TK-Maxx was?'

'A place to buy designer-label clothing at reasonable prices?'

He laughed.

'The very idea! Next you'll be telling me that IKEA just sells furniture you have to build yourself.'

'Isn't it?'

'Of course not. Here she is.'

We had approached the checkout, where a sphere of warm light about eighteen foot wide encompassed most of the till and a queue of bored-looking shoppers. Right at the back of the queue was a familiar face: Aornis Hades, younger sister of Acheron. She was a mnemonomorph – someone with the ability to control memories. I'd defeated her good and proper; twice in the real world and once in my head. She was slim, dark and attractive and dressed in the very latest fashions – but only from when she was looped seven years earlier. Mind you, because of the vague meanderings of the fashion industry, she'd been in and out of high fashion twenty-seven times since then, and was currently 'in' – although she'd never know it. To a looped individual, time remains the same.

'You know she can control coincidences?'

'Not any more,' replied Friday with a grimness that I found disconcerting in one so young.

'Who are they?' I asked, pointing at the other women in the queue for the checkout.

'They're not prisoners – just real shoppers doing real shopping at the time of her enloopment; Miss Hades is stuck in an eight-minute zone, waiting to pay for goods, but she never does. If it's true what they say about her love of shopping, this punishment is *particularly* apt.'

'Do I have anything to bargain with?'

Friday looked at the file.

'You can stretch her loop by twenty minutes.'

'How do I get to talk to her?'

'Just step inside the sphere of influence.'

I took a deep breath and walked into the globe of yellow light. All of a sudden normality returned with a jerk. I was back in what seemed like real life. It was raining outside, which was what must have been happening when she was looped. Aornis, well used to the monotonous round of limited dialogue during her eight-minute existence, noticed me immediately.

'Well, well,' she murmured sarcastically. 'Is it visiting day already?'

'Hello, Aornis,' I said with a smile, 'remember me?'

'Very funny. What do you want, Next?'

I offered her a small vanity case with some cosmetics in it that I had picked off a shelf earlier. She didn't take it.

'Information.'

'Is there a deal in the offing?'

'I can give you another ten minutes. It's not much, but it's something.'

She looked at me, then all around her. She knew people were outside the sphere looking in, but not how many, and who. She had the power to wipe memories, but not read minds. If she could, she'd know how much I hated her. Mind you, she probably knew that already.

'Next, please!' said the checkout girl, and Aornis put two dresses and a pair of shoes on the counter.

'How's the family, Thursday – Landen and Friday and the girls?'

'Information, Aornis.'

She took a deep breath as the loop jumped back to the beginning of her eight minutes and she was once more at the rear of the queue. She clenched her fists so tightly her knuckles went white. She had been doing this for ten years without respite. The only thing worse than a loop was a loop in which one suffered a painful trauma, such as a broken leg. But even the most sadistic judge could never find it in themselves to order that. Aornis calmed herself, looked up at me and said:

'Give me twenty minutes and I'll tell you what you want to know.'

'I want to know about Felix8.'

'That's not a name I've heard for a while,' replied Aornis evenly. 'What is your interest in that empty husk?'

'He was hanging around my house with a loaded gun yesterday,' I told her, 'and I can only assume he was wanting to do me harm.'

Aornis looked mildly perturbed.

'You saw him?'

'With my own eyes.'

'Then I don't understand. After Acheron's untimely end, Felix8 seemed rather at a loss. He came round to the house and was making a nuisance of himself, very like an abandoned dog.'

'So what happened?'

'Cocytus put him down.'

'I'm assuming you don't mean in the sense of "to humiliate".'

'You think correct.'

'And when was this?'

'Nineteen eighty-six.'

'Did you witness the murder? Or see the body?'

I stared at her carefully, trying to determine whether she was telling the truth.

'No. He just *said* he had. You could have asked him yourself, but you killed him, didn't you?'

'He was evil. He brought it upon himself.'

'I wasn't being serious,' replied Aornis. 'It's what passes for humour in the Hades family.'

'This doesn't really help me,' I murmured.

'That's nothing to do with me,' replied Aornis. 'You wanted intel and I gave it to you.'

'If I find out you've lied,' I said, getting ready to leave, 'I'll be back to take away the twenty minutes I gave you.'

'If you've seen Felix8 how could you think otherwise?' pointed out Aornis with impeccable logic.

'Stranger things have happened.'

I stepped out of the loop-cell and was back in the bluey-greenness of TK-Maxx among the time-frozen customers, with Friday at my side.

'Think she's telling the truth?' he asked.

'If she is, it makes no sense at all, which is a point in her favour.

If she'd told me what I wanted to hear, I'd have been more suspicious. Did she say anything else to me she might have made me forget?'

Aornis, with her power of memory distortion and erasure, was wholly untrustworthy – she could tell you everything only to make you forget it a few seconds later. At her trial the judge and jury were merely actors – the real judge and jury watched it all on CCTV. To this day the actors in the courtroom still have no idea why that 'frightfully pleasant girl' was in the dock at all. Friday ran over what he had witnessed her saying, and we managed to find an exchange that she'd erased from my recollection: that she was going to bust out of TK-Maxx with the help of someone 'on the outside'.

'Any idea who that might be?' I asked. 'And why did she shield it from me?'

'No idea – and it's probably just her being manipulative; my guess is the recollection will be on time release – it'll pop into your head in a few hours.'

I nodded. She'd done something similar to me before.

'But I shouldn't worry,' added Friday. 'Temporal enloopment has a hundred per cent past-present-future escape-free record; she'd have to bend the Standard History Eventline to get out.'

I left Aornis to her never-ending wait at the checkout and Friday powered down the visitors' interface. The manager popped back into life as time started up again.

'Did you get all you need?' she asked pleasantly.

'I hope so,' I replied, and followed Friday from the store.

'Thanks,' I said, giving him a motherly hug and a kiss.

'Mum,' he said in a serious tone.

'What?'

'There's something I need to suggest to you and you're going to have to think really carefully before you reply.'

'What is it?'

'It's Friday. The *other* Friday. We've got three and a half days to the end of time. Does it seriously look like he's going to join the ChronoGuard?'

'It's possible.'

'Mum – truthfully?'

'No.'

'We're fast running out of options. My Director General older self is still absent at the end of time, so I had a word with Bendix and he suggested we try . . . *replacement.*'

'What do you mean?'

'That your Friday is removed, and I take his place.'

'Define "removed"?'

Friday scratched his head.

'We've run several timestream models and it looks good. I'm precisely the same age as him, and I'm what he *would* be like if he hadn't gone down the bone-idle route. If "replacement" isn't a good word for you, why not think of it as just rectifying a small error in the Standard History Eventline.'

'Let me get this straight,' I said, 'you want to murder my son and replace him with yourself? I only met you ten minutes ago.'

'I'm your *son*, Mum. Every memory, good or bad, is as much part of me as it is of the Friday at home. You want me to prove it? Who else knows about the BookWorld? One of your best friends is Melanie Bradshaw, who's a gorilla. It's true she let me climb all over the furniture and swing from the light fixtures. I can speak **Courier Bold**, Lorem Ipsum and even unpeel a banana with my feet – want me to show you?'

'No,' I said, 'I accept that you're my son. But you can't kill the other Friday – he's done nothing wrong. I won't let you.'

'Mum! Which Friday would you rather have? The feckless lazy arse or me?'

'You don't understand what it is to be a mother, Friday. The answer's no. I'll take the Friday I'm dealt.'

'I thought you might say that,' he said in a harsher manner. 'I'll report back to Mr Scintilla but if they feel there's no alternative, we might decide to go ahead anyway – with or without your permission.'

'I think we've spoken enough,' I said, keeping my anger at bay. 'Do one thing for me: how long do you think I have until they might take that action?'

He shrugged.

'Forty-eight hours?'

'Promise?'

'I promise,' said Friday. 'By the way, have you told Dad about all your Jurisfiction work? You said you were going to.'

'I will – soon, I promise. Goodbye, darling.'

And I kissed him again and walked away, boiling with inner rage. Fighting with the ChronoGuard was like fighting City Hall. You couldn't win. Every way I looked at it, Friday's days were numbered. But paradoxically, they weren't – the Friday I had just spoken to was the one I was meant to have and the one who I had met in the future, the one who made sure he escaped Landen's eradication and the one who whipped up the timephoon in the Dark Ages to cover up St Zvlkx's illegal time fraud. I rubbed my head. Time travel was like that – full of impossible paradoxes that defied explanation and made theoretical physicists' brains turn to something resembling guacamole. But at least I still had two days to figure out a way to save the lazy good-for-nothing loafer that was my son. But before then, I needed to find out just how Goliath had managed to send a probe into fiction.

19

The Goliath Corporation

'The Isle of Man had been an independent corporate-
state within England since it was appropriated for the
greater fiscal good in 1963. It had hospitals and schools, a
university, its own fusion reactor and also, leading from Douglas
to Kennedy Graviport in New York, the world's only privately
run Gravitube. The Isle of Man was home to almost 200,000
people who did nothing but support, or support the support of,
the one enterprise that dominated the small island: the Goliath
Corporation.'

I hopped on the Skyrail at the Brunel Centre and went the three
stops to Swindon's Clary-LaMarr travelport, where I caught the
next bullet train to Saknussum International. From there I jumped
on the next Overmantle Gravitube with seconds to spare, and was
at James Tarbuck International in Liverpool, a journey time of just
over an hour. The country's hyper-efficient public transport network
was the Commonsense Party's greatest achievement so far. Very few
people used cars for journeys over ten miles these days. The system
had its detractors, of course – the car-parking consortiums were
naturally appalled, as was the motorway service industry, which had
taken the extraordinary step of producing good food in order to
win back customers.

I made good use of the time by calling Landen and telling him
all about the alternative Friday's offer: to replace our idle and mostly
bedridden headbanger of a son with a well-groomed, upright and
responsible member of society, and Landen had agreed with me –
that we'd keep the smelly one we had, thank you very much. Once

I'd tubed to Tarbuck I took the hi-speed Ekranoplane all the way to the distinctly unimaginatively titled Goliathopolis on what had once been the Isle of Man. Despite losing nearly everything during the dramatic St Zvlkx adventure back in 1988, the vast multinational had staged an impressive comeback – mostly, it was said, by hiding their net worth and filing for bankruptcy on a subsidiary company that conveniently emerged from the distant past to take a lot of the flak. 'Timefoolery' was suggested but despite an investigation by the ChronoGuard's Fiscal Chronuption Unit, which looked very closely at such matters, no wrongdoing had been found – or could be proved. After that it didn't take long for the Corporation to re-establish itself, and Goliathopolis was once again the Hong Kong of the western hemisphere, a forest of glassy towers striding up the hillside towards Snaefell.

Even before we left the dock at Tarbuck International, I had the idea that I was being watched. As the Goliath ground-effect transport jetted across the Irish Sea, several of the Goliath employees on the craft looked at me cautiously, and when I sat down in the coffee shop, the people near me moved away. It was kind of flattering, really, but since I had trounced the Corporation in the very biggest way possible at least once, they clearly regarded me as something of a threat. How big a threat was revealed to me when we docked at Goliathopolis forty minutes later. There was a welcoming committee already waiting for me. But I don't mean 'welcoming committee' in the ironic sense of large men with no necks and coshes – they had laid out the red carpet, bedecked the jetty with bunting and put on a baton-twirling demonstration by the Goliathopolis Majorettes. More importantly, the entire upper echelons of Goliath management had turned out to greet me, including the president, John Henry Goliath V, and a dozen or so of his executive officers, all of whom had a look of earnest apprehension etched upon their pasty faces. As someone who had cost the company dear over the past two decades, I was clearly feared – and possibly even revered.

'Welcome back to Goliathopolis,' said John Henry politely, shaking my hand warmly. 'I hope that your stay is a happy one and that whatever brings you here can be a matter of mutual concern to us both. I hardly need to stress the respect in which we hold you, and would hate that you might find reason to act upon us without first entertaining the possibility of a misunderstanding.'

He was a large man. It looked as though someone had handed his parents a blueprint of a baby and told them to scale it up by a factor of one and a quarter.

'This is a joke, right?'

'On the contrary, Ms Next. Based on past experiences, we have decided that complete and utter disclosure is the only policy worth pursuing as far as your good self is concerned.'

'You'll excuse me if I remain unconvinced by your perceived honesty.'

'It's not honesty, Ms Next. You *personally* cost us over a hundred billion pounds in lost revenue, so we regard our openness as a sound business strategy – albeit of an abstract nature. Because of this there is no door closed to you, no document unreadable, no member to whom you may not speak. I hope I am candid?'

'Very,' I replied, put off my guard by the Corporation's attitude. 'I have a matter I'd like to discuss with you.'

'Naturally,' replied John Henry. 'The majorettes would like to perform, if that's all right with you?'

'Of course.'

So we watched the majorettes march up and down for twenty minutes to the music of the Goliath Brass Band, and when it was over I was driven in John Henry's Bentley towards the Goliath head office, a mighty one-hundred-and-ten-storey building right at the heart of Goliathopolis.

'Your son and family are well?' asked John Henry, who aside from a few more grey hairs didn't seem to have aged a great deal since we had last met. He fixed me with his piercing green eyes, and poured on the natural charm he had been blessed with.

'I expect you know full well they are,' I replied, 'and everything else about me.'

'On the contrary,' protested John Henry. 'We thought that if even the sniff of surveillance was detected you might decide to take action, and action from you, as we have seen to our cost, is never less than devastating to our interests.'

'Ah,' I murmured, suddenly realising why there had been a deafening silence from Goliath over the years.

'So how can we help?' asked John Henry. 'If,' he added, 'we can help at all.'

'I want to find out what advances you have made in transfictional travel.'

John Henry raised his eyebrows and smiled genially.

'I never thought it would remain a secret from you for ever.'

'You've been leaving Outlander probes scattered all over the BookWorld.'

'The research and development on the Book Project has been somewhat hit or miss, I'll admit that,' replied John Henry candidly. 'To be honest, I had expected you to call on us sooner than you have.'

'I've been busy.'

'Of course. And since you are here, perhaps you would grace us with your comments on the technical aspects of our project.'

'I promise nothing, but I'd certainly like to see what you're up to.'

The car drove towards the modern glassy towers of the corporate centre of the multinational and past well-tailored executives going about their administrative business. A few minutes later we pulled up outside the front entrance of the Goliath headquarters, which was comfortably nestled into the hillside.

'I don't suppose that you would want to "freshen up" or anything before we show you around?' asked John Henry hopefully.

'And miss something that you might try and hide from me?' I answered. 'No, if it's all the same to you, I'd really like to see how far you've got.'

'Very well,' said John Henry without any sense of concern, 'come with me.'

We walked into the expansive lobby and crossed, not to the elevators or the Apologorium where I had been last time, but to where a golf cart was at readiness. A curious crowd of Goliath employees had gathered to watch our progress with undisguised inquisitiveness. I couldn't think it was just me – I don't suppose many of them had ever seen John Henry Goliath, either.

We drove out of the lobby and into a tunnel that led directly back into the hillside. It was crudely utilitarian after the simple elegance of the entrance vestibule, with roughly concreted walls and lit by overhead strip-lights. The roadway was smooth concrete and there were cable conduits attached to the walls. The subterranean vaults of Goliath R&D were at least half a mile inside the hill, and on the journey John Henry and I chatted amiably about national politics and global economics. Surprisingly, a more intelligent and well-informed conversation about current affairs I have yet to have. I might even have liked him, but for the utter ruthlessness and singularity of purpose that ran through his speech. Excusable in a person of little or no power, but potentially devastating in one such as John Henry Goliath.

We encountered three different levels of security on the way, each of them waved aside by John Henry. Beyond the third security checkpoint was a large set of steel blast-doors, and after abandoning the golf cart, we proceeded on foot. John Henry had his tie knot scanned to confirm his identity, and the doors slid open to let us in. I gasped at the sight that met my eyes. Their technology had gone beyond the small metal probe I had already seen. It had gone farther – *much* farther.

20

The Austen Rover

'I had been aware of Goliath's endeavours to enter fiction for many years. Following their abortive attempt to use the fictional world to "actualise" flawed technology during the plasma rifle debacle of '85, they had embarked upon a protracted R&D project to try to emulate Mycroft's Prose Portal. Until the appearance of the probe, the farthest I thought they'd got was to synthesise a form of stodgy gunge from Volumes 1 to 8 of *The World of Cheese*.'

In the centre of the room and looking resplendent in the blue-and-yellow livery of some long-forgotten bus company was a flat-fronted single-decker coach that to my mind dated from the fifties. Something my mother, in her distant and now much-embellished youth, might have boarded for a trip to the seaside, equipped with hampers of food and gallons of sunblock. Aside from the anachronistic feel, the most obvious feature of the coach was that the wheels had been removed and the voids covered over to give the vague appearance of streamlining. Clearly, this wasn't the only modification. The vehicle in front of me now was probably the most advanced piece of transport technology known to man.

'Why base it on an old coach?' I asked.

John Henry shrugged.

'If you're going to travel, do it in style. Besides, a Rolls-Royce Phantom II doesn't have enough seats.'

We walked down to the workshop floor and I took a closer look. On both sides at the rear of the coach and on the roof were small faired outriggers that each held a complicated engine with which I was not familiar. The tight-fitting cowlings had been removed and the engines were being worked on by white-coated technicians who had stopped what they were doing as soon as we walked in, but now resumed their tinkering with a buzz of muted whispering. I moved closer to the front of the coach and ran my fingers across the Leyland badge atop the large and very prominent radiator. I looked up. Above the vertically split front windscreen was a glass-covered panel that once told prospective passengers the ultimate destination of the bus. I expected it to read 'Bournemouth' or 'Portsmouth' but it didn't. It read: *Northanger Abbey*.

I looked at John Henry Goliath, who said:

'This, Ms Next, is the Austen Rover – the most advanced piece of transfictional technology in the world!'

'Does it work?' I asked.

'We're not entirely sure,' remarked John Henry. 'It's the prototype, and has yet to be tested.'

He beckoned over the technician who seemed to be in charge, and introduced us.

'This is Dr Anne Wirthlass, the project manager of the Austen Rover. She will answer any questions you have – I hope perhaps you will answer some of ours?'

I made a non-committal noise and Wirthlass gave me a hand to shake. She was tall, willowy and walked with a rolling gait. Like everyone in the lab, she wore a white coat with her Goliath ID badge, and although I could not see her precise ladder number, she was certainly within four figures – the top one per cent *Seriously* important.

'I'm pleased to meet you at last,' she said in a Swedish accent. 'We have much to learn from your experience.'

'If you know *anything* about me,' I responded, 'you'll know exactly why it is that I don't trust Goliath.'

'Ah!' she said, somewhat taken aback. 'I thought we'd left those days behind us.'

'I'll need convincing,' I returned without malice. It wasn't her fault, after all. I indicated the tour bus. 'How does it work?'

She looked at John Henry, who nodded his permission.

'The Austen Rover is a standard Leyland Tiger PS2/3 under a Burlingham body,' she began, touching the shiny coachwork fondly, 'but with a few . . . *modifications*. Come aboard.'

She stepped up into the coach and I followed her. The interior had been stripped out and replaced with the very latest state-of-the-art technology, which she attempted to explain in the sort of technical language in which it is only possible to understand one word in eight, if lucky. I came off the bus ten minutes later having only really absorbed the fact that it had twelve seats, carried a small thirty-megawatt fusion device in the rear, and couldn't be tested – its first trip would be either an utter failure or a complete success, nothing in between.

'And the probes?'

'Yes, indeed,' replied Wirthlass. 'We've been using a form of gravity wave inducer to catapult a small probe into fiction on a one-minute free-return trajectory – think of it like a very large yo-yo. We aimed them at the *Dune* series as it was a large and very wordy target that was probably somewhere near the heart of Science Fiction, and after seven hundred and ninety-six sub-fictional flights we hit paydirt: the probe returned with a twenty-eight-second audio-visual recording of Paul Atreides riding a sandworm.'

'When was this?' I asked.

'Nineteen ninety-six. We fared better after that and by a system of trial and error have managed to figure out that individual books seemed to be clumped together in groups. We've started plotting a map – I'll show you if you like.'

We walked into a room next door, which seemed to be filled to capacity with computers and their operators.

'How many probe missions have you sent?'

'About seventy thousand,' said John Henry, who had followed us. 'Most come back without recording anything, and over eight thousand never returned at all. In total, we have had four hundred and twenty successful missions. As you can see, getting into fiction for us is at present a somewhat haphazard affair. The Austen Rover is ready for its first trip — but by simple extrapolation of the probe figures, every journey has a one in eight chance of not returning, and only a one in *one hundred and sixty* possibility of hitting something.'

I could see what they were up against — and why. They were hurling probes into a BookWorld that was eighty per cent Nothing. The thing was, I could pretty much draw from memory a genre map of the BookWorld. With my help, they might actually make it.

'This is the BookWorld as we think it exists,' explained John Henry, laying out a large sheet of paper on a desk. It was patchy in the extreme and full of errors. It was a bit like throwing ping-pong balls into a dark furniture store and then trying to list the contents by the noises they made.

'This will take you a long time to figure out,' I murmured.

'Time that we don't really have, Ms Next. Despite my position as president, even I have to concede that the amount spent will never be recouped. All funding for this project will be withdrawn in a week.'

It was the first time I had felt any sort of relief since I arrived. The idea of Goliath even stepping so much as a toe inside fiction filled me with utter dread. But one question still niggled me.

'Why?'

'I'm sorry?'

'Why are you trying to get into fiction at all?'

'Book tourism,' replied John Henry simply. 'The Austen Rover was designed to take twelve people around the high points of Jane

Austen's work. At five hundred pounds for a twenty-minute hop around the most loved works we thought at the time it would be highly profitable. Mind you, that was nine years ago when people were still reading books.'

'We thought it might reinvigorate the classics,' added Wirthlass.

'And your interest in the classics?'

It was John Henry who answered.

'We feel publishing in general and books in particular are something well worth hanging on to.'

'You'll excuse me if I'm not convinced by your supposed altruism.'

'No altruism, Ms Next. The fall in revenue of our publishing arm has been dramatic, and since we own little in the way of computer games or consoles, the low reading rate is something that affects us financially. I think you'll find that we're together on this one. What we want is what *you* want. Even though our past associations have not been happy and I understand your distrust, Goliath in its reborn shape is not quite the all-devouring corporation that you think it is.'

'I haven't been in the BookWorld since the days of *The Eyre Affair*.'

John Henry coughed politely.

'You knew about the probes, Ms Next.'

Damn.

'I have . . . contacts over there.'

I could see they didn't believe me, but that was tough. I'd seen enough.

'Looks like you've wasted a lot of money,' I said.

'With or without you we're going to test it on Friday evening,' announced Wirthlass. 'I and two others have decided to risk all and take her out for a spin. We may not return, but if we do, then the data gained will be priceless!'

I admired her courage, but it didn't matter – I wasn't going to tell them what I knew.

'Just explain one thing,' said Wirthlass. 'Is the force of gravity entirely normal in the BookWorld?'

'What about the universality of physical laws?' piped up a second technician who had been watching us.

'And communication between books – is such a thing possible?'

Before long there were eight people all asking questions about the BookWorld which I could have answered with ease – had I any inclination to do so.

'I'm sorry,' I said, as the questions reached a climax, 'I can't help you!'

They were all quiet and stared at me. To them, this project was everything, and to see its cancellation without fruition was clearly a matter of supreme frustration – especially as they suspected I had the answers.

I made my way towards the exit and was joined by John Henry, who had not yet given up trying to charm me.

'Will you stay for lunch? We have the finest chefs available to make whatever you want.'

'I run a carpet shop, Mr Goliath, and I'm late for work.'

'A carpet shop?' he echoed with incredulity. 'That sells carpets?'

'All sorts of floor coverings, actually.'

'I would offer you discounted carpets for life in order for you to help us,' he said, 'but from what I know of you, such a course would be unthinkable. My private Dakota is at Douglas airfield if you want to use it to fly straight home. I ask for nothing but say only this: we are doing this for the preservation and promotion of books and reading. Try to find it in your heart to consider what we are doing here in an objective light.'

We had by now walked outside the building and John Henry's Bentley pulled up in front of us.

'My car is yours. Good day, Ms Next.'

'Good day, Mr Goliath.'

He shook my hand and then departed. I looked at the Bentley and then at the ranks of cabs a little way down the road. I shrugged and climbed in the back of the Bentley.

'Where to, madam?' asked the driver.

I thought quickly. I had my TravelBook on me and could jump to the Great Library from here – as long as I could find a quiet spot conducive to bookjumping.

'The nearest library,' I told him, 'I'm late for work.'

'You're a librarian?' he enquired politely.

'Let's just say I'm really into books.'

21

Holmes

'I don't know what it was about travelling to and from the BookWorld that dehydrated me so much. It had got progressively worse, almost without me noticing, a bit like a mildly increased girth and skin that isn't as elastic as it used to be. On the upside, however, the textual environment kept all the aches and pains at bay. I hardly noticed my bad back in the BookWorld, and was never troubled by headaches.'

A few minutes and several pints of rehydrating water later, I walked into the Jurisfiction offices at Norland Park. Thursday5 was waiting for me by my desk, and looked decidedly pleased with herself.

'Guess what!' she enthused.

'I have no idea.'

'Go on, guess!'

'I don't want to guess,' I told her, hoping the tedium in my voice would send out a few warning bells. It didn't.

'No, you *must* guess!'

I sighed. 'Okay. You've got some new beads or something.'

'Wrong,' she said, producing a paper bag with a flourish. 'I got you the bacon roll you wanted!'

'I never would have guessed *that*,' I replied, sitting down to a desk that seemed to be flooded with new memos and reports, adding, in an unthinking moment: 'How are things with you?'

'I didn't sleep very well last night.'

I rubbed my forehead as she sat down and stared at me intently, hands clasped nervously in front of her. I didn't have the heart to tell her that my enquiry over her health was merely politeness. I didn't actually want to know. Quite the reverse, in fact.

'Really?' I said, trying to find a memo that might be vaguely relevant to something.

'No. I was thinking about the Minotaur incident yesterday and I want to apologise . . . again.'

'It's past history. Any messages?'

'So I'm sorry.'

'Apology accepted. Now: any messages?'

'I wrote you a letter outlining my apology.'

'I won't read it. The matter is closed.'

'Yes – well – right,' she began, flustered that we weren't going to analyse the previous day at length, and trying to remember everything she'd been told that morning. 'Mr Buñuel called to say that he'd completed the refit of *Pride and Prejudice* and it was online again this morning. He's got *Northanger Abbey* in the maintenance bay at the moment, and it should be ready on time as long as Catherine stops attempting to have the book "Gothicised".'

'Good. What else?'

'The Council of Genres,' she announced, barely able to control her excitement. 'Senator Jobsworth's secretary *herself* called to ask you to appear in the debating chamber for a policy directive meeting at three this afternoon!'

'I wonder what the old bore wants now? Anything else?'

'No,' replied Thursday5, disappointed that I didn't share her unbridled enthusiasm over an appearance at the CofG. I couldn't. I'd been there so many times I just saw it as part of my duties, nothing more.

I opened my desk drawer to take out a sheet of headed notepaper and noticed Thursday5's assessment letter where I'd left it the night before. I thought for a moment and decided to give her one more chance. I left it where it was, pulled out a sheet of paper and wrote a letter to Wing Commander Scampton-Tappett, telling him to get out of *Bananas for Edward* since Landen wasn't currently working on it, and move instead to *The Mews of Doom*, which he was. I folded up the letter, placed it in an envelope and told Thursday5 to deliver it to Scampton-Tappet in person. I could have asked her to send it by courier, but twenty minutes' peace and quiet had a great deal of appeal. Thursday5 nodded happily and vanished.

I had just leaned back in my chair and was thinking about Felix8, the possible end of time and the Austen Rover when a hearty bellow of 'Stand to!' indicated the imminence of Bradshaw's daily Jurisfiction briefing. I dutifully stood up and joined the other agents who had gathered in the centre of the room.

After the usual apologies for absence, Bradshaw climbed on to a table, tingled a small bell and said: 'Jurisfiction meeting number 43,370 is now in session. But before all that we are to welcome a new agent to the fold: Colonel William Dobbin!'

We all applauded as Colonel Dobbin gave a polite bow and remarked in a shy yet resolute manner that he would do his utmost to further the good work of Jurisfiction to the best of his ability.

'Jolly good,' intoned Bradshaw, eager to get on. 'Item one: an active cell of bowdlerisers have been at work again, this time in Philip Larkin and "This Be the Verse". We've found several editions with the first line altered to read: *They tuck you up, your mum and dad*, which is a gross distortion of the original intent. Who wants to have a go at this?'

'I will,' I said.

'No . . . what about you, King Pellinor?'

'Yes-yes what-what hey-hey?' said the white-whiskered knight in grubby armour.

'You've had experience of dealing with bowdlerisers in Larkin before – cracking the group who altered the first line of "Love

Again" to read: *Love again: thanking her at ten past three* was great stuff – fancy tackling them again?'

'What-what to go a-mollocking for the Bowdlers?' replied Pellinor happily. ''twill be achieved happily and in half the time.'

'Anyone want to go with him?'

'I'll go,' I said.

'Anyone else?'

The Red Queen put up her hand.

'Item two: the 287th Annual BookWorld Conference is due in six months' time and the Council of Genres have insisted we need to have a security review after last year's . . . *problems.*'

There was a muttering from the assembled agents. BookCon was the sort of event that was too large and too varied to keep all factions happy, and the previous year's decision to lift the restriction on Abstract Concepts attending as delegates opened the floodgates to a multitude of Literary Theories and Grammatical Conventions who spent most of the time pontificating loftily and causing trouble in the bar, where fights break out at the drop of a participle. When Post-structuralism got into a fight with Classicism they were all banned, something that upset the Subjunctives no end; they complained bitterly that 'if it *were* the case that they had been fighting, they would have won'.

'Are the Abstracts allowed to attend this year?' asked Lady Cavendish.

'I'm afraid so,' replied Bradshaw. 'Not to invite them would be seen as discriminatory. Volunteers?'

Six of us put up our hands and Bradshaw diligently scribbled down our names.

'Top notch,' he said at last. 'The first meeting will be next week. Now – item three, and this one is something of a corker. We've got a Major Narrative Flexation brewing in *The Memoirs of Sherlock Holmes.*'

'Is it the Watson bullet wound problem again?' asked Mr Fainset.

'No, it's more serious than that. Sherlock Holmes . . . *has been murdered*!'

There was a spontaneous cry of shock and outrage from the assembled agents. The Holmes series was a perennial favourite and thus of particular concern – textual anomalies in unread or unpopular books were always lower priority, or ignored altogether. Bradshaw handed a stack of papers to Lady Cavendish, who distributed them.

'It's in *The Final Problem*. You can read it yourself, but essentially Sherlock travels to Switzerland to deal with Professor Moriarty. After the usual Holmesian escapades, Watson follows Sherlock to the Reichenbach falls where he discovers that Holmes has apparently fallen to his death – and the book ends twenty-nine pages before it was meant to.'

There was a shocked silence as everyone took this in. We hadn't had a textual anomaly of this size since Lucy Pevensie refused to get into the wardrobe at the beginning of *The Lion, The Witch, and The Wardrobe*.

'But *The Memoirs of Sherlock Holmes* was the fourth volume,' observed Mrs Tiggy-Winkle, looking up from her ironing. 'With Sherlock dead at the Reichenbach it would render the remaining five volumes of stories narratively unsustainable.'

'Partly right,' replied Bradshaw. '*The Hound of the Baskervilles* was written after *Memoirs* but is set earlier – I think we can keep hold of that one. But yes, the remaining four in the series will start to spontaneously unravel unless we do something about it. And we will, I assure you – erasure is not an option.'

This was not as easy as it sounded despite Bradshaw's rhetoric, and we all knew it. All books in the Sherlock Holmes series were closed; unavailable to enter until someone had actually booksplored their way in – and the Holmes canon had continuously resisted exploration.

Gomez was the first Jurisfiction booksplorer to try by way of Conan Doyle's *The Lost World*, but he mistakenly became involved in the narrative and was shot dead by Lord Roxton. Harris Tweed tried it next and was nearly trampled by a herd of angry stegosauri.

'I want everyone in on this problem. The Cat formerly known as Cheshire will be keeping a careful eye on the narrative corruption of the series up at Text Grand Central, and I want Beatrice, Benedict, Zhark and Tiggy-Winkle to try and find a way in using the other books in the Conan Doyle oeuvre – I suggest the Professor Challenger stories. Fainset and Foyle, I want you to explore the possibility of communication with anyone inside the Holmes series – they may not even know they have a problem.'

'They're well outside the footnoterphone network,' said Mr Fainset. 'Any suggestions?'

'I'm relying on Foyle's ingenuity. If anyone sees Hamlet or Peter and Jane before I do, send them immediately to me. Any questions?'

'What do you want me to do?' I asked, wondering why I had been left out of everything important so far.

'I'll speak to you later. Okay, that's it. Good luck, and . . . let's be *careful* out there.'

The collected agents instantly started chattering. We hadn't had anything like this for years, which made it seem even more stupid that Bradshaw wasn't including me on the assignment. I caught up with him as he sat at his desk.

'What's going on?' I asked. 'You need me on this.'

'Hello, my dear! Not like you to nearly miss a session – problems in the Outland?'

'I was up at Goliath.'

He raised an eyebrow.

'How do things look?'

I explained at length what I had seen, ending with the observation that it wasn't likely that they'd perfect a transfictional machine any time soon, if at all – but we needed to keep our eyes on them.

Bradshaw nodded sagely, and I reiterated my feeling that I was being somehow 'left out' of the Holmes inquiry.

'How's Friday? Still a bed slug?'

'Yes – but nothing I can't handle.'

'Have you told Landen about us yet?'

'I'm building up to it. Bradshaw, you're flannelling – *why aren't I on the Holmes case?*'

He gestured for me to sit and lowered his voice.

'I had a call from Senator Jobsworth this morning. He's keen to reinstate a certain cadet that we recently . . . had to let go.'

I knew the cadet he was referring to. There was a sound reason for her rejection – she had been euphemistically categorised *unsuitable*. Not in the way that my nice-but-a-bit-dopey cadet was unsuitable, but unsuitable as in obnoxious. She'd gone through five tutors in as many days. Even Emperor Zhark said that he'd prefer to be eaten alive by the Snurgg of Epsilon-7 than spend another five minutes in her company.

'Why has Jobsworth requested her? There are at least ten we rejected that are six times better.'

'Because we're light on agents in contemporary fiction, and the CofG thinks she ticks all the genre boxes.'

'He's wrong, of course,' I said quite matter-of-factly, but people like Jobsworth are politicians, and have a different set of rules, 'but I can see his point. The question is, what are you going to do about it? She's exhausted all the agents licensed to take apprentices.'

Bradshaw said nothing and stared at me. In an instant, I understood.

'Oh, no,' I said, 'not me. Not in a thousand years. Besides, I've already got a cadet on assessment.'

'Then get rid of her. You told me yourself that her timidity would get her killed.'

183

'It will – but I feel kind of responsible. Besides, I've already got a full caseload. The Mrs Danvers that went berserk in *The God of Small Things* still needs investigating, the Minotaur tried to kill me – not to mention about thirty or so cold cases, some of which are potentially solvable – especially the Drood case; I think it's possible Dickens was . . . *murdered.*'

'In the Outland? And for what reason?'

'To silence Edwin Drood – or someone else in the book.'

I wasn't sure about this, of course, and any evidence was already over a hundred years old, but I would do anything not to take this apprentice. Sadly, Bradshaw wasn't taking no for an answer, or softening to my pleas.

'Don't make me order you, old girl, it will embarrass us both. Besides, if you fail her – as I'm sure you shall – then we really *have* run out of tutors and I can tell Jobsworth we did everything in our power.'

I groaned.

'How about me taking her next week? That way I can get to grips with the Holmes death thing.'

'Senator Jobsworth was *most* insistent,' said Bradshaw. 'He's been on the footnoterphone three times this morning already.'

I knew what he meant. When Jobsworth got his teeth into something, he rarely let go. The relationship between us was decidedly chilly and we were at best only ever cordial. The crazy thing was, we both wanted the best for the BookWorld – we just had different methods of trying to achieve it.

'Very well,' I said at last. 'I'll give her a day – or a morning, if she lasts that.'

'Good lass!' exclaimed Bradshaw happily. 'Appreciate a woman who knows when she's being coerced. I'll get her to meet you outside Norland.'

'Is that all?' I asked, somewhat crossly.

'No. It seems someone's made an ass of themselves over at resource management regarding maintenance schedules and we've got a . . . well, see for yourself.'

He handed me a report and I flicked through the pages with a rising sense of despair. It was always the same. Someone at admin screws up and we have to pick up the pieces.

'The Piano Squad has been on the go for eight hours straight,' he added, 'so I'd like you to step in and relieve them for a rest period. Take your cadets with you. Should be a useful training session.'

My heart sank.

'I've got to appear at the CofG later this afternoon,' I explained, 'and if I've a second cadet to nursemaid—'

'I'll make it up to you,' interrupted Bradshaw. 'It'll be a doddle – a walk in the park. How much trouble can anyone get into with pianos?'

'TransGenreTaxis was one of several BookWorld taxi companies, and the only firm that could boast an accident rate that was vaguely acceptable. Taxis were a good way to get around the BookWorld if you weren't that good at jumping or had lots of luggage, but in comparison to the instantaneous bookjump they were like snails. They didn't so much jump as creep. Getting all the way across the BookWorld – from Philosophy to Poetry, for instance – could take as long as an hour.'

'You're kidding me?' I said into my mobile footnoterphone, twenty minutes later. I was outside the main entrance to Norland Park, as the sun began its downward slope from midday heat into the rare beauty of an Austen literary afternoon. The warm rural environment was rich with the sounds of the plough-horses' bridles jingling in the fields, the bees buzzing merrily in the hedgerows, and young ladies a-twitter with gossip regarding the genteel ensnarement of monied husbands.

'Well,' I added crossly, 'just send it as soon as you can.'

I snapped the mobile shut.

'Problems?' asked Thursday5, who had been making daisy chains while sitting cross-legged on the warm grass.

'Those twits at TransGenreTaxis,' I replied. 'More excuses. They claim there are long tailbacks owing to a traffic accident inside *The Great Gatsby* and our cab will be at least an hour.'

'Can't we just jump straight to wherever it is we're going?' She stopped and thought for a moment. 'Where *are* we going?'

'The Piano Squad. But we're waiting for someone.'

'Who?'

'We're waiting,' I said, unsure of how to break the news, 'for a cadet who is under reappraisal.'

'*Another* cadet?' repeated Thursday5, who seemed vaguely miffed at first, but soon recovered. 'If only I'd known I could have baked a welcome cake.'

'I don't think she's a cake sort of person,' I murmured, as a noise like the scrunching of cellophane heralded her arrival. She appeared looking somewhat out of breath, and we all three stared at one another for some moments in silence until both cadets said at precisely the same time:

'What's *she* doing here?'

'Listen,' I said to them both, 'I know this is an awkward situation – and a little weird too if you want to know my opinion – and if either of you don't like it you can just go straight back to your respective books.'

My latest apprentice glared at me, then at Thursday, then at me again before saying with a forced smile:

'In that case I should probably introduce myself and say what an *incredible* honour it is to be apprenticed to the *great* Thursday Next.'

'Why don't you save your breath – and your sarcasm?' I retorted. I liked a challenge but this was probably one or two challenges too far. For this, of course, was the *other* Thursday Next, the one from the first four books in the series – the violent ones full of death and gratuitous sex.

'Well, whoop-de-do,' she said quietly, looking at us both. 'If this is how the day starts, it can only get better.'

Thursday5 and I stared at the newcomer with a curious kind of fascination. Unlike Thursday5, who always dressed in Fairtrade cotton and woollens, this Thursday preferred aggressive black leather –

leather trousers, jacket and a greatcoat that swept to the floor. So much, in fact, that she squeaked when she walked. Her hair was the same length as ours but was pulled back into a ponytail more sharply, and her eyes were hidden by small dark glasses. Attached to her belt were two automatic pistols with the butts facing in so she could cross-draw – heavens knows why. Aside from this, and despite featuring in books that were set between 1985 and 1988, she looked exactly as I did – even to the flecks of grey hair that I *still* pretended I didn't care about.

But she wasn't me. She was less like me, in fact, than the talking-to-flowers version, if such a thing were possible. I'd read the books and although she *attempted* to do things for the right reason, her methods could best be described as dubious, and her motivations suspect. Thursday5 was mostly thought with very little action; Thursday1–4 was mostly action with very little thought. The series had sacrificed characterisation over plot, and humour over action and pace. All atmosphere had evaporated, and the books were a parade of violent set-pieces interspersed with romantic interludes, and when I say 'romantic', I'm stretching the term. Most famous was her torrid affair with Edward Rochester and the stand-up cat fight with Jane Eyre. I had thought it couldn't get any worse until Mrs Fairfax turned out to be a ninja assassin and Bertha Rochester was abducted by aliens. And all that was just in the first book. It got more far fetched after that. By Book 4 it felt as though the first draft had been torn apart by wolves and then stuck back together at random before publication. I took a deep breath, inwardly cursed Commander Bradshaw and said:

'Thursday . . . meet Thursday.'

'Hello!' said Thursday5 brightly, offering a hand in reconciliation. '*So* pleased to meet you, and happy birthday – for yesterday.'

Thursday looked at Thursday's outstretched hand and raised an eyebrow.

'I've had the misfortune to read *The Great Samuel Pepys Fiasco*,' she said in an unfriendly tone. 'If you took the "Samuel Pepys" out of the title it would be a lot more honest. A bigger crock of shit I've yet to find. I kept on waiting for the shoot-outs to begin and there weren't any – just a load of hugging, vitamins and people saying they loved one another.'

'There's nothing wrong with hugging,' retorted Thursday defensively. 'Perhaps if you were to try—?'

She put out her arms but was met with the curt response:

'Lay your muesli-smelling paws on me and I'll break your nose.'

'Well—!' said Thursday5 in an indignant huff. 'I'm almost sorry I wished you a happy birthday – and I'm *very* glad I didn't bake you a cake.'

'I'm devastated.'

'Listen,' I said before this descended into blows, 'I'm not going to ask you to get along, I'm *telling* you to get along. Okay?'

Thursday1–4 gave a lackadaisical shrug.

'Right,' I began, addressing Thursday1–4, 'there are three simple rules if you want to train with me. Rule one: you do exactly as I tell you. Rule two: you speak when you're spoken to. Rule three: I shall call you "Thursday1–4" or "Thur1–4" or "Onesday" or . . . anything I want, really. You will call me ma'am. If I call for you, you come running. Rule four: you give me any crap and you're history.'

'I thought you said there were only three rules?'

'I make it up as I go along. Do you have any problem with that?'

'I suppose not.'

'Good. Let's start at the beginning. How much classroom theory have you done?'

'Six weeks. Took my finals last Tuesday and came third.'

'That's not bad.'

'How many in the class?' asked Thursday5, who was still smarting over the possibility that her hands smelled of muesli, let alone the threat of a broken nose. Thursday1–4 glared at her and mumbled:

'Three, and two per cent above the minimum pass mark, before you ask. But I scored ninety-nine per cent on the range. Pistol, rifle, machine gun, grenade launcher – you name it.'

This was the main reason I didn't like the Thursday Next series – far, far too many guns and a body count that would be the envy of the cinematic Rambo. Thursday1–4 unholstered an aggressive-looking automatic and showed it to us both.

'Glock nine-millimetre', she said proudly, 'sixteen in the clip and one up the spout. *Severe* stopping power. I carry two to make quite sure.'

'Only two?' I murmured sarcastically.

'No, since you're asking.' She lifted up the back of her leather greatcoat to show me a large shiny revolver stuffed down the back of her trousers.

'What do you carry?' she asked. 'Beretta? Browning? Walther?'

'Nothing,' I said. 'Charge into a room with a gun and someone ends up dead.'

'Isn't that how it's meant to work?'

'In *your* books, perhaps. If someone dies during an assignment, then the assignment was a failure. No exceptions.'

'Diplomacy and using your head,' put in Thursday5 bravely, 'are better than waving a gun around.'

'And what would you know about it, your supreme bogusness?'

'You don't have to insult me *all* the time,' she replied, visibly upset, 'and besides, I'm not sure "bogusness" is a word.'

'Well, listen here, veggieburger,' said the leather-clad Thursday in a sneering tone of voice, 'I *do* have to insult you all the time. Firstly because it's fun, and secondly because . . . no, I don't need a second reason.'

'Jeez,' I said, shaking my head sadly as all patience left me, 'you're still revolting, aren't you?'

'Revolting?' she retorted. 'Perhaps. But since I'm mostly you, I guess you're partly to blame, right?'

'Get this straight in your head,' I said, moving closer. 'The only thing you share with me is a name and a face. You can have a go at *The Great Samuel Pepys Fiasco* all you want, but at least it's not a constant orgy of comic-book violence and abundant, meaningless sex.'

'Oh, I'm sorry – is that a criticism? Or just wishful thinking on your part? Because I was having a look at the figures the other day and I'm still selling strongly.' She turned to the *Pepys* Thursday. 'How many books have *you* sold in the past five years?'

It was a pointed yet strictly rhetorical remark. *The Great Samuel Pepys Fiasco* had been remaindered less than six months after publication.

'You don't hate *me*,' said Thursday1–4 to Thursday5, 'you secretly want to be like me. If you want to hate anyone, hate *her*.'

She directed this comment at me.

'Why would I?' asked Thursday5, close to tears. With a creaking of leather Thursday1–4 moved closer to her and said in a low voice:

'Because she insisted that your book should be full of touchy-feely family values – pet dodo, gardening, a husband, two lovely kids—'

'Three.'

'Whatever. They asked me to do Book Five but I took one look at the script and told them to stick it.' She pointed a gloved finger at me. 'Her personal vanity condemned you to the slow death of being unread, unreviewed, undiscussed and out of print. The real Thursday is as single minded as I am – even to the ultimate vanity of rewriting herself into the guise of little Miss Granola Tree-Hugger here – with no other reason than to protect her own fragile vanity, Z-class celebrity status and inconsequential public opinion. She and I are more alike than she thinks.'

She stopped talking with a triumphant smile on her face. The other Thursday looked at me with tears in her eyes. I was feeling hotly indignant myself, mostly because what she was saying was *true*. The only reason I'd taken Thursday5 on at all was because I felt responsible. Not just because she *was* an insufferable drip, but because she was an unread one as well.

'Oh, *no*!' said Thursday5, giving out a heavy sob. 'Now all my chakras are *completely* unaligned – can I have the rest of the day off?'

'Good idea,' said Thursday1–4 with an unpleasant chuckle. 'Why not go and meditate? After all, it's better than doing nothing all day.'

Thursday5, gave another cry of indignation. I told her she could leave and she did so with a faint *pop*.

'Listen,' I said, also moving closer and lowering my voice, 'you can do your character assassination crap all day if you want but that's not important. What *is* important is that the CofG in all its misguided wisdom seem to think you might be good enough for Jurisfiction. Five previous tutors don't agree. *I* don't agree. I think you're a viper. But it's not up to me. It's up to you. For you to join Jurisfiction you need to learn how to survive in the hostile and dynamic textual environment. You and I are going to spend the next few days together whether I like it or not, and since my conduct review of you is the only thing that counts towards your final acceptance at Jurisfiction, you need to try *really* hard not to piss me off.'

'Ahh!' she murmured patronisingly. 'She does speeches. Listen, sister, you may be a big cheese at Jurisfiction *today* but if I were you I'd show a keen sense of diplomacy. I'll have the Bellman's job one day – and I'll be looking out only for my friends. Now, are you going to be a friend or not?'

'Good Lord,' I said in a quiet voice. 'The Cheshire Cat was right – you really are *completely* obnoxious. Is that your final word?'

'It is.'

'Then you can piss off back to your boxed set right now. Give me your badge.'

She seemed perturbed for an instant. Her all-consuming arrogance had not even *once* entertained the notion she might actually be fired. But true to form, instead of even attempting conciliation, she went into more threats:

'The CofG cadet selection subcommittee won't be happy.'

'Screw *them*. Your badge?'

She stared at me with a sense of rising confusion.

'You'd fire . . . *me*?'

'Just have. Give me your badge or I'll place you under arrest.'

She took the Jurisfiction cadet's shield from her pocket and slapped it in my open palm. Without that or a travel permit she was technically a PageRunner and could be erased on sight.

'Good day,' I said. 'I won't say it's been a pleasure because it hasn't.'

And I walked away, pulling out my mobile footnoterphone as I did so.

'Hello, Bradshaw? I've just fired Thursday 1–4. I'm amazed anyone lasted more than ten minutes with her – I didn't.'[1]

'Yes, already. Tell Jobsworth we did our best.'[2]

'Too bad. I'll take the flak for it. This one's a serious piece of—'

'Wait, wait!' yelled Thursday, holding her head in a massive display of self-control. 'That was my last chance, wasn't it?'

1 'Goodness! Already?'

2 'This is really awkward. Jobsworth just called – he's overjoyed that you're taking Thursday and said that if we do a *really* good job, he would give Jurisfiction's extra funding his especial attention.'

'Yes.'

She massaged her temples.

'I can do this. I'm sor— I'm sor— *soooor*—'

'You can say it.'

'I can't.'

'*Try.*'

She screwed up her face and forced the word out.

'I'm ... *so-rry*. I'll be your apprentice. Jurisfiction has need of people like me and I am willing to run the gauntlet of your overbearing mediocrity in order to achieve that.'

I stared at her for a moment.

'Vague apology accepted.'

I moved away so Thursday1–4 couldn't hear me and spoke into my mobile footnoterphone again.

'Bradshaw, how badly do we need to suck up to Jobsworth right now?'[3]

I told Bradshaw to rely on me, he thanked me profusely, wished me well and rang off. I snapped the mobile shut and placed it back in my bag.

'Right,' I said, tossing Thursday1–4's badge back at her, 'for your first assignment you are to get Thursday5 back here, chakras realigned or not, and apologise to her.'

Thursday1–4 stared at me for a moment, then dialled her own mobile. I turned away and walked down the gravel drive, trying to relax. What a start.

I sat on an ornamental lion at the foot of the entrance steps and watched from a distance as Thursday5 reappeared. After the briefest of altercations, they shook hands. There was a pause and then a few raised voices until finally, incredibly, her bearing as stiff as a poker,

---

[3] 'Bundles, old girl. Do this as a favour to old Bradders, eh? Just until the end of the day.'

Thursday1–4 allowed herself to be hugged. I smiled to myself, got up and walked back to where the pair of them were standing, Thursday5 looking optimistically positive, and Thursday1–4 brooding stonily.

'Have you two sorted yourselves out?'

They both nodded.

'Good,' I said, consulting my watch. 'We've got a few hours before we attend the Council of Genre's policy directive meeting, but before that—'

'*We* are attending the CofG meeting?' asked Thursday5 with eyes like saucers.

'Yes – but only as in the sort of "we" that means you stand at the back and say nothing.'

'Wow! What will they be discussing?'

'BookWorld policy. Such as whether we should be supplying characters to video games to give them added depth. It's particularly relevant as publishing these days doesn't necessarily restrict books to being just books. It's said that Harry Potter will make a rare appearance. Now, we've got to—'

'Will we really meet Harry Potter?' she asked in a soft whisper, her eyes going all dewy at the mention of the young wizard. Thursday1–4 looked to heaven and stood, arms crossed, waiting for us to get on with the day's work.

I sighed. 'It depends if you pay attention or not. Now for this afternoon's assignment: relieving the staff who are dealing with the BookWorld's ongoing piano problem. And for that, we need to go to Text Grand Central.'

23

The Piano Problem

'The piano was thought to have been invented by
Bartolomeo Cristofori in the early eighteenth century,
and was originally called the *Gravicèmbalo col piano e forte*,
which was thankfully reduced to *pianoforte*, then more
simply to *piano*. Composed of 550lbs of iron, wood, strings and
felt, the 88-key instrument is capable of the most subtle of
melodies, yet stored up in the tensioned strings is the destructive power of a family saloon moving at 20 miles per hour.'

If Jurisfiction was the policing agency inside books and the Council
of Genres were the politicians, Text Grand Central was the bureaucracy that bridged the two. Right up until the Ultraword™ debacle
TGC had remained unimpeachably honest, but after that the Council
of Genres – on my advice – took the harsh but only possible course
of action to ensure that Text Grand Central would be too inefficient and unimaginative to pose a threat. They appointed a committee
to run it.

As we walked on to one of the main storycode engine floors, I
heard Thursday5 gasp. The proportions of the room were more in
keeping with a factory that made Very Large Things, and the stone
walls, vaulted ceiling and flickering gas lamps betrayed the room's
provenance as something borrowed from an unpublished Gothic
Horror novel. Laid in serried ranks across the echoing vastness of
the room were hundreds of storycode engines, each one the size of
a coach and built of shiny brass, mahogany and cast iron. A convo-
luted mass of pipes, valves and gauges, they looked like a cross
between an espresso machine, a ship's engine and a euphonium on

acid. They were so large they had a catwalk running around the upper section for easy maintenance, with a cast-iron spiral staircase at one end for access.

'These are ImaginoTransference storycode engines. The most important piece of technology we possess. Remember the pipe leading out of Core Containment in *Pinocchio*?'

Thursday5 nodded.

'The throughput is radiated across the inter-genre Nothing and ends up here, where it is then transmitted into the reader's imagination.'

I hadn't the vaguest notion of how it worked, and was suspicious that perhaps there wasn't an explanation at all – or indeed any need for one. It was something we called an 'abstract narrative imperative': it works solely because it's expedient that it does so. The BookWorld is like that. Full of wholly improbable plot devices that are there to help grease the storytelling cogs.

I paused so they could both watch the proceedings for a moment. Thursday5 made no secret of her fascination, but Thursday1–4 stifled a faux yawn. Despite this, she still looked around. It was hard not to be impressed – the machines stretched off into the hazy distance almost as far as you could see. Technicians scurried like ants over the whirring machinery, checking dials, oiling, venting off steam and filling out reports on clipboards. Others moved between machines with trolleys full of papers to be filed, and the air was full of the smell of hot oil and steam. Above our heads a series of clanking shafts and flapping leather belts brought power to the engines, and the combined clatter and hum in the vast chamber sounded like a cascading waterfall.

'Five hundred machines on each floor,' I shouted above the tumult, 'with each one capable of handling up to fifty thousand concurrent readings. The ones in the blue overalls are the storycode technicians known affectionately as word monkeys. They keep the engines running smoothly, clean out the dialogue injectors and make sure there isn't a build-up of irony on the compressors. The man dressed in the white labcoat is the text collector. There is a "reader echo" that pings back to the engine to throughput the next word, so we can use that to check if the book is running true to the author's original wishes. Any variance is termed a "textual anomaly" and is caught in the waste-gate of the echo skimmers, which are those large copper things on the top.'

'This is all *really* fascinating technological stuff,' observed Thursday1–4 drily, 'but I'm waiting to see how it relates to pianos.'

'It doesn't, O sarcastic one. It's called ed-u-cation.'

'Pointless exposition, if you ask me.'

'She's not asking you,' retorted Thursday5.

'Exactly,' I replied, 'and some people enjoy the techie stuff. Follow me.'

I opened an arched oak door that led off the engine floor and into the administrative section of Text Grand Central, a labyrinth of stone corridors lit by flaming torches affixed to the walls. It was insufferably gloomy, but economic – part of the unfinished Gothic Horror novel from which all of TGC was fashioned. As soon as the door closed, the noise from the main engine floor ceased abruptly.

'I was just trying to explain,' I said, 'how we find out about narrative flexations. Most of the time the anomalies are just misreads and lazy readers getting the wrong end of the stick, but we have to check everything, just in case.'

'I can get this on the Text Grand Central tour for twenty shillings and better company,' said Thursday1–4, looking pointedly at Thursday5.

'*I'm* interested, ma'am.'

'Creep.'

'Slut.'

'What did you call me?'

'Hey!' I shouted. '*Cut it out.*'

'She started it,' said Thursday1–4.

'I don't care who started it. You'll *both* be fired if you carry on like this.'

They fell silent and we walked along the echoing corridors, past endless oak doors, all relating to some textual activity such as word meanings, idea licensing and grammasite control.

'The problem with pianos,' I began, 'is that there aren't enough to go around. Lots of people in the BookWorld play them, they frequently appear in the narrative and are often used as plot devices. Yet for an unfathomable reason that no one can fully explain, there are only fifteen to cover the entire BookWorld.'

'Fifteen?' snorted Thursday1–4, who was lagging behind in a petulant manner. 'How do they manage that, then?'

'With a lot of difficulty. Have a look.'

I opened a door off the corridor. The room was much like a psychiatrist's office, full of bookshelves and with diplomas on the wall. There was a desk, two chairs and a couch. Two men were sitting in the chairs: a beard and pipe identified the first man immediately as a psychiatrist, and the second, who seemed desperately nervous, was obviously the patient.

'So, Mr Patient,' began the psychiatrist, 'what can I do for you?'

'Well, Doc,' muttered the patient unhappily, 'I keep on thinking I'm a dog.'

'I see. And how long has this been going on?'

'Since I was a puppy.'

'Excuse me,' I interrupted, 'I'm looking for the Piano Squad.'

'This is Very Old Jokes,' explained the psychiatrist apologetically. 'Pianos are down the corridor, first on the left.'

'Sorry,' I muttered somewhat sheepishly, and quietly closed the door.

'I keep on doing that,' I murmured. 'They should really label these doors better.'

We walked along the corridor, found the correct door and opened it to reveal a room about fifty foot square. The walls were rough plastered, and the stone vaulted ceiling was supported in the centre of the room by a sturdy pillar. Set into the wall to our right was an aperture the size of a single garage, painted bright white and illuminated from within by several hundred light bulbs. As we watched there was a faint buzz, a flicker and an ornate cabinet piano suddenly appeared in the aperture. Almost instantly, a workman dressed in brown overalls and with a flat cap moved forward to wheel it out on well-oiled castors. Facing the bright white opening was a control desk that looked like a recording studio mixing console, and behind this were two men of youthful countenance dressed in linen suits. They were wearing headsets and had the harried look of men under great pressure.

'Upright Rosewood returned from *Sons and Lovers*,' whispered the one who was standing. 'Stand by to send the Goetzmann into *Villette*.'

'Check!' shouted the other man as he adjusted the knobs and sliders on the console. The workman pushed a Goetzmann grand into the empty aperture, stepped back, called 'Clear' and, with another buzz, the piano vanished.

They looked at us as soon as we entered and I nodded a greeting. They nodded one back and returned to their work.

'Observe,' I said to the Thursdays, and pointed to a large indicator panel on the wall behind the men. The fifteen pianos were listed down the left-hand side, and in columns next to them were indicator lights and illuminated panels that explained what was happening to each. The uppermost piano on the list we noted was a 'generic' grand and was currently inside *Bleak House*. It would be available in a few minutes and was next due to appear in *Mill on the Floss*, where it would stay for a number of scenes until departing for *Heart of Darkness*. As we watched, the indicator boards clicked the various changes as the two operators expertly moved the pianos back and forth across fiction. Below the indicator boards were several other desks, a water cooler, a kitchenette and a coffee bar. There were a few desultory potted plants kicking around, but aside from several rusty filing cabinets, there was not much else in the room.

'Fifteen pianos is usually ample,' I explained, 'and when all pianos are available for use, the Piano Squad just trots along merrily to a set timetable. There are a few changes here and there when a new book requires a piano, but it generally works – eighty-six per cent of pianos appear in nineteenth- and early-twentieth-century literature.'

I pointed to the indicator board.

'But if you notice, eight pianos are "status unavailable", which means that they have been pulled out of front-line service for maintenance.' I waved the report Bradshaw had handed me. 'There was an administrative mix-up; we usually have one piano offline at a time but some clot had them all refitted at once to save costs.'

The Thursdays looked at the two operators again and, as we watched, an upright piano made of rosewood and with inlaid brass was moved from *Sons and Lovers* to *Mayor of Casterbridge* and then on to *The Turn of the Screw*.

'That's right,' I said. 'Charles and Roger are having to spread seven pianos around the entire canon of English fiction. Hang on, it looks as though we're coming to a break.'

They did indeed seem to be about to stop work for a few minutes. The two operators relaxed, stopped what they were doing, removed their headsets and stretched.

'Hello, Thursday,' said the younger of the two in a quiet whisper, 'brought your family into work?'

I laughed. 'Not a chance. Jurisfiction cadets Thursday5 and Thursday1–4, meet Charles and Roger of the Piano Squad.'

'Hello!' yelled Roger, who appeared not to be able to converse at anything less than a shout. 'Come up and have a look-see.'

The Thursdays went to join Roger at the console. Thursday5 because she was genuinely interested, and Thursday1–4 because Roger was actually quite attractive.

'Just how many piano mentions are there in fiction?' asked Thursday5.

'Thousands,' he replied, 'but in varying degrees. Much of nineteenth-century literature, and the Brontës, Hardy and Dickens in particular, are literally *awash* with pianos – but they are rarely played. Those are the easy ones to deal with. Our pianos one to seven are non-functioning and are for description only. They are simply on an automatic circuit of the BookWorld, appearing momentarily in the text before flashing off to appear elsewhere.' He turned to the indicator board. 'If you look at the panel, our trusty old P-6 Broadwood upright is currently on page 339 of *The Lost World*, where it occupies a space near the standard lamp in the Potts' villa in Streatham. In a few moments it will jump automatically to the sub-basement on page 91 of *Howards End*, where it will sit beneath a Maud Goodman painting. A moment later it will jump off to page 161 of *Huckleberry Finn* and the Grangerford parlor.'

'But,' added Charles in a whisper, 'Eliot, Austen and Thackeray are not only knee deep in pianos, but working ones, which in many instances are the hinge-pin of a scene. And *those* are the ones we have to be most careful with regarding supply and demand. Amelia Sedley's piano in *Vanity Fair* is sold at auction and repurchased by Dobbin to be given to her as a gift, and the singing and accompaniment within Austen do much to add to the general atmosphere.'

Thursday5 nodded enthusiastically and Thursday1–4, for the first time that day, actually expressed a vague interest and asked a question.

'Can't someone just make some more pianos?'

'There is a measure of economy that runs throughout the BookWorld,' Charles replied. 'We count ourselves lucky – pianos are positively *bountiful* compared to the number of real dusty-grey-and-wrinkly elephants.'

'How many of those are there?'

'One. If anyone needs a herd the Pachyderm Supply Division have to make do with cardboard cut-outs and a lot of off-page trumpeting.'

The Thursdays mused upon this for a moment, as Charles and Roger donned their jackets and prepared to take a few hours off while I took over. I'd done it before, so it wasn't a problem.

'Everything's pretty much set on automatic,' explained Charles as they headed out of the door, 'but there are a few manual piano movements you'll need to do – there's a list on the console. We'll be back in two hours to take care of the whole *Jude the Obscure* letter-in-the-piano plot device nonsense, and to somehow juggle the requirements of a usable piano in *Three Men in a Boat* with the destruction of a Beulhoff grand in *Decline and Fall*.'

'Sooner you than me,' I said. 'Enjoy your break.'

They assured me that they would and departed with the man in overalls, whose name, we learned, was Ken.

'Right,' I said, sitting down and putting my feet up on the console, 'get the coffee on, Thursday.'

Neither of them budged an inch.

'She gave *you* an order,' said Thursday1–4, 'and I take mine black and strong.'

'Humph!' muttered Thursday5, but went off to put the kettle on nonetheless. Thursday1–4 took off her greatcoat, hung it on a peg and sat down in one of the other chairs.

'So ... we just sit here and watch pianos move around the BookWorld?' she asked in a somewhat sneering tone of voice. Mind you, she usually spoke like that, so it was nothing unusual.

'That's *exactly* what we do. Much of Jurisfiction's work is like this. Boring but essential. Without an uninterrupted supply of pianos, much essential atmosphere would be lost – can you imagine *The Woman in White* without Laura's playing?'

Thursday1–4 looked blank.

'You don't know what I'm talking about, do you?'

'The classics are too slow for me,' she replied, idly taking one of her automatics from its holster and removing the clip to stare at the shiny rounds, 'not enough action. I'm more into David Webb.'

'You've read Robert Ludlum?' I asked in surprise. Most bookpeople didn't read. It was too much like a busman's holiday.

'Nope. It's Dave I like, *especially* when he's Jason Bourne. Knows how to show a lady a good time and can pop a head shot from a thousand yards.'

'Is there anyone in fiction you *haven't* slept with?'

'I love *The Woman in White*,' put in Thursday5, who had returned with a tray of coffees – but with a glass of water for herself, I noticed. 'All that Mozart to express her love for Hartright – dreamy!'

I took my coffee and we watched the lights flicker on the console as a non-functioning Bösendorfer was moved from *Our Mutual Friend* to *Persuasion*, where it jumped rapidly between the twelve different scenes in which it was mentioned before vanishing off into *Wives and Daughters*.

'I think atmosphere in novels is overrated,' said Thursday1–4, taking a sip of coffee before she added patronisingly: 'Good coffee, Thursday – jolly well done.'

'That's put my mind at rest,' replied Thursday5 sarcastically, something that Thursday1–4 missed.

'Are there any biscuits?' I asked.

'Yes,' echoed Thursday1–4, 'are there any?'

Thursday5 huffed, got up, found some Jaffa cakes and placed them on the console in front of me, glaring at Thursday1–4 as she did so.

'Don't underestimate atmosphere,' I said slowly, helping myself to a Jaffa cake. 'The four opposing forces in any novel are atmosphere, plot, character and pace. But they don't have to be in equilibrium. You can have a book without any plot or pace at all, but it has to make up for it in character and a bit of atmosphere – like *The Old Man and the Sea*. Most thrillers are plot and pace and nothing else, such as *Where Eagles Dare*. But it doesn't matter; each to a reader's own—'

I stopped talking because a warning light was flashing on the console in front of us.

'Hmm,' I murmured as I leaned closer, 'they're overrunning in *Dubliners* and *Ulysses* needs an upright piano for Mr Dedalus to comment upon at the Ormond Hotel in less than a minute's time.'

'Isn't there a spare piano at Norland Park?' asked Thursday5.

'No – Marianne took it with her to Devon and it's currently one of those being overhauled.'

I scanned the knobs and switches of the console, looking for a spare piano that could be redirected. I eventually found one in *Peter Pan*. It was only referred to in a line of dialogue, so I redirected it to *Ulysses* as quickly as I could. Too quickly, to be honest, and I fumbled the interchange.

'Shit,' I muttered under my breath.

'What?'

'Nothing,' I replied, knowing full well that no one would notice. I'd placed it in the wrong part of the Ormond Hotel. I didn't have time to worry about this, however, as another warning light was flashing. This was to alert us that the first manual piano movement that Roger and Charles had left us with was approaching. I picked up the handwritten note and read it.

'We've got the Goetzmann grand returning from *Villette* and it has to be sent with piano stool 87B into Agatha Christie's *They Do It with Mirrors*. Who can see a piano stool anywhere?'

Neither of the Thursdays moved an inch. Thursday5 eventually tapped Thursday1–4 on the arm and said: 'Your turn. I did the coffee.'

'In that case,' replied Thursday1–4 with impeccable twisted logic, 'it must have been *my* turn to do the Jaffa cakes?'

'I suppose.'

'Then since you very kindly undertook that task on my behalf, it's your turn to do something again – so find the sodding piano stool and stop bothering me with your bleating.'

I laid a hand on Thursday1–4's arm and said:

'Find the piano stool, Thursday.'

She tutted haughtily in a manner that Friday would have approved of, but got up and had a look around the room, eventually finding it near a heap of sheet music, a few music stands and a dusty bassoon.

'Here,' she said in a bored tone, lifting the lid to look inside. Just at that moment, there was a buzzing noise and the Goetzmann grand appeared in the brightly lit aperture in the wall.

'Right on time.'

I twiddled a few knobs to set its onward journey, told Thursday1–4 to put the piano stool with it, which she did, and then with a buzz I sent it on to the Great Hall of Stonygate House inside Agatha Christie's *They Do It with Mirrors*.

'Good,' I muttered, crossing that first task off the list, 'we've got nothing else for a half-hour.'

But my troubles weren't nearly over, as Thursday5 had sat in the chair recently vacated by Thursday1–4.

'You're in my seat.'

'It's not your seat.'

'I sat in it first so it's mine.'

'You can't bagsy seats and besides, you don't *own* it.'

'Listen,' growled Thursday1–4, 'do you like doing crochet?'

'Yes—?'

'Then perhaps you can imagine how tricky that might be . . .
with broken fingers.'

Thursday5's lip trembled for a moment.

'I'm . . . I'm . . . sure we can discuss this like rational adults before
resorting to anything so crude as violence.'

'Perhaps we could,' returned Thursday1–4, 'but it's far easier with
me telling you how it's going to be. Now: get your tie-dyed butt
out of my seat.'

'Thursday?' I said.

'I can deal with this,' snapped Thursday5 in a rare show of annoyance. 'I don't need to be rescued like a child every single time Miss
Slagfest here opens her gob!'

'I'm not meddling,' I replied, 'all I want to know is where
Thursday1–4 got that pistol.'

'This?' she said, holding up the small black automatic that I'd
noticed she had in her hand. 'It's really cool, isn't it? A Browning
.26-calibre standard single-action automatic with slide-and-grip
safety.'

'Where did you get it?'

'I found it,' she retorted defensively, 'so I'm keeping it.'

I didn't have time for this.

'Tell me where you found it or you'll be its next victim.'

She paused, then said:

'It was . . . in that piano stool.'

'Idiot!' I yelled, getting up and demanding she hand it over,
which she did. 'That's an essential plot point in *They Do It with
Mirrors*! Why can't you just leave things alone?'

'I thought—'

'That's the problem. You don't. Stay here while we sort this out and don't touch anything. I repeat: touch *nothing*. Do you understand?'

'Yes, yes, of course I understand – what do you think I am, a child?'

I didn't have time to argue, so after telling Thursday5 to follow me closely, I jumped out of the Piano Squad to the Great Library, and from there we made our way into Agatha Christie's *They Do It with Mirrors*.

We arrived at Stonygates in the short length of dimly lit corridor that connected the square lobby with the Great Hall. We pressed ourselves into the shadows, and I looked inside the hall. It was a large room that oozed Victorian Gothic gloominess, with dark wood and minimal lighting. There were a half-dozen or so people chattering, but more importantly, directly ahead of us, was the Goetzmann grand that we had dispatched not two minutes before. And in front of this, the piano stool to which the weapon had to be returned. I was about to chance my luck and sneak in but had not got two paces when a young man came and sat on the piano stool and began to play. I retreated into the shadows and felt Thursday5 grip my arm nervously as the lights flickered and went out, leaving the house in the semi-dark. We backed farther into the shadows as a large man with a sulky expression came out of the door and vanished into the gloom, muttering about the fuses. A few minutes later an elderly woman tottered to the dining room and back to retrieve something, and almost immediately the front door was pushed violently open and a young man strode into the hall in an overdramatic manner. This was followed by an argument, the sound of the study door opening and closing, more muffled shouting and eventually two shots. With the characters in the room thus distracted,

I padded softly to the man seated at the piano and tapped him lightly on his shoulder. He looked up with some surprise, and I showed him my Jurisfiction badge. I raised my eyebrows, placed a finger to my lips and gestured him to join the people on the other side of the room. He did as I asked, and once his back was turned I slipped the small automatic into the piano stool, between a copy of Handel's *Largo* and Chopin's *Preludes*.

I quickly and noiselessly retraced my steps to where Thursday5 was waiting for me and within a few minutes we had returned to the Piano Squad's headquarters.

As we re-entered, the squad room was in chaos. Warning lights were flashing, klaxons were going off and the control console was a mass of flickering indicator lights. I was relieved – if such a word could be used in such uproar – to see that Roger and Charles had both returned and were trying to bring some sort of semblance of order back to the piano distribution network.

'I need the Thürmer back from *Agnes Grey*,' yelled Roger, 'and I'll swap it for a non-working Streicher . . .'

'What the hell's going on, Thursday?'

It was Commander Bradshaw, and he didn't look very happy.

'I don't know. When I left everything was fine.'

'You *left*?' he echoed incredulously. 'You left the piano room unattended?'

'I left—'

But I stopped myself. I was responsible for any cadet's actions or inactions, irrespective of what they were and where they happened. I'd made a mistake. I should have called Bradshaw to cover for me or to get someone to go into *Mirrors*. I took a deep breath.

'No excuses, sir – I screwed up. I'm sorry.'

'*Sorry?*' repeated Bradshaw. 'That's it? You're *sorry*? I've got a dead

Holmes on my hands; one of the Outland's most favourite series is about to unravel and I really don't need one of your idiot cadets suddenly thinking that she's God of all the pianos.'

'What did she do?'

'If you'd have been supervising properly, you'd know!'

'Okay, okay,' I retorted, seriously beginning to get pissed off, 'this one's down to me and I'll face the music, but I'd like to know what she's done before I wipe the smirk off her face for good.'

'She decided,' he said slowly, and with great restraint, 'to do her own thing with piano supply in your absence. Every single piano reference has been deleted from Melville, Scott and Defoe.'

'*What?*' I said, looking around the room and finally catching sight of Thursday1–4 on the other side of the room, where she was standing, arms folded and apparently without a care in the world.

'As I said. And we don't have the time or the pianos to replace them. But that's not the worst bit.'

'It gets worse?'

'Certainly. For some reason known only to herself, she dropped an upright Broadwood straight into Miss Bates's drawing room inside Austen's *Emma*.'

'Have they noticed?'

'Pianos aren't generally the sort of things one can miss. As soon as it arrived speculation began on where it might have come from. Miss Bates agrees with Mrs Cole that it's from Colonel Campbell but Emma thinks its from Mrs Dixon. Mrs Weston is more inclined to think it was from Mr Knightley, but Mr Knightley believes it's from Frank Churchill. Quite a mess, wouldn't you agree?'

'Can we get it out?'

'It's embedded itself now. I'm going to get Churchill to take the rap and it shouldn't inflict too much damage. But this is down to you, Thursday, and I've got no choice but to suspend you from Jurisfiction duties pending a disciplinary inquiry.'

'Let's keep a sense of perspective on this, Bradshaw. I know I'm responsible but it's not my fault – besides, you told me to do this and I said I couldn't.'

'It's my fault, is it?'

'Partly.'

'Humph,' replied Bradshaw, and bristled his moustache in anger. 'I'll take it under advisement – but you're still suspended.'

I jerked a thumb in the direction of Thursday1–4. 'What about her?'

'She's your cadet, Thursday. *You* deal with it.'

He took a deep breath, shook his head, softened for a moment to tell me to look after myself and departed. I told Thursday5 to meet me up at the CofG and beckoned Thursday1–4 into the corridor.

'What the *hell* did you think you were doing?'

'Oh, c'mon,' she said, 'don't be such a hard-arse. It's not like there's any seriously lasting damage. So I dropped a piano into *Emma* – it's not like it landed on anyone.'

I stared at her for a moment. Even allowing for Thursday1–4's supreme arrogance, it still didn't make any sense.

'You're not stupid. You *knew* it would get you fired once and for all, so why do it?'

She stared at me with a look of cold hatred.

'You were going to fire me anyway. There wasn't a ghost's chance I'd have made it.'

'The chance was slim,' I admitted, 'but it was there.'

'I don't agree. You hate me. Always have. From the moment I was first published. We could have been friends but you never even *visited*. Not once in four entire books. Not a postcard, a footnote, nothing. I'm closer to you than family, Thursday, and you treated me like crap.'

And then, I understood.

212

'You put the piano into *Emma* just to drop me in the shit, didn't you?'

'After what you've done to me, you deserve far worse. You had it in for me the moment I arrived at Jurisfiction. You all did.'

I shook my head sadly. She was consumed by hate. But instead of trying to deal with it, she just projected it on to everyone around her. I sighed.

'You did this for revenge over some perceived slight?'

'That wasn't revenge,' said Thursday1–4 in a quiet voice. 'You'll know revenge when you see it.'

'Give me your badge.'

She dug it from her pocket and then tossed it on to the floor rather than hand it over.

'I quit,' she spat. 'I wouldn't join Jurisfiction now if you *begged* me.'

It was all I could do not to laugh at her preposterous line of reasoning. She couldn't help herself. She was written this way.

'Go on,' I said in an even tone, 'go home.'

She seemed surprised that I was no longer angry.

'Aren't you going to yell at me or hit me or try to kill me or something? Face it: this isn't much of a resolution.'

'It's all you're going to get. You really don't understand me at all, do you?'

She glared at me for a moment, and then bookjumped out.

I stood in the corridor for a few minutes, wondering whether there was anything else I might have done. Aside from not trusting her an inch, not really. I shrugged, tried and failed to get TransGenreTaxis to even *answer* the footnoterphone, and then, checking the time so I wouldn't be late for the policy directive meeting, made my way slowly towards the elevators.

24
Policy Directives

'The Council of Genres is the administrative body that look after all aspects of BookWorld regulation, from policy decisions in the main debating chamber to the day-to-day running of ordinary BookWorld affairs, supply of plot devices and even control of the word supply coming in from the Text Sea. They control the Book Inspectorate, which governs which books are to be published and which to be demolished, and also control Text Grand Central and Jurisfiction – but only as regards policy. For the most part they are even handed, but need to be watched, and that's where I come into the equation.'

I didn't go straight to either Jurisfiction or the Council of Genres but instead went for a quiet walk in Wainwright's *Pictorial Guide to the Lakeland Fells*. I often go there when in pensive mood, and although the line drawings that I climbed were not as beautiful nor as colourful as the real thing, they were peaceful and friendly, imbued as they were with a love of the fells that is seldom equalled, or surpassed. I sat on the warm sketched grass atop Haystacks, threw a pebble into the tarn and watched the drawn ripples radiate outwards. I returned much refreshed an hour later.

I found Thursday5 still waiting for me in the seating area near the picture window with the view of the other towers. She stood up when I approached.

'I'm sorry,' she said.

'Why?' I returned. 'It wasn't your fault.'

'But it certainly wasn't yours.'

'That's the thing,' I replied, 'it was. She's a cadet. She has no responsibility. Her faults are mine.'

I stopped to think about what I had just said. She was impetuous, passionate and capable of almost uncontrollable rage. Her faults really *were* mine.

I took a deep breath and looked at my watch.

'Show time,' I murmured despondently, 'time for the policy directive meeting.'

'Oh!' exclaimed Thursday5, and then searched through her bag until she found a small yellow book and a pen.

'I hope that's not what I think it is.'

'What do you think it is?'

'An autograph book.'

She said nothing and bit her lip.

'If you even *think* about asking Harry Potter for an autograph, your day ends right now.'

She sighed and dropped the book back into her bag.

The policy meeting was held in the main debating chamber. Jobsworth's chair was the large one behind the dais, with the seats either side of him reserved for his closest aides and advisers. We arrived twenty minutes early and were the first ones there. I sat down in my usual seat to the left of where the genres would sit, and Thursday5 sat just behind me. The Read-O-Meter was still clicking resolutely downwards, and I looked absently around the chamber, trying to gather my thoughts. Along the side walls were paintings of various dignitaries who had distinguished themselves in one way or another during the Council of Genre's rule – my own painting was two from the end, sandwiched between Paddington Bear and Henry Pooter.

'So what's on the agenda?' asked Thursday5.

I shrugged, having become somewhat browned off with the

whole process. I wanted to just go home – somewhere away from fiction and the parts of me I didn't much care for.

'Who knows?' I said in a careless fashion. 'Falling read-rates, I imagine – fundamentally, it's all there is.'

At that moment the main doors were pushed open and Jobsworth appeared, followed by his usual retinue of hangers-on. He saw me immediately and chose a route that would take him past my desk.

'Good afternoon, Next,' he said. 'I heard you were recently suspended?'

'It's an occupational hazard when you're working in the front line,' I replied pointedly – Jobsworth had always been administration. If he understood the remark he made no sign of it. I added: 'Are you well, sir?'

'Can't complain. Which one's that?' he asked, pointing to Thursday5 in much the same way as you'd direct someone to the toilet.

'Thursday5, sir.'

'You're making a mistake to fire the other one,' said Jobsworth, addressing me. 'I'd ask for a second or third opinion about her if there was anyone left to ask. Nevertheless, the decision was yours and I abide by it. The matter is closed.'

'I was down in the maintenance facility recently,' I told him, 'and Isambard told me that the CofG had insisted on upgrading all the throughput conduits.'

'Really?' replied Jobsworth vaguely. 'I do wish he'd keep himself to himself.'

He walked to the raised dais, sat in the central chair and busied himself with his notes. The room fell silent, aside from the occasional click of the Read-O-Meter as it heralded another drop in the Outland read-rate.

The next delegate to arrive was Colonel Barksdale, head of the CofG Combined Forces. He sat down four desks away without looking at me. We had not seen eye to eye much in the past as I disliked his constant warmongering. Next to arrive was Baxter, the senator's chief adviser, who flicked a distasteful look in my direction. In fact, all eight members of the directive panel, aside from the equestrian senator, Black Beauty, didn't much like me. It wasn't surprising. I wasn't just the only Outlander member on the panel, I was the LBOCS and consequently wielded the weapon that committees always feared – the veto. I tried to discharge my duties as well as I could, despite the enmity it brought.

I could see Thursday5 move expectantly every time the door opened, but aside from the usual ten members of the committee and their staff, no one else turned up.

'Good afternoon, everyone,' said Jobsworth, standing up to address us. There weren't many of us in the debating chamber but it was usually this way – policy meetings were closed-door affairs.

'Sadly, I have to advise you that Mr Harry Potter is unable to attend owing to copyright restrictions, so we're going to leave the "supplying characters from video games" issue for another time.'

There was a grumbling from the senators, and I noticed one or two put their autograph books back into their bags.

'Apologies for absence,' continued Jobsworth. 'Jacob Marley is too alive to attend, the Snork Maiden is at the hairdresser's and Senator Zigo is once more unavailable. So we'll begin. Item one: the grammasite problem. Mr Bamford?'

Senator Bamford was a small man with wispy blond hair and eyes that were so small they almost weren't there. He wore a blue boiler suit very obviously under his senatorial robes, and had been in charge of what we called 'The Grammasite Problem' for almost four decades, seemingly to no avail. The predations of the small parasitical beasts upon the books on which they fed was damaging and a constant drain on resources. Despite culling in the past their numbers were no smaller now than they had ever been. Mass extermination was often suggested, something the Naturalist genre were violently against. Pests they might be, but the young were cute and cuddly and had big eyes, which was definitely an evolutionary edge to secure survival.

'The problem is so well known that I will not outline it here again, but suffice to say that numbers of grammasites have risen dramatically over the years, and in order to keep the naturalists happy I suggest we undertake a programme of textualisation whereby representative specimens of the seven hundred or so species will be preserved in long-winded accounts in dreary academic tomes. In that way we can preserve the animal and even, if necessary, bring them back from extinction – yet still exterminate the species.'

Bamford sat down again, and Jobsworth asked for a show of hands. We all agreed. Grammasites were a pest, and needed to be dealt with.

'Item two,' said Jobsworth, 'falling readership figures. Baxter?'

Baxter stood up and addressed the room, although to be honest, the other delegates – with the possible exception of Beauty – generally went with Jobsworth on everything. The person Baxter really needed to address was me. As the holder of the only veto, I was the one he would have to swing.

'The falling readership figures have been a matter of some concern for a number of years now, and increased expenditure in the Well of Lost Plots to construct thrilling new books has failed to grasp the imagination of the reading public. We of the Readership Increasement Committee have been formulating some radical ideas to rekindle interest in novels.'

He turned over a paper and coughed before continuing.

'After a fact-finding mission conducted in the real world, we have decided that *interactivity* is the keyword of the new generation. For many readers, books are too much of a one-sided conduit of information, and a new form of novel that allows its readers to choose where the story goes is the way forward.'

'Isn't that the point of books?' asked Black Beauty, stamping his hoof angrily on the table and upsetting an inkwell. 'The pleasure lies in the *unfolding* of the plots. Even if we know what must happen, how one *arrives* there is still entertaining.'

'I couldn't agree with you more,' remarked Baxter, 'but our core readership is ageing and the world's youth is growing up without being in the habit of reading books.'

'So what's your suggestion?' asked Jobsworth.

'To create a new form of book – an *interactive* book which begins blank except for ten or so basic characters. Then, as it is written, chapter by chapter, the readers are polled on who they want to keep, and who they want to exclude. As soon as we know, we write the new section, and at the end of the new chapter poll the readers again. I call it a "reality book show" – life as it *really* is, with all the human interactions that make it so rich.'

'And the boring bits as well?' I asked, recalling my only experience with reality TV.

'I don't suggest that *every* book should be this way,' added Baxter hurriedly, 'but we want to make books hip and appealing to the youth market. Society is moving on, and if we don't move with it, books – and we – will vanish.'

As if to reinforce his argument, he waved a hand at the Read-O-Meter, which dropped another seventeen books by way of confirmation.

'Why don't we just write better books?' I asked.

'Because it's expensive, time-consuming and there's no guarantee it will work,' said Senator Aimsworth, speaking for the first time. 'From what I've seen of the real world, interactivity is a sure-fire hit. Baxter is right. The future is reality book shows based on democratic decision-making shared by the creators and the readers. Give people what they want, and in just the way they want it.'

'Once the ball starts rolling downhill it can't be stopped,' I remarked. 'This is the wrong route – I can feel it.'

'Your loyalty is misplaced, Ms Next. What could be wrong with offering reader choice? I say we vote on it. All those in favour of directing funds and resources to an interactive reality book project?'

Everyone raised their hands – except me and Senator Beauty. Me because I didn't agree with them and Beauty because he had a hoof. It didn't matter. He was against it.

'As usual,' growled the senator, 'the contrarian among us knows better. Your objections, Ms Next?'

I took a deep breath.

'The point is, ladies and gentleman, that we're *not* in the book industry. This isn't a publishing meeting with sales targets, goals, market research and focus groups. The book may be the delivery medium but what we're actually peddling here is *story*. Humans like stories. Humans *need* stories. Stories are good. Stories *work*. Story clarifies and captures the essence of the human spirit. Story, in all its forms – of life, of love, of knowledge – has marked the upward surge of mankind. And story, you mark my words, will be with the last human to draw breath, and we should be there, supporting that one last person. I say we place our faith in good stories well told and leave the interactivity as the transient Outlander fad that it is. Instead of being subservient to reader opinion, we should be leading it.'

I paused for a moment and stared at the sea of unconvinced faces. The Read-O-Meter clicked down another twenty-eight books.

'Listen, I'm as worried about falling reading rates as anyone, but wild and desperate measures are not the answer. We've got to go back to the root cause and figure out why people prefer watching *Samaritan Kidney Swap* to reading a good book. If we *can't* create better books, then we should be doing a lot more than simply dreaming up gimmicks to pander to the lowest common denominator.'

There was silence. I meant about seventy-five per cent of it, but needed to get the message across. There should be room on this planet for *Dr Zhivago* and *Extreme Spatula Makeover*, but the scales had tipped far enough – and I didn't want them to go any farther. They all stared at me in silence as Jobsworth drummed his fingers on the desk.

'Does this mean you are exercising your veto?'

'It does.'

There was a collective groan from the other delegates and I suddenly wondered whether I had gone too far. After all, they had the good of the BookWorld as their priority, as did I – and it wasn't as though I could come up with anything better.

'I'd like to conduct my own study group,' I said, hoping that by using their own corporate buzzword language they might go for it, 'and see if I can throw up any strategies to pursue. If I can't we'll go with your interactive idea, no matter how dumb it sounds.'

'Very well,' intoned Jobsworth as they all exchanged annoyed looks, 'since I know you too well to expect you to change your mind, we'll reappraise the situation in a week's time and move on. Next item?'

Colonel Barksdale stood up and looked at us all in the sombre manner in which he always imparted bad news. He never had anything else. In fact, I think he *engineered* bad news in order to have the pleasure to give it. He had been head of BookWorld defence for the past eight years and clearly wanted to raise his game to include an inter-genre war or two. A chance to achieve *greatness*, if you like.

'I expect you've all heard about Speedy Muffler's recent threat to the stability of the BookWorld?'

We all mumbled our agreement.

'Good. Well, as security is my province, I want you all to agree to a plan of action that is both decisive and *final*. If Muffler can deploy a dirty bomb then none of us are safe. Hardliners in Ecclesiastical and Feminist are ready to mobilise for war to protect their hard-won ideologies, and it is my opinion that a pre-emptive strike will show those immoral bastards that we mean business. I've three brigades of Danverclones ready and waiting to stream across the border. It won't take long – Racy Novel are a ramshackle genre at best.'

'Isn't war a bit hasty?' I asked. 'Muffler will try anything to punch above his weight. And even if he *has* developed a dirty bomb, he still has to deliver it. How's he going to smuggle something like that into Feminist? It's got one of the most well-protected frontiers in the BookWorld.'

'We have it on good authority that they might disguise it as a double entendre in a bedroom farce and deliver it up the rear entrance at Comedy.'

'Pure conjecture. What about good old-fashioned diplomacy? You could offer Muffler some Well-surplus subtext or even dialogue to dilute the worst excesses of the genre – he'd probably respond well to it. After all, all they want to do is develop as a genre.'

Colonel Barksdale drummed his fingers impatiently and opened his mouth to speak, but Jobsworth beat him to it.

'That's the worry. Ecclesiastical are concerned that Racy Novel want to undertake an expansionist policy – there is talk of them wanting to reoccupy the dehumorised zone. Besides,' he added, 'subtext and dialogue are up to almost seven hundred and fifty guineas a kilo.'

'Do we know if they even *have* a dirty bomb?' I asked. 'It might all be a bluff.'

Jobsworth signalled to Colonel Barksdale, who handed me a dossier marked 'Terribly Secret'.

'It's no bluff. We've been sent some rather disturbing reports regarding outbreaks of incongruous obscenity from as far away as Drama – Charles Dickens, no less.'

'*Bleak House*,' I read from the sheet of paper I'd been handed, 'and I quote: "Sir Leicester leans back in his chair and breathlessly ejaculates".'

'You see?' said Barksdale, as the rest of the delegates muttered to themselves and shook their heads in a shocked manner. 'And what about this one?'

He handed me another sheet of paper, this time from Thomas Hardy's *Mayor of Casterbridge*.

'. . . the Mayor beheld the unattractive exterior of Farfrae's erection.'

'And,' he added decisively, 'we've got a character named "Master Bates" turning up all over *Oliver Twist*.'

'Master Bates has always been called that,' I pointed out. 'We used to giggle over the name at school.'

'Despite that,' replied Colonel Barksdale with no loss of confidence, 'the other two are quite enough to have this taken *extremely* seriously. The Danverclones are ready. I only need your approval—'

'It's called word drift.'

It was Thursday5. The meeting had never seen such a flagrant lapse of protocol, and I would have slung her out myself – but for the fact she had a point.

'I'm sorry,' said Senator Jobsworth in a sarcastic tone, 'I must have missed the meeting where the other Thursday was elected to the Security Council. Jurisfiction cadets must train, so I will overlook it this once. But one more word—!'

Unabashed, Thursday5 added:

'Did Senator Muffler send those examples to you?'

Senator Jobsworth wasted no time and called over his shoulder to one of the many Danverclones standing close by.

'Security? See that Thursday with the flower in her hair? She is to be returned to her—'

'She's with me,' I said, staring at Jobsworth, who glared back dangerously, 'and I vouch for her. She has opinions that I feel are worth listening to.'

Jobsworth and Barksdale went silent and looked at one another, wondering whether there wasn't some sort of rule they could invoke. There wasn't. And it was for precisely these moments that the Great Panjandrum had given me the veto – to slow things down and make the Council of Genres think before they acted.

'Well?' I said. 'Did Speedy Muffler send those examples to you?'

'Well, not perhaps . . . as such,' replied Colonel Barksdale with a shrug, 'but the evidence is unequivocally compelling and totally, absolutely without doubt.'

'I contend,' added Thursday5, 'that they are simply words whose meanings have meandered over the years and those books were written with *precisely* the words you quoted us now. Word drift.'

'I hardly think that's likely, my dear,' replied Jobsworth patronisingly.

'Oh no?' I replied. 'Do you mean to tell me that when Lydia from *Pride and Prejudice* thinks of Brighton and ". . . the glories of the camp – its tents stretched forth in beauteous uniformity of lines, crowded with the young and the gay", she might possibly mean something else?'

'Well, no, of course not,' replied the senator, suddenly feeling uncomfortable under the combined baleful stare of Thursday5 and me. There was a mumbling among the other delegates, and I said:

'Words change. Whoever sent these examples to you has an agenda which is more about confrontation than a peaceful outcome to the crisis. I'm going to exercise my veto again. I suggest that a diplomatic resolution be attempted until we have irrefutable evidence that Muffler really has the capabilities he claims.'

'This is bad judgement,' growled Jobsworth with barely controlled rage, as he rose from his seat and gathered his papers together. 'You're on morally tricky ground if you side with Racy Novel.'

'I'm on morally *trickier* ground if I don't,' I replied. 'I will not sanction a war on misplaced words in a few of the classics. Show me a blatantly unsubtle and badly written sex scene in *To the Lighthouse* and I will personally lead the battle myself.'

Jobsworth stared at me and I stared back angrily.

'By then the damage will have been done. We want to stop them before they even get started.'

He paused and composed himself.

'Two vetoes in one day,' he added. 'You must be particularly pleased with yourself. I hope you have as many smart answers when smutty innuendo is sprinkled liberally across *The Second Sex*.'

And without another word he stormed out of the meeting, closely followed by Barksdale, Baxter and all the others, each of them making 'tut tut' noises and shaking their heads in a sickening display of inspired toadying. Only Senator Beauty wasn't with them. He shook his head at me in a gesture meaning 'sooner you than me', and then trotted out.

We were left in silence, aside from the Read-O-Meter, which ominously dropped another thirty-six books.

'That "word drift" explanation was really very good,' I said to Thursday5 when we were back in the lift.

'It was nothing, really.'

'Nothing?' I echoed. 'Don't sell yourself short. You probably just averted a genre war.'

'Time will tell. I meant to ask. You said you were the "LBOCS". What does that mean?'

'It means I'm the council's Last Bastion Of Common Sense. Because I'm from the Outland I have a better notion of inde-

226

pendent thought than the generally deterministic BookWorld. Nothing happens without my knowledge or comment.'

'That must sometimes make you unpopular.'

'No,' I replied, 'it makes me unpopular *all* the time.'

We went back down to the Jurisfiction offices for me to formally hand over my badge to Bradshaw, who took it from me without expression and returned to his work. I returned despondently to where Thursday5 was waiting expectantly at my desk. It was the end of her assessment, and I knew she wanted to be put out of her misery one way or another.

'There are three recommendations I can make,' I began, sitting back in my chair. 'One: for you to be put forward for further training. Two: for you to be returned to basic training. And three: for you to leave the service entirely.'

I looked across at her and found myself staring back. It was the look I usually gave to the mirror, and it was disconcerting. But I had to be firm, and make my decision based on her performance, and suitability.

'You were nearly eaten by a grammasite and you would have let the Minotaur kill me,' I began, 'but on the plus side, you came up with the "word drift" explanation, which was pretty cool.'

She looked hopeful for a moment.

'But I have to take all things under consideration, and without bias – either in your favour, or against. The Minotaur episode was too important a failing for me to ignore, and much though I like your mildly eccentric ways, I'm sorry, but I'm going to have to recommend that you do not join Jurisfiction, either now or in the future.'

She didn't say anything for a while, and looked as though she was about to cry, which she did, a second or two later. She might have made a decent Jurisfiction agent, but the chances of her getting

227

herself killed were just too high for me to risk. On my graduation assignment I was almost murdered by a bunch of emotion junkies inside *Shadow the Sheepdog*. Given the same situation, Thursday5 wouldn't have survived, and I wasn't going to have that on my conscience. She wasn't just a version of me, she was something closer to *family*, and I didn't want her coming to any harm.

'I understand,' she said between sniffs, dabbing at her nose with a lacy handkerchief.

She thanked me for my time, apologised again for the Minotaur, laid her badge on my desk and vanished off into her book. I leaned back in my chair and sighed – what with firing both Thursdays, I had really been giving myself a hard time today. I wanted to go home, but the power required for a transfictional jump to the Outland might be tricky on an empty stomach. I looked at my watch. It was only four, and Jurisfiction agents at that time liked to take tea. And to take tea, they generally liked to go to the best tea rooms in the BookWorld – or anywhere else, for that matter.

25

The Paragon

———

'There are three things in life that can make even the worst problems seem just that tiniest bit better. The first is a cup of tea – loose-leaf Assam with a hint of Lapsang and poured before it gets too dark and then with a dash of milk and the smallest hint of sugar. Calming, soothing and almost without peer. The second, naturally, is a hot soaking bath. The third is Puccini. In the bath with a hot cup of tea and Puccini. Heaven.'

It was called the Paragon, and was the most perfect 1920's tea room, nestled in the safe and unobserved background fabric of P.G. Wodehouse's *Summer Lightning*. To your left and right upon entering the carved wooden doors were glass display cases containing the most sumptuous home-made cakes and pastries. Beyond these were the tea rooms proper, with booths and tables constructed of a dark wood that perfectly matched the panelled interior. This was itself decorated with plaster reliefs of Greek characters disporting themselves in matters of equestrian and athletic prowess. To the rear were two additional and private tea rooms; one of light-coloured wood and the other in delicate carvings of a most agreeable nature. Needless to say it was inhabited by the most populous characters in Wodehouse's novels. That is to say it was full of voluble and opinionated aunts.

There were two Jurisfiction agents sitting at the table we usually reserved for our 3.30 tea and cakes. The first was tall and dressed in jet-black, high-collared robes buttoned tightly up to his throat. He had a pale complexion, high cheekbones and a small and very precise goatee. He sat with his arms crossed and was staring at all the other customers in the tea rooms with an air of haughty superiority, eyebrows raised imperiously. This was truly a tyrant among tyrants, a ruthless leader who had murdered billions in his never-ending and inadequately explained quest for the unquestioned obedience of every living entity in the known galaxy. The other, of course, was a six-foot-high hedgehog dressed in a multitude of petticoats, apron and bonnet, and carrying a wicker basket of washing. There was no more celebrated partnership in Jurisfiction either then or now – it was Mrs Tiggy-Winkle and Emperor Zhark. The hedgehog from Beatrix Potter, and the emperor from the 'Zhark' series of bad science fiction novels.

'Good afternoon, Thursday,' intoned the emperor when he saw me, a flicker of a smile attempting to crack through his imperialist bearing.

'Hi, Emperor. How's the galactic domination business these days?'

'Hard work,' he replied, rolling his eyes heavenward. 'Honestly, I invade peaceful civilisations on a whim, destroy their cities and generally cause a great deal of unhappy mayhem – and then they turn against me for absolutely no reason at all.'

'How senselessly irrational of them,' I remarked, winking at Mrs Tiggy-Winkle.

'Quite,' continued Zhark, looking aggrieved and not getting the sarcasm. 'It's not as though I put them *all* to the sword, anyway – I magnanimously decided to spare several hundred thousand as slaves to build an eight-hundred-foot-high statue of myself striding triumphantly over the broken bodies of the vanquished.'

'That's probably the reason they don't like you,' I murmured.

'Oh?' he asked with genuine concern. 'Do you think the statue will be too small?'

'No, it's the "striding triumphantly over the broken bodies of the vanquished" bit. People generally don't like having their noses rubbed in their ill fortune by the person who caused it.'

Emperor Zhark snorted.

'That's the problem with inferiors,' he said at last, 'no sense of humour.'

And he lapsed into a sullen silence, took an old school exercise book from within his robes, licked a pencil stub and started to write.

I sat down next to him.

'What's that?'

'My speech. The Thargoids kindly accepted me as God-Emperor of their star system and I thought it might be nice to say a few words – sort of thank them, really, for their kindness – but under-score the humbleness with veiled threats of mass extermination if they step out of line.'

'How does it begin?'

Zhark read from his notes.

'"Dear Worthless Peons – I pity you your irrelevance." What do you think?'

'Well, it's definitely to the point,' I admitted. 'How are things on the Holmes case?'

'We've been trying to get into the series all morning,' said Zhark, laying his modest acceptance speech aside for a moment and taking a spoonful of the pie that had been placed in front of him, 'but all to no avail. I heard you got suspended. What was that all about?'

I told him about the piano and *Emma*, and he whistled low.

'Tricky. But I shouldn't sweat it. I saw Bradshaw writing up the duty rosters for next week and you're still on them. One moment.' He waved a carefully manicured hand at the waitress and said: 'Sugar on the table, my girl, or I'll have you, your family and all your descendants put to death.' The waitress bobbed politely, ignored his manner entirely and said: 'If you killed me, Your Imperial Mightiness, I wouldn't have any descendants, now, would I?'

'Yes, well, *obviously* I meant the ones now living, girl.'

'Oh!' she said. 'Well, just so we're clear on the matter,' and with a cute bob, she was gone.

'I keep on having trouble with that waitress,' muttered Zhark after she had departed. 'Do you think she was . . . mocking me?'

'Oh no,' said Mrs Tiggy-Winkle, hiding a smile, 'I think she was terrified of you.'

'Has anyone thought of redirecting the Sherlock Holmes throughput feeds from the Outland?' I asked. 'With a well-positioned textual sieve we could bounce the series to a storycode engine at TGC and rewrite the ending with the Holmes and Watson from *The Seven Percent Solution*. It will hold things together long enough to give us time to effect a permanent answer.'

'But where *exactly* to put the sieve?' enquired Zhark, not unreasonably.

'What exactly *is* a textual sieve?' asked Mrs Tiggy-Winkle.

'It's never fully explained,' I replied.

The waitress returned with the sugar.

'Thank you,' said Zhark kindly. 'I have decided to . . . spare your family.'

'Your Highness is overly generous,' replied the waitress, humouring him. 'Perhaps you could just torture one of us – my younger brother, for instance?'

'No, my mind is made up. You're to be spared. Now begone or I will— Oh no. You don't trick me that way. Begone or I will *never* torture your family.'

The waitress bobbed again, thanked him, and was gone.

'Perky, that one, isn't she?' said Zhark, staring after her. 'Do you think I should make her my wife?'

'You're thinking of getting married?' asked Mrs Tiggy-Winkle, almost scorching a collar in her surprise.

'I think it's high time that I did,' he said. 'Slaughtering peaceful civilisations on a whim is a lot more fun when you've got someone to do it with.'

'Does your mother know about this?' I asked, fully aware of the power that the Dowager Empress Zharkina IV wielded in his books. Emperor Zhark may have been the embodiment of terror across innumerable star systems, but he lived with his mum – and if the rumours were correct, she still insisted on bathing him.

'Well, she doesn't know *yet*,' he replied defensively, 'but I'm big enough to make my *own* decisions, you know.'

Mrs Tiggy-Winkle and I exchanged knowing looks. Nothing happened in the imperial palace without the empress's agreement.

Zhark chewed for a moment, winced and then swallowed with a look of utter disgust on his face. He turned to Mrs Tiggy-Winkle.

'I think you've got my pie.'

'Have I?' she replied offhandedly. 'Now you come to mention it, I thought these slugs tasted sort of funny.'

They swapped pies and continued eating.

'Ms Next?'

I looked up. A confident middle-aged woman was standing next to the table. She had starburst wrinkles around the eyes and greying brown hair, a chickenpox scar above her left brow and asymmetric dimples. I raised an eyebrow. She was a well-realised character but I didn't recognise her – at least, not at first.

'Can I help?' I asked.

'I'm looking for the Jurisfiction agent named Thursday Next.'

'That's me.'

Our visitor seemed relieved at this and allowed herself a smile.

'Pleased to meet you. My name's Dr Temperance Brennan.'

I knew who she was, of course; the heroine of her own genre – that of the forensic anthropologist.

'Very pleased to meet you,' I said, rising to shake her hand. 'Perhaps you'd care to join us?'

'Thank you, I shall.'

'This is Emperor Zhark, and the one with the spines is Mrs Tiggy-Winkle,' I said, introducing them both.

'Hello,' said Zhark, sizing her up for matrimony as he shook her hand. 'How would you like the power of life or death over a billion godless heathens?'

She paused for a moment and raised an eyebrow.

'Montreal suits me just fine.'

She shook Mrs Tiggy-Winkle's claw and exchanged a few pleasantries over the correct method to wash linens. I ordered her some coffee and after asking about her Outlander book sales, which were impressively large compared to mine, she admitted to me that this wasn't a social call.

'I've got an understudy covering for me so I'll come straight to the point,' she said, looking with apparent professional interest at Zhark's high cheekbones. 'Someone's trying to kill me.'

'You and I have much in common, Dr Brennan,' I replied. 'When did this happen?'

'Call me Tempe. Have you read my latest adventure?'

'*Grave Secrets*? Of course.'

'Near the end I'm captured after being slipped a Mickey Finn. I talk my way out of it and the bad guy kills himself.'

'So?'

'Thirty-two readings ago I was drugged for *real* and nearly didn't make it. It was all I could do to stay conscious long enough to keep the book on its tracks. I'm first-person narrative so it's all up to me.'

'Yeah,' I murmured, 'that first-person thing can be a drag. Did you report it to Text Grand Central?'

She pushed the hair away from her face and said: 'Naturally. But since I kept the show going it was never logged as a textual anomaly, so according to TGC there's no crime. You know what they told me? "Come back when you're dead and *then* we can do something."'

'Hmm,' I said, drumming my fingers on the table. 'Who do you think is behind it?'

She shrugged.

'No one in the book. We're all on very good terms.'

'Any skeletons in the cupboard? If you'll excuse the expression.'

'Plenty. In Crime there's always at least one seriously bad guy to deal with per book – sometimes more.'

'*Narratively* speaking that's how it appears,' I pointed out, 'but with you dead everyone else in your books would become redundant overnight – and with the possibility of erasure looming over them, your former enemies actually have some of the best reasons to keep you alive.'

'Hmm,' said Dr Brennan thoughtfully, 'I hadn't thought of it that way.'

'The most likely person to want to kill you is someone outside your book – any thoughts?'

'I don't know anyone outside my books – except Kathy and Kerry of course.'

'It won't be them. Leave it with me,' I said after a moment's pause, 'and I'll see what I can do. Just keep your eyes and ears open, yes?'

Dr Brennan smiled and thanked me, shook my hand again, said goodbye to Zhark and Mrs Tiggy-Winkle, and was gone, muttering that she had to relieve a substandard and decidedly bone-idle understudy who was standing in for her.

'What was that all about?' asked Zhark.

'No idea,' I replied. 'It's kind of flattering that people bring their problems to me. I just wish there was another Thursday to deal with it.'

'I thought there was.'

235

'Don't even joke about it, Emperor.'

There was a crackle in the air and Commander Bradshaw suddenly appeared just next to us. Zhark and Tiggy-Winkle looked guilty all of a sudden and the hedge-pig washerwoman made a vain attempt to hide the ironing she was doing.

'I thought I would find you here,' he said, moustache all a-twitch as it was when he was a bit peeved. 'That wouldn't be moon-lighting, would it, Agent Tiggy-Winkle?'

'Not at all,' she replied. 'I spend so much time at Jurisfiction I can hardly get through the ironing I need to do for my own book!'

'Very well,' said Bradshaw slowly, turning to me. 'I have a job that I think you should do.'

'I thought I was suspended?'

He passed me my badge.

'You hadn't been suspended for at least a week, and I thought you might think you'd fallen out of favour. The disciplinary paper-work was accidentally eaten by snails. Most perplexing.'

I smiled.

'What's up?'

'A matter of great delicacy. There were a few minor textual irreg-ularities in . . . the Thursday books.'

'Which ones?' I asked, suddenly worried that Thursday5 might have taken her failure to heart.

'The first four. Since you know them quite well and no one else wants to touch them or her with a bargepole, I thought you might want to check it out.'

'What sort of irregularities?'

'Small ones,' said Bradshaw, handing me a sheet of paper. 'Nothing you'd notice from the Outland unless you were a committed fan. I'm thinking it might be the early stage of a breakdown.'

He didn't mean a breakdown in the Outlander sense. In the BookWorld a breakdown meant an internal collapse of the char-

236

acter's pattern of reason – the rules that made them predictable and understandable. Some, like Lucy Deane, collapsed spontaneously and with an annoying regularity; others just crumbled slowly from within, usually as a result of irreconcilable conflicts within their character. In either case, replacement by a fully trained-up generic was the only option. Of course, it might be nothing and very possibly Thursday1–4 was just angry about being fired and venting her spleen on the co-characters in the series.

'I'll check her out.'

'Good,' said Bradshaw, turning to Zhark and Tiggy-Winkle. 'And you two – I want you all kitted up and ready to try and get into *The Speckled Band* by way of *The Disintegrator Ray* by eighteen hundred hours.'

Bradshaw looked at his clipboard and then vanished. We all stood up.

'Do you want us to come with you?' asked Zhark. 'Strictly speaking you checking up on Thursday1–4 is a "conflict of interest" transgression.'

'I'll be fine,' I said, and the pair of them wished me well and vanished, like Bradshaw, into thin air.

26

Thursday Next

'I was only vaguely consulted when the first four of the Thursday Next books were constructed. I was asked about my car, my house, and even lent them a photo album (which I never got back). I was also introduced to the bland and faceless generic who would eventually become Thursday1–4. The rest was created from newspaper reports and just plucked out of the air. If I'd cared more about how it all was going to turn out, perhaps I would have given them more time.'

After another fruitless argument with the dispatcher at TransGenreTaxis, who told me they'd got two drivers off sick and it wasn't their fault but they would 'see what could be done', I took the lift down to the sixth floor of the Great Library and walked to the section of shelving that carried all five of the Thursday books, from *The Eyre Affair* all the way through to *The Great Samuel Pepys Fiasco*. There was every edition, too – from publisher's proof to hardback, large-print and mass-market paperback. I picked up a copy of *The Eyre Affair*, and looked carefully for a way in – I knew the book was first-person narrative, and having a second me clearly visible to readers would be wildly confusing – if the book wasn't confusing enough already. I soon found what I was looking for: a time lapse of six weeks after Landen's death near the beginning of the book. I scanned the page for the correct place, and using an oblique non-appearing entry method taught to me by Miss Havisham, I slipped unseen into the end of Chapter 1.

I arrived in the written Swindon just as the sun was dipping below the horizon, and I was standing opposite our house in the

239

old town. Or at least it was the *remains* of our house. The fire had just been put out and the building was now a blackened ruin, the still-hot timbers steaming as they were doused with water. Through the twinkling of blue and red emergency lights I could see a small figure sitting in the back of an ambulance, a blanket draped across her shoulders. The legal necessity of removing Landen from the series was actually a blessing in disguise for the publishers. It freed their Thursday up romantically and also gave a reason for her psychotic personality. Boy, was this book ever *crap*.

I waited in the crowd for a moment until I could sense the chapter was over, then approached Thursday1–4, who had her back to me and was talking to a badly realised version of Bowden, who in this book was known by the legally unactionable name Crowden Babel.

'Good evening,' I said, and Thursday jumped as though stuck with a cattle-prod.

'What are you doing here?' she asked without turning round.

'Text Grand Central saw a few wrinkles in the narrative and you're too unpleasant for anyone other than me to come and have a look.'

'Yes,' she said, 'everything's fine. It's probably a storycode engine on the fritz. A build-up of irony on the dialogue injectors or something.'

She seemed jittery, but still didn't want to turn and look at me face to face.

'You sure?'

'Of course I'm sure – do you think I don't know my own book? I'm afraid I must go – I've got to run through some lines with the replacement Hades.'

'Wait,' I said, and grabbed her arm. I pulled her round to face . . . *someone else entirely*. It wasn't Thursday1–4. It was a woman with the same colouring and build, clothes and general appearance, but it wasn't her.

'Who the hell are you?' I demanded.

She sighed heavily and shrugged.

'I'm . . . I'm . . . a character *understudy*.'

'I can see that. Do you have a name?'

'Alice-PON-24330,' she replied resignedly.

'This series isn't up for maintenance for years. What are you doing here?'

She bit her lip, looked away and shifted her weight uneasily.

'If she finds I've talked – well, she has a *temper*.'

'And I don't?'

She said nothing. I turned to Crowden Babel.

'Where is she?'

He rubbed his face but said nothing. It seemed I was the only person not frightened by Thursday1–4.

'Listen,' I said to Babel, pointing at Alice-PON-24330, 'she's just an understudy and is like a phone number – replaceable. You're in every book and have a lot more to lose. Now: either you talk to me right here and now and it goes no further or we go to Jurisfiction and thirty tons of prime-quality shit is going to descend on you from a very great height.'

Babel scratched the back of his head.

'She does this every now and then. She thinks the series is too small for her.'

Babel and the ersatz Thursday glanced nervously at one another. There was something else going on. This wasn't just a simple substitution so Thursday1–4 could have a break.

'Somebody better start talking or you'll discover where she gets her temper from. Now: *where has she gone*?'

Babel looked nervously around.

'She came back *furious*. Said you'd fired her on false pretences and she wanted to get some . . . serious payback.'

'What sort of payback?'

241

'I don't know.'

'If you're lying to me . . . !'

'I swear on the life of the Great Panjan—'

'I know where she is,' said the ersatz Thursday in a quiet voice. 'What the hell, when she discovers I've talked to you I'll be dead anyway. She's out . . . in the *real world*!'

This was serious. Substitution and illegal pagerunning was one thing, crossing over to the real world was quite another. I could legally erase her on sight, and the way I felt right now, I—

My thoughts were interrupted because both Crowden and the understudy had looked anxiously towards the burned-out shell of the house. I suddenly had a very nasty thought, and my insides changed to lead. I could barely say the word, but I did:

'*Landen?*'

'Yes,' said the understudy in a soft voice. 'She wanted to know what it was . . . to *love*.'

I felt anger well up inside me. I pulled out my TravelBook and read as I walked towards the house. As I did so, the evening light brightened, the emergency vehicles faded back into fiction and the house, though burned to a husk in *The Eyre Affair*, was suddenly perfect again as I moved back into the real world. My mouth felt dry after the jump and I could feel a headache coming on. I broke into a panicky sweat and dumped my jacket and bag in the front garden but kept my pistol and slipped a spare eraserhead into my back pocket. I very quietly stepped up to the front door and silently slipped the key in the lock.

The house was silent aside from the thumping of my heart, which in my heightened state of anxiety was almost deafening. I had planned to lie in wait for her but a glance down at the hall table made me reappraise the situation. My house keys and distinctive grammasite key fob were already lying where I had left them – *but I still had mine in my hand*. I felt powerfully thirsty, too, and was badly dehydrated – the most annoying side effect of my return to the Outland. I looked through to the kitchen and could see a jug of half-finished squash on the draining board. If I didn't drink something soon, I'd pass out. On the other hand, Thursday1–4 was somewhere in the house, waiting for Landen or rummaging in our sock drawer or something. I silently trod along the downstairs hallway, checked the front room, then went through to the dining room beyond and from there to the kitchen. The only thing I noticed out of place was a book of family holiday snaps open on the coffee table. I moved into the kitchen and was about to take a swig of juice straight from the jug when I heard a noise that turned my blood to ice. I dropped the pitcher, which shattered on the kitchen floor with a concussion that echoed around the house.

Pickwick woke up in her basket and started plocking at everything in sight until she saw who it was, and then went back to sleep. I heard voices upstairs and the sound of footsteps padding across the bedroom floor. I held my pistol at arm's length and walked slowly down the hall to the stairs. The sound that had made me drop the pitcher was Landen, but he had made the sort of sound that only I ever heard him make – something that was for me and me alone.

I rounded the newel post and looked up. Almost immediately Thursday1–4 stepped on to the landing, completely naked and holding her automatic. Fictional she may have been, but out here she was as deadly as any real person. We stared at one another for a moment and she fired. I felt her shot whine past me and embed itself in the door frame. At almost exactly the same time I fired my pistol. There was a low thud and the air wobbled as though momentarily seen through a milk bottle. She jumped back into the bedroom as the wide spread of the eraserhead impacted harmlessly on the walls and stairs – the charge only affected anything textual. She'd know my weapon was single-shot, so I turned on my heels and ran back through the front room, breaking the pistol open to reload. The cartridge ejected with a soft *thwup* and I pulled the spare out of my back pocket and pushed it into the breech. There was a detonation and another whine of a near-miss as I jumped across the breakfast table and snapped the pistol shut with a flick of my wrist. I pulled over the heavy oak kitchen table to shield me and three shots thudded into the wood. I heard the sound of footsteps running away and rose to fire at her retreating form. The dull thud of the eraserhead echoed round the room and there was a mild hiss as it struck its mark. I heard the front door open and I got up – slightly too quickly – and the room went squiffy. I staggered to the sink and drank from the running tap and then, still feeling light headed but tolerably alert, stumbled up the hall to the open front door. There was a small scattering of fine text on the doorstep, and more leading out into the front garden, where I saw her automatic lying on the garden path. I turned and yelled upstairs: 'Stay where you are, Land!' then followed the trail of text to the front gate, where there was a random scattering of letters. I cursed. There wasn't enough here to be fatal – I'd probably just clipped her and caused a small part of her to unravel. It was no big deal – she could have another body part written exclusively for her down in the Well.

My shoulder bag was still where I'd left it in the front garden and I rummaged inside for a spare eraserhead. I slipped the shiny cartridge into the barrel, then stopped. Something was *wrong*. I searched the bag more frantically, then all around the area near by, but found only a light smattering of text. The wounded Thursday1–4 had been here – *and taken my TravelBook*. I looked around, closed the pistol and followed the small trail of letters to the garden gate, where they ended abruptly. I looked out into the empty street. Nothing. She had jumped out, back to where she belonged – and with my TravelBook. My *TravelBook*. I wiped the sweat from my brow and muttered:

'Shit-shit-shit-*SHIT*.'

I turned and ran back to the house but then stopped as I suddenly had a series of terrible thoughts. Thursday1–4's adventures ranged across several years, so she wasn't particularly age specific, so Landen couldn't know that it was not me but my fictional counterpart he'd just made love to. I didn't bear him any malice – I mean, it was not as if he'd slept with another woman or anything. But because he knew nothing about Jurisfiction and it was better for our relationship that he *never* knew, there was only one course of action I could take.

'Hang on, Land,' I yelled upstairs, 'I'm okay. Just stay where you are.'

'Why?' he yelled back.

'Just do as I ask, sweetheart.'

I grabbed the dustpan and brush and hurriedly swept up the text that littered the front step and the path, and as I heard the distant wail of the police sirens I went back indoors, took off all my clothes, stashed them behind the sofa and ran upstairs.

'What's going on?' asked Land, who had just got his leg and trousers on. I wrapped myself in a dressing gown but couldn't look at him, and just sat at the dressing table, clenching and unclenching my fists to try to control the violent thoughts. Then I realised: after what she'd done, I could think about wringing her badly written neck as much as I wanted. I was a woman wronged. Dangerously violent thoughts were *allowed*. I'd get her for this, but I was in no hurry. She had nowhere to go. I knew *exactly* where I could find her.

'Nothing's going on,' I said in a quiet voice, 'everything's fine.'

Bound to the Outland

'Although we never really saw eye to eye with the local police force when we were SpecOps, we always used to help them out if they got into a jam, and the young ones never forgot it. It would be hard to, really, when some lunatic plucks you from the jaws of a werewolf or something. Because of this I was still granted favours in return. Not parking tickets, unfortunately – just the big stuff.'

By the time the police had arrived I had regained control of myself. I picked up Thursday1–4's clothes with a disdainful finger and thumb and deposited them in the laundry basket. I would take them out and burn them later that evening. I went through the pockets of her jacket but found only an empty wallet and a few coins. I knew I was going to have to admit owning her automatic, so had to hope they would take my previous exemplary conduct into account before citing me on any illegal firearms charges. While I explained it all to the cops, Landen called Joffy's partner Miles to get him to pick up the girls from school, and we eventually tracked Friday down to Mum's, where he had been discussing the merits of the guitar riff on the second track of *Hosing the Dolly* with his aunt.

'So let me get this straight,' said Detective Inspector Jamison an hour later, thumbing through his notes, 'you were both upstairs – er – *naked* when you heard a noise. You, Mrs Parke-Laine-Next, went downstairs to investigate with an illegally held Glock nine-millimetre. You saw this man whom you identified as "Felix8", an associate of the deceased Acheron Hades you last met sixteen years ago. He was armed and you fired at him once when he was standing at the door, once when he was running to the kitchen, then three times as he hid behind the kitchen table. He then made his escape from the house without firing a single shot. Is that correct?'

'Quite correct, Officer.'

'Hm,' he said, and his sergeant whispered something in his ear and handed him a fax. Jamison looked at it, then at me.

'You're *sure* it was Felix8?'

'Yes – why?'

He placed the fax on the table and slid it across.

'The body of missing father-of-two Danny Chance was discovered in a shallow grave in the Savernake forest three years ago. It was skeletal by then and only identifiable by his dental records.'

'That's not possible,' I murmured, with good reason. Even if he hadn't been in the house this afternoon, I had certainly seen him yesterday.

'I know Hades and Felix are tied up in all manner of weird shit, so I'm not going to insist you *didn't* see him, but I thought you should know this.'

'Thank you, Officer,' I muttered, reading through the report, which was unequivocal; it even said the bones had been in the ground a good ten years. Aornis had been right – Cocytus *had* killed him like a stray dog.

Inspector Jamison turned to Landen.

'Mr Parke-Laine? May we speak to you now?'

They finally left at nine in the evening and we called Miles to bring the kids back. We'd been given the all-clear to tidy up, and to be honest it didn't sound as though they were going to make a big deal of it. It didn't look as if they would even bother to prosecute; they knew about Felix8 – everyone did. He, Hades and Aornis were as much a part of popular culture as Robin Hood. And that was it. They took the Glock 9mm, privately told me that it was an honour to meet me and that I could expect their report to be lost before being passed to the prosecutor, and were gone.

'Darling?' said Landen as soon as the kids had been safely returned home.

'Yes?'

'Something's bothering you.'

'You mean aside from having an amoral lunatic who died fifteen years ago try to kill us?'

'Yes. There's something else on your mind.'

Damn. Rumbled. Lucky I had *several* things on my mind I could call upon.

'I went to visit Aornis.'

'You did? Why?'

'It was about Felix8. I should have told you: he was hanging around the house yesterday. Millon spotted him and Spike nabbed him – but he escaped. I thought Aornis might have an idea why he's suddenly emerged after all these years.'

'Did Aornis . . . say anything about us?' asked Landen. 'Friday, Me, Tuesday, Jenny?'

'She asked how everyone was, but only in an ironic way. I don't think she was concerned in the least – quite the opposite.'

'Did she say anything else?'

I turned to look at him. He was gazing at me with such concern that I rested a hand on his cheek.

'Sweetheart – what's the matter? She can't harm us any longer.'

'No,' said Landen with a sigh, 'she can't. I just wondered if she said anything – anything at all. Even if you only remembered it later.'

I frowned. Landen knew about Aornis's powers because I'd told him, but his specific interest seemed somehow *unwarranted*.

'Yeah. She said that she was going to bust out with the help of someone "on the outside".'

249

He took my hands in his and stared into my eyes.

'Thursday – sweetheart – promise me something?'

I laughed at his earnestness but stopped when I saw he was serious.

'Two minds with but a single thought,' I told him, 'two hearts that beat as one.'

'That was good – who said that?'

'Mycroft.'

'Ah! Well, here it is: don't let Aornis out.'

'Why should I want to do that?'

'Trust me, darling. Even if you forget your own name, remember this: *don't let Aornis out.*'

'Babes—'

But he rested his finger on my lips, and I was quiet. Aornis was the least of my worries. Without my TravelBook I was marooned in the Outland.

We had dinner late. Even Friday was vaguely impressed by the three bullet holes in the table. They were so close they almost looked like one. When he saw them he said:

'Nice grouping, Mum.'

'Firearms are no joking matter, young man.'

'That's our Thursday,' said Landen with a smile. 'When she shoots up our furniture she does as little damage as possible.'

I looked at them all, and laughed. It was an emotional release and tears sprang to my eyes. I helped myself to more salad and looked at Friday. There was still the possibility of his replacement by the Friday-that-could-have-been hanging over him. The thing was, I couldn't do anything about it. There's never anywhere to hide from the ChronoGuard. But the other Friday had told me I had forty-eight hours until they might attempt such a thing, and that wasn't up until mid-morning the day after tomorrow.

'Fri,' I said, 'have you thought any more about the Time Industry?'

'Lots,' he said, 'and the answer's still no.'

Landen and I exchanged looks.

'Have you ever wondered,' remarked Friday in a languid monotone from behind a curtain of oily hair, 'how nostalgia isn't what it used to be?'

I smiled; dopey witticisms at least showed he was *trying* to be clever, even if for the greater part of the day he was asleep.

'Yes,' I replied, 'and imagine a world where there were no hypothetical situations.'

'I'm *serious*,' he said, mildly annoyed.

'Sorry!' I replied. 'It's just difficult to know what you're thinking when I can't see your face; I might as well converse with the side of a yak.'

He parted his hair so I could see his eyes. He looked a lot like his father did at that age. Not that I knew him then, of course, but from photographs.

'Nostalgia used to have a minimum twenty years before it kicked in,' he said in all seriousness, 'but now it's getting shorter and shorter. By the late eighties people were doing seventies stuff, but by the mid-nineties the eighties revival thing was in full swing. It's now 2002 and already people are talking about the nineties – soon nostalgia will catch up with the present and we won't have any need for it.'

'Good thing too, if you ask me,' I said. 'I got rid of all my seventies rubbish as soon as I could and never regretted it for a second.'

There was an indignant *plock* from Pickwick.

'Present company excepted.'

'I think the seventies are underrated,' said Landen. 'Admittedly fashion wasn't terrific, but there's been no better decade for sitcoms.'

'Where's Jenny?'

'I took her dinner up to her,' said Friday. 'She said she needed to do her homework.'

251

I frowned as I thought of something, but Landen clapped his hands together and said:

'Oh yes: did you hear that the British bobsleigh team has been disqualified for using the banned force "gravity" to enhance performance?'

'No!'

'Apparently so. And it transpires that the illegal use of gravity to boost speed is endemic within most downhill winter sports.'

'I wondered how they managed to go so fast,' I replied thoughtfully.

Much later that night, when the lights were out, I was staring at the glow of the street lights on the ceiling, and thinking about Thursday1-4 and what I'd do to her when I caught her. It wasn't terribly pleasant.

'Land?' I whispered in the darkness.

'Yes?'

'That time we . . . made love today.'

'What about it?'

'I was just thinking. How did you rate it – y'know, on a one to ten?'

'Truthfully?'

'Truthfully.'

'You won't be pissed off at me?'

'Promise.'

There was a pause. I held my breath.

'We've had better. *Much* better. In fact, I thought you were pretty terrible.'

I hugged him. At least there was one piece of good news today.

28

The Discreet Charm of the Outland

> **'The real charm of the Outland was the richness of detail
> and the *texture*.** In the BookWorld a pig is generally just pink
> and goes "oink". Because of this most fictional pigs are simply a
> uniform flesh colour without any of the tough bristles and innu-
> merable scabs and skin abrasions, shit and dirt that make a pig a
> pig. And it's not just pigs. A carrot is simply a rod of orange.
> Sometimes living in the BookWorld is like living in Legoland.'

The Stupidity Surplus had been beaten into second place by the
news that the militant wing of the no-choice movement had been
causing trouble in Manchester. Windows were broken, cars over-
turned and there were at least a dozen arrests. With a nation driven
by the concept of 'choice', a growing faction of citizens who
thought life was simpler when options were limited had banded
together into what they called the 'no-choicers' and demanded the
choice to have no choice. Prime Minister Redmond Van de Poste
condemned the violence but explained that the choice of 'choice'
over 'just better services' was something the *previous* administration
had chosen, and was thus itself a 'no-choice' principle for the current
administration. Alfredo Traficcone, MP, leader of the opposition
'Prevailing Wind' party, was quick to jump on the bandwagon,
proclaiming that it was the inalienable right of every citizen to have
the choice over whether they had choice or not. The no-choicers
had suggested that there should be a referendum to settle the matter
once and for all, something that the opposition 'choice' faction had
no option but to agree with. More sinisterly, the militant wing
known only as NOPTION were keen to go farther, and demanded

that there should be only one option on the ballot paper – the no-choice one.

It was 8.30 and the girls had already gone to school.

'Jenny didn't eat her toast again,' I said, setting the plate with its uneaten contents next to the sink. 'That girl hardly eats a thing.'

'Leave it outside Friday's door,' said Landen. 'He can have it for lunch when he gets up – *if* he gets up.'

The front doorbell had rung, and I checked on who it might be through the front-room windows before opening it to reveal . . . Friday. The *other* Friday.

'Hello!' I said cheerily. 'Would you like to come in?'

'I'm in a bit of a hurry,' he replied. 'I just wondered whether you'd thought about my offer of replacement yesterday? Hi, Dad!'

Landen had joined us at the door.

'Hello, son.'

'This,' I said by way of introduction, 'is the Friday I was telling you about – the one we were meant to have.'

'At your service,' said Friday politely. 'And your answer? I'm sorry to push you on this but time travel has still to be invented and we have to look very carefully at our options.'

Landen and I looked at one another. We'd already made up our mind.

'The answer's no, Sweetpea. We're going to keep *our* Friday.'

Friday's face fell and his manner changed abruptly.

'This is so typical of you. Here I am, a respected member of the ChronoGuard, and you're still treating me like I'm a kid!'

'Friday—!'

'How stupid can you both be? The history of the world hangs in the balance and all you can do is worry about your lazy shitbag of a son.'

'You talk like that to your mother and you can go to your room.'

'He *is* in his room, Land.'

'Right. Well – you know what I mean.'

Friday snorted, glared at us both, told me that I really shouldn't call him 'Sweetpea' any more and walked off, slamming the garden gate behind him. I turned to Landen.

'Are we doing the right thing?'

'Friday told us to dissuade him from joining the ChronoGuard, and that's what we're doing.'

I narrowed my eyes, trying to remember.

'He did? When?'

'At our wedding bash? When Lavoisier turned up looking for your father?'

'Shit,' I said, suddenly remembering. Lavoisier was my least favourite ChronoGuard operative and on that occasion he had a partner with him – a lad of about twenty-five who had looked vaguely familiar. We figured it out several years later. It was Friday *himself*, and his advice to us was unequivocal: 'If you ever have a son who wants to be in the ChronoGuard, try and dissuade him.' Perhaps it wasn't just a moan – perhaps it had been . . . a *warning*.

Landen placed a hand on my waist and said:

'I think we should follow his best advice and see where it leaves us.'

'And the end of time?'

'Didn't your father say that the world was *always* five minutes from total annihilation? Besides, it's not until Friday evening. It'll work itself out.'

I took the tram into work and was so deep in thought I missed my stop and had to walk back from MycroTech. Without my TravelBook I was effectively stuck in the real world, but instead of feeling a sense of profound loss as I had expected, I felt something more akin to *relief*. In my final day as the LBOCS I had scotched any chance of book interactivity or the pre-emptive strike on

255

Speedy Muffler and the ramshackle Racy Novel, and the only worrying loose end was dealing with slutty bitchface Thursday1–4. That was if she hadn't been erased on sight for making an unauthorised trip to the Outland. Well, I could always hope. Jurisfiction had got on without me for centuries and would doubtless continue to do so. There was another big plus point too: I wasn't lying to Landen quite as much. Okay, I still did a bit of SpecOps work, but at least this way I could downgrade my fibs from 'outrageous' to a more manageable 'whopping'. All of a sudden, I felt really quite happy – and I didn't often feel that way. If there hadn't been a major problem with Acme's overdraft and the potential for a devastating chronoclasm in two and a half days, everything might have been just perfect.

'You look happy,' said Bowden as I walked into the office at Acme.

'Aren't I always?'

'No,' he said, 'hardly at all.'

'Well, this is the new me. Have you noticed how much the birds are singing this morning?'

'They always sing like that.'

'Then . . . the sky is always that blue, yes?'

'Yes. May I ask what's brought on this sudden change?'

'The BookWorld. I've stopped going there. It's over.'

'Well,' said Bowden, 'that's *excellent* news!'

'It is, isn't it? More time for Landen and the kids.'

'No,' said Bowden, choosing his words carefully, 'I mean excellent news for Acme – we might finally get rid of the backlog.'

'Of undercover SpecOps work?'

'Of *carpets.*'

'You mean you can make a profit selling carpets?' I asked, having never really given it a great deal of thought.

'Have you seen the order books? They're full. More work than we can handle. Everyone needs floor coverings, Thurs – and if you can give some of your time to get these orders filled, then we won't need the extra cash from your illegal cheese activities.'

He handed me a clipboard.

'All these customers need to be contacted and given the best deal we can.'

'Which is?'

'Just smile, chat, take the measurements and I'll do the rest.'

'Then *you* go.'

'No, the big selling point for Acme is that Thursday Next – the Z-4 *celebrity* Thursday Next – comes and talks to you about your floor-covering needs. That's how we keep our heads above water. That's how we can support all these ex-SpecOps employees.'

'C'mon,' I said doubtfully, 'ex-celebrities don't do retail.'

'After the disaster of *The Eyre Affair* movie, Lola Vavoom started a chain of builder's merchants.'

'She did, didn't she.'

I took the clipboard and stared at the list. It was long. Business *was* good. But Bowden's attention was suddenly elsewhere.

'Is that who I think it is?' he asked, looking towards the front of the store. I followed his gaze. Standing next to the cushioned linoleum display stand was a man in a long dark coat. When he saw us watching him he reached into his pocket and flashed a badge of some sort.

'Shit,' I murmured under my breath, 'Flanker.'

'He probably wants to buy a carpet,' said Bowden with a heavy helping of misplaced optimism.

Commander Flanker was our old nemesis from SO-1, the SpecOps department that policed other SpecOps departments. Flanker had adapted to the disbanding of the service well. Before, he made life miserable for SpecOps agents he thought were corrupt, and now he made life miserable for *ex*-SpecOps agents he thought were corrupt. We had crossed swords many times in the past, but not since the disbandment. We regarded it as a good test of our discretion and secrecy that we had never seen him at Acme Carpets. Then again, perhaps we were kidding ourselves. He might know all about us but thought flushing out renegade operatives just wasn't worth his effort – especially when we were actually offering a service that no one else wanted to offer.

I walked quickly to the front of the shop.

'Good morning, Ms Next,' he said, glancing with ill-disguised mirth at my name embroidered above the company logo on my jacket. 'Literary Detective at SO-27 to carpet fitter? Quite a fall, don't you think?'

'It depends on your point of view,' I said cheerfully. 'Everyone needs carpets – but not everyone needs SpecOps. Is this a social call?'

'My wife has read all your books.'

'They're not *my* books,' I told him in an exasperated tone. 'I had no say at all in their content – for the first four, anyway.'

'Those were the ones she liked. The violent ones with all the sex and death.'

'Did you come all this way to give me your wife's analysis of my books?'

'No,' he said, 'that was just the friendly breaking-the-ice part.'

'It isn't working. Is there a floor covering I could interest you in?'

'Axminster.'

'We can certainly help you with *that*,' I replied professionally. 'Living room or bedroom? We have some very hard-wearing wool/acrylic at extremely competitive prices – and we've a special this week on underlay and free fitting.'

'It was Axminster *Purple* I was referring to,' he said slowly, staring at me intently. My heart jumped but I masked it well. Axminster Purple wasn't a carpet at all, of course, although to be honest there probably *was* an Axminster in purple, if I looked. No, he was referring to the semi-exotic cheese, one that I'd been trading in only a couple of days earlier. Flanker showed me his badge. He was CEA – the Cheese Enforcement Agency.

'You're not here for the carpets, are you?'

'I know you have form for cheese smuggling, Next. There was a lump of Rhayder Speckled found beneath a Hispano-Suiza in '86, and you've been busted twice for possession since then. The second time you were caught with six kilos of Streaky Durham. You were lucky to be only fined for possession and not trading without a licence.'

'Did you come here to talk about my past misdemeanours?'

'No. I've come to you for information. While cheese smuggling is illegal, it's considered a low priority. The CEA has always been a small department more interested in collecting duty than banging up harmless cheeseheads. That's all changed.'

'It has?'

'I'm afraid so,' replied Flanker grimly. 'There's a new cheese on the block. Something powerful enough to make a user's head vanish in a ball of fire.'

'That's a figure of speech for "really powerful", right?'

'No,' said Flanker with deadly seriousness, 'the victim's head really *does* vanish in a ball of fire. It's a killer, Next – and addictive. It's apparently the finest and most powerful cheese ever designed.'

This was worrying. I never regarded my cheese smuggling as anything more than harmless fun, cash for Acme and to supply something that should be legal anyway. If a cheese that I'd supplied had killed someone, I would face the music. Mind you, I'd tried most of what I'd flogged and it was, after all, only cheese. Okay, so the taste of a particularly powerful cheese might render you unconscious or make your tongue numb for a week, but it never killed anyone – until now.

'Does this cheese have a name?' I asked, wondering whether there had been a bad batch of Machynlleth Wedi Marw.

'It only has a code name: X-14. Rumour says it's so powerful that it has to be kept chained to the floor. We managed to procure a half-ounce. A technician dropped it by mistake and this was the result.'

He showed me a photograph of a smoking ruin.

'The remains of our central cheese-testing facility.'

He put the photograph away and stared at me. Of course, I *had* seen some X-14. It had been chained up in the back of Pryce's truck the night of the cheese buy. Owen had declined to even show it to me. I'd traded with him every month for over eight years and I never thought he was the sort of person to knowingly peddle anything dangerous – he was like me: someone who just loved cheese. I wouldn't snitch on him; not yet – not before I had more information.

'I don't know anything,' I said at length, 'but I can make enquiries.'

Flanker seemed to be satisfied with this, handed me his card and said in a stony voice: 'I'll expect your call.'

He turned and walked out of the store to a waiting Range Rover and drove off.

'Trouble for us?' asked Bowden as soon as I had returned.

'No,' I replied thoughtfully, 'trouble for me.'

He sighed. 'That's a relief.'

I took a deep breath and thought for a moment. Communications into the Socialist Republic of Wales were non-existent – when I wanted to contact Pryce I had to use a short-wave wireless transmitter at prearranged times. There was nothing I could do for at least forty-eight hours.

'So,' continued Bowden, handing me the clipboard with the list of people wanting quotes on it, 'how about some Acme celebrity carpet stuff?'

'What about SpecOps work?' I asked. 'How's that looking?'

'Stig's still on the case of the Diatrymas and has at least a half-dozen outstanding chimeras to track down. Spike has got a few biters on the books and there's talk of another SEB over in Reading.'

It was getting desperate. I loved Acme, but only insofar as it was excellent cover and I never had to actually do anything carpet related.

'And us? The ex–Literary Detectives?'

'Still nothing, Thursday.'

'What about Mrs Mattock over in the Old Town? She still wants us to find her first editions, surely?'

'No,' said Bowden, 'she called yesterday and said she was selling her books and replacing them with cable TV – she wanted to watch *England's Funniest Chainsaw Mishaps*.'

'And I felt so good just now.'

'Face it,' said Bowden sadly, 'books are finished. No one wants to invest the time in them any more.'

'I don't believe you,' I replied, an optimist to the end. 'I reckon if we went over to the Booktastic! megastore they'd tell us that books are still being sold hand over fist to hardcore story aficionados. In fact, I'll bet you that tin of biscuits you've got hidden under your desk that you think no one knows about.'

'And if they're not?'

'I'll spend a day fitting carpets and pressing flesh as the Acme Carpets celebrity saleswoman.'

It was a deal. Acme was on a trading estate with about twenty or so outlets but, unusually, it was the only carpet showroom – we always suspected Spike might have a hand in scaring off the competition, but we never saw him do it. Between us and Booktastic! there were three sporting goods outlets all selling exactly the same goods at exactly the same price, since they were three branches of the same store, with the same sales staff, too. The two discount electrical shops actually *were* competitors, but still spookily managed to sell the same goods at the same price, although 'sell' in this context actually meant offering 'brief custodianship between outlet and landfill'.

'Hmm,' I said as we stood inside the entrance of Booktastic! and stared at the floor display units liberally stacked with CDs, DVDs, computer games, peripherals and specialist magazines. 'I'm sure there was a book in here last time I came in. Excuse me?'

A shop assistant stopped and stared at us in a vacant sort of way.

'I was wondering if you had any books.'

'Any *what*?'

'Books. Y'know – about so big and full of words arranged in a specific order to give the effect of reality?'

'You mean DVDs?'

'No, I mean *books*. They're kind of old fashioned.'

'Ah!' she said. 'What you mean is *videotapes*.'

'No, what I mean is *books*.'

We'd exhausted the sum total of her knowledge, so she went into default mode:

'You'll have to see the manager. She's in the coffee shop.'

'Which one?' I asked, looking around. There appeared to be three – and it wasn't Booktastic!'s biggest outlet, either.

'That one.'

We thanked her and walked past boxed sets of obscure sixties TV series that were better – and safer – within the rose-tinted glow of memory.

'This is all so wrong,' I said, beginning to think I might lose the bet. 'Less than five years ago this place was all books and nothing else. What the hell's going on?'

We arrived at the coffee shop and couldn't see the manager, until we noticed that they had opened a smaller branch of the coffee shop actually *inside* the existing one, and named it 'X-press' or 'On-the-Go' or 'More Profit' or something.

'Thursday Next,' I said to the manager, whose name we discovered was Dawn.

'A great pleasure,' she replied. 'I did *so* love your books – especially the ones with all the killing and gratuitous sex.'

'I'm not really like that in real life,' I replied. 'My friend Bowden and I wondered if you'd sold many books recently, or failing that, if you have any, or know what one is?'

'I'm sure there're a few somewhere,' she said, and with a 'woman on a mission' stride we went over most of the outlet. We walked past computer peripherals, stationery, chocolate, illuminated world globes and pretty gift boxes to put things in until we found a single rack of long-forgotten paperbacks on a shelf below the boxed set of *Hale & Pace Out-takes Volumes 1–8* and *The Very Best of Little and Large*, which Bowden said was an oxymoron.

'Here we are!' she said, wiping away the cobwebs and dust. 'I suppose we must have the full collection of every book ever written?'

'Very nearly,' I replied. 'Thanks for your help.'

And that was how I found myself in an Acme van with Spike, who had been coerced by Bowden to do an honest day's carpeting in exchange for a week's washing for him and Betty. I hadn't been out on the road with Spike for a number of years, either for the weird shit we used to do from time to time, or any carpet-related work, so he was particularly talkative. As we drove to our first fitting, he told me about a recent assignment:

'. . . so I says to him: "Yo, Dracula! Have you come to watch the eclipse with us?" You should have seen his face. He was back in his coffin quicker than shit from a goose, and then when he heard us laughing he came back out and said with his arms folded:

"I suppose you think that's funny?" and I said that I thought it *was* perhaps the funniest thing I'd seen for years, especially since he tripped and fell head first in his coffin, and then he got all shitty and tried to bite me, so I rammed a sharpened stake through his heart and struck his head from his body.'

He laughed and shook his head.

'Oh, man, did *that* crease us up.'

'My amusement might have ended with the sharpened stake thing,' I confessed, 'but I like the idea of Dracula falling flat on his face.'

'He did that a lot. Clumsy as hell. That "biting the neck" thing? He was going for the *breast* and missed. Now he pretends that's what he was aiming for all along. Jerk. Is this number eight?'

It was. We parked up, got out and knocked at the door.

'Major Pickles?' said Spike as a very elderly man with a kindly expression answered the door. He was small and slender and in good health. His snow-white hair was immaculately combed, a pencil moustache graced his upper lip, and he was wearing a blazer with a regimental badge sewn on the breast.

'Yes?'

'Good morning. We're from Acme Carpets.'

'Jolly good!' said Major Pickles, who hobbled into the house and ushered us to a room that was devoid of any sort of floor covering. 'It's to go down there,' he said, pointing at the floor.

'Right,' said Spike, who I could tell was in a mischievous mood. 'My associate here will begin carpeting operations while I view the selection of tea and biscuits on offer. Thursday – the carpet.'

I sighed and surveyed the room, which was decorated with stripy green wallpaper and framed pictures of Major Pickles' notable wartime achievements – it looked as if he had been quite a formidable soldier. It seemed a shame that he was in a rather miserable house in one of the more run-down areas of Swindon. On the plus side, at least he was getting a new carpet. I went to the van and brought in the toolbox, vacuum cleaner, grippers and a nail gun. I was just putting on my knee pads when Spike and Pickles came back into the room.

'Jaffa cakes,' exclaimed Major Pickles, placing a tray on the windowsill. 'Mr Stoker here said that you were allergic to anything without chocolate on it.'

'You're very kind to indulge my partner's bizarre and somewhat disrespectful sense of humour,' I said. 'Thank you.'

'Well,' he said in a kindly manner, 'I'll leave you to get on, then.'

And he tottered out of the door. As soon as he had gone Spike leaned close to me and said: 'Did you see that!?!'

'See what?'

He opened the door a crack and pointed at Pickles, who was limping down the corridor to the kitchen.

'His *feet*.'

I looked, and the hair on the back of my neck rose. There was a reason Major Pickles was hobbling – just visible beneath the hem of his trouser leg were *hoofs*.

'Right,' said Spike as I looked up at him. 'The cloven one.'

'Major Pickles is the *Devil*?'

'*Nah!*' said Spike, sniggering as if I were a simpleton. 'If that was Mephistopheles you'd *really* know about it. Firstly, the air would be thick with the choking stench of brimstone and decay and we'd be knee deep in the departed souls of the damned, writhing in perpetual agony as their bodies were repeatedly pierced with the barbed spears of the tormentors. And secondly, we'd never have got Jaffa cakes; probably Rich Tea or those ones with "Nice" written on them – but which aren't.'

'Yeah, I hate them too. But listen, if not Satan, then who?'

Spike closed the door carefully.

'A demi-devil or junior demon or something, sent to precipitate mankind's fall into the eternal river of effluent that is the bowels of hell. Let's see if we can't get a make on this guy. Have a look in the backyard and tell me if you see anything unusual.'

I peered out of the window as Spike looked around the room.

'I can see the old carpet piled up in the carport,' I said, 'and an almost brand-new washing machine.'

'How does the carpet look?'

'It seems perfect.'

'Figures. Look here.'

He pointed to an old Huntley & Palmer biscuit tin that was sitting on the mantelpiece. The lid was half off and clearly visible inside was a wad of banknotes.

'Bingo!' said Spike, drawing out the hefty wad. They were all £50 pound notes – easily a grand. 'This is demi-demon Raum, if I'm not mistaken. He tempts men to eternal damnation by the sin of theft.'

'Come on!' I said, mildly sceptical. 'If Lucifer has everyone that had stolen something, he'd have more souls than he'd know what to deal with.'

'You're right,' agreed Spike, 'the parameters of sin have become blurred over the years. A theft worthy of damnation has to be deceitful, cowardly and *loathsome* – like from a charming and defence-less pensioner war veteran. So what Raum does is stash the real Major Pickles in a cupboard somewhere, assume his form, and leave the cash in plain sight until some poor boob chances his luck. He counts his blessings, has a few nights on the tiles and forgets all about it until Judgement Day. And then – *shazam!* He's having his eyeballs gouged out with a spoon. And then again. And again . . . and *again.*'

'I . . . get the picture. So this Raum guy's a big deal, right?'

'Nah – pretty much a tiddler,' said Spike, replacing the money. 'First sphere, tenth throne – any lower and he'd be in the second hierarchy and confined to hell rather than doing the cushy number up here, harvesting souls for Lucifer and attempting to engineer the fall of man.'

'Is there a lot of this about?' I asked. 'Demons, I mean – hanging around ready to tempt us?'

Spike shrugged.

'In Swindon? No. And there'll be even less if I can do anything about it.'

He flipped open his mobile and dialled a number, then pointed at the floor.

'You'd better get those grippers down if we're to finish by lunchtime. I'm kidding. He doesn't want a carpet; we're only here to be tempted – remember all that stuff in the backyard? Hi, Betty? It's Dad. I've got a five-five in progress with a tenth-throner name of Raum. Will you have a look in Wheatley's and see how to cast him out? Thanks.' He paused for a moment, looked at me and added: 'Perhaps it wasn't Felix8 at all. Perhaps he was . . . *Felix9*. After all, the linking factor between the Felixes was only ever his face, yes?'

'Good point,' I said, wondering quite how Spike could be so relaxed about the whole demon thing he could be thinking about the Felix problem at the same time.

'Betty?' said Spike into his mobile. 'I'm still here . . . Cold steel? No problem. Have you done your homework? . . . Well, you'd better get started. One more thing: Bowden said he'd do the washing for us, so get all the curtains down . . . Love you too. 'Bye.'

He snapped his mobile shut and looked around the room for something made of steel. He picked up the nail gun, muttered 'Damn, sherardised' then rummaged in the toolbox. The best he could find was a long screwdriver but rejected this because it was chrome plated.

'Can't we just go away and deal with Raum later?'

'Thursday,' said Spike in a quiet voice, 'I think he's on to us.'

'Doesn't work that way,' he said, peering out of the window to see whether there was anything steel within reach, which there wasn't. 'We deal with this clown right now or not at all.'

He opened the door a crack and peered out.

'Okay, he's in the front room. Here's the plan: you gain his attention while I go into the kitchen and find something made of steel, then I send him back to the second sphere.'

'What if you're mistaken?' I asked. 'He might be suffering from some – I don't know – rare genetic disorder that makes him grow hoofs.'

Spike fixed me with a piercing stare.

'Have you even *heard* of such a thing?'

'No.'

'Then let's do it. I hope there's a Sabatier or a tyre iron or something – it'll be a pretty messy job with an egg whisk.'

So while Spike slipped into the kitchen, I went to the door of the front room, where Major Pickles was watching TV. He was seated on a floral-patterned settee with a cup of tea and a slice of fruitcake on a table near by.

'Hello, young lady,' he said amiably, 'done already?'

'No,' I said, trying to appear unflustered, 'but we're going to use the nail gun and it might make some noise.'

'Oh, that's quite all right,' he said. 'I was at Tobruk, you know.'

'Really? What was it like?'

'My dear girl, the *noise* – and you couldn't get a decent drink anywhere.'

'So a nail gun is no problem?'

'Nostalgic, my dear – fire away.'

Spike hadn't yet reappeared, so I carried on:

'Good. Right, well – hey, is that *Bedazzled* you're watching?'

'Yes,' he replied, 'the Brendan Fraser version – *such* a broad head, but very funny.'

269

'I met him once,' I said, stalling for time, 'at the launch party for *The Eyre Affair* movie. He played the part of—'

'Thursday?'

It was Spike, calling from the kitchen. I smiled and said to Major Pickles:

'Would you excuse me for just one moment?'

Pickles nodded politely and I walked to the kitchen, which was, strangely enough, empty. Not a sign of Spike anywhere. It had two doors and the only other entrance, the back door, had a broom leaning up against it. I was about to open the fridge to look for him when I heard a voice.

'I'm up here.'

I looked up. Spike was pinned to the ceiling with thirty or so knives, scissors and other sharp objects, all stuck through the periphery of his clothing and making him look like the victim of an overenthusiastic circus knife-thrower.

'What are you doing?' I hissed. 'We're meant to be dealing with the Raum guy.'

'What am I *doing*? Oh, just admiring the view – why, what do you *think* I'm doing?'

I shrugged.

'Thursday,' added Spike in a quiet voice, 'I think he's on to us.'

I turned to the door and jumped in fright because Major Pickles had crept up without me realising. But it wasn't the little old gent I had seen a few moments ago; this Pickles had two large horns sticking out of his head, yellow eyes like a cat's, and was dressed in a loincloth. He was lean, muscular and with shiny bright red skin – a bit like those ducks that hang in Chinese restaurant windows. He also smelled strongly of sewage.

'Well,' said Raum in a deep rasping voice that sounded like a tin of rusty nails, 'Thursday Next. What a surprise!' He looked up.

'And Mr Stoker, I presume – believe me, you are *very* unpopular where I come from!'

I made a move to thump him but he was too quick and a moment later I was thrown to the ceiling with a force so hard it cracked the Artex. I didn't drop; I was held, face pointing down, not by any knives or scissors, but the action of an unearthly force that made it feel as if I were being sat upon by a small walrus.

'Two unsullied souls,' growled Raum sadly. 'To His Infernal Majesty, *worthless*.'

'I'm warning you,' said Spike, with a masterful display of misplaced optimism, 'give yourself up and I'll not be too hard on you.'

'SILENCE!' roared Raum, so loudly that two of the kitchen windows cracked. He laughed a deep, demonic cackle, then carried on: 'Just so that this morning hasn't been a complete waste, I am prepared to offer a deal: either you both die in an exceptionally painful manner and I relinquish all rights to your souls, or one gives himself to me . . . and I free the other!'

'How about a game of chess?' suggested Spike.

'Oh no!' said Raum, wagging a reproachful finger. 'We don't fall for *that* one any more. Now, who's it going to be?'

'You can take me,' said Spike.

'No!' I cried, but Raum merely laughed. He laughed long and loud. He laughed again. Then some more. He laughed so long, in fact, that Spike and I looked at one another. But still Raum laughed. The plates and cups cracked on the dresser, and glasses that were upside down on the draining board shattered. More laughter. Louder, longer, harder, until suddenly and quite without warning he exploded into a million tiny fragments that filled the small kitchen like a red mist. Released from the ceiling, I fell to the floor via the kitchen table, which was luckily a bit frail, and had nothing on it. I was slightly dazed but got up to see . . . the *real* Major Pickles, standing

271

where Raum had been, still holding the steel bayonet that had dispatched the demon back to hell.

'Hah!' said the elderly little gent with an aggressive twinkle in his eye. 'They don't like the taste of cold steel up 'em!'

He had several days of stubble, was dressed in torn pyjamas and covered in soil.

'Are you okay?'

'He thought he could keep me prisoner in the garden shed,' replied the pensioner resolutely, 'but it was only fifteen yards nor'-nor'-east under the patio to the geranium bed.'

'You dug your way out?'

'Yes, and would have been quicker too if I'd had a dessert spoon instead of this.'

He showed me a very worn and bent teaspoon.

'Or a spade?' I ventured.

'Hah!' he snorted contemptuously. 'Spades are for losers.' He looked up and noticed Spike. 'I say, you there, sir – get off my ceiling this minute.'

'Nothing I'd like better.'

So we got Spike down and explained as best we could to the sprightly nonagenarian just who Raum was, something that he seemed to have very little trouble understanding.

'Good Lord, man!' he said at last. 'You mean I killed a demon? There's a notch for the cricket bat and no mistake.'

'Sadly, no,' replied Spike, 'you just relegated him to the second sphere – he'll not reappear on earth for a decade or two, and will get a serious lashing from the Dark One into the bargain.'

'Better than he deserves,' replied Major Pickles, checking the biscuit barrel. 'The rotten blighter has pigged all my Jaffa cakes.'

'Spike,' I said, pointing at a desk diary I had found on the counter, 'we're not the only people to have had an appointment this morning.'

He and Major Pickles bent over to have a look, and there it

was. This morning was the first of three days of soul entrapment that Raum had planned for the home-call professionals of Swindon, and we had been the third potential damnees. The first, an electrician, Raum had crossed out, and he had made a note: 'sickeningly pleasant'. The next, however, was due to install a new washing machine, and Raum had written three ticks next to the name of the company: Wessex Kitchens. I rummaged through the papers on the countertop and found a job sheet – the workman had been someone called Hans Towwel.

'Blast!' said Spike. 'I *hate* it when Satan obtains a soul. Don't get me wrong, some people deserve to be tortured for all eternity, but damnation without the possibility of salvation – it's like a three-strike life sentence without the possibility of parole.'

I nodded my head in agreement. Obscene though the crime was, eternal damnation was several punishments too far.

'All this defeatist claptrap is making me sick to the craw,' growled Major Pickles. 'No one is going to hell on my account – what happens if we get the money back?'

Spike snapped his fingers.

'Pickles, you're a genius! Mr Towwel doesn't join the legion of the damned until he actually makes use of his ill-gotten gains. Thursday, call Wessex Kitchens and find out where he is – we need to get to him before he spends any of the cash.'

Ten minutes later we were heading at high speed towards the Greasy Monk, a popular medieval-themed eatery not far from the rebuilt cathedral of St Zvlkx. I had tried to call Towwel's mobile but it was switched off, and when I explained that there was a substantial sum of money missing from Major Pickles' house, the boss of Wessex Kitchens said he was horrified – and promised to meet us there.

The restaurant was filled to capacity as the cathedral of St Zvlkx had just been nominated as the first GSD drop-round-if-you-want-but-hey-no-one's-forcing-you place of worship/contemplation/meditation, and the many followers/adherents/vaguely interested parties of the single unified faith were having lunch and discussing ways in which they could best use the new multi-faith for over-whelming good.

As soon as we pushed open the doors Spike yelled: 'Hans Towwel?' in his most commanding voice, and in the silence that followed a man in a navy blue boiler suit signalled to us from behind a wooden plate of bread and dripping.

'Problems?' he said as we walked up.

'Could be,' said Spike. 'Did you pay for the meal with the money you pinched from Major Pickles?'

'You what?'

'You heard him,' I said. 'Did you pay for that meal with the money you stole from Major Pickles?'

'Bollocks to you!' he said, getting up. Spike, who was pretty strong, pushed the man hard back down into his seat.

'Listen,' said Spike in a quiet voice, 'we're not cops and we don't give a shit about the money and we don't give a shit about you – but we do give a shit about your *soul*. Now just tell us: have you spent any of the cash or not?'

'That's well sweet, isn't it?' growled Towwel. 'Some cash is missing so you blame the working man.'

'Towwel?' said a crumpled and untidy-looking man in a crumpled and untidy-looking suit who had just arrived. 'Is what they say true?'

'Who are you?' asked Spike.

'Mr Hedge Moulting of Wessex Kitchens,' said the untidy man, offering us a business card. 'I must say I am shocked and appalled by our employee's behaviour – how much was taken?'

'Now look here—!' said Towwel, growing angrier by the second,

274

which caused Mr Moulting of Wessex Kitchens to flinch and hide behind Spike. 'I don't steal from people. Not from customers, not from pensioners, not from you, not from *anyone*!'

'You should be ashamed of yourself!' said Moulting, still half hidden behind Spike. 'You're *fired* – and don't expect a reference.'

'How do we know *you* didn't take it?' demanded Towwel.

'Me?' exclaimed Moulting. 'How dare you!'

'*You* made a random inspection of my work this morning and you're a sleazy piece of crap – I say *you* took it.'

'An outrageous accusation!' yelled Moulting, waving a threatening finger in his direction. 'You'll never fit a washing machine in this town again, and what's more I will make it my duty, nay pleasure, to see you convicted of this heinous crime. A thousand pounds? From a *war veteran*? You deserve all you're going to get!'

There was silence for a moment.

'Mr Moulting,' said Spike, 'we never said how much was stolen. As I said to Mr Towwel here, we don't give a shit about the money, we're here to save a soul from the torment of eternal damnation. It was a diabolical entrapment from one of Old Scratch's accomplices. If you've got the money and haven't spent any of it, then just drop it in the nearest poor box and your soul is clear. If you *have* spent some of the cash, then there's nothing anyone can do for you.'

I turned to Mr Towwel.

'Sorry to have accused you unjustly, sir. If you need a job call me any time at Acme Carpets.'

And we walked out, bumping aside Moulting as we went. His shaking hand reached for a chair-back to steady himself. He had turned pale and was sweating, trembling with the fear of the man who is condemned to eternal hellfire, and knows it.

We recarpeted Major Pickles' entire house with the finest carpet we had. We also did his shopping, his washing and bought two dozen packets of Jaffa cakes. After that, the three of us sat down and nattered all afternoon, drinking tea and telling stories. We parted the best of friends and left our phone numbers on his fridge so he could call us if he needed anything. I even suggested he give Polly a call if he wanted some company.

'I never realised carpet laying could be so much fun,' I said as we finally drove away.

'Me neither,' replied Spike. 'Do you think Bowden will be pissed off that we've done this one for free and it took us all day?'

'Nah,' I replied with a smile, 'I'm sure he'll be just fine about it.'

29
Time out of Joint

'I never did get my head around time's carefree propensity for paradox. My father didn't exist, yet I was born, and time travel had never been invented but they still hoped that it might. There were currently two versions of Friday and I had met myself and him several times in the past – or was it the future? It gave me a dull ache in the head when I thought about it.'

'How was work?' asked Landen when I walked in the door.

'Quite good fun,' I replied. 'The floor-covering business is definitely looking up – how are things with you?'

'Good, too – lots of work done.'

'On *The Mews of Doom*?' I asked, still hopeful about Scampton-Tappett, and remembering that I had sent a note down to *Bananas for Edward* for him to swap books. He'd cost me a thousand book-guineas and I was sure as hell going to get my money's worth.

'No. I've been working on Spike's weird-shit self-help book: *Collecting the Undead*.'

Damn and blast again.

I recalled a news item I had overheard on the tram home.

'Hey, do you know what Redmond Van de Poste's Address to the Nation is all about?'

'Rumour says it's going to be about the Stupidity Surplus. Apparently his top advisers have come up with a plan that will deal with the excess in a manner that won't damage economic interests, and might actually generate new business opportunities.'

'He'll top the ratings with that one – I only hope he doesn't generate more stupidity – you know how stupidity tends to breed off itself. How are the girls?'

'They're fine. I'm just playing Scrabble with Tuesday. Is it cheating for her to use Nextian geometry to bridge *two* triple word scores with a word of only six letters?'

'I suppose. Where's Jenny?'

'She's made a camp in the attic.'

'Again?'

Something niggled in my head again. Something I was meant to do.

'Land?'

'Yuh?'

'Nothing. I'll get it.'

There was someone at the door, and they had knocked, rather than rung, which is always mildly ominous. I opened the door and it was Friday, or at least it was the clean-cut, non-grunty version. He wasn't alone, either – he had two of his ChronoGuard friends with him, and they all looked a bit serious. Despite the dapper light blue ChronoGuard uniforms they all looked too young to get drunk or vote, let alone do something as awesomely responsible as surf the timestream. It was like letting a twelve-year-old do your epidural.

'Hello, Sweetpea!' I said. 'Are these your friends?'

'They're *colleagues*,' said Friday in a pointed fashion. 'We're here on official business.'

'Goodness!' I said, attempting not to patronise him with motherly pride and failing spectacularly. 'Would you all like a glass of milk and a biscuit or something?'

But Friday, it seemed, wasn't in much of a mood for milk – or a biscuit.

'Not now, Mum – we *still* haven't invented time travel.'

'Maybe you can't,' I replied, 'maybe it's impossible.'

'We used the technology to get here,' said Friday with impeccable logic, 'so the possibility still exists, no matter how slight – we've got every available agent strung out across the timestream doing a fingertip search of all potential areas of discovery. Now, where is he?'

'Your father?'

'No; *him*. Friday – the other, different me.'

'Don't you know? Isn't this all ancient history?'

'Time is not like it should be. If it was, we'd have solved it all by now. So where is he?'

'Are you here to replace him?'

'No – we just want to talk.'

'He's out practising with his band.'

'He is *not*. Would it surprise you to learn that there was no band called the Gobshites?'

'Oh no!' I said with a shudder. 'He didn't call it the Wankers after all, did he?'

'No, no, Mum – *there is no band.*'

'He's definitely doing his band thing,' I assured them, inviting them in and picking the telephone off the hall table. 'I'll call Toby's dad. They use their garage for practice. It's the perfect venue – they're both partially deaf.'

'Then there's not much point in phoning them, now, is there?' said the cockier of Friday's friends.

'What's your name?'

'Nigel,' said the one who had spoken, a bit sheepishly.

'No one likes a smart-arse, Nigel.'

I stared at him and he looked away, pretending to find some fluff on his uniform.

'Hi, is that Toby's dad?' I said as the phone connected. 'It's Friday's mum here . . . No, I'm not like that – it only happens in the book. My question is: are the boys jamming in your garage?'

I looked at Friday and his friends.

'Not for at least three months? I didn't know that. Thank you – goodnight.'

I put the phone down.

'So where is he?' I asked.

'We don't know,' replied the other Friday, 'and since he's a free radical whose movements are entirely independent of the SHE, we have no way of knowing where or when he is. The feckless dopey teenage act was a good one and had us all fooled – you especially.'

I narrowed my eyes. This was a new development.

'What are you saying?'

'We've had some new information and we think Friday might be actually *causing* the non-discovery of the technology – conspiring with his future self to overthrow the ChronoGuard!'

'Sounds like a trumped-up bullshit charge for you to replace him,' I said, beginning to get annoyed.

'I'm serious, Mum. Friday is a dangerous historical fundamentalist who will do whatever it takes to achieve his own narrow agenda – to keep time as it was originally meant to run. If we don't stop him, then the whole of history will roll up and there will be nothing left of any of us!'

'If he's so dangerous,' I said slowly, 'then why haven't you eradicated him?'

Friday took a deep breath.

'Mum? Like . . . *duh*. He's a younger version of me and the future Director General. If we get rid of him we get rid of ourselves. He's clever, I'll grant him that. But if he can stop time travel being discovered, then he knows how it was invented in the first place. We need to speak to him. Now – where is he?'

'I don't rat on my son, son,' I said in a mildly confusing way.

'*I'm* your son, Mum.'

'And I wouldn't rat out on you either, Sweetpea.'

280

Friday took a step forward and raised his voice a notch.

'Mum, this is important. If you have any idea where he is, then you're going to have to tell us – and don't call me "Sweetpea" in front of my friends.'

'I don't know where he is – Sweetpea – and if you want to talk to me in that tone of voice, you'll go to your room.'

'This is beyond room, Mother.'

'Mum. It's *Mum*. Friday always called me Mum.'

'I'm Friday, Mum – *your* Friday.'

'No,' I said, 'you're *another* Friday – someone he *might* become. And do you know, I think I prefer the one who can barely talk and thinks soap is a type of TV show.'

Friday glared at me angrily.

'You've got ten hours to hand him over. Harbouring a time terrorist is a serious offence, and the punishment unspeakably unpleasant.'

I wasn't fazed by his threats.

'Are you sure you know what you're doing?' I asked.

'Of course!'

'Then by definition, *so does he.* Why don't you take your SO-12 buddies and go play in the timestream until dinner?'

Friday made a *harrumph* noise, turned on his heels and departed with his friends following quickly behind.

I closed the door and joined Landen who was leaning on the newel post, staring at me. He'd been listening to every word.

'Pumpkin, just what the hell's going on?'

'I'm not sure myself, darling, but I'm beginning to think that Friday's been making a monkey out of the pair of us.'

'Which Friday?'

'The hairy one that grunts a lot. He's not a dozy waster after all – he's working undercover as some sort of historical fundamentalist. We need some answers, and I think I know where to find

281

them. Friday may have tricked his parents, the SHE and half the ChronoGuard, but there's one person no teenage boy ever managed to fool.'

'And that is?'

'His younger sister.'

'I can't believe it took you so long to figure out,' said Tuesday, who agreed to spill the beans on her brother for the bargain price of a new bicycle, a £30 gift token to MathsWorld and lasagne three nights in a row. 'He didn't stomp on Barney Plotz either – he forged the letters and the phone call. He needed the time to conduct what he called his . . . *investigations*. I don't know what they were, but he was at the public library a lot – and over at Gran's.'

'Gran's? Why Gran's? He *likes* his food.'

'I don't know,' said Tuesday, thinking long and hard about it. 'He said it was something to do with Mycroft and a chronuption of staggering proportions.'

'That boy,' I muttered grimly, 'has got some serious explaining to do.'

30
Now Is the Winter

——

'One of the biggest wastes of money in recent years was the "Anti-Smote Shield", designed to protect mankind (or Britain, at the very least) from an overzealous deity eager to cleanse the population of sin. Funded initially by Chancellor Yorrick Kaine, the project was halted after his ignominious fall from grace. Cancelled but not forgotten, the network of transmission towers still lies dotted about the country, a silent testament to Kaine's erratic and somewhat costly administration.'

My mother answered the door when we knocked and she seemed vaguely surprised to see us all. Landen and I were there as concerned parents, of course, and Tuesday was there as she was the only one who might be able to understand Mycroft's work, if that was what was required.

'Is it Sunday lunchtime already?' asked my mother.

'No, Mother. Is Friday here?'

'Friday? Goodness me, no! I haven't seen him for over—'

'It's all right, Gran,' came a familiar voice from the living-room door, 'there's no more call for subterfuge.'

It was Friday – *our* Friday, the grunty, smelly one, who up until an hour ago had been someone we thought wouldn't know what 'subterfuge' meant, let alone be able to pronounce it. He had changed. There seemed to be a much more upright bearing about him. Perhaps it was because he wasn't dragging his feet when he walked, and he actually looked at us when he spoke. Despite this, he still *seemed* like a sad teenage cliché: spots, long, unkempt hair, and with

283

clothes so baggy you could dress three people out of the material and still have enough to make some curtains.

'Why don't you tell us what's going on?' I asked.

'You wouldn't understand.'

I fixed him with my best 'son, you are in *so* much trouble' look.

'You'd be amazed what I can understand.'

'Okay,' he said, drawing a deep breath. 'You've heard that the ChronoGuard are using time travel technology now in the almost certain knowledge that it's invented in the future?'

'I get the *principle*,' I replied, somewhat guardedly, as I still had no idea how you could use something that had yet to be invented.

'As weird as it might seem,' explained Friday, 'the principle is sound. Many things happen solely because of the curious human foible of a preconceived notion altering the outcome. More simply put: if we convince ourselves that something is possible, it becomes so. It's called the Schrödinger Night Fever principle.'

'I don't understand.'

'It's simple. If you go to see *Saturday Night Fever* expecting it to be good, it's a corker. However, if you go *expecting* it to be a crock of shit, it's that too. Thus *Saturday Night Fever* can exist in two mutually opposing states *at the very same time*, yet only by the weight of our expectations. From this principle we can deduce that *any* opposing states can be governed by human expectation – even, as in the case of retro-deficit engineering, the present use of a future technology.'

'I *think* I understand that,' said Landen. 'Does it work with any John Travolta movie?'

'Only the artistically ambiguous ones,' replied Friday, 'such as *Pulp Fiction* and *Face/Off*. *Battlefield Earth* doesn't work because it's a stinker no matter how much you think you're going to like it, and *Get Shorty* doesn't work either because you'd be hard pressed not to enjoy it, irrespective of any preconceived notions.'

284

'It's a beautiful principle,' I said admiringly. 'Yours?'

'Sadly not,' replied Friday with a smile. 'Much as I'd like to claim it, the credit belongs to an intellect far superior to mine – Tuesday. Way to go, sis.'

Tuesday squirmed with joy at getting a compliment from her big brother, but still none of it made any real sense.

'So how does this relate to Mycroft and time travel?'

'Simple,' said Friday. 'The obscenely complex technologies that the ChronoGuard use to power up the time engines contravene one essential premise that is at the very core of science: that disorder will always stay the same, or increase. More simply stated, you can put a pig in a machine to make a sausage, but you can't put a sausage in a machine to make a pig. It's the second law of thermo-dynamics. One of the most rigid tenures of our understanding of the physical world. You can't reverse the arrow of time to make something *un*happen – whether it be unscrambling eggs or unmaking a historical event.'

'The recipe for unscrambled eggs,' I murmured, suddenly remem-bering a family dinner we had about the time of the *Jane Eyre* episode. 'He was scribbling it on a napkin and Polly made him stop; they had an argument – that's how I remember it.'

'Right,' said Friday. 'The recipe was actually an equation that showed how the second law of thermodynamics could be modi-fied to allow a reversibility of time's arrow. That you *could* unbake a cake with almost breathless simplicity. The recipe for unscram-bled eggs is at the heart of reversing the flow of time – without it, *there is no time travel!*'

'So,' I said slowly, 'the whole of the ChronoGuard's ability to move around in time rests on them getting hold of this recipe?'

'That's about the tune of it, Mum.'

'So where is it?' asked Landen. 'Logically it *must* still exist or the likelihood of time travel drops to zero. Since your future self just popped up twenty minutes ago to make veiled threats, the possibility remains that it will be discovered some time before the end of time – some time in the next forty-eight hours.'

'Right,' said Friday, 'and that's what I've been doing with Polly for the past two weeks – trying to find where Mycroft put it. Once I've got the recipe I can destroy it: the possibility of time travel drops to zero, and it's "Goodnight, Vienna" for the ChronoGuard.'

'Why would you want that?'

'The less you know, Mum, the better.'

'They say you're a dangerous historical fundamentalist,' I added cautiously, 'a terrorist of time.'

'But they would say that, wouldn't they? The Friday you met – he's okay. He's following orders, but he doesn't know what I know. If he did he'd be trying to destroy the recipe, the same as me. The Standard History Eventline is bullshit and all they're doing is trying to protect their temporal-phoney-baloney jobs.'

'How do you know this?'

'I become Director General of the ChronoGuard when I am thirty-six. In the final year before retirement at seventy-eight, I am inducted into the ChronoGuard Star Chamber – the ruling elite. It was there that I discovered something so devastating that if it became public knowledge it would shut down the industry in an instant. And the time business is worth six hundred billion a year – *minimum*.'

'Tell them what it is,' said Polly, who had been standing at his side. 'If anything happens to you then at least one of us might be able to carry on.'

Friday nodded his head and took a deep breath.

'Has anyone noticed how short attention spans seem to have cast a certain lassitude across the nation?'

'Have I ever,' I replied, rolling my eyes and thinking of the endlessly downward clicking of the Read-O-Meter. 'No one's reading books any more – they seem to prefer the mind-numbing spectacle of easily digested trash TV and celebrity tittle-tattle.'

'Exactly,' said Friday. 'The Long View has been eroded. We can't see beyond six months if that, and short-termism will spell our end. But the thing is, it needn't be that way – there's a *reason* for it. The time engines don't just need vast quantities of power – they need to run on time. Not punctuality, but time *itself*. Even a temporal leap of a few minutes will use up an infinitesimally small amount of the abstract concept. Not the hard *clock* time, but the soft stuff that keeps events firmly embedded in a small cocoon of prolonged event – the *Now*.'

'Oooh!' murmured Tuesday, who twigged it first. '*They've been mining the Now!*'

'Exactly, sis,' said Friday, sweeping the hair from his eyes. 'The Short Now is the direct result of the Time Industry's unthinking depredations. If the ChronoGuard continue as they are, within a few years there won't be any Now at all, and the world will move into a dark age of eternal indifference.'

'You mean TV could get *worse*?' asked Landen.

'*Much* worse,' replied Friday grimly. 'At the rate the Now is being eroded, by this time next year *Samaritan Kidney Swap* will be considered the height of scholarly erudition. But easily digestible TV is not the cause – it's the effect. A short Now will also spell the gradual collapse of forward planning, and mankind will slowly strangulate itself in a downward spiral of uncaring self-interest and short-term instant gratification.'

There was a bleak silence as we took this on board. We could see it all now. Short attention spans, a general malaise, no tolerance, no respect, no rules. Short-termism. No wonder we were seeing Outlander read-rates go into free-fall. The short Now would hate books; too much thought required for not enough gratification. It brought home the urgency of finding the recipe, wherever it was:

without unscrambled eggs, there was no time travel, no more depredation of the Now and we could look to a brighter future of long-term thought – and more reading. Simple.

'Shouldn't this be a matter for public debate?' asked Landen.

'What would that achieve, Dad? The ChronoGuard don't have to *disprove* that the reduction of the Now is caused by humans – they only have to create doubt. They'll always be Short Now deniers, and the debate will become so long and drawn-out that as soon as we realise there *is* a problem, we won't care enough to want to do anything about it. This issue is not for debate – the ChronoGuard *cannot* get hold of that recipe. I'm staking my career on it. And believe me, I would have had an excellent career to stake.'

There was silence after Friday's speech. We all realised that he was right, of course, but I was also thinking about how proud I was of him, and how refreshing it was to hear such eloquence and moral lucidity from such a grubby and dishevelled individual, who was wearing a *Wayne Skunk Is the Bollocks* T-shirt.

'If only Mycroft were alive,' sighed Polly, breaking the silence, 'we could ask him where he put it.'

And then, I *understood*.

'Aunt,' I said, 'come with me. Friday – you too.'

It was dusk by now and the last rays of the evening light were shining through the dusty windows of Mycroft's workshop. It seemed somehow more shabby in the twilight.

'All those memories!' breathed Polly, hobbling across the concrete floor with Friday holding her arm. 'What a life. Yes indeed, what a life. I've not been in here since before he . . . you know.'

'Don't be startled,' I told her, 'but I've seen Mycroft twice in here over the past two days. He came back to tell us something, and until now I had no idea what it was. Polly?'

Her eyes had filled with tears as she stared into the dim emptiness of the workshop. I followed her gaze and as my eyes became accustomed to the light, I could see him too. Mycroft's opacity was low, and the colour seemed to have drained from his body. He was barely there at all.

'Hello, Poll,' he said with a smile, his voice a low rumble, 'you're looking positively *radiant*!'

'Oh, Crofty!' she murmured. 'You're such a fibber – I'm a doddering wreck ready for the scrapheap. But one that has missed you *so* much!'

'Mycroft,' I said in a respectful whisper, 'I don't want to keep you from your wife, but time is short. I know why you came back.'

'You mean it wasn't Farquitt or the chairs?'

'No. It was about the recipe for unscrambled eggs.'

'We need to know,' added Polly, 'where you left it.'

'Is that all?' laughed Mycroft. 'Why, goodness – I put it in my jacket pocket!'

He was beginning to fade and his voice sounded hollow and empty. His post-life time was almost up.

'And *after* that?'

He faded some more – I was worried that if I blinked he'd go completely.

'Which jacket, my darling?' asked Polly.

'The one you gave me for Christmas,' came an ethereal whisper, 'the blue one . . . with the large checks.'

'Crofty?'

But he had vanished. Friday and I rushed to support Polly, who had gone a bit wobbly at the knees.

'Damn!' said Friday. 'When does he next come back?'

'He doesn't,' I said, 'that was it.'

'Then we're no closer to knowing where it is,' said Friday. 'I've been through all his clothes – there isn't a jacket with blue checks in his cupboard.'

'There's a reason for that,' said Polly, her eyes glistening with tears. 'He left it on the *Hesperus*. I scolded him at the time, but now I see why he did it.'

'Mum? Does this make any sense to you?'

'Yes,' I said with a smile. 'It's somewhere the ChronoGuard can't get to it. Back in 1985, before he used the Prose Portal to send Polly into "I Wandered Lonely as a Cloud", he tested it on himself. The jacket is right where he left it – in the teeth of an Atlantic gale inside Henry Longfellow's poem "The Wreck of the *Hesperus*".'

'Inside the *BookWorld*?'

'Right,' I replied, 'and nothing, repeat *nothing*, would compel me to return there. In two days the ChronoGuard will be gone, and the slow repair of the Now can begin. You did good, Sweetpea.'

'Thanks, Mum,' he said, 'but please – don't call me Sweetpea.'

31

Spending the Surplus

***

**'The Commonsense Party's first major policy reversal
of perceived current wisdom was the scrapping of
performance targets, league tables, and the attempt to
make subtle human problems into figures on a graph
that could be solved quickly and easily through "initiatives".** Arguing that important bodies such as the Health Service
should have the emphasis on "care" and not on "administration", the Commonsense Party forced through legislation that
essentially argued: "If it takes us ten years to get into the shit,
it will take us twenty years to get out – and that journey starts
now."'

We stayed at Mum's for dinner, although 'dinner' in this context
might best be described as a loose collection of foodstuffs tossed
randomly into a large saucepan and then boiled for as long as it
took for all taste to vanish, never to return. Because of this, we
missed Redmond Van de Poste's Address to the Nation, something
that didn't really trouble us as the last address had been, as they
always were, unbelievably dreary but astute and of vital importance.
It was just so good to talk to Friday again on a one-to-one. I'd
forgotten how pleasant he actually was. He lost no time in telling
me that he was going to have to stay undercover as a lazy good-
for-nothing until the ChronoGuard had ceased operations – and
this meant that I shouldn't even *attempt* to wake him until at least
midday, or two at the weekends.

'How convenient,' I observed.

Tuesday had been thoughtful for some time and finally asked:

'But can't the ChronoGuard go back to the time between when Great-Uncle Mycroft wrote the recipe and when he left it on the *Hesperus*?'

'Don't worry,' said Friday with a wink, 'it was only twenty-eight minutes, and the older me has it covered at the other end. The only thing we have to do is make sure the recipe stays in "The Wreck of the *Hesperus*". We can win this fight with nothing more than in-action, which as a teenager suits me just fine.'

It was only as we were driving home that I suddenly thought of Jenny.

'Oh my God!' I said in a panic. 'We left Jenny at home on her own!'

Landen took hold of my arm and squeezed it, and I felt Friday rest his hand on my shoulder.

'It's all right, darling, calm down. We left her with Mrs Berko-Boyler.'

I frowned.

'No we *didn't*. You said she was making a camp in the attic. We came straight out. How could we have forgotten?'

'Sweetheart,' said Landen with a deep breath. 'There is no Jenny.'

'What do you mean?' I demanded, chuckling at the stupidity of his comment. 'Of course there's a Jenny!'

'Dad's right,' said Friday soothingly, 'there has never been a Jenny.'

'But I can *remember* her—!'

'It's *Aornis*, Mum,' added Tuesday. 'She gave you this mindworm seven years ago and we can't get rid of it.'

'I don't understand,' I said, beginning to panic, 'I can remember everything about her! Her laugh, the holidays, the time she fell off her bicycle and broke her arm, her birth – *everything*!'

'Aornis did this to you for *revenge*,' said Landen. 'After she couldn't wipe me from your memory, she left you with this – that's what she's doing her thirty-year stretch for.'

'The bitch!' I yelled. 'I'll kill her for this!'

'Language, Mum,' said Tuesday, 'I'm only twelve. Besides, even if you did kill her, we think Jenny would still be with you.'

'Oh, *shit*,' I said as reason started to replace confusion and anger, 'that's why she never turns up at mealtimes.'

'We pretend there *is* a Jenny to minimise the onset of an attack,' said Landen. 'It's why we keep her bedroom as it is and why you'll find her stuff all around the house – so when you're alone, you don't go into a missing-daughter panic.'

'The evil little cow!' I muttered, rubbing my face. 'But now I know we can do something about it, right?'

'It's not as easy as that, sweetheart,' said Landen with a note of sadness in his voice. 'Aornis is truly vindictive – in a few minutes you won't remember any of this and you'll believe that you have a daughter named Jenny again.'

'You mean,' I said slowly, 'I've done this before?'

We pulled up outside the house and Landen turned off the engine. There was silence in the car.

'Sometimes you can go weeks without an attack,' said Landen quietly, 'at other times you can have two or three an hour.'

'Is that why you work from home?'

'Yeah. We can't have you going to school every day expecting to pick up a daughter who isn't there.'

'So . . . you've explained all this to me before?'

'Many times, darling.'

I sighed deeply.

'I feel like a complete twit,' I said in a quiet voice. 'Is this my first attack today?'

'It's the third,' said Landen, 'it's been a bad week.'

I looked at them all in turn, and they were all staring back at me with such a sense of loving concern for my well-being that I burst into tears.

293

'It's all right, Mum,' said Tuesday, holding my hand, 'we'll look after you.'

'You are the best, most loving, supportive family anyone could ever have,' I said through my sobs. 'I'm so sorry if I'm a burden.'

They all told me not to be so bloody silly. I told them not to swear, and Landen gave me his handkerchief for my tears.

'So,' I said, wiping my eyes, 'how does it work? How do I stop remembering the fact there's no Jenny?'

'We have our ways. Jenny's at a sleepover with Ingrid, okay?'

'Okay.'

He leaned across and kissed me, smiled and said to the kids: 'Right, team, do your stuff.'

Friday poked Tuesday hard in the ribs. She squealed.

'What was *that* for!?'

'For being a geek!'

'I'd rather be a geek than a duh-brain. And what's more, Strontium Goat are rubbish and Wayne Skunk couldn't play a guitar if his life depended on it!'

'Say that again!'

'Will you two cut it out!' I said crossly. 'Honestly, I think Friday's proved he's no duh-brain over the Short Now thing, so just pack it in. Right. I know your gran gave us some food, but does anybody want anything proper to eat?'

'There's some pizza in the freezer,' said Landen, 'we can have that.'

We all got out of the car and walked up to the house with Friday and Tuesday bickering.

'Geek.'

'Duh-brain.'

'Geek.'

'Duh-brain.'

'I said *cut it out*.'

I suddenly thought of something.

'Land, where's Jenny?'

'At a sleepover with Ingrid.'

'Oh, yeah. Again?'

'Thick as thieves, those two.'

'Yeah,' I said with a frown, 'thick as thieves those two.'

Bowden called during dinner. This was unusual for him but not totally unexpected. Spike and I had crept away from Acme like naughty schoolkids as we didn't want to get into trouble over the cost of Major Pickles' carpet, not to mention that it had taken us both all day and we'd done nothing else.

'It's not great, is it?' said Bowden in the over-serious tone he used when he was annoyed, upset or angry. To be honest, I had the most shares in Acme, but he *was* the managing director, so day-to-day operations were down to him.

'I don't think it's all *that* bad,' I said, going on the defensive.

'Are you insane?' replied Bowden. 'It's a disaster!'

'We've had bigger problems,' I said, beginning to get annoyed. 'I think it's best to keep a sense of proportion, don't you?'

'Well, yes,' he replied, 'but if we let this sort of thing take a hold, we never know where it might end up.'

I was pissed off now.

'Bowden,' I said, 'just cool it. Spike got stuck to the ceiling by Raum and if Pickles hadn't given the demi-devil the cold steel, we'd both be pushing up the daisies.'

There was silence on the line for a moment until Bowden said in a quiet voice:

'I'm talking about Van de Poste's Address to the Nation — what are *you* talking about?'

'Oh — nothing. What did he say?'

'Switch on the telly and you'll see.'

295

I asked Tuesday to switch channels. OWL-TV was airing the popular current affairs show *Fresh Air with Tudor Webastow* and Tudor, who was perhaps not the best but was certainly the tallest reporter on TV, was interviewing the Commonsense minister of culture, Cherie Yogert, MP.

'. . . and the first classic to be turned into a reality book show?'

'*Pride and Prejudice*,' announced Yogert proudly. 'It will be renamed *The Bennets* and will be serialised live in your household copy the day after tomorrow. Set in starchy early-nineteenth-century England, it features Mr and Mrs Bennet and their five daughters, who will be given tasks and then voted out of the house one by one with the winner going on to feature in *Northanger Abbey*, which itself will be the subject of more "readeractive" changes.'

'So what Van de Poste is sanctioning,' remarked Webastow slowly, 'is the wholesale plunder of everything the literary world holds dear.'

'Not *everything*,' corrected Ms Yogert, 'only books penned by English authors. We don't have the right to do dumb things with other nations' books – they can do that for themselves. But,' she went on, 'I think "plunder" would be too strong a word – we would prefer to obfuscate the issue by using nonsensical jargon such as "market-led changes" or "user-choice enhancements". For too long the classics have been dreary, overlong and incomprehensible to anyone without a university education – reality book shows are the way forward, and the interactive book council are the people to do it for us!'

'Am I hearing this right?'

'Unfortunately,' murmured Landen, who was standing next to me.

'For too long we have suffered under the yoke of the Stalinist principle of one-author books,' continued Ms Yogert, 'and in the modern world we must strive to bring democracy to the writing process.'

'I don't think any authors would regard their writing process as creative totalitarianism,' said Webastow uneasily. 'But we'll move on. As I understand it, the technology that will enable you to alter the storyline of a book will change it permanently, and in every known copy. Do you not think it would be prudent to leave the originals as they are and write *alternative* versions?'

Yogert smiled at him patronisingly.

'If we did that,' replied Yogert, 'it would barely be stupid at all, and the Commonsense Party take the Stupidity Surplus problem *extremely* seriously. Prime Minister Van de Poste has pledged to not only reduce the current surplus to zero within a year, but to also cut all idiocy emissions by seventy per cent in 2020. This requires unpopular decisions, and he had to compare the interests of a few diehard elitist dweeby bespectacled book fans with those of the general voting public. Better still, because this idea is *so* idiotic, the loss of a single classic – say, *Jane Eyre* – will offset the entire nation's stupidity for an entire year. Since we have the potential to over-write *all* the English classics by reader choice, we can do *really* stupid things with impunity. Who knows? We may even run a stupidity *deficit* – and could then afford to take on other nations' idiocy at huge national profit. We see the UK as leading the stupidity-offset-trading industry – and the idiocy of *that* idea will simply be offset against the annihilation of *Vanity Fair*. Simple, isn't it?'

I realised I was still holding the phone.

'Bowden, are you there?'

'I'm here.'

'This stinks to high heaven. Can you find out something about this so-called Interactive Book Council? I've never heard of such a thing. Call me back.'

I returned my attention to the TV.

'And when we've lost all the classics and the Stupidity Surplus has once again ballooned?' asked Webastow. 'What happens then?'

'Well,' said Ms Yogert with a shrug, 'we'll cross that bridge when we come to it, eh?'

'You'll forgive me for saying this,' said Webastow, looking over his spectacles, 'but this is the most hare-brained piece of unadulterated stupidity that any government has ever undertaken *anywhere*.'

'Thank you very much,' replied Ms Yogert courteously. 'I'll make sure your compliments are forwarded to Mr Van de Poste.'

The programme moved on to a report on how the 'interactive book' might work. Something about 'new technologies' and 'user-defined narrative'. It was all baloney – I knew what was going on. It was Senator Jobsworth. He'd pushed through the interactivity book project of Baxter's. Worse, he'd planned this all along – witness the large throughput conduits in *Pride and Prejudice* and the recent upgrading of all of Austen's work. I wasn't that concerned with how they'd managed to overturn my veto or even open an office in the real world – what worried me was that I needed to be in the BookWorld to stop the nation's entire literary heritage being sacrificed on the altar of popularism.

The phone rang. It was Bowden. I made a trifling and wholly unbelievable excuse about looking for a hammer, and vanished into the garage so Landen couldn't hear the conversation.

'The Interactive Book Council is run out of an office in West London,' Bowden reported when I was safely perched on the lawn-mower. 'It was incorporated a month ago and has the capacity to take a thousand simultaneous calls – yet the office itself is barely larger than the one at Acme.'

'They must have figured out a way to transfer the calls en masse to the BookWorld,' I replied. 'I'm sure a thousand Mrs Danvers would be overjoyed to be working in a call centre rather than bullying characters or dealing with rampant mispelings.'

I told Bowden I'd try and think of something, and hung up. I stepped out of the garage and went back into the living room, my heart thumping. This was why I had the veto – to protect the BookWorld from the stupefyingly short-sighted decisions of the Council of Genres. But first things first. I had to contact Bradshaw and see how Jurisfiction was taking to the wholesale slaughter of literary treasures – but how? JurisTech had never devised a two-way communication link between the BookWorld and the Outland, as I was the only one ever likely to use it.

'Are you all right, Mum?' asked Tuesday.

'Yes, poppet, I'm fine,' I said, tousling her hair. 'I've just got to muse on this a while.'

I went upstairs to my office, which had been converted from the old boxroom, and sat down to think. The more I thought, the worse things looked. If the CofG had discounted my veto and forced the interactive issue, it was entirely possible that they would also be attacking Speedy Muffler and Racy Novel. The only agency able to police these matters was Jurisfiction – but they worked to Text Grand Central's orders, which were *themselves* under the control of the Council of Genres, so Jobsworth was ultimately in command of Jurisfiction – and he could do with it what he wanted.

I sighed, leaned forward and absently pulled out my hair-tie, then rubbed my scalp with my fingertips. Commander Bradshaw would never have agreed to this interactive garbage and would resign out of principle – as he had hundreds of times before. And if I were there, I could reaffirm my veto. It was a right given me by the Great Panjandrum, and not even Jobsworth would go against *her* will. This was all well and good but for one thing – I'd never even *considered* the possibility of losing my TravelBook, so never worked out an emergency strategy for getting into the BookWorld without it.

The only person I knew who could bookjump without a book was Mrs Nakajima, and she was in retirement at Thornfield Hall. Ex-Jurisfiction agent Harris Tweed had been banished permanently to the Outland, and without his TravelBook he was as marooned as I was. Ex-Chancellor Yorrick Kaine, real these days and currently licking his wounds in a cell at Parkhurst, was no help at all, and neither was the only other fictionaut I knew still living, Cliff Hangar. I thought again about Commander Bradshaw. He'd certainly want to contact me and was a man of formidable resource – if *I* were him, how would I go about contacting someone in the real world? I checked my e-mails but found nothing, then looked to see whether I had any messages on my mobile, which I hadn't. My mobile footnoterphone, naturally, was devoid of a signal.

I leaned back in my chair to think more clearly and let my eyes wander around the room. I had a good collection of books, amassed during my long career as a Literary Detective. Major and minor classics, but little of any great value. I stopped and thought for a moment, then started to rummage through my bookshelf until I found what I was looking for – one of Commander Bradshaw's novels. Not one he wrote, of course, but one that *featured* him. There were twenty-three in the series, written between 1888 and 1922, and all featured Bradshaw either shooting large animals, finding lost civilisations or stopping 'Johnny Foreigner' causing mischief in British East Africa. He had been out of print for over sixty years and hadn't been read at all for more than ten. Since no one was reading him he could say what he wanted in his own books, and I would be able to read what he said. But there were a few problems: one, twenty-three books would take a lot of reading; two, Text Grand Central would know if his books were being read; and three, it was simply a one-way conduit, and if he *did* leave a message, he would never know whether it was me who had read it.

I opened *Two Years amongst the Umpopo* and flicked through the pages to see whether anything caught my eye, such as a double line space or something. It didn't, so I picked up *Tilarpia, the Devil-fish of Lake Rudolph*, and after that *The Man-eaters of Nakuru*. It was only while I was idly thumbing through *Bradshaw Defies the Kaiser* that I hit pay dirt. The text of the book remained unaltered but the *dedication* had changed. Bradshaw was smart; only a variation in the *story* would be noticed at Text Grand Central – they wouldn't know I was reading it at all. I took the book back to my desk and read:

Thursday, D'girl

If you can read this you have realised that something is seriously squiffy in the BookWorld. Plans had been afoot for weeks and none of us had seen them. Thursday1–4 (yes, it's true) has taken your place as the CofG's LBOCS and is rubber-stamping all of Jobsworth's idiotic schemes. The interactivity idea is going ahead full speed and even now Danverclones are massing on the borders of Racy Novel, ready to invade. Evil Thursday has loaded Text Grand Central with her toadies in order to keep a careful watch for any textual anomalies that might give them – and her – a clue as to whether you have returned. For it is this that Evil Thursday fears more than anything: *that you will return, unmask her as an impostor and retake your place*. She has suspended Jurisfiction and had all agents confined to their books, and now commands a legion of Danverclones who are waiting to capture you should you appear in the BookWorld. We stole back your TravelBook and have left it for you with Captain Carver inside *It Was a Dark and Stormy Night* if you can somehow find a way in. This dedication will self-erase in two readings. Good luck, old girl – and Melanie sends her love.
Bradshaw

I read the dedication again and watched as the words slowly dissolved from the page. Good old Bradshaw. I had been to *It Was a Dark and Stormy Night* a couple of times, mostly for training. It was a maritime adventure set aboard a tramp steamer on the Tasman Sea in 1924. It was a good choice because it came under the deregulated area of the library known as Vanity Publishing. Text Grand Central wouldn't even know I was there. I replaced *Bradshaw Defies the Kaiser* on the shelf, then unlocked the bottom drawer and took out my pistol and eraserhead cartridges. I stuffed them in my bag, noted that it was almost ten, and knocked on Friday's door.

'Darling?'

He looked up from the copy of *Strontmania* he was reading.

'Yuh?'

'I'm sorry, Sweetpea, but I have to go back to the BookWorld. It may put the unscrambled eggs recipe in jeopardy.'

He sighed and stared at me.

'I knew you would.'

'How?'

He beckoned me to the window and pointed to three figures sitting on a wall opposite the house.

'The one in the middle is the other me. It shows there is still a *chance* they'll get hold of the recipe. If we'd won, they'd be long gone.'

'Don't worry,' I said, laying a hand on his, 'I know how important the length of the Now is to all of us. I won't go anywhere near "The Wreck of the *Hesperus*".'

'Mum,' he said in a quiet voice, 'if you get back home and I'm polite, well mannered and with short hair, don't be too hard on me, hey?'

He was worried about being replaced.

'It won't come to that, sweetheart. I'll defend your right to be smelly and incommunicative . . . with my *life*.'

We hugged and I said goodbye, then did the same to Tuesday, who was reading in bed, giggling over the risible imperfections of the Special Theory of Relativity. She knew I was going somewhere serious, so got out of bed to give me an extra hug just in case. I hugged her back, tucked her in, and told her not to make Einstein look *too* much of a clot in case 'it made her look cocky'. I then went to say goodbye to Jenny, and can remember doing so, although for some reason Friday and Tuesday picked that moment to argue about the brightness of the hall light. After sorting them out, I went downstairs to Landen.

'Land,' I said, unsure of what to say, since I rarely got emergency call-outs for carpet laying and to pretend I did now would be such an obvious lie, 'you do know I love you?'

'More than you realise, sweetheart.'

'And you trust me?'

'Of course.'

'Good. I've got to go and—'

'—do some emergency carpet fitting?'

I smiled.

'Yeah. Wish me luck.'

We hugged, I put on my jacket and left the house, hailing a cab to take me to the Clary-LaMarr travelport. When I was safely on the bullet train to Saknussum, I took out my mobile and keyed in a number. I stared out at the dark Wessex countryside which zipped past so fast the few street lamps I could see were almost orange streaks. The call was picked up, and I paused, heart thumping, before speaking.

'My name's Thursday Next. I'd like to speak to John Henry Goliath. You're going to have to wake him. It's a matter of some importance.'

32

The Austen Rover Roving

'The basis for the Austen Rover, I learned much later, was a coach that the Goliath Corporation had bought in 1952 to transport their employees to the coast on "works days out", a lamentable lapse in Goliath's otherwise fine record of rampant worker exploitation. The error was discovered after eight years and the day trips discontinued. True to form, Goliath docked the wages of everyone who attended and charged them for the trip – with backdated interest.'

'The Austen Rover has two separate systems,' explained Dr Anne Wirthlass, 'the transfictional propulsion unit and the book navigation protocol. The former we have worked out – the latter is something you need to update us on.'

It was almost noon of the following day, and I was being brought up to speed on the Rover's complexities by the brilliant Dr Wirthlass, who had thanked me profusely for changing my mind so close to the time before they were to fire themselves off into the unknown.

'It was the least I could do,' I replied, keeping the real reason to myself.

There had been an excited buzz among the technicians in the lab that morning, and I had been introduced to more specialists in an hour than I'd met in a lifetime. John Henry Goliath himself was on hand to smooth over any problems we might have, and there had already been a propulsion test. The Austen Rover had been chained to the floor and the engines had been spooled up. With a deafening roar the Rover had flexed at the chains while an inky black void had opened up in front of it. The engines had been throttled back and the void had closed. It didn't have the quiet subtleness of Mycroft's Prose Portal, but it had certainly been impressive.

That had been three hours ago. Right now we were in the control room, and I had been trying to explain to them just what form the BookWorld takes, which was a bit odd as it was really only *my* interpretation of it, and I had a feeling that if they accepted *my* way it would become *the* way, so I was careful not to describe anything that might be problematical later. I spread a sheet of paper on the table and drew a rough schematic of the various genres that made up the BookWorld, but without too many precise locations – just enough for them to get us inside, and then to *It was a Dark and Stormy Night* without any problems.

'The Nothing is a big place,' I said without fear of understatement, 'and mostly empty. Theoretical storyologists have calculated that the readable BookWorld only makes up twenty-two per cent of visible reading matter – the remainder is the unobservable remnants of long-lost books, forgotten Oral Tradition and ideas still locked in writers' heads. We call it "Dark Reading Matter".'

'Why so much of it unread and untold?'

I shrugged.

'We're not altogether sure, but we think ninety-eight per cent of the world's fiction was wiped out by the accidental death of an Iron Age storyteller about three thousand years ago. It was what we call a mass erasure – we wouldn't see anything of that size until human perfidy, fire and mould wiped out seventy-five per cent of Greek drama at the CE boundary. The reason I mention it is because navigating through the Nothing could be more treacherous than you imagine – colliding with a lost work of Aeschylus or being pulled apart by the Hemingway "lost suitcase of manuscripts" could bring your trip to a painfully verbose. And punctuated. End.'

Dr Wirthlass nodded sagely.

I drew a rough circle near the Maritime Adventure (Civilian) genre.

'We think that this area is heavy with detritus from an unknown genre – possibly Squid Action/Adventure – that failed to fully form a century ago. Twice a year Maritime is pelted with small fragments of ideas and snatches of inner monologue regarding important invertebrate issues which don't do much harm, but bookjumping through this zone has always been a bit bumpy. If we wanted to go from Maritime to Frontier quickly and easily we wouldn't jump direct but go through Western.'

We talked along these lines for a good four hours; it surprised me that I knew so much about the BookWorld without really having to have sit down and learn it, and it also surprised me how much the Goliath Transfictional Project had progressed. By agreement they would drop me on page sixty-eight of *It Was a Dark and Stormy Night* before slingshotting back to Goliath, then await my return and a debrief before attempting any further travel. I had made my demands clearly when I had spoken to John Henry the previous evening. They would do this my way or not at all, something that he was happy to agree to. He also proposed some sort of business partnership in which I could direct the whole Austen Rover project, and in what direction book tourism would go. I still didn't like the idea of it, but if the alternative was the wholesale loss of all the classics through reality book shows, then I'd pretend to go along. I told John Henry we could discuss the precise details upon my return. Throughout the day I had been having nagging doubts about cosying up to Goliath, despite their entreaties, and in an afternoon rest break I wandered into the employees' canteen area, where there was a TV showing a programme all about the upcoming *Pride and Prejudice* reality show.

'Welcome to *Bennetmania*,' said a lively young man with painfully fashionable facial hair. He was presenting one of several 'reality book

TV shows' that had been rushed on to the schedules to cater for the latest fad. '. . . and our studio panel will be here to give an up-to-date analysis of the book's unfolding drama as soon as it begins. Dr Nessecitar, our resident pseudo-psychologist, will point out the bleeding obvious about the Bennet housemates' progress, and our resident experts will give their opinions and advice on who should be voted out. But first, let's have a rundown on who the house-mates actually are.'

I stood and stared with a kind of numb fascination as a jaunty tune started up with an annoyingly buoyant voiceover that accompanied 'artists' impressions' of the family.

'Mr Bennet is the father of the clan, and when he's not chastising his younger daughters for their silliness or teasing his wife, he likes nothing better than to sit in his study and conduct his affairs. His wife is Mrs Bennet, who has a brother in trade and is convinced that her daughters should marry up. This old bunny is highly unstable, prone to panic attacks and socially awkward, so keep your eyes fixed on her for some seriously good fireworks.'

The illustration changed to that of the sisters, with each being highlighted in turn as the voiceover described them.

'None of the daughters will inherit Longbourn owing to the lack of an heir, and the apparent absence of any suitable males in Meryton makes the issue of potential husbands a major concern. Curvaceous, doe-eyed Jane, twenty-two, is the beauty of the family, with a kindly temperament to match. And if Bingley looks at another woman, watch out for the waterworks! Next in line is the thinker of the house and Mr Bennet's favourite: Lizzie, who is twenty. Wilful, skilful and adept with words, she is certainly one to watch – never mind the looks, check out the subtext! Third eldest is Mary, who just likes to read and criticise the rest of them. Dreary and unappealing, we don't think she'll last long. Kitty and Lydia are the two youngest of the Bennets and the most silly and excitable of them all, especially when there is a uniform around, or even the sniff of a party. Impetuous and uncontrollable, these are the two that all eyes will be riveted upon!'

The music ended and the annoying presenter came back on screen.

'There you have it. Seven Bennets, one house, three chapters, one task, one eviction. Bookies are already taking bets as to who's for the bullet. Tune in tomorrow with your book in hand to read the housemates' first task as it is set and join us for the live reading of *The Bennets – live*!'

I switched off the set and walked back to the Book Project lab, all doubts over the wisdom of my actions dispelled from my mind.

By six that evening the Austen Rover was primed and ready to go. Although there was seating for twelve, the crew was to be only the four of us – myself, Dr Wirthlass and two technicians, whose sole function was to monitor the systems and collect data. I called Landen before we left, and told him I'd be home before bedtime. I didn't see any problems. After all, I had been prancing around the inside of the BookWorld for nigh on twenty years and had faced almost all the terrors that could be thrown in my direction. I felt as safe and confident inside fiction as I did walking down the street in Swindon. I'd turn up at the CofG, reveal Thursday1–4 as an impostor, put everything to rights and be back in time to take Jenny to her piano lesson. Simple. But if it *was* that simple, why did my insides feel so leaden?

John Henry Goliath came to see us off and we all shook hands before the door closed and sealed itself with a hermetic hiss. The doctor and the two technicians were too busy to be worried about the risks, something that I felt myself, but tried not to show. After a half-hour countdown, Wirthlass fired up the main reactors, released the handbrake, rang the bell twice and engaged the gravity engines.

And with a mild tingling sensation, we were somewhere else entirely.

33
Somewhere Else Entirely

'The BookWorld was generally agreed to be only part of a much larger Bookverse, but quite how big it was and what percentage was unobservable was a matter of hot debate among booklogians. The fundamental rules of the Bookverse were also contentious. Some factions argued that the Bookverse was constantly expanding as new books were written, but others argued convincingly for a "steady state" Bookverse where ideas were endlessly recycled. A third faction, who called themselves "simplists", argued that there was a single fundamental rule that governed all story: that if it works, it works.'

The darkness drifted away like morning mist, leaving us hovering above a slate-grey sea with empty horizons in all directions. The sky was the same colour as the sea, and stretched across the heavens like a blanket, heavy and oppressive. A light breeze blew flecks of foam from the top of the waves, and positioned not thirty feet below us was an old steamer of riveted construction. The vessel was making a leisurely pace through the waves, a trail of black smoke issuing languidly from her funnel and the stern trailing a creamy wake as the ship rose and fell in the seas.

'That'll be the *Auberon*,' I said, craning my neck to see whether I could spot Captain Carver in the wheelhouse. I couldn't, so asked Wirthlass to move closer and try to land the Rover on the aft hold cover so I could step aboard. She expertly moved the coach in behind the bridge and gently lowered it on to the boards, which creaked ominously under the weight. The door of the coach hissed open and a strong whiff of salty air mixed with coal smoke drifted in. I could feel the rhythmic thump of the engine through the decking, and the swell of the ocean. I took my bag and stepped from the Rover, but I hadn't gone three paces when all of a sudden I realised there was something badly wrong. This ship wasn't the *Auberon*, and if that was the case, this book certainly wasn't *Dark and Stormy Night*.

'Okay, we've got a problem,' I said, turning back to the Rover only to find Dr Wirthlass standing in the doorway – holding a pistol and *smiling*.

'*Bollocks*,' I muttered, which was about as succinct as I could be, given the sudden change of circumstance.

'Bollocks indeed,' replied Dr Wirthlass. 'We've waited over fifteen years for this moment.'

'Before now I'd always thought patience was a virtue,' I murmured, 'not the secret weapon of the vengeful.'

She shook her head and smiled again.

'You're *exactly* how he described you. An ardent moralist, a goody-two-shoes, pathologically eager to do what's best and what's right.' She looked around at the ship, which heeled in the swell. 'So this place is particularly apt – and the perfect place for you to spend the rest of your pitifully short life.'

'What do you want?'

'Nothing. Nothing at all. With you trapped here we have everything I want. We'll be off to the *Hesperus* now, Ms Next – to find that recipe.'

'You know about the unscrambled eggs?' I asked, shocked at the sudden turn of events.

'We're Goliath,' she said simply, 'and information is power. With the End of Time due tomorrow evening it will be something of a challenge, but listen: I like a challenge, and I have the knowledge of your defeat to freshen my mind and make the task that much more enjoyable.'

'You'll never find it,' I said. 'Longfellow is at the other end of the BookWorld and Poetry is the place you'll discover . . .'

I checked myself. I wasn't helping these people, no matter how acute the perils.

'Discover what?' asked Wirthlass with a frown.

'Never mind.'

'We'll be fine,' she replied. 'We just needed your expertise to make the initial jump. We're not *quite* as stupid as you think.'

I couldn't believe that I'd been hoodwinked by Goliath again. I had to hand it to them, this plan had been hatched and executed *beautifully*.

'How long have you known about the recipe?'

'That's just the weirdest thing about it.' Dr Wirthlass smiled. 'On the one hand only a day, but on the other . . . over fifteen years.'

'Retrospective investment,' I whispered, suddenly understanding. In their desperation, the ChronoGuard were breaking every single rule they'd ever made.

'Right! The Star Chamber lost confidence in your son's ability to secure the future so they called Lavoisier out of retirement to see if there weren't *other* avenues to explore. He approached John Henry yesterday at breakfast-time to ask him if the long-abandoned Book Project could be brought up to speed. Since it couldn't, Lavoisier suggested that they restart the project fifteen years ago so it could be ready for the End of Time. John Henry agreed with certain *conditions*, and I must say, we only just made it.'

'This is something of a mindf**k,' I replied, with no possibility of understatement. 'What does Goliath get out of it?'

'How do you think we survived being taken over by the Toast Marketing Board? Two days ago Goliath was just a bad memory with John Henry in debtor's prison, and I was working for International Pencils. When you have friends in the Time Industry, anything is possible. The ChronoGuard will be willing to offer us

313

almost untold patronage for the recipe to unscramble eggs, and with it the secret to travel in time. And in return? A corporation allowed to speculate freely in *time*. Finally, we will be able to bring our "big plan" to fruition.'

'And that plan is . . . ?'

'To own . . . everything.'

'In a world with a short Now?'

'Of course! With a compliant population only interested in the self and instant gratification, we can flog all manner of worthless crap as the "latest thing to have". There'll be big profits, Next – and by subtly choosing from whom the Now is mined, the Long Now Überclass can sit back and enjoy the benefits that will be theirs and theirs alone.'

I stared at Wirthlass, wondering whether I could rush her. It seemed doubtful since I was at least ten feet away, and the two technicians still on board the Rover also looked as if they had weapons.

'Okay,' said the doctor, 'we're all about done here. Enjoy your imprisonment. You'll know what it was like for my husband. Two years in *The Raven*, Next – *two years*. He still has nightmares, even today.'

'You're Jack Schitt's *wife*?'

She smiled again.

'Now you're getting it. My full name is Dr Anne Wirthlass-Schitt, but if you'd known it might have been a bit of a giveaway, hmm? Bye-bye now.'

The door swung shut, the bell rang twice, there was a low hiss and the Austen Rover lifted off. It hovered for a moment and then slowly rotated, expertly missed the crane derrick, rose above the height of the funnel and then became long and drawn out like a piece of elastic before vanishing with a faint 'pop'. I was left standing on the deck, biting my lip in frustration and anger. I took a deep breath and calmed myself. The reality book show of *The Bennets* wasn't due to start until tomorrow morning, so there was always hope. I looked around. The steamer rolled gently in the swell, the smoke drifted across the stern past the fluttering red ensign and the beat of the engine echoed up through the steel deck. I knew I wasn't in *Dark and Stormy Night* because the ship wasn't a rusty old tub held together by paint, but I was certainly *somewhere*, and somewhere was better than nowhere – and it was only when I arrived *there* and was out of ideas, time and essential metabolic functions that I was going to give up.

I trotted up the companionway, ducked into the galley and made my way up the ladder to the bridge, where a boy not much older than Friday was holding the ship's wheel.

'Who's in command?' I asked, a bit breathless.

'Why *you*, of course,' replied the lad.

'I'm not.'

'Then why are you a-wearin' the cap?'

I put up my hands to check and strangely enough, I *was* wearing the captain's cap. I took it off and stared at it stupidly.

'What book is this?'

'No book I knows of, Cap'n. What be your orders?'

I looked out of the wheelhouse ahead but could see nothing but a grey sea meeting a grey sky. The light was soft and directionless and for the first time I felt a shiver of dread. Something about this place was undeniably *creepy*, but I couldn't put my finger on it. I went to the navigation desk and looked at the chart. There was nothing on it but the pale blueness of open ocean, and a quick look in the drawers of the desk told me that all the charts were the same. Whatever this place was, this was all there was of it. I had to assume I was somewhere in the Maritime genre, but a quick glance at my mobile footnoterphone and the absence of any signal told me that I was several thousand volumes beyond our repeater station in the Hornblower series, and if that was the case, I was right on the periphery of the genre – as good as lost. I tapped my finger on the desk and thought hard – panic was the mind-killer and I still had several hours to figure this out. If I was no farther on in ten hours' time – *then* I could panic.

'What are your orders, Cap'n?' asked the lad at the wheel again.

'What's your name?'

'Baldwin.'

'I'm Thursday. Thursday Next.'

'Good to know you, Cap'n Next.'

'Have you heard my name? Or of Jurisfiction?'

He shook his head.

'Right. Tell me, Baldwin, do you know this ship well?'

'As well as I know meself,' he replied proudly.

'Is there a Core Containment Room?'

'Not that I knows of.'

So we weren't in a published work.

'How about a storycode engine anywhere on board?'

He frowned and looked confused.

'There's an *ordinary* engine room. I don't know nuffin 'bout no *storycode*.'

I scratched my head. Without a storycode engine we were either non-fiction or something in the Oral Tradition. Those were the upbeat possibilities: I might also be in a forgotten story, a dead writer's unrealised idea, or even a handwritten short story stuck in a desk drawer somewhere – the Dark Reading Matter.

'What year is this?'

'Spring of 1932, Cap'n.'

'And the purpose of this voyage?'

'Not for the likes of me to know, Cap'n.'

'But *something* must happen!'

'Oh, aye,' he said, more confidently, 'things most *definite* happen!'

'What sort of things?'

'*Difficult* things, Cap'n.'

As if in answer to his enigmatic comment, someone shouted my name. I walked out on to the port wing, where a man in a first officer's uniform was on the deck below. He was in his mid-fifties and looked vaguely cultured, but somehow out of place; as though his service in the merchant navy was intended to remove him from problems at home.

'Captain Next?' he said.

'Yes, sort of.'

'First Officer William Fitzwilliam at your service, ma'am – we've got a problem with the passengers!'

'Can't you deal with it?'

'No, ma'am – *you're* the captain.'

I descended and found Fitzwilliam at the foot of the ladder. He led me into the panelled wardroom, where there were three people waiting for us. The first man was standing stiffly with his arms folded and looked aggrieved. He was well dressed in a black morning coat and wore a small pince-nez perched on the end of his nose. The other two were obviously man and wife. The woman was of an unhealthy pallor, had recently been crying and was being comforted by her husband, who every now and then shot an angry glance at the first man.

'I'm very busy,' I told them, 'what's the problem here?'

'My name is Mr Langdon,' said the married man, wringing his hands. 'My wife Louise here suffers from Zachary's syndrome and without the necessary medicine, she will die.'

'I'm very sorry to hear that,' I said, 'but what can I do?'

'That man has the medicine!' cried Langdon, pointing an accusatory finger at the man in the pince-nez. 'Yet he refuses to sell it to me!'

'Is this true?'

'My name is Dr Glister,' said the man, nodding politely. 'I have the medicine, it is true, but the price is two thousand guineas and Mr and Mrs Langdon have only a thousand guineas, and not the capacity to borrow more!'

'Well,' I said to the doctor, 'I think it would be a kindly gesture to lower the price, don't you?'

'I wish that I could,' replied Dr Glister, 'but this medicine cost me everything I possessed to develop. It destroyed my health and damaged my reputation. If I do not recoup my losses, I will be forced into ruin, my property will be repossessed and my six children become destitute. I am sympathetic to Mrs Langdon's trouble, but this is a fiscal issue.'

'Listen,' I said to the Langdons, 'it's not up to me. The medicine is Dr Glister's property for him to dispose of as he wishes.'

'But she needs the medicine *now*,' pleaded Mr Langdon. 'If she doesn't get it, she will die. You are the captain of this ship so have the ultimate authority. You *must* make the decision.'

I sighed. I had a lot more important things to deal with right now.

'Dr Glister, give him the medicine for a thousand guineas. Mr Langdon, you will work to repay Dr Glister *no matter what*. Understand?'

'But my livelihood!' wailed Glister.

'I place Mrs Langdon's *definite* death above the *possibility* of your penury, Dr Glister.'

'But this is nothing short of theft!' he replied, outraged at my words. 'And I have done nothing wrong — only discovered a cure for a fatal illness. I deserve better treatment than this!'

'You do, you're right. But I know nothing of you, nor the Langdons. My decision is based only on the saving of a life. Will you excuse me?'

Baldwin had called from the wheelhouse and I quickly scooted up the stairs.

'What is it?'

He pointed to something about a mile off the starboard bow. I picked up a pair of binoculars and trained it on the distant object. Finally, some good luck. It looked like a turmoil, the name we gave to a small, localised disruption in the fabric of the written word. This was how heavy weather in the BookWorld got started; a turmoil would soon progress into a powerful wordstorm, able to uproot words, ideas and even people, then carry them with it across the empty darkness of the Nothing, eventually dumping them on distant books several genres away. It was my way out. I'd never hitched a ride on a wordstorm before, but it didn't look too difficult – Dorothy, after all, had no real problems with the tornado.

'Alter course thirty degrees to starboard,' I said. 'We're going to intercept the wordstorm. How long do you think it will take for us to get there, Baldwin?'

'Twenty minutes, Cap'n.'

It would be a close thing. Turmoils increase their pace until a rotating tube rises up into the heavens, filled with small sections of plot and anything else it can suck up, then, with a flurry of distorted sense, it lifts off and vanishes. I wouldn't get this chance again.

'Is that wise, Captain?' asked First Officer Fitzwilliam, who had joined us on the bridge. 'I've seen storms like that. They can do serious damage – and we have forty souls on board, many of them women and children.'

'Then you can lower me in a lifeboat ahead of the storm.'

'And leave us without a lifeboat?'

'Yes – *no* – I don't know. Fitzwilliam?'

'Yes, Captain?'

'What is this place?'

'I don't know what you mean, Captain.'

'I mean—'

'Cap'n,' said Baldwin, pointing to the port side of the ship, 'isn't that a lifeboat?'

I turned my attention to the area at which he pointed. It *was* a lifeboat, with what looked like several people, all slumped and apparently unconscious. *Damn.* I looked again, hoping for confirmation that they might already be dead, but saw nothing to tell me either way. I frowned to myself. Did I just hope for them to be dead?

'You can pick them up after you've dropped me off,' I said. 'It'll only mean an extra forty minutes for them and I really need to get out of here.'

I saw Fitzwilliam and Baldwin exchange glances. But as we watched, the lifeboat was caught by a wave and capsized, casting the occupants into the sea. We could see now that they *were* alive, and as they scrabbled weakly to cling to the upturned boat, I gave the order.

'Turn about. Reduce power and stand by to pick up survivors.'

'Aye aye, Cap'n,' said Baldwin, spinning the wheel as Fitzwilliam rang up 'slow ahead' on the engine room telegraph. I walked out on to the starboard wing and watched despondently as the turmoil developed into a wordstorm. Within the twenty minutes it took to intercept the lifeboat, the whirling mass of narrative distortion lifted off, taking part of the description of the ocean with it. There was a ragged dark hole for a moment and then the sea washed in to fill the anomaly, and in a few moments everything was back to normal. Perhaps I should have left the lifeboat. After all, the Long Now and the classics were more important than several fictional castaways. Mind you, if I'd been on that lifeboat, I know what I would have wanted.

'Captain!'

It was Dr Glister.

'I don't want to know about your arguments with the Langdons,' I told him.

'No, no,' he replied in something of a panic, 'you *cannot* pick up these castaways!'

'Why not?'

'They have Squurd's disease.'

'They have *what*?'

We walked into the wheelhouse and out again on to the port wing, where Fitzwilliam was directing the rescue operation. The lifeboat was still at least a hundred yards ahead of us. The ship was moving ahead slowly, a cling net had been thrown over the side, and several burly sailors were making ready to pick up the castaways.

'Look carefully at the survivors,' urged Dr Glister, and I trained my binoculars on the small group. Now that they were closer I could see that their faces were covered with unsightly green pustules. I lowered the binoculars and looked at Dr Glister.

'What's the prognosis?'

'One hundred per cent fatal, and highly contagious. Bring them on board and we'll be looking at a minimum of twenty per cent casualties. We don't reach port for six months and these poor wretches will already have died in agony long before we could get any help to them.'

I rubbed my temples.

'You're completely sure of this?'

He nodded. I took a deep breath.

'Fitzwilliam?'

'Yes, Captain?'

'Break off the rescue.'

'What?'

'You heard me. These people have a contagious fatal illness, and I won't risk my passengers' lives saving castaways who will die no matter what we do.'

'But, Captain!' he protested. 'We *never* leave a man in the water!'

'We're doing it today, Fitzwilliam. Do you understand?'

He glared at me menacingly, then leaned over the rail and repeated my order, making sure the men knew who had made it. After that, he went into the wheelhouse, rang up 'full ahead' and the vessel shuddered as we made extra speed and steamed on.

'Come inside,' said Dr Glister.

'No,' I said, 'I'm staying here. I won't hide from the men I've condemned to death.'

And I stood there and watched as the lifeboat and the men drifted astern of the ship and were soon lost to view in the seas.

It was with a heavy heart that I walked back into the wheelhouse and sat in the captain's chair. Baldwin was silent, and gazed straight ahead.

'It was the right thing to do,' I muttered to no one in particular, 'and what's more, I could have used the wordstorm to escape after all.'

'Things happen here,' muttered Baldwin, '*difficult* things.'

I suddenly had a thought, but hoped upon hope I was wrong. 'What's the name of this ship?'

'The ship?' replied Baldwin cheerily. 'It's the steamship *Moral Dilemma*, Cap'n.'

I covered my face with my hands and groaned. Anne Wirthlass-Schitt and her obnoxious husband had not been kidding when they said they'd chosen this place especially for me. My nerves were already badly frayed and I felt the heavy hand of guilt pressing upon me. I'd only been here an hour – what would I be like in a week, or a month? Truly, I was trapped in an unenviable place: adrift on the Hypothetical Ocean, in command of the *Moral Dilemma*.

'Captain?'

It was the cook this time. He was unshaven and wearing a white uniform that had so many food stains on it that it was hard to say where stain ended and uniform began.

'Yes?' I said, somewhat wearily.

'Begging your pardon, but there's been a gross underestimation on the provisions.'

'And?'

'We don't get into port for another six months,' the cook continued, referring to a grubby sheet of calculations he had on him, 'and we only have enough to feed the crew and passengers on strict rations for two-thirds of that time.'

'What are you saying?'

'That all forty of us will starve long before we reach port.'

I beckoned Fitzwilliam over.

'There wouldn't be another port closer than that, would there?'

'No, Captain,' he answered. 'Port Conjecture is the only port there is.'

'I thought so. And no fish, either?'

'Not in these waters.'

'Other ships?'

'None.'

I got it now. These were the 'difficult things' Baldwin had spoken of, and they were mine and mine alone to deal with. The ship, the sea and the people on it might be hypothetical – but they could suffer and die the same as anyone.

'Thank you, Cook,' I said, 'I'll let you know of my decision.'

He gave a lazy salute, and was gone.

'Well, Fitzwilliam,' I said, doing some simple maths on a piece of paper, 'there is enough food for twenty-six people to survive until we reach port. Do you think we could find fourteen volunteers to throw themselves over the side to ensure the survival of the rest?'

'I doubt it.'

'Then I have something of a problem. Is my primary duty as captain to ensure that as many people as possible survive on my ship, or is it my moral obligation to not conduct or condone murder?'

'The men in the lifeboat just now wouldn't see you as anything but a murderer.'

'Perhaps so, but this one's harder; it's not a case of *inaction* to bring about a circumstance, but *action*. This is what I'm going to do. Anyone under eighteen is excluded as are six essential crew to keep the ship going. All the rest will choose straws – thirteen will go over the side.'

'If they don't want to go?'

'Then I will throw them over.'

'You'll hang for it.'

'I won't. I'll be the fourteenth.'

'Very . . . *selfless*,' murmured Fitzwilliam, 'but even after your crew and age exclusions, thirty-one passengers are still under eighteen. You will still have to select seven of them. Will you still be able to throw them overboard, the children, the innocents?'

'But I save the rest, right?'

'It's not for me to say,' said Fitzwilliam quietly, 'I am not the captain.'

I closed my eyes and took a deep breath, my heart thumping and a cold panic rumbling inside me. I had to do terrible things in order to save others, and I'm not sure I could even do it – thus imperilling everyone's life. I stopped for a moment and thought. The dilemmas had been getting progressively worse since I arrived. Perhaps this place – wherever it was – was quirkily responsive to my decisions. I decided to try something.

'No,' I said, 'I'm not going to kill anyone simply because an abstract ethical situation demands it. We're going to sail on as we are, and trust to providence that we meet another ship. If we don't, then we may die, but we will have at least done the right thing by one another.'

There was a distant rumble of thunder in the distance and the boat heeled over. I wondered what would be next.

'Begging your pardon, Captain, but I bring bad news.'

It was a steward who I hadn't seen before.

'And—?'

'We have a gentleman in the wardroom who claims there is a bomb on board the ship – and it's set to go off in ten minutes.'

I allowed myself a wry smile. The rapidly changing scenarios seemed to have a clumsy intelligence to them. It was possible this was something in the Oral Tradition, but I couldn't be sure. But if this small world was somehow sentient, it could be beaten – but for it to be vanquished, I needed to find its weakness, and it had just supplied one – *impatience*. It didn't want a long, drawn-out starvation for the passengers; it wanted me to commit a hands-on murder for the greater good – and soon.

'Show me.'

I followed the steward down into the wardroom, where a man was sitting on a chair in the middle of the room. He looked sallow, had fine, wispy blond hair and small eyes that stared intently at me as I walked in. A burly sailor named McTavish who was tattoo and Scotsman in a 3:4 ratio was standing guard over him. There was no one else in the room – there didn't need to be. It was a hypothetical situation.

'Your name, sir?'

'Jebediah Salford. And I have hidden a bomb—'

'I heard. And naturally, you won't tell me where it is?'

'Naturally.'

'This bomb,' I went on, 'will sink the ship, potentially leading to many deaths?'

'Indeed, I hope so,' replied Jebediah cheerily.

'Your own included?'

'I fear no death.'

I paused for thought. It was a classic and overused ethical dilemma. Would I, as an essentially good person, reduce myself to torturing someone for the greater good? It was a puzzle that had been discussed for many years, generally by those for whom it has no chance of becoming real. But the way in which the scenarios came on thick and fast suggested that whoever was running this show had a prurient interest in seeing just how far a decent person could be pushed before they did bad things. I could almost feel the architect of the dilemma gloating over me from afar. I would have to stall him if I could.

'Fitzwilliam? Have all passengers go on deck, close all watertight doors and have every crew member and able-bodied passenger look for the bomb.'

'Captain,' he said, 'that's a waste of time. There *is* a bomb but you can't find it. The decision has to be made here and now, in this wardroom.'

Damn. Outmanoeuvred.

'How many lifeboats do we have?' I asked, getting increasingly desperate.

'Only one left, sir – with room for ten.'

'Shit. How long do we have left before this bomb goes off?'

'Seven minutes.'

If this was the real world and in a situation as black and white as this, there wasn't a decision to make. I would use all force necessary to get the information. But most importantly, submit myself to scrutiny afterwards. If you permit or conduct torture, you must be personally responsible for your actions – it's the kind of decision for which it's best to have the threat of prison looming behind you. But the thing was, on board this ship here and now, it didn't look as though torturing Salford would actually achieve anything at all. He would eventually tell me, the bomb would be found – and the next dilemma would begin. And they would carry on, again and again, worse and worse, until I had done everything I would never have done, and the passengers of this vessel were drowned, eaten or murdered. It was hell for me, but it would be hell for them, too. I sat down heavily on a nearby chair, put my head in hands and stared at the floor.

'Captain,' said Fitzwilliam, 'we only have five minutes. You *must* torture this person.'

'Yeah, yeah,' I mumbled incoherently, 'I know.'

'We will all die,' he continued, '. . . *again*.'

I looked up into his eyes. I'd never noticed how incredibly blue they were.

'You all die in the end, don't you?' I said miserably. 'No matter what I do. It's just one increasingly bad dilemma after another until everyone's dead, right?'

'Four minutes, Captain.'

'Am I right?'

Fitzwilliam looked away.

'I asked you a question, Number One.'

He looked at me, and he seemed to have tears in his eyes.

'We have all been drowned,' he said in a quiet voice, 'over a thousand times each. We have been eaten, blown up and suffered fatal illnesses. The drownings are the worst. Each time I can feel the smothering effect of water, the blind panic as I suffocate—!'

'Fitzwilliam,' I demanded, 'where is this damnable place?'

He took a deep breath and lowered his voice.

'We're Oral Tradition but we're not in a story – we're an ethics seminar.'

'You mean, you're all hypothetical characters during a lecture?'

Fitzwilliam nodded miserably. The steward somewhat chillingly handed me a pair of pliers, while reminding me in an urgent whisper that there were only three minutes left.

I looked down at the pliers in an absent sort of way, at Jebediah, then back to Fitzwilliam, who was staring at the floor. So much suffering on board this ship and for so long. Perhaps there *was* another way out. The thing was, to take such radical action in the Oral Tradition risked the life of the lecturer giving the talk. But what was more important? The well-being of one real-life ethics professor, or the relentless torture of his subjects, who had to undergo his sadistic and relentless hypothetical dilemmas for two-hour sessions three times a week? When you tell a tragic story, someone dies for real in the BookWorld. I was in the Oral Tradition. Potentially the best storytelling there was – and the most destructive.

'McTavish, prepare the lifeboat for launching. I'm leaving.'

McTavish looked at Fitzwilliam, who shrugged, and the large Scotsman and his tattoos departed.

'That isn't one of the options,' said Fitzwilliam, 'you can't do it.'

'I have experience of the Oral Tradition,' I told him. 'All these scenarios are taking place only because I am here to preside in judgement upon them. This whole thing only goes one way: in a downward spiral of increasingly impossible moral dilemmas which will leave everyone dead except myself and one other, who I will be forced to kill and eat or something. If I take myself out of the equation you are free to sail across the sea unhampered, unimpeded – and safe.'

'But that might, that might—'

'—harm the lecturer, even kill him? Possibly. If the bomb goes off, you'll know I've failed, and he's okay. If it doesn't, you'll all be safe.'

'And you?' he asked. 'What about you?'

I patted him on the shoulder.

'Don't worry about me. I think you've all suffered enough on account of the Outland.'

'But surely – we can pick you up again if all goes well?'

'No,' I said, 'that's not how it works. It can't be a trick. I have to cast myself adrift.'

I trotted out of the wardroom and to the side of the ship, where McTavish had already lowered the lifeboat. It was being retained against the scramble net by lines fore and aft held by deckhands, and it thumped against the hull as the waves caught it. As I put my leg over the rail to climb down, Fitzwilliam held my arm. He wasn't trying to stop me – he wanted to shake me by the hand.

'Goodbye, Captain – and thank you.'

I smiled.

'Think you'll make Port Conjecture?'

He smiled back.

'We'll give it our best shot.'

I climbed down the scramble net and into the lifeboat. They let go fore and aft and the boat rocked violently as the bow wave caught it. For a moment I thought it would go over, but it stayed upright, and I rapidly fell behind as the ship steamed on.

I counted off the seconds until the bomb was meant to explode, but thankfully it didn't, and across the sea I heard the cheer of forty people celebrating their release. I couldn't share in their elation because in a university somewhere back home the ethics lecturer had suddenly keeled over with an aneurism. They'd call a doctor and, with a bit of luck, he'd pull through. He might even lecture again, but not with this crew.

The *Moral Dilemma* was at least a quarter-mile away by now, and within ten minutes it was just a smudge of smoke on the horizon. In another half-hour it had vanished completely, and I was on my own in a grey sea that extended for ever in all directions. I looked through my shoulder bag and found a bar of chocolate which I ate in a despondent manner, and then just sat in the bows of the lifeboat and stared up at the grey sky, feeling hopelessly lost. I leaned back and closed my eyes.

Had I done the right thing? I had no idea. The lecturer couldn't have known the suffering he was putting his hypothetical characters through, but even if he had, perhaps he'd justify it by reasoning that the suffering was worth the benefits to his students. If he survived I'd be able to ask him his opinion. But that wasn't likely. Rescue seemed a very remote possibility, and that was at the nub of the whole ethical dilemma argument. You never come out on top, no matter what. The only way to win the game is not to play.

34

Rescue / Capture

'There was only one Jurisfiction agent who worked exclusively in the Oral Tradition. He was named Ski, rarely spoke and wore a tall hat in the manner of Lincoln – but that was the sum total of his recognisable features. When appearing at the Jurisfiction offices he was always insubstantial, flickering in and out like a badly tuned TV. Despite this he did some of the best work in the Oraltrad I'd seen. Rumour had it that he was a discarded Childhood Imaginary Friend, which accounted for his inconsolable melancholy.'

When I awoke, nothing had changed. The sea was still grey, the sky a dull overcast. The water was choppy but not dangerously so, and had a sort of twenty second pattern of movement to it. With nothing better to do I sat up and watched the waves as they rose and fell. By fixing my eyes on a random part of the ocean, the same wave would come round again like a loop in a film. Most of the BookWorld was like that. Fictional forests had only eight different trees; a beach five different pebbles; a sky twelve different clouds. It was what made the real world so rich by comparison. I looked at my watch. The reality book show of *The Bennets* would be replacing *Pride and Prejudice* in three hours, and the first task of the household would be unveiled in two. Equally bad, that worthless shit Wirthlass-Schitt might well have the recipe by now, and would be hoofing it back to Goliath. But then again, she might not. I'd visited enough poetry to know that it's an emotionally draining place and on a completely different level. Whereas *story* is processed in the mind in a straightforward manner, poetry bypasses rational thought and goes straight to the limbic system and lights it up like a bushfire. It's the crack cocaine of the literary world.

My mind, I knew, was wandering. It was intentional. If I didn't let it, it returned like an annoying default setting to Landen and the kids. Whenever I thought of them my eyes welled up, and that was no good for anything. Perhaps, I mused, instead of lying to Landen after the Minotaur shot me in 1988, I should have just stayed at home and led a blameless life of unabashed domestication. Washing, cleaning and making meals. Okay, with *some* part-time work down at Acme in case I went nuts. But no SpecOps stuff. None. *Except* maybe dispatching a teensy-weeny chimera. Or two. And if Spike needed a hand? Well, I couldn't say no, now could— [4]

My thoughts were interrupted by my mobile footnoterphone. Until now, it had been resolutely silent. I dug it out of my bag and stared at it hopefully. There was still no signal, which meant that *someone else* was within a radius of about ten million words. Not far in a shelf of Russian novels, perhaps, but out here in the Oral Tradition it could mean covering a thousand stories or more. It was entirely possible that they weren't friends at all, but anything was better than slow starvation, so I keyed the mike and pretended I was a communications expert from OFF-FNOP, the watchdog responsible for overseeing the network.

'OFF-FNOP tech number – um – 76542: request user ident.'

I looked carefully all around me but the horizon was clear. There was nothing at all; just endless grey. It was like— [5]

I paused. Footnoterphones weren't like normal phones – they were textual. It was impossible to tell who was talking. It was a bit

4 'fffffgghuhfdffffffggggoooonpicUp..passs1cccccwwww'
5 'kkkkkcar45kAR45%%%%%bloody hellfire!>>>sodding jjjjjjjjjj Bureaucrats even out here+eeee'

like text messages back home, but without the dopey 'CUL8R' shorthand nonsense.

'I say again: request user ident.'

I looked around desperately, but still nothing. I hoped it wasn't another poor twit like me, compelled to take over the reins as ethical arbiter.[6]

My heart suddenly leapt. Whoever it was, they were somewhere close – and they didn't read like anyone who would do me harm. I needed to tell them how to find me, but the only direction I could think of was 'I'm near a wave,' which was only marginally less useful than 'I'm in a boat'. Then, I had an idea.

'If you can hear me,' I said into my mobile, 'head for the rainstorm of text.'

I tucked the phone in my pocket and took out my pistol. I released the safety, pointed it into the air and fired. There was a low thud and the air seemed to wobble as the eraserhead arced high into the sky. It was a risky move as it would almost certainly be picked up by the weather stations dotted around the genres, and from there would be transmitted to Text Grand Central. If they were looking for me, they'd know instantly where I was.

It took a few seconds for the charge to reach the thick stratus of cloud, but when it hit, the effect can only be described as spectacular. There was a yellow and green starburst and the textual clouds changed rapidly from grey to black as the words dissolved, taking the meaning with them. A dark cloud of letters was soon fluttering down towards the sea like chaff, a pillar of text that could be seen for miles. They landed on me and the boat but mostly the sea, where they settled like autumn leaves on a lake.

I looked up and saw that the hole in the clouds was already healing

6 'jjjjjjjjahagssffffffssss–Is anyone out there? All I dddddddd can see is endless BLEEDING ocean–*llllllll*'

itself, and within a few minutes the text would start to sink. I opened the pistol and reloaded, but I didn't need to fire a second time. On the horizon and heading towards me was a small dot that gradually grew bigger and bigger until it was overhead, then circled twice before it slowed to a stop, hovering in the air right next to the lifeboat. The driver rolled down his window and consulted a clipboard.

'Are you Ms Next?' he asked, which was mildly surprising, to say the least.

'Yes, I am.'

'And you ordered me?'

'Yes, yes I did.'

'Well, you'd better get in then.'

I was still in mild shock at the turn of events, but quickly gathered my thoughts and my belongings and climbed into the yellow vehicle. It was dented and dirty and had the familiar TransGenreTaxis logo on the door. I'd never been so glad to see a cab in my entire life. I settled myself in the back seat as the driver switched on the meter, turned to me with a grin and said:

'Had the devil's job finding you, darling – where to?'

It was a good point. I thought for a moment. *Pride and Prejudice* was definitely in dire peril, but if the Now got any shorter, then *all* books were in danger – and a lot more besides.

'Longfellow,' I said, 'and make it snappy. I think we're going to have some unwanted company.'

The cabby raised his eyebrows, pressed on the accelerator and we were soon scooting across the sea at a good rate of knots. He caught my eye in the rear-view mirror.

'Are you in some kind of trouble?'

'The worst kind,' I replied, thinking that I was going to have to trust this cabby to do the right thing. 'I'm subject to a shoot-to-kill order from the CofG, but it's bullshit. I'm a Jurisfiction agent and I could seriously do with some help right now.'

'Bureaucrats!' he snorted disparagingly, then thought hard for a moment and added: 'Next, Next – you wouldn't be *Thursday* Next, would you?'

'That's me.'

'I like your books a lot. Especially the early ones with all the killing and gratuitous sex.'

'I'm not like that. I'm—'

'Whoa!'

The cabby swerved abruptly and I was thrown violently to the other side of the taxi. I looked out of the rear window and could see a figure in a long black dress hitting the sea in a cascade of foam. They were on to me already.

'That was strange,' said the cabby, 'but I could have sworn that was a fifty-something creepy-looking housekeeper dressed entirely in black.'

'It was a Danverclone,' I said. 'There'll be more.'

He clicked down the central locking and turned to stare at me.

'You've really pissed someone off good and proper, haven't you?'

'Not without good reason – look out!'

He swerved again as another Danvers bounced off the bonnet and stared at me in a very unnerving way as she flew past the window. I watched her cartwheel across the waves behind us. That was the thing about Danverclones. They were wholly expendable.

A moment later there was a heavy thump on the roof that shook the cab. I looked behind but no one had fallen off, and then heard a noise like an angle grinder from above. It was another Danverclone on the roof, and she was planning on getting in.

'This is too heavy for me,' said the cabby, whose sense of fair play was rapidly departing. 'I've got a livelihood and a very expensive backstory to support.'

'I'll buy you a fleet of new cabs,' I told him somewhat urgently, 'and Master Backstoryist Grnksghty is a personal friend of mine; he'll spin you a backstory of your choice.'

Before the cabby could answer another Mrs Danvers landed heavily on the bonnet near the radiator. She stared at us for a moment and then, by pushing her fingers into the steel body-work, began to crawl up the bonnet towards us, lips pursed tightly, the slipstream flapping her clothes and tugging at her tightly combed black hair. She wore the same small dark glasses as the rest of them, but you didn't need to see her eyes to guess her murderous intent.

'I'm going to have to turn you in,' said the cabby as another Danverclone landed on the taxi with a crash that shattered the side window. She hung on to the roof guttering and flapped around for a bit before finally getting a hold and then, reaching in through the broken window, she fumbled for the door handle. I reached across, flicked off the lock and kicked the door open, dislodging the Danverclone, who seemed to hang in the air for a moment before a large wave caught her and she was left behind the rapidly moving taxi.

'I'm not sure I can help you any further,' continued the cabby. 'This is some seriously bad shit you've got yourself into.'

'I'm from the Outland,' I told him as another two Danvers fell past, vainly flailing their arms as they attempted to catch hold of the taxi. 'Ever wanted something Outlandish? I can get it for you.'

'Anything?' asked the cabby. There was a screech of metal from above as the Danverclone on the roof began to cut her way in; sparks began to fall from the roof as the angle grinder bit into the metal.

'*Anything!*'

'Well, now,' said the cabby, ignoring another Danvers, who landed on the one crawling up the bonnet. There was the sort of sound a squeaky toy makes when you sit on it heavily and they both bounced off and were gone. 'What I'd really like,' he continued, completely unfazed, 'is an original Spacehopper.'

It seemed an unusual request until you realised just how valuable Outlander memorabilia were. I'd once seen two generics almost kill each other over a traffic cone.

'Orange and with a face on the front?'

'Is there any other? You'll find a seat belt in the back,' he said. 'I suggest you use it.'

I didn't have time to even search for it before he suddenly pointed the cab straight up and went into a vertical climb towards the clouds. He turned to look at me, raised his eyebrows and smiled. He thought it was something of a lark; I was . . . well, *concerned*. I looked behind me as the Mrs Danvers fell from the roof along with the petrol-driven grinder and tumbled in a spiralling manner towards the sea, which was now far below. A few moments later, we were enveloped by the soft greyness of the clouds, and almost immediately, but without any sensation of having righted ourselves, we left the cloud on an even keel and were moving slowly between a squadron of French sailing ships and a lone British one. That might have been nothing to worry about except that they were both armed naval vessels and were firing salvos at one another, and every now and again a hot ball of iron would sail spectacularly close to the cab with a whizzing noise.

'I had that Admiral Hornblower in the back of my cab once,' said the taxi-driver, chatting amiably to me in that curious way that cabbies do when they talk over their shoulder and look at the road at the same time. 'What a gent. Tipped me a sovereign and then tried to press me into service.'

'Where are we?' I asked.

'C. S. Forester's *Ship of the Line*,' replied the cabby. 'We'll hang a left after the HMS *Sutherland* and move through *The African Queen* to join the cross-Maritime thoroughfare at *The Old Man and the*

Sea. Once there we'll take a back-double through *The Sea Wolf* and come out at *Moby-Dick*, which neatly sidesteps *Treasure Island* as it's usually chocka at this hour.'

'Wouldn't it be better to go via *20,000 Leagues under the Sea* and hang a left at *Robinson Crusoe*?'

I could see him staring at me in the rear-view mirror.

'You want to try it that way?' he asked, annoyed that I might question his judgement.

'No,' I replied hastily, 'we'll do what you think best.'

He seemed happier at this.

'Okey-dokey. Whereabouts in Longfellow were you wanting to go?'

'"The Wreck of the *Hesperus*".'

He turned round to stare at me.

'*Hesperus*? You're one whole heap of trouble, lady. I'll drop you off at "Psalm of Life" and you can walk from there.'

I glared at him.

'An original Spacehopper, was it? *Boxed?*'

He sighed. It was a good deal, and he knew it.

'Okay,' he said at last, '*Hesperus* it is.'

We moved slowly past a small steam launch that was shooting some rapids on the Ulanga, and the cabby spoke again:

'So what's your story?'

'I was replaced by my written other self who is rubber-stamping the CofG's most hare-brained schemes with the woeful compliance of our prime minister back home. You've heard about *Pride and Prejudice* being serialised as a reality book show called *The Bennets*? That's what I'm trying to stop. You got a name?'

'Colin.'

We fell silent for a moment as we followed the Ulanga down-river to where it joined the Bora and then into the lake, where the gunboat *Königin Luise* lay at anchor. I busied myself reloading my pistol and checking the last two eraserheads. I even took the pistol's holster and clipped it to my belt. I didn't like these things, but I was going to be prepared. Mind you, if they decided to send in the clones, I'd be in serious shit. There were seven thousand Danvers and only one of me. I'd have to erase over three thousand per cartridge, and I didn't think they'd all gather themselves in a convenient heap for me. I pulled out my mobile and stared at it. We were in full signal range but they'd have a trace on me for sure.

'Use mine,' said Colin, who had been watching me. He passed his footnoterphone back to me and I called Bradshaw.

'Commander? It's Thursday.'[7]

'I'm in a taxi heading towards *Moby-Dick* via *The Old Man and the Sea*.'[8]

'Apparently not. How are things?'[9]

'No; I've got to destroy something in *Hesperus* that will hopefully raise the Outlander read-rates. As soon as I'm done there I'll be straight on to Jobsworth.'[10]

I looked out of the window. We were over the sea once again, but this time the weather was brighter. Two small whaling boats, each with five men at the oars, were pulling towards a disturbance in the water, and as I watched a mighty, grey-white bulk erupted from beneath the green water and shattered one of the small boats, pitching the hapless occupants into the sea.

'I'm just coming out the far end of *Moby-Dick*. Do you have anything for me at all?'[11]

---

7 'Thursday! Great Scott, girl! Where are you?'

8 'Wouldn't it be better to go via *20,000 Leagues under the Sea* and hang a left at *Robinson Crusoe*?'

9 'Not good. Can you get up to the CofG straight away?'

10 'Good luck, old girl. You'll need it. Where are you now?'

11 'Not a thing. I'm under house arrest. You're all alone on this one, Thursday. Best of British and all that.'

I closed the mobile and handed it back. If Bradshaw was short on ideas, the situation was more hopeless than I had imagined. We crossed from Maritime to Poetry by way of 'The Rime of the Ancient Mariner', and after hiding momentarily in the waste of wild dunes, marram and sand of 'False Dawn' while a foot patrol of Danvers moved past, we were off again and turned into Longfellow by way of 'The Lighthouse'.

'Hold up a moment,' I said to Colin, and we pulled up beneath a rocky ledge on a limestone spur that led out in the deep purple of the twilight to a lighthouse, its beam a sudden radiance of light that swept around the bay.

'This isn't a "wait and return" job, is it?' he asked nervously.

'I'm afraid it is. How close can you get me to the actual wrecking of the *Hesperus*?'

He sucked air in through his teeth and scratched his nose.

'During the gale itself, not close at all. The reef of Norman's Woe during the storm is not somewhere you'd like to be. Forget the wind and the rain – it's the cold.'

I knew what he meant. Poetry was an emotional rollercoaster of a form that could heighten the senses almost beyond straining. The sun was always brighter, skies bluer, and forests steamed six times as much after a summer shower and felt twelve times more earthy. Love was ten times stronger, and happiness, hope and charity rose to a level that made your head spin with giddy well-being. On the other side of the coin it also made the darker side of existence twenty times worse – tragedy and despair were bleaker, more malevolent. As the saying goes, 'They don't do nuffing by half-measures down at Poetry'.

'So how close?' I asked.

'Daybreak, three verses from the end.'

'Okay,' I said, 'let's do it.'

He released the handbrake and motored slowly forward. The

light moved from twilight to dawn as we entered 'The Wreck of the *Hesperus*'. The sky was still leaden and a stiff wind scoured the foreshore, even though the worst of the storm had passed. The taxi drew to a halt on the sea-beach and I opened the door and stepped out. I suddenly felt a feeling of strong loss and despair, but knowing full well that these were simply emotions seeping out of the over-charged fabric of the poem, I attempted to give it no heed. Colin got out as well, and we exchanged nervous looks. The sea-beach was littered with the wreckage of the *Hesperus*, reduced to little more than matchwood by the gale. I pulled my jacket collar up against the wind and trudged up the shoreline.

'What are we looking for?' asked Colin, who had joined me.

'Remains of a yellow tour coach,' I said, 'or a tasteless blue jacket with large checks.'

'Nothing too specific, then?'

Most of the flotsam was wood, barrels, ropes and the odd personal artefact. We came across a drowned sailor, but he wasn't someone from the Rover. Colin became all emotional over the loss of life and lamented about how the sailor had been 'sorely taken from the bosom of his family' and had 'given his soul to the storm' before I told him to pull himself together. We reached some rocks and chanced across a fisherman, staring with a numbed expression at a section of mast that gently rose and fell in the sheltered water of an inlet. Lashed to the mast was a body. Her long brown hair was floating like seaweed and the intense cold had frozen her features in the expression she'd last worn in life – of abject terror. She was wearing a heavy seaman's coat which hadn't done much good, and I waded into the icy water to take a closer look. Ordinarily I wouldn't have, but something was *wrong*. This should have been the body of a young girl – the skipper's daughter. But it wasn't. It was a middle-aged woman. It was *Wirthlass-Schitt*. Her eyelashes were encrusted

341

with frozen salt and she stared blankly out at the world, her face suffused with fear.

'She saved me.'

It was a little girl's voice and I turned. She was aged no more than nine and was wrapped in a Goliath-issue duvet jacket. She looked confused, as well she might; she hadn't survived the storm for over one hundred and sixty-three years. Wirthlass-Schitt had underestimated not only the power of the BookWorld and the raw energy of poetry . . . but also *herself*. Despite her primary goal of corporate duty, she couldn't leave a child to drown. She'd done what she thought was right, and suffered the consequences. It was what I was trying to warn her about. The thing you discover in poetry . . . is your *true* personality. The annoying thing was, she'd done it all for nothing. A clean-up gang from Jurisfiction would be down later, putting everything chillingly to rights. It was why I didn't like to do 'the rhyming stuff'.

Colin, overcome by the heavy emotions that pervaded the air like fog, had begun to cry.

'O, wearisome world!' he sobbed.

I checked Anne's collar and found a small necklace on her cold flesh. I pulled it off and then stopped. If she'd been on the *Hesperus*, perhaps she had picked up Mycroft's jacket?

The seaman's coat was like cardboard and I eased it open at the collar to look beneath. My heart fell. She wasn't wearing the jacket, and after checking her pockets I found that she wasn't carrying the recipe, either. I took a deep breath, and my emotions, enhanced by the poem, suddenly fell to rock bottom. Wirthlass-Schitt must have given the jacket to her crewmates – and if it was back at Goliath I'd have a snowball's chance in hell of getting to it. Friday had entrusted me with the protection of the Long Now and I had failed him. I waded back to shore and started sniffing as large salty tears started to run down my face.

'Oh, *please* dry up,' I said to Colin, who was sobbing into his hanky next to me, 'you've got me started off now.'

'But the sadness drapes heavily on my countenance!' he whimpered.

We sat on the foreshore next to the fisherman, who was still looking aghast, and sobbed quietly as though our hearts would break. The young girl came and sat down next to me. She patted my hand reassuringly.

'I didn't *want* to be rescued anyway,' she announced. 'If I survive, the whole point of the poem is lost – Henry will be *furious*.'

'Don't worry,' I said, 'it'll all be repaired.'

'And everyone keeps on giving me their jackets,' she continued in a huffy tone. 'Honestly, it gets harder and harder to freeze to death these days. There's this one that Anne gave me,' she added, thumbing the thick pile on the blue Goliath jacket, 'and the one the old man gave me seventeen years ago.'

'Really, I'm not interested in—'

I stopped sobbing as a bright shaft of sunlight cut through the storm clouds of my melancholia.

'Do . . . you still have it?'

'Of course!'

And she unzipped the Goliath jacket to reveal . . . a man's blue jacket in large checks. Never had I been happier to see a more tasteless garment. I quickly rummaged through the pockets and found a yo-yo string, a very old bag of jelly babies, a domino, a screwdriver, an invention for cooking the perfect hard-boiled egg and . . . wrapped in a plastic freezer bag, a paper napkin with a simple equation written upon it. I gave the young girl a hug, my feeling of elation quadrupled by the magnifying effect of the poetry. I breathed a sigh of relief. *Found!* Without wasting a moment I tore the recipe into small pieces and ate them.

'Riublf,' I said to Colin with my mouth full, 'leb's get goinf.'

'I don't think we're going anywhere, Ms Next.'

I looked up and saw what he meant. Occupying every square inch of space, on the sea-beach, the foreshore, the dunes and even standing in the sea, were hundreds upon hundreds of identical black-clad Mrs Danvers, staring at me malevolently. We'd killed five of their number recently so I guessed they wouldn't be that pleased. Mind you, they were always pretty miserable, so it might have had nothing to do with it. I instinctively grasped the butt of my pistol but it was pointless – like using a peashooter against a T-54 battle tank.

'Well,' I said, swallowing the last piece of the recipe and addressing the nearest Danverclone, 'you'd better take me to your leader.'

35
The Bees, the Bees

**'The Danverclones had advanced a good deal from their
accidental creation from the original Mrs Danvers in
Rebecca.** Originally they had simply been creepy fifty-something
housekeepers with bad attitude, but now they had weapons training
as well. A standard Danverclone was a fearless yet generally vapid
drone who would willingly die to follow orders. But just recently
an elite force of Danverclones had arisen, with not only weaponry
but a sound working knowledge of the BookWorld. Even I would
think twice before tackling this bunch. We called them the SWAT
team.'

The Danverclones moved in silently. With bewildering speed and
a tentacle-like movement of their bony limbs, four of them grasped
my arms while another took my shoulder bag and a sixth removed
my pistol. A seventh, who appeared to be the platoon commander,
spoke briefly into a mobile footnoterphone:

'Target number one located and in custody.'

She then snapped the mobile shut and used a brief series of hand
signals to the other Mrs Danvers, who began to jump out of the
poem, beginning with the ones right at the back. I looked across at
Colin, who was also being held tightly. A Danverclone had pulled
his taxi licence from his wallet and held it up in front of him before
tearing it in two and tossing the halves in the air. He glanced at me
and looked severely annoyed, but not with me – more with the
Danverclones and the circumstances. I was just wondering where
they would take me when there was a faint crackle in the air and
my recently appointed least favourite person was standing right in

front of me. She was dressed in all her black leather finery, twin automatics on her hips and a long black greatcoat that fell to the shingle. She leered at me as she appeared and I thought about spitting in her eye but decided against it – she was too far away and if I'd missed I would just have looked even more enfeebled.

'Well, well,' said Thursday1–4, 'the great Thursday Next finally brought to book.'

'Wow!' I replied. 'Black is surely the colour of choice today.'

She ignored me and continued:

'Do you know, it's going to be fun being you. Senator Jobsworth has extended to me all the rights that are usually yours – you in the BookWorld, you at the CofG, you in the much awaited and now greenlighted *Thursday Next Returns – This Time It's Personal*, and you in the Outland. That's the bit I like best. As much Landen as I want.' She leaned closer and lowered her voice. 'And believe me, I want a *lot*.'

I gave an almighty howl of anger and struggled to break loose from the Danvers but without any luck. The clones all sniggered and Thursday1–4 smiled unpleasantly.

'It's time for you to vanish, Thursday,' she growled.

She tossed a pair of handcuffs to the Danvers, who pulled my arms behind my back and secured them. Thursday1–4 held on to me, took my shoulder bag from a nearby clone and was about to walk away when the commander of the Mrs Danvers contingent said:

'I have orders to take her direct to the Île Saint-Joseph within *Papillon* as per your original plan, Ms Next1–4.'

The other me turned to the Mrs Danvers, looked her up and down, sneered and said:

'You've done your job, Danny – you'll be rewarded. This is *my* prisoner.'

But Mrs Danvers had an order, and Danvers only do one thing: they do as they're told – and until their instructions are countermanded by a written order, they do it rather well.

'I have my *written* instructions,' she said more firmly, and the other Danvers took a menacing step towards us, three of them producing weapons from within the folds of their black dresses.

'I'm countermanding your order.'

'No,' said Mrs Danvers, 'I have my orders and I *will* carry them out.'

'Listen here, shitface,' said Thursday1–4 with a snarl, 'I'm the new Mrs de Winter now – *geddit*?'

Mrs Danvers took a step back in shocked amazement, and in that short moment Thursday1–4 held tightly to my arm and jumped us both out.

I was expecting a ready-dug grave – or, worse, a shovel and a place for *me* to dig one – but there wasn't one. Instead, the place where we'd arrived looked more like the sitting room of a Georgian country house of moderate means, and thankfully there wasn't a shovel in sight – but there was a Bradshaw, five Bennet sisters and Mr Bennet, who were all staring at me expectantly, which was somewhat confusing.

'Ah!' said Bradshaw. 'Thank goodness for that. Sorry to keep you in the dark, old girl, but I knew my footnoterphone was bugged. We've got to get you across to the CofG, but right now we have a serious and very pressing problem.'

'*O-kay*,' I said slowly and in great puzzlement. I looked across at Thursday, who was rapidly divesting herself of the weapons and leather apparel.

'I actually *swore*,' she muttered unhappily, holding one of the automatics with a disdainful finger and thumb, 'and these clothes! Made from *animal skins* . . .'

My mouth may have dropped open at this.

'Thursday5?' I mumbled. 'That's *you*?'

She nodded shyly and shrugged. Underneath the leathers, I noticed, was her usual attire of naturally dyed cotton, crocheted jumper and Birkenstocks. She had taken her failure over the Minotaur

347

to heart and made good. Perhaps I had been too hasty over her assessment.

'We knew you were in the BookWorld but then you disappeared off the radar,' said Bradshaw. 'Where have you been the past ten hours?'

'I was trapped in a moral dilemma. Any news from the Outland? I mean, are people buying into this whole reality book thing?'

'And how!' exclaimed Bradshaw. 'The news from the CofG is that a half-million people are waiting to see how *The Bennets* will turn out, as the idea of being able to change a major classic has huge appeal — it's the latest fad in the Outland, and you know how the Outland like fads.'

'Sometimes I think they enjoy little else.'

Bradshaw looked at his watch.

'There's only six minutes before *Pride and Prejudice* as we know it is going to be rewritten and lost for ever, and we don't have a seriously good plan of action. In fact,' he added, 'we don't have *any* plan of action.'

Everyone stared at me. Twenty seconds earlier I had thought I was almost certainly dead; now I was expected at short notice to fashion a plan of infinite subtlety to save one of our greatest novels from being reduced to a mind-numbing morass of transient popular entertainment.

'Right,' I said as I attempted to gather my thoughts, 'Lizzie?'

'Here, ma'am,' said the second-eldest Bennet sister, bobbing respectfully.

'Fill me in. How does this "reality book" thing work? Have you been given any instructions?'

'We've not been told much, ma'am. We are expected to gather in the house, but instead of looking for husbands and happiness we are to undertake a preset task of an altogether *curious* nature. And as we do so,' she added sorrowfully, 'our new actions and words are indelibly burned into the new edition of our book.'

348

I looked around the room. They were *still* all staring at me expectantly.

'Let me see the task.'

She handed me a sheet of paper. It had an Interactive Book Project letterhead and read:

TASK ONE
Chapters 1–3 (one hour's reading time)
All housemates <u>must</u> participate

The housemates will gather in the parlour of Longbourn and make bee costumes. After that, the housemates will be expected to act like bees. One of the housemates, dressed as a bee, will ask Mr Bingley to organise a fancy-dress costume ball where everyone is required to dress as bees. The housemate who is judged to have made the best bee costume and to have done the most satisfactory bee impersonation will win the first round and be allowed to put up two housemates for eviction. The voting Outlander public will decide who is to go. Housemates will be expected to go to the diary room and talk about whatever comes into their heads no matter how dreary.

I put down the sheet of paper. This was a good deal worse than I had expected, and my expectations hadn't been high.

'I'm *not* dressing up as a bee,' announced Mr Bennet indignantly. 'The very idea. You girls may indulge in such silliness, but *I* shall withdraw to my study.'

'Father,' said Lizzie, 'remember we are doing this to ensure that the Outland read-rates do not continue to fall in the precipitous manner that has marked their progress in recent years. It is a sacrifice, to be sure, but one that we should shoulder with determination, and dignity – for the good of the BookWorld.'

'I'll dress as a bee!' cried Lydia excitedly, jumping up and down.

'Me too!' added Kitty. 'I will be the finest bee in Meryton!'

'You shall not, for I shall!' returned Lydia, and they joined hands and danced round the room. I looked at Mary, who turned her eyes heavenwards and returned to her book.

'Well,' said Jane good-naturedly, 'I shall dress as a bee if it is for the greater good – do you suppose Mr Bingley will *also* be required to dress as a bee? And shall we,' she added somewhat daringly, 'get to see one another again, as bees?'

'It doesn't state as such,' replied Mr Bennet, looking at the task again, 'but I expect Mr Bingley will be requested to make an idiot of himself in the fullness of time – and Darcy too, I should wager.'

'Where's Mrs Bennet?' I asked, having not seen her since I'd arrived.

'We had to put poor Mama in the cupboard again,' explained Lizzie, pointing at a large wardrobe which Thursday5 opened to reveal that, yes, Mrs Bennet was indeed inside, stock still and staring with blank eyes into the middle distance.

'It calms her,' explained Jane as Thursday5 closed the cupboard door again. 'We have to commit dear Mama to the wardrobe quite often during the book.'

'Yes,' added Lizzie thoughtfully, 'I fear she will not take to the bee task. While there are daughters unmarried, Mama has only one thing on her mind, and she is liable to get . . . *agitated* and cause a dreadful scene. Do you think that will spoil the task?'

'No,' I said wearily, 'the worse it gets the better reality it is, if you see what I mean.'

'I'm afraid I don't.'

'Thursday, old girl,' interrupted Bradshaw, who had been staring at his watch, 'how's this for a suggestion? Everyone hides so there's no book at all.'

'Out of the question!' intoned Mr Bennet. 'I will not hide my family from view and skulk in my own home. No indeed. No matter how silly we may look, we shall be here in the front room when the new book begins.'

'Wait a moment,' I said. 'This first section lasts an hour's reading time, yes?'

Lizzie nodded.

I took the piece of paper with the task written on it and pulled a pen from my top pocket, put three broad lines through the task and started to write my own. When I had finished, I handed it to Lizzie, who looked at it thoughtfully and then passed it to her father.

'Oh, boo!' said Lydia, crossing her arms and jutting out a lip. 'And I did *so* want to become a bee!'

'I'm going to read this out loud,' announced Mr Bennet, 'as we must all, as a family, agree to undertake this new task – or not.' He looked around at everyone; they nodded their agreement, except Lydia and Kitty, who were poking one another, and Mrs Bennet, who couldn't, as she was still 'relaxing' in the cupboard.

'"First task Chapters One to Three",' he began. '"Mr Bennet, of Longbourn house in Meryton, should be encouraged by his wife to visit Mr Bingley, who has taken up residence at nearby Netherfield Park. Mr Bingley shall return the visit without meeting the daughters, and a ball must take place. In this ball Mr Bingley and Jane Bennet are to dance together. At the same time Mr Darcy is also to attend, and he shall be considered rude, proud and aloof by Lizzie and the rest of the family. At the same time, we are to learn much of the Bennet marriage, and their daughters, and their prospects. The reading public can vote on whether Jane and Bingley are to dance a second time. Mrs Bennet is free to do 'her own thing' throughout."'

Mr Bennet stopped reading, gave a smile and looked around the room.

'Well, my children?'

'It sounds like an *excellent* task,' said Jane, clapping her hands together. 'Lizzie?'

'I confess I cannot fault it.'

'Then it is agreed,' opined Mr Bennet with a twinkle in his eye.

'Truly an audacious plan – and it *might just work*. How long before we begin?'

'Forty-seven seconds,' answered Bradshaw, consulting his pocket-watch.

'I don't understand,' said Lydia. 'This new task. Isn't that what usually happens?'

'Duh,' replied Kitty, pulling a face.

'Places, everyone,' said Mr Bennet, and they all obediently sat in their allotted chairs. 'Lizzie, are you ready to narrate?'

'Yes, Father.'

'Good. Mary, would you let Mrs Bennet out of the cupboard? Then we can begin.'

Myself, Thursday5 and Bradshaw scurried out into the corridor as Lizzie began the reality book show with words that rang like chimes, loud and clear, in the canon of English literature:

'It is a truth universally acknowledged,' we heard her say through the closed door, 'that a single man in possession of a good fortune, must be in want of a wife.'

'Thursday,' said Bradshaw as he, Thursday5 and I walked to the entrance hall, 'we've kept the book exactly as it is – but only until the Council of Genres and the interactive book people find out what we've done – and then they'll be down here in a flash!'

'I know,' I replied, 'so I haven't got long to change the CofG's mind over this interactivity nonsense. Stay here and try to stall them as long as possible. It's my guess they'll let this first task run its course and do the stupid bee thing for Task Two. Wish me luck.'

'I do,' said Bradshaw grimly, 'and you're going to need it.'

'Here,' said Thursday5, handing me an Emergency TravelBook and my bag, 'you'll need these as much as luck.'

I didn't waste a moment. I opened the TravelBook, read the required text and was soon back in the Great Library.

36
Senator Jobsworth

'Appointees to senatorial positions in the Council of
Genres are generally pulled from the ranks of the indi-
vidual book council members who officiate on all internal
book matters. They are usually minor characters with a lot of
time on their hands, so aside from a few notable exceptions, the
Council of Genres is populated entirely by unimaginative D-4s.
They meddle, but they don't do it very well. It is one of the
CofG's strengths.'

I impatiently drummed my fingers on the wall of the lift as I rose
to the twenty-sixth floor of the Great Library and the Council of
Genres. I checked in my bag and found I still had two eraserheads,
but wasn't sure whether a show of force was the correct way to go
about this. If what Bradshaw had said was true and Evil Thursday
was commanding a legion of Danvers, I might not even have a
chance to plead my own case, let alone *Pride and Prejudice*'s.

I decided that the best course of action was to simply wing it,
and was just wondering how I should approach even this strategy
when the lift doors opened and I was confronted by *myself*, staring
back at me from the corridor. The same jacket, the same hair,
trousers, boots – everything except a black glove on her left hand
which covered the eraserhead wound, I imagined. Bradshaw was
right – Thursday1–4 had divested herself of her own identity and
taken mine, along with my standing, integrity and reputation – an
awesome weapon for her to wield. Not only as the CofG's LBOCS
and as a trusted member of Jurisfiction, but *everything*. Jobsworth,
in all his dreary ignorance, probably thought that this *was* me, having

353

undergone a bizarre – and to him – entirely fortuitous change of mind regarding policy directives.

We stared at one another for a moment, her with a sort of numbed look of disbelief and me – I hope – with the expression that a wife rightly reserves for someone who has slept with their husband.

'Meddling fool!' she said at last, waving a copy of *Pride and Prejudice* that she had been reading. 'I can only think this is your doing. You may have won the first round, but it's merely a post-ponement – we'll have the reality book show back on track after the first three chapters have run their course!'

'I'm going to erase you,' I said in a quiet voice, 'and what's more, *enjoy it.*'

She stared at me with a vague look of triumph.

'Then I was wrong,' she replied, 'we *are* alike.'

I didn't have time to answer. She took to her heels and ran off down the corridor towards the debating chamber. I followed; if we were externally identical then the first to plead their case to the CofG had a clear advantage.

Thinking about it later, the pair of us running hell for leather down the corridors must have been quite a sight, but probably not *that* unusual, given the somewhat curious nature of fiction. Annoyingly, we were evenly matched in speed and stamina, and her ten-foot head start was still there when we arrived at the main debating chamber's door two minutes and many startled CofG employees later. She had to slow down at the door and as she did so I made a flying tackle and grabbed her round the waist. Toppled by the momentum, the pair of us went sprawling headlong on the carpet, much to the astonishment of three heavily armed Danverclones who were just inside the door.

The strange thing about fighting with yourself is that not only are you of equal weight, strength and skill, but you both know all the same moves. After we had grappled and rolled around on the carpet

354

carpet for about five minutes and achieved nothing but a lot of grunting and strained muscles, my mind started to shift and think about other ways in which to win – something that my opponent did at *exactly* the same time, and we both switched tactics and went for each other's throats. The most this achieved was that Landen's birthday locket was torn off, something that drove me to a rage that I never knew I had.

I knocked her hand away, rolled on top of her and punched her hard in the face. She went limp and I climbed off, breathing hard, picked up my bag and locket and turned to Jobsworth and the rest of the Security Council, who had come into the corridor to watch.

'Arrest her,' I panted, wiping a small amount of blood from my lip, 'and bind her well.'

Jobsworth looked at me and the other Thursday, then beckoned to the Danverclones to do as I asked.

She was still groggy, but seemed to regain enough consciousness to yell:

'Wait, wait! She's not the real Thursday – I am!'

Jobsworth, Barksdale and Baxter all swivelled their heads to me, and even the Danverclones took notice. In the CofG my veto counted for everything, and if there was any doubt at all over which was the correct Thursday, I had to quash it here and now.

'Want me to prove it?' I said. 'Here it is: the book interactivity project stops *now*.'

Jobsworth's face fell.

'Stop it? But you were all for it not less than an hour ago!'

'That wasn't me,' I said, pointing an accusing finger at the dishevelled and now defeated Thursday, who was at that moment being cuffed by the Danverclones, 'it was the *other* Thursday, the one from the crap-as-hell TN series who has been trying, for reasons of her own personal vindictiveness, to screw up everything I have worked so hard to achieve.'

355

'She's lying!' said the other Thursday, who now had her arms secured behind her back and still seemed unsteady from when I had hit her. 'She's the ersatz Thursday – I'm the real one!'

'You want more proof?' I said. 'Okay. I'm also reinforcing my veto on the insane decision to invade the Racy Novel genre. Diplomacy is the key. And I want all Jurisfiction agents released from their books and returned to work.'

'But that was your idea!' muttered Jobsworth, who, poor fellow, was still confused. 'You said there was a bad apple at Jurisfiction and you needed to flush them out!'

'Not me,' I said, 'her. To keep me from returning. And if you need any more proof, here's the clincher: we're not going to have her reduced to text. She's going to spend the next two years contemplating her navel within the pages of The Great Samuel Pepys Fiasco. She's smart and resourceful so we'll keep her in isolation so she doesn't try to be me again, and if she even attempts to escape, she'll be reduced to text.'

Jobsworth needed no further convincing.

'It shall be so,' he said in a faintly pompous way, and the other Thursday was dragged off, still uselessly proclaiming her unbogusness.

I took a deep breath and sat down. I could feel a bruise coming up on the side of my neck and my knee hurt. I stretched my hand and rubbed it where I had struck her.

'Well,' said Baxter, 'I can't say I'm glad you've decided against invading Racy Novel, but I am a lot happier that you are the one making the wrong decisions and not some poorly written wannabe. What the hell was she up to?'

'As you say. Just a jumped-up generic who wanted to be real. Better put a textual sieve lockdown on The Great Samuel Pepys Fiasco both in and out – I don't want to even entertain the possibility of someone rescuing her.'

Jobsworth nodded to one of his aides to do as I had asked, and also – very reluctantly – to put a halt to the interactivity project and the Racy Novel invasion plans.

'But look here,' said Colonel Barksdale, who seemed to be somewhat miffed that he wasn't going to spearhead an invasion of Racy Novel, 'we can't just ignore Speedy Muffler and those heathens.'

'And we shan't,' I replied. 'After we have pursued all possible diplomatic channels, *then* we will have a look at other means of keeping them in check – and I rule out nothing.'

Barksdale stared at me, unconvinced.

'Trust me,' I said, 'I'm Thursday Next. I know what I'm doing.'

He seemed to find some solace in this – my name counted for a lot.

'Right,' I said, 'I'm bushed. I'm going to go home – we'll discuss things tomorrow, right?'

'Very well,' replied Jobsworth stonily, 'we can talk at length about the falling read-rates and what you intend to do about them then.'

I didn't reply and left the debating chamber. But instead of going back to Swindon, I took a walk in the corridors of power at the CofG. Everything was busy as usual, the debating chamber in full swing, and there was little – if any – evidence that we were no longer at war and rewriting the classics. I stopped by the large picture window that looked out on to the other towers. I'd never really looked out of here for any length of time before, but now, with time and the BookWorld as my servant, I stared out, musing upon the new responsibilities that I had, and how I would exercise them first.

I was still undecided twenty minutes later when Bradshaw tapped me lightly on the shoulder.

'Old girl?'

He startled me and I looked round, took one glance at who was with him, and drew my automatic.

'Whoa, whoa!' said Bradshaw hurriedly. 'This is Thursday5.'

'How do you know?' I barked, pointing my gun directly at her, my sensibilities keenly alert to any sort of lookalike subterfuge. 'How do we know it isn't the evil Thursday back here in disguise or something?'

Bradshaw looked mildly shocked at my suggestion.

'Because she's not left my side since we last saw you, old girl.'

'Are you sure?'

'Absolutely! Here, I'll prove it.' He turned to Thursday5. 'What were the names of the Von Trapp children in *The Sound of Music*?'

Thursday5 didn't pause for an instant and recited in one breath: 'Kurt, Friedrich, Louisa, Brigitta, Marta, Gretl and Liesl.'

'You see?'

'You're right,' I said, 'only a total drip like Thursday5 would know *that* – or at least,' I added hurriedly, 'that's what Evil Thursday would think.'

I clicked on the safety and lowered the gun.

'I'm sorry,' I said. 'It's been a tough day and my nerves are in shreds. I need to get home and have a long hot bath and then a martini.'

Thursday5 thought for a moment.

'After you've drunk the long hot bath,' she observed, 'you'll never have room for the martini.'

'You what?'

'Never mind.'

'We just came to congratulate you,' said Bradshaw, 'on re-reversing the vetoes. *Pride and Prejudice* is running precisely as it should, and without the interactive book idiots to set any new tasks, we're in the clear. The Bennets wanted me to send you their very best and to tell you to drop round for tea some time.'

'How very proper of them,' I said absently, feeling a bit hot and bothered and wanting them to go away. 'If there's nothing else—?'

'Not really,' replied Bradshaw, 'but we wondered: why did you lock her up in *The Great Samuel Pepys Fiasco*?'

I shrugged.

'Punishment to fit the crime, I guess – are you questioning my judgement?'

'Of course not, old girl,' replied Bradshaw genially, exchanging a glance with Thursday5.

'*That* explains why I can't get back in,' murmured Thursday5 in dismay. 'Is this permanent? I know my book's unreadable – but it's home.'

'Listen,' I said, rubbing my scalp, 'that's your problem. Since when were you part of the decision-making process?'

Bradshaw's mobile footnoterphone rang.

'Excuse me,' he said, and wandered off to answer it.

'It's been a long day,' murmured Thursday5, staring out of the window at the view, 'you must be tired. Do you want me to fetch you a chai?'

'No, I don't drink any of that rubbish. What were you saying about the hot bath and the martini again?'

She didn't have time to answer.

'That was Text Grand Central,' said Bradshaw as he returned. 'We've been getting some major textual flexations inside *The Great Samuel Pepys Fiasco*. It seems the entire first chapter has broken away from the rest of the book.'

'*What?*'

'As I said. It's a good job no one reads it these days. We've tracked Thursday to page two hundred and eight.'

I took a deep breath and looked at Bradshaw and Thursday5 in turn. 'This is unfinished business,' I said quietly. 'I'm going to put an end to her once and for all.'

They didn't try to argue with me. I should have killed her there and then in the corridor. What *was* I thinking of?

'The book's been two-way sieved,' said Bradshaw. 'Call me when you're about to jump and I'll get Text Grand Central to open you a portal. As soon as you're in we'll close it down and you'll both be trapped. Do you have your mobile footnoterphone?'

I nodded.

'Then call me when you're done. Use Mrs Bradshaw's middle name so I know it's you and *really* you. Good luck.'

I thanked them and they walked off down the corridor before evaporating from view. I tried to calm my nerves and told myself that facing Thursday couldn't be *that* bad, but the consequences if I failed were serious indeed. I took another deep breath, wiped my sweaty palms on my trousers, made the call to Bradshaw and jumped all the way to page two hundred and eight of *The Great Samuel Pepys Fiasco.*

37

The Great Samuel Pepys Fiasco

'The *real* adventure that came to be known as *The Great Samuel Pepys Fiasco* was my first proper sojourn in non-fiction, and was, as the title suggests, one of my more embarrassing failures. I don't really know why, but nothing ever went right. I tried to convey a sense of well-meaning optimism in the book, where I was caught between two impossible situations, but it came across as mostly inept fumbling with a lot of hugging and essential oils.'

I came to earth in Swindon. Or at least, the *Fiasco* touchy-feely version of Swindon, which was sunny, blue-skied and where every garden had an annoying splash of bright primary colours that gave me a headache. The houses were perfect, the cars clean and everything was insanely neat and orderly. I pulled out my automatic, removed the clip to check it, replaced it and released the safety. There would be no escape for her this time. I knew she was unarmed but somehow that didn't fill me with much confidence; after all, she was almost infinitely resourceful. The thing was, *so was I*. After I'd killed her I would just jump out and everything would be right – for ever. I could reinstate the reality book project before the readers had finished the first three chapters – then go to the Outland and savour the joys of Landen once more. Following that, and after paying a small amount of lip-service to diplomacy, I could also deploy two legions of Mrs Danvers into Racy Novel. I might even lead the attack myself. That, I had discovered, was the best thing about being Thursday Next – you could do anything you damn well pleased and no one would, could or dared oppose you.

I had only two problems to deal with right now: disposing of the *real* Thursday Next and trying to figure out Mrs Bradshaw's middle name, the code word to get out. I hadn't a clue – I'd never even met her.

I pulled the glove off my hand and looked at where the mottled flesh still showed signs of the eraserhead. I rubbed the itchy skin, then moved to the side of the street and walked towards where this version of Thursday's house was located. It was the same as the one that was burned down in the first chapter of my book, so I knew the way. But the strange thing was, the street was completely deserted. Nothing moved. Not a person, not a cat, a squirrel, *nothing*. I stopped at a car that was abandoned in the street and looked through the open passenger door. The key was still in the ignition. Whoever had once populated this book had left – and in a hurry.

I carried on walking slowly down the road. That pompous fool Bradshaw had mentioned something about a chapter breaking away from the main book – perhaps that was where all the background characters were. But it didn't matter. Thursday was here now and she was the one I was after. I reached the garden gate of Landen5's house and padded slowly up the path, past the perfectly planted flowers and windows so clean and sparkly they almost weren't there. Holding my gun outstretched, I stepped quietly inside the house.

Thursday5's idea of home furnishing was different from mine and the real Thursday's. For a start the floor covering was seagrass, and the curtains were an odiously old-fashioned tie-dye. I also noticed to my disgust that there were Tibetan mantras in frames upon the wall and dreamcatchers hanging from the ceiling. I stepped closer to the pictures on the mantelpiece and found one of Thursday5 and Landen5 at Glastonbury. They had their faces painted as flowers and were grinning stupidly and hugging one another, with Pickwick5 sitting between them. It was quite sickeningly twee, to be honest.

'I would have done the same.'

362

I turned. Thursday was leaning on the doorway that led through to the kitchen. It was an easy shot, but I didn't take it. I wanted to savour the moment.

'What would you have done the same?' I asked.

'I would have spared you, too. I'll admit it, your impersonation of me was about the most plausible I'll ever see. I'm not sure there's anyone out there who would have spotted it. But I didn't think you could keep it up. The *real* you would soon bubble to the surface. Because like it or not, you're not enough of me to carry it off. To be me you need the seventeen years of Jurisfiction experience – the sort of experience that means I can take on people like you and come out victorious.'

I laughed at her presumption.

'I think you overestimate your own abilities, Outlander. I'm the one holding the gun. Perhaps you're right a little bit, but I *can* and *will* be you, given time. Everything you have, everything you are. Your job, your family, your *husband*. I can go back to the Outland and take over from where you left off – and probably have a lot more fun doing it, too.'

I pointed my gun at her and began to squeeze the trigger, then stopped. She didn't seem that troubled, and that worried me.

'Can you hear that?' she asked.

'Hear what?'

She cupped a hand to her ear.

'That.'

And now she mentioned it, I *could* hear something. A soft thrumming noise that seemed to reverberate through the ground.

'What is it?' I asked, and was shocked to discover that my voice came out cracked, and . . . *afraid*.

'Take a look for yourself,' she said, pointing outside.

I wiped the sweat from my brow and backed out of the door, still keeping my gun firmly trained on her. I ran down to the garden gate and looked up the street. The houses at the end of the road seemed to have lost definition and were being eaten away by a billowing cloud of sand.

'What the hell's that?' I snapped.

'You'd know,' she replied quietly, 'if only you'd gone to Jurisfiction classes instead of wasting your time on the shooting range.'

I looked at the pillar box on the corner of the street, and it seemed to crumble to fragments in front of my eyes and then be taken up into the cloud of dust and debris that was being sucked into a vortex high above us. I pulled out my footnoterphone and frantically dialled Bradshaw's number.

'But you don't know Melanie Bradshaw's middle name,' observed Thursday, 'do you?'

I lowered the phone and stared at her uselessly. It was a set-up. Thursday must have spoken to Bradshaw and together they tricked me into coming here.

'It's *Jenny*,' she added. 'I named my second daughter after her. But it won't help you. I told Bradshaw not to lift the textual sieve on any account, password or not. As soon as you were inside and the generics were safely evacuated, he was instructed to begin . . . the *erasure* of the entire book.'

'How did you contact him?' I asked.

'He contacted *me*,' she replied. 'Thursday5 suggested to Bradshaw that you might have pulled the same trick as she did. I couldn't get out, but we could trick you *in*.'

She looked at her watch.

'And in another eight minutes this book and everything in it – you included – will be gone.'

I looked around and saw to my horror that the erasure had crept up without me noticing, and was less than ten feet away – we were standing on the only piece of remaining land, a rough circle a hundred feet across in which stood only Landen's house and its neighbours. But they wouldn't stay for long, and even as I watched the roofs were turning to dust and being whirled away, consumed by the erasure. The dull roar was increasing and I had to raise my voice to be heard.

'But this will erase you, too!'

'Maybe not – it depends on you.'

She beckoned me back into the house as the garden gate turned to smoke and was carried away into the dust cloud. As soon as we were in the kitchen she turned to me.

'You won't need that,' she said, pointing at my gun. I fumbled the reholstering clumsily, and it fell to the floor with a clatter. I didn't stoop to pick it up. I looked out of the window into the back garden. The shed and the apple tree had both gone, and the erasure was slowly eating its way across the lawn. The ceiling was starting to look blotchy and, as I watched, the front door turned to dust and was blown away in the wind.

'*Bollocks*,' I said, as realisation suddenly dawned. Not that I was going to be erased; no. It was the cold and sobering revelation that I wasn't nearly as smart as I thought I was. I'd met a foe immeasurably superior to me, and would suffer the consequences of my own arrogance. The question was: would I give her the pleasure of knowing it? But on reflection, she didn't want or need that sort of pleasure, and everything suddenly seemed that much more peaceful. I said instead:

'I'm truly flattered.'

'Flattered?' she enquired. 'About what?'

The ceiling departed in a cloud of swirling dust, and the walls started to erode downwards with the pictures, mantel and furniture rapidly crumbling away to a fine debris that was sucked up into the whirlwind directly above us.

'I'm flattered,' I repeated, 'because you'd erase a whole book and give your own life just to be rid of me. I must have been a worthy adversary, right?'

She sensed my change of heart and gave me a faint smile.

'You almost defeated me,' said Thursday, 'and you still might. But if I *do* survive this,' she added, 'it is my gift to you.'

The walls had almost gone and the seagrass flooring was crumbling under my feet. Thursday opened a door in the kitchen where a concrete flight of steps led downwards. She beckoned me to follow, and we trotted down into a large subterranean vault shaped like the inside of a barrel. Upon a large plinth there were two prongs across which a weak spark occasionally fired. The noise of the wind had subsided, but I knew it was only a matter of time before the erasure reached us.

'This is the Core Containment room,' explained Thursday. 'You'd know about that if you'd listened at class.'

'How,' I asked, 'is your survival a gift to me?'

'That's easily explained,' replied Thursday, removing some pieces of packing case from the wall to reveal a riveted iron hatch. 'Behind there is the only method of escape – across the emptiness of the Nothing.'

The inference wasn't lost on me. The Nothing didn't support textual life – I'd be stripped away to letters in an instant if I tried to escape across it. But Thursday wasn't text: she was flesh and blood, and *could* survive.

'I can't get out of here on my own,' she added, 'so I need your help.'

I didn't understand to begin with. I frowned, and then it hit me. She wasn't offering me forgiveness, a second chance or rescue – I was far too bitter and twisted for that. No, she was offering me the one thing that I *would* never, *could* never have. She was offering me redemption. After all I had done to her, all the things I had *planned* to do, she was willing to risk her life to give me one small chance to atone. And what was more, *she knew I would take it*. She was right. We were more alike than I had thought.

The roof fell away in patches as the erasure started to pull the containment room apart.

'What do I do?'

She indicated the twin latching mechanisms which were positioned eight feet apart. I held the handle and pulled it down on the count of three. The hatch sprang open, revealing an empty black void.

'Thank you,' she said as the erasure crept inexorably across the room. The sum total of the book was now a disc less than eight foot across, and we were in the middle of what looked like a swirling cloud of dirt and debris, while all about us the wind nibbled away at the remaining fabric of the book, reducing it to an undescriptive textdust.

'What will it be like?' I asked as Thursday peered out into the inky blackness.

'I can't tell you,' she replied, 'no one knows what happens after erasure.'

I offered her my hand to shake.

'If you ever turn this into one of your adventures,' I asked, 'will you make me at least vaguely sympathetic? I'd like to think there was a small amount of your humanity in me.'

She took my hand and shook it. It was warmer than I had imagined.

'I'm sorry about sleeping with your husband,' I added as I felt the floor grow soft beneath my feet, '. . . and I think this is yours.'

And I gave her the locket she had lost when we fought.

As soon as Thursday1–4 returned my locket I knew that she had finally learned something about me and, by reflection, herself. She was lost and she knew it, so helping me open the hatch and handing over the locket could only be altruism – the first time she had acted thus, and the last time she acted at all. I climbed partially out

367

of the hatch into the Nothing. There was barely anything left of the book at all – just the vaguest crackle of the book's spark growing weaker and weaker. I was still holding Thursday1–4's hand as I saw her body start to break up, like sandstone eroded by wind. Her hair was being whipped by the currents of air, but she looked peaceful. She smiled and said:

'I just got it.'

'Got what?'

'Something Thursday5 said about hot baths and a martini.'

Her face started to break down and I felt her hand crumble within mine like crusty sun-baked sand. There was almost nothing left of *Fiasco* at all, and it was time to go.

She smiled at me and her face fell away into dust, her hand turned to sand in mine and the spark crackled and went out. I let go and was—

369

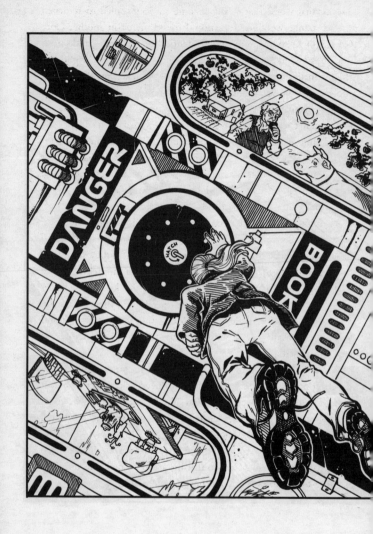

372

The textual world that I had become so accustomed to returned with a strange wobbling sensation. I found myself in another Core Containment room pretty much identical to the first – aside from the book's spark, which crackled twenty times more brightly as readers made their way through the book. I picked myself up, shut and secured the hatch and made my way up the steps and towards the exit, securing the locket around my neck as I did so.

I couldn't really say I was saddened by Thursday1–4's loss as she would almost certainly have killed me and done untold damage if she'd lived. But I couldn't help feeling a sense of guilt that I might have done more for her. After all, it wasn't strictly her fault – she had been written that way. I sighed. She had found a little bit of me in her, but I knew there was some of her in me, too.

I cautiously opened the containment room door and peered out. I was in a collection of farm buildings constructed of red brick and in such a dilapidated state of disrepair it looked as if they were held together only by the moss in the brickwork and the lichen on the roof. I spotted Adam Lambsbreath through the kitchen window where he was scraping ineffectually at the washing-up with a twig. I made the sign for a telephone through the window at him and he pointed towards the woodshed across the yard. I ran across and pushed open the door.

There was something nasty sitting in the corner making odd slavering noises to itself but I paid it no heed other than to reflect that Ada Doom had been right after all, and found the public foot-noterphone that I needed. I dialled Bradshaw's number and waited impatiently for him to answer.

'It's me,' I said. 'Your plan worked: she's dust. I'm in *Cold Comfort Farm*, page sixty-eight. Can you bring a cab to pick me up? This is going to be one serious mother of a debrief.'

38

The End of Time

'No one ever did find out who the members of the ChronoGuard "Star Chamber" were, nor what their relationship with the Goliath Corporation actually was. But it was noted that some investment opportunities by the multinational were so fortuitous and so prudent and so long sighted that statistically they seemed impossible. There were never any whistle-blowers, so the extent of any Chronuption was never known, nor ever would be.'

By the time I arrived back home it was dark. Landen heard my key in the latch and met me in the hallway to give me a long hug, which I gratefully received – and returned.

'What's the news over the reality book show?'

'Cancelled. Van de Poste has been on the TV and wireless explaining that, owing to a technical error, the project has been shelved – and that the Stupidity Surplus will be discharged instead by reinvigorating the astronomically expensive and questionably useful Anti-Smote shield.'

'And *Pride and Prejudice*?'

'Running exactly as it ever did. But here's the good bit: all the readers who bought copies of the book to see the Bennets dress up as bees continued reading to see if Lizzie and Jane would get their men, and if Lydia would come to a sticky end. Naturally, all the new readers were delighted at what happened – so much so that people with the name of Wickham have had to go into hiding.'

'Just like the old days,' I said with a smile.

The passion for books was returning. I thought for a moment

and walked over to the bookcase, pulled out my copy of *The Great Samuel Pepys Fiasco* and riffled through the pages. They were blank, every single one.

'How are Friday and the girls?' I asked, dropping the book into the wastepaper basket.

'Friday is out – the girls are in bed.'

'And Pickwick?'

'Still bald and a bit dopey. So . . . you managed to do what you set out to do?'

'Yes,' I said quietly, 'and Land, I can't lie to you any more. The Acme Carpets stuff is just a front.'

'I know,' he said softly. 'You still do all that SpecOps work, don't you?'

'Yes. But Land, that's a front too.'

He placed a hand on my cheek and stared into my eyes.

'I know about Jurisfiction as well, Thurs.'

I frowned. I hadn't expected this.

'You knew? Since when?'

'Since about three days after you'd said you'd given it up.'

I stared at him.

'You *knew* I was lying to you all those years?'

'Pumpkin,' he said as he took my hand in his, 'you do love me, don't you?'

'Yes, but—'

He put a finger to my lips.

'Hang on a minute. I know you do and I love it that you do. But if you care *too* much about upsetting me then you won't do the things you have to do, and those things are important – not just to me but to *everyone*.'

'Then . . . you're not cross I've been lying to you for fourteen years?'

'Thursday, you mean *everything* to me. Not just because you're

376

cute, smart, funny and have a devastatingly good figure and boobs to die for, but because you do right for right's sake – it's what you are and what you do. Even if I never get my Magnum Opus published I will still die secure in the knowledge that my time on this planet was well spent – giving support, love and security to someone who actually *makes a difference.*'

'Oh, *Land,*' I said, burying my head in his shoulder, 'you're making me go all misty!'

And I hugged him again, while he rubbed my back and said that everything was all right. We stood like this for some time until I suddenly had a thought.

'Land,' I said slowly, '*how* much do you know?'

'Mr and Mrs Bradshaw tell me quite a lot, and Spike and Bowden often call to keep me updated.'

'The rotten swines!' I said with a smile. 'They're always telling me to spill the beans to you!'

'We *all* care about you, Thursday.'

This was abundantly true, but I couldn't get Thursday1–4 and her brief sojourn in the real world out of my mind.

'What about . . . *other* stuff?'

Landen knew exactly what I was talking about.

'I only figured out she was the *written* Thursday when you came back upstairs.'

'How?'

'Because it was only then I realised she hadn't been wearing the necklace I gave you for your birthday.'

'Oh,' I said, fingering the locket around my neck. There was silence for a moment as we both considered what had happened. Eventually I said:

'But she was a terrible lay, right?'

'*Hopeless.*'

And we both laughed. We would never mention it again.

'Listen,' said Landen, 'there's someone to see you in the front room.'

'Who?'

'Just go in. I'll make some tea.'

I walked into the living room, where a tall man was standing at the mantelpiece with his back to me, looking at the framed pictures of the family.

'That's us holidaying on the Isle of Skye,' I said in a soft voice, 'at the Old Man of Storr. Jenny's not there because she was in a huff and sat in the car, and you can just see Pickwick's head at the edge of the frame.'

'I remember it well,' he said, and turned to face me. It was Friday, of course. Not *my* Friday, but his older self. He was about sixty, and handsome with it. His hair was greying at the temples and the smile wrinkles round his eyes made me think of Landen. He was wearing the pale blue uniform of the ChronoGuard, the shoulder emblazoned with the five gold pips of Director General. But it wasn't the day-to-day uniform, it was ceremonial dress. This was a special occasion.

'Hi, Mum.'

'Hi, Sweetpea. So you *did* make it to Director General after all!'

He shrugged and smiled.

'I did and I didn't. I'm here but I can't be. It's like everything else that we've done in the past to change the present – we were definitely there but we couldn't have been. The one thing you learn about the time business is that mutually opposing states can comfortably coexist.'

'Like *Saturday Night Fever* being excellent and crap at the same time?'

'Kind of. When it comes to travelling about in the timestream, paradox is always a cosy bedfellow – you get used to living with it.'

He looked at his watch.

'You destroyed the recipe, didn't you?'

'I ate it.'

'Good. I've just come to tell you that with only twenty-three minutes to go until the End of Time and without the equation for unscrambling eggs, the Star Chamber has conceded that the continued existence of time travel is retrospectively insupportable. We're closing down the time engines right now. All operatives are being demobilised. Enloopment facilities are being emptied and places found for the inmates in conventional prisons.'

'She was right after all,' I said quietly.

'I'm sorry?'

'Aornis. I *did* get her out of the loop.'

'We're making quite sure that all prisoners with "special requirements" are being looked after properly, Mum.'

'I hope so. What about the other inventions built using retro-deficit engineering?'

'They'll stay. The microchip and Gravitube *will* be invented so it's not a problem – but there won't be any new retro-deficit technologies. More importantly, the Standard History Eventline will stay as it was when we switch off the engines.'

'None of the history-rolling-up-like-a-carpet, then?'

'Possibly – but not very likely.'

'And Goliath get to stay as they are?'

'I'm afraid so.'

He paused for a moment, and sighed.

'So many things I could have done, might have done – have done and haven't done. I'm going to miss it all.'

He looked at me for a moment. This was my son but it wasn't. It was him as he *might* have turned out, but never would. I still loved him, but it was the only time in my life when I was glad to say goodbye.

'What about the Now?'

'It'll recover, given time. Keep people reading books, Mum, it helps to reinforce and strengthen the indefinable Moment that anchors us in the here and now. Strive for the Long Now. It's the only thing that will save us. Well,' he added with finality, giving me a kiss on the cheek, 'I'll be off. I've got to do some paperwork before I switch off the last engine.'

'What will happen to you?'

He smiled again.

'The Friday *Last*? I wink out of existence. And do you know, I'm not bothered. I've no idea what the future will bring to the Friday *Present*, and that's a concept I'll gladly die for.'

I felt tears come to my eyes, which was silly, really. This was only the possibility of Friday, not the actual one.

'Don't cry, Mum. I'll see you when I get up tomorrow and . . . you know I'm going to sleep in, right?'

He hugged me again and in an instant, he was gone. I wandered through to the kitchen and rested my hand on Landen's back as he poured some milk into my tea. We sat at the kitchen table until, untold trillions of years in the future, time came to a halt. There was no erasure of history, no distant thunder, no 'we interrupt this broadcast' on the wireless – nothing. The technology had gone for good and the ChronoGuard with it. Strictly speaking, neither of them had ever been. But as *our* Friday pointed out the following day, they *were* still there, echoes from the past that would make themselves known as anachronisms in ancient texts and artefacts that were out of place and out of time. The most celebrated of these would be the discovery of a fossilised 1956 Volkswagen Beetle preserved in Precambrian rock strata. In the glove box they would find the remains of the following day's paper featuring the car's discovery – and a very worthwhile tip for the winner of the 3.30 at Kempton Park.

'Well, that's it,' I said after we had waited for another five minutes and found ourselves still in a state of pleasantly welcome existence. 'The ChronoGuard have shut themselves down and time travel is as it should be: technically, logically and theoretically . . . *impossible*.'

'Good thing too,' replied Landen. 'It always made my head ache. In fact, I was thinking of doing a self-help book for SF novelists eager to write about time travel. It would consist of a single word: *don't*.'

I laughed and we heard a key turn in the front door. It turned out to be Friday, and I recoiled in shock when he walked into the kitchen. He had short hair and was wearing a suit and tie. As I stood there with my mouth open he said:

'Good evening, Mother, good evening, Father. I trust I am not too late for some sustenance?'

'Oh my God!' I cried in horror. 'They *replaced* you!'

Neither Landen nor Friday could hold it in for long and they both collapsed into a sea of giggles. He hadn't been replaced at all – he'd just had a haircut.

'Oh, very funny,' I said, arms folded and severely unamused. 'Next you'll be telling me Jenny is a mindworm or something.'

'She is,' said Landen, and it was my turn to burst out laughing at the ridiculousness of the suggestion. They didn't find it at all funny. Honestly, some people have no sense of humour.

39
A Woman Named
Thursday Next

'The Special Operations Network was instigated to handle
policing duties considered either too unusual or too
specialised to be tackled by the regular force. There were
thirty departments in all, starting at the more mundane Neighbourly
Disputes (SO-30) and going on to Literary Detectives (SO-27) and
Art Crime (SO-24). Anything below SO-20 was restricted information so what they got up to was anyone's guess. What *is* known
is that the individual operatives themselves were slightly unbalanced.
"If you want to be a SpecOp," the saying goes, "act kinda weird."'

My father had a face that could stop a clock. I don't mean that he
was ugly or anything; it was a phrase the ChronoGuard used to
describe someone who had the power to reduce time to an ultra-
slow trickle. Dad had been a colonel in the ChronoGuard and kept
his work very quiet. So quiet, in fact, that we didn't know he had
gone rogue at all until his timekeeping buddies raided our house
one morning clutching a Seize & Eradication order open dated at
both ends and demanding to know where and when he was. Dad
had remained at liberty ever since; we learned from his subsequent
visits that he regarded the whole service as 'morally and historically corrupt' and was fighting a one-man war against the bureaucrats within the Office for Special Stemporal Temp . . . Tability.
Temporal . . . stemp . . . Special—

'Why don't we just hold it right there?' I said before Thursday5
tied her tongue in knots.

'I'm sorry,' she said with a sigh, 'I think my biorhythms must be out of whack.'

'Remember what we talked about?' I asked her, raising an eyebrow.

'. . . or perhaps it's just a tricky line to say. Here goes: Special . . . Temporal . . . *Stability*. Got it!' She smiled proudly at her accomplishment, then a stab of self-doubt crossed her face. 'But aside from that, I'm doing okay, right?'

'You're doing fine.'

We were standing in the opening chapter of *The Eyre Affair*, or at least, the refurbished first chapter. Evil Thursday's erasure caused a few ruffled feathers at Text Grand Central, especially when Alice-PON-24330 said that while she was happy to keep the series running for the time being, she was not that keen taking on the role permanently – what with all the sex, guns, swearing and stuff. There was talk of scrapping the series until I had a brainwave. With the erasure of *The Great Samuel Pepys Fiasco* Thursday5 was now bookless and needed a place to live; *she* could take over. Clearly there had to be a few changes – quite a lot actually – but I didn't mind; in fact, I welcomed them. I applied for a whole raft of internal plot adjustments and Senator Jobsworth, still eager to make amends and keep his job after the reality book farrago, was only too happy to accede to my wishes – as long as I at least *tried* to make the series commercial.

'Can we get a move on?' asked Gerry, the first assistant imaginator. 'If we don't get to the end of this chapter by lunchtime, we're going to get behind schedule for the scene at Gad's Hill tomorrow.'

I left them to it, and walked to the back of Stanford Brookes' café in London, faithfully recreated from my memory and the place where the new *Eyre Affair* starts, rather than at a burned-out house belonging to Landen, where, in point of fact, I didn't live for another two years. I watched as the imaginators, characters and technicians translated the story into storycode text to be uploaded to the engines at TGC – and eventually to replace the existing TN series. Perhaps, I mused to myself, life might be getting back to normal after all.

It had been a month since we'd erased *Pepys Fiasco*, and Racy Novel, despite all manner of threats, had to admit that dirty bomb technology was still very much in the early stages, so Feminist and Ecclesiastical breathed a combined sigh of relief and returned to arguing with each other about the malecentricness of religion.

At the same time the gentle elongation of the Now was beginning to take effect: the Read-O-Meter had been steadily clicking upwards as read-rates once again began to rise. In the Outland the reality TV craze was now thankfully on the wane – *Samaritan Kidney Swap* had so few viewers that by the second week they became desperate and threatened to shoot a puppy on live TV unless a million people phoned in. They had two million complaints and were closed down. Bowden and I visited Booktastic! a week ago to find they now had two entire sections of books because, as the manager explained, 'there had been a sudden demand'.

As part of the whole ChronoGuard decommissioning process Dad had been reactualised from his state of quasi-non-existence and turned up at Mum's carrying a small suitcase and a bunch of flowers. We had a terrific reunion for him and I invited Major Pickles along; he seemed to hit it off rather well with Aunt Polly.

On other matters, I travelled to Goliathopolis to meet Jack Schitt and return his wife's necklace, with an explanation of what had happened to her on board the *Hesperus*. He took the jewellery and the details of her death in stony silence, thanked me and was gone. John Henry Goliath made no appearance, and I didn't tell them that the Austen Rover was, as far as we knew, still adrift without power in intergenre space somewhere between Poetry and Maritime. I didn't know whether this was the end of the

Book Project or not, but TGC were taking no chances and had erected a battery of textual sieves in the direction of the Outland and marked any potential transfictional incursions as 'high priority'.

I walked out of the café to where Isambard Kingdom Buñuel was waiting for me. We were standing in Hangar 3 among the fabric of *Affair*, which was ready to be bolted in. Buñuel had already built a reasonable facsimile of Swindon, which included my mum's house and the Literary Detectives' office, and was just getting started on Thornfield Hall, Rochester's house.

'We've pensketched the real Thornfield,' he explained, showing me some drawings for approval, 'but we were kind of thinkworthing how your Porsche was painted?'

'Do you know Escher's *Reptiles*?'

'Yes.'

'It's like that – only in red, blue and green.'

'How about the Prose Portal?'

I thought for a moment.

'A sort of large leather-bound book covered in knobs, dials and knife switches.'

He made a note.

'And the unextincted Pickwick?'

'About so high and not very bright.'

'Did you bring some snapimagery?'

I rummaged in my shoulder bag, brough out a wad of snaps and went through them.

'That's Pickers when she still had feathers. It's blurred because she blinked and fell over but it's probably the best. And this is Landen, and that's Joffy, and that's Landen again just before his trousers caught fire – that was *hilarious* – and this is Mycroft and Polly. You don't need pictures of Friday, Tuesday or Jenny do you?'

'Only Friday birth-plus-two for *Something Rotten*.'

'Here,' I said, selecting one from the stack, 'this was taken on his second birthday.'

Buñuel recoiled in shock.

'What's that strangeturbing stickbrownymass on his face? Some species of alien facehugger or somewhat?'

'No, no,' I said hurriedly, 'that's chocolate cake. He didn't master the fine art of cutlery until . . . well, he's yet to figure it out, actually.'

'Can I temporown these?' asked Buñuel. 'I'll have them snoodled up to St Tabularasa's to see what they can do.'

'Be my guest.'

The book pre-production had been going on for about two weeks now, and as soon as Buñuel had constructed everything for *The Eyre Affair* he could move on to the more complex build for *Lost in a Good Book*.

'Is there anything you'll be able to salvage from the old series?' I asked, always thinking economically.

'Indeedly so,' he answered, 'Acheron Hades and all his heavisters can be brought across pretty much unaltered. Delamare, Hobbes, Felix7 and 8, Müller – a few different lines here and there and you'll never know the difference.'

'You're right,' I said slowly as an odd thought started to germinate in my mind.

'A few of the other iddybiddyparts we can scavenge,' added Buñuel, 'but most of it will be a newbuild. The warmspect the Council of Genres holds for you is reflected in the high costcash.'

'What was that?' I asked. 'I was miles away.'

'I was mouthsounding that the budget for the new TN series—'

'I'm sorry,' I replied in a distracted manner, 'would you excuse me for a moment?'

I walked over to where Colin was waiting for me in his brand-new taxi. Under the TransGenreTaxis logo they had added *By*

Appointment to Thursday Next in an elegant cursive font. I didn't ordinarily endorse anything, but they had told me I would always be 'priority one', so I figured it was worth it.

'Where to, Ms Next?' he asked as I climbed in.

'Great Library, Floor Six.'

'Right–o.'

He pulled off, braked abruptly as he nearly hit a shiny black Ford motor car, yelled at the other driver, then accelerated rapidly towards the wall of the hangar, which opened like a dark void in front of us.

'Thanks for the Spacehopper,' he said as the hole closed behind us and we motored slowly past the almost limitless number of books in the Great Library. 'I'll be dining out on that for months. Any chance you can get me a lava lamp?'

'Not unless you save my life again.'

I noted the alphabetically listed books on the shelves of the Library and saw that we were getting close.

'Just drop me past the next reading desk.'

'Visiting Tom Jones?'

'No.'

'*Bridget* Jones?'

'No. Just drop me about . . . *here.*'

He stopped next to the bookcase and I got out, told him he didn't need to wait and to put the fare on my account, and he vanished.

I was in the Great Library standing opposite the original Thursday Next series, the one kept going by Alice-PON-24330, and I was here because of something Buñuel had said. Spike and I had never figured out how Felix8 had managed to escape, and since his skeletal remains were found up on the Savernake, Spike had suggested quite rightly that he had been not Felix8, but *Felix9*. But Spike could have been wrong. What if the Felix I had met was the *written* Felix8?

It would explain how he got out of the Weirdshitorium – he just melted back into his book.

I took a deep breath. I didn't want to go anywhere near the old TN series, but this begged further investigation. I picked up the first in the series and read myself inside.

Within a few moments the Great Library was no more, and I was instead aboard an airship floating high over the Home Counties. But it wasn't one of the small fifty-seaters that plied the skies these days, it was a 'Hotel-class' leviathan, designed to roam the globe in style and opulence during the halcyon days of the airship. I was in what had once been the observation deck, but many of the perspex windows had been lost and the shabby craft rattled and creaked as the lumbering bulk pushed through the air. The icy slipstream blew into the belly of the craft where I stood and made me shiver, while the rush of air and the incessant flap of loose fabric were a constant percussive accompaniment to the rhythmic growl of the eight engines. The aluminium latticework construction was apparent wherever I looked, and to my left a door gave access to a precipitous veranda where first-class passengers would once have had a unique bird's-eye view of the docking and landing procedure. In the real world these monsters had been melted down into scrap long ago, the job of repeater stations for TV and wireless signals now taken over by pilotless drones in the upper atmosphere. But it was kind of nostalgic to see one again, even in this illusory form.

I wasn't in the main action, the 'better dead than read' adage as important to me as to anyone else. The narrative was actually next door in the main dining room, where Thursday aka Alice-PON-24330 was attempting to outwit Acheron Hades. This wasn't how it *really* happened, of course – Acheron's hideout had actually been in Merthyr Tydfil's abandoned Penderyn Hotel in the Socialist Republic of Wales. It was dramatic licence – and fairly bold dramatic licence at that.

389

There was a burst of gunfire from next door, some shouting and then more shots. I positioned myself behind the door as Felix8 came running through as he usually did, escaping from Bowden and myself once Acheron leapt into the pages of *Jane Eyre*. As soon as he was inside he relaxed since he was officially 'out of the story'. I saw him grin to himself and click on the safety of his machine pistol.

'Hello, Felix8.'

He turned and stared at me.

'Well, well,' he said after a pause, 'will the real Thursday Next please stand up.'

'Just drop the gun.'

'I'm not really violent,' he said, 'it's just the part I play. The real Felix8 – now that's someone you should keep an eye on.'

'Drop the gun, Felix. I won't ask you again.'

His eyes darted around the room and I saw his hand tighten around the grip of his gun.

'Don't even *think* about it,' I told him, pointing my pistol in his general direction. 'This is loaded with eraserhead. Put the gun on the floor – but *really* slowly.'

Felix8, fully aware of the destructive power of an eraserhead, gently laid his weapon on the ground, and I told him to kick it to one side.

'How did you get into the real world?'

'I don't know what you mean.'

'You were in the *real* Swindon five weeks ago. Do you know the penalty for pagerunning?'

He said nothing.

'I'll remind you. It's erasure. And if you read the papers, you know that I'll erase a whole book, if required.'

'I've never been out of *The Eyre Affair*,' he replied, 'I'm just a C-3 generic trying to do my best in a lousy book.'

'You're lying.'

'That it's not a lousy book?'

'You know what I mean. Keep your hands in the air.'

I walked behind him and, keeping my pistol pressed firmly against his back, searched his pockets. Given the obsession that members of the BookWorld had with the Outland, I reckoned it was impossible that he had been all the way to Swindon and not returned with a few Outlandish mementoes to sell or barter. And so it proved. In one pocket I found a joke rubber chicken and a digital watch, and in the other a packet of Bachelors Cup-a-Soup and a Mars bar. I chucked them on the floor in front of him.

'Where did you get these, then?'

He was silent, and I backed off a few yards before telling him to turn slowly around and face me.

'Now,' I said, 'let's have some answers. You're too mediocre to have hatched this yourself so you're working for someone. Who is it?'

Felix8 made no answer and the airship banked slightly as it made a trifling correction to its course. The aluminium-framed door to the exterior promenade walkway swung open and then clattered shut again. It was dusk, and two miles below the small orange jewels that were the street lights had begun to wink on.

'Okay,' I said, 'here's the deal: you tell me what you know and I'll let you go. Play the hard man and it's a one-way trip to the Text Sea. Understand?'

'I've only *eighteen* words and one scene,' he said at last. 'One lousy scene! Do you have any idea what that's like?'

'It's the hand you were dealt,' I told him, 'the job you do. You can't change that. Again: *who sent you into the Outland to kill me?*'

He stared at me without emotion.

'And I would have done it too, if it wasn't for that idiot stalker. Mind you, Johnson blew it as well so I'm in good company.'

This was more worrying. 'Mr Johnson' was the pseudonym used by the Minotaur – and he'd referred to my murder as 'a job', so this looked to be better organised than I'd thought.

'Who ordered my death? And why me?'

Felix8 smiled.

'You *do* flatter yourself, Ms Next. You're not the only one they want, you're not the only one they'll get. And now, I shall take my leave of you.'

He moved towards the exterior door, which clattered in the breeze, opened it and stepped out on to the exterior promenade. I ran forward and yelled 'Hold it!' but it was too late. With a swing of his leg Felix8 slipped neatly over the rail and went tumbling off into space. I ran to the rail and looked down. Already he was a small figure spiralling slowly downwards as the airship droned on. I felt a curious sickly feeling as he became nothing more than a small dot and then disappeared from view.

'Damn!' I shouted, and slapped the parapet with my palm. I took a deep breath, went inside out of the chill wind, pulled out my mobile footnoterphone and pressed the speed-dial connection to the Cheshire Cat, who had assumed command of Text Grand Central.[12]

'Chesh, it's Thursday.'[13]

'I've lost a C-3 generic, "Felix8", from page two hundred and seventy-eight of *The Eyre Affair*, ISBN–0–340–820470. I'm going to need an emergency replacement asap.'[14]

'No.'[15]

---

12 '*Prego! Il Gatto del Cheshire?*'
13 'Sorry – just practising for my holidays in Brindisi this year. What can I do for you?'
14 'Sure. Say, did you order a textual sieve lockdown on *The Eyre Affair?*'
15 'Well, you've got one. Mesh is set to ultra-fine and time-locked – not even a full stop is going to get out of that book for at least twenty minutes.'

'Blast,' I muttered. 'Can you find out who's been dicking around with the textual sieves and get it lifted? I've no urge to hang around a cold airship for any longer than I have to.'[16]

I told him that I'd be fine if he'd just call me back when the sieve was lifted, and snapped the mobile shut. I pulled my jacket up around my neck and stamped my feet to keep warm. I leaned against an aluminium girder and stared out at the mauve twilight in which even now I could see stars begin to appear. Felix8 would have hit the ground so hard his text would have fused with the surrounding description; when we found him we'd have to cut him from the earth. Either way he'd not be doing any talking.

I started thinking of people who might want to kill me, but stopped counting when I reached sixty-seven. This would be harder than I thought. But . . . what did Felix8 say: that I shouldn't flatter myself . . . *it wasn't just me*? The more I thought about it, the stranger it seemed until suddenly, with a flash of realisation, I knew what was going on. Sherlock Holmes, Temperance Brennan, the Good Soldier 'vejk and myself – kill us and you kill not *just* the individual, but the *series*. It seemed too bizarre to comprehend but it had to be the truth – *there was a serial killer loose in the BookWorld.*

I looked around the airship and my heart fell. They'd tried to kill me twice already, and who was to say they wouldn't try again? And here I was, trapped ten thousand feet in the air by a textual sieve that no one ordered, hanging beneath twenty million cubic feet of highly inflammable hydrogen. I pulled out my mobile and hurriedly redialled the cat.[17]

'No questions, Chesh – I need a parachute and I need it *now*.'

As if in answer, there was a bright flare from the rear of the airship as a small charge exploded in one of the gas cells. Within a

16 'No problemo, Outlander amiga. Do you want me to keep you company?'
17 '*Prego! Il Gatto del Cheshire?*'

393

second this had ignited the cell next to it and I could see the bright flare arc out into the dusk; the airship quivered gently and started to drop at the stern as it lost lift.

'I need that parachute!' I yelled into my mobile as a third gas cell erupted, vaporising the fabric covering and sending a shower of sparks out on either side of the craft. The tail-down attitude increased as the fourth gas cell erupted, followed quickly by the fifth and sixth, and I grabbed a handrail to steady myself.

'Goddamit!' I yelled to no one in particular. 'How hard can it be to get a parachute around here?!' The airship trembled again as another explosion ripped through the envelope, and with an unpleasant feeling of lightness I felt the craft very slowly begin to fall. As I looked down to see where we were heading and how fast, twelve parachutes of varying styles, colours and vintage appeared in front of me. I grabbed the most modern-looking, stepped into the leg straps and quickly pulled it on to my back as the ship was again rocked by a series of explosions. I clicked the catch on the front of the webbing and, without even pausing for breath, leapt over the rail and out into the cold evening air. There was a sudden feeling of rapid acceleration and I tumbled for a while, eventually coming to rest on my back, the air rushing past me, making my clothes flap and tugging at my hair. Far above me the airship was now a chrysanthemum of fire which looked destructively elegant, and even from this distance I could feel the heat on my face. As the airship grew smaller I snapped out of my reverie and looked for a toggle or something to deploy the chute. I found it across my chest and pulled as hard as I could. Nothing happened for a moment and I was just thinking that the chute had failed when there was a *whap* and a jerk as it opened. But before I had even *begun* to sigh with relief there was a thump as I landed on the ground, bounced twice and ended up inside the lines and the canopy, which billowed around me. I scrambled clear, released the harness, pulled out my mobile and pressed the speed dial for Bradshaw, running as fast as I could across the empty and undescribed land as the flaming hulk of the airship fell slowly and elegantly in the evening sky, the blackened skeleton of the stricken ship showing dark and silhouetted against the orange fireball above it, an angry flaming mass that even now was beginning to spread to the fabric of the book, as the clouds and sky started to glow with the green iridescence of text before it spontaneously combusts.

'It's Thursday,' I panted, running to get clear of the airship before it hit the ground, 'and I think we've got a situation . . .'

My thanks to:

My very dear Lipali **Mari Roberts**, for countless hours of research, assistance and for looking after her writer and partner in the throes of creation. I hope that in the fullness of time I might do the same for her.

Molly Stern and **Carolyn Mays**, the finest editors in the galaxy, and to whom I am always grateful for support and guidance. And by extension, to the hordes of unsung heroes and heroines at Hodder and Penguin who diligently support and promote me and my work.

My grateful thanks go to **Kathy Reichs** for allowing Dr Temperance Brennan to make a guest appearance in this book.

With kind thanks to Agatha Christie Limited (A Chorion company) for reference to *They Do It with Mirrors* © 1952 AGATHA CHRISTIE LIMITED (a Chorion company), all rights reserved.

Jordan Fforde, my own teenage son, who is a fine, upstanding young man and displays nothing like the worst excesses of Friday's idleness, and who served only vaguely as any sort of reference material.

Bill Mudron and **Dylan Meconis** of Portland, Oregon, for their outstanding artwork completed in record time and with an understanding of the author's brief that left me breathless. Further examples of their work and contact details for commissions can be found at: www.thequirkybird.com (Dylan) and www.excelsiorstudios.net (Bill).

Professor **John Sutherland** for his Puzzles in Fiction series of books, which continue to fascinate and inspire.

The Paragon tea rooms exist in the same or greater splendour as that described in the pages of this novel. They can be found on the main street of Katoomba, in the Blue Mountain region of New South Wales, Australia, and no visit to the area would be complete without your attendance. Who knows – you may even see a giant hedgehog and a tyrannical leader of the known universe sharing a booth and discussing Irritable Vowel Syndrome in hushed tones.

Special thanks to the **residents of Thirlestane-Green** for their generous hospitality to my other half.

Thanks to **June Haversham** for support beyond the call of fiction.

This novel was written in BOOK V8.3 and was sequenced using an Mk XXIV ImaginoTransferoDevice. Harley Farley was the imaginator. Generics supplied and trained by St Tabularasa's. Holes were filled by apprentices at the HoleSmith's Guild, and echolocation and post-creative grammatisation were undertaken by Outland contractors at Hodder and Penguin.

The 'galactic cleansing' policy undertaken by Emperor Zhark is a personal vision of the emperor's, and its inclusion in this work does not constitute tacit approval by the author or the publisher of any such projects, howsoever undertaken.

Thursday Next will return in:

The War of the Words

or

Last Among Prequels

or

Apocalypse Next

or

Dark Reading Matter

or

Paragraph Lost

or

Herrings Red

or

The Palimpsest of

Dr Caligari

or

The Legion of the Danvers

or

Some Other Title Entirely

Expensive Cheese?

Annoyed by your decadent, corrupt, capitalist pigdog government bleeding you white over the very mildest cheddar?

Want clean air, sweet song, decent rugby and the finest cheeses known to man?

Then you need a cheese tasting holiday in the

Socialist Republic of Wales

Wales: not always raining.

See your local tourist office for details.

Get into the Classics
...aboard the *Austen Rover!*

Bronte * Trollope * Austen * Thackeray * Dickens

Goliath proudly presents the very latest in advanced tourist technology. Visit all your favourite books from the comfort and safety of our transfictional tour bus and see the classics as you've never seen them before. Tours begin March 2003 and bookings are now being taken at Goliath Holidays, inc.

Read on for a sneak preview of
Jasper Fforde's new book . . .

SHADES OF
GREY

It is a lush and green, long-depopulated, post-apocalyptic Britain.

All notion of history has been quietly forgotten, and all that remains are tea and scones, politeness, cricket, queues, sensible haircuts, talk of weather and an almost fanatical devotion to the avoidance of social embarrassment. Governance has been replaced by the all-encompassing LAWS, which look suspiciously as though they have been lifted unchanged from a Public School Rule-book. The nation is strictly run by a network of Prefects, Monitors, Oiks, Swots, Bullies and Snitches, who use the threat of de-merits to keep the population in line.

If only it were all that simple.

Hierachy is established not by position or cash, but by the colour you can see, with the Violets at the top of the chromatic scale, and Reds at the bottom. Below them are the Achromatic Greys - the hardworking unrepresented drones of the collective. In a small village on the outer fringes of the nation, Eddie Russett is looking for social advancement but instead finds something much more unexpected: a defiant Grey named Jane who has dangerously radical ideas. Together they embark on a journey to discover the dark nature of the Rules – but they will have to defy the Prefects and overcome everything they once feared: darkness, swan attack, lightning, Beigistan and the feral subhumans known only as the Riffraff. It won't be easy. They're not allowed past the boundary without first signing the outings-book, and supper is at 7:00PM *sharp*.

SHADES OF GREY –
a story of love, social revolution and scones.

Welcome to the new world
from comic and creative genius

JASPER FFORDE

SHADES OF GREY

In a black and white world,
colour is a privilege . . .

OUT IN HARDBACK JANUARY 2009